1 MONTH OF FREE READING

at

www.ForgottenBooks.com

By purchasing this book you are eligible for one month membership to ForgottenBooks.com, giving you unlimited access to our entire collection of over 1,000,000 titles via our web site and mobile apps.

To claim your free month visit:
www.forgottenbooks.com/free119786

* Offer is valid for 45 days from date of purchase. Terms and conditions apply.

ISBN 978-0-267-65232-7
PIBN 10119786

This book is a reproduction of an important historical work. Forgotten Books uses state-of-the-art technology to digitally reconstruct the work, preserving the original format whilst repairing imperfections present in the aged copy. In rare cases, an imperfection in the original, such as a blemish or missing page, may be replicated in our edition. We do, however, repair the vast majority of imperfections successfully; any imperfections that remain are intentionally left to preserve the state of such historical works.

Forgotten Books is a registered trademark of FB &c Ltd.
Copyright © 2018 FB &c Ltd.
FB &c Ltd, Dalton House, 60 Windsor Avenue, London, SW19 2RR.
Company number 08720141. Registered in England and Wales.

For support please visit www.forgottenbooks.com

TRAVELS AND JOURNALS

PRESERVED IN THE

BOMBAY SECRETARIAT.

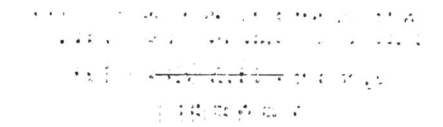

EDITED BY

GEORGE W. FORREST, C.I.E.,
EX-DIRECTOR OF RECORDS, GOVERNMENT OF INDIA.

BOMBAY
PRINTED AT THE GOVERNMENT CENTRAL PRESS
1906

[*Price*—*Rs.* 7 or 10s. 6d.]

UNIV. OF CALIFORNIA
AT LOS ANGELES
LIBRARY

PREFACE.

The documents in this volume were brought together by me when I was Director of Records, Bombay Government. They have been buried in the archives of that Government or in old journals not easily accessible. To bring them to light and to preserve them "from the greedy and devouring jaws of oblivion" is the object of this work. They have been printed, letter for letter, exactly as they are in the original papers. Many words occur which are not easily accounted for, many names are spelt contrary to orthodox rules, many sentences war against the laws of grammar. It has been suggested that the text should be edited and the geographical information brought down to the present time. To alter the text would, however, destroy the old flavour of these travels and their main charm. It was proposed to give a list of *errata*, but after much labour it was abandoned as an impossible task. No two experts agreed as to what the list should contain. Under these circumstances, being but an amateur student of Central Asian geography, I sought the advice of Sir Thomas Holdich, one of the greatest living authorities on the subject, and he most kindly read the volume for me and came to the decision that it should be published exactly as it has been printed. He writes: "I am glad to find that so useful a series is now put together under one cover. They are all of them most valuable, although there is hardly any part of the regions dealt with that has not been recently either explored thoroughly or actually surveyed." If the lands which these adventurous pioneers first opened have now become familiar fields of enterprise, the freshness of the tales of their exploits still remains, for they are as simple, strong and masculine as the great men who wrote them.

I have to thank Professor Margoliouth for having kindly read the proofs of the Introduction and for having provided me from his vast store of knowledge with notes essential to the quotations from some of the travels.

It affords me much pleasure to acknowledge the valuable assistance rendered me in the preparation of this volume by my former Head Assistant Mr. Balvant Mahadev whose labours as Custodian of the Bombay Records can only be appreciated by those who have seen their results.

The introduction has no official character or authority.

GEORGE WILLIAM FORREST.

IFFLEY, OXON.,
28th July 1905.

CONTENTS.

	PAGES.
Introduction	i to xxviii
Itinerary from Yezd to Herát and from Herát to Kábul *viâ* Kandáhár	1
Report of a Journey from Herát to Simla *viâ* Kandáhár, Kábul and the Punjáb, by Major D'Arcy Todd	19
Notice on Herát with a sketch of the State of Affairs in the surrounding countries	33
Narrative of a Journey from Khelát to Sonmeani in November 1839, by Captain Outram ...	43
Account of an Embassy to the King of Persia from the Ameer of Kábul in 1837, Part I ...	51
Do. do. do. do. II ...	61
Letters from Major D'Arcy Todd	77
Letters from Lieutenant Pottinger	95
Masson's Journals	101
Narrative of a Journey from the Tower of Ba-'l-Haff, on the Southern Coast of Arabia, to the Ruins of Nakab-al-Hajar, 1835	189
Account of an Excursion in Haḍramaut by Adolphe Baron Wrede	203
Memoir of the South Coast of Arabia from the entrance of the Red Sea to Misenat, 1839 ...	209
Narrative of a Journey from Mokhá to San'á by the Tarik-esh-Shám, or Northern Route, in July and August 1836	235
Narrative of a Journey to Shoa	253
Index	i—xxix

INTRODUCTION.

The first record in these selections is an Itinerary from Yezd to Herát and from Herát to Kábul *viâ* Kandáhár. In a letter, dated Kábul, 29th August 1839, Major Neil Campbell, Acting Quartermaster-General of the Army, requests the Secretary to the Bombay Government to submit to the Honourable the Governor in Council the journal of a ride from Yezd to Herát and again from Herát to Kábul *viâ* Kandáhár. The journey, he informs us, was undertaken in 1826 by a French Officer now in " the Sikh service at the request, I believe, of Count Yermal, the Russian Governor of Georgia." The translation was made by Major Campbell himself. The journal gives a graphic account of the places visited by the traveller, and though nearly eighty years have rolled on since it was written, the information has not been superseded by modern travellers.

The second paper in the volume is the account of a journey made by Major D'Arcy Todd from Simla to Herát in the year 1838. Major D'Arcy Todd accompanied John McNeill, the British Envoy at the Court of Persia, on the march to Herát from Tehrán. The object of the mission was to dissuade the Sháh from continuing the siege of Herát. The story of that long siege is of perennial interest to Englishmen, because a single young British subaltern was the life and soul of the defence. Early in 1837, Eldred Pottinger, a Lieutenant in the Bombay Artillery, started in the disguise of a Cutch horse-dealer to explore the then unknown regions of Afghanistan. On reaching Kábul he determined to push through the wild mountainous country inhabited by fanatic hordes to Herát, the famous frontier city of Afghanistan. He assumed the disguise of a Syud or holy man from Hindustan, and, accompanied by a guide, started forth on his perilous venture. Through hardships and imprisonments, suspected of being an infidel (which if confirmed meant death), the valiant English lad held his way, and on the 18th of August he reached Herát. A month later the news came that the Shah of Persia acting under Russian influence was about to advance on Herát. The fall of that city, Pottinger saw, would be calamitous to the Afghan people and inimical to British interests. As an Artillery Officer he might be of service to the defenders. He therefore made himself known to the ruler of the state, Shah Muhammad, and his Vuzier Yar Muhammad, who saw the advantage of having the advice and assistance of a skilled English officer. The Persians invested Herát, and it was mainly due to the fortitude, ability and judgment of the young artillery officer that it did not fall into their hands. The siege had gone on for some weary months when the English Minister arrived in the Persian Camp. He at once sent Major Todd to negotiate with the Herátees, and as it was the first time a British officer had appeared in Herát in full uniform, "a vast crowd went out to gaze at him. The tight fitting coat, the glittering epaulettes and the cocked-hat all excited unbounded admiration." The negotiations failed and Todd was sent by McNeill to convey despatches to the Governor-General and to inform him what was the actual state of affairs. On the 8th of May 1838 he wrote : " I am now

B 903—1

under sailing orders and shall weigh anchor in the course of a few days charged with dispatches to Lord Auckland. The route which I now contemplate is that which leads through Kandáhár, Kábul, Pesháwar, Attock, and thence through the Punjáb to Ludiana, whence Simla is distant only a night's or a couple of night's dâk. I shall travel as an Englishman, but in the dress of an Afghán, without luggage or other encumbrances, save a pair of saddle-bags on the horse I ride. This mode I believe to be the best in every respect. All the difficulties that Europeans have encountered in these countries have arisen from their foolishly endeavouring to personate natives." On the 22nd of July he wrote from Simla: " I left the Persian Camp before Herát on the 22nd of May and after a very interesting journey of about sixty days viâ Kandáhár, Kábul, Pesháwar and the Punjáb, I arrived without accident at this place on Friday last the 20th. People tell me that I have made a very rapid journey—a fact with which I am pretty well acquainted, knowing as I do the difficulties and detentions and dangers which a traveller must meet with in the countries which I have lately traversed."

Two months had not elapsed after Todd had arrived at Simla to report the failure of the negotiations when Eldred Pottinger wrote to W. H. Macnaghten, Esquire, Political Secretary, Supreme Government, Calcutta: " Thanks be to the Almighty God, I have the honour to report the cessation of hostilities in this quarter for the information of His Lordship the Governor-General. In consequence of the Persian King having agreed to the message brought to him by Lieutenant-Colonel Stoddart from Her Majesty's Envoy at Tehrán, the Persian Army yesterday broke up from their quarters and commenced their retreat towards their territory." Two other letters from Lieutenant Eldred Pottinger discovered in the Bombay Archives, now printed for the first time, recall to memory a striking episode and one of those characters which give a dramatic life to the annals of our Empire.

When the first Afghan war was declared, Major D'Arcy Todd was gazetted as Political Assistant and Military Secretary to the Envoy and Minister at the Court of Shah Sujah, the ill-fated monarch whom we were about to place again on " the throne of his ancestors " by British bayonets. Todd accompanied the Army of the Indus, which reached Kandáhár in April 1839, and Shah Sujah was proclaimed King of Kábul. As Yar Muhammad, the Vuzier of Herát, was the first to congratulate the monarch on his restoration to the throne, it was considered an opportune moment for sending a special mission to Herát to make a treaty with the ruler. After the Shah of Persia had abandoned the siege " Lieutenant Eldred Pottinger of the Bombay Artillery had been appointed to be Political Agent at Herát, subject to the orders of the Envoy and Minister of the Court of Shah Sujah-ul-mulk." In June, Todd started for Herát, accompanied by Captain Sanders of the Engineers and Lieutenant James Abbott of the Artillery, with Lieutenant C. F. North and Assistant Surgeon Login. On the 25th of July, the special mission reached the city, and was " received with every mark of respect by the Monarch and his Prime Minister." A treaty of friendship and alliance with Shah Kamran was concluded. The ruler of Herát was to receive from the Indian Government twenty-five thousand rupees a month on certain conditions, the chief being that he should hold no intercourse with Persia without the knowledge and consent of the British Envoy. In September, 1839, Pottinger left Herát and Todd succeeded him as Political Agent. Three months later he sent James Abbott on a friendly mission to the Khan of Khiva. " An opening was offered me," he wrote, " so I took advantage of it on my own responsibility and I am happy to say that the Governor-General has approved of the measure. James Abbott was well received by the Khán, and has been employed as a mediator between Khiva and Russia, the troops of the latter being on their march towards the Khan's capital. James Abbott will probably have to proceed to St. Petersburg ! I cannot guess what the powers will think of this bold step, but I have done my best to defend it." One of the objects of Abbott's mission was to release from cruel bondage the Russian captives in Khiva and to put a stop to man-slavery and the traffic in human beings. But Yar Muhammad and the Central Asian Chiefs were all engaged in a trade that yielded profits large enough to counteract its perils, and their stern bigotry went hand in hand with their thirst for gain. Slavery was sanctioned by their creed and Abbott's action was regarded as a blow to their religion by an infidel sect. Todd, like Burnes at Kábul, did not understand the nature of the man with whom he had to deal. " All is quiet here," he wrote on the 1st of April 1840. "We are on the best possible terms with the authorities of the place, and I believe that Yar Mahomed Khan, who is the *de facto* ruler of the country, is beginning to understand that honesty is the best policy." The letter had hardly been despatched before Todd received substantial proof of the Vuzier's treachery. A copy of a letter written by the Vuzier, in the name of Shah Kamran, to the King of Persia was sent to him by the British representative at the Persian Court. The ruler of Herát " declared himself to be the faithful servant of the Shah-in-Shah (King of Kings), that he merely tolerated the presence of the English Envoy from expediency, although to give him his due, he was by no means niggardly in the expenditure of money, jewels, etc., and that his (Shah Kamran's) hopes were in the Asylum of Islam." It did not suit the policy of the British Government to have an open rupture with the Vuzier and his master, and their treachery was condoned. A policy of this yielding tentative order bore its natural fruit. Matters grew worse month by month, Yar Muhammad's aim was to blind the British Government without sacrificing the liberty of the state, and he played the game with marvellous skill. The Afghan is a master in political lying, but in the profusion and recklessness of his lies Yar Muhammad stood without a peer. Todd writes to Sir W. H. Macnaghten on the 29th of January 1841 that the Vuzier had sent a secret Mission to Meshed. "On ascertaining the fact, I immediately addressed a note to the Vuzier, expressing my regret at his having taken this extraordinary step and my fear that it would be attended with the most disastrous consequences to himself." Yar Muhammad in answer to the note " expressed great surprise at the serious view which I had taken of this trivial matter, and asserted in excuse that I had given him permission to send a man to Meshed for the purpose of demanding the restoration of Ghoriani, which had been the reason of his despatching Fyz Mahomed Khan." Todd had given him permission to send a man or a letter, "but this could never be applied to the departure of his most confidential servant with a train of 40 or 50 followers." The British Envoy adds: " I may here mention that there is but one opinion in the town of the real object of his mission, namely an alliance with Persia based on our ejectment from Herát. A strong and general feeling of insecurity prevails ; many persons are preparing to send their families to Kandáhár, and the only question about our treatment is whether we are to be seized and plundered to-day or to-morrow."

On the 24th of January Todd had an interview with the Minister. " In excuse for his conduct he pleaded his fears of our ultimate intentions, thereby admitting his guilt, although he declared most solemnly that the only message with which he had charged Fyz Mahomed was that previously stated. He said that he had yesterday heard of the arrival of 20,000 men at Shikárpur, and asked me whether it was true. I answered that I had only received intelligence of preparations being made for subsisting 17,000. He then stated that all his advisers and correspondents warned him that the destination of these troops was Herát, and that the English wished to involve him in hostilities with Persia, merely to enable them to crush him with greater facility. I observed that I considered my word of greater weight and more worthy of belief than the reports and speculations of all his correspondents and advisers; that the authorities of Herát were the only people in the world who doubted our word or distrusted us in any way; and that if he had enquired of me regarding the destination of these troops, I could have set his mind perfectly at rest on the subject. I added that, had he reflected for a moment, he could never have feared us, for our conduct towards him up to this moment had been uniformly liberal and friendly, and had we wished to destroy him we should have done so either openly, on our first arrival in the country previously to strengthening him, or secretly by the expenditure amongst his enemies of one-tenth of the sum that had been lavished on him. This, he said, could not be denied, but observed that it was natural for the weaker to fear the stronger, and he therefore requested me to give him a paper of assurance (khatur jum) in order to remove his apprehensions. I replied that it was out of my power to furnish him with the paper he required; that if what we had already done in and for the country had not satisfied him of our disinterested friendship, nothing could; and that it rested with him to counteract the evil he had done and to satisfy us for the future."

On the day following the interview, Yar Muhammad sent his three most confidential advisers to endeavour to procure from Todd the paper of assurance. "This I steadily refused to give for the reasons which I had assigned to the Minister the day before, and to themselves on a former occasion. I consented, however, to take no decided step until the receipt of the intelligence from Meshed." The crafty Minister was in want of a large sum of money, and he was afraid that the handsome monthly allowance paid by the Government would be stopped. He therefore sent two days later his principal adviser to endeavour to discover what terms would be granted to him.

"The Khan made several propositions, none of which, however, appeared to me to promise any security for the future, and at length he stated that if I would give the Minister confidence there would be no objection to our introducing a brigade of British troops into the country, or even into the town, with the express proviso that His Majesty Shah Shujah should not interfere in the matter, and that Shah Kamran should remain as nominal ruler. I was careful not to manifest any anxiety on the subject of the introduction of our troops, although this was the point on which I was desirous of ascertaining the Minister's sentiments, and I therefore dismissed Nujjoo Khan with the promise that I would give further consideration to the question. It is possible, and even probable, that the hint thrown out regarding our troops was merely intended as a feeler."

On the 1st of February the British Envoy intimated to the Prime Minister that he could "under existing circumstances only disburse the monthly allowance (25,000 Company's rupees) to the King and Chiefs, which had been promised for the present year, provided the Herát authorities acted in conformity to the wishes of the British Government. As it seemed to me that a manifest breach of treaty had been committed, I did not feel myself authorized to continue the allowance. In reply, the Minister acknowledged that he had no claim to further pecuniary assistance in the present state of affairs, but expressed a hope of being able to make it appear that my suspicion of the want of faith had been groundless." And Yar Muhammad did his best to persuade the British Envoy that he was a faithful ally. The 3rd of February, a festival was celebrated, and Todd went to the citadel with the Officer of the Mission. "Dresses of honour were given us by the King and we rode with His Majesty as usual." Two Muhammadans attached to the Mission establishment were, however, grossly and shamefully insulted by two dependents of the Vuzier's establishment. "On being made acquainted with the circumstances," Todd writes, " which had taken place in the presence of a vast concourse of people, I sent several witnesses of it to the Vuzier and advised, especially with reference to the present state of feeling in the town, that the punishment of the offenders should be summary and public. Their guilt was proved, and after being bastinadoed in the market-place, their faces being smeared with mud, they were led through the different streets of the city, while a crier proclaimed with a loud voice their offence and punishment." Having appeased the British Envoy by the punishment of the offenders, the Minister again attempted to gain the money by diplomatic pressure backed by a threat. On the afternoon of the 7th he sent a deputation with a letter in which he stated : " Now this is the last letter that I shall write to you. To-day you will either give me perfect assurance and confidence or take from me all hope. Henceforward into whatever well I may throw myself I have thrown myself. Let there be no complaint on either side." The British Envoy addressed a letter to the Vuzier stating that after what had occurred he was anxious to discuss with him personally the questions under consideration, but that if he objected to an interview, he would treat with anyone to whom he gave written credentials. The next morning the deputation returned with a letter from the Vuzier giving them full powers to adjust matters on his behalf. The British Envoy " opened the conference by begging them to state the requisitions with which they were charged." They mentioned the following :

" (1) A written assurance on the part of the British Government relieving the Vuzier from all apprehensions for the future.

(2) The immediate payment of the Vuzier's debts, amounting to nearly two lákhs of Company's rupees.

(3) A liberal monthly allowance, far exceeding that at present given, to be guaranteed to the Herát Government for one year.

(4) A written promise that the British Government would not embroil that of Herát in any foreign war, until after the present harvests, which are reaped in June and July.

(5) The fortifications of the city to be repaired and strengthened at our expense.

(6) Loans of money to be advanced to enable the Herát Government to recover entire possession of the Char Vilayut, Ghorian, Seestaun and the Tymunee country, and the Herát troops to be subsidised in the field so long as engaged in these operations. I asked what the Herát Government was prepared to grant in the event of the above demands being acceded to by my Government, and in reply was requested to mention what I deemed an equivalent."

It was impossible for the British Envoy to accede to these proposals. He held the opinion that it was both necessary and politic to acquire a supremacy in Herát, but this could only be done, as he had informed the Indian Government, by the occupation of the citadel by a Brigade of British troops with artillery. He promptly told the deputation that "the treaty having been again broken by the authorities of Herát and their promises having been found valueless, it was for the British Government now to demand security for the future, and that in his opinion " the only satisfactory mode of giving this was by admitting a brigade of British troops with artillery into the citadel of Herát, and the immediate deputation of the Vuzier's son to Girishk to accompany the troops to Herát. Under these circumstances I promised, pending the sanction of Government, to give a written assurance to the Vuzier guaranteeing to him the Vuzarat of Herát during his life-time, the payment of his debts to the amount of one lákh of Company's rupees on the arrival of our troops, and an allowance to the Herát Government, for one year, of one lákh of Herát rupees, Company's Rs. 33,333⅓, per mensem, to commence on the arrival of the Vuzier's son at Girishk, up to which date the present allowance of 25,000 Company's rupees a month would be continued. I also agreed to the repair of the fortifications, provided our troops were admitted into the citadel, but in the event of their being located outside the town, I stated that the expense of fortifying a post for their accommodation would be considerable, and in this case the Herátees must repair their own works. This was said with reference to a long discussion which took place on the subject of our troops being quartered in the citadel, to which the deputation objected in the strongest terms as a measure to which they were certain the Vuzier would never agree. On reflection it seemed to me that our object would be equally gained by our holding a strong position in the immediate vicinity of the city; indeed there were considerations which pointed this out as the more desirable arrangement. I waived for the present the discussion of articles Nos. 4 and 6."

This interview, which lasted nearly the whole day, was brought to a close by the deputation informing the British Envoy that they did not think it possible the Vuzier would agree to his terms : "that the Vuzier's wife could not be persuaded to part with her son, and that an immediate payment of money would be required." Finding that Todd was not disposed to make the required concessions, the deputation informed him that " I might select my Mehmandar, as any further stay at Herát would be useless, and that my Hindustáni, Kábul and Kandáhár servants would be allowed to accompany me, but that those of Herát would not be permitted to leave the place. I selected Sirdar Fatteh Khan as my Mehmandar, and remarked that I did not require the permission of the Vuzier to take with me the natives of India or the subjects of Shah Shoojah, and that by the laws of Nations I had a right to retain in my service, at least until I reached the frontier, all my Herát servants who were willing to accompany me."

Yar Muhammad was greatly troubled and much disconcerted at the British Envoy so promptly consenting to withdraw the Mission from Herát. It was, however, the only course open to a Minister who had a due regard for the dignity of the Government which he represented, and the safety of his staff. To withdraw the Mission on his own responsibilty was a grave step, but, in his letter to Macnaghten, Todd states : " I must state my conviction that our further stay at Herát would have been productive of no good, and that with the examples of Major Pottinger, Colonel Stoddart and Lieutenant Loveday before me, I should not have been justified in exposing the officers of the mission to insult and danger by remaining at Herát in opposition to the expressed wishes of the Vuzier." And Todd had good ground for his conviction. When it became known that the Mission was about to depart, " the greatest excitement prevailed throughout the town, the inhabitants armed themselves, guns were discharged in every direction, and large crowds collected round the residence of the

Mission. Our followers and servants were threatened with death, and their families with dishonour; and it was generally believed that we were to be seized and our property plundered." On the afternoon of the 9th of February the Mission set forth from Herát. " Dense crowds had assembled to witness our departure, and I apprehended personal insult, if not violence, being offered to us by some of the Vuzier's lawless soldiery, but by leaving the town at a different gate from that which we had named we avoided the crowd and reached our first place of encampment about four miles from Herát without being molested." Here they halted the next day in order to enable the servants to bring their families from the city and to negotiate the release of Kazi Mullah Muhammad Hussein who had incurred the deadly enmity of the Vuzier on account of the services he and his sons had rendered the British Government. Yar Muhammad who had placed the Kazi under strict surveillance, threatened that he should be put to the most awful tortures, "that the women of his family should be given over to the soldiery, and that the males should, after having been tortured, be paraded through the streets, a crier proclaiming that such was the punishment of all who served infidels." Todd knew he was dealing with a tyrant who would not hesitate to carry his worst threats into execution. He also justly felt " that our abandonment of these families whose only crime in the eyes of the Vuzier was the service they had rendered our Government, would have been as injurious to the British name in these countries as our stepping forward in behalf of persons thus situated would be honourable," and he offered the Vuzier a substantial sum for their release. The love of money is stronger than the passion for revenge. The offer was accepted. On the night of the 12th the Kazi and his brother " with the males of their families, the females having been placed in safety in the harems of their relations," joined the British camp. Next morning arrangements having been made for the payment of the ransom, the Mission made their first regular march to a spot 42 miles from the city. On the 22nd of February they reached the Fort of Girishk about two miles from the right bank of the Helmund, " having performed the journey, nearly 300 miles, in nine days, and though our baggage, cattle, camels and mules suffered much from the long march we were obliged to make, I am happy to say that we sustained no loss of property, public or private, on the road." While waiting at Girishk to hear the policy which the Government intended to pursue towards Herát, Todd learnt that his withdrawal of the Mission had proved fatal to his own interests. Lord Auckland condemned his proceedings and summarily dismissed him from political employment. The Governor-General wrote " What we have wanted in Afghanistan has been repose under an exhibition of strength, and he has wantonly and against all orders done that which is most likely to produce general disquiet, and which may make our strength inadequate to the calls upon it." The policy of the hour was that we might secure safety and peace by gratifying the avarice of a brave and fanatical race. In Herát and Afghanistan money was freely spent. Todd saw that the policy of repose was a policy of weakness and must end in disaster. He withdrew his Mission without the loss of a single life. In less than a year the head of the British Mission at Kábul was slain, and then came that memorable disaster which shook the foundation of our Indian Empire. D'Arcy Todd returned to regimental life, and he devoted with characteristic zeal and energy his whole time to the executive duties of a Captain of an artillery company. His pride in the profession dignified by danger was a solace for the hard measure dealt out to him. At the bloody contest of Ferozeshar he came to the best end a gallant soldier could know. He was struck by a round shot when leading his troop of Horse Artillery into action. The letters now printed do tardy justice to the memory of a brave soldier. They show that in the most critical affair of his career he acted as the envoy of a great government with clear vision and genuine public spirit.

The documents in this volume bear witness not only to the courage and enterprise of that valiant band of pioneer explorers who, belonging to an army which won for England an Empire, revealed to us by their labours and privations the geographical features of Central Asia, but also to the chivalrous enthusiasm and love of adventure of the officers of the old Indian Navy, a service on whose great actions time can never efface the writing. The first paper is a " Narrative of a journey from the Tower of BA-'L-HAFF on the Southern Coast of Arabia to the Ruins of NAKAB-AL-HAJAR in April 1835." " During the progress of the survey of the south coast of Arabia by the East India Company's surveying vessel the *Palinurus* while near the tower called Ba-'l-haff, on the sandy Cape of Ras-ul-Aseidá, in latitude 13° 57' north, longitude $46\frac{3}{4}°$ east nearly," the Bedouins stated that there were some extensive ruins erected by infidels and of great antiquity some distance from the coast. " It was an opportunity of seeing the country not to be lost." On the afternoon of the 29th of April 1835, Lieutenant Wellsted and Mr. Cruttenden, a midshipman, having filled their water skins, mounted their camels and set forward accompanied by two Bedouins. After proceeding along the shore for some distance they left the coast and wound their way between a broad belt of low sand hills. At midnight they were in the territories of the " Diyabi Bedouins, who from their fierce and predatory habits are held in much dread by the surrounding tribes. Small parties, while crossing this tract, are not unfrequently cut off, and we were therefore cautioned by our guides to keep a good look-out for their approach. But after spreading our boat-cloaks in the sand, we were little annoyed by any apprehensions of this nature, and slept there very soundly until the following morning, Thursday April 30th." At dawn they proceeded on their journey and after marching for a couple of hours, they ascended a ledge about 400 feet in elevation, from the summit of which they obtained an extensive but dreary view of the surrounding country. " Our route lay along a broad valley, either side being formed by the roots or skirts of a lofty range of mountains. As these extend to the northward they gradually approach each other, and the valley there assumes the aspect of a narrow deep defile. But on the other hand, the space between our present station and the sea gradually widens, and is crossed by a barrier about thirty miles in width, forming a waste of low sandy hillocks ; so loosely is the soil here piled that the Bedouins assure me that they change their outline, and even shift their position with the prevailing storms. How such enormous masses of moving sand, some of which are based on extensive tracts of indurated clay, could in their present situation become thus heaped together, affords an object of curious inquiry. They rise in sharp ridges, and are all of a horse-shoe form, their convex side to seaward. Our camels found the utmost difficulty in crossing them, and the Bedouins were so distressed that we were obliged to halt repeatedly for them. The quantity of water they drank was enormous. I observed on one occasion a party of four or five finish a skin holding as many gallons."

After noon they passed a sandstone hill called Jebel Másinah, and leaving the sandy mounds they crossed over " table ridges elevated about 200 feet from the plains below and intersected by numerous valleys, the beds of former torrents, which had escaped from the mountains on either hand. The surface of the hills was strewn with various sized fragments of quartz and jasper, several of which exhibited a very pleasing variety of colours." At 4 p.m. they descended into Wadi Meifah and halted near a well of good light water. "The change which a few draughts produced in the before drooping appearance of our camels, was most extraordinary. Before we arrived here, they were stumbling and staggering at every step; they breathed quick and audibly, and were evidently nearly knocked up, but directly they arrived near the water, they approached it at a round pace, and appeared to imbibe renovated vigour with every draught. So that browsing for an hour on the tender shoots of the trees around, they left as fresh as when we first started from the sea-coast, notwithstanding the excessive heat of the day, and the heavy nature of the road."

After an hour's halt they mounted again their camels and proceeded in a west-north-westerly direction along the valley. "It is about one and a half mile in width; the bank on either side, and the ground over which we were passing, afford abundant evidence of a powerful stream having but a short time previous passed along it." The country now began to assume a different aspect. "Numerous hamlets, interspersed amidst extensive date groves, verdant fields of jowári * and herds of sleek cattle show themselves in every direction, and we now for the first time since leaving the sea-shore fell in with parties of inhabitants. Astonishment was depicted on the countenance of every person we met, but as we did not halt, they had no opportunity of gratifying their curiosity by gazing for any length of time on us." When darkness fell the Bedouins lost track of the road and they found themselves clambering over the high embankments which enclose the jowári fields. "The camels fell so frequently while crossing these boundaries, that the Bedouins at last lost all patience, took their departure, and left us with an old man and a little boy, to shift for ourselves." As they were about to bivouac in the fields they met an old woman who guided them to "a sort of caravansera, one or more of which are usually found in the towns of Yemen, and other parts of the East" and here they slept soundly "after a hearty supper of dates and milk." The earliest dawn gave to their view fields of millet and tobacco as far as the eye could reach; their verdure of the darkest tint. "Mingled with these we had the soft foliage of the acacia, and the stately, but more gloomy, aspect of the date palm, while the creaking of the numerous wheels with which the grounds are irrigated, and several rude ploughs, drawn by oxen in the distance; together with the ruddy and lively appearance of the people (who now flocked towards us from all quarters) and the delightful and refreshing coolness of the morning air, combined to form a scene, which he who gazes on the barren aspect of the coast could never anticipate being realized."

At 6 a.m. on the 18th of May, they again mounted their camels. Three hours later they passed over a hill about 200 feet high from the summit of which the ruins were pointed out to them. An hour's march brought them to their goal.

"The ruins of Nakab-al-Hajar,† considered by themselves, present nothing therefore than a mass of ruins surrounded by a wall; but the magnitude of the stones with which this is built, the unity of conception and execution, exhibited in the style and mode of placing them together, with its towers, and its great extent, would stamp it as a work of considerable labour in any other part of the world. But in Arabia, where, as far as is known, architectural remains are of rare occurrence, its appearance excites the liveliest interest. That it owes its

---

* Jowári. Hind *jowár, juár*, one of the best and most frequently grown of the tall millets of southern countries. Yale and Burnell, *Hobson-Jobson.*

† Nakabu-l-Hajar (more correctly Nakbu'l-ḥajar) signifies "the excavation from the rock" (rather 'the stony pass').

origin to a very remote antiquity (how remote it is to be hoped the inscription will determine)*
is evident, by its appearance alone, which bears a strong resemblance to similar edifices
which have been found amidst Egyptian ruins. We have (as in them) the same inclination
in the walls, the same form of entrance, and the same flat roof of stones. Its situation and
the mode in which the interior is laid out, seem to indicate that it served both as a magazine
and a fort, and I think we may with safety adopt the conclusion that Nakab-al-Hajar, as
well as the other castle which we have discovered, were erected during that period when the
trade from India flowed through Arabia towards Egypt, and from thence to Europe, and
Arabia Felix, comprehending Yemen, Saba, and Hadramaut, under the splendid dominion
of the Sabaean or Homerite dynasty, seems to have merited the appellation she boasted of."

The day was spent in observing the ruins and the surrounding country. "It stands,"
says Lieutenant Wellsted, " in the centre of a most extensive valley called by the natives
Wadi Meifah, which, whether we regard its fertility, its populousness, or its extent, is the
most interesting geographical feature we have yet discovered on the southern coast of Arabia.
Taking its length from where it opens out on the sea-coast, to the town of 'Abbán, it is
four days' journey or seventy-five miles. Beyond this point I could not exactly ascertain the
extent of its prolongation, various native authorities fixing it from five to seven days more
throughout the whole of this extent. It is thickly studded with villages, hamlets and
cultivated grounds." He was struck with the attention paid to agriculture. "The fields are
ploughed in furrows, which for neatness and regularity would not shame an English peasant.
The soil is carefully freed from the few stones which have been strewn over it, and the whole
is plentifully watered morning and evening by numerous wells. The water is drawn up by
camels (this is a most unusual circumstance, for camels are rarely used as draught animals in
any part of the East),† and distributed over the face of the country along high embankments.
A considerable supply is also retained within these wherever the stream fills its bed. Trees
and sometimes houses are also then washed away, but any damage it does is amply compensated
for by the muddy deposit it leaves, which although of a lighter colour, and of a harder nature,
is yet almost equally productive with that left by the Nile in Egypt. But beyond what I
have noticed, no other fruits or grain are grown."

On the 1st of May at 4 p.m. they started on their return journey and travelled until
near sunset when they halted outside one of the villages and were most hospitably treated by
the inhabitants. Shortly after midnight they again started and travelled until four, when
finding they had lost their way they halted until day-light.⁕ "At this time a heavy dew was
falling, and Fahrenheit's thermometer stood at 58°; it was consequently so chilly that we were
happy to wrap ourselves up in our boat-cloaks." When the day broke they resumed their
journey and halted at a well to replenish their skins previous to again crossing the sandy
hillocks. The march tried their power of endurance to the utmost degree. "From 9 a.m.
this morning until 1 h. 30 m. we endured a degree of heat I never felt equalled. Not a breath
of wind was stirring, and the glare produced by the white sand was almost intolerable. At
2 h. our guides were so much exhausted, that we were obliged to halt for an hour. At 5 h.
30 m. we arrived at the date groves, near to 'Aïn Abú Mabuth, where there is a small
village and some fountains of pure water about fifteen feet square and three deep." At 7 h.
they arrived at the beach which they followed until they came opposite to the vessel.

---

* The inscription was interpreted by Praetorius in the *Teitschift der morgen landischen Gesellschaft*, xxvi.
(1872), p. 434. It does not determine the date.

† Their use seems to have been common in earlier times in Arabia.

" It was, however, too late to care about making a signal to those on board for a boat, and I was, moreover, desirous, from what we overheard passing between the Bedouins who were with us, to defer our departure until the morning. Any disturbance we might have with them had better happen then than during the night. We, therefore, took up our quarters amidst the sand-hills, where we could light a fire without fear of being observed by those on board." The next morning they were discovered from the ship and a boat was immediately despatched for them. " Strengthened now with the boat's crew, we settled with the Bedouins, without any other demand being made on us, and in the course of a few minutes we were on board the vessel, where we received the congratulations of all on our return." It was a bold exploit and it extended the bounds of knowledge. Mr. D. G. Hogarth in the *Penetration of Arabia** writes : " The inscription of Nakab-al-Hajar, together with two others found by officers of the *Palinurus* in the previous year on rocks at Hisn Gorab near Makalla, furnished Europe with its first decisive proof that Himyaritic records survived from the great days of Arabian civilisation. Niebuhr had heard of more than one such text in the hill country, and apparently been shown an actual copy at Mokha in 1764; but sick as he was then, he took it for cuneiform, and left to a later generation the fame of the first discovery of a class of inscriptions, now numbered by thousands, and of immense historical value. Himyaritic studies have had most important influence on our knowledge not only of ancient Arabia, but of modern. The present science of no land, except perhaps Asia Minor, owes more to explorers inspired by curiosity about the past. The officers of the *Palinurus* were the forerunners of Wrede, Arnaud, Halevy, Doughty, Huber, Euting, Glaser, Hirsch, and Bent, names with which is associated nearly all the romantic element in the history of Arabian exploration."

The next paper is an " Account of an excursion in Hadramaut by Adolphe Baron Wrede " a mere recital by Captain J. B. Haines, Indian Navy. Baron Wrede, a soldier of fortune, of good Bavarian family, who is said to have resided in Egypt, sailed from Aden disguised as a Muhammadan on the 22nd of June 1843 for Osurum.† On arriving there he travelled by land to Makalla and on the 26th June he set forth for the interior under the protection of a Bedouin of the powerful tribe Akábre.‡ Their route lay through "a continued succession of deep and narrow dales bounded by bare granitic mountains which elevate their serrated summits about 2,000 feet above the level of the sea." On the fourth day the Baron ascended the great mountain of Sidara 2,000 feet above its fellows. "The sides of this mountain are covered with aromatic plants : on arriving at its summit I found myself at the foot of two peaks called Choreibe and Farjalat, which on the right and left rose perpendicularly to the height of 800 feet above my position, and being hardly 10 minutes asunder they looked like colossal pillars of a gigantic gate." The following day he ascended some terrace-like ridges rising one above the other, " the highest of which is named Gebel Drôra."§ He was now about 8,000 feet above the level of the sea and the "view from west to north-east ranged over a yellowish plain of immense extent, on which rose every here and there conical hills and ridges. In the east the summit of the colossal Kar Seban‖ towered beyond the plain. Towards the south is seen a labyrinth of dark granitic cones and the view is lost in the misty atmosphere

---

* The Penetration of Arabia : by D. G. Hogarth, M.A., p. 148.
† Apparently a misprint for Borum or Ras Borum, in some maps written Burum.
‡ Spelt by Wrede *Aqaybere.*
§ In Wrede's narrative *Tsahura.*
‖ In Wrede Kaur *Sayban.*

of the ocean." Across this immense plain with neither bush nor village to break the monotony the road runs till it suddenly reaches the Wadi Doân. "The ravine 500 feet wide and 600 feet in depth, is enclosed between perpendicular rocks, the debris of which form in one part a slope reaching to half their height. On this slope towns and villages rise contiguously in the form of an amphitheatre; while below the date-grounds, covered with a forest of trees, the river about 20 feet broad, and enclosed by high and walled embankments, is seen first winding through fields, laid out in terraces, then pursuing its course in the open plain, irrigated by small canals branching from it. From the description you will, I trust, form a correct idea of the Wadi Doân, of the extent, situation, and character of which travellers have given such contradictory statements." The road that led down to the Wadi was of the steepest and most dangerous description. "On the right, in some places are precipices from 300 to 400 feet in depth, whilst a rocky wall on the left nearly stops up the road, leaving it scarcely 4 feet in breadth; and to add to the difficulty it is paved with pebblestones, which, having been constantly trodden by men and animals, have become as smooth as a looking glass. No kind of parapet or railing whatever has been constructed to prevent accidents."

At Choreibe the Baron was received with all possible hospitality by a local Sheikh who owing to his sanctity had great influence in the country. From thence the traveller made several expeditions into the adjoining Wadis. The account of a visit to the desert El-Ahkaf is given with equal spirit and freshness of colouring.

"After a 6 hours' journey in a north-westerly direction I reached the borders of the desert, which is about 1,000 feet below the level of the high land. A melancholy scene presented itself to my astonished sight! Conceive an immense sandy plain strewed with numberless undulating hills, which gave it the appearance of a moving sea. Not a single trace of vegetation, be it ever so scanty, appears to animate the vast expanse. Not a single bird interrupts with its note the calm of death, which rests upon this tomb of the Sabaean army. I clearly perceived three spots of dazzling whiteness, the position and distance of which I measured geometrically. 'That is Bahr el Saffi,' said my guide to me; 'ghosts inhabit those precipices, and have covered with treacherous sand the treasures which are committed to their care; every one who approaches near them is carried down, therefore do not go.' I of course paid no attention to their warnings, but requested to be led to those spots in accordance with the agreement I had made with my Bedouins. It took my camels full 2 hours' walk before we reached the foot of the high plateau, where we halted at sunset, in the vicinity of two enormous rocky blocks. On the following morning I summoned the Bedouins to accompany me to the places alluded to above, but they were not to be induced; and the dread of ghosts had obtained such complete mastery over them, that they scarcely ventured to speak; I was therefore determined to go alone, and taking with me a plummet of half a kilo's weight and a cord of 60 fathoms, I started on my perilous march. In 36 minutes I reached, during a complete lull of the wind, the northern and nearest spot, which is about 30 minutes long and 26 minutes broad, and which towards the middle takes by degrees a sloping form of 6 feet in depth, probably from the action of the wind. With the greatest caution I approached the border to examine the sand, which I found almost an impalpable powder; I then threw the plumb-line as far as possible; it sank instantly, the velocity diminishing, and in 5 minutes the end of the cord had disappeared in the all-devouring tomb. I will not hazard an opinion of my own, but refer the phenomenon to the learned who may be able to explain it, and restrict myself to having related the facts."

On his return to Choreibe the Baron accompanied by two sons of his host started on a visit to the country of Kubr-el-Hud "which historically and geologically is highly interesting." The party "rested the first night at Grein,* a considerable town on the right bank of the Wadi Doân," and on the following day the Baron arrived at Scef about an hour after his companions who had preceded him.

"A multitude of people had assembled in the town to celebrate the feast of the Sheïkh Saïd ben Issa ibn Achmudi,† who was buried in Gahdun,‡ situated in the vicinity of Seef. As soon as I had arrived among the crowd they all at once fell upon me, dragged me from my camel, and disarmed me; using me very roughly, they tied my hands behind my back and carried me, with my face covered with blood and dust, before the reigning Sultan Mohammed Abdalla ibn ben Issa Achmudi. The whole of my captors raised a horrible cry and declared me to be an English spy exploring the country, and demanded my instantly being put to death. The Sultan being afraid of the Bedouins, on whom he, like all the Sultans of the Wadi, is dependent, was about to give orders for my execution, when my guides and protectors came in haste and quieted the Bedouins' minds by means of the moral influence they had over them. In the meantime I remained confined to my room with my feet in fetters. I was imprisoned for three days, but provided with every necessary; on the evening of the third day my protectors came to me with the news that they had pacified the Bedouins under the condition that I was to return to Macalla and that I should give up all my writings. At night I concealed as many of my papers as I could, and delivered only those which were written in pencil, with which they were contented. After my notes were given up, the Sultan wished to see my luggage, from which he selected for himself whatever pleased him. The next morning I set out on my return to Macalla, which town I reached on the 8th of September, after a journey of 12 days, and thence took a boat for Aden."

Captain Haines besides forwarding the report from Wrede to the Bombay Government communicated it to the Royal Geographical Society in 1844. Mr. D. G. Hogarth, in *The Penetration of Arabia* writes: "The great Prussian geographer, Karl Ritter, then finishing the Arabian volumes of his 'Description of Asia,' welcomed Wrede's report as an immense gain to knowledge." But neither a map nor a copy of the inscription of Wadi Ubne accompanied the report. The existence of these, however, as well as of certain water-colour sketches and notes was attested by Fresnel, who had talked with the author after his return to Cairo; and this learned Arabist, as well as Ritter, Murchison and other authorities, made no doubt of Wrede's good faith. But the famous Humboldt, who met him after his return to Westphalia, called in grave question the account of the Bahr-el-Ṣaffi, quoted above, and so prevailed on scientific and public opinion that Wrede fell under general suspicion of having compiled a sensational report from hearsay; and that although Arnaud had spoken not only of knowing him before and after his exploit, but of having talked in Marib with a man of Hadramaut who had just come from his native district and seen Wrede there. His story passed into the same category as Du Couret's "Mystères du Desert," a fabulous concoction concerning Marib and the Hadramaut, put together from various sources, notably the narrative of Arnaud, and published in 1859.

---

* Grein should be Karrain.
† Issa ibn Achmudi should be Ed Ahmud.
‡ Gahdun should be Kahdum.

The result was that Wrede published no more, but emigrated to Texas, and there, is said to have killed himself about 1860. Thirteen years later Baron Heinrich von Maltzan, who had made the Mecca pilgrimage in disguise in 1860, and had since occupied himself with Arab studies, issued Wrede's journal in full, with map, inscription, notes and a vindicatory preface, but no sketches. The words of the original report appeared here and there with a mass of new matter concerning Bedouin custom, recent history, and personal adventure. Notably the passage concerning Bahr-el-Ṣaffi recurred unaltered. Von Maltzan states that he obtained the manuscript from Dr. Karl Andree into whose possession it had come. The map was reissued in a revised form, in 1872, in Petermann's "Mittheilungen."

Humboldt's attitude notwithstanding, there is no real doubt as to the authenticity of either Wrede's journey in Hadramaut, or his journal. To the first an even better authority than Arnaud and Haines bears witness, namely, Van den Berg, in the masterly essay on Hadramaut (1886), which he based on examination of numerous colonists from that country settled in Java. He states that he himself had talked to an Arab of Hanin, who was an eye-witness of the arrest of this "'Abd-al-Hud," (sic) a stranger who comported himself like a madman, and was only saved from the populace by the intervention of the Sheikh.

The next paper is the "Memoir of the South Coast of Arabia from the entrance of the Red Sea to Misena't, in 50° 43' 25" E., by Captain S. B. Haines, Indian Navy." Haines, who had few superiors in seamanship and the art of command, states that his object was "to give a description of about 500 miles of the southern coast of Arabia hitherto almost unknown— and such an account of its population, Government and commerce as was obtained, during the survey of those shores by myself and the officers of the E. I. Company's ship *Palinurus*, in the years 1834, 1835 and 1836: premising that the longitudes were determined by meridian distances, measured from the flag-staff at Bombay, assumed to be in 72° 54' 26" E., by the means of 5 and also of 8 chronometers at different times, and by quick and direct measurements."

He describes Aden, now one of the most famous stages in the world's great highway, then almost unknown to the European world. But that barren rock, as Haines reminds us, was in the time of Constantine considered "a Roman emporium, and celebrated for its impregnable fortifications, its extended commerce, and excellent ports, in which vessels from all the then known quarters of the globe might be met with." Three centuries ago the city ranked among the foremost of the commercial marts of the East. It fell to ruin in the revolutions which followed the British conquest. At the period of Haines' visit, it was a ruined village of 600 persons, "250 are Jews, 50 Banians and the rest Arabs: here is a Dowlah or Assistant-Governor, a Collector of Customs, and a guard of 50 Bedawi soldiers. The present Sultan of the Abdáli territory in which Aden is situated is an indolent and almost imbecile man, 50 years of age, who resides at Lahaj." In January 1838, Haines on behalf of the Government of Bombay demanded from the Sultan restitution for an outrage on the passengers and crew of a native craft under British colours wrecked in the neighbourhood of Aden. The Sultan undertook to make compensation for the plunder of the vessel and also agreed to sell the port and town to the English. But his son refused to ratify the agreement made with his father. On the 16th of January 1839, Aden was captured by Her Majesty's steamer *Volage*, 28 guns, and a cruiser of 10 guns, with 300 Europeans and 400 Native troops under Major Baillie.

The next paper is a "Narrative of a Journey from Mokhá to San'á by the Tarik-Esh-Shám or Northern Route in July and August 1836, by Mr. Charles J. Cruttenden, Indian

Navy." On the 13th of July 1836, accompanied by Dr. Hulton, "two servants who also acted as interpreters, and four muleteers, all well armed," Cruttenden quitted Mokha at sunset, and travelled along the shores of the Red Sea in a northerly direction about two miles from the beach. After a march of about 15 miles they halted at the small village of Ruweis. The next day, gradually diverging from the shore, they reached, after a march of twenty miles, Múshij or Maushij,* a large village "celebrated for the quantity of '*yasmin*' or jessamine, which grows there; its flower, stripped of its stalks, and strung upon thread, is daily carried to Mokha, where it is eagerly purchased by the women as ornaments for their hair. In each thicket of jessamine there is a well of pure and sweet water, so that these bowers form a very delightful retreat during the intense heat of the day." The journey next day in a north-north-east direction to the hamlet of Sherjah was through "an arid sandy plain covered with a coarse kind of grass and stunted bushes, here and there intersected by the dry bed of a mountain torrent." The next day's march from Sherjah to Zebid was through a country in many places carefully cultivated. "This valley is mentioned by Niebuhr as the 'largest and most fruitful in the whole of Tehameh;' and in a prosperous season it certainly would deserve that appellation. Four years of continued drought had, however, completely burned up the soil, and the husbandman could not but despond, when he had placed the grain in the ground, and saw no prospects of a return for his labour." At midnight they reached Zebíd, once the Capital of Tehameh.†

"Zebid is a city of moderate size, not quite so large as Mokha. It had a peculiarly gloomy appearance, owing to the dark colour of the bricks with which the houses are built, and the ruinous state of many of them. It is, I believe, considered as being the most ancient town in Tehameh. The Arabs have a tradition that it has been three times washed away by floods, with the exception of the Mesjid el Jami, or principal mosque, which certainly wears a venerable appearance.

That edifice is very large, and has an octagonal menáreh, which is ornamented with a light net-work of stone, giving it a very elegant appearance. The interior is the same as in other mosques, and consists of one large room, with the kiblah pointing out the direction of Mekkah, and several small adjoining oratories branching off in different directions, containing the tombs of deceased 'welis', or saints. The 'suk', or market, is remarkably well arranged and divided into three compartments for fish, flesh and vegetables. The supplies are ample for the garrison of 700 men, and the inhabitants, who may amount to 7,000 persons."‡

---

* Also called Mauched, in Niebuhr's *Arabia*, Vol. I.

† The territory of Yemen is naturally divided into two distinct provinces. That part which borders on the Arabic gulph is a sandy plain, which as it spreads backward, rises by a gradual ascent, into hills, and terminates in a lofty range of mountains. The place is called *Tehameh*. *Niebuhr's Travels*, Vol. I., page 263.

‡ Zebíd is situate near the largest and most fertile valley in all Tehameh. It was dry when I visited it, but in the rainy season a large river runs through it, and being, like the Nile, conducted by the canal through the neighbouring fields, communicates to them a high degree of fertility. Zebíd was once the place of a sovereign's residence and the most commercial city in all Tehameh. But, since the harbour of Ghalefka was choked up, its trade has been transferred to Beit-el-Fakeh and Mokha; and that city now retains nothing but the shadow of its former splendour. Viewed from a distance it appears to some advantage, by means of the mosques and kubbets of which it is full. Several of these mosques were erected by different Pachas who resided here, during the short period while this part of Arabia was in the possession of the Ottoman Porte. *Niebuhr's Travels*, Vol. II, page 282.

xvi

On the 17th of July they left Zebíd in the afternoon and after " a very long and fatiguing stage of nine hours and a half or nearly thirty miles, in a north-easterly direction " they reached the city of Beit-el-Fakih * an hour after midnight.

" We found Beit-el-Fakih, a large town of 8,000 persons, with a citadel of some strength in the centre of it. The town itself was unwalled, and consisted generally of a large kind of houses, built partly of brick and partly of mud, and roofed with branches of the date-tree. It is the frontier-town of the Egyptian Government, and as such is of some importance, it being the emporium of all the coffee that comes from the interior. The principal articles of trade in Zebíd and Beit-el-Fakih are piece-goods from India, consisting chiefly of coarse, blue and white cloth, English shawls, which are in great request, spices from Java, and sugar from Mauritius, which are bartered for money, wax, gums and frankincense, and a small quantity of coffee that the neighbouring Bedawis bring down in preference to sending it to the San'á market. Indian Banias are the principal merchants in the place; they are very numerous, but they have to pay a very heavy tax to the Governor, and one of them declared, with tears in his eyes, that they could not make near so much profit as in India under the Government of the English. A heavy duty is here levied upon all káfilahs (caravans) of coffee that arrive from San'á on their way to Hodeïdah or Mokha, and so vexatious are the continual demands upon the San'á merchants that it will end, in all probability, in their carrying their coffee to Aden, more especially as it is now under the British flag. The distance is nearly the same, and we frequently heard while in San'á that the merchants contemplated changing the route, if practicable: though of course, when this was said, they knew nothing of the treaty since formed by the Bombay Government with the Sultan of Aden."†

At 6 p.m. on July the 18th they left Beit-el-Fakih and "travelled in a north-east direction for eight hours, immediately towards the mountains" till they reached a pass, and crossing over a low shoulder of the mountain they "descended by a densely-wooded ravine into the beautiful valley of Senniff. Dark as it was, it was evident that the scene was changed. Tall, majestic elm trees mingled with the wide-spreading tamarind, and forming a natural avenue met our view. The babbling of a brook was heard, and the sound of our footsteps was lost in the grass. To us, who for six days had been travelling in a comparative desert, the change was delightful in the extreme." Senniff then formed a large village "built entirely of conical straw huts, with the exception of the Sheikh's house, which was a large barn-like building." Senniff, however, ranked as a market town and was also called "Suk-el-Jum'ah" or Friday market. There are seven market-towns between this place and San'á, in each of which the market is held on a different day of the week, and they are a night's ourney distant from each other. The Sheikhs of the different villages levy a tax upon all merchandise, and take the merchants under protection for the time." At Senniff they first saw the " Bedawis " of the mountains.

" They are very slightly but elegantly formed, and their average height is five feet six inches; their colour is lighter than that of the Bedawis on the southern coast, and they have

---

* Niebuhr writes: Beit-el-Fakih meaning the house or dwelling of the sage. Niebuhr's Travels, Vol. II, page 271. He also states: " I arrived early in the morning at Zebíd; having travelled in a short time five German miles, which is the computed distance between this town and Beit-el-Fakih."

† The city of Beit-el-Fakih is in a favourable situation for trade.

long, black, curling hair. The dress of the higher classes among them consists of a blue frock or shirt, with very wide sleeves, bound tight round the waist by the belt of their yambé (jambiye) or dagger, and no sash or, as it is termed in India, 'kamarband.' The dagger is different from any other that I have seen, being much longer and nearly straight. Their turban is of blue cloth, with several folds of cotton of the same colour bound round it, the Bedawi disdaining to wear the straw hat used by the cultivators of the soil. They carry a short sword with a very broad, spoon-shaped point, if I may use the term, and a long matchlock. When on horse-back they carry a very long spear, having a tuft of horse hair close to the steel head. They appear to be very quick in taking offence, but their quarrels seldom last long. I have seen a man deliberately draw his sword and endeavour to cut down another with whom he was disputing, nothing but the folds of his turban saving his life, and I have been surprised to see, the very same men quietly smoking their pipes together on the evening after the quarrel. We found them inquisitive, but not impertinently so. They would collect round us when we halted and listen to our accounts of 'Wiláyat' or England, or to what they infinitely preferred, the musical box which we had with us. Some, indeed, after hearing the box for a minute or two, would exclaim, "'Audhá Billah min Sheïtáne rájim!'—'God preserve us from the power of the devil!'—and walk away, but they were generally laughed at for their folly. They all expressed the utmost detestation of the Turks, or ' El Ahmarán ' (the red men), as they designated them, and laughed at the idea of their endeavouring to penetrate into the interior through the intricate mountain-passes."

At Senniff they were joined by the leader of a large kafilah which was awaiting them twenty miles further and two San'á merchants " mounted on two very beautiful Abyssinian mules." At day light, 20th July, they left Senniff and proceeded through a very romantic valley called "Wadi Koleibah" on their way to Hajir.

" As we gradually ascended, the scenery hourly became more striking and magnificent. The hills were thickly clothed with wood, and we recognised several trees that we had formerly seen in the Jebel Hajjïyeh of Socotra. The villages became more numerous, and the sides of the mountains being in their natural state too steep to admit of grain being cultivated, they are cut away so as to form terraces, which in many places gives them the appearance of an immense amphitheatre. The hamlets are generally built of loose stones with flat mud roofs, and, perched upon overhanging rocks as they generally are, they add considerably to the romantic beauty of the scene. After a halt of an hour during the hottest part of the day at one of these villages called Abu Kirsh, we again pursued our way up a steep ravine where we had to dismount. We here observed many large trees, one in particular, of a spongy nature, the stem about two feet six inches in diameter, and the leaves very large and of a leathery texture. It is called by the natives the 'Tolak-tree' (Ficus Bengalensis) and is generally covered with the nests of the 'baia,' a small kind of sparrow. I have seen upwards of 300 nests upon one tree. They are of a pear shape, having a long funnel-like aperture at the base, and the interior divided into two compartments, one for the male and the other for the female and her progeny."

A very steep climb brought them to the fortified serai of Hajir on the side of a mountain commanding the pass on both sides. " On another ridge immediately above Hajir is a fortress of considerable strength belonging to the Beni Dhobeïbi tribe though nominally one of the frontier garrisons of the Imam." At sunrise they again set forth and descending the ravine on the east-north-east side of Hajir, pursued their way through a broad and cultivated valley called Wadi Sehan till they reached Dakra, "a very strong hill fort on a conical shaped mountain" where it opened out into a broad plain. "The mountains on the north side of this plain are known as Jebel Harráz and on the other side they are called Jebel Burrá." In the ravine bordering on Jebel Harráz resided a small tribe who were in the habit of waylaying any unfortunate straggler and murdering him. "This dreaded part of the plain is known as Khubt ibn Deran, and we were shown several graves which remained as monuments of the cruelty and ferocity of the miscreants." The travellers halted for the night at the village of Samfur and the next day they entered the Harráz mountains.

"The valley now became much narrower, in many places not exceeding twenty yards in width, while the mountains on either side rose to the height of 1,200 or 1,400 feet above the plain, thickly wooded to within 200 feet of their summit, where they presented a barren sheet of grey limestone rock. Under a huge mass which had fallen and completely blocked up the valley, we found a coffee-house and two or three small huts. Understanding that there was a coffee plantation in the neighbourhood, and of the very best quality, we gladly availed ourselves of the suggestion of Sheïkh el Jerádí, and halted there for the day. A scrambling walk over the before-mentioned rock, by means of steps cut in it, brought us to the coffee-plantation of Dórah.* It was small, perhaps not covering half an acre, with an embankment of stone round it to prevent the soil from being washed away."

They found the "fig, plantain, orange, citron, and a little indigo growing among the coffee." The following morning the travellers left Dórah and took the road to Mofḥak.

"The valley of Dórah through which we travelled in an east-north-east direction, opened, after three or four miles, upon a large plain, in the midst of which was the village of Seïhan.† The country was the same as that we had hitherto passed through, though not so mountainous. At three we reached the village of Mofḥak,‡ and found good quarters in a simsereh. This village of 50 huts is situate on the crest of an oblong hill, about 300 feet high,§ the sides of which are too steep for any beast of burden to ascend. It presents the appearance of an immense fort, and with a little care might be rendered impregnable. We here found another plantation of coffee of the 'Uddeïni sort. The trees were about twelve feet in height; but, owing to a scarcity of water in the immediate neighbourhood, looked sickly and faded."

The next day they made a short march of four hours to the village of El Hudein ¶ from whence they sent on a courier to Saná with a letter of introduction to one of the principal merchants. On the morning of July the 25th they set forth and ascended gradually for about two hours, when they reached the ridge of the mountain, and from the summit a most magnificent view burst upon them.

---

* Coffee-plantage Eddóra —Niebuhr, *Reise* I, 433.

† Sehân, Niebuhr, Voy. I, 432.

‡ "We travelled this day onward to Mofhak, a small town situate on the summit of a precipitous hill. The houses in which the travellers lodge stand at the foot of the hill." *Niebuhr, Descr.*, page 250, *Voy*.

"An hour or so later we passed under the strange fortress of Mofhak grandly situated on the pinnacle of a rock some five hundred feet above the valley; and, leaving a large encampment of Turkish troops on our left, once more began to ascend." *A Journey through the Yemen.* By Walter B. Harris (1893).

§ According to Glaser 1690 meters above sea level.

¶ According to Glaser (Petermann's Mittheilungen, 1886, page 39) its correct name is Al-Hauḍaim ('the two cisterns').

"The hills formed an immense circle, like the crater of a huge volcano, and the sides of which from the top to the bottom were cut regularly into terraces. I counted upwards of 150 in uninterrupted succession; and the *tout-ensemble* was most extraordinary. At the bottom of this basin ran a small stream, which, from the height at which we were, looked like a silver thread. Small hamlets each with its little white mosque, were scattered over the sides of the mountains, and added greatly to the beauty of the scene." * After skirting "the edge of this natural amphitheatre" they reached a long table land "very barren and stony," that extended to the village of Motteneh. Here they halted for the night. The next day they continued their march over a table land till they reached the village of Assur "seated at the eastern verge of this plateau, and saw the city and beautiful valley of San'á stretched before us."

Cruttenden was the first to reveal to the European world the beauty and prosperity of the Yemen Capital, the character of its architecture and the grandeur of its public buildings. The two palaces of the Imam are well described.

"The Imam of San'á has two large palaces with extensive gardens adjoining; the whole walled round and fortified. The first and largest is called Bustán el Sultán, or the Garden of the Sultán; the other, which is the most ancient, Bustán el Metwokkil. They are built of hewn stone, plastered over with a grey-coloured mortar, having the windows and cornices of a bright white colour, which gives the house a very light and airy appearance. Fountains appear to be indispensable in the houses at San'á, and in the Bustán el Metwokkil there are several. The Imam has a stud of very fine horses that are always piqueted in front of the palace. They come from the desert of Jóf, to the north of San'á, and for the first four years of their life rarely taste anything but dates and milk. They are larger than the 'Nejdi' breed, but I believe are not considered as inferior to them in symmetry or speed."

He then gives a picturesque account of the visit of the Imam to the great mosque on Friday.

"Troops were called into the town to assist at the ceremony and during the time of the procession the city gates were, as usual, closed. About fifty armed Bedawis formed the commencement of the cavalcade. They walked six abreast, and sang in chorus. The principal people of the town followed, mounted on horseback, each carrying a long spear with a small pennon. The Imam next followed on a splendid white charger, and very superbly dressed. He held in his hand a long spear with a silver head, having the shaft gilt. His left hand rested on the shoulder of a confidential eunuch, and two grooms led his horse. A very magnificent canopy, much like an umbrella in form, was carried over his head, having the fringe ornamented with silver bells. The Seïf el Khalifah came next, having a canopy held over his head likewise, but smaller and less costly. The commander of the troops and the Imam's relations and principal officers followed, and about 100 more Bedawis closed the procession. On reaching the square in front of the palace, the footmen ranged themselves round it, and the Imam, followed by his nearest relations, galloped repeatedly round the square, brandishing

---

* "The track was leading us along the summit of a mountain top, which to the north looked straight down into a great valley, thousands of feet below. What a wonderful valley it was, full of coffee-groves, and luxuriating in all the glories of gorgeous vegetation, amongst which banana-leaves could be plainly distinguished, waving their great green heads! Amongst all this verdure, clinging as it seemed to the mountain-sides, were villages each crowned by its *burj* or fort, the whole perched on some over-hanging rock." *A Journey through the Yemen.* By Walter B. Harris, page 327.

his spear, and making a feint of attacking the nearest horsemen. After this had lasted some minutes, the Imam stood still in the centre of the square, and the people rushed from every quarter to kiss his knees. He then retired towards the palace, and as he passed under the archway, a gun was fired to give notice that the ceremony was at an end."

Cruttenden discusses the physical features of the country and the climate and estimates the population to be about 40,000 and " in the four towns of the valley, *viz.*, San'á, Rōdah, Wadi Dhar, and Jeráf there are not less than 70,000 people."* The merchants formed the principal body of men in the town. " They are generally wealthy and live in good style. The Banias are also numerous, but they are compelled, like the Jews, to conceal what they really possess and however wealthy they may be, to put on an outward show of abject poverty." The Jews of the Yemen are believed to have come from India, and the ghetto was then as it is now separate from the city.†

Cruttenden and his companions went about the city in their uniforms, and not only was no insult offered them but great courtesy was shown them by the inhabitants, as he states in his clear description of the town.

" The old city of San'á is walled round and, including Bïr el Azab, is 5½ miles in circuit: it has some guns, but in a very bad condition. The houses are large, and the windows of those of the higher classes are of beautiful stained glass. A handsome stone bridge is thrown across the principal street, as in wet weather a stream of water runs down it. The streets are narrow, though broader than those of Mokhá and Zébíd. Great hospitality was shown us on entering their houses; we were always pressed to stay, and never allowed to go without taking a cup of coffee, or rather of an infusion of the coffee husk, called ' Keshr ; ' for, strange to say, though in the heart of the coffee country, coffee is never taken as a beverage, being considered as too heating.‡ The infusion of the husk is very palatable; and we found it much more refreshing, and nearly as powerful a stimulant as the infusion of the bean itself."

During their rambles through the city, the travellers discovered some Himyaritic inscriptions and copied them on the spot. "On close inquiry, we found that the stones had been brought from Máreb, about two days journey to the north-east, and that there were many more to be found there. The longest inscription was on a slab of white marble, and, when we saw, it served to cover a hole in the roof of a mosque. A bribe of a dollar had a magical effect on the scruples of a servant, and the stone was brought to our lodgings that night to be copied and carefully replaced before daylight." The two travellers determined to visit Máreb, but they could not accomplish it, as the Imam grew jealous of their proceedings and Dr. Hulton was smitten with a severe illness. As soon as he could be moved they left San'á (20th August), after having resided there for a month. In fourteen days they reached the gates of Mokha. Dr. Hulton died very shortly after he reached the *Palinurus*. He was a man of considerable

---

* " The population of San'á, although there is no official census to base one's calculation upon, probably numbers some forty or fifty thousand, of whom twenty thousand are said to be Jews." *A Journey through the Yemen*, by Walter B. Harris, page 312.

" Manzoni's estimate of the population is half that of Harris, made after a lapse of fifteen years, and is probably still the more correct." *The Penetration of Arabia.* By D. G. Hogarth, page 198.

† " The principal artizans are the Jews : these amount to about 3,000 persons, and live in a quarter of the city appropriated to them." *Cruttenden's journey*, page 250.

A chapter on the Yemen Jews is given by Maltzan Reiser in Arabia, i, 172-181. He holds that their condition has been improved owing to the growth of British influence.

‡ Glaser from " Hudaida to San'á " in Petermann's Mittheilungen, 1886, page 2, confirmed this.

scientific attainments, an intrepid traveller, and of a modest and unselfish nature, which caused him to be loved by all his shipmates.*

The last paper in this volume is a "Narrative of a Journey to Shoa." On the 24th of April 1841, the Secretary to the Bombay Government writes as follows to Captain W. C. Harris, Bombay Engineers.

"I am directed to inform you that the Honourable the Governor in Council having formed a very high estimate of your talents and acquirements, and of the spirit of enterprise and decision, united with prudence and discretion, exhibited in your recently published Travels 'Through the Territories of the Chief Moselekalse to the tropic of Capricorn', has been pleased to select you to conduct a Mission, which the British Government has resolved to send to Sahela Selássie, the King of Shoa, in Southern Abyssinia, whose capital, Ankóbar, is computed to be about four hundred miles inland from the port of Tajura, on the African Coast."

The embassy was composed of Captain W. C. Harris; Captain Douglas Graham, Bombay Army, Principal Assistant; Assistant-Surgeon Rupert Kirk, Bombay Medical Service; Dr. J. R. Röth, Natural Historian; Lieutenant Sydney Horton, H. M. 49th Foot, as a volunteer; Lieutenant W. C. Barker, Indian Navy; Assistant-Surgeon Impey, Bombay Medical Service; Mr. Martin Bernatz, Artist; Mr. Robert Scott, Surveyor and Draftsman; Mr. J. Hatchatoon, British Agent at Tajura. A German Missionary, a Mr. Krauff, acted as Interpreter. The escort consisted of ten European soldiers, Volunteers from the Bombay Artillery, and Her Majesty's 6th Foot. The presents and baggage required 180 camels, and besides they had 33 mules and 17 horses. The embassy first disembarked at Aden, and it was not till the 17th of May that it reached Tajura, a deep bay which runs fifty miles inland at the entrance of the Red Sea. Here they had to stay for some time, in order to procure the necessary number of camels to carry the presents, and they did not commence their journey till the evening of the 1st of June 1841, "the anniversary of one of our greatest naval battles, and hence we considered that we had launched into the desert under rather favourable auspices." The road from Tajura to Shoa crosses the desert for two hundred miles. Shortly after leaving Tajura they encamped on the borders of Bahar Assal, the Salt lake, "six hundred feet below the level of the sea."

"Never shall I forget this day. The heat was indeed fearful, the glare oppressive; in vain we looked for shelter, a few stunted acacias, scattered here and there, as if in very mockery of nature, was all that could be obtained, and even there we were not allowed to remain under in peace, for both camels and mules, throwing off their accustomed fear of the 'lords of the creation,' crowded together and were with difficulty kept off." At 11 p.m. they departed from "the furnace" and had not proceeded far " before man and beast began to sleep by the wayside from sheer exhaustion: in vain every encouragement was held out, their sufferings were too great."

"Our road lay over a broken mass of lava for some distance, and again we gradually ascended, till as the day dawned the foremost of our party arrived at some small pools of water the most refreshing man ever tasted. A supply was instantly sent back to the sufferers, and the party pushed forward, descending again to the south-east corner of the Salt Lake. We there

---

* An account of Mr. Cruttenden's visit to San'á was published in Volume II of the transactions of the Bombay Geographical Society. It differs from the present text, which is the same as the account published in Volume VIII, Journal of the Royal Geographical Society.

B 903—6

crossed over a mass of salt hard as ice, and at length reached our halting-place about eight o'clock in the morning. The whole party, however, did not get up till late in the afternoon."

A low belt of hills forms the western bank of this field of salt and opens into a mountain ravine. They proceeded up this ravine till they reached Goongoonteh, their halting place. For two days and a half "our cattle had not tasted a drop of water. A small stream of water issuing from some hot springs in the head of the ravine was murmuring along when we arrived: nothing could restrain our animals from making to it: they would not wait to have their bridles removed." The dire Tehameh, an iron-bound waste, had been passed. The gloomy ravine was not a verdant spot. No forage or fuel could be got there. But the animals and men had suffered so greatly that it was determined to halt there for an extra day. Every precaution was taken against being surprised by the Bedouins. "A portion of our Native escort was stationed some yards in advance, and an English sentinel kept watch and ward in our immediate vicinity." All passed quietly the first night. During the day they found shelter in some caves by the side of the ravine, and in the evening moved down to their encampment. The same precautions were taken. "An hour before midnight a sudden and violent sirocco scoured the Wady, the shower of dust and pebbles raised by its hot blast being followed by a few heavy drops of rain with a calm as still as death."* At three in the morning the stillness was broken by a loud scream. Hurrying to the spot Harris and Graham found Sergeant Walpole and Corporal Wilson, H.M. 6th Foot, lying weltering in their blood. "One had been struck with a crease in the carotic artery immediately below the ear, and the other stabbed through the heart; whilst speechless beside their mangled bodies was stretched a Portuguese follower with a frightful gash across the abdomen." Three men belonging to a tribe on the opposite coast had crept down the ravine and when the sentry was at the other end of his beat had swiftly committed the foul deed. The object was not plunder but to prove their manhood. ".For every victim, sleeping or waking, that falls under the murderous knife of one of these fiends in human form, he is entitled to display a white ostrich plume in the woolly hair, to wear on the arm an additional bracelet of copper, and to adorn the hilt of his reeking crease with yet another stud of silver or pewter—his reputation for prowess and bravery rising amongst his clansmen in proportion to the attendant circumstances."† As the day broke, were borne enveloped in a blood-stained winding sheet the remains of the two soldiers to the graves dug by the Native escort. A portion of the burial service was read and three volleys of musketry, the soldiers' last tribute, rang among the dark recesses of the defile. Then the party wound up the ravine till they reached their halting place at Aloolie—signifying fresh water. "To us this place appeared a perfect paradise after what we had suffered in crossing the Tehameh, a large pool of water teeming with wild duck, which ere long garnished our table."

On the 10th of July, after weary marches through the low country of the Adail, they encamped on the eastern bank of the river Hawash. "As we approached its banks the country gradually improved, and game became abundant. Here on its banks the vegetation was most luxuriant, and our weary animals at length, for the first time since quitting the coast, had abundance of grass." However, on crossing the stream, the country again displayed much the same character as to the eastward—a barren desert. The climate was, however,

---
* *The Highlands of Aethiopia* by Major Cornwallis Harris, Vol. I, p. 123.
† *The Highlands of Aethiopia* by Major Cornwallis Harris, Vol. I, p. 125.

much cooler. On the 14th of July they arrived at the frontier station of his Most Christian Majesty Sahela Selássie (Bounty of the Trinity) " King of Shoa, Efat and the Galla—a high-sounding title."

"Verily, I do think that there is not a more inhospitable desert than we have just traversed. *On one occasion only*, on the banks of the Hawash did we ever have grass, wood and water at the same time; out of seventeen horses one only was in a state fit to mount; our mules were almost as bad, for, poor animals! on several occasions they were two and even three days without water. All that can be said of the country is that it is worthy of its possessors, a wild race, whose hand is against every man, who fear neither God nor man—indeed, whose whole life is spent in bloodshed, murders of the most atrocious kind being of daily occurrence. Nature appears to have set her curse upon the country and its inhabitants, for it is scorched and burnt up, the greater portion having been at one time subject to volcanic action, as thermal waters are to be found scattered all about the place. The inhabitants are liars and murderers from their youth."

The embassy had now mounted two thousand feet above the level of the sea, and their camp was pitched at the foot of the lofty mountains of Shoa, which towered some six thousand feet above them. On the 17th having delivered over all the baggage to the authorities, to be carried on men's shoulders, they began their ascent of the Abyssinian Alps.

"What a contrast to the country we had just left! Our road wound round the sides of the mountains, across running streams of the most clear and delicious water—a great treat to us—the hills crowned with villages whose inhabitants greeted us with loud shouts of joy, for we were 'the King's strong strangers,' and accompanied by the Royal troops, the principal of his Governors, and the General of the Gunmen. Our hearts felt quite light as we wound our way cheerily along, for all around smiled peace, and the country had a refreshing appearance. They had had a few showers, though the rainy season had not fairly set in, which caused the green grass to show itself; we heard the warbling of birds; verily it appeared to us a perfect paradise. Who has not read of the happy valley in Johnson's Rasselas? We fancied that he had chosen this very spot for the scene of his tale."

After ascending three thousand feet they halted at the market town of Alio Amba upon the crest of a scarped prong formed by the confluence of two mountain streams. Here they had to stay in some " wretched barn-looking place swarming with vermin" until the 1st August when his Most Christian Majesty consented to receive them at his private residence at Muklewans " only about three miles from this, and about the same distance from his Capital." His Majesty had repented of having invited so large a body of " gypsies" as they termed them. Many were the tales told of their conquests of foreign lands. "True they are few in number," said they, " but they have with them guns, and fire (alluding to the rockets), which, if thrown upon the ground, will destroy whole armies." The next day the Mission was ushered into the Royal presence. "The apartment was a rude thatched building." In a sort of alcove reclined His Majesty, supported by silken cushions. He " had no head-dress or covering for his feet; his hair was frizzled up and well greased; he had silken small clothes, and the usual Abyssinian robe, but adorned with several broad red stripes at each end and also in the middle. He had evidently determined to receive us with reserve, and, as we entered, he glanced at each of us with his one eye (be it observed that he had lost the use of the other), returned our salutation in a scarce audible tone, and then begged us to be covered and seated. We had previously sent our chairs, which were placed in front of the throne." After the letter from the Bombay Government had been delivered, and the usual compliments, the presents were brought.

"A magnificent musical clock, musical boxes, a Brussells carpet, dress, swords, silks, muslins, Delhi scarves, *ad infinitum*, were displayed before the King, to each of which the answer given was "May God reward thee! May God restore it unto thee!" with the utmost gravity. The European escort then made their appearance and went through the manual and platoon exercise. At the moment when the movement was made to receive cavalry, the King exclaimed, "Ah, that will do here, but would they thus kneel before the cavalry of the Galla?" They retired and brought in the muskets; hitherto the King had retained his gravity, but about the time the hundredth musket, with its bright polished bayonet, was laid before him, he gave vent to his feelings in a prolonged shrill whistle. "Ye gods! what an unkingly act! Shortly after we took leave, and were that evening regaled with all the luxuries the royal kitchen afforded." The next day they had a private audience of the King, when the remainder of the costly gifts were spread out for His Majesty's acceptance, with the ammunition and the three pounder field-piece. "To initiate him into the use thereof we had some artillery practice in the evening, at which he appeared perfectly delighted." On the 5th of August, after having another private audience, they took leave and set forth for Ankobar, which they reached after a ride of about an hour along very narrow pathways. Here they were detained, "scarcely ever moving a yard from the house," until the 23rd of September when they were invited to pay His Majesty a visit at Debra Berhan, about twenty miles from Ankobar, to be present at a review of a portion of his troops. On reaching Debra Berhan they were graciously received "and accommodated with bread, raw meat, and mead in abundance." The review commenced "by Itoo Kotama bringing forth his gallant band of gunmen, in number about six hundred, chanting forth songs in praise of the 'Bounty of the Trinity,' and shouting defiance to his enemies, the worthy General, in his cracked voice, screaming 'Behold in me the King's great warrior! I have slain the Galla till their blood flowed like water! I am the King's slave' to which his worthy followers replied by a loud shout of 'Wo—Wo—Wo' in a kind of chant." Having discharged their muskets and matchlocks they advanced to the foot of the throne, bared themselves to the waist and fell prostrate to the earth. They then arose, and marched past, shouting and singing as they came.

"These are the King's favourite troops, and were the only portion allowed to come up to the very foot of the throne, the others not being permitted to approach nearer than three hundred yards. Itoo Kotama was clad in silken small clothes, his loins girded up with some sixty or eighty yards of cloth, wearing a particoloured chintz waistcoat, and the skin of the lion buttoned round the neck and hanging over the left shoulder. He had a silver-sheathed sword, his shield (carried by a young man, his shield-bearer) was studded with silver devices, the Cross predominating. On his arm he wore a silver gauntlet, and armlets of the same metal and ivory above his elbow, and his appearance altogether was the very type of the savage warrior."

Thirteen Governors passed by in the same order as the matchlock men with their several contingents and lastly the Galla Cavalry, under Itoo Maretch, which had been drawn up on one side of the ground.

"These were the finest body of men, in number about two thousand. They came forward at a hard gallop in a double line, and pulled up so suddenly that their horses were almost thrown upon their haunches. 'I have slain men!' shouted forth Itoo Maretch as he approached to make his obeisance; he then galloped off along the line of his followers, and returning shouted 'I am the King's slave! Behold in me the Father of Warriors!' and then throwing his spears at some imaginary foe (which were nimbly picked up by his shield-bearer) and throwing his sword, his men gave a loud shout, then galloped past, and were soon lost in a cloud of dust."

Itoo Maretch was dressed like the Infantry General, but in addition to the ornaments worn by the latter, he had the "Akoo Dama," which was worn only by the bravest of the brave. "It is a silver bar which is fastened across the forehead, and to which there is appended a row of silver chains reaching below the eyes, and at each extremity of the bar down to the shoulders, imparting a peculiarly wild appearance to their swarthy features." Shortly before the Galla Cavalry advanced the European escort were requested to take their places by the gun, in order that "the King's strong strangers" might be seen and to fire the gun quickly. "We fired about thirty rounds, till the little gun danced about in fine style. These valleys had never before been disturbed by the roar of cannon. Great astonishment was depicted on every countenance." A few days after the review the envoy informed the King that he had been ordered to return to his country and requested his assistance to enable him to return to Harrar. The King gave his consent to his returning and promised him a letter to the Emir of that country. Barker went back to Ankōbar to prepare for his journey to Harrar and the King set forth on his expedition against a tribe of the Gallas. The success of the foray was complete. "The royal forces fell upon them by surprise, and it is said slew about four thousand men, women and children, drove off all their cattle, to the number of nearly twelve thousand, and destroyed the whole of their crops by fire." On the 18th of November the King made his triumphal entry into Ankobar. "Not having my uniform with me I could not witness it. For the first time the glorious ensign of old England was displayed at the *Residency*." The envoy reminded the King of his promise to give him a letter of introduction and after a considerable pressure the document was drafted. "He tried to dissuade me from attempting the journey, and begged I would remain in his country; but at length, finding me determined, he carefully perused the letter to the Emir of Harrar which had been written in Amharic, having a translation in Arabic, ordered his seal to be brought, and attached it to the document." The letter was as follows:

"May this letter from Sahela Selassie, King of Shoa, Efat, and the Galla, reach the hands of Aboo Bekr, the Ruler of Harrar! How are you? Are you well? Are you quite well? I am well. The bearer of this letter is Captain Barker; he is an Englishman and commands a vessel in the sea of Tajura. He has been ordered by his Queen to return soon to his country; now, in order that he might do this, he wished to return by the nearest road, and begged of me a letter of recommendation to you. I am thinking of him very much; and I wish that on his road, and when he passes through your country, nothing should do him harm. I therefore wish that you should protect him perfectly, and assist him in all that he wants. The love which you show to him I will consider as shown to myself, and it will give me pleasure to hear that he has reached the sea-coast in safety by your assistance. He came to me by order of his Queen, and I am in great friendship with her; if you will show kindness to him, my name as well as yours will be honoured beyond the Great Sea. A traveller when in a far country has no father, no mother, no relations; it is therefore becoming in the watchmen of kingdoms, in the Kings and Rulers of Provinces, that they should protect travellers and assist them in all that they desire. If they do this they will be blessed by God and honoured by men. I command you this; I command you this."

Having obtained this important document Barker returned to the village of Alio Amba about five miles from Ankōbar where he had resided for some time. It was chiefly inhabited by Harrar Merchants, " who reside here until they have disposed of their merchandise, and then return with slaves to their native country, a fresh swarm taking their place." It was these Harrar merchants who raised the greatest obstacles against Barker travelling through their country. However, by patience, courage and tact the difficulties were surmounted, and on the 15th January, he left Alio Amba "accompanied for several miles by the villagers, who evinced great sympathy with us, many of them crying bitterly." The sailor had won their hearts by attending on them when sick and curing their simple ailments. A caravan left Alio Amba at the same time for Tajura, and Barker joined it. It consisted of about fifteen of the natives of that place, who had with them fifty camels laden with provision for the journey, about fifty male and twenty female slaves (mostly children of from six to ten years of age). After a tedious journey of eight days, they arrived at the lake Yoor Erain Murroo where they fell in with a great number of Bedouins, "who were watering their cattle, to the amount of at least three thousand head of horned cattle, and sheep innumerable." Datah Mahomed, to whose charge Barker had been entrusted, was fortunately their Chief, and he invited Barker and the caravan to pay a visit to his village. "We accordingly set out thither, and found him, with the principal people of his tribe, seated under the shade of a venerable acacia, indulging in a luxurious feast of raw beef. Six bullocks were slaughtered immediately on our arrival and we were desired to 'eat and be merry'." The next day they were summoned to the dwelling of the old chief to witness his marriage with a new wife. They found the bride "a comely maiden, well formed and of moderate stature" about fourteen years of age, seated on a wicker frame about six inches from the ground.

"After the opening chapter of the Korán had been recited by a venerable sage, to which all devoutly responded 'Ameen,' a large bowl of sour milk was produced, thickly sprinkled with red pepper, not at all savoury in smell or pleasing to the eye. What was the surprise of the old man when I declined partaking thereof! Not drink sour milk! 'There is no God but God! God is great!' he exclaimed; however, he had the civility to send for a bowl of fresh milk, and I partially regained his favour by the ample justice I did to this, almost equal to the relish evinced by my Tajuran friends to the former bowl. Fresh ghee (clarified butter) was then handed round, with which all anointed their bodies, and we then took our departure."

Soon after the ceremony the old chief returned the visit and said to Barker, "My son, you see I have treated you with great honour, I have feasted you with meat and milk in plenty; now I want a mule and plenty of cloth, for all my people want cloth and as yet you have given me nothing." I became angry, and told him that I had given him the horse and cloth, etc.; he smiled and said "Yes, I know that, but I want a mule; my horse has been stolen." He also said he wanted some blue cloth, and he took a great fancy to my Arab cloak, my only covering at night. My portmanteau being torn, he thrust his fingers in between the outer leather and the lining, and said, with a most avaricious grin, "What have you here?" Upon this I arose and said, "I see now that you are no longer my father. The Wulasma Mohamed said you would be kind to me; is this your kindness?" He begged pardon, and said, "Don't be afraid, my son; I will take nothing but what you give freely. People have been telling you bad things of me, but don't believe them. I am an old man now, and have given up plundering people."

The Bedouin Chief dared not infringe the rites of hospitality so sacred in the East. "Had we not feasted together at Gouchoo, had we not eaten salt together, this man would assuredly have plundered me, aye, and have thought as little of murdering me as of killing any animal by whose death he would have been benefited." At 2 p.m. on the 26th of January "the welcome order was given to load the camels and prepare once more to move forward." But Captain Barker had to abandon all idea of reaching Harrar. " By remaining with the Bedouins I should but be bandied about from one chief to another, and the constant demands of Datah Mahomed for tobacco, cloth, etc., in fact, for all that his covetous eyes lighted upon did not give me any encouragement to trust myself with him after the departure of the Tajurans." The Tajurans also all begged of him not to think of remaining with the Bedouins. "Think not of your property alone" cried out Ibrahim, " but also of your life and the lives of your servants. Remember the belly of the 'Bedoo' is never filled. Come on with us; we will share with you our provisions and travel with speed." And the Tajurans proved true to their word. After six days' journey, Barker, leaving his luggage with the Kafilah people, pushed forward for Tajura with a small party. It consisted of " Ibrahim, the Ras-el-Kafilah; Deeni, the interpreter; a Bedouin of the Assoubah tribe (a sub-tribe of the Adaiel) who rejoiced in the designation of 'Adam the Black'; John, a Greek; Adam, an Indian; Mahomed, an Arab (my servants); and myself; altogether seven, all mounted on mules and well armed." At a rapid pace they passed through the Wady Dalaboyeh and descended on the 4th of February to the plains of Gingaddi.

"As we had to pass near several encampments, the fires of which we could see in the distance, we halted and sent the Bedouin ' Adam the Black ' forward as a scout, to ascertain whether they were friends or foes. Dismounting from his mule, stripping himself perfectly naked, and grasping his crease or dagger in the right hand and his shield in the left, the wily savage crept along on his hands and knees. We awaited in breathless suspense the return of our scout : at last Ibrahim whispered to me 'They have found him out; let us go forward : he is a Bedoo and will take care of himself.' We had moved but a few yards, however, when he was in the midst of us—he had approached so cautiously. The encampment nearest to us, he said, was one of the Debeni. Although a friendly tribe, it was deemed advisable to pass them as quietly as we could. We succeeded in doing so without disturbing one of them, and having got a respectful distance by half-past eight we halted in a clear space, so that we could see any one approaching."

The next day they crossed the Salt Lake not by the route which the embassy had taken ; they " struck off to the right, over broken masses of lava and volcanic remains, and had a splendid view of the lake from summit of the hills. At one o'clock I found the heat so very oppressive that I was obliged to halt for a couple of hours under the shade of some detached rocks. The wind was blowing with such violence that it considerably retarded our progress, so that we did not arrive at Dahfurri till sunset. Here we found a large pool of fresh water, clear as crystal ; this we must have passed, on going to Shoa, within a few hundred yards, at a time when we suffered so much from the want of water, and only four miles from our halting-place at the Salt Lake. However, Ibrahim declared to me that at that time it was a mere pool of filth, but that the late rains had filled it as we found it now."

Having filled their water-skins, they retired to some distance from the pool, and kept a most vigilant watch till one o'clock next morning, when they started again, "so as to clear the Ra Esa pass before day-light," as they had heard that the Bedouins were hovering about its vicinity, on the look out for their customary toll from the Kafilah.

"As we wound up this dreadful pass the barking of dogs betrayed the vicinity of the Bedouins—indeed they were encamped but a short distance above us. Not a word was spoken, but each urged his mule forward by sundry kicks, and as the day dawned we ascended to the elevated plain of Wady Lissan, where we halted for about two hours, and shared the last of our provisions about a handful of parched grain and a cup of coffee! Indeed we were so hard pushed that we were glad to eat some *jowari* or millet we had kept for the mules."

Shortly after resuming their journey they got a glimpse of the sea. "How delighted I was! 'All danger is over now!' I exclaimed; 'now I am at home!'" On Sunday morning, the 6th of February, they reached Tajura where they were "received with demonstrations of joy by rich and poor." The Sultan, who took Barker to his house, was most civil and asked him whether he would remain at Tajura till the arrival of the East India Company's vessel from Aden or whether he would hire a boat. "I replied that my desire was to return instantly to Aden, but that I had neither funds nor food, and further that the Bedouin objected to going across to Aden and I had not the means of paying him." Upon this the Sultan said "Do as seems best to you: the town is yours if you wish to stay; if you wish to go, there is Aboo Bekr's boat at your service; and as for the Bedouin, I will advance what you will require for him. Your food I will also care for, and if you go to Aden I will take care of your mules till you return or send for them." The money was advanced, and on the morning of the 10th of February Barker set sail from Tajura and about noon anchored in Mersa Munger Duffa, on the opposite coast. "In the evening I went on shore to bathe. A number of the Eesah had collected, and were disposing of their goods, to the no small advantage of the Tajurans. The instant they saw me they shouted out ' The Lord preserve us from Satan the stoned!' and were seized with such a panic at the sight of a white man that they one and all took flight, and it was some time before they could be persuaded to return." On the 15th of February the boat anchored at Berbera. Barker was carried ashore as he was suffering from a severe attack of fever. An Arab merchant received him in his home and "if kindness could have cured me I should have soon been well." On the evening of the 21st Barker embarked in one of the boats belonging to the hospitable merchant and early on the 25th he anchored "under Seerah southward of Aden."

"I had so far rallied that I was enabled to land and walk up to the house of the Political Agent, Captain Haines. I was quite worn-out, and this, together with the fact of my having adopted the Turkish costume, and presenting a wild appearance from not having allowed the razor to touch my face for upwards of ten months, prevented his recognising me for some time. For many subsequent days and nights I could not sleep. It is impossible to describe the state of mind I was in from the constant excitement of the past five weeks."

Here ends the last of the tales of the exploits of the soldiers and sailors of the East India Company and these plain narratives of facts show that in searching the most opposite corners and quarters of the Eastern World they faced the dangers and distresses which beset them with calm courage and made good use of the opportunities of their calling for the furtherance of knowledge.

ITINERARY FROM YEZD TO HERÁT

AND

FROM HERÁT TO KÁBUL VIÂ KANDÁHÁR.

ITINERARY FROM YEZD TO HERAT AND FROM HERAT TO KÂBUL VIÂ KANDA'HA'R.

The distance from Yezd to Herat is reckoned at 200 pharsacs.[1]

The direction of the route is N.E. as far as the town of Toon, from thence generally E. with a little northing, if the road by Gownabad is followed, but if you pass by Birdjan it is S.E. as far as that place, and from thence N.E. to Herát.

Caravans of camels use this route, they take from 35 to 50 days in performing it; horsemen however, do it easily in 12 or 15 days. The road is in reality nothing more than a well defined foot-path, but as it generally passes over a level country, it could be easily traversed by wheeled carriages as far as the city of Toon. There are caravanserais at each halting place, erected by pious persons for the accommodation of Persian travellers, who go on pilgrimage to the tomb of Emaum Reza in Mushed, the capital of Khorássán. You also meet with at certain distances, wells that have been sunk for passers-by to allay their thirst; but owing to the want of care on the part of the Government they are almost all at the present day unfortunately filled up.

The plains to pass over are dry barren deserts, and seem from a distance like a sea of salt; of this description are those of Ali-abad, Shah-abbas, Shiardil and Garidj, where one meets with considerable tracts of country, the earth strongly tasting of nitre and salt; the only vegetation to be observed is a few saline plants. You have also to cross some low ranges of hills of an easy access as far as the sandy mountains called "*Rég Shuturán*", which are about fifty pharsacs N.E. of Yezd. You traverse the dependencies of this latter city, keeping on your right the great desert of Kabis or Kermania, having on your left the salt desert, shown in the present maps of Persia, as being bounded by the cities of Kochan, Kayn, Sernman, Torkis, Toon and Tabos, and which the inhabitants state to be twenty-four pharsacs in length and breadth. The mountains of Bix Barrik are seen in the middle of this desert, and what is not least remarkable, is that they are studded with villages, whose cultivated lands (sufficiently productive), offer a pleasing contrast to the frightful wastes which surround them.

On leaving the mountains of "*Rég Shuturán*" you enter upon the eastern possessions of Khorássán, which extend as far as Herát. You first pass over the dependencies of Tubbas,

---

[1] The length of a pharsac (fursung) in this paper must be much underrated. In a work called the Durra Muktai its length is computed as follows:—

6 Barley corns (say ¼ Inch)	=	1 Finger's breadth doubled.
24 fingers' breadth doubled	=	1 Gaz of 36 inches.
4,000 Gazs ,,	=	1 Meel kroh or koss.
3 Meels ,,	=	1 porasung, equal to 6 miles 1 furlong and 4 yards.

But by examining the survey which accompanies this journal the distance from Yezd to Herát cannot be more than 400 miles and the fursung must be taken at 2 miles only.

which may be the Tahren of the Greeks, then follow those of Toon, which is no other, I presume, than the Parthanils of the ancients, and there still are the remains of tombs, which very possibly may be those of the Parthian kings: subsequently traversing the lands of Kagis, which you quit at the hills of Guisk to enter on the vast deserts, which end at Herát; the length being about forty pharsacs.

The ranges of hills which are passed during this route, are for the most part isolated, and of no great height, excepting those of Ecchdakan, Khanjuen, Kon and Guisk; they have a barren appearance throughout, and their want of vegetation is a strong proof of their richness in metals. It is much to be wished, that an able mineralogist would explore these countries; at every step he would make many useful discoveries. There is still a lead mine near the village of Ecchkidur, about six pharsacs W. of Yezd. The hill of Derind presents many traces of lead and silver ore. The earth of Posht-Badam produces some grains of gold. In the district of Toon, there is a lead mine near the village of Khok; one of copper on the other side of Khanjuerkan; and another of silver at a place called Shia-Nagree. All these mines were formerly worked, but from the oppression of the present Government, which smothers all industry, they are now entirely abandoned.

I found on the surface of the earth between Buseriah and Toon many handsome specimens of agate; above all, they are plentiful near Shiah-Dera.

On the range of hills near the castle of Fourk, you are still shown the copper mines, formerly worked by Meerza Rajik Khán, the metal from which was employed in casting several pieces of cannon now to be seen at Birdjan.

The hills of Guisk are of a light red, which seems to prove them of a volcanic nature, and on the western side near the tomb of Sultan Ibrahim Roza, flows a moderately warm mineral spring, to which the inhabitants of the country go on pilgrimage, and drink the water for the benefit of their health. Many snakes are to be met with on this range, the bite of which is fatal.

Not far from the ruins of Gazun, is a stream the water of which has a strong acid taste; near to Tubbus is another of a corroding nature.

Upon all the ranges of hills which extend from Batal to Herát the people of the country gather a sort of gum called "Terendjebin" of which the Persian medical practitioners make great use: it exudes from a small thorny shrub which grows in tufts, and which resembles the plant the camels are so fond of. The flower is whitish, like that of the lettuce, which on dropping off gives place to a milky substance that congeals into yellow drops, which is the gum. For the purpose of collecting it the inhabitants cut the bush, allow it to dry, and then sift it. This plant grows wild in most of these sterile plains.

The greatest quantity of this gum is gathered in the district of Engoonzik, where also is found the assafœtida; the plant which produces the latter, grows in almost all these hills, particularly those of Kelmond, Tabas Khilike and those which extend to the west of Herát. The plant grows to two or three feet high, the stem is straight and resembles very much the coarse fennel of Corsica; it has thick roots, which extend to a considerable distance. To extract the assafœtida, it is necessary, in spring time, to cut the stem close to the earth to prevent its shooting, when during this season, a milky gum flows from it, which becomes hard. Every night this is removed with the blade of a knife, and every ten or twelve days a fresh incision is made to allow the gum to flow freely. Those who follow this avocation, take the precaution to cover the plants, to preserve them from the heat of the sun. It is sold to the Hindus of Herát who send it on to India where it is much used in cooking.

In addition to these two plants, many are found in the hills, said to possess medicinal properties, and annually collected by the druggists of the country.

The only wild animals to be found in the hills are wolves, antelopes, a few hares, and some partridges; bears are rarely seen; it is only towards the hills of Guisk that traces of them are to be met with. We killed two enormous ones near the salt spring of Kaband. On this route, you come upon troops of wild asses that abound in Seistan. This beast, much smaller than the horse, resembles in form the domestic ass, from which it differs only in the colour of its hair, which is reddish. Its speed is great, and they are long winded, seldom allowing itself to be approached sufficiently near to be shot; the Afghans are fond of its flesh.

Amongst the very few trees to be seen near the hamlets, there is a bush in the district of Gosk, that produces the zerisk which the Persians are so fond of in their pilau. The tree is like the pomegranate: its branches in September are adorned with scarlet berries, which have a pleasing effect.

The whole country which extends from Yezd to Herát is subject from May to October to violent gales of wind. The heat is suffocating in summer. During this season you are also exposed to the hot wind of the desert, but which in this country is not of a fatal nature. It rains in March, April and December; it snows a little in winter. Notwithstanding that there are two crops annually, the produce is barely sufficient for consumption.

What is most remarkable during the fatiguing journey is the total absence of any natural streams of water. Here and there are a few springs, in a *karez*,[1] which are often brackish, and do not allay the traveller's thirst; and what does flow from them barely suffices to water a few acres of ground, and for which purpose the inhabitants keep it in reservoirs that are only opened two or three times a day, and distributed with great care. Their miserable looking dwelling places take off but little in appearance from the frightful sterility of the country, a small patch of verdure only distinguishing them at a distance. The people are generally sedentary in their habits, but you meet with some wandering tribes such as Shrondanes, the Kazunees, the Banikazals, Beni-Assad and Beni-Kafodges, who inhabit the lands of Tobas and Toon. Towards the dependencies of Kayin are the Falahies, the Sahbis, the Heeroonees, the Yakoobees, and the Elabousails. All these tribes are of Arabic origin. A great many are colonies settled by Shah-Abbas, others of the time of Tamerlane, who on his return from his conquests established them in this country. These Arabs have neither preserved the customs nor manners of their ancestors except that of living in tents; they have even forgotten all traces of the language; all their wealth consists in cattle; they possess a greater mildness of manner than the inhabitants of the villages; the latter give themselves up without exertion to their miserable lot, cultivating only a few acres of land, the produce of which hardly suffices to exist upon.

In place of cultivating much, the inhabitants pass their time in spinning wool, consequently they are often subject to famine, besides being plundered by the Turkomans and Beloochees. Their fields produce wheat, barley, radishes, beetroot and oil of sesamum. From a want of grain, forage and water, it would be impossible for an army to march through this country: consequently from time immemorial there are only two instances of this having been done. Shah-Abbas was the first who had the hardihood to do so with a portion of his troops on his return from the conquest of Kandáhár. This great monarch astonished at the sterility of the sandy mountains, and the dangers which travellers were put to, halted and directed wells to be sunk, besides building small pyramids at certain distances as guides across the country of moving sand the passage of which is so dangerous. The inhabitants of Robad still point out an elevated spot where this restorer of his country pitched his tent, and from whence he was delighted to watch the progress of his works. Most of the wells and caravanserais from Yezd to Toon owe

---

[1] An aqueduct which brings the melted snow or a spring from the hills.

B 1485—2

their existence to him. The sand hills are formed by violent gales, which blow in this country at certain periods, and which continually heap up the sand of the desert against the sides of these low ranges. They extend from N.W. to S.E. This route is a point of communication between the great salt desert and that of Kobis, and by which Meer Mahomed ventured in 1722, with a hoard of Afghans, when he dethroned Shah Sultan Hussein, king of Persia.

This route since 1812 has become very dangerous for caravans on account of the gangs of Beloochees that lie in wait to plunder them. Since that time the pillage collected by these marauders has amounted to immense sums: often on finding nothing to capture on this route they have extended their incursions as far as Kerman, Ispahan and Kochan, but with little success, many of their company being killed. As soon as one has collected sufficient plunder, he returns, and his place is filled by another. To arrive at these places they traverse the desert of Kobis on the backs of camels, often making from twenty to thirty pharsacs a day. The gangs are never less than thirty, and seldom amount to one hundred men. The greater part of them are under a chief called Khán Dejun, who lives in the fortress of Shaknápur on the borders of Seistan; he it is who sends them on these expeditions and receives one-third of their booty as his share. These ferocious fellows have a sun-burnt complexion. Their dress consists of a long cotton frock wound round the waist with a thong of camel's hide; their heads enveloped in turbans. They shave part of the upper lip, leaving only the end of their moustaches, and allow two long locks of hair to fall on each side of the face, which reach to their shoulders. When they visit these sandy mountains, they halt and encamp at Shia Bactiára, or rather near the source of a spring, about two pharsacs to the right of the road which leads to Chontoran. Here they leave their camels and advance upon the road on foot to attack the caravans. They lie in ambush in all places, but the principal spot is in a defile near Godin Komber to the north of the sand-hills. The Beloochees hiding themselves behind the heights, allow the caravans to enter the defile, when possessing themselves of both outlets, they pounce upon their prey sword in hand. Those who make the least resistance are sure to be massacred without pity. By their unheard of cruelties they have made themselves so much feared that twenty or thirty of them have been known to plunder a caravan of two hundred persons with impunity, the greater part of them armed. The murders they have committed are without number. The most dreadful took place in 1823, when they put to death a hundred or more pilgrims going to pay their devotions to the tombs at Mushed. There is still to be seen near the third pyramid a heap of the remains of these unfortunate creatures as a warning to other travellers. At the time we passed we saw the bodies of five persons that had recently been murdered, and their assassins were encamped at Shia Bactiára as we passed, but as they were few in number, they were afraid to attack our caravan which was a strong one. We were well armed, besides having an escort with us. A detachment belonging to them, six in number, returning from a plundering excursion, fell in by mistake with our advance guard and were sabred; two of them that were not killed were taken on to Robad Khán, where they were tied to a tree and shot. The people of the village that witnessed their execution showed signs of discontent, but they were not attended to; this makes me believe that they are in league with the Beloochees, and that it is from them the latter purchase their provisions whenever they are obliged to stay any time here to wait for a favourable opportunity of attack, and what confirms me in this idea, is, that they never plunder on the lands belonging to Robad Khán, whilst there is no sort of violence that they have not committed on those of Sogan and Pusht-Bodam.

The Governor of the country, who has every means in his power to put a stop to this pillaging, makes no attempt to do so, beyond going through the form of having a detachment of cavalry at Robad, with orders from time to time to patrol as far as the sand-hills. One is equally astonished to find that the Prince at Yezd allows his territory to be plundered with impunity.

FROM HERÁT TO KA'BUL VIÁ KANDÁHÁR.

Those in power, that he has placed at Kharam Segan and other places, are more to gather a tax from those that pass by, than any thing else. The only precaution they take, is to prevent a caravan from going on when they hear that the Beloochees are out plundering; for this purpose they have videttes posted on the highest places, who by signs or fires, warn the inhabitants to take to their villages. Under a better administration it would be easy to put a stop to this rapine. Detachments of cavalry posted at the most dangerous places, would preserve the tranquillity of the country, and protect travellers, who now, during this fatiguing journey, are always in fear and inquietude. This danger is not the only one to be feared during this march; one is also exposed to that of meeting with Turkomans, which is still more terrible, as in case you fall into their hands, you are carried off to slavery. The Turkomans, who are addicted to plundering are generally of the Imak tribe, the chief of whom lives at a place called Mei-moneh, about eight days' march from Herát. From time immemorial, their hordes have been in the habit of plundering with impunity both Khorássan and Herát, without the Princes at the head of these provinces being able to oppose them. Their incursions are rapid and unexpected. They plunder all that they encounter, and carry into slavery men, women and children, that are subsequently sold at Bokhára. It is not only the prospect of plunder which induces them to undertake these forays, but also the desire to satisfy their hatred to the Persians; being Soonees, they believe they are performing a meritorious action in the eyes of the Prophet in taking the Persians into slavery and in obliging them to abandon the sect of Sheeas to which they belong, to adopt their own. The dangers from the Turkomans commence on the territory of Koon, and only finish at the gates of Herát; the worst part is between Kayn and Kauf. To avoid this part our caravan conductor took another route more to the south, and which led through the district of Birdjan, but this precaution nearly proved fatal to us, for about three days' journey before reaching Herát we were attacked by a band of Beloochees, that were only driven off by an obstinate resistance on our part.

The inhabitants of these countries have neither security nor repose; the poor wretches in cultivating their land are always kept in a state of alarm and often obliged to abandon the fruits of their labour, that they may not fall into the hands of the Turkomans. To live in some sort of security, they are forced to build small watch-towers in their fields, to which they fly in case of pressing danger, and which can only be entered but by a ladder. Not a family to be met with but has to complain of one of its members being carried off into slavery by the Turkomans; but what is surprising to learn is, that those who have been so taken away, make no exertion to return to their native land; on the contrary they write to their friends, that finding themselves comfortably settled, it would be madness on their part to make any sacrifices in attempting to restore them at liberty: some of them even act as guides to the Turkomans on their expeditions. At the time we travelled this route the greatest ravages were being committed by them. The district of Herát was so infested, that Prince Kamran was obliged to seek the alliance of the Prince of Khorássan for them, in common cause to attempt to put down so great a scourge. To avoid this danger I parted from the caravan at Sedik, and went to Birdjan to see if I could not procure an escort from the Governor, whom I had known well at the Persian Court at Tehrán. He was astonished to see me, received me with great kindness and loaded me with presents. I learnt from him that Mr. Oms, who has left the Persian service in 1824 to go on to India, had been arrested by his people, stripped of all his effects and confined in the citadel at Fourk from whence he had contrived to escape. So different was the treatment I received, that I appreciated the advantage of acquaintances in a strange land. The Khán furnished me with an escort of cavalry, which I sent to my friend and fellow traveller Avitabile, and who directed the march of the caravan upon Avaz, passing by the stages of Dejisk, Gosk and Nahkop; as for myself I followed the road by Fourk, accompanied by a son of the Governor, who did not separate from me until we arrived at Avaz. In passing by Fourk he took me to see the copper mine that his forefathers discovered, the metal from which was used in casting some guns that are now in the castle of that place.

On our arrival at Herát we found the province exposed to a civil war. Prince Kamran having in the month of April 1826 driven out his father Mahomed Sháh, two parties declared themselves and waged a furious war, the King, with the assistance of Boonia Khán, head of the Azeris, besieged the fort of Herát during the month of June, but the desertion of some of his troops obliged him to fall back upon Farrah, from whence he was taking fresh measures to drive his son from this province. These preparations obliged Kamran to seek an alliance with Hoosain Ali Mirza, Prince of Khorássan, who, flattered by this submission on the part of one, who up to this time had refused to acknowledge his authority, and foreseeing the advantages to be gained to himself, sent to his support six thousand men and four guns under his own son Orghan Mirza. Their united forces were encamped on the banks of the Morgab, with the intention of opposing the Khán of Meimaneh, who was coming to the support of Mahomed Sháh.

The city of Herát, which is no other than Aria of the Greeks, was, it is said, built by Alexander the Great. The inhabitants state that the plain upon which it now stands was formerly a lake formed by the waters of the Heriz, and kept in by the range of hills called Sinjer D'jun, through which Alexander having cut a passage for the water to flow, the plain was left dry, and the beauty of the country induced him to found this city—one thing certain that the castle, situated about six pharsacs to the east of Herát, was built by this conqueror.

The city of Herát is small, and enclosed in a high wall built of mud, flanked by towers falling in ruins, surrounded by a deep and broad ditch always full of water. The city contains about six thousand houses, twenty caravanserais, thirty public baths, four bázárs, six colleges and the Prince's palace, which may be considered its castle. There is nothing remarkable to be seen but the palace of Ibrahim Khan D'Jamshed, and a large and deep cistern which supplies the greater part of the population with water; it is filled by an underground aqueduct (karez), which comes from the hills. The population amounts to about forty thousand souls: about two thirds of whom are Persians, the rest Afghans. The commerce which is carried on with Bo-- khara, Kandáhár, Mushed and Yezd attracts a great many strangers to it. Its productions are silk and cotton. It was pillaged by D'Jenghis Khán in the year of the Higira 619, and again by Tamerlane, whose descendants for a long time made it their residence. This city gave birth to the celebrated historian Khandenur, author of an abridged Universal History, also to the poet Djami, who flourished during the reign of Sultan Hussain Bookara, of the race of Tamerlane, and to whom he dedicated his "Bahoristan". The environs of Herát are exceedingly agreeable. Among other places are the country seats of Takli, Sofer, Goozerja, and the garden of Shahzada Mulik Kossouree, which are situated to the north-east of the city. On this same side is also the famous mosque of Moosa Hola, which is close to the royal garden, such an edifice is rarely to be met with in Persia. It is now in ruins. It has six minarets and a large college, and what remains is sufficient to show that its architecture, though simple, was elegant and well adapted to the climate. The richness of the ceilings and domes is surprising. The walls for the most part are mosaic, built of glazed bricks; which from their embellishments present an agreeable appearance to the eye: the minarets above all, from their lightness and height to which they have been erected are most pleasing to behold. One of these has an inclination towards the Tomb of Imam Roza in Mushed, which the over-religious ascribe to a miracle, and which is shown with great display to travellers. This superb edifice was erected by Sultan Hussan Mirza Bairam at the entreaty of his favourite slave Goher Shah; regarding which the inhabitants tell a marvellous tale; others give the credit of building it to Gaistuddeen of the Gawridean Dynasty; it was destroyed by the Tartars of D'Jenghis Khán.

Not far from Gouzherab, upon the hills near where this garden is situated, is a ruby mine, which was formerly worked, but has since been abandoned in consequence of these precious stones being latterly found full of very minute holes, which took so much from their value. Further to the east on the same range is a lead mine, which Prince Kamran works on his own account. The mountains which extend to the north are said to be wooded, and among many kinds of trees is to be found the pistachio and other fruit trees in a wild state. The druggists also gather many herbs from these hills, and the dyers also find seeds and roots which they use with advantage in dyeing their clothes and in which they excel us Europeans. The valley of Herát is of a fertility seldom to be met with in Asia; in approaching it the richness of its enclosures and the number of villages gladden the traveller's sight after the fatiguing journey he has to make over barren deserts to reach it. It must be about four pharsacs in breadth from north to south, and about thirty from east to west; the inhabitants are calculated to possess twelve thousand pair of bullocks for agricultural purposes. The fruits are in great numbers, and most excellent. They reckon as high as thirty-two kinds of grapes, of which the best are the Kaye-Goramun and the Resil Baba. I observed that the vine is cultivated in a manner peculiar to this place. The country is everywhere intersected by canals, fed by the Heri river, which almost leave the latter dry. The principal one is called the Eedzil canal which, passing by the royal garden, fills the ditch of the fort. The Heri river has its source in the hills to the east, its course is to the west and loses itself in the desert which stretches to the north of Khorassan; it is therefore a mistake in some geographers making it discharge itself in the Zeri Lake. It is crossed by a bridge called the *Pool-i-Malán* to go to Kandáhár; on the Mushed road it is crossed several times.

The city of Herát from the time of Nádir Sháh has always been an apple of discord between the Persians and the Afghans, who have disputed each other's right to it by sanguinary wars, the latter having almost always the advantage. In 1818 the Persians, wishing to take advantage of the troubles which then existed in Afghanistan, did their utmost to reconquer it; in consequence of which a battle took place at Kafir-Kala, where the Persians, although victorious, were obliged to give up the attempt. Since that time it has remained with the Afghans, who have not been molested, from the frequent insurrections in Khorassan keeping the Persian troops in check. Soon after this, the Barukzyes, having dethroned Mahomed Shah, this city only and its dependencies remained the property of this unfortunate king, who had again the weakness to allow himself to be despoiled of this by his son Kamran Shah, who now governs it. This Prince, who is nearly fifty years of age, is brave and full of courage, of a determined mind and great activity. There is no means that he does not use to attempt the recovery of his father's kingdom, but the want of money obliges him to wait until providence offers a more favourable opportunity. It might not, however, be a difficult task for him to accomplish, considering that the Barukzye Chiefs do not act in concert, and even make war between themselves; and further their rule is so selfish that all the tribes are disgusted with their avarice, and ripe for revolt.

The city of Herát is capable of being better fortified. This place in the hands of Persia would, from its geographical position, have a great influence over any expedition sent from Russia in the direction of India. As an ally, it would keep in awe the people of Bokhara, Balk and Kandáhár, and by preserving its communication with the rear permit it to advance without fear to conquest; but occupied by an enemy it could cause insurmountable obstacles.

On leaving Herát two routes present themselves leading to Kábul, one by the Huzareh country which does not take more than eight or ten days, the other is that of Kandáhár which is much more circuitous. Our anxiety to reach the end of our journey made us incline to follow the first, but after taking the opinion of some merchants we were obliged to give up our intention of following that route, not only on account of the roads being so bad in this mountainous country, but also from the dangers to be run from the oppressive conduct of those who govern it, towards travellers passing through. We therefore gave the preference to that by Kandáhár. This latter route passes along the western side of the Firooz Khan chain of mountains, which extend as far as Kandáhár, dividing Seistan from the province of Gauz, and the distance is about one hundred and twenty-five pharsacs: it is almost entirely over open plains, occasionally crossing the low ranges of hills, which are in no way difficult for guns to traverse. The only inconvenience that troops would find on this road, is, that it is thinly inhabited and but few supplies to be had, besides the want of water at some of the usual stages, which would oblige them at times to make double marches. Supplies could be drawn from Farrah and Giriskh. The caravans that use this road are composed of camels; rarely are mules to be met with. They pay a tax of three sequins, and horses six, with a present from the conductor of the caravan. Camels generally travel the distance in twenty-five days; horses in eight, or at most ten. The latter march day and night, and only halt during the time necessary to rest their laden beasts. They commence to march generally at midday and do not halt until midnight. They always rest at places some distance off the road to avoid any thieves that may be abroad. At daybreak they are again in motion to arrive at the next stage about two or three hours after sunrise: here some hasten to get a little rest, while others are employed in cooking and giving their horses a feed. At 12 in the day they again are in motion and continue the same time as the preceding day. This manner of travelling is slow and most tiresome for a person who is not accustomed to it. Before commencing our journey, we laid aside our Persian costume to assume that of the Afghans: this precaution was indispensable, as the latter being Soonees and detesting the Persians, we should have been constantly in trouble. The better to deceive them we had our beards and mustaches fashioned after theirs, and during the whole of the journey we conformed to their ways. We left Herát the 1st of October 1826: our first halt was at a caravanserai of Shákhábad, which is after passing the defile called Mir Dooad; in passing through which I was imprudent enough to separate from the caravan, and my friend Avitable and myself would most assuredly have been assassinated by some of the Noorzye tribe, who inhabited these hills, had we not owed our escape to the fleetness of our Arabs. It is in these gorges that commences the lower range of Firauz Khan mountains; its direction is from north-west to south-east: they are not however to be compared in height to those which extend further to the north. The most elevated spot is called Firoug, from whence branch off two ranges, that of Karek and Kasserman, which run towards the west. These valleys are some of them cultivated and others not. They are inhabited by pastoral people, who live in tents, and who generally encamp near the source or by the side of a rivulet. They communicate by a number of paths accessible to horsemen.

On quitting Sháhábad, we left the high road to the right, and took a cross route. The reason which induced our guide to this, was, that he wished to avoid the troops of Mahomed Shah which were encamped in the plain beyond, and who were committing dreadful ravages. The country we passed over was very hilly: it was intersected by two small streams, the Ghag and the Adraskán which coming from the north-east are said to fall into that of Farrah. At the time of our crossing them they were nearly dry, but at the melting of the snow they swell to that size that the caravans are often obliged to halt for many days. This country was covered with the wild pistachio, which in autumn, is covered with a rich fruit. This tree seems to flourish best in barren spots; it gives forth a quantity of gum in white drops, of which the people make no use. They gather the fruit which they take as a stomachic. After making two marches, we descended into the plain of Dowlatabad, debouching from the Karek chain of hills by rather a difficult descent. More to the west, there is a much easier descent, by which goes the high road leading to Farrah, birth-place of the famous Rustam, the Hercules of Persia, and who is so often made mention of, in the Shah Namah of Firdose. The plain upon which this place stands, is, for the most part uncultivated, if we except its immediate environs. It is intersected from east to west by a small river, which, having its source in the Firouz Khan mountains, passes through a part of Seistan, and finally empties itself in the lake of Zeri, which may be the Ariapolis of the ancients. I presume that this river is no other than the Pharnacotes of the Greeks, and that the city of Farrah is the Phra of antiquity. At the time we crossed this river, it had but little water in it, but in spring it is said to be full and rapid, the bed is pebbly, and its banks covered with tents inhabited by Noorzyes. On quitting this plain, we left the high road to the left, to follow a bye-path which led through a pass called Rendzye Endgousht—a terrible road for our poor laden beasts, and bad enough for those on foot. This defile is remarkable on its eastern side for having its entrance like a gateway formed by two enormous rocks. A small stream which rises here, gives a picturesque appearance to the place. The high road leads through the Kasserman pass, about six pharsacs higher up, and which is no way difficult. From this we entered upon an extensive plain opening as far as the eye could reach towards the south, through the middle of which was running a small stream, called the Ibrahim, and which waters the lands of Bakora, an isolated village. The plain was covered with hares, antelopes and wild asses ; this last species of quadruped is always in herds. In the middle of the plain stands a small hill called Kou-Doug. Passing to the north we found ourselves attacked, without warning, by a band of Beloochees, some on horseback and others riding upon camels. They succeeded in carrying six beasts that were laden fromt he rear of the caravan. During this time we rallied and opposed them, but continued moving on with our ranks well closed up. Returning to the attack, they made another attempt to overpower us, but a volley that we discharged obliged them to retire and permit us to continue our route unmolested, which we did as far as the Koshroud River. From thence we entered again into the passes of this hilly country, moving with the greatest caution for fear of encountering more Beloochees, but happily we met with no more disasters. Our next stage was at the village of Vorachenk, which is encircled by a mud wall ; it is inhabited by Noorzyes who have the character of being very expert thieves. They are in the habit like, the rest of the Afghans, of collecting and mixing with the caravans under the pretext of seeking for news, and committing every sort of pilfering ; it is necessary therefore for travellers to keep a sharp look out, or they are sure to be plundered. The country which extends to the north of this village is neither cultivated nor inhabited. The river Kosháb passes through it, coming from the north, which is no other than a strong torrent which at the time we crossed it was nearly dry. In these hills, according to Kondemir, lived the noted imposter Hakim-ben-Hasheen who, from natural causes, produced effects which astonished the inhabitants of these countries, and who looked upon him as a man inspired.

On leaving Vorachenk, we descended through a mountainous country into the plain of Sar inhabited by the tribe of Subjezyes, having always in sight the Dohor hills, which form part of the Firouz Khan range, and which are inhabited by Alizyes. This country of Dohosi may very possibly be Dat, where Alexander passed through after having defeated the Scythians. Prom this we moved upon Girisk. In approaching this town a great change for the better was observed in the surrounding country : we saw a district well cultivated and watered by the Helmund river. This river has its source in the province of Gour, entering on the low country through the Dohor hills, it runs here from the north-east to south-west, but lower down to the west passing through Seistan, and eventually losing itself in the Zeri Lake. On leaving the hills the Helmund is a rapid stream and, having very confined banks, it is subject to overflows. During some time in 1825 this occurred, when it swept away more than ten thousand tents, including inhabitants and their flocks that were encamped upon its banks. The water is very clear from passing over a gravelly bottom. Excepting during the rainy season, it is fordable in some places. The best is that by which we crossed and which is about three miles above Giriskh, it is known from there being a number of high poplar trees close upon the left bank. Here the river divides into three branches, the eastern one of which is deepest. Artillery might cross over but not without unloading the wagons. It is surprising that there are no ferry boats, considering it would not be difficult to construct them, as the neighbouring hills would furnish sufficient wood, but the Afghans have not sufficient foresight to see the utility of it.

Giriskh is a good sized place, situated about three-quarters of a mile from the Helmund, but which formerly washed its walls, the intervening space being now rice fields; it is defended by a fort, on an elevated site, and which commands it; it is of no great strength and could offer no resistance to artillery. The side which faces to the east is on level ground, but the ground which faces the other three is much broken, and by taking advantage of the ravines, they can be approached to a very short distance; in addition to which the fort might be mined. It was built by Peerdill Khan, one of the present rulers of Kandáhár: it is the principal seat of the Barákzaes who inhabit the banks of the Helmund. This tribe has become the most powerful in Afghanistan; its chiefs having dethroned Mahomed Shah, have divided amongst themselves the provinces of the kingdom, which they rule despotically and live in a perfect state of independence. Here we were subject to a most rigorous examination, the people of the custom house actually searching us to the very skin, and for every sequin found on us taking at the rate of five per cent., and every laden animal was taxed at two sequins, the vagabonds practising every kind of fraud to impose upon the merchants, and even confiscating a part of their wares. From Giriskh to Kandáhár is not more than 20 pharsacs; the road is generally over a very barren soil. The Firauz mountains are still in sight and which here join the Sháh Maeesoond mountains. From these latter two other ridges branch off to the south-west and which enclose the district of Maeevend, famous for its fruits, and above all the pomegranate. On reaching Koosh-i-Nakhúd we found ourselves upon a spot which was admirably calculated to defend the city of Kandáhár on the west. From this is visible the Argandáb river running to the west and which empties itself into the Helmund about four pharsacs below Giriskh. The country which extends to the south, is covered with sandy hillocks for about forty pharsacs as far as Núshki and Karon, situated in Beloochistan and from whence the Kandáhárians procure camels and dates. The right bank of this river shows many rich villages, the principal are Sung Hissár, Kolk and Pachemour. On examining the course of the Argandáb I could not fail to remark the great error into which Danville has fallen in making a pretended river rise at Kandáhár, to which he gives an eastern course eventually falling into the Indus. Foster has likewise given to this river a false direction.

I observed that all the rivers which are in this province, such as the Argandáb, the Turnuk, the Arkassan and the Doree pass, to the west and discharge their waters into the Helmund. I presume the Argandáb is no other than the Arachotus of the Greeks, because they say it fell into a lake; its source is at the Goolkoo mountain in the district of Naoor.

After having forded the Argandáb, we entered the plain of Kandáhár, through the pass of "Chahalzeená," so called from forty steps which lead to a grotto situated at the end of a hill close to the right, and which the Afghans say was excavated by a descendant of Tamerlane. This point also presents an admirable defence to the city of Kandáhár; the numerous canals which intersect it would be difficult to pass. There are still to be seen the ruins of a small fort which formerly defended this entrance. From the end of the hill, the view is most picturesque; on one side you have below you a superb valley covered with meadows and gardens, and on the other the vast plain of Kandáhár. Nature here has been prodigal, the water of the Argandáb fertilizing the country by innumerable canals, the principal of which are the Noodseezan and Patab, the last before reaching the city passes by the village of Shah Dukteran and is full of grains of mica.

The city of Kandáhár was built by Ahmed Shah; in the construction of its buildings, which in general are of no solidity, and with little taste, it is easy to see that they were erected in haste, and without any ornament. Two principal streets run through it, crossing each other at right angles, and meeting in the centre of the town, which is called the " Chár Sú," over which is a lofty dome, from whence the streets face the four cardinal points ; they are broad and are intended to have been grand bázárs, but have never been completed, and in their places have been built miserable huts. The only building in Kandáhár worth noticing is the tomb of Ahmed Shah, which is surmounted by a handsome octangular dome. The garden that surrounded it has been entirely neglected.

The population of this city may be reckoned at twenty-five thousand souls, composed of Afghans, Persians, Beloochees and Hindus, who are distinguished from each other by the form of their head-dress ; the first are most numerous. I observed that the females are kept more secluded than in Persia. It is very rare to encounter women in the streets; those that go abroad are of a tribe that practise medicine and bleed the sick. Among the crowd that are seen in the bázárs, are many half-witted creatures that are perfectly naked and whom the Afghans treat with great consideration, considering them to be inspired by God. They are called " Houlliads", that is to say, " saints." At their death, tombs are built over them, which eventually become places of pilgrimage to the people of the country ; this is why so many places of this kind are to be met, particularly at Kandáhár; the principal ones are those of Shah Maksúd, Baba Wullee and Huzrutgee ; the first is about ten pharsacs to the north upon the range of hills which bears the same name. They there find small yellow stones, transparent and like amber, with which chaplets are made and are in great request among the Afghans ; other colours are found, but not of so fine a water as the first. Kandáhár is not commanded from any point; it has a wall of defence flanked by towers, and in pretty good order, but which could offer little resistance to artillery. The ditch which encircles it is not deep; it is filled from the Patab Canal, which would be easy to turn in another direction by a besieging army and thereby reduce the inhabitants to their wells, of which there are very few within the town. The ancient city is situated close under the eastern side of a hill, which bounds the plain of Kandáhár to the west. The remains of the citadel are still to be seen from some distance; it is now entirely in ruins and deserted, Nadir Shah having destroyed it. There is to be seen at the end of the hill the small fort Kola-tool from whence this monarch battered it with his artillery. The siege lasted six months, and would have continued longer, but that the daughter of Shah Hossain betrayed and delivered the fort into Nadir's hands, who, as the price of her crime, had her quartered in the presence of her father. From this fort a number of walls for defence branch off and continue to the foot of the hill, which were built to resist the attacks of the Persians. It is supposed that this city is that which Alexander built in the Arachasia.

The city Nadir Sháh built is about three miles south of Kandáhár which is now also in ruins. The ground of Kandáhár is very rich and well adapted for the growth of vines, which are not, however, sufficiently cultivated, and much less than at Herát ; its principal productions are wheat, barley, tobacco and madder ; they also grow maize, peas, beans and oil of sesamum. The banks of the Arghandab are studded with orchards, which produce a great quantity of fruit, above all pomegranates, mulberries, apples, plums and apricots; this abundance would allow of an army halting here for many months ; they are all remarkably cheap. Spring is the pleasantest time at Kandáhár, the heat is great in summer, and above all, when there is a southerly

B 1485—4

wind. It is remarked that it only snows here about once in seven years. The climate is considered healthy excepting in autumn when fevers are very common.

Amongst the several tribes that inhabit this country the Barukzyes are the most powerful; then the Achikzyes; and after them the Populzyes. The first reside in villages, and the others are nomads; the riches of the latter consists in their sheep and camels.

The true character of the Afghans is better observed at Kandáhár than at Herát, Kábul or Peshawar, as in the three last places, the number of strangers mixed with them has softened their national traits. If you compare their customs and usages with the Persians, you will find them very similar, as they both follow the precepts of the Koran; but as a nation one cannot help remarking that they are much rougher and coarser in their manners. The want of civilization amongst them proves that their rulers are always occupied in defending themselves against attacks of their neighbours, and have never thought of ameliorating their laws. The Afghan has neither the vanity nor the politeness of a Persian; so far from resembling him in his easy way and empty compliments, he is grave, distant, cold in his replies, and even a little too rude in his manners. Beyond the respect he pays to his master, he looks upon all as his equals and addresses them without ceremony. A European travelling in Afghanistan, must be immediately struck with the familiarity which exist between the high and low, nevertheless an Afghan is a slave to his master; beyond this, however, he would rather suffer himself to be killed than subjected to a foreign yoke. Deriving his origin from a wandering tribe he practises hospitality equal with the Arab. He is courageous, and believes himself to be the bravest soldier in the world. On this point he is quite convinced; he delights in recounting the exploits of the Dooranees that adorned the armies of Nadir, and conquered India under Ahmed Shah. He delights in times of disorder, as it gives him an opportunity of gratifying his inclination to plunder. In religion he is a fanatic, and is as superstitious as a Turk or Persian, being a Soonee in the strictest sense of the word, he detests the Persians who are Sheahs. Beyond this he is tolerant towards other persuasions, above all to Christians, as he believes in the Gospel and looks on it as an inspired work. Like the Persian he puts great faith in dreams and astrology, and possesses equally with him all the prejudices of the Mahomedan, but still will partake of food with any one of a different sect to his own. He has no education. With them their rulers and priests are the only persons that can read or write; their books are in Persian. From their youth they are taught to use the "spear and the sword," to take a true aim, and to ride well, and this is all the instruction they receive. An Afghan is a good swordsman; his food is bread, rice, meat and milk. "Kouroot" (a kind of curd) is his favourite dish. He does not indulge in wine, his religion prohibiting it; but he delights in drinking bháng, and smoking intoxicating drugs, the use of which for the time produces a sort of stupor which delights the senses, but the excessive use of which soon brings an imbecility of mind; his dwelling is like the Persians, with this difference that it is more simply furnished. Their luxuries consist in having fine horses, splendid trappings, rich attire, and above all many retainers. Their costume is much the same as the Persians, only differing in the head-dress. The sheep skin cap is here substituted by an unbecoming cap wound round by a large blue turban with a red border, which by the manner of putting it on points out the particular tribe to which they belong. The beard they look upon as sacred; nevertheless, in place of allowing it to grow naturally, they cut it to a fantail shape: they also clip the centre of their mustache, allowing the sides only to grow to any length.

The province of Kandáhár since 1818 has been governed by five brothers: Peer Dil Khan, Khondil Khan, Sherdil Khan, Ramdil Khan, and Meer Dil Khan; the principal authority is now in the hands of Peer Dil Khan on the death of the latter in 1826. Their troops are about six thousand Cavalry, and four of Infantry; with more revenue it would be easy to double this force. The Kandáháris are good swordsmen, but not being disciplined, have no steadiness; they receive but small pay, and only assemble when wanted. The Infantry are armed with sword and matchlock, long but of small bore; they have about twenty pieces of cannon, almost useless and without artillerymen to serve them. The rulers of this country seem to have adopted for maxim, " to know no other law than their own absolute authority. " Grasping for money there are no means to procure it, that they are not capable of. With them to be rich is a crime which soon brings on confiscation and ruin. They have debased their coin until the alloy preponderates. All merchants and strangers arriving here, before being allowed to circulate any foreign money, are obliged to get it stamped, paying a tax of five per cent, or run the risk of its being confiscated; also every merchant before leaving this is forced to have each article marked by an agent of Government on which there is a fixed rate, evading which his whole property is seized and lost to him for ever. It follows that the commerce of this place, which was once so flourishing, has become almost nothing. Kandáhár was once the "entrepôt" of the produce of India and Persia; it still receives from India supplies viâ Shikárpur; shawls from Cashmere by way of Kábul which are sent on to Persia, paying a transit duty which is generally arbitrary. Silk and cottons that are manufactured here barely suffice for home consumption. The principal trade is in madder, tobacco and dried fruits, which are sent to India.

The road which leads to Shikárpur is not much frequented by merchants; it is a difficult and dangerous route and about 360 kos long. At the end of this journal will be found an abstract of the route given to me by a native of Kandáhár who has often travelled it. This route cannot be considered practicable for an army during summer, a great portion would perish for want of water; if it was to be attempted under all hazard it would be necessary to establish at different points depôts of supplies, besides each soldier being furnished with an iron plate to cook his cakes, as is done in the East, and every company supplied with a small hand-mill to grind flour; without these precautions they would run the risk of perishing of hunger after the first few marches. These difficulties have compelled the merchants to select a new line of route which further to the north passing by Kelat-i-Nahsir Khan (Khelat-i-Ghilzie) through a country inhabited by Beloochees, ends at Dera Ghazi Khan, situated on the banks of the Indus. That which leads from Kandáhár to Kábul, offers none of these difficulties, excepting, that it is not practicable in winter, from the quantity of snow which lies. Although passing through a hilly country, it presents no obstacle to the march of artillery; it winds through a rich valley closed in by two ranges of hills having a north-easterly direction as far as Kábul, and running nearly parallel the whole way. The northern range, which is no other than the mountains of Paropamisan of the Greeks, is very much more elevated than the southern one; this latter seems to abound in metals. The valley is most fertile, and traversed as far as Makur by the Turnak river, which joins the Arghandab. It enjoys a bracing and healthy climate, and this is the reason that between Pootee and Julduk are still to be seen the ruins of an ancient city called Sher-i-Soofa, meaning the city of health. The mountains which extend to the north of the province of Kandáhár, and the sand-hills which go off to the south, make this city the point from whence the two routes to India by Shikárpur and Kábul lead. Any army from the north marching to the conquest of Hindustan must necessarily pass this; halt, and take proper measures to support its further advance.

After forty days' detention a caravan being about to start for Kábul we hastened to take advantage of its protection, and quitted Kandáhár on the 28th of October, and in four days found ourselves forty kos in advance, and arrived at Mookur. Our halting places were Pootee, Julduk, Tajee and Mooknee; so far I observed that we passed very few villages, but in their places an infinite number of black tents inhabited by tribes of Sudoozyes, Alikzyes and Gilzies. I remarked that their women did not cover their faces with that care that those in the villages did; however they still wear a veil, which partly conceals their countenances. Their dress is of a peculiar shape, which somewhat approaches to the European. Their hair is divided in front by two long plaits, which with married women are allowed to hang negligently over their shoulders; but before marriage they are studded with coins, and partly cover the face before strangers.

At Fazi we were stopped by a chief of the Gilzyes, who, living independently and under no control, assumes the right of levying toll upon all caravans. The tax is not fixed, but taken according to his own will and pleasure. He was most arbitrary with us, seizing any of our arms to which he took a fancy, and seeming to be much surprised as well as offended at our attempting to prevent it. The plain about Fazi was the scene of a bloody battle between Shah Zamoon and Mahomed Shah, sons of Timour, who disputed the throne of Afghanistan; the former in losing the battle was also deprived of his eye-sight by his brother.

A stranger in passing this country on the approach of winter, would remark the number of poles erected in all the villages, to which are suspended the carcases of sheep, salted and hung to dry, as their food during this season, which practice they probably learnt from their Tartar neighbours.

The village of Mookur is situated close under the southern face of the Goolkun chain, which defends it from the strong wind of the north; near the village is the source of the Turnuk River in which are found plenty of fish of a good kind.

The people of this hamlet are exceedingly obliging, lodging all strangers in their houses; and their cleanliness, so unusual in the East, would make one fancy they were settlers from another country. Six kos beyond the hills, which border the plain towards the south, is the salt lake of Zourmal. From Mookur we continued our journey to Guznie in traversing the plains Kuzabak and Nanee; in advance of this the country is covered with a number of small villages each enclosed by a mud wall with small towers at the angles. This manner of protecting the villages is very common in Asia, but above all in Afghanistan, where the number of civil wars that have constantly taken place have rendered this mode of defence necessary, as in case of danger, it offers a place of refuge, and enables them to keep what they possess in safety.

Before arriving at Guzni the conductor of our caravan, receiving very discouraging accounts of the state of the affairs of the country before us, judged it prudent not to halt there, but turned aside, and took the caravan to his own village, which is about six miles from this city. My friend Avitabile and a few merchants, who preceded the main body, not being aware of this alteration in our movements, pushed on and slept that night at Guzni. The next morning at day dawn we were surprised to see several horsemen enter the village, whose sinister appearance boded us no good, and shortly after they were followed by another party that possessed themselves of all the outlets of the place. By order of their Chief we were seized, our arms and property taken from us, and the caravan and every person belonging to it conducted to Guzni. On our arrival there we were made to enter a caravansarai, a strong guard put over us, and our effects removed to another place, and had to undergo a rigorous search to ascertain if we had nothing secreted on our persons. What surprised me most was to find that they took no notice of my papers, which I carried about my person in the way Asiatics usually do, and which gave me reason to believe the vagabonds were only anxious to secure our money. The few sequins found upon me were seized with great delight. Fortunately before quitting Kandáhár, we had exchanged our money for bills upon Kábul, given to us by, a merchant, to whom I had been particularly recommended by some acquaintance at Herát, without which my friend and myself would have been put to great distress. The next day I was taken before the Governor of Guzni, who strictly questioned me as to who I was, from whence I came, and to what place I was going. I answered him rapidly and with confidence that I was a Georgian on my way to India in search of one of my relatives. On this he commenced bantering me, wishing me to understand that he was aware of my being a European. He then made me open out all my papers, and showed me some mathematical instruments and my watch, that had been found with my effects, asking me to tell him the use of them. I pleaded ignorance, and said that they had been given to my care by an Englishman at Teheran, to be delivered to a friend of his in India. On this he became very serious, desiring under pain of the severest punishment to tell him where I had secreted my money. I answered him that having been made a prisoner, searched, and all my effects taken from me, that I had nothing more in my possession. This seemed to satisfy him, and I was dismissed under a strong escort to the caravansarai, where I had the pleasure to find my friend, whom I found had been questioned as well as myself. Our accounts of ourselves were found to tally, as before leaving Ispahan, we had agreed upon what should be said, and had also instructed our servants.

That night we concerted measures to attempt our escape; we could hit upon no other plan than to despatch the servant to Kábul that our " companions in arms " had sent us from India. He was to find out Nawab Jubber Khan, brother of the rulers of Afghanistan, and with whom our friends were on intimate terms, who no doubt would interest himself in our favour. As a further measure of prudence my friend Avitabile determined, if possible, to escape and accompany him. Taking advantage of our people being absent with the horses to water, he scaled the walls of the caravansarai, and contrived to secure two for himself and servant, and managed to effect his escape.

Eight days after, I was agreeably surprised at the Governor sending for me, overwhelming me with apologies for the treatment I had received, and reproaching me for having disguised from him the truth. I at first thought it was a trap he had laid for me, but I soon felt myself at ease when he presented me with a letter from my friend. From this time he was kind in his attentions, restored all my property, and started me for Kábul, where I arrived on the 13th of November. I took up my abode with the noble " Nawab Jubber Khan" (where I found my friend Avitabile), whose kind hospitality soon made me forget all the privations that I had lately suffered under his brother.

There are three stages for caravans from Guzni to Kábul. Their names are Chesgoo, Shekabad and Maidan; before reaching this latter you have to cross a small clear stream which comes from Azeres, which after fertilizing the valley of Languerd falls into the Kábul River. At Maidan you come upon a river which is the same as the one that flows to Kábul. From this the line of road to Kábul is well adapted to defensive operations, but it might be turned if the precaution was taken of marching from Guzni by Goidez and Londgerd. It was at Shekabad that Futtee Khan was put to death. Kamran Shah having a hatred to him, took advantage of his defeat at Kaffir Kola, to deprive him of his eye-sight, but not satisfied with this revenge he subsequently had him put to death at this place. This man's fall is still regretted by the Afghans, who speak in terms of praise of his courage and the able manner in which the affairs of Government were conducted under him. Born a Barakzye he preserved amidst all his greatness the simple manners of his tribe, which won the hearts of all about him. To this was added an unbounded liberality. At his death his brothers, to the number of twenty-one, who were almost all in high situations, revolted; called around them the tribe of Barakzyes, of which they were the Chiefs, and assumed supreme power in dethroning Mahomed Shah. Since that time they have divided amongst themselves the provinces of Afghanistan, which they govern without fear of opposition.

Translated by
NEIL CAMPBELL, Major,
Acting Quarter Master General.

Kábul, 29th August 1839.

REPORT

OF A

JOURNEY FROM HERÁT TO SIMLA VIÂ KANDÁHÁR, KÁBUL
AND THE PANJAB,

By

MAJOR D'ARCY TODD.

REPORT

OF A

JOURNEY FROM HERA'T TO SIMLA VIA KANDA'HA'R AND THE PUNJAB

UNDERTAKEN IN THE YEAR 1838 BY ORDER OF

HIS EXCELLENCY JOHN McNEILL, Esq.,

H. B. M.'s ENVOY EXTRAORDINARY AND MINISTER PLENIPOTENTIARY AT THE COURT OF PERSIA.

By MAJOR D'ARCY TODD.

The circumstances under which this journey was undertaken, the short time (sixty days which it occupied, and the disturbed state of some of the districts on my route prevented my taking more than a hasty survey of the countries through which I passed or obtaining any information beyond what chance threw in my way.

The following rough notes were mostly jotted down either on horseback or after being in the saddle from twelve to fifteen hours out of the twenty-four :—

I left the Persian Camp before Herát on the 22nd May and arrived at Simla on the 20th of July.

The city and valley of Herát have been minutely described by successive travellers. It may however be required that I should say a few words on the defences of a place which garrisoned by a small band of determined men had up to the date of our latest authentic intelligence successfully resisted the whole concentrated power of Persia for upwards of seven months.

The strength of the besieging army be estimated at from 12 to 15 thousand regular Infantry, 7 or 8 thousand Irregular Horse and about 50 pieces of brass ordnance, 24, 18, 14, 12, 6 and 4-pounders, about half of which being of the two last-mentioned calibre with half a dozen 5½ inch mortars. I do not think that the besieged mustered more than 2,500 fighting men actually under arms; they had no Artillery and their horsemen had been sent away to Korook Subzawaur and other places soon after the commencement of the siege.

The city of Herát is of an oblong shape, about 1,600 yards in length and 13 or 14 hundred yards in breadth. The place is encircled by an artificial mound of earth varying from 40 to 60 feet in height, on the summit of which stands the wall of the town. There are about thirty bastions on each face circular and built of unburnt brick, those at the angles of the place being much larger and higher than the intermediate ones. The height of the bastions and walls above the mound varies from 25 to 35 feet.

The following rude section of the defences will illustrate my description of them :—

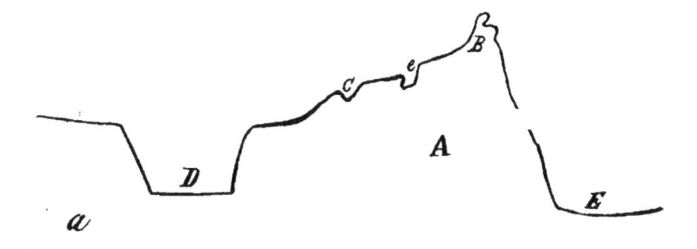

A. The artificial mound mentioned above which forms the real circle of defence.
B. The walls of the place.
C.C. Trenches cut in the mound, or what may be called the exterior slope of the rampart, about 6½ or 7 feet deep, and running entirely round the place. These are called the upper and lower Sheer Hajee, or Sheeradah, and in them are stationed nearly the whole of the garrison. The Sheer Hajees communicate with one another and with the town by subterranean passages, and since the commencement of the siege they have been partly traversed.
D the ditch.
E the town.

I saw the ditch only at two points, at the S. E. angle of the place, it was about nine yards broad, with water in it but not filled. The Afghans had established a covered way or place of arms on the counterscarp communicating with the scarp by means of a plank thrown across the ditch. The Persians had worked up to within ten or twelve yards of this work, and both parties were incessantly engaged in mining and countermining. I also saw the ditch between the S. W. angle and the Kandáhár gate, which is situated in the centre of the Southern face. It was dry at this point and about twelve yards broad. The Persians had here advanced a covered gallery half way across the ditch.

The exterior slope of the artificial mound or rampart is at an angle of from 35 to 45, forming in most places too steep an ascent for men encumbered with arms, in face of a determined enemy. The breadth of this mass of earth, at its base, may be from 90 to 100 feet. There are some places where the ascent is not so steep, and at one of these, the Persians in a late attempt at assault, clambered up to the upper Sheer Hajee, of which they kept possession for some time.

The citadel of Herát is built upon a mound at the northern end of the town, surrounded by a wet ditch, said to be of considerable depth, and about 36 feet wide, and flanked by large massive towers of burnt brick, 60 or 70 feet high. The position is a strong one, and might be held for some days, or even weeks, after the fall of the town. The only entrance to the citadel is on its southern face, over a bridge which might be destroyed in a few minutes. On the northern face of the town, an outwork has of late years been constructed, called the Ark-i-no or new citadel. This covers the citadel and one of the gates of the town.

From the above rough sketch of the defences of Herát, some idea may be formed of its strength. It would be very difficult if not impossible to breach it with artillery, and the immense quantity of powder which would be necessary in order to establish such a mine as would effect a praticable breach, may be estimated from the dimensions of the rampart above given. From the size of the place it would require an army of 25 or 30 thousand men to invest it effectually.

Herát is not, however, without its weak points. The ruined walls of houses and gardens surround the place, and afford shelter to the besiegers, almost up to the edge of the ditch. On the northern side of the town is an immense mound called the "Tull-i-bunjee", which was thrown up, I believe by Nadir Sháh, about 4 or 5 hundred yards from the walls, and behind which a couple of Regiments might be encamped completely screened from the fire of the town. The very size of Herát is also a weakness; it would require a garrison of at least 10,000 men to defend it against an active and enterprising enemy.

The Sheer Hajees are not traversed throughout their whole extent, and might therefore by an enfilading ricochet fire be rendered in some places untenable.

Nearly all the weak points above mentioned, might however be remedied by a skilful Engineer, and if time were allowed for this, the place supplied with guns and a sufficiency of ammunition, and the works defended with common bravery, the capture of Herát even with European troops would be a tedious and difficult enterprize.

Names of Towns, Villages, Stations.	Distance in Miles.	Direction.	Remarks.
Herát	...	...	On leaving the town the road to Kandáhár leads due south through a succession of gardens and fields intersected by numerous water-courses. About three miles from the town the Herirood or Pul-i-Malaum River is crossed. Formerly a fine bridge of burnt brick spanned the stream at this point, but the river has formed for itself a new channel, and now flows round one end of the bridge. The breadth of the river at the place where I crossed was about 150 yards, the stream was exceedingly rapid, and the water reached to our saddle flaps. Several fatal accidents had lately occurred to persons who had attempted to ford the stream when it had been swollen by a fall of rain in the adjacent mountains. To the south of the river is a fine tract of pasture land thickly studded with villages and gardens.
Houz (Reservoir of water)...	14	S.	Situated in an opening of the range of hills to the south of the town.
Meer Daoud	4	S.	Caravanserai in good repair in a fine stream of clear water from a kahreez or succession of wells connected by an underground passage which conducted the stream from its source.
Sháh Beg	12	S.	Ruined caravanserai, abundance of water.
Meer Allah	12	S.	Ruined caravanserai. $5\frac{1}{2}$ miles beyond Shah Beg a spring of sweet water on the left of the road. The caravanserai of Meer Allah surrounded by cultivation, and a fine stream of water runs under the walls.
Rood-i-Guz	6	S.	A rapid stream 15 or 20 yards broad.
Rood-i-Adruscund	5	S.	Stream one mile beyond Rood-i-Adruscund, a rocky pass with springs of fresh water.
Khajeh Ourieh ...	6	S.	A ziaret gáh or place of pilgrimage, a ruin perched on the summit of a rocky hill at the foot of which runs a stream slightly brackish.
	4	S.	Road turns off to Subzawaur, leaving that which leads direct to Kandáhár on the left.
Houz	7	S.W.	Reservoir of water ruined.
Subzawaur	10	S.S.W.	A small mud fort, 200 or 250 yards square, with seven circular bastions on each face, one gate on the southern face, scarcely any ditch, the walls in a state of dilapidation. A small ark or citadel, the residence of the Prince Governor, in the centre of the place. Subzawaur is a place of no strength, and might be taken with little loss by a *coup de main*. It is situated in the midst of a richly cultivated tract of country studded with innumerable villages which are inhabited by Noorzyes; each village is about sixty yards square, surrounded by a mud wall with towers at the angles, a range of hills of inconsiderate elevation to the south of the town, distant about two miles. The road between Herát and Subzawaur is good and level, and passable for wheel carriages of every description. Abundance of fresh water in every part of this route, but provisions are not procurable at any point between Herát and Subzawaur. Shahzadeh Iskunder, a son of Sháh Kamran, was nominally the Governor of this district; when I passed through it he possessed, however, little weight or influence anywhere, and none beyond the walls of his fort; he seemed to be a half-witted and imbecile person. He had made no attempt to succour his father, or even to divert the attention of the Persians. The surrounding country was in a state of utter disorder. Bands of plunderers were roving about in every direction, and those men were described as acknowledging neither God nor king.
	13	E.	At this point the road from Subzawaur joins the main road between Herát and Kandáhár. The range of hills to the south of Subzawaur terminates four miles from the town in a long spur, upon which the remains of an extensive fort are visible. This is called the "Killa Dookhter", or maiden's castle, and at a short distance from it on a mound in the plain are the ruins of another castle called "Killa-i-Pisr", or the youth's fort. The plain is thickly studded with villages and khails (encampment) of Noorzyes, abundance of water. Road perfectly level.

Names of Towns, Villages, Stations.	Distance in Miles.	Direction.	REMARKS.
Kharuck	30	S.E.	A grove of Khunjuck trees with a fine stream of water situated under a range of hills running W. S. W. and E. N. E. Wells or springs at every six or eight miles, but no provisions procurable. For the last four or five miles the road hilly and difficult for wheel carriages, but a road, which is described as being good and level, strikes off to the right three miles before Kharuck, and after turning the Kharuck range crosses the plain to Davlatabad, where it again joined the road which I followed. Encampments of Noorzyes are occasionally found in the vicinity of Kharuck, but these cannot be depended on for furnishing supplies, even to a small force.
Summit of pass	3	S.	Road or rather pathway impassable for wheel carriages.
Davlatabad	15	S.E.	A ruined fort on the right bank of the Furrah road. Several large encampments in the vicinity. The valley of the Furrah road runs from north-east to south-west, and is said to be richly cultivated in the vicinity of the town of Furrah about 40 miles below Davlatabad. Supplies to almost any extent and of every description might be drawn from the district of Furrah. A son of Kamram with the title Suadat-ool-Moolk resides at Furrah and is the Governor of the district. He like the Subzawaur Prince has not attempted to aid his father.
Checkaub	22	S.E. by E.	On the 29th of May the river was fordable at a point where it was divided into five streams. About 300 yards above, a large solitary tree which stands on the water edge is remarkable as being the only tree near Davlatabad. Checkaub is the name given to a fine spring of water near which was an encampment of Noorzyes. The road from Davlatabad is passable for wheel carriages; no water between the Furrah road and Checkaub, except a few brackish streams. Abundance of water and a good deal of cultivation, wheat and barley in the immediate vicinity of Checkaub.
Largebur Kahreez	9	E.	Gardens half mile to the right of road with abundance of water; some encampments at Chikzyes in the vicinity.
Carvan Cazee	4	S.E.	Water.
Toot-i-Gusserman	10	E.	Several encampments near some mulberry trees which are said to mark the half-way distance between Herát and Kandáhár. Abundance of water and cultivation. Road from Largebur Kahreez hilly and stony, difficult for wheel carriages.
	8	S.	
Gunneemurgh	6	E.	Gardens and encampments of Atchikzyes near a fine stream. Country hilly, but road good.
Ibrahim joee (River)	7	S.S.E.	We turned off the main road at this point and ascended the right bank of the stream.
Tull-i-Kumân	7	N.E.	Mud fort belonging to Memkhan, a Chief of Noorzyes, on the left bank of the stream. There are about thirty other forts higher up the stream inhabited by the Barizye branch of the Noorzyes. There are two branches of the Noorzyes, the Chulakzyes and the Badirzye. The head of the former is Mahomed Haleemkhan (at present in the Persian camp before Herát; he was with Sheer Mahomed Khan when Ghorian was given up to Mahomed Shah) and Hassan Khan, at present in Herát, is the head of the latter. It is said that the two branches of this tribe muster from 600 to 700 families. There is no such fort as "Killa Suffeed" as mentioned by Lieutenant Conolly and inserted in Arrowsmith's map; but I was told that the Tull-i-Kumân was built upon the site of what had once been the Killa Suffeed which like all other Killa Suffeeds is assigned to the days of Rustam and the white demon.

Names of Towns, Villages Stations.	Distance in Miles.	Directions.	REMARKS.
	9	S.E. & S.	The Tull-i-Kuman is surrounded by encampments, and is used as a keep for the flocks and herds of the Chief and his people. In time of danger these people retired to caves and hiding places in the adjacent hills. The Tull-i-Kuman and its dependent forts are nominally under the authority of the Fyfool Moolk, a son of Shah Kamran, who resides at Ghore, said to be about 35 miles north of Toot-i-Gusserman, but he has not been able for a long time past to extract any thing from them in the shape of revenue or taxes, and they enjoy their fields and their flocks without paying any regard to the constituted authority, which is too weak to enforce its demands. Came again upon the high road; abundance of water on the roads between the Tull-i-Kuman and this point; passed several gardens and encampments.
Khaushrod (river)	6	E.S.E.	A fine stream 20 or 30 yards broad running from the north, fordable. This is the boundary between Kamran's territory and that of the Kandáhár Sardárs.
Washeer	14	E. by S.	Four forts situated on a fine stream and surrounded by rich cultivation and gardens.
Byabanck	24	E.	Village with a stream from a Kahreez. The road in some places rugged but passable for wheel carriages. No fresh water during the first 10 or 12 miles This road is to the south of that followed by Lieutenant Conolly which leads through the villages of Poosand and Numzand.
Dooshaukh	5	E.	Village surrounded by a mud wall and towers.
Lur	3½	E.	Deserted fort with a stream from Kahreez. No encampments in the vicinity.
	7	E.S.E.	Stream near a deserted fort and some encampments of Barukzyes. Road perfectly level.
Sadant	4	E.S.E.	Fort small but strong, in good repair. This fort was built by Fattekhán Barukzye for his mother who is said to have held a petty court here; abundance of water.
Girishk	21	S.E.	The fort of Girishk is built upon a mound about two miles from the right bank of the Helmund. Girishk is a place of considerable strength, and if properly garrisoned would require a force of three or four thousand men with a small train of Artillery (4 iron guns and 2 or 3 Mortars would be sufficient) to ensure its capture. There are four or five old guns in the fort, but they appeared to be in an unserviceable state. Between the river and the fort is a fine Chummun (pasture land) intersected by water-course and dotted with gardens and groves and villages. The country round the fort might be easily flooded and the approach to it thus rendered exceedingly difficult to a besieging force. Mahomed Siddikkhán, a clever intelligent young man, one of the sons of Sardár Kohimdilkhán (the eldest of the Kandáhár brothers) rules at Girishk and is the Governor of the Frontier District. He is attempting to form a corps of Infantry to be drilled and disciplined after the European manner. I saw about a hundred of his recruits armed with sticks in lieu of muskets being drilled by a fellow who looked very much like a runaway sepoy dressed in a gay English uniform when I passed through Girishk. Mahomud Omarkhán and Mahomud Oosmankhán, two sons of Kohimdilkhán, were encamped in the vicinity with about two hundred followers on the way to join the Persian army before Herát. The measure was most unpopular and it was given out that after a sufficient force had been collected the young Chiefs would in the first instance undertake a plundering expedition against Furrah and Subzawaur.
Rood-i-Helmund (River)	2	E.	The *Etymander* of the ancients. Broad and exceedingly rapid river, not fordable at this season. The distance between the banks is about a thousand yards, but in spring it is said to spread itself over the low ground on its right bank and sometimes to approach within a few hundred yards of the walls of Girishk. The Helmund takes its rise on the mountains to the west of Kábul and after a

B 1485—7

Names of Towns, Villages, Stations.	Distance in Miles.	Direction.	Remarks.
			course of 600 miles, during which it is joined by several considerable streams, the principal of which are the Turunk, the Urghundáb, the Shahbund and the Khaushrood, it falls into the lake of Tumah.
There is usually a small boat at this place by which travellers cross the river when the stream is not fordable, but this had been destroyed a short time before our arrival, and we crossed the river on an elephant, the water being in some places about seven feet deep, in June..
Khak-i-Chaupan	24	E.S.E.	A grove of mulberry trees with a small stream; there is no water between Helmund and this place.
Kooshk-i-Nakhood or Khoorsh Nakhood.	7	E. by S.	A great deal of rich cultivation and several fine gardens in the vicinity; abundance of water. The ruins of an ancient fort called the Kulla-i-Nader, which must have been a place of considerable strength in its day, about two miles to the west of Khoorsh Nakhood.
Houzi Muddudkhán	14	E.	A large tank on the right of road.
Kandáhár	26	E.	The Urghundáb, a fine stream about $\frac{1}{2}$ a mile to the right of road; the banks of the river thickly studded with gardens and villages. The Urghundáb after passing Kandáhár takes a westerly course as far as the Houzi Muddudkhán and then turns to the south not as it is laid down in Arrowsmith's map. The road from the Houzi to Kandáhár passes through a succession of fields and gardens and villages which cover this fertile and delightful valley, the breadth of which varies from 3 to 9 miles. Nearly the whole of the water of the Urghundáb is taken up by canals for the purpose of irrigation.
The route by which I travelled from Herát to Kandáhár was nearly by the same as that followed in 1828 by Lieutenant Connolly, to the accuracy of whose statements and descriptions I can bear ample testimony. I calculated the distance to be $380\frac{1}{2}$ miles by the average rate of fast walking horse which I found to be 4 miles an hour on level ground.
The journey is performed by horsemen in ten and sometimes in nine days, but caravans of laden mules are usually from sixteen to eighteen days between Herát and Kandáhár. The country is occupied by pastoral tribes chiefly of the Noorzye, Atchikzye and Barukzye branches of the Dooranee Afghans. They are possessed of numerous flocks and herds and in the vicinity of their *Khails* or encampments they raise a sufficiency of grain for their own consumption. These Khails, which generally are from fifteen to fifty tents, are scattered over the face of the country, and as they are usually at some distance from the road it is impossible for a mere traveller even to mark a rough guess at the extent of population or the amount of the resources of the country.
To the south of the route above described is another which passed through Bakwa and which was followed by Forster in 1783, since which time I believe no European has travelled it. This southern or Dilaram road as it is usually called is described as being perfectly level and not more than forty or fifty miles longer than the northern or more direct one, but there is a scarcity of water on it, some of the halting places being upwards of 30 miles apart. It is however travelled by caravans and horsemen, and for an army it would have the advantage of passing within a short distance of Furrrah and Subzawaur, from which places supplies almost to any extent are procurable.
The city of Kandáhár is of an oblong shape; the length, north and south, being about 2,000, and the breadth 1,600 yards. The city is enclosed by a mud wall with circular bastions at regular intervals. The height of the walls may be about thirty feet, the ditch is dry and from ten to sixteen feet deep and fifteen broad in some places, besides a wall loopholed for musketry about six feet high runs round the scarp of the ditch between which and the main wall is

Names of Towns, Villages, Stations.	Distance in Miles.	Direction.	REMARKS.
			a level space or *faussebraye* eight or ten feet in breadth. The works are in a tolerable repair. Kandáhár is surrounded by gardens and enclosed fields which would afford cover to a besieging force almost up to the edge of the ditch. About a hundred yards from the south-west angle is a large walled garden which was taken possession of by Shah Shooza in attempt upon Kandáhár in 1834 and which formed a strong advanced post for his troops.
Killa-i-Khalekdad Khan	13	E. and E. N.E.	A half ruined village. Road for the first two or three miles led through gardens and cultivation, after which we travelled over an open uncultivated plain. Good level road free from stones; water only amongst the gardens and cultivation.
Kulla-i-Azmi Khán	3	E. by N.	A small fort in tolerable repair with a stream of clear water.
	8	E. by N.	Opening in a low range of hills.
Khail-i-Akhoond or Dominies Khail	7	E.N.E.	Road good but stony.
	...	N.E. by E.	A few houses built round the tomb of a sainted school-master situated on the right bank of the river Turnuk (N.E. & S.W.) is marked by green line of tamarisk trees. A good deal of cultivation round the village.
Bivouac on the right bank of the Turnuk.	20	N.E.	Road excellent; cultivation the whole way; but no villages or Khails to be seen, the people having retired from vicinity of the high way to avoid the extortions of the great men who frequent the road.
Teer Andaz	4	N.E.	A minaret about 40 feet high on the right of the road said to mark the spot where an arrow of Ahmed Shah's fell when that monarch was shooting from an eminence which is pointed out on the left of the road.
Khower Taneh	16	N.E.	No habitation to be seen. Bivouac on the right bank of the Turnuk in the district of Khawer Tauch two or three miles beyond the minár at a place called Jalloogeer or the bridle full the road bad and stony for a short distance; with this exception the road perfectly level and good following the right bank of the Turnuk. The valley of the Turnuk is now (12th June) a sheet of waving corn ripe for the sickle.
Julduk	4	N.E.	A village surrounded by gardens about a mile to the left of the road.
Ford	8	N.E.	Crossed the Turnuk near a mill which marks the boundary between the country of the Dooranees and that of the Ghiljees. Here we diverged from the direct road, which leads along the right bank of the Turnuk and passes Kelat-i-Ghiljee, but which is now seldom taken by travellers in consequence of its being infested by robbers or lawless Ghiljee Chiefs who either send their followers to attack caravans or levy contributions themselves under various pretences. The principal of these are the sons of one Shahabadeen Khán and are considered as the Chiefs of this part of the country. They are upward of twenty in number and are seldom mentioned by their own names, being generally called " Buchahad Shahabadeen," the sons of Shahabadeen. They reside at Kelat-i-Ghiljee and in the forts of this district between the territories of the Ameer and the Sardárs and are uncontrolled by either of them. Nominally their country is under the rule of the latter.
Kulla-i-Ramazan Khán	8	E. by N. E. N. E.	A small fort. Our route from the river lay amongst low hills, road stony, but passable for wheel carriages. Black mail was levied upon us at this place by Shahabadeen's men who had heard of our being in the vicinity.
Koorrum	22	N.E.	Small garden and Kahreez in the district of Koorrum; passed several forts and Khails with slips of cultivation. At the 14 mile Deewalik a ruined fort which is said to have been once a considerable place. As far as Deewalik, the country is inhabited by the Hoteekee branch of the tribe of Ghiljee. The district of Koorrum is inhabited by Tokhees; the river Turnuk 2 or 3 miles distant behind some low hills to the westward.

Names of Towns, Villages, Stations.	Distance in Miles.	Direction.	Remarks.
Kulla-i-Jaafferee	30	N.E.	Several forts. The road from Koorum over undulating ground passable for wheel carriages, Khails; and forts on either side but at some distance from the road. At the 8th mile Gloondee* said to be a large village (we passed it in the dark) the residence of one of the sons of Shahabadeen. At the Kulla Jaafferee we again entered the valley of the *Turnuk*. Forts and Khail are seen in every direction—rich fertile tract of country on the banks of the stream.
Ford	11	N.E.N.	Crossed the Turnuk, water reaching to horses' knees.
Gadhar Ghar	1	N.E.	The first fort of the district of Mookoor which forms the part of the Government of Kábul.
Source of the Turnuk	16	N.N.E.	Several fine springs under a range of hills. Road for the last ten miles lay through fields of waving corn (wheat and barley) clover and madder. Forts thickly spread over the country and abundance of water at every step. These forts form the district of Mookhoor; road level and free from stones.
Kahreez in the district of Obeh or Oba.	14	N.N.E.	Road sandy. Obeh is a pastoral district; the whole plain covered with flocks of sheep and goats and droves of camels. But few forts are to be seen; some Khails under the hills on either side of the road at the distance of 6 or 8 miles.
Chardeh	16	N.N.E.	One of the thousand forts of the fertile district of Karabagh which is chiefly peopled by Hazarehs. The whole country as far as the eye can reach is one large field of wheat. The harvest is gathered early in July.
Khareez	6	N.E.	Good level road.
Khareez	2	N.E.	Road execrable sand and large round stones.
Water Mills	16	...	In the district of Nánee between this district and Karrabagh is that of Moorakee which is said to be very populous and to contain many forts, but I saw nothing of it as I passed it in the dark.
Chehl Buchagan	8	N.E.	Fine groves; a place of pilgrimage; road good. Numerous villages, chiefly on the right, inhabited by the Undiri division of the Ghiljees, the whole plain covered with green wheat and fine clumps of trees. Abundance of water.
Ghuznee	4	N.N.E.	The present town of Ghuznee is a small place, not more than four hundred yards square, said to have been the citadel of a former town. It was built by the Jagatars four hundred years ago and is situated on the south slope of a hill to the S. W. of two minárs which are said to mark the spot upon which or near which stood the bázár of Sultán Mahmood's city. The walls of modern Ghuznee are lofty and stand upon a khakreez or *faussebraye* of considerable elevation; but the ditch is narrow and of no depth, and the whole of the works are commanded by some hills to the N. E. and N. of the place. At the northern and the upper end of the town is a hill upon which has been constructed a small citadel forming the palace of the Governor (Gholam Hyder Khán, a son of Ameer Dost Mahomed Khán). I saw one large unmanageable gun and four smaller ones as I passed from the gate of the town to the citadel. I had no opportunity, however, of examining their state; the approach to Ghuznee from the south is highly picturesque and the citadel from its great height looks formidable. The river of Ghuznee flows from the north under the western face of the town which supplies the place and the surrounding country with an abundance of water. Ghuznee may contain from 900 to 1,000 families—Tanjiks, Dooranees and Hindu shop-keepers and merchants. As Ghuznee commands the high road between Kandáhár and Kábul, it would be necessary that a force advancing from the former upon the latter place should take possession of it, but this would be easily accomplished as the works are of no strength and are commanded as above mentioned.
Tomb of Sultan Mahomed	2	N.E.	This celebrated place of pilgrimage is situated in the midst of a large village surrounded by fine gardens with several running streams.

TO SIMLA BY MAJOR D'ARCY TODD IN 1838.

Names of Towns, Villages, Stations.	Distance in Miles.	Direction.	Remarks.
	6	N.E.	A narrow defile called the "Tung-i-Sheer", a very strong position, but I believe it may be turned.
	1½	N.E.	End of pass.
Shusgao	2½	N.E.	Village. Water and cultivation.
Sydabad	23	W.	Village. The country between Shusgao and Sydabad highly cultivated; a fine valley between low hills; villages at every step; abundance of water; road good but stony in some places.
Logur River	4		Bridge called the Pul-i-Shaikabad. The Logur river runs from N.W. to S.E. crossing the valley and entering some hills to the eastward.
Top	6	N.	Village.
River of Kábul	12	N.	Ford, rapid stream, about 20 yards broad; water at the season (June) stirrup deep. The Kábul river comes from a break in the hills to N.W. of this point and runs in a south-easterly direction through a similar break called the Tung-i-Lullunder in the easterly range.
Mydán	½	N.	A collection of villages to the left of the road; rich cultivation; abundance of water. The country between Ghuznee and Mydán is chiefly inhabited by Wardeks who claim descent from Emaum Teiralabadeen; they number about 12,000 families and pay Rs. 90,000 to Government; they are divided into three branches— 1 Malyar, Chief Koorum Khán. 2 Nooree ,, Tein Khán. 3 Meerkhail ,, Ján Mahomed Khán.
Urghundee	9½	E.N.E.	Several fine villages forming the district of Urghundee about a mile to the north of the high road.
Kábul	14	E.	Half way from Urghundee the village of Kulla-i-Hazee. From this place to the city the road passes through a succession of gardens and fields; the whole country intersected by water-courses brought from the river of Kábul. Road excellent and gardens as far as the eye can reach. The approach to Kábul from the west is through a narrow defile which forms as it were the western gate of the city and through the defile runs the river of Kábul which afterwards flows through the centre of the city. The hills on both sides been fortified with lines of wall, flanked at regular intervals by massive towers, but the works, which have fallen to decay, are too extensive to be properly defended, and the height may be easily turned. The citadel or Bala Hissar, situated at the eastern extremity of the city, is a place of no strength, being commanded by heights in the vicinity. There are about 40 guns in Kábul, most of which are in a serviceable state. The route between Kandáhár and Kábul above described is generally blocked up by snow during four months of winter, but at the other seasons is good and passable for all descriptions of wheel carriages. Water is abundant and supplies are procurable at any seasons for an army of 20 or 30,000 men. A caravan travels between Kandáhár and Kábul in fifteen days, but horsemen perform the journey in 8 days and couriers in 6. I estimated the distance at 317 miles, but the direct route viá Kelat-i-Ghiljee is shorter by about ten or fifteen miles.
Kábul Bool	12	E. by N.	Village. Road through gardens and fields.
Khak Teezee	25	S.E. & E.	Do. situated on the skirt of a range of lofty hills. At the 4th mile entered a defile called Tung-i-Khoord Kábul, about 3 miles in length; ascended a small stream which is crossed by the road every 50 yards; after passing the defile the road enters an open country, the villages of Khoord Kábul. Two miles to the right, twelve miles beyond Bootlchak, another defile. Road hilly and stony, in some places impassable for guns. Between the second defile and Teizee the road passes over the "Huft Kothul" or seven passes. Khooda Buksh Khán is the Chief of this district.
Hissaruk (Pissaruk of Arrowsmith's map).	17	E. by S.	Cluster of villages on the Soorkhoud stream. After leaving Teizee steep ascent for about 5 miles, mountains covered with pine and holly-oak; magnificent scenery; road impassable for guns; abrupt

B 1485—8

Names of Towns, Villages, Stations.	Distance in Miles.	Direction.	Remarks.
			descent for about two miles; the road or pathway in the bed of a mountain stream. The Soorkhoud flowed from a break in the mountains to the east of Hissaruk. The skirt of the mountains covered with gardens and villages.
Isphan	4	E.S.E.	Village on the left of the road. Between Kábul and this place the country is inhabited by Ghiljees, but we here enter the districts peopled by Khogianees. Forded the Soorkhoud, a clear rapid stream near Hissaruk; water at this season (June) stirrup deep and about 20 yards broad. The Soorkhoud after being fed by numberless mountain streams which come down from the ranges called Suffeed Karh joins the Kábul river near Jallalabad.
Mookoor Khail	12	E. by S.	Large Village; abundance of water; fine cultivation; road strony but passable for wheel carriage; crossed several mountain streams running from south to north.
Wurzeh	14	E. & S.E.	Village in a valley ruuning down from the Suffeed Karh; abundance of water; gardens and cultivation. After leaving Mookoor Khail the road descends into a valley. At the sixth mile passes the celebrated garden of *Memla*, about a mile to the left. At the tenth mile villages and gardens on the skirts of the Suffeed Karh range.
Agaum	7	E. S. E. & S. E.	Village situated in a valley similar to that of Wurzeh. Fine stream, gardens and rich cultivation; villages as far as the eye can reach; road stony, but passable for guns. Sardar Mahomed Akber Khán, a son of Ameer Dost Mahomed Khán, was encamped with his troops in the valley of Agaum. This young man although not the eldest is said to be possessed of more power and influence than any of the other sons. He has acquired a high character for courage, and he certainly displayed this quality in the affair of Jumrood. The Government of Jallalabad has been entrusted to him, and if he is not greatly respected by the people, he is certainly the least unpopular of the family. His immediate dependants are said to be devoted to him. His troops were scattered in the different villages near Agaum when I passed through that place; but I believe he has twelve guns, chiefly 6-pounders, in a serviceable condition. A corps of 1,500 Jazarjurchees, a fine body of men, armed with long heavy guns which are fired from a rest and will carry a ball four hundred yards with precision, and two or three thousand good horses.
Jallalabad	24	N.N.E.	Village. The road or rather pathway for the first 6 miles led through gardens and rice fields; the whole country flooded for the purpose of irrigation, impassable for guns; there is however a gun road which makes a circuit of some miles between Agaum and Jallalabad; the remainder of the road passable for wheel carriages. Jallalabad is situated on the right bank of the Kábul river which is here a stream of considerable volume and about half a mile broad. Round Jallalabad are the remains of a wall of considerable extent, but the place is now reduced to a mere village, surrounded by extensive ruins. The various routes between Jallalabad and Peshawar have been already minutely described. At this season of the year (June) the river route is generally followed as being the safest and most expiditious. Rafts are formed of splinters of wood, which hold together from twenty to a hundred inflated bullock skins and an accident rarely happens during the months of May, June and July, when the water is of a sufficient depth to cover the rocks which are dangerous at other seasons. Near Jallalabad, the river runs in a broad bed with low banks on each side. Distant hills with snow on their summits on either hand. The space between the foot of these hills and the river covered with villages and green fields. Fine groves of trees scattered along the banks. The stream when I passed down was running at the rate of six or seven miles an hour. A few miles below Jallalabad the Kábul river is joined by a broad and rapid stream of considerable volume called

Names of Towns, Villages, Stations.	Distance in Miles.	Direction.	REMARKS.
			Durya-i-Koower. This distance between Jallalabad and Peshawar by the river route is about 90 miles. This distance is performed on a raft of 25 skins impelled by two large oars in about 12 hours. Half way is the large village of Lalpur, situated on the left bank of the river, the residence of Soadat Khan, Chief of the Momund tribe, which is said to number 40,000 families. After passing Lalpur the river flows for about 30 miles in a deep narrow channel walled in by precipitous rocky mountains of great height. In this part of the river are most of the whirlpools and dangerous places. One called the *Shutr Gurdun* or "camel's neck", 26 or 27 miles below Lalpur, is particularly dreaded by the raftsmen, and is considered, even in the best season, a place of peril. Two or three miles below *Shutr Gurdun* the river diverges from the mountains and enters an open cultivated country. At the village of Muchnee on the left bank tolls are levied on rafts passing down the river. From Muttee, a small village on the right bank of the river, seven or eight miles below *Shutr Gurdun*, Peshawur is distant about 14 miles. The country was overflowed for the purpose of irrigation, and the road, which passed through a succession of rice fields, was scarcely passable to laden ponies.
			I need say nothing of the present state of Peshawar or of the route through the Punjab from that place to Loodiana, both having been minutely described by others.

(Signed) E. D. TODD, Major,

Acting Secretary of H. B. M.'s Legation at the Court of Persia.

NOTICE ON HERAT

WITH A

SKETCH OF THE STATE OF AFFAIRS IN THE SURROUNDING COUNTRIES.

NOTICE ON HERA'T WITH A SKETCH OF THE STATE OF AFFAIRS IN THE SURROUNDING COUNTRIES.

1. *Object of the Report.*—While Persia prosecutes her designs against Herát, it is desirable to take a cursory view of the state of affairs in Herát itself, and the countries adjacent to it, as well to understand the resistance which they can offer as the facilities which they afford to an invading army. The variety of subjects treated only admits of this document being a sketch, in which light I give it.

2. Herát has been already described by so many travellers that any minuteness would be superfluous. It is situated in one of the richest countries in the East. It is a walled town with a citadel surrounded by a deep wet ditch, which is supplied with water from springs in it, and may also be filled from the river. The ditch is in good, and the walls in tolerable, repair. The size of Herát has been greatly overrated. The limited space occupied prevents its having the population assigned to it, and it is not considered half the size of Kábul. Asiatics are not good judges of the number of people in a city, but in comparing one place with another they may be relied on. The importance of its situation is very great, and it has always exercised considerable influence over the affairs of Central Asia. The most polished Court in the west of Europe could not at the close of the 15th century vie in magnificence with that of Herát.[1]

3. *Its Government and Politics.*—Kamran, the present ruler, is the last remaining scion of the Sudavzye princes in Afghánistán. He is a man of bad passions, cruel and dissipated, entirely in the hands of Yár Mahomed Khán Alckozye, an Afghán, who has raised himself to eminence at Herát by getting rid of all the other Chiefs. He is now Vazir and would remove Kamran himself or substitute a son in his stead were he not afraid of the great Huzara Chief Shere Mahomed Khán, who resides to the north and is a devoted supporter of Kamran's interests. The great tribe of the Berdooránees, who were removed from Eastern Afghánistán to Herát by Nadir, are nearly extinct in Herát. Of 3,000 families about one-fourth remain, and their Chief Meer Sidick Khán has been lately put to death for real or supposed intrigues in Persia and Kandáhár. Shumsoodeen Khán Populzye, who distinguished himself in the last war with Persia, and had the Government of Fura, has now gone over to that power in disgust—an unfortunate and ill-timed defection. The Chief of Lash, Sháh Pusund Khán, has also repaired to the Persian camp.

4. *Garrison.*—The garrison in Herát consists of about 10,000 men. The Vazir and his family muster 1,500, and the dependants of Kamran about 200 more. 6,000 Dooránees and other Afgháns have been removed from Fura into the city, and besides these are 3,000 foot, known by the name of "Doutulub." These are also Afgháns, and a description of troops first established by Ahmed Sháh Dooránee. They were obliged to furnish a horseman for every pair of ploughs, but Kamran last year converted the levy into foot, fixing two individuals for each plough. It caused a great deal of dissatisfaction, but this, it is believed, is now removed, The Kuzzelbash, or Shiáh inhabitants, have been either sold by the minister or fled the country, with the exception of about 1,200 families, who have been removed to a place called Jakera outside the city to prevent treason. Many of the Soonee residents have been also sold, but the rest remain. Provisions have been plentifully stored, and to this time the city cannot be correctly said to be besieged, since two of its gates are open. There are but 10 guns in Herát, and none of any calibre. The strength of the place consists more in its position than garrison.

---

* Erskine's Baber.

In 1833 when the present Sháh of Persia, then Mahomed Mirza, attacked Herát, the operations were interrupted by the death of A'bbás Mirza, and the Persians made a disastrous retreat to Tehrán.

5. *Siege of Herát.*—The Persian Army has been before Herát for the last 60 days without making any impression upon it. Ghorian, the frontier town and a strong place, was betrayed into their hands, and this has enabled them to procure provisions and make good their footing, otherwise the subsistence of the army would have been very difficult; as it is the defections of Shumsodeen Khán and others have been most fortunate for them. The season chosen for the attack is favourable to Persia in one respect, because it prevents Kamran being succoured by the Khivans, Toorkmáns, and other nations of Toorkistán. If Herát can hold out till the equinox (Nowroz), it is supposed that this aid may be procured, as will be hereafter stated. If the Persians are obliged to raise the siege it will prove most calamitous to them; if Herát falls, the power of the Afgháns as a nation will be much broken. In Ghorian Persia has secured a great stronghold which may hereafter enable her to hold her position and contribute to her ultimate success.

6. *Extent of Herát Revenue.*—At the present time the chiefship of Herát extends eastward to the Khanshrood, a river half way to Kandáhár. To the north it has but a few miles of territory, the country in that quarter belonging to Shere Mahomed Khán Huzara. To the west to the district of Ghorian which, before its capture, exercised an influence over the Persian canton of Khaf. To the south Herát is bounded by the Helmund and Seistán, Kamran having subdued this latter province about four years ago. Herát has four districts called "wilayuts" and nine called "belooks." The "wilayuts" are Obé and Ghorian on the east and west, Kurokh or Kila-i-Nan on the north, and Sabizwar on the south. Its "belooks" are the lands cultivated by so many canals and bear their names. Two-thirds of the produce is generally taken by Government. It is doubtful if the revenue amounts to 13 lákhs of rupees; but Kamran is rich in jewels and hoarded treasure. Tyranny and trade do not exist together.

7. The territories of Herát need not be further described. I shall commence from the south and give, in succession, an account of the circumjacent countries. Seistan, though now a province of Herát, will deserve a short notice from its former fame. The ruling family of this province, descended from the line of Kyánee, has lately lost its power. To Behrám Khán Kyánee a son succeeded to the Government and ruled over three Chiefs, two of whom were Seistánees and Shiáhs, the other a Belooch. A brother rebelled and sought the assistance of the Belooch Chief, the son of Khán Ján by an intermarriage. The rightful heir died or was put to death and the Beloochees ill-using the rebellious brother, he fled to Herát and sued for the aid of Kamran. He immediately invaded Seistan, plundered it and drove off 6,000 of its inhabitants captive, whom he sold into slavery or exchanged to the Toorkmáns for horses. He assigned to the Kyánee family the town of Jahánábád south of the Helmund, where they now reside, and fixed his own Governor at Chukunsoor north of the river. Little regular revenue is derived from Seistán except camels, cows and sheep; it is thinly peopled and altogether a poor possession.

8. *Geography of Seistán.*—The most remarkable feature of this old province is the intersection by the Helmund and its tributary rivers. In summer all these are greatly swollen, and it has been said that they form a lake called "Zurrah"; but the natives whom I interrogated were unacquainted with this name and described the rivers to be lost in a vast swampy region, full of reeds called "Hamoo." Many of the places on the map are also quite unknown; but this will be sufficiently accounted for when it is stated that ancient forts are often laid bare by the blowing away of the sand, while modern ones are overwhelmed. This is to the people a constant source of wonder, and castles of a former age are said to show themselves as newly from the hands of the architect. The singular appearance of the waters of the Helmund and this changeable face of nature would account for the many fabulous descriptions of Seistán. Among

innumerable ruins which I heard of, one in particular, that of an old city called Zdedum in the "Loote" or desert, yields many antiquities—rings, coins, &c.,—which are taken by the finders to Fura for sale. One curious property of the climate is that the horse cannot live in it and probably there are not 100 of these in Seistán. Kamran lost nearly all his cavalry in his campaign, most of the horses dying from a disease of the digestive organs contracted in it, which makes it very unfavourable for military operations; but the camels of Seistán are celebrated.

9. *Lásh.*—To the north of Seistán and south of Fura, one of the governments under Herát is the small district of Lásh held by Sháh Pusund (or Saloo) Khán, a Sakzye Dooránee. Lásh itself is a place of considerable strength in these parts, being a fort on a scarped hill or rock, which has resisted all Kamran's endeavours to take it. It is situated on the Fura road and, with seven or eight small forts, forms all the possession of this Chief. Kamran, unable to seize it, destroyed its "kahreezes" or water-courses. This hostile disposition has driven Sháh Pusund Khán from his natural friends the Afgháns to Persia, with which he is leagued in hopes of warding off danger from himself. The Chief is well spoken of in these countries. He received the ex-king Shooja-ool-Moolk after his last defeat at Kándahár, who fled there in hopes of support from Kamran; but though these members of the Sudarzye family exchange presents with each other there is no cordiality, since in the success of either, one must fall, and at present Kamran has power of which Shooja has been deprived.

10. *Kayu.*—Kayu is the first Persian province to the west of Fura and lies on the frontier of the kingdom. It is entirely inhabited by Shiáhs, which has led the Toorkmáns to seek for slaves in it during their "chupows" or forays. The inhabitants are a timid race and live in small forts, the number of which is very great. Kayu is a country badly watered, and the bair tree, which always flourishes in arid countries, is common. Birgind and Kayu are the principal places, and the district is ruled by a Governor of its own, whose subjection to the Sháh however is complete, since he furnishes a quota of three or four thousand infantry when called upon. They form part of the force at present before Herát. The Chief of Herát had designs on Kayu, and on a difference between that and the neighbouring canton of Tubbus, which arose six years ago, Kamran lent his aid to the Governor of Kayu, but the dispute was adjusted. Kayu was never subdued by Kamran, and it refused also to accept a governor of A'bbás Mirza's appointment in 1832. It is now held by a son of Meer Alum Khán, its former Governor.

11. *Tubbus.*—Adjoining Kayu and further to the west is Tubbus, which is also subject to Persia and inhabited by Shiáhs. Its principal places are Tubbus, Toon and Goonabad. Of them Toon is the largest. It has its own Governor, Meer Ali Naghee Khán, and very much resembles Kayu in soil and productions, though the orange tree is not found in any other part of Khorásán. Its quota of troops is also furnished in infantry, and both places are noted for the carpets which form part of their tribute.

12. *Toorshish.*—North of Tubbus is Toorshish, a district which is well watered and peopled yielding good fruit. It is smaller than Kayu and furnishes about 3,000 troops to the Sháh, and has a governor appointed over it. It lies south from Meshed.

13. *Khaf.*—Between Toorshish and Herát, and south of the road which leads from Meshed to that city, is the district of Khaf, a miserable tract with a climate very incongenial from the high winds. It has been nearly depopulated by the Toorkmáns. The principal place is Killa Rohee, which is held by Nussur Collah Teimoree, who is a Shiáh. Khaf could scarcely be said to be dependent on Persia till the present campaign. The Shiáh population is also outnumbered by the Soonees, who are Teimurees. Kamran's minister had, in some degree, subdued Khaf and very imprudently garrisoned the frontier town of Ghorian by its natives, who were Shiáhs, which led to its being betrayed into the hands of the Sháh.

14. The hilly country between Meshid and Herát, on both sides of the high road, to within 40 miles of that city, has been subject to Persia since 1833, and is held directly under Meshid. Previous to that period, many petty Chiefs, who were robbers, occupied the tract. Of these Mahomed Khán Kuráee of Toorbut Hyderee was the most notorious. He is now in the service of the Sháh, and Toorbut and Sungan, his strongholds, are garrisoned by Persians. Toorbut-i-Shakh Jam, a place of pilgrimage, was held by the Huzaras, as also Mahmoodabad and Shuhr-i-no. On the approach of the Persians the population was marched further east, and the few residents in these places only cultivate within a gun-shot of their villages from fear of the Toorkmáns. Water and forage abound.

15. *Shurukhs.*—North of this tract, and about 100 miles from Meshid, lies Shurukhs, long the seat of Toorkmáns, who plundered Khorásán. In 1832 I saw it rich in the spoils of others, but a few months after it was surprised by A'bbás Meerza in person, who either captured or killed its entire population. Those who were ransomed returned to Shurukhs; but in the following year the Khivans, who claim some power over it, insisted on their removing further into the desert to Merv,. where they are located. Shurukhs has abundance of cultivable land on the banks of the Tijend; but the excesses of its population scared away the traveller and the merchant, and if not now the residence of robbers, it lies on the route by which these children of the desert issue to plunder on the frontiers of Persia.

16. *Moorghab and the Soonee Huzaras.*—Immediately north of Herát lies the country of the Soonee Huzaras, and that portion of the tribe ruled by Shere Mahomed Khán of Killa-i-no, an adherent of the Chief of Herát. This country includes Obé, and extends to the Moorghab. On the last invasion of Herát, he removed about 4,000 Tajik families from their seats nearer Herát, to the more fertile lands east of Punjdeh on the bank of that river, that if his enemies triumphed over him near Herát, he might still have subjects. This Chief has great power in these countries, and besides his attachment to Kamran has connections with the Khivans, Toorkmáns and Chiefs in and about Maimuna, all of whom would only assist Herát through him. He plunders the country of its property and inhabitants as far west as Meshid and Nishapur, and the petty Chiefs of Khaf, Toorshish and Tabbus are glad to send him annual presents to spare in some degree their people. He is a man of about 45 years of age and of a better disposition than his cruel occupation would lead to the belief. He is a nephew of Mahomed Khán Begler-begec and now holds that title. He can take the field with 6,500 horse; 2,000 of these are constantly present and 2,000 more from his "Ooloos" can be assembled in a few days, 1,500 are furnished from the Feerozkohees, who are his subjects, and the Jamsheedee Kimaks, who are his friends and co-adjutors, will send 1,000 more. He can also command two or three thousand horse from Maimuna, and on the former invasion of the Persians Toorkmáns co-operated with him. Without the aid of Shere Mahomed Khán, Herát could have no hope against Persia, but that Chief will not aid Kamran against Kandáhár or any other power. Though cordial with Kamran, he is inimical to his minister, whom he considers to have supplanted him in authority.

17. *Maimuna.*—Across the Moorghab and towards Balkh, which city is in the territories of the king of Bokhára, lie the small states of Maimuna, Andkho, Shibbergan, Siripool and Akchu. A connection, as I have before stated, subsists between them and Herát, but since they are divided against each other, their aid is of small avail, as a minute account of them will better exhibit. All of them are engaged in the slave trade and independent, though they send presents of horses, both to Herát and Bokhára. Maimuna is the most important of the whole. The Chief is Mizrab Khán, an Uzbek of the tribe of Wun, and his country extends from Maimuna to the Moorghab and adjoins that of Shere Mahomed Khán Huzara. Maimuna itself is an open town or rather village

of about 500 houses, but the strength of the Chief consists in his "Ils" or moving population who frequent Ulmar, Jankira, Sorbagh, Kafir Kilar, Khyrabad, Kusar, Chuchaktoo, Tukht-i-Khatoom and other sites which can scarcely be called villages. He also numbers Arabs among his subjects, many of that tribe having been long settled here. With his whole adherents drawn out he could muster about 6,000 horse and three small guns; but he could never quit his territories with half the number, as he is on bad terms with the Chief of Seripool, who is much feared though less powerful. Mizrab Khán is about 40 years of age; he succeeded to his brother about six years ago, whom he poisoned—a common mode of disposing of people in these countries, and a fate which his own father also met.

18. *Andkho.*—Andkho or Andkhoee is ruled by Sháh Wullee Khán, an Ufshur Toork who settled here, with others of his tribe, in the time of Nádir. They were then Shiáhs, but are now Soonces. The "Ils" of the Chief, besides his own race, are Arabs, and he can furnish 500 horse, and is on good terms with Maimuna. Andkho has a larger fixed population than Maimuna being on one of the high roads to Bokhára; but there is a scarcity of water in this canton. It is here that the wheat is a triennial plant. Andkho is the place where Moorcroft perished.

19. *Shibbergam.*—Shibbergam belongs to an Uzbeck Chief named Roostam Khán, who has a character for moderation; he can muster five or six hundred horse and is on good terms with both Maimuna and Koondooz. Shibbergam is considered to be a very ancient place, being given to the days of the Kaffirs (Greeks?) and still the strongest fort in these parts. The "ark" or citadel is built of brick and mortar and surrounded by walls of mud. Kilick Ali Beg, the late Chief of Balkh, besieged it for seven years without success; but it must only be understood to be strong against Uzbeks, who are badly supplied with artillery. Water is conducted to it from the rivulet of Siripool.

20. *Siripool.*—Toolfkar Shere, an Uzbek of the tribe of Achumuclee, governs Siripool and is known as a brave and determined man. He is on bad terms both with Koondooz and Maimuna, and though he has only one thousand horse, he resists the attacks of both and plunders all round. His feud with Maimuna arises on account of his daughter, a wife of the former Chief, being seized by Mizrab Khán. His "Ils" are in Sungcharuk, Paogan, Goordewan and Dughdrab, and if he can enlarge their number, which is not improbable, his power will be increased. Siripool itself is as large as Maimuna.

21. *Akhchu and Balkh.*—Akhchu is a dependency of Balkh and held by a son of Eshan Khoja, the governor of that once vast city. It is consequently tributary to Bokhára. The Governor of Balkh through fear lately permitted Moorood Beg of Koondooz to establish himself on one of the canals of Balkh; but the king of Bokhára sent a force of 8,000 men and has just dislodged him; half of this body was raised in Balkh and the rest from Bokhára. The Koondooz Chief offered no resistance to the king.

22. *Supplies, Roads and nature of these Chiefships.*—All of these chiefships are situated in the plain country which in general is well watered by rills or canals and has abundance of forage for camels and horses which are numerous. The soil is dry, but there are many gardens near the towns. The style of building, from a scarcity of wood, is that of the bee-hive shape. There is a good open caravan road from Meshid to Balkh, which is a journey of 16 days; thus from Meshid to Shurukhs 4, to the Moorghab 3, to Maimuna 4, and to Balkh in 5 days. This is much the nearest route to Kábul from the west.

23. *Huzaras between Herát and Kábul.*—Between Herát and Kábul and south of these chiefships, lies the mountainous country of the Huzaras. The journey between the cities has been performed in 12 days by Sháh Zumán with a body of horse and is said to be passable for aillery of small calibre. Caravans also travel it in summer, but the ascents and descents of

innumerable hills are such that it is very fatiguing to the cattle, and the roads from Kábul by Maimuna or Kandáhár are always preferred. Towards Herát the Huzaras are Soonces, while those near Kábul are Shiáhs, which is a singular reversal, since the people of Kábul are of the former and those of Persia of the latter persuasion. About Khojee Chist, east of Obé and Herát the Teimuneer are partially submissive to Shere Mahomed Khán and will assist Herát. Those who are near Maimuna and the adjoining States are plundered by them, while Moorád Beg of Koondooz plunders the country to Yokoa-bung over three of the passes of Hindoo Koosh and near Bamian. The eastern portion about Bamian, and west of the road between Ghuzni and Kandáhár, are subjects of Kábul and pay a regular tribute. They are the Huzaras of Besoot, Dih-Zunghee (in part), Kava Bagh and Jaghooree. The Kuzzilbashes of Kábul have orders given, on the greater part of this tract, for their allowances, the people being Shiáhs; but the revenues of Besoot are generally collected by one of the Ameer's sons. The Huzaras of Taloda Hoojoo-ristán, which is west of Jaghooree, as well as those of Deh Koondee, secure independence from their remote position. The whole race is without a head, or it might prove very formidable; at present they are driven off in every direction and sold like sheep. At no period did the kings of Kábul derive so much revenue from them as is now procured by Dost Mahomed Khán. The Eastern Huzaras are bigoted Shiáhs, and devotedly attached to the Persian party in Afghánistán.

24. *Kandáhár.*—South of the territories of the Huzaras we have the Chiefship of Kandáhár, but its affairs require a more extended notice than can be here given to them. It will be sufficient to observe, that if Herát were not crippled by Persia, Kandáhár could not resist an attack from it without the aid of Kábul. The position of Kandáhár is isolated, and its cordial union with Kábul is therefore necessary for its existence and preservation. The chiefs themselves are perfectly aware of their danger, and in seeking an alliance with Persia, have no security in their solicitude, but the object of security against Herát. Their position is further endangered by differences which are unhappily too frequent among the ruling brothers, and which foreign threats do not always extinguish.

25.—*Probable effects of Persian invasion and ascendancy.*—Having thus passed in review the state of Herát itself and the countries around it, they certainly would not appear to be in a condition likely to offer much resistance to a power which had any consolidation. If Persia fails in the present attack, the result may be disastrous to her, but if enabled to establish an ascendancy in Herát, she could in course of time bring under subjection the petty States to the north. She could never advance a step further east without paralyzing or conquering them. The Afgháns themselves view with concern, and many of them with despair, the present invasion by Persia; the whole resources of that country, say they, have never of late years been arranged under the Sháh, and that this attack differs in consequence from all others. If it prove successful they anticipate the removal of the Afgháns round Herát into the interior of the kingdom according to a usage very common in these countries, which will let in upon its fertile plains the neighbouring Shiáh subjects of Persia and thus fix its supremacy and supplant the feelings of the Afgháns in religion and policy by those of Persia. Should these opinions turn out well founded, the result of the campaign will be most calamitous to the Afghán people, though the progress of Persia towards Kábul itself would even in that case be still impeded by the number of chiefships, though their number and their disunion would ensure their ultimate fall. It is fortunate that the Huzaras about Herát are enemies, in creed, to Persia and that the whole country to the Indus is inhabited by rigid Soonees; still with a tolerant policy that interfered not with their religion, any power might overrun and maintain the region lying between India and Persia. Had Runjeet Sing, in the outset of his career, permitted the Mahomedans to pray aloud and kill cows, he might have possessed himself of the entire kingdom of Ahmed Sháh Dooránee. But Persia is not likely to pursue more enlightened views, and the present reigning family in Afghánistan, the Barukzyes, may avail themselves of the opportunity to secure their possessions by submitting to this power, for, since Persia cannot govern them herself, they may do it under her. Should however the Afgháns, circumscribed though they now are, by narrow limits, be freed from apprehension on the East, instead of following the destinies of Persia, on the fall of Herát, they might without difficulty be united, when their country would form a barrier not to be forced by future aggressors. The materials are, by no means, so incoherent as they at first sight appear, but without measures that will ensure their union as a nation (whatever independence may be allowed to each chiefship) this country must sink under one of even inferior resources.

(Signed)   A. BURNES.

Kábul, 7th February 1838.

NARRATIVE

OF A

JOURNEY FROM KHELÁT TO SONMEANI IN NOVEMBER 1839

By

CAPTAIN OUTRAM.

NARRATIVE

OF

A JOURNEY FROM KHELA'T TO SONMEANI IN NOVEMBER 1839.

It being a point of importance to ascertain the practicability, or otherwise, of a direct road for troops from Kandáhár and Shawl, through Beluchistan, to the sea, viâ Khelát, I determined on exploring that through Nal, said to be the best káfilla route, the only other road having been reported on by Colonel Pottinger 30 years previously.

Accordingly, being relieved from military duty, by the successful termination of hostilities consequent on the capture of Khelát on the 13th November, and honored by General Wiltshire's despatches for the Bombay Government, I left camp (before Khelát) at midnight on the 15th November disguised in Afghán costume, and accompanied by three holy Syuds of Shawl, two armed attendants of theirs, and one of my own, the whole party of six persons being mounted on four ponies and two camels carrying provisions for the road, and as much grain for the animals as we could conveniently take.

My preparations being scarcely completed on the 15th, I had intended to delay till next day, but that forenoon the Syuds came to urge immediate departure, in order, they said, to precede, if possible, the news of the death of the Chiefs Wully Mahomed of Wudd, and Shahdost of Nal who were slain in the combat of the 13th November. It being considered advisable to depart as secretly as possible, we agreed to leave camp at midnight.

16th November, nineteen hours in the saddle.—Halted at 4 P.M. for an hour at Rodrinjoe, after a pleasant march of four hours in bright moonlight but bitterly cold; not a soul in the village, it being usual for the inhabitants to emigrate to the warmer climate of Cutch Gundava for the winter. At daybreak continued our journey to Sohrab, a cluster of villages also deserted for the same reason, with the exception of one or two families remaining in each to look after the premises. On this day's march passed many groupes of fugitive women from Khelát, the men who ought to have protected them either having been killed in fight, or outstripped them in flight! One party, however, was better attended than the rest, having several armed men with it (but all the females except one old lady, were on foot), on coming up to which my friends the Syuds were recognized as old acquaintances, and a long detail of the hardships they had endured was entered into by the ladies, who, it appeared, were the families of the Khan's brother, and of the principal minister, Mahomed Hussan, who, poor things, had never been beyond the precincts of a harem before. It behoved us to remain with them a sufficient time to listen to their griefs while we kept the same road; and especially was I called upon in my holy character of *Pir* (as which my companions had announced me, and I had afterwards to support throughout the journey), to display sympathy, which I did by apparent attention, though not understanding a word they said, while one of my companions relieved the mother for a time of the burden of Mahomed Hussan's child, by carrying it on horseback before him. My situation during the time we accompanied this party was by no means enviable, for, independent of the fairness of my complexion being calculated to excite suspicion, (although concealed as much as possible by a large turban tied over the chin,) it so happened that I had equipped myself and servant in apparel taken from Mahomed Hussan's own wardrobe, from which the prize agents had permitted me to select what was necessary for my disguise. Fortunately,

I had considered the humblest garb most suited to the character I was to assume, and the clothes I selected were probably of too common a description to have passed through the harem, the fair hands of whose inmates embroidered the more costly suits. Whether from that cause, or that their cares diverted their thoughts from such trifles, our garments were not recognized, and we took the first opportunity of pleading an excuse to leave the poor creatures behind. We were pestered however, throughout the journey by horsemen, galloping up from different directions to enquire into the particulars of the Khelát disaster; but my friends the Syuds always managed to place themselves in such a position as to be first questioned, and had then so much of interest to communicate to the enquirers that I remained unnoticed. The sensation created by the news of the fall of Khelát and death of Mehrab Khán, and the other chiefs, was very great, and as far as I could understand, many were the curses showered on the Firangis, and vows of vengeance; while national vanity induced them to seek every means of excusing the defeat of their countrymen. The more they questioned, however, the more were they downhearted at the undeniable evidence of the superiority of Pirangi prowess; and I suspect their ardour to avenge their brethren was considerably cooled by what they learnt, and will soon evaporate entirely, though we were told that the Khán's brother and his spiritual adviser, who yesterday had passed in flight, gave out they were only going to assemble the tribes to assail our troops in their descent through the passes.

We selected for our bivouac that night the shelter of the walls of a deserted village, but our arrival was observed, and, notwithstanding the apparently deserted state of the country, people flocked to us from all quarters to enquire regarding relatives and friends engaged at Khelát; among others, were agents sent back by the Khán's brother to meet and escort his and the minister's families, which we had passed in the morning. My companions, the Syuds, were not sparing in their taunts at the conduct of the Khán's brother for leaving his family behind to walk on foot, while he and his companions fled on horseback. They also hinted that he must have been very precipitate in leaving Khelát, as there was no egress from the place for an hour before Mehrab Khán fell in the citadel. This indignation on the part of my friends elicited much applause in the assembly, and the emissaries of the Khán's brother (I forget his name) looked very foolish, but they talked big, and said he was only gone to raise the clans to cut off the Firangis in the pass. I afterwards asked the Syuds if this was likely, as in that case I should wish to send back some warning to the General that such was contemplated. They assured me however that the blow struck on the 13th prevented any chance of an obstruction to the English being attempted, that no body of Beluchees would now dare to unite to oppose us, and that the Khán's brother merely urged that pretext to cover his own cowardice. During these discussions I avoided the inconvenience of being personally questioned by pretending to sleep, but my companions had to satisfy a succession of inquirers till night was well advanced, when the moment we were relieved from their presence we determined on pushing on immediately, instead of resting till morning as we had intended, to avoid detention and inconvenient questioning by fresh visitors we might expect to be assailed by in the morning. A poor man was persuaded to engage with us as guide, but only on condition that I would furnish a charm to insure a sick camel from harm during his absence, accordingly a tuft of the animal's hair was brought to me and I was obliged in support of my assumed characters to go through the farce of apparently muttering cabalistic words over it. God forgive the hypocrisy.

Travelled six hours further that night to a stream of clear water, where we bivouacked till daybreak. In the morning we were delighted to find the traces of the horses and camels of the Khán's brother and other fugitives which we had hitherto followed. Struck off to the left, taking the road to Wudd, their being in our front having caused us considerable anxiety here-to-fore.

17th November, 10 hours.—Continued our journey for 10 hours to Parkoo, a village lately destroyed by the Khán for some contumacy of its inhabitants, where we found comfortable shelter for the night amidst the ruins, and were spared the society of strangers, of whom we fortunately met none during this day's march. The few hamlets we passed being at this time entirely deserted.

18th November, 17 hours.—Departed at daybreak and crossed a high range of hills by a goat-path impracticable for any laden cattle, my companions having heard of persons being on the high road to Nal, whom they thought it prudent to avoid; occupied five hours in reaching that place, but passed it and rested in the jungles three miles beyond, sending one of the Syuds and two attendants into the village for horse gram; unfortunately the latter missed our hiding place and passed on, for whom, having waited till evening, we became alarmed and the other Syud went back to the village to enquire about them, leaving me with no one, but my servant Hoossain. As neither of us could speak a word of the Belluch language should have been awkwardly situated had we been discovered and addressed by any of the people, several of whom passed close to us on their way home from the fields. Nearly an hour elapsed and darkness was coming on without any appearance of the Syud, whereupon I could not but conclude that my journey had been discovered and that Fakeer Mahomed, the Chief of Nal, whose near relation had been killed, had adopted the plan of detaining my companions to oblige me to come and seek them. Under these circumstances I considered what was best to be done, the provisions and money were with the other parties, without which, without guide or knowledge of the language, murder was inevitable by the first Beluchees we meet, who must immediately detect who we were; I determined therefore at once to proceed to the village where the holy influence of my Syud friends might still prove of some avail, if I failed to terrify the chief into civility by threats of the consequences of maltreating a British Officer. We were on our way accordingly and I was comforting poor Hoossain with the assurance that his life as a Mahomedan was at all events secure, when a cry from behind caused us to look round, and we joyfully recognized our friend the Syud, who having missed our place of concealment had long been hunting for us, a most happy reprieve from what I considered almost certain destruction. The Syud informed us that the rest of our party had left the village some hours before, and had doubtless gone on thinking we had preceded them. We therefore now went in search of them, and after two hours tracing from village to village where we ascertained they had been enquiring for us, we found them at last in a small fort, assisting at the wake of its chief the news of whose death at Khelát had arrived that afternoon. We could hear the wailing of the women long before we reached the village, which sounded very plaintively in the still night. The relations of the deceased urgently invited us to enter the house of mourning but we protested against intruding in the hour of such distress, and were glad of the excuse for proceeding on after resting for an hour, determined at last to outstrip the news of the Khelát catastrophe by pushing on all night, which we did till near day-break (8 hours), at an amble of at least five miles an hour, being a perfectly level smooth road and beautiful moonlight, also now quite mild, a most agreeable change from the bitter cold we had so lately experienced, and a proof how much we must have descended since leaving Khelát. It was satisfactory to find also that we were now out of the haunts of man, having seen no trace of habitation for the last thirty miles, and it was with a feeling of greater security than we had yet experienced that we lay down to sleep for a couple of hours on the bank of a river.

19th November, 8 hours.—On awaking about 7 A.M. were much vexed to find that our guide had decamped. He having been paid in advance for the whole trip to Beila, and tired probably of our long journeys (though riding on a camel) as well as ourselves, had taken advantage of our sound sleep to walk off, carrying nothing with him however as we always slept on the little kit we possessed, and with our bridles in our hands. Fortunately some flocks were observed grazing at a little distance and we persuaded a shepherd to accompany us. Our journey this day occupied eight hours by a good road passing over a high range of mountains the "Oornach" by easy ascent and descent; bivouacked in the bed of the Oornach river generally dry but here some small springs trickled into it from the side of a hill, affording a little green grass for our horses, the first forage we had had time or opportunity to give them, they having hitherto subsisted on a scanty allowance of grain brought with us, from Khelát in the first instance and renewed at Nal. The camels also had green tamarisk to feed on, a luxury they had enjoyed for the first time yesterday in the Nal Valley, on entering which the sight of the luxuriant green tamarisk bushes was quite refreshing, contrasted with the stuff we had seen in Afghanistan stunted and brown, as if burnt by fire or blighted by frost. Indeed this was the first green foliage we had yet seen since leaving Kábul with the exception of a few juniper bushes in the Karkar hills; and its appearance, as also that of several well known Indian shrubs, lost sight of since we entered Afghanistan, cheered me much on my last night's moonlight march, such as the babool and keim trees, also bulrushes, &c. Even the scanty yellow grass on the hill sides in the Sohrab valley was a pleasing sight to me, for nowhere between that and Kábul is grass to be found growing wild except occasionally fringing water streams. No habitations seen, or people met, on this march.

20th November, 18 hours.—Marched at midnight, almost full moon, passed some hamlets and fields of ripe jovári (the first seen since leaving India) in a retired dell in the midst of the hills seemingly quite isolated from the world by the wildness of mountains surrounding it; passed on silently without communicating with or awaking the inhabitants, said to be a wild race notwithstanding the peaceful appearance of their valley. Surmounted the Pooralloo range, higher apparently than that of the Oornach. Here were dashed any hopes of the practicability of this route, which latterly had become sanguine, for the road over this pass, which I saw no means of otherwise turning, is a path so narrow, steep, and rocky, sometimes winding along the side of precipitous hills, at others through narrow fissures of hard rock, as to be utterly impracticable for guns, and incapable of being made so but at immense cost of time and labour if at all. After eleven hours' march dismounted and passed the day in a ravine affording a scanty supply of water and a little green pasture for the cattle; under pretence of the heat separated to a little distance from my companions for the shelter of a bush, but in reality to indulge in the pleasure of reading a Bombay Times of the 12th October which I had secreted for the purpose of beguiling an hour but had hitherto had no opportunity of looking at. The history of this paper is somewhat curious. After the storm of Khelát while the place was yet uncleared of the prisoners, and some were still holding out, a person of consideration among the Beluchees held up the paper to the soldier who probably would have sacrificed him on the spot considering it a barefaced avowal of one of the acts by which his race had most vexed us, *i. e.* robbing our Dâks. Luckily Major Campbell passing at the time inquired into the matter, and ascertained that this personage having sent to tender his submission to the Political Agent, and to request a safe conduct, that officer returned this paper (received that morning) to be used as a signal of protection in the absence of a written one, there being no writing materials at hand to furnish it. While occupied with my paper, hearing a rustling above me, I looked up, and was not a little startled to see a ferocious looking wild Beloochee with a long matchlock observing me from the top of the bank, who made off however on seeing my companions get up from a little distance on my calling to them; how he came there or what his intentions were, I know not, but the circumstance warned me not to separate from my companions and to be more careful in future of displaying the paper. In the evening continued our journey for seven hours over another range of mountains, but both ascent and descent easy, generally along smooth fine sandy beds of dry water channels, which in the descent gradually widened to the expanse of a magnificent river but quite devoid of water, the banks varying from sloping hills shaded with gigantic tamarisk trees, to perpendicular bare rock of stupendous height, generally opening to wide valleys in the former case, and contracting to narrow channels in the latter. The scenery throughout this march heightened by bright moonlight was very beautiful. I here had the pleasure to recognize an old Indian acquaintance in the "prickly-pear" which brought pleasing recollections of Hog and Tiger hunts to "while the weary way." Not a trace of inhabitants the whole of this day's march except in the secluded dell above mentioned.

21st November, 9½ hours.—Arose from our bivouac at daybreak, for two hours our road still continued along dry water channels, on emerging from which glad I was to find my view to the outward unconfined by hills. All before me was now open, all difficulties surmounted, and [but little danger remaining, for the tidings of Khelát had not yet travelled so far. One easy march of nine and half hours brought us to a hamlet on the opposite bank of the Purali (a fine river with much cultivation for the last six miles along the right bank), where we bivouacked, my companions indulging in a fatted lamb and free intercourse with the people, concealing however the events at Khelát, and fate of Mehrab Khán, to whose daughter the Beila Chief is married, or of Wully Mahomed his (the Beila Chief's) uncle. My own fare however continued as heretofore to consist of dates and water, which was attributable to the abstinence becoming my holy character.

22nd November, 10½ hours.—Started at 3 A.M. so as to pass Beila before daybreak. Had to pass through a large kafillah from Bombay encamped under its walls, the leaders of which roused by their dogs and seeing the direction from which we had come were most importunate for information as to what was going on at Khelát, having heard at Bombay that the English Army was expected there, and fearing that they might suffer in passing through the country in case of warfare. The Syuds were prudently uncommunicative however, declaring that we had only come from Nal and that when we left that place it was unknown how the Firangis would settle with Mehrab Khán. The kafillah people evidently suspected that we knew more about it, and plied us with numerous questions, but we at last got away from them as the day broke, my friends being particularly anxious to avoid recognition by people at Beila, who would have insisted on detaining us from motives of hospitality which might have led to very unpleasant consequences. Pursued our journey till 1 P.M. and rested on the bank of the Purali; no village. From Beila two roads branch off, one direct to Sonmeani, the other viâ Lyari to Sonmeani, the latter most circuitous, which, however, I chose, as the other had been seen by Pottinger.

23rd November, 14 hours.—Marched at 8 P.M. On the 22nd travelled all night and till 10 this forenoon, when we arrived at Sonmeani, passing Lyari, a paltry village. Indeed the country from Beila to the sea though perfectly level, a rich soil, and well watered by the Purali, is almost a desert owing to the scantiness of its population; besides Beila, Lyari and Sonmeani, I did not see above half a dozen hamlets, and those consisting of but a few huts each, the whole way from the hills to the sea.

Ascertained and made myself known to the Hindu agent of Naomull Seth of Karáchi, who treated me and my companions most hospitably and furnished me with a boat in which I embarked in the evening for Karáchi, taking with me my Afghan yaboo, which though only 13 hands, had carried me and saddle bags, altogether weighing upwards of 16 stones, the whole distance (355 miles) in 7½ days, having during that time been 111 hours on his back.

(Signed) J. OUTRAM, Captain.

P S.—12th December 1839.—A batch of horses landed from Somneani, the Beloochi dealers with which state, at midnight of the day I sailed from that port, the son of Wully Mahomed (the Chief of Wudd slain at the storm of Khelát) arrived with a party in pursuit of me and displayed much irritation on learning of my escape. It appears that information of my journey and disguise was received by this Chief the night after I passed Nal.

(Signed)   **J. OUTRAM.**

ACCOUNT

OF AN

EMBASSY TO THE KING OF PERSIA

FROM THE

AMEER OF KÁBUL IN 1837.

PART I

ACCOUNT

OF AN

EMBASSY TO THE KING OF PERSIA

FROM THE

AMEER OF KA'BUL IN 1837-38.

WRITTEN BY MAHOMED HOOSAIN KASHEE, THE ELCHEE, AT THE REQUEST OF CAPTAIN BURNES.

PART I.

After praising God be it known that I, Mahomed Hoosain, known by the name of Kashee, the Tribe of Fulee, born at Vhooramábád and educated at Kashan, had from my youth been in the service of His Highness the late Prince Mahomed Ali Mirza, the ruler of Kashan Shahan. After his death, I, in company with his beloved son Juhma Mirza, who was also Abbas Mirza's son-in-law, entered the service of His Majesty Abbas Mirza and spent ten years in serving him through all his struggles with Russians and Turks with extreme zeal and deligence. At length being displeased with the disagreeable words of his minister, Mirza Abdool Kasim, "Vazir Toork," spoken to me I determined to travel into different countries and become acquainted with the world, for as the old proverb goes, "Travelling takes off the imperfections of man": "Meat will not be roasted without being turned": "Till a man has not experience of the world and kept company with wise and prudent persons he will not be called learned by the learned." The Maulama Jala-loodin Roomee gives an example of this in his work (Musnuvee). He states that a few ignorant and inexperienced persons being desirous of looking at an elephant which they had never seen before, went to its shed. But as it was too dark and nothing could be seen, each of them touched a part of his body and satisfied himself of thus obtaining perfect knowledge of that animal. On their return they were asked what an elephant was? One of them said it was a pillar strong enough to support a building, another asserted it to be a rope, and the third a fan; in short every one had a separate idea of his own, while none of them gave the true one.

As these examples teach us the necessity of travelling, I proceeded to the holy city of Meshed as a merchant, and from thence passing through Maimuna and Andhoe advanced to Bokhara. After staying some time there, I went to Russia by way of Orgunge, Khiva and Kufnak, and spent eleven months in its Capital of Moscow in acquiring Russian literature. An account of the adventures which I met with in this country has been narrated in another volume. Leaving that country I returned to Kábul, where I was introduced to Ameer Dost Mahomed Khan by the late Mahomed Rahim Khan Ameen-ul-Mulk, the only person I was acquainted with. The Ameer was in the habit of calling me now and then into his company and treating me very kindly.

After his success against Sha Shooja, and being assisted by the Crusaders, he proceeded to Peshawar to oppose the Sikhs; but on Sultan Mahomed Khan and other Afghan Chiefs deserting him and joining the Sikhs, as well as a scarcity of grain ensuing, he abandoned his enterprise and was compelled to return to Kábul. After some days he called me in secret, where there was only one confidential person, Aga Mahomed, present, and said that "you know that my Peshawar brothers leaving me have joined my enemy (the Sikhs), and are ready to raise their arms against me. Therefore I think it advisable to commence correspondence with His Majesty Mahomed Sháh the King of Persia, and shelter myself under his protection. For executing such an

B 1485—14 +

important duty you are the only person I find capable. Therefore I wish you to undertake a mission to Persia and accomplish my objects." I replied—" You still retain your Afghan usages or is it otherwise?" He asked—" What are those usages?" I said, the Afghans always use the word "Dugha" in their conversation, which signifies merely this and that, but it also means deceit in your language; therefore whoever interferes in your affairs is always cheated and consequently reduced to misery. He answered, "I have left off all the Afghan customs since my youth, and am like the ancient kings strict in fulfilling my word. Believe whatever I say, and, on your return from Persia bring a confidential person from that Court to me." I said it was impossible for a Persian Ambassador to come either by way of Bokhara or Kandáhár, because in the first instance the people of Orgunge who are living in Merv, the Turkomans and the Bokharians will also hinder him, in the other Huzaras the people of Herát are the chief obstacles. The Ameer said, "bring him in the disguise of a merchant." I said it will be a great disgrace for the King of Persia, he ought to come with pomp and dignity, which will make your enemies tremble and put them in confusion. But I am afraid that your brothers may disturb you before I return, get rid of their wickedness if you can. He said, "I know my affairs better than you. Go and make a draft of a letter from me to Mahomed Shah, and after showing it to me take it to Mirza Abdoo-Sameca Khan, who will copy it." According to his order I wrote a letter to this effect: "I with a small force, composed of 20,000 horse, 10,000 foot and Juzailchees, together with 50 pieces of artillery have many times opposed the Sikh army consisting of 100,000 horse and 300 guns and often repulsed them. But at present I am involved in a very disastrous state on account of the want of money and the union of my brothers with the Sikhs. Therefore I think it necessary to unite my interest with some powerful State. It is very irreligious to make alliance either with the Sikhs or with the British Government; but as you are a Mahomedan prince and also had this country formerly united to the kingdom of Persia, I adhere to you and ask your assistance. But in case you do not aid me I must make terms with the British Government and give seven hundred thousand Afghan houses into its power." I showed this letter to the Ameer, who approved of it and ordered Mirza Abdoo-Sameca to copy it. I said to the Ameer that before I return, there are two probabilities, that of Runjeet Sing's dying and your taking possession of Peshawar, and the other of his attacking Kábul and driving you from it. In both cases you ought to be firm in fulfilling the contents of this letter. The Ameer assured me he would do so, and gave a letter to Kuhruman Mirza, the ruler of Khorasan, and also for Alla-zar-khan (Asefoodaulah). I requested also a letter for the Ameer of Bokhara. He said, "I have sent many letters together with presents to that Ameer and his Vazir the Kooshbegee through Moola Budroodin, a merchant, but have received no answer." I replied that if I communicate your letter to him, be satisfied that you will receive an answer together with handsome presents in return on my arrival here. He said "You are now an Agent on the part of Afghans and I will be much obliged if you will manage my affairs properly." At the time of dismissal I observed to the Ameer—your brothers Peer Mahomed Khan who is at Kabul now and Mahomed Zaman Khan are both useless and unserviceable fellows. The latter, I think, is worthy of wearing a coarse woollen garment, to have a stick in hand with a rope tied round his head and so tend seven camels given for the purpose. Observing his abilities I believe that at evening he would bring five of the camels home and leave two in the wilderness. The good disposition of the people towards him is merely on account of wealth, otherwise he is a fraudulent and disloyal man.

Intelligence of this conversation having reached Mahomed Zaman Khan it provoked him to the highest measure and made him ardent to take his revenge. Accordingly he sent a letter to Moola Dauran "Kakuree," the Agent at Bamiyan, which he holds as a Jághír, stating that he had sent twenty horsemen to kill me wherever I should be found. He must also be careful not to lose the opportunity of putting me to death. After departing from Kábul I halted at Surcushma, two marches from the city, on account of the severity of cold and the falling of snow, when I received a letter from the writer of the Nabab, a Kizilbash, informing me of this affair. Being frightened at this horrid intelligence I remained twenty days in that very place watching on account of the Afghans. They came every night to take my life, but returned unsuccessful. I despatched a cassid to Meers Abbas, Abyas, and Kázim, requesting them to send twenty Huzara (foot soldiers) for which I would pay at the rate of twenty rupees each, to accompany me as far as Bamiyan. After few days the agent of Meer Abbas, known by the name of Buchui Moghool, with the twenty foot soldiers arrived at Surcushma. Seeing my miserable condition he advised me to write to the Ameer, but I did not think it advisable to do so, for I thought he would not believe me and have a bad opinion of all Kizilbash people. Buchui Moghool stated that the road was fit for footmen alone, but impassable for horse on the snow. I took three horses with me as far as the Kotali (pass of) Onnee. The snow was increasing step by step, and when we arrived close to the foot of Onnee the horses sunk down so that their ears alone were visible. sent for the people of the fort and by their assistance dragged the horses out and sent them back to Kábul. I was obliged to travel on foot and carry my baggage on Huzaras. The Afghans exerted all their efforts to kill me, but were disappointed in every attempt. No sooner I had arrived at Gurdun Deewar than a man brought a letter from Mahomed Zumán Khán to Meer Kazim, stating that I had enticed away some persons from Kumuruk and Churkh and that he should delay me few days there, till he receives further intelligence. Meer Kazim instead of detaining me flogged the man severely and imprisoned him, but he escaped at night and fled to Kábul. Leaving that place I went to the fort of Kázár, where I was hospitably entertained by the son of Yuzdan Bukhsh. From this fort I proceeded to Kaloo, but the pass of Kaloo being deeply covered with snow I went to Bamiyan by way of Mooree. After leaving Mooree a body of about twenty persons, considering us merchants, hindered our progress and consequently a fight took place, in which about fifteen guns were fired, but no one wounded or killed. At length a person from our party went to converse with them and put a stop to the contest. Continuing my march I arrived at Bamiyan, where Moola Douran, who was my old friend, informed me about the letter which he had received from Mahomed Zuman Khán, and said that he would not injure me the least, and took care of me day and night as long as I was there.

From Bamiyan I advanced to Khoollum. From Khoollum to Bokhára, and I did not meet with any important event worthy of notice. On my arrival at Bokhára I concealed the letters of Dost Mahomed Khán under my arm, and kept that of Jubbar Khán in my hand, and delivered them all to Sayid Mirza, a person from Teheran. The merchants of Kábul had sent letters to their agents at Bokhara declaring that I was Dost Mahomed Khán's Agent sent to Mahomed Saheb. The Ameer of Bokhára being informed of this, mentioned it to the Kooshbegee, his minister, who sent for me and asked whether I was really Dost Mahomed Khán's Agent or not. I denied being so. The next day he sent his servants to my resting place to search for the letters in my baggage, where they only found Jubbar Khán's letter, which they took to the Ameer. The Ameer sent for me at night, and after conversing on different subjects demanded Dost Mahomed Khan's letters, promising to return them after reading. I denied having any letters and declared that Jubbar Khán had sent me his letters after my departure from Kábul. Being provoked by my denial the Ameer began to speak with anger. When I observed a change in his countenance I amused him by narrating some histories of ancient kings and thus pacified him. I returned home, but the Ameer sent for me the following night again, when there was only Shukoor Beg, a confidential person, present and demanded the letters. I denied as before. He said I should be punished by being thrown from the Nakkarkhana (a high place where kettle-drums are beaten), because I was giving power to infidels and weakening the religion of Mahomed. I observed that if His Majesty would order me to be killed it would be advantageous to myself in every respect. If I was really weakening the Mahomedan religion, then by being punished in this world, I would rid myself of the torments of the next. But if I was not really so, then I would through innocence be killed by the Commander of the Faithful and enjoy the happiness of paradise; while you a king in this world will be indebted to me in the world to come. The Ameer laughed, and observed that a person of such abilities was worthy to be an Agent, and began to speak mildly. I then stated that even our Lord Mahomed the Prophet as well as the ancient Mahomedan kings did always correspond with infidels. The Persians had also sent an Ambassador to Bokhára to condole on the death of Ameer Hydar Ghází, and congratulate on the succession of the late Ameer Hoosain. There would be no harm if your Majesty also sent a person to Mahomed Shah to condole on the death of Futeh Alee Sha and Abbas Mirza, and to congratulate him on his accession to the throne, and likewise to bring authentic accounts of the intentions of that king, the number of his troops and guns, state of the country, &c. And as to Dost Mahomed Khán's intentions I may now tell you that he considering me a confidential person has entrusted his letters to me. I would never give them to any person though I may be killed. The Ameer being highly pleased with these arguments called me close to him, and putting his hand upon my forehead caressed and applauded me very kindly. Turning towards Shukroo Beg the Ameer remarked, that God depriving the Europeans and the Kazilbash people of the true religion has bestowed on them wisdom and intellect in its stead. He consulted Shukoor Beg which of his officers was fit for sending on a mission to Persia. He named some, but the Ameer did not approve. At last the Ameer himself chose Kabil Beg the 'Kurawool Begec' for the Ambassador.

After two months he sent Kabil Beg with two pairs of shawls and a copy of the Korán, written by the most elegant writers, to Mahomed Shah, and Allah Koolee Beg ("Chuhgutta Begu"), who had formerly been sent to Russia, as an ambassador to the Sultan of Room (Turkey)—the former accompanied by twenty horsemen and the latter by thirty. We all left for the holy city of Mushhud in company with a caravan which had two hundred camels laden with lamb skins and indigo. We gave our horses to be led by servants, rode on panniers on camels to Merv. On our arrival at that city Neaz Mahomed Khán, the agent of Allah Koolee Khán, the ruler of Orgunge, had employed four thousand Turkuman in building a fort on the banks of the river of Merv, some of whom were engaged in procuring wood and other materials, and some in bringing earth. The caravan was detained for four days on account of gathering the duties, during which period I could not come out of the panniers except at night, and my servants lived apart from me. At length Neaz Mahomed Khán calling upon me in person took me to the fort, and said : "I have learned from the letters of the Bokhára merchants that you have been deputed by Dost Mahomed Khán to Mahomed Shah; I will send this intelligence to Allah Koolee Khán; you must wait here until I receive the answer." I denied being an agent, and after holding a long conversation returned home. He sent his servant to Allah Koolee Beg telling him to go whenever he pleased, but desired Kabil Beg to remain. Kabil Beg, being much perplexed at this message, refused to do so. Neaz Mahomed Khán appointed four hundred horsemen to watch him. No sooner did Kabil Beg receive this intelligence than he went to Khaleefa Sofee Islam (a Turkuman), who was at the distance of a league from the city, to sue for his good offices. The Khaleefa immediately went to Neaz Mahomed and stated that peace between the people of Bokhára and Orgunge had just been established, and that he should not again cause a war by detaining a Bokhára agent. Neaz Mahomed Khán replied, who will be answerable to Allah Koolee Khán when he asks me? The Khaleefa said I will be responsible to the Khán. The Aksukals (officers) also favoured Kabil Beg. After a long conversation he permitted him to proceed to his destination. I went to Neaz Mahomed Khán at night, and presented through a merchant, who was his sincere friend, a Kashmeer shawl together with twenty lamb skins, five maunds of Russian sugar, and two maunds of tea, entreating him to let me go. He told me to come to-morrow and explain my case in presence of the Aksukals; then he would answer me, which I accordingly did. He told the authorities that I was not the man mentioned in the letter, and that the real person might have passed before, or will come hereafter. I was dismissed, and thanked God for delivery, because had I been sent to Orgunge, and the letters taken from me, I would have been obliged to tend the flocks of camels all my life. I was in constant fear for three days of being called back; after that time I felt myself free.

Before my arrival at Merv the Governor of Orgunge had sent four thousand horsemen to Kelat-i-Nadirée. The son of Saed Mahomed Khán, the ruler of Kelat, had not yet come out of that fort, when the people of Orgunge set some stocks of grain, which were around Kelat, on fire. The son of Saed Mahomed Khán pursued them, killed and wounded many, and returned back. As I was leaving Merv the people of Orgunge entered it. When I arrived at a place about one league from Surukhs, the son of Saed Mahomed Khán, Mahomed Ali Khán, had plundered about forty houses of Turkumans and led them away captives. His horsemen were ready to reduce us to the same condition; but as I had acquaintance with Saed Mahomed Khán at Mushhud, and Mahomed Ali Khán was also aware I did not allow them to oppress caravans, I pursued my way to Mushhud, and on my arrival at the pass of Muzdooran pitched tents and picketed my horses, seeing which the Turkumans were astonished. From this place I sent a Turkuman to Mushhud to Asifoodaula informing him of the arrival of two ambassadors from Bokhara—one deputed to Mahomed Sháh and the other to the Sultan of Turkey. The A'sif sent his man about three leagues from the city to receive us; but as I had previously left Meshed displeased, I did not accept his compliments, and accordingly halted outside the city for two days without the knowledge of A'sif. At length the A'sif being apprised of this affair sent his agent, Zainool Abideen, to take me in with him, which I refused. The A'sif then sent a note requesting I would come along with baggage, which I did, and he gave me a commodious place and paid me great respect and attention. The second day the A'sif sent for me and made inquiries about Kábul and its ruler, and I was then dismissed. The third day Zainool Abideen came and advised me to go this night to the A'sif, and after having consulted with him departed for the Sháh's camp, which was then near Kálposh, five stages from Meshed. On my calling on him at night, he advised that when I got to the presence of the Sháh I should speak with His Majesty deliberately. Having obtained my leave I remained three days more in the city, during which time the A'sif was very kind and hospitable. He also sent along with me his agent, Zainool Abideen Beg, to His Majesty's camp at Jahazán. Hunuf Koolee Khán, the son of Nujuf Ali Khán, feasted us, and after travelling four stages in a peopled country we arrived at Kalposh, the fifth stage, where we did not find the Sháh's camp. Leaving this place we passed on in search of our destination for two days, and, observing the impressions of gun-carriages on the ground, were led for two stages through a desert, and on the third entered a forest, passing now and then through trees and plain ground void of any grain for our horses or food for ourselves. We fed the horses on grass and ourselves on a little dry bread that we had fortunately saved. On the seventh day we missed trace of the carriage wheels and entered an interminable jungle, in which we wandered for two days without finding a road. The trees were immense in size, some of them being a hundred guz high and having a diameter of about eight. On the third day the Azbuks of our party were very tired, and declared that if we could find no end to this wilderness we must to-day prepare ourselves to perish, for our provisions are exhausted and we can subsist no longer. At length to our great joy we espied two footmen advancing, and who were awed with fear by our great numbers; we pacified them, and on asking the name of this thicket were answered that it was called the Plain of Mazinduran (Dushti Mazrinduran). We also demanded of them some information about the king, who they said was on the banks of the

F 1485—15

river Goorgan. In the meantime three other men with two camels and a cow appeared in sight ; the latter we found they had obtained by plunder. We took one of the men as a guide, who reluctantly agreed to follow us. Pursuing our way and a little before me, when we were descending from a height, the guide concealed himself in a hollow and made his escape Here we found water and plenty of grass for the horses, and halted for the night. In the morning we mounted our horses and came to a Turkuman residence where the houses were burned down and destroyed, and we found dead bodies of men, horses and camels in abundance. Amongst the grass was a cow which we slaughtered and ate, hoping by the next day to reach the king's camp. At the end of the following day we came to a village deserted and burned down, near which we met with the traces of gun wheels which we lost some days ago ; we followed, discovering on the way five or ten Turkuman horsemen, who fled on seeing us. This day we subsisted on a camel which we luckily met with. We also found a pit containing about fifty maunds of Tubrezee wheat, which in some degree supplied our wants.

The next morning two minarets came in sight from a great distance, while the plain was so level that no tree could be seen within ten leagues, and at the foot of these we halted that evening. We found one of them to be a tower of immense size, and the other about eighty guz high and thirty in diameter, surrounded by water and a thicket of bamboos. In this place there were about a thousand dogs alive, two thousand dead, and numerous bodies of camels, cows, sheep, &c., scattered around. There must have been no less than five thousand Turkumans here. In the morning we found a man amongst the reeds, and on my asking him the name of the minaret and tower, also where the camp of the king was, and the reason why the place was deserted, he replied that " two hundred Kizilbash horsemen came to attack this village, and on being opposed by the natives fifty of them were killed, but a reinforcement overpowering the villagers obliged them to leave their habitations. I sought an asylum in this thicket, but discovered to you because you were a Somnee. This minaret is called (Chihil Zeena) or the forty steps, and the tower Boorji Kafirán or the Tower of the Infidels ; both were erected by Alexander the Great. It is two days since the camp left this place."

Leaving that minaret we proceeded to search for the camp, travelled the whole day and halted at evening in a plain. We did not meet with a single stone during the sixteen days we had been travelling. In the morning the horses were so much fatigued as to be unable to walk without flogging. We were in consequence obliged to travel on foot and led them by the bridle. At noon we were much afflicted by the oppressive heat of the sun and lost all hopes of reaching the camp ; when on ascending a height we discovered, by means of a telescope, a number of horsemen at a distance. Kabil Beg said he did not know whether those horsemen were Kajars (Persians) or Turkumans. Therefore leaving our baggage with Balta Koolu Beg and those whose horses were quite tired, I and Kabil Beg, with forty horsemen, went in front to ascertain who these people were. On proceeding half a league we found out from their caps that they were men of Mahomed Sháh's army and about five thousand in number. On seeing us they retraced their steps about half a coss and halted. Approaching within an arrow's flight we called aloud for a man of their party to come and speak with us, but received no answer. I wished to gallop my horse and go alone to them, but Kabil Beg would not allow me. At length leaving all our horsemen behind, I and Kabil Beg, taking each of us a horseman, went forward. The four hundred Persians fled at our approach. Seeing no other remedy I alone proceeded, upbraiding them for their cowardice, told them to look at my turban that I was an Elchee-i-Bokhara with whom two of you should come and converse. Ten men of the party separated from the main body, and having heard all I had to say, returned. That night we halted on the banks of a stream, and Balta Koolee Beg as well as Zainool Abideen, who were left behind with the baggage, joined. Each of us sent his servants to the camp for some provisions: they brought two maunds of flour and the same quantity of barley. On asking the price of grain we heard that both these articles were sold at the rate of four kurans (rupees) per maund. Next morning Abbas Khán Hiratee came from the camp to receive us about a league. We pitched near Mirza Musood's tent, the Minister for Foreign Affairs, who sent a man to demand of me Dost Mahomed Khán's letters, stating that it was a custom of the court for the minister to peruse the letters previous to their being laid before His Majesty. I replied that the letters in my charge were for Mahomed Sháh, and he was not the king that I should deliver them to him. On Mirza Musood's informing the king of my answer His Majesty was pleased to call me in person the next day.

ACCOUNT

OF AN

EMBASSY TO THE KING OF PERSIA

FROM THE

AMEER OF KÁBUL IN 1837.
PART II.

ACCOUNT
OF AN
EMBASSY TO THE KING OF PERSIA
FROM THE
AMEER OF KA'BUL IN 1837.

WRITTEN BY MAHOMED HOOSAIN KASHEE, THE ELCHEE, AT THE REQUEST OF CAPTAIN BURNES.

PART II.
INTRODUCTION TO SHA'H.

I was taken by the minister into the court. When the king came in sight the Mirza saluted him, and signed to me to do the same. I declined, and on proceeding a few paces further he again made a sign to me to make my obeisance, which I did not attend to. When the king was about five paces distant we both made our obeisance, and stood. His Majesty, not recognizing me, asked whether I was an Afghán or a Kizilbash. I declared myself to be a Kizilbash of the tribe of Feelee, a native of Persia, born at Khuramabad. Are you not Mahomed Hoosain Khán, the son of Abdool Kaháb Khán? said the king. I replied, yes. His Majesty then asked where I had been so long. I gave some account of my adventures. The king then talked to Mirza Musood in Turkish. I also replied in that language. He then spoke to the Russian. I also answered in that tongue. His Majesty then asked where I had learned the latter language. I said I had been for two years in Russia, and was engaged for one year in acquiring that language. He then applauded me and asked about Dost Mahomed Khán. I stated I had been in his service for eight years. His Majesty asked what was the number of Runjit Singh's army. I replied that the force which he brings into the field amounts to fifty thousand foot and a similar number of horsemen, with two hundred pieces of artillery. Meanwhile I attempted to describe Dost Mahomed Khán's power and determination in the field of battle, when the king observed that the power of Runjit Singh was not ancient; how has he acquired such immense wealth and influence in so short a period? I answered that as His Majesty could not manage all things alone, and as is the case with every monarch that the affairs of the kingdom are consigned to experienced and active ministers, so His Highness Runjit Singh is furnished with able and prudent officers and counsellors, and his wealth and country improved. His Majesty observed that his officers have been instructed by himself. I said undoubtedly, for if a man is naturally ch ar he can be easily taught; otherwise he may have Plato and Galen for his tutors, and will derive no benefit. The king said that he heard that a man Abdool Aziz (Azeezoodeen) by name is Runjit's minister. I stated that he was a native of Kashmeer, a dealer of shawls and well acquainted with the trade of every sort; therefore His Highness has entrusted his moveables to him, and he does not meddle with political affairs,[1] and Runjit Singh has got many other respectable officers. The king observed that the people of India are very indolent and cowardly, because Nádir Sháh, Ahmed Sháh and many other kings went against India and subdued it. I remarked that the Indian forces are now disciplined and regular, and that its troops and artillery surpass those of Persia. The king then laughed, and observed; "Please God, we shall see."

---

[1] The king was right and the elchee is wrong. Uzeez Deen Fakeer is the person alluded to.—(*Note by Burnes.*)

After this conversation the king opened Dost Mahomed Khán's letter with his own hands, and began to read. When he got to the sentence "and give seven hundred thousand Afghán houses into the British power" he remarked "Please God, it will not be." It was getting late; the king dismissed me and returned home.

As my conversation with His Majesty regarding the ministers showed the incompetency of Mirza Agásee, the first minister, who was also Mirza Masood's enemy, it pleased the latter exceedingly. He feasted me that night, and entertained me very hospitably. I found him a man of amiable disposition, and his good conduct to be worthy of the dignity of a minister, prudent and wise. All the officers in the court were pleased with him.

On the next evening Mirza Agásee invited me and the Bokhára Agent to a party at his house, where conversation on many subjects took place. In the morning the king ordered the whole of his troops and artillery, consisting of eighty-five pieces, for parade, and took me, Kabil Beg, and Balta Koolee Beg with him to the field to look at the military exercise. While we were inspecting the forces His Majesty asked, since I had seen the Russian army and also that of Runjit Singh, what was the difference between his and them. I did not answer; he put the same question again, to which I did not still reply. The third time he asked why I did not answer him? I said, should I flatter or tell the real truth? He laughed, and ordered me to let him know the fact. I observed that the arrangement of His Majesty's force was a mere name, because a military and a medical officer were absolutely necessary, to regulate the force and cure the sick of the army, and the medicine should be granted by the Government. I also added that His Majesty had once inspected the army on quitting Teheran, and till he reviewed the forces again he would not know how many of the soldiers were sick. I saw about two thousand soldiers sick on the way, many of whom were walking lamely, and others even unable to travel, and about five thousand were begging among the tents. An army is like a family which should always be protected and supported, but if the income is deficient, the army should be kept low in proportion. When this coversation began I had begged the king to order the Bokhára Agent to retire, which His Majesty was pleased to do.

On hearing these expressions the Sháh was much confused and became very angry, sent for Hájee Mirza Agásee, and said to him that he had put a question to me to which I had answered, and he should listen to what I said. I repeated His Majesty's question and my reply to it, all which he acknowledged as true. The Sháh then was silent and retired to his tent. He did not send for me for three days, after which he removed the camp three koses further, on account of its becoming offensive.

The Prince Faredoon Mirza together with Messrs. Lindsay and Baronsky at the head of four thousand horse and six thousand foot was sent five koses ahead to conquer the fortress of Bag. At that fort there were about ten thousand Turkumans, who on being informed of the Kizilbash's attacking them prepared themselves to oppose, but being unable to stand against the ordnance were obliged to flee. The Kazilbash began to plunder the baggage. The Turkumans, seeing their enemy dispersed and engaged in plunder, returned to destroy it, but were defeated again: about one thousand of them were killed and about two thousand taken as captives. The fort was subdued, and about four thousand men, women and children were taken as prisoners of war, and about thirty thousand cows, sheep and camels were plundered and sent to the Sháh's camp. The Sháh halted for ten days there, and on the tenth day the Turkumans assembling together came at night to attack our camp, and I heard two shots fired. In the morning the camp was removed three koses to the rear, halted for one day, and then returned towards Sharoot and Boostam.

In the road we met with narrow passages and thick jungles impassable for two horsemen together, and the road was also bad from mud washed down by the rain. It being too difficult for the gun carriages the Sháh ordered all his officers to drag them with their own hands, which they did, and trailed out all the guns safe. The Sháh then reminded me of the late harsh observations I had made to His Majesty, acknowledging them as true.

I expressed my astonishment about His Majesty's undertaking an enterprise—to seize freebooting Turkumans; for all the world expected that on His Majesty's accession to the throne he would first endeavour to attack some foreign possession, while the Sháh having only plundered Turkumans wanted to return home. A single officer with about ten thousand soldiers was sufficient to destroy the Turkumans. I also added that it was very improper for a king to oppose any one but a king; His Majesty replied of course it was so, but he left Meshed on account of the cholera prevailing there. I observed that I never believed all my life what I had not verified, and I could not believe His Majesty's word, though he killed me; and I asserted that this inconvenience was caused by His Majesty's inexperienced and imprudent officers. The Sháh was then silent, and did not talk to me for about a league; after which I pulled the reins of my horse and wanted to go behind him, but His Majesty looking towards me ordered me to come along. After travelling a league more we arrived at the halting place, where the Sháh went to his tent and I to mine.

His Majesty had not taken off his boots when he sent for Hájee Mirza Agásee, and told him that His Majesty never assented to any of his officer's requests, but that Mahomed Hoosain Khán, a foreigner, had put a question to His Majesty which he could not reply to, and he (Hájee Agásee) should answer it. I was sent for by the Sháh where Mr. Stoddart, an Englishman, was also present, and requested by His Majesty to repeat the past observations again, which I did. Hájee Agásee, the minister, asked me where I had acquired ability to interfere in political matters. I replied that His Majesty sits before us, and is at liberty to send for such judges as will decide the truth of my statement; if wrong, His Majesty can punish me, and should I be right he (the Hájee) should then suffer punishment. The Sháh agreed, and ordered the Russian minister, Mirza Mahomed Tukee, Mirza Masood, the Minister for Foreign Affairs, the head physician, and many other learned officers to be called into his presence.

The king ordered me to repeat what I had to say against His Majesty's minister. I accordingly stated fully the extent of my accusation, in his having informed the people of the army, when they applied for their pay, that there was no money in the treasury, and that the drums beaten in honour of the treasure were merely to show that the chests were not empty, remarking that if he had said so intentionally he was guilty of unworthy behaviour to his master, and if otherwise he was unworthy to hold the office of a prime minister. The Russian minister said that he also had heard this report, and likewise other officers verified the truth of my assertion. I accused him of many other disloyal acts, to write which would be rather too long and tedious.

After this the king got enraged, and reviled Hájee Agásee. I was dismissed, and returned to my tent. We travelled three marches, and on the fourth I was summoned by the Sháh, and asked my opinion of how His Majesty should act towards Ameer Dost Mahomed Khán. I answered that it was advisable to send some confidential person with suitable presents to the Ameer, and make it appear to Runjit Singh and other enemies of the Ameer that the interests of Persia and Afghánistán were one, and, should the Ameer be in want of assistance either of money or men, to state he would get the needful from Persia, and, should this report gain circulation, any power wishing to invade Afghánistán will be cautious in making the attempt.

The Sháh approved of my suggestion, and said he would surely depute a man to Kábul. I observed that Kumher Alee Khán, the head of the musketeers, was a proper person for that office. The Sháh said very well, and then asked what presents would be suitable for Dost Mahomed Khán. I answered that it would be proper to give him some weapons belonging to the late king. His Majesty smiled, and said that he would send him a sword set with diamonds. On this day no more conversation took place.

From the fort of Bag, where the Turkoman battle was fought, we arrived at Boostam in twelve days. When we were entering this city His Majesty saw me from a distance, summoned me, and said that he was now going to dismiss the Elchee of Bokhára, Kabil Beg, and that in case His Majesty undertook the intended expedition to Herát, His Majesty would dismiss me at Meshed. We halted at Boostam for two days, and then set out for Sháh Rode, where the Sháh reviewed his troops, and finding them all in a broken-down and miserable state abandoned the enterprise.

One day His Majesty sent for me, and said that he would depute Kumber Alee Khán lightly equipped to Dost Mahomed Khán. I observed that he was a Persian ambassador, and ought to go with pomp and dignity to show to the Afgháns and the people of Runjit Singh the splendour of the Persian throne. The court was dismissed, and I returned to my tent. We halted for ten days at Sháh Rode, during which time the Sháh did not send for me again. Kabil Beg was dismissed at this place.

In the journey to Kargan the scarcity of grain was such that one Tubrez maund of barley was sold for one ducat, and rice and all other sorts of grain and bread in a similar manner.

My daily expense paid by the Sháh was three scores of rupees of Irak, equal to twenty rupees Se Abbase of Kábul, where, as I had ten horsés and six loading ponies, the daily expense of which amounted to fifteen ducats besides the dinner expenses of myself and servants, which also came to fifteen ducats, I did not think it proper to accept three ducats for my daily expense from His Majesty while I was spending thirty. In consequence I received it for ten days, and after that when the officers of the Sháh brought the ducats I returned them. After a few days this intelligence reached the Sháh's ears. His Majesty spoke to me when riding along the road that he supposed I was ashamed to accept his Persian bread. I replied that I was amply supplied by the liberality of Ameer Dost Mahomed Khán, and although he may be considered in poverty his people are wealthy and enjoy affluence. His Majesty looked to Nusroola Khán, the head of the body guard, and remarked that a servant should be like me, and requested I would state the expenses of my maintenance that they might be supplied to me. I inadvertently uttered an oath by the head of His Majesty that I would not receive any expense, and accordingly for want of money I was obliged to sell the land, which I possessed in the fort of Bák, to Furrookh Khán, who had often applied to me for its purchase, for seven hundred toománs, equal in value to six thousand rupees.

The enmity between myself and the minister daily increased, until we arrived at Sháh Rode. One day previous to our starting for Teherán the Hájee asked me over to his tent, and quietly expressed his dissatisfaction at my behaviour in having spoken against him before the king. I apologized as I thought proper. I took two cups of tea at the Hájee's house, and on returning home fell sick.

At the time of my discussion with Hájee Mr. Stoddart was also present. He used to call upon me twice every day to enquire after my health as far as Simnan. I became so weak in body that I was tumbling down from my horse at every five steps, and my servants had to assist me up again.

On our arrival at Simnan Mr. Sheel, the Agent of the English, joined us. Mr. Stoddart had informed Mr. Sheel about my sickness; they both came over to my tent. The latter, having opened his box, took some medicine out, and gave it to me to take, and remained with me during the day. The medicine operated much. Next day both the gentlemen again visited, and presented me with some tea.

In my familiar conversation with these gentlemen on topics favourable to the English Government I was listened to by Mahomed Alee (Nazir of the Minister for Foreign Affairs) from behind the tent walls, who went and informed Hájee, the minister. He, taking advantage of this, informed the king that I was negotiating with the English for the Afghán nation, and to prevent my going to Teherán, because the English minister was there. The Sháh made inquiries, and found that I had some correspondence with the English. Accordingly I was ordered to appear. Being sick at the time I was unable to mount my horse without being supported by two servants, one on each side of me. When I came before the king I was ordered to depart in company with Kumber Alee Khán. I begged His Majesty would favour me with an answer to the letter of Nawáb Jubbar Khán and also some presents for him. His Majesty was pleased to order Hájee Agásee to procure a fur "chogha" or pelisse and a letter for Jubbar Khán. The Hájee to gain his own ends and procure my speedy departure immediately brought the articles in question, and I was ordered to proceed by the route of Kandáhar. I urged that some presents for the Kandáhar Chiefs were also necessary. The Sháh ordered a sword and a pair of plain Persian pistols for Kohun Dil Khán, and a Cashmeer shawl chogha each for Mehr Dil and Ruhim Dil Khán, and ordered Hájee Agásee to appear before the king next day with letters for the three chiefs. I returned to my tent. The next day I attended, still being very unwell. I received a white Cashmeer shawl chogha from the king, and before being dismissed begged I might be allowed to go to Teherán for medical aid, as my infirm state of health made me think that I would not survive two days longer. The king refused my request, and directed that I should remain at Simnan, and be attended on by the king's physician. After repeated requests on my part and refusals on the king's, His Majesty ordered a place to be cleared out and allotted for my accommodation, suspecting the former report against me by the Hájee to be true, and departed. Mahomed Alee, the steward of the Minister for Foreign Affairs, escorted me and my baggage to Simnan, and the day following brought one hundred and fifty toománs as a present from the king, which I declined accepting, observing that I had refused His Majesty's former favour of aid, and in the present I would do the same. He made me over to a physician and followed the king. I remained at Simnan for two days, and then hastened on to Teherán, although against the king's commands. The first stage on my way was Lasgurd, governed by Sháhzáda Saifoola, the son of the late king. This prince had gone to meet the king two stages distant, and while there was informed by Hájee, the minister, that I had some intentions of going to Teherán, and if so to detain me on the way. The Governor shortly arrived, and found me at Lasgard. He sent Syfoola Mirza to my halting place, intimating that the king had left me with Kumber Alee Khán at Simnan, and as Kumber Alee had joined the king, I should also go there. I replied that I was unwell, and must go to Teherán. After a short discussion on both sides it was agreed that we should both write to the minister and await the result. I therefore wrote to the minister to the effect that as I had a mother and two children at Kashan, I should proceed there, and it was immaterial whether I received his permission or not. A mounted courier arrived next day with the answer granting me permission to go.

I was entertained for two days by the Sháhzáda, and on the third Syfoola Mirza returned to Simnan, and I proceeded to Kashan. I was accompanied on my way by Sháhzáda Buhmun, who being a friend of my father, treated me kindly as far as Kum, where I took my leave of him and advanced further on. I remained twenty five days at Kashan, and taking my children along with me then proceeded to Teherán.

Within one stage of Teherán I sent a man to the Hájee or Minister for Foreign Affairs to prepare a house for me. On reaching the gates of the city I met my servant, who informed me the place for my abode was not ready, and that I should remain out until the next day. I was much disappointed at the message, and in the meantime I met Mr. Stoddart, who was out riding. He apprised the British ambassador of my arrival, who prepared the house of Mirza Abbas, one of his own writers, for my reception. Mr. Stoddart kindly assisted with his own hands in spreading the carpet, and after making me welcome and comfortable returned home, and in the evening sent me two bottles of wine. In the morning Mr. Sheel came to visit me, and in the evening the British ambassador also paid me the same honour. When I first saw him I was surprised, and took him from his demeanour to be of the tribe of Feelee, Soor, or Zindea; his polished language and learned arguments were so perfect as made me think him to be a scholar of the famous Mirza Muhdee, and superior to Mahomed Hosen Murnee and Ibrahim Kháni-Sheerazee. I drew him into conversation merely to admire his ability. I was informed by him that what had passed between me and the king had all been brought to his notice.

Next day I waited on the English ambassador, and from what I have seen of him in every aspect I have not words sufficient to express my sentiments of his several qualities; in fact, he is a firm supporter of, and honour to the English Government.

I sent some fruit and few other things to Hájee the minister as a present, and a little while after I went to see him in person. He took as little notice of me as would a camel when taken uselessly to the shop of a farrier. Mirza Masood, the Minister for Foreign Affairs, paid some outward civilities to me, but merely in words.

Two days before my arrival at Teherán Taj Mahomed Khán, the son of Munsoor Khán Barukzan deputed by Kohun Dil Khán, reached Teherán, and Hájee the minister was treating him very friendly.

A few days after the news of my being at Teherán reached the ears of the king, and I was sent for. His Majesty desired that I should leave my son as Peshkhidmut in his service. I replied that my son was too young, and not possessed of abilities for the situation.

The Sháh asked by whose means I got a house from the English. I replied that I first sent a man to the minister to get me a place, and on his saying that it was not ready when I arrived, the English ambassador procured me one, because it very often happens that English gentlemen come to Kábul, and are very well received and entertained, and expecting such treatment they make a like return.

The Sháh inquired what conversation I had had with Mr. Sheel in my tent at Simnan. I answered that, being unwell at the time, he came to give me medicine, there was no conversation on politics.

The king ordered me to leave my son in his service, and that he should come and pay respects at the time of salutation in company with Furrookh Khán and remain with him. On this I was dismissed.

After a few days Táj Mahomed Khán was dismissed, and received eight thousand rupees, four pieces of cloth, three horses, and one English gun as a present. The one hundred and fifty "toománs", which were offered to me and rejected formerly, were again proffered. I swore not to accept.

During my travel I had presented one pair of Cashmeer shawls and two maunds of fine Bara rice of Pesháwar to Hájee, the minister, and to the Minister for Foreign Affairs two bundles of lamb skins of Bokhara and a quantity of Bara rice, and many small presents of fruit to both of them, and received not a copper in return. I halted at Teherán for forty days, during which time the only means of my happiness was the British ambassador.

The sword and the pair of pistols which the Sháh had promised to send to Kohun Dil Khán at my request were but plain, and on the arrival of Táj Mahomed Khán His Majesty ordered fifty ducats to be spent in ornamenting the sword and twenty on the pistols.

Kumber Alee Khán, Táj Mahomed Khán and I were dismissed, and having an objection to leaving my son behind in the king's service I advised my companions to proceed, stating that I would follow them in a few days after, during which time the English ambassador summoned me to his house. I informed him as I had refused the Sháh's pecuniary assistance and presents, and now being totally destitute of means, I could not proceed. The next day he sent me a hundred toománs of Irak, equal in value to a hundred and eleven ducats. Upon this I waited upon him, and in the first instance begged to decline his offer; but as I was in want of money I would accept his favour on condition of the British minister receiving a note of hand from me payable to any gentleman at Kábul. He replied that I should give a writing on Ameer Dost Mahomed Khán payable to any European at Kábul, to which I assented, and gave the receipt. Six days after I departed for Kashan, and on my arrival there I found that Kumber Alee Khán had reached three days previously. We remained one day at Kashan, and on the next started for Yezd.

On the way to Yezd our horses were fatigued and unable to walk for three marches, and my children were obliged to travel on foot.

From Yezd I proceeded to Kerman, and on arriving there I found that Aga Khán, the Governor, had rebelled and placed his standard at Bampoor. Soorab Khán was ordered by the king to vanquish the rebel. Water and supplies were scarce in the royal army, and in consequence they were detained for twenty-five days at Kerman, during which time all the officers were summoned, and a muster made. It was found that the army consisted of four thousand horse, two thousand foot, and four pieces of artillery. I also accompanied the army. Within a league of the fort of Bampoor, Mirza Abdool Hoosain Khán, the brother of Aga Khán, sallied out with a body of about eighty horsemen and a hundred foot, made a rush against the king's army, and defeated it. In my younger days the rebel governor was my school-fellow, and his father Khubeloollá Khán and Mirza Abdool Husain Khán were the friends of my father. In this affair I ran my horse up to Mirza Abdool Hoosain Khán, who taking me for an enemy pointed his gun. I no sooner observed this than I called out aloud. He recognized me, and put his hand on his head as a mark of welcome. I admired his bravery and expertness, and cried bravo. He pursued the king's army for about half a league, but the death of his most beloved friend Alee Khán Bukhtiyaree put a stop to his pursuit, and accordingly he returned to his fort. The next day Shahro Khán and Mirza Hádee Khán went at night near the fort and threw up an entrenchment. The day following Aga Khán sent me two trays of sweetmeats and two of meals as an entertainment, and asked me to pay him a visit; but Kumbur Alee Khavdia advised me not to meet Aga Khán's request, because he was a rival of the Sháh. The next day we removed our camp and encamped closer to the fort, and there we remained for ten days. Mirza Abdool Hoosain Khán used to sally out every day, kill and wound many, and return. On account of the scarcity of the grass and grain in the camp I myself and Táj Mahomed Khán proceeded to Nurmsher, and left Kumbur Alee Khán in the camp, who joined us fifteen days after. From this place we advanced to the fort of Kázee, where we halted for five days, and after taking supplies for fifteen days along with us started to Loot. Our first stage was Sher Guz. In this place we put up in a ruined shed. There were two wells about three guz in depth, but their water being impure we dug two others, and the two hundred men of Seestan who had accompanied me from Kerman drew water for themselves and their horses from them : every one took a water-bag full of water along with him, and then started at midday. At evening a minaret, about hundred guz in length and ten in diameter, came in sight in the desert, having no water within thirty koses around it. Here we stopped for a while, took our meals, fed our horses, and set out again. Travelling the whole night till twelve o'clock in the morning we arrived at a high eminence, showing some traces of an ancient fort, and having a few trees around, and a karez (subterraneous water-course) near it. Here we halted till evening, fed and watered our horses, and set off again. Travelling till six o'clock in the morning we arrived at some wells, where we rested for a while, watered our horses, and again continued our journey till sunset. After feeding our horses we started again at twelve o'clock in the morning; we reached a pass of a mountain, having immense trees and a fountain. Taking some water along with us we advanced. Travelling about fifty cosses in twenty-four hours we halted at a thicket of reeds, having some fountains around ; a march of two days more brought us to the water of Seestan, where we spent two days more in travelling along the bank to find out a ferry, and on the third we were guided by the natives of Seestan to the ferry, where we crossed on rafts. The ferry could not be crossed more than twice during the day. The horses and camels crossed by swimming. After a march of three days we arrived at Seestan. Mahomed Ruza Khán, the Governor of Seestan, sent his brother to receive me, and gave me place of accommodation out of the fort, and entertained me for three days. The citadel (ark) of the fort of Seestan is very strong, containing about three thousand houses in a ruinous condition. Leaving Seestan I journeyed two marches, and arrived at the bank of a large river interspersed with jungle of brush-wood, and a ruined fort situated near. Two stages on we came to a fort of Beloochees, which I passed without molestation, and emerged out of the boundary of Seestan. Entering the territory of Gurmser I encamped on the bank of a river, on the opposite side of which was a fort belonging to Hájee Dost Mahomed, who sent some provisions to me. Performing two marches more, I learned that Kohun Dil Khán had encamped in the environs of Guesk, and I bent my steps towards his camp. When we arrived within a march, Alla Dád Khán Burdooránee came with two loads of sweetmeats, a tent and the tent walls which were plundered from Shojáool Moolk, to receive us. The tent was pitched for Kumbur Alee Khán. We stopped here for two days, and were well entertained by our host, and on the third day proceeded to the camp according to the Sardár's request. Within a kos Mahomed Siddeck Khán, the son of Sardár Kohun Dil Khán, came with a thousand well-equipped horsemen, and took us to the camp. Kumbur Alee Khán went on horseback to Kohun Dil Khán, and presented with his own hands the sword, the pistols and pelisses (chogas) sent by his master to the Sardárs, and receiving much respect and a satisfactory welcome from Kohun Dil Khán returned to his tent. We were sent on to the hills of Chihilzeena (forty steps), and the Sardár joined us the next day. Kohun Dil Khán had some difference with Sardár Rahim Dil Khán, and in order to reconcile them, their well-wishers made Kohun Dil Khán stop at Chihilzeena for two days till Sardár Rahim Dil Khán, Sardár Mehr Dil Khán and Meer Afzul Khán came out of Kandáhar with all their horsemen to meet Kohun Dil Khán, and so the matter was made up. Kumbur Alee Khán was received with much respect, having the Sardár's horsemen and guns on both sides as a mark of honour. Kumbur Alee Khán was ordered to put up at Yuhuya Khán's house, and I had a separate lodging distant from him. I sent a secret communication unknown to the Sardárs of Kandáhár to Dost Mahomed Khán, to this effect, that I have delivered your messages to the King of Persia, and in answer to which His Majesty was pleased to give his royal consent and has deputed Kumber Alee Khán to you with a sword made by Hájee Mahomed Hoosain Isfahanee for the late king, and that His Majesty will come on Teermah (the fourth Persian month) to besiege Herát, when His Majesty will send an officer with twelve thousand men and a crore of rupees to Ameer Dost Mahomed Khán. Though this last information was false, "an untruth told advisedly is better than a truth which foments disturbance," as the old proverb runs, because Sardár Mahomed Akbár Khán was opposing Runjeet Singh's army at that time, and this intelligence would give them strength of mind. I also desired the Ameer to send a respectable man to receive Kumber Alee Khán. Forty days elapsed before I received the answer by Sháhghassee Painda. While I was at Kandáhár the Sardárs were endeavouring to breed animosity between Kumber Alee Khán and Ameer Dost Mahomed, and in consequence delayed his going to Kábul, and also prevented Sháhghassee Painda by bribe and flattery from seeing us. I assured Kumher Alee Khán that the Sardárs did not wish the prosperity of Dost Mahomed Khán, and they therefore detained him. Kumber Alee Khán always informed me of the conversation that passed between him and the Sardárs. I despatched two letters more by messengers to Dost Mahomed Khán, apprising him of the Kandáhár Chiefs detaining the Persian ambassador and other affairs which were going on at Kandáhár, and requesting him again to send another confidential person.

In a few days I had the opportunity of visiting Mehr Dil Khán, and after conversing on different subjects, I declared, that the Sardárs should not cause their overthrow by fomenting mutual disturbances, because if Dost Mahomed Khán were defeated at Kábul, they were unable to stand, and their defeat at Kandáhár was inevitable if Dost Mahomed Khán should fall, adding that although the Ameer was their sincere friend, they were endeavouring to destroy him, which was a matter of injustice. While we were speaking, Sardár Kohun Dil Khán entered, and inferring the substance of our conversation observed, that "we considered ourselves better qualified than Dost Mahomed"; whereas Alexander Burnes has been deputed by the English Government to the Ameer, and if Kumber Alee Khán should also go to him, then he will gain pre-eminence over us in the eyes of the people, which cannot be endured. Being much dejected at this observation I returned home. The next day Sardár Kohun Dil Khán summoned Kumber Alee Khán, and told him that Alexander Burnes had come to Kábul, and Dost Mahomed Khán was negotiating with him; that if he should go also there, he would surely return with disgrace and bring dishonour to the King of Persia; that in such a case he would not advise him to proceed to Kábul; that it was more advisable to take his (Kohun Dil Khán's) son accompanied by a hundred horsemen and Alla Dád Khán Burdooránee, and return to the service of His Majesty. He also added that I was an ally of the English, and that Alexander Burnes was come through my means. Kumber Alee Khán was aware of my previous conversation with the British ambassador, and Kohun Dil Khán's expressions convinced him of the fact. Kumber Alee Khán agreed to what Kohun Dil Khán had set forth, and the next day mentioned all that passed between them. The day after I waited upon the Sardár, and said I had heard of the sentiments expressed to Kumber Alee Khán, and requested that he should give me a hearing; if he was right I will be convinced, and if otherwise, he was at liberty to act according to his pleasure. The Sardár told me to state what I had to say. I expressed—that you have appointed your son to go to Persia and detained Kumber Alee Khán from proceeding to Kábul; it is true that Mahomed Sháh has got wealth, and an army sufficient to assist you, but I assure you that you will not get it before the lapse of a year, and if Dost Mahomed Khán is apprised of your intentions, he will prepare himself to cause your overthrow; and if Alexander Burnes, who is now at Kábul, hears this, he will strengthen his alliance with Dost Mohomed Khán and wrest Kandáhár from you in three months. Moola Rusheed Akhunzada approved of my sentiments. Sardár Mehr Dil Khán, who was also present at the time, said that he was afraid, if he should go to Kábul, and Alexander Burnes and Kumber Alee Khán be in Dost Mahomed Khán's presence and he should be questioned as to his (Dost Mahomed's) superiority, if he should answer that he (the Sardár) was superior, Dost Mahomed would ruin him, and if otherwise he would be telling a falsehood, because he was not under him. I replied, that I would give it to them in writing that the ambassador will not put any such question in Dost Mahomed Khán's presence. He said that he was aware of my friendship with Alexander Burnes, and Kumbur Alee Khán also was of my party, and if I would deal fairly with him, he would accompany me to Kábul, and gave me his hand as a mark of promise in presence of Moola Rusheed. I also gave my word, that I would be his well-wisher and would do much for his good. Sardár Mehr Dil Khán retired to Kumber Allee Khán to change his former intention and direct him to proceed to Kábul. On hearing this, Kumber Alee Khán showed his outward displeasure, and observed that you are a curious set of people, being so fickle and changing your mind in an instant. Sardár Mehr Dil Khán apologized and satisfied him. It was settled that we should depart from Kandáhár, and put up at the Tukhya (a place near the city), and that Sardár Mehr Dil Khán would proceed to Kábul with five hundred horsemen the next day. The Sardár's baggage was accordingly sent to the Tukhya, and we halted at Mehr Dil Khán's garden and from hence to the Tukhya. Next morning we marched towards Shorab. On arriving here I found that neither Mehr Dil Khán nor his men had made any preparations for leaving Kandáhár, and received a message from Sardár Mehr Dil Khán to stop at Shorab for two days, that he may join us, which we accordingly did. After two days a mounted courier arrived at Kandáhár from Ghuznee with information that Shumsoodeen Khán, the son of Ameer Mahomed Khán, was seized by Dost Mahomed Khán, and Guznee, which he held as a jághír, was confiscated. On hearing this intelligence the Sardárs were much broken-hearted, and accordingly they sent Alla Dád Khán Burdooránee and Táj Mahomed Khán to Kumber Alee Khán, desiring him to come back again to the Tukhya, and the Sardárs would act according to his pleasure. Kumber Alee Khán complied with this request, and went back to the Tukhya, and after a long conversation between him and Mehr Dil Khán it was settled that Mahomed Ameer Khán should accompany Kumber Alee Khán to the Court of Persia, and the ambassador believing in their oaths returned from the way, and I also accompanied him to the garden of Mehr Dil Khán. After two days I waited upon the Sardárs, and by adducing reasonable arguments and historical proofs I changed their intentions again, and it was agreed that Kumber Alee Khán should leave his baggage at Ahmud Sháhee (Kandáhár) and proceed lightly equipped together with Sardár Mehr Dil Khán at the head of thirty horsemen to Kábul. The next day was appointed for their departure, when the intelligence, that Moola Jubbar Achukzaees was coming to the Sardárs from Dost Mahomed Khán, arrived at Kandáhár, and our departure was delayed for a few days till he came. He used such quarrelsome language to the Sardárs, that they entirely gave up the design of proceeding to Kábul, and destroyed the relation of brotherhood with Dost Mahomed Khán. The Sardárs spoke to me decidedly that Kumber Alee Khán must not go to Kábul, and desired me to live with him, and he would share whatever bread he had with me, and said that Dost Mahomed Khán would not appreciate the services I had performed for him, and that if I liked I should accompany Mahomed Omur Khán to Persia as a "naib" (deputy) instead of Alla Dád Khán. I replied that it was far from justice and loyalty to do so, and that, in order to get rid of the reproach of the people, I would first go to Kábul, and, further, that Dost Mahomed Khán was at liberty to do me good or harm.

Moola Jubbar spoke to Mehr Dil Khán that Dost Mahomed Khán was talking in his court that he had sent a letter through me to Mahomed Sháh asking of him some pecuniary assistance, because he was a Mahomedan king; and that if Kumber Alee Khán had brought some money for him, he might advance, otherwise there was no need of his coming here

This intelligence Mehr Dil Khán communicated to Kumber Alee Khán, who being much surprised and afflicted sent for me, and related the whole story. I said that I did not believe such to be Dost Mahomed Khán's observations, but that the Sardár himself had instructed Moola Jubbar to say so, because none of the Afgháns have a wish for Dost Mahomed Khán's greatness but the Kizilbashes. However, continued I, he should remain at Kandáhár, and I would proceed to Kábul, and ascertain the state of affairs: if favourable I would send him a messenger in twenty-five days, and he should advance to Kábul; otherwise he should return to Persia. Having settled this I departed to Kábul the next morning.

Mehr Dil Khán had promised to give me two hundred rupees a month. I remained at Kandáhár for five months, during which time I only received one month's expenses—two hundred rupees, and that, too, by the recommendation of Sardár Kohun Dil Khán, and also a pony, since I had lost some of my horses on the road from Seestan and Loot, and my servants were on foot; at the time of my departure Akhmand Moola Rusheed gave me twenty rupees.

In my progress to Kábul I did not meet with any thing worthy of notice. Arriving within a march of Kábul I sent a man to the Ameer Dost Mahomed Khán, informing him of my arrival. The Ameer sent Mirza Alee Akbar Khán, the son of Aga Sayad Mahomed, and Aga Mahomed, the head servant, to receive me, and gave me a dwelling at the Nawab Jubbar Khán's house. The following night I waited upon the Ameer, and related the adventures of my travelling. He turned his face towards the people in the court, and said that those that had received ten hundred thousand rupees from him had not performed such services as I had done for him. After a few days I spoke to the Ameer requesting him to write to Kumber Alee Khán to come on to Kábul. He ordered me to go to Mirza Abdool Sumee Khán, make a draft of the letter and bring it to his presence, all of which I did. Since the letter showed the superiority of Mahomed Sháh over Dost Mahomed Khán he was much perplexed on hearing it, and ordered it to be torn and another to be written, asserting that he was equal to Mahomed Sháh and not inferior. To this I made no reply and returned home. The next day a person came to me with the Ameer's letter for Kumber Alee Khán, and a message that I should forward it with my own letters to that ambassador. I opened the letter, and on reading I did not think it proper to send it on, because in the event of Kumbur Alee Khán showing it to Mahomed Sháh it would produce differences between him and Mahomed Sháh. Therefore I dismissed the messenger kept the letter by me, and wrote to Kumber Alee Khán on my own part that I had not found Dost Mahomed Khán as I had expected, and it was better for him to go back to Persia. I used to go every day to the Ameer's Darbár and heard nothing more but evil-speaking of Mahomed Sháh, for which purpose I entirely abstained waiting upon the Ameer for two months. Mirza Abdool Sumee Khán, Mirza Imám Verdee and Mirza Alee Akber called at my place one night, and earnestly desired me to go to the Ameer's presence, but I did not comply with their request. On the day of the festival, Eed of Ramzan, Mirza Abdoo Sumee called me to his house, and from thence compelled me to wait upon the Ameer. After that I used to wait upon the Ameer every fourth day. I had all along been most anxious to see Alexander Burnes, because he was my old friend in the journey to Bokhára, but Mirza Abdool Sumec prevented me from waiting upon him without the permission of Dost Mahomed Khán, till the time when I had access to the Ameer, and I asked his leave on the subject. After a short silence he answered yes, but I should not tell anything out of the way. I replied, that I should have nothing to do with political conversation. After this I called upon Alexander Burnes: from what I had before seen of him he had now made great progress in politics, arguments, &c., being perfect before, he had now become more perfect. He asked me some news. I told him whatever I knew for the good of the English Government. After this I waited upon the Ameer, who asked me about the nature of the con-

B 1485—19

versation that passed between me and Alexander Burnes. I answered that that gentleman would exert all his efforts for the benefit of the Ameer, and the English Government will do according to their discretion. He then said, would Mr. Burnes satisfy his wishes? I asked, what he wanted? He said, first to be put in possession of Peshāwar; second, to obtain thirty or forty lakhs of rupees, after which he would go and face Mahomed Shāh. I replied that his wish could be attained by requesting twenty regiments either from Runjeet Singh's force or the British Army, because Mahomed Shāh's troops are regular and disciplined, and he could not cope with him, without being on the same footing; and even receiving thirty lākhs of rupees he still required efficient officers from the English Government to regulate his army, and he would not, after all be able to oppose the Persians before three years, because he had no experienced officers, and his army was irregular and wild, on which very little reliance would be placed. I also added that my speaking so freely on such a matter arose from a consciousness of my being acquainted with military tactics. On hearing this remark the Ameer looked serious, changed colour, and said "Please God I will show you." I replied, if God preserve my life I will see, and advised him to make over the reins of his Government into the hands of the English, and they would manage for themselves and also for his benefit. He said he would not give over charge of his affairs to any one. This interview was over, and after a moment the Ameer said again he did not know what would be the result of the negotiation between himself and Alexander Burnes. I asked him if the above gentleman had promised him anything, or had given him an assurance to accomplish his views. He replied, no, and as often as he had sent his Mirza to Alexander Burnes to ascertain that matter, he answered nothing but that he had written all the propositions to his Government, and until he received an answer from it he could settle nothing. I said Alexander Burnes was right; being an experienced politician how should he give any such pledges. After some time the Governor General's letter arrived, when the Ameer sent for me, and said that his request from the English had not met with a favourable reception, and in consequence he would depute me to Mahomed Shāh. I replied that I had performed one service, which was enough for me till the day of resurrection, that I was not acquainted with him first, but now I would be a mad man if I interfered in his affairs. He used to upbraid Mahomed Shāh before, and now he scandalized the English and Alexander Burnes. One day Ameer Dost Mahomed Khán sent for me in private, talked about Mahomed Shāh and evil to the English. I said, that a man cannot procure a friend in ten years, whereas he can make a thousand enemies in a moment; that if he could not make friends he should not make enemies; that it was far from the law of wisdom to entertain such notions; that his object was that the English should give him money; that how could they trust him, that who of the Afghan nation has ever kept his oath; that I who had served him with so much faithfulness had received nothing but rebukes. To these expressions the Ameer gave no answer. I said that I presumed to say so much merely for his own good, that he ought to be considerate, and leave off talking nonsense. Upon this he said I spoke the truth, and he went over to Alexander Burnes in person and began to speak mildly. After this he kept himself quiet, and did not speak against the English in any society. He sent a communication with the original of the Governor General's letter to the Sardárs of Kandáhár, upon which Sardár Mehr Dil Khán came to Kábul. After having three or four interviews with Alexander Burnes, they (the Ameer and Mehr Dil Khán) were convinced that their object could not be attained from the English, and that they should consequently settle matters with Vitkievitch, and asked him that if they connected themselves with the Russians, and the English and Runjeet Singh should come with their united forces upon them how should they act. Vitkievitch, who was somewhat void of sense, replied that he would bring twenty regiments from Russia into Kábul in two months. I hinted to the Ameer whether such could be the case. The Ameer said to me afterwards that it was untruth, and that he was merely confronting Vitkievitch with Alexander Burnes in order to procure money from the latter. I did not believe the Ameer, and told him that I would never sit in his company, or talk to him on any subject.

I travelled for two years, and remained for seven months at Kábul, during which time I spent thirty thousand rupees from my own pocket, and on the day of my departure from Kábul I did not receive a single rupee or anything of the value of a pice from the Ameer. During my stay at Kábul I was supplied with expense by Nawab Jubbar Khán, and Alexander Burnes also assisted me on account of the friendship I had with him.

The Afgháns are so foolish that, notwithstanding such ill-treatment, Ameer Dost Mahomed Khán expected faithfulness and good service from me, sometimes desiring me to go to Persia, and sometimes to Russia to make arrangements with these powers. I always pray to God for getting an opportunity to serve the English, and to liquidate the debt of gratitude I owe to them, because had I not been supplied by the English I would have not been master of horses and men at this time. The curse of God and his servants be on those who believe in an Afghán's word, or assist them in any matter, and curse be on him who, if able, does not injure that nation; and whoever says that he has found rectitude in them, especially in Dost Mahomed Khán, is the greatest liar in the world. I cannot give a full account of the Afghán nation.

Translated by Akhwundzada Abdool Kureem under the supervision of

(Signed)   A. BURNES,
Late on a Mission to Kábul.

Camp at Rorce Bukhur, 1st February 1839.

LETTERS

FROM

MAJOR D'ARCY TODD.

LETTERS FROM MAJOR D'ARCY TODD.

To
 Sir W. H. MACNAGHTEN, Bart.,
  Envoy and Minister,
   &c., &c., &c.,
    Jallálábád.

Sir,—In continuation of my letter to your address, No. 94, dated 30th November, and reporting the state of affairs at Herát, I have the honour to submit to your notice some circumstances which have lately occurred, and to lay before you the observations which I deem it my duty to offer on the subject of our relations with this Government.

2. Some time ago Moosa Beg, a messenger from the Persian Ausef-ood-Dowlah, arrived at Herát, the ostensible object of his visit being to deliver complimentary letters to the Vuzeer and myself, as I had lately written to the Ausef regarding the detention of our packets at Meshed, thereby giving him a pretext for sending a messenger to this place. I did not take any notice of Moosa Beg's arrival, although I had repeatedly warned the Vuzeer against even complimentary intercourse with the Persian authorities as tending to raise reports prejudicial to his interests, and to give the British Government grounds of suspicion as to his intentions. During Moosa Beg's stay at Herát it was not suspected that he had been charged with any mission on the part of the Ausef, but I have now reason to believe that he was the bearer of proposals of friendship and alliance with the Vuzeer. In order to avoid suspicion the Persian messenger was not admitted to any private conference with Yár Mahomed Khán, but I have ascertained that he was allowed to converse with the Vuzeer's sister in the inner apartments, one other woman only being present at the interview. Friendship between the Persian and Herátees and a family alliance between the Ausef and the Vuzeer were the subjects discussed on that occasion.

3. About the time of the occurrence above mentioned Yár Mahomed Khán was preparing to send his son, Syud Mahomed Khán, on a mission to the Chiefs of the Huzáreh and Jumsheedee tribes, to which I had objected, principally on the ground of its involving him in unnecessary expense. Objects inimical to our interests had, however, been generally attributed to the proposed measure. The departure of Syud Mahomed Khán was delayed from day to day and from week to week, and at length the Vuzeer gave out that Fyz Mahomed Khán, his Master of Ceremonies, would proceed, in place of his son, with letters and presents to the Rlmauk Chiefs. On the 17th instant Fyz Mahomed Khán left Herát, and on that day it was first intimated that his destination instead of being Khooslik and Kulla-i-No, as was supposed, was in reality Meshed. So secret had this been kept that most of Fyz Mahomed's followers were ignorant of their destination until they had left the city. On ascertaining the fact I immediately addressed a note to the Vuzeer expressing my regret at his having taken this extraordinary step and my fear that it would be attended with the most disastrous consequences to himself.

4. Fyz Mahomed Khán is a person of some influence, being a confidential servant of the Minister, to whose tribe he belongs, and has been notorious since my arrival at Herát for his hatred to the English, which he has more than once displayed in an insulting manner. The deputation of this individual with a train of 40 or 50 followers, and, it is believed, presents, to the Persian authorities, could therefore only be looked upon as a manifest breach of treaty, even setting aside the suspicious fact of its having been devised and executed with the most careful secrecy. The Vuzeer, in answer to my note, expressed great surprise at the serious view which I had taken of this trivial matter, and asserted, in excuse, that I had given him permission to send a man to Meshed for the purpose of demanding the restoration of Ghoriani, which had been the reason of his despatching Fyz Mahomed Khán.

5. Finding that his excuse was not deemed admissible, the Vuzeer sent several of his confidential advisers with oaths and protestations and declarations of readiness to remedy by any means in his power the evil that had been done, swearing by all that is held sacred among Mahomedans that the only object of Fyz Mahomed's mission was to demand the restoration of Ghoriani, and offering to abide by the heaviest penalty should any other question be discussed at Meshed by his messenger. It was, however, admitted that the step which had been secretly taken bore a very bad appearance, and that it would have been better had Fyz Mahomed never left Herát, but no promise or offer was made immediately to recall him.

It is true that I had some time ago given the Vuzeer permission to send a man or a letter to Meshed for the purpose mentioned in the concluding part of the 4th paragraph, but this could never be applied to the departure of his most confidential servant with a train of 40 or 50 followers. To use the expression of an intelligent A'fghán, when he heard of the circumstance, "the excuse is worse than the fault."

6. I may here mention that there is but one opinion in the town of the real object of his mission, namely an alliance with Persia based on our ejectment from Herát. A strong and general feeling of insecurity prevails; many persons are preparing to send their families to Kandáhár, and the only question about our treatment is whether we are to be seized and plundered to-day or to-morrow.

7. My reply to the Vuzeer's messages and to the urgent supplications of his sycophants to prevent a rupture was to the effect that whatever might have been the instructions of Yár Mahomed Khán to Fyz Mahomed, I feared, from my knowledge of the character of the latter, that he would compromise his principle beyond redemption and that my interference would be unavailing. The matter had in fact been taken out of my hands, for the British Government would doubtless hear of this Mission from other sources, and would take such measures as might seem advisable with reference to any report I might make on the subject, unless, indeed, the Vuzeer by some immediate and undisguised act of hostility towards the Persians, such as attacking Ghoriani, proved beyond the slightest doubt that the general belief regarding the object of Fyz Mahomed's mission was utterly groundless.

8. On the 24th instant, at an interview with the Minister which immediately succeeded these occurrences, I held the same language. In excuse for his conduct he pleaded his fears of our ulimate intentions, thereby admitting his guilt, although he declared most solemnly that the only message with which he had charged Fyz Mahomed was that previously stated. He said that he had yesterday heard of the arrival of 20,000 men at Shikárpur, and asked me whether it was true. I answered that I had only received intelligence of preparations being made for subsisting 17,000. He then stated that all his advisers and correspondents warned him that the destination of these troops was Herát, and that the English wished to involve him in hostilities with Persia merely to enable them to crush him with greater facility. I observed that I considered my word of greater weight and more worthy of belief than the reports and speculations of all his correspondents and advisers; that the authorities of Herát were the only people in the world who doubted our word or distrusted us in any way; and that if he had enquired of me regarding the destination of these troops, I could have set his mind perfectly at rest on the subject. I added that, had he reflected for a moment he could never have feared us, for our conduct towards him up to this moment had been uniformly liberal and friendly, and had we wished to destroy him we should have done so either openly, on our first arrival in the country previously to strengthening him, or secretly by the expenditure amongst his enemies of one-tenth of the sum that had been lavished on him. This, he said, could not be denied, but observed that it was natural for the weaker to fear the stronger, and he therefore requested me to give him a paper of assurance (khatur jum) in order to remove his apprehen-

sions. I replied that it was out of my power to furnish him with the paper he required ; that if what we had already done in and for the country had not satisfied him of our disinterested friendship, nothing could ; and that it rested with him to counteract the evil he had done and to satisfy us for the future.

9. On the following day (the 25th) the Vuzeer sent his three most confidential advisers to endeavour to procure from me the paper to the effect above mentioned. This I steadily refused to give for the reasons which I had assigned to the Minister the day before and to themselves on a former occasion. I consented, however, to take no decided step until the receipt of intelligence from Meshed.

10. The greatest possible state of alarm was excited in the mind of the Vuzeer by my continuing to hold this language, and fearing that the immediate result of his conduct would be the cessation of all pecuniary assistance, he, on the 27th, sent his principal adviser, Nujjoo Khán, to endeavour to discover what terms would be granted him.

The Khán made several propositions, none of which, however, appeared to me to promise any security for the future, and at length he stated that if I would give the Minister confidence there would be no objection to our introducing a brigade of British troops into the country, or even into the town, with the express proviso that His Majesty Sháh Shoojáh should not interfere in the matter and that Sháh Kamrám should remain as nominal ruler. I was careful not to manifest any anxiety on the subject of the introduction of our troops, although this was the point on which I was desirous of ascertaining the Minister's sentiments, and I therefore dismissed Nujjoo Khán with the promise that I would give further consideration to the question. It is possible, and even probable, that the hint thrown out regarding our troops was merely intended as a feeler.

11. Nujjoo Khán came again this morning (29th) to learn my final decision. I informed him that before settling a question of such magnitude and importance it would be necessary that he should bring written credentials from the Vuzeer.

There are many circumstances chiefly connected with Yár Mahomed Khán's character, but too numerous to be detailed here, which would lead me to prefer negotiating with the Vuzeer through the medium of an accredited third person, rather than with himself, and Nujjoo Khán is certainly in every respect the fittest of all Yár Mahomed Khán's confidential advisers for the office of mediator.

12. I will here state the only terms which should in my opinion be granted to Yár Mahomed Khán as the alternative to our undertaking a hostile movement against Herát, and it is my intention to offer this alternative for reasons which I will endeavour to explain in the concluding part of my letter :—

1. A brigade of British troops with artillery to occupy the citadel of Herát.
2. The revenues of Seestan to be appropriated to the maintenance of these troops.
3. The present Government of Herát to remain unchanged during the lifetime of Sháh Kamrán.
4. Three lákhs of Company's rupees per annum to be given as assistance to the Government of Herát during the lifetime of the Vuzeer, and after his death maintenance to be guaranteed to his son. Amongst minor arrangements it would be necessary that the Vuzeer's son should immediately proceed to Girusht, there to remain until the decision of Government is known, when he will either accompany the brigade to Herát, or be allowed to report on the retirement of our Mission from this place.

13. Before detailing my reasons for recommending that any terms should be offered the Herát Government on the present occasion, I will submit a few observations on the nature and value of our relations with this petty state.

14. It is either politic and necessary to obtain a commanding influence at Herát or it is not. If the former be granted, our experience of the last two years and the present state of affairs at Herát sufficiently prove that we must have recourse to very different measures from those which we have hitherto adopted to obtain that influence. If the latter be the case, the money which we have already expended on this country must be considered as having been spent in the great cause of humanity—a noble cause—in which British gold has been freely sacrificed in every corner of the globe to the unfading glory of the British name; but further pecuniary assistance is not required except for the purpose of maintaining our influence at Herát, and I would therefore recommend that we abandon the post, for we cannot hold it, even on our present insecure tenure, without a considerable expenditure of treasure. I am clearly of opinion, as I have frequently before stated, that it is both necessary and politic to acquire a supremacy at Herát.

15. Recent events on the Russian frontier of Turkastán might seem to diminish the value of this position, but I am of opinion that its importance has been by those very events rather enhanced than lessened, for the Russians having been foiled in their attempt to advance towards our Indian empire by the route of Khiva and the Oxus, after having experienced its almost insurmountable difficulties, will naturally turn their attention more seriously to the only remaining line of advance, namely, that on which Herát is situated.

16. The influence of Russia is now paramount in Persia, and any extension of the Persian frontier towards India must be considered as an approach made by Russia. Herát cannot remain independent between Kábul and Persia; it must be, *de facto*, subject to one or the other. If we abandon Herát, it will be occupied by the Persians, and the Perso-Russian frontier will then be brought within 150 miles of Kandáhár, or 400 miles nearer than it now is to the yet unsettled kingdom of Kábul. This cannot, I think, be permitted.

17. The question, therefore, in my mind is resolved into one of expenditure. Supposing the measure now advocated be carried into effect Herát becomes virtually ours at an expense which may be easily calculated, whereas that of undertaking an expedition against this place is indefinite and would certainly be enormous. Even after the successful result of hostile operations against Herát we must, in order to reap the fruits of our campaign, subject ourselves to an outlay, equal at least to that of the proposed arrangement, and in the mean time we should have incurred throughout Central Asia the odium which such an expedition would necessarily bring upon us, our efforts to restore this country to prosperity would have been marred, and a great sacrifice of human life would have been made.

18. The departure of our Agent from Herát would be the signal for the worst species of cruelty and outrage being again perpetrated on every individual supposed to possess wealth. All classes would alike suffer, and if to these horrors were added the evils of invasions, Herát would soon be the wilderness it was left by Mahomed Sháh. It could again only be rendered valuable at an expense equal to that already incurred.

19. It may not be considered advisable to garrison such a distant and isolated part as Herát with our own troops, but I am convinced that insuperable objections would be raised to the admission of those of Sháh Shoojáh or to the use of his name in the proposed arrangement, which, however, might be easily set aside on the death of Sháh Kamrán when our troops might be relieved by those of His Majesty Sháh Shoojáh, Herát being re-annexed to Kábul should such a measure be desirable.

20. In conclusion I would strongly urge the expediency of concentrating troops at Kandáhár with as little delay as possible, for I feel confident that their services will be required before summer either for the attack or for the occupation of Herát, unless indeed it be determin-

ed to abandon the position. I may add thát under any circumstances I do not apprehend violence being offered to the officers or servants of the Mission.

I have the honour to be, &c.,
(Signed) E. D. A. TODD,
Herát, 29th January 1841.
Envoy to Herát.

To
    J. P. WILLOUGHBY, Esquire,
        Secretary to Government in the Political Department,
            Bombay.

Sir,—I have the honour to forward for the information of the Honourable the Governor of Bombay copy of a Despatch (No. 106, dated 4th February,) to the address of the Envoy and Minister at Kábul, being a continuation of a report on the present state of affairs at Herát.

I have the honour to be, &c.,
(Signed) E. D. A. TODD,
Herát, 5th February 1841.
Envoy to Herát.

Copy.
No. 136.

To
    Sir W. H. MACNAGHTEN, Bart,
        Envoy and Minister at the Court of Sháh Shoojáh-ool-Moolk,
            Jállálábád.

Sir,—In continuation of my letter No. 103, under date the 29th ultimo, I have the honour to report for your information that the Vuzeer has evinced considerable anxiety to defer the discussion of the subject of our future relations with this Government until news shall have been received of the proceedings of Fyz Mahomed Khán at Meshed, and in the meantime has declined giving to Nujjoo Khán the paper alluded to in the 11th paragraph of my letter above mentioned. I have therefore not yet brought forward the terms which I proposed offering, although the Vuzeer seems to be perfectly aware that he can no longer play a double part, and that he must submit himself to the power either of England or of Persia. I hope, in the course of a day or two, to ascertain, by means of agents whom I have despatched to Meshed, all the particulars of Fyz Mahomed's mission to that place.

2. On the 1st instant I intimate to Yár Mahomed Khán that I could under existing circumstances only disburse the monthly allowance (25,000 Company's rupees) to the King and Chiefs which had been promised for the present year, provided the Herát authorities acted in conformity to the wishes of the British Government. As it seemed to me that a manifest breach of treaty had been committed I did not feel myself authorized to continue the allowance. In reply the Minister acknowledges that he had no claim to further pecuniary assistance in the present state of affairs, but expressed a hope of being able to make it appear that my suspicion of his want of faith had been groundless.

3. Yesterday the festival of Koorham was celebrated, and no demand or request was made for money on the occasion. I went to the citadel with the officers of the Mission as on former festivals. Dresses of honour were given to us by the King and we rode with His Majesty as usual. In the course of the day an event occurred which might have led to serious consequences. Kázi Moolláh Mahomed Hussein and his son Aukun Ladáh Mahomed Dáood, who are attached to the Mission establishment, and who are known as being devotedly attached to our interests, were grossly and shamefully insulted by two dependants of the Vuzeer's family. On being made

acquainted with the circumstances which had taken place in the presence of a vast concourse of people, I sent several witnesses of it to the Vuzeer, and advised, espicially with reference to the present state of feeling in the town, that the punishment of the offenders should be summary and public. Their guilt was proved, and after being bastinadoed in the market-place, their faces being smeared with mud, they were led through the different streets of the city, while a crier proclaimed with a loud voice their offence and punishment.

4. I have received intelligence from Erzeroom, dated the 7th December, when the British Mission was still at that place, and there did not appear to be any immediate prospect of the settlement of our differences with the Persian Government. Meerza Massood, the Persian Secretary of State for Foreign Affairs, and his son who has lately been officiating in that capacity, had been disgraced, in consequence of the latter having forged the King's signature. Meerza Abdool Hussun Khán, formerly Ambassador to England and for many years past a pensioner of the British Government, has been appointed Foreign Minister.

I have the honour to be, &c.,
(Signed) E. D. A. TODD,
Herát, 4th February 1841.   Envoy to Herát.

To
    Lieutenant E. K. ELLIOTT,
        Political Assistant, Girishk.

Sir,—I have the honour to inform you that our relations with Herát are broken off and that I see no prospect of their re-establishment by negotiation. The officers and servants of the British Mission were obliged to withdraw from the city yesterday afternoon, and we shall probably make our first and regular march towards Kandáhár to-morrow morning. No violence or insult has been as yet offered us, and we have succeeded in bringing with us the greater part of our property. Sirdár Futteh Khán, a cousin of the Vuzeer, has been appointed to escort us with a party of 40 and 50 horsemen to the frontier, which I hope to reach on the 18th instant.

2. It is not impossible, from the excited state of feeling in the country, the treacherous character of these people, and the belief which prevails of our being possessed of a large sum of money, that attempts will be made to plunder us on the road, most probably when we have crossed or are near the frontier. May I therefore request that you will, if convenient, despatch from Girishk a strong escort of horse to Washeer, or even to the dák station on the Khonah river, there to await our arrival. I hoped moving by the route of Gurmec, Gurmal and Buckwa. If you could arrange to send one day's provisions for our party consisting of about 80 mounted followers, with 30 or 40 baggage mules to Shoorawuk, and the same, if possible, to Delárám, it will obviate the necessity of our marching by the circuitous route of Washeer.

3. I think it probable that this rupture will be followed up on the part of Yár Mahomed Khán by an immediate hostile movement in the direction of Kandáhár, and that an attempt will be made to surprise the fort of Girishk.

4. May I beg the favour of your forwarding a copy of this letter to the Political Agent at Kandáhár for his information and for transmission to the Envoy and Minister? The dák which left Herát on the 30th ultimo and which contained a detailed account of the circumstances which led to this crisis, was plundered near Gurmah. I will endeavour to forward a copy of the last despatches with further particulars as soon as possible.

I have, &c.,
(Signed) E. D. A. TODD,
Camp at Joghara, 4 miles south of Herát,   Envoy to Herát.
6 A.M., 10th Feburary 1841.

To

Sir W. H. MACNAGHTEN, Bart., K.D.,
Envoy and Minister,
&c., &c., &c.,
Jallálábád.

Sir,—In continuation of my letter, No. 106, under date the 4th instant, I have the honor to lay before you a statement of the circumstances which led to my withdrawal of the British Mission from the Herát territory and of the occurrences which have taken place in connection with this measure up to the present time.

2. On the afternoon of the 7th instant I was waited on by a deputation consisting of the Topohee Bashee, Ishuk Aghassee and Uruz Beggee, who brought a letter from the Vuzeer, of which the enclosed is a translation. In this letter Yár Mahomed Khán requested that I would immediately either give him full security for the future, or take from him all hope; in the latter case he stated that I must not be surprised at his committing some desperate act. As the three persons above mentioned were not authorized by the Vuzeer to negotiate on his part, I wrote in reply that after what had occurred I was anxious to discuss with himself the questions under consideration, but that if he objected to a personal interview I would treat with any one to whom he gave written credentials.

3. On the morning of the 8th instant the three persons mentioned in the foregoing paragraph brought a letter from the Vuzeer giving them full powers finally to adjust matter on his behalf. I had previously learnt the result of a consultation which had been held the night before by the Vuzeer and his advisers and the demands which the two were instructed to make on the present occasion. I therefore opened the conference by begging them to state the requisitions with which they were charged. These they informed me were as follows:—

1. A written assurance on the part of the British Government relieving the Vuzeer from all apprehensions for the future.
2. The immediate payment of the Vuzeer's debts amounting to nearly two láks of Company's rupees.
3. A liberal monthly allowance, far exceeding that at present given, to be guaranteed to the Herát Government for one year.
4. A written promise that the British Government would not embroil that of Herát in any foreign war until after the present harvests which are reaped in June and July.
5. The fortifications of the city to be repaired and strengthened at our expense.
6. Loans of money to be advanced to enable the Herát Government to recover entire possession of the Char Viláyut, Ghorian, Seestaun and the Tymunee country, and the Herát troops to be subsidised in the field so long as engaged in these operations. I asked what the Herát Government was prepared to grant in the event of the above demands being acceded to by my Government, and in reply was requested to mention what I deemed an equivalent.

4. I stated that the treaty having been again broken by the authorities of Herát and their promises having been found valueless, it was for the British Government now to demand security for the future, and that in my opinion the only satisfactory mode of giving this was by admitting a brigade of British troops with artillery into the citadel of Herát and the immediate deputation of the Vuzeer's son to Girishk to accompany the troops to Herát. Under these circum-

b 1485—22

stances I promised, pending the sanction of Government, to give a written assurance to the Vuzeer guaranteeing to him the Vuzárat of Herát during his life-time, the payment of his debts to the amount of one lákh of Company's rupees on the arrival of our troops, and an allowance to the Herát Government for one year of one lákh of Herát rupees, Company's Rs. 33,333½, per mensem, to commence on the arrival of the Vuzeer's son at Girishk, up to which date the present allowance of 25,000 Company's rupees a month would be continued. I also agreed to the repair of the fortifications, provided our troops were admitted into the citadel, but in the event of their being located outside the town, I stated that the expense of fortifying a post for their accommodation would be considerable, and in this case the Herátees must repair their own works. This was said with reference to a long discussion which took place on the subject of our troops being quartered in the citadel, to which the deputation objected in the strongest terms as a measure to which they were certain the Vuzeer would never agree. On reflection it seemed to me that our object would be equally gained by our holding a strong position in the immediate vicinity of the city; indeed there were considerations which pointed this out as the more desirable arrangement. I waived for the present the discussion of articles Nos. 4 and 6. This interview, which occupied nearly the whole day, and throughout which Lieutenant North and my Persian Secretary were present, was concluded by the deputation informing me that they did not think it possible the Vuzeer would agree to my terms; that the Vuzeer's wife could not be persuaded to part with her son; and that an immediate payment of money would be required. It was evident to me that the object of the discussion was merely to gain time, and, if possible, to induce me to advance money before the result of Fyz Mahomed Khán's mission to Meshed became known. Finding that I was not disposed to make the required concessions, the deputation informed me, on the part of the Vuzeer, that I might select my Mehmándár, as any further stay at Herát would be useless and that my Hindustáni, Kábul, and Kandáhár servants would be allowed to accompany me, but that those of Herát would not be permitted to leave the place. I selected Sirdár Fatteh Khán as my Mehmándár, and remarked that I did not require the permission of the Vuzeer to take with me the natives of India or the subjects of Sháh Shoojáh, and that by the laws of Nations I had a right to retain in my service, at least until I reached the Frontier, all my Herát servants who were willing to accompany me. I will not here recapitulate the reasons which induced me to offer any terms to the Vuzeer after what had occurred; for these I beg to refer you to my letter of the 29th ultimo. With regard to my consenting to withdraw the British Mission from Herát on my own responsibility, I must state my conviction that our further stay at Herát would have been productive of no good, and that with the examples of Major Pottinger, Colonel Stoddart and Lieutenant Loveday before me, I should not have been justified in exposing the officers of the Mission to insult and danger by remaining at Herát in opposition to the expressed wishes of the Vuzeer.

5. Very early in the morning of the 9th I received a note from the Topehee Bashee informing me that the Vuzeer would not agree to any one of my terms; that Sirdár Futteh Khán had been appointed my Mehmándár; and that our Herát camel-drivers, grooms and muleteers would be permitted to accompany us to Kandáhár. At this time the gates of the city had been closed, the shops of the bázárs shut, and the caravanserais sealed. The greatest excitement prevailed throughout the town, the inhabitants armed themselves, guns were discharged in every direction, and large crowds collected round the residence of the Mission. Our followers and servants were threatened with death, and their families with dishonour; and it was generally believed that we were to be seized and our property plundered.

6. I have on several occasions had the honour to bring to your notice the services of Kázi Moolláh Mahomed Hussun and his family. In the time of Major Pottinger they were the only

persons in the country who had the hardihood to oppose the nefarious practice of kidnapping and selling the inhabitants although it was sanctioned by all the other members of the priesthood and even followed by some of them. The Kázi was the means of our first opening negotiations with Khyva, and by the favourable ideas which he instilled into the mind of the Khán Huzrut regarding our power and policy induced that Chief to depute an Envoy to Herát for the purpose of allying himself with the British Government. Lieutenant Shakespear has mentioned in several letters the valuable services performed by the Kázi throughout the negotiations of that officer for the release of the Russian slaves. The Kázi's eldest son was the person as you may remember, who rescued Captain Abbott from the hands of the Kuzzaks, and is now with Captain Conolly at Khyva. His second son accompanied Lieutenant Shakespear to Dash Kulla and rendered important services during that officer's difficult and dangerous journey to the Russian frontier. For the known adherence of this family to the interests of the British Government they had incurred the ruinous enmity of the Vuzeer and his advisers, and threats had often been held out that they would be made the first victims of his displeasure on our retirement from the city. I therefore felt the greatest anxiety and apprehension on account of Kázi Moollah Mahomed Hussun and his family, especially as it had been intimated to me that they would not be permitted to leave the city, and, indeed, that the restriction regarding our Herát servants applied principally to them.

7. Under these circumstances I addressed a letter to the Vuzeer, expressing a hope that his last act towards me would be one of personal friendship, and that he would permit the Kázi and his family, together with the whole of my Herát servants and their families, to accompany me to Kandáhár, and I promised, in the event of his acceding to my request, to pay the allowances of the King and Chiefs for the present month, the disbursement of which had been suspended in consequence of the deputation of Fyz Mahomed Khán to Meshed. The Vazir replied that I might take with me the whole of my Herát servants and their families, but that he would not allow the Kázi or any of his family to leave the city. At the same time he declined to receive the monthly allowance. The cause of his apparent indifference to money on the part of the Vuzeer will be explained hereafter.

8. We passed the forenoon in preparation for our journey and in endeavouring to allay the fears of our servants. During this time several unsuccessful attempts were made to plunder the Mission premises. About midday Sirdár Futteh Khán made his appearance and shortly afterwards I was waited upon by Sirdár Syud Mahomed Khán, the Vuzeer's son Sirdár Sheer Mahomed Khán, the Vuzeer's brother and several of the Vuzeer's principal adherents who came to conduct our party from the city. Dense crowds had assembled to witness our departure, and I apprehended personal insult, if not violence, being offered to us by some of the Vuzeer's lawless soldiery, but by leaving the town at a different gate from that which we had named we avoided the crowd and reached our first place of encampment about four miles from Herát without being molested.

9. On the 10th instant we halted at Jagharra for the purpose of enabling our servants to bring their families from the city and of continuing our negotiations for the release of the Kázi. We learnt this morning that our communication with Kandáhár had been cut off by order of the Vuzeer, and that Envoys were about to be sent in all directions for the purpose of procuring assistance in money and troops. I was visited by the son and the principal advisers of the Vuzeer. The chief point of difference was carefully avoided, and it was evident that their object was to delay me in the vicinity of the city by holding out hopes of the Vuzeer eventually agreeing to my terms. In the course of the day I learnt that the Vuzeer, immediately on our

leaving the town, had placed the Kázi and his brother Moolláh Mahomed Omar under strict surveillance, and had threatened them and their families with the most horrible tortures. At the same time he demanded the Kázi's second son, Mahomed Daood, who being a servant of the Mission, had accompanied us from the city. To this demand I replied that I would not and could not give up any servant of the establishment who claimed our protection without force being used. I again made the offer mentioned in the 4th paragraph of this letter to pay the allowance for the present month to the Sháh and Chiefs, provided the Vuzeer would release the Kázi and his family, but as the amount had already been advanced to the Vuzeer by a merchant in the city to whom I had promised to pay the allowance when due, and as no part of this sum would consequently reach the Vuzeer, my offer was declined. I was, however, informed that if I paid the amount of the monthly allowance, 25,000 Company's rupees, into the hands of the Vuzeer, the Kázi and his family would be allowed to accompany me. To this exorbitant demand I could not accede, as I had promised the merchant above mentioned, Syud Oman Oollah, a person of great respectability and influence in the city, that the first money I disbursed to the Herát Government should be paid to him.

10. I am sensible that my conduct in offering money for the release of persons attached to our interests may be severely censured; but it should be borne in mind that I was dealing with a barbarian and a tyrant who would not have hesitated to carry his worst threats* into execution, and that our abandonment of these families whose only crime in the eyes of the Vuzeer was the service they had rendered our Government, would have been as injurious to the British name in these countries as our stepping forward in behalf of persons thus situated would be honourable. Under these circumstances I was led to offer a thousand Herát tomauns; about 6,500 Company's rupees, in addition to what was due to the Syud for the monthly allowance, on condition that the Kázi and his family should be released and permitted to proceed to Kandáhár, and persuaded the Syud to give five hundred tomauns for the same purpose. I may here mention that nearly the whole of the money I offered was in the hands of a Hindoo banker in the city who had been seized with the other merchants and bankers on the 9th instant and whose property had been confiscated. I had therefore no hope of realising it by any other means.

11. On the morning of the 11th I was informed that the Vuzeer had agreed to my proposal of yesterday, and I determined, chiefly by the advice of my Mehmándar, who apprehended treachery on the part of the Vuzeer, to make a short march across the river. This was accomplished in the afternoon although several messages were sent to detain us. I had ascertained that with one exception, Ishikaghassee Abdoomheem Khán, the whole of the Vuzeer's advisers were strenuously urging on Yár Mahomed Khán the policy of seizing and plundering us and the folly of allowing so valuable a prey to escape. The next day we marched to Meer Daood, a caravanserai about 16 miles from the city. Here we were joined in the night by the Kázi and his brother with the males of their families, the females having been placed in safety in the harems of their relations. On the morning of the 13th we concluded our

---

*One of the threats held out by the Vuzeer was that the Kázi should be tortured more cruelly than Meer Sedik Khán; that the women of his family should be given over to the soldiery, and that the males should, after having been tortured, be paraded through the streets, a crier proclaiming that such was the punishment of all who served infidels.

Meer Sedik Khán, a rival of the Vuzeer was about seven years ago put to the most horrid tortures. He was placed naked upon a red hot copper tray until his testicles burst; he was then boiled over a slow fire, and when nearly dead, his body was cut into small pieces.

The terror of the Kázi and his brother at the purport before them was heart-rending and perfectly indescribable.

arrangements for the payment of the ransom money and made our first regular march to a spot about 42 miles from the city.

12. On the 19th instant we crossed the Frontier and were met by a party of horse under Sirdár Sooltán Mahomed Khán Bárukzái, who had been sent by Lieutenant Elliot to escort us to Girishk. The conduct of our Mehmándár, Sirdár Futteh Khán, has been admirable. I have brought him on to this, and I shall dismiss him with a handsome present in shawls and money. Had he not accompanied us it would have been impossible for us to have passed through the country between Herát and the Khaush river, notorious for plunderers of every description, without, at least, the loss of our property. We reached this place yesterday afternoon, having performed the journey, nearly 300 miles, in nine days; and though our baggage cattle, camels and mules suffered much from the long march we were obliged to make, I am happy to say that we sustained no loss of property, public or private, on the road. The officers of the Mission were, however, obliged to leave at Herát much of their heavy baggage, such as furniture, books, and some tents, and I would respectfully suggest that compensation be allowed to Leiutenant North and Dr. Login on this account. It was also found impossible to bring away the whole of the public property, but the amount lost is inconsiderable compared to what has been saved.

13. I cannot close this letter without expressing my grateful sense of the valuable services rendered by Lieutenant North and Dr. Login, to whose cheerful exertions and assistance under the trying circumstances in which we have been lately placed I am chiefly indebted, under Providence, for the successful manner in which our retreat has been effected. There are many circumstances which would seem to render my presence as near the Frontier as possible desirable, and I shall therefore remain at Girishk pending your orders.

I have the honour to be, &c.,

(Signed)   E. D. A. TODD,
Envoy to Herát.

Girishk, 22nd February 1841.

Translation of a note addressed by the Vuzeer of Herát to Major E. D. A. Todd, 7th February 1841.

After compliments,—I know not whether it be from my evil destiny or from want of kindness on your part that from the day you returned from the Bund (meaning the journey towards Ghorian in June last), although you yourself prevented the expedition against Ghorian, all my efforts during the last six months to propitiate your favour have failed. I again sent the Topohee Bashee and the Ishukaghassee to you with a message that I would attack Ghorian, but you would not consent to it. At length I proposed to you to send a person (Yek Nuffer Adum) to Meshed that the Asuf-ood-Dowlah might have an excuse) for coercing Ghorian. You consented, but after the messenger departed you were angry. You may now have learnt that he has not uttered a word except in the matter of Ghorian, yet you will not take the same road with me (beech rahhumrahee ma na mee geereed). Yesterday I sent to you the Ishukaghassee and Uruz Beggee, but you answered them plainly that you would not, under any circumstances, be reconciled to me, and you deprived me of all hope from the British Government. Now this is the last letter that I shall write to you. To day you will either give me perfect assurance and confidence or take from me all hope. Henceforward into whatever well I may throw myself I have thrown myself. Let there be no complaint on either side.

(True Translation.)
(Signed) E. D'ARCY TODD,
Envoy to Herát.

To
    J. P. WILLOUGHBY, Esquire,
        Secretary to Government in the Political Department,
                Bombay.

SIR,—I have the honour to forward for the information of the Honble the Governor of Bombay copy of a letter which I have this day addressed to the Envoy and Minister at Kábul.

I have the honor to be, &c.,
(Signed) E. D. A. TODD,
Political Agent, Herát.

Girishk, 26th February 1841.

"*Girishk, 1st March 1841.*

MY DEAR OUTRAM,—The dâk is being closed and I have not time to say a word in forwarding copy of my official letter of the 26th ultimo to the Envoy and Minister. Every thing here is in *statu quo;* the rebels of Tanim Damer Ail said to be dispersing, but I think it probable that it will be found necessary to send out a force against them. I am of course most anxious to learn the Envoy and Minister's opinion of my late proceedings. What do you think of the state of affairs?

Yours very sincerely,
(Signed) E. D. A. TODD."

To
    SIR W. H. MACNAGHTEN, BART.,
        Envoy and Minister,
           &c.,   &c.,   &c.,
                Kábul.

SIR,—In continuation of my letter to your address, under date the 22nd instant, I have the honour to lay before you my opinions on the course likely to be pursued by the Herát Government consequent to the withdrawal of the British Mission, and on the measures which seem called for under the altered aspect of affairs in Western Afghánistán.

2. Yár Mahomed Khán was probably influenced in sending his confidential servant on a mission to Meshed by the hope that we should be alarmed at the prospect of his allying himself with Persia, and induced to comply with his demands for further pecuniary assistance, in order to ward off the evil which we were supposed to apprehend from such an alliance. The

immediate result of this step was very different from that which the Vuzeer had been led to expect, and when he became aware of the false and dangerous position in which he had placed himself, his fears led him to require assurances of safety which could not be granted; to propose terms, the palpable object of which was to gain time, and finally to hasten a rupture, which he believed, to the last moment of our stay in the vicinity of Herát, we should be glad to avoid by the payment of a large sum of money.

3. It does not seem to me probable that the Mission of Fyz Mahomed Khán to Meshed will lead to any alliance being contracted between Persia and Herát. The overtures of the Vuzeer will be received with strong suspicion, and if any terms are offered him, they will be such as evidently to involve his ultimate destruction; indeed I have learnt on good authority since my arrival at Girishk that the Persian authorities, in reply to the proposals brought by Fyz Mahomed Khán, declared that they could place no faith in the Vuzeer's word, and that as a preliminary to negotiation he must send his son as a hostage to Meshed. The intelligence of our departure from Herát will have reached Meshed shortly after we left the city, and whatever terms may be then offered by the Persians will be based on the admission of Persian troops into the citadel of Herát. The rancorous hatred, embittered by sectarian animosity, existing between the Persians and the Herátees would seem to form an insurmountable barrier to their coalescing against us, except in the event of a religious war being proclaimed by the Mahomedan world; but even if this feeling could be overcome and the Herát Government were willing to purchase assistance of Mahomed Sháh by the surrender of their independence, the Persian King would hardly place himself in a hostile attitude towards the British Government unless he is certain of direct assistance in money and troops from the Russians. In the present state of European politics such open interference on the part of Russia is not, I think, to be apprehended.

4. One of the first acts of the Vuzeer on finding that he had been taken at his word and that the British Mission was about to withdraw from Herát, was to levy a heavy and arbitrary imposition on the bankers and merchants, Hindoo and Mahomedan, in the city, and to seize the whole of their property until the amount, upwards of two lákhs of rupees, should be realized. The promise held out to these people by the Vuzeer was that the money should be repaid when he obtained possession of Kándáhár, or in the possible event of his being unsuccessful in that direction, when he received the pecuniary assistance which he expected from Persia. About the time that the British Mission quitted the valley of Herát the Vuzeer sent out his Peshkhána, or advanced tents, a short march in the direction of Kándáhár, and one of Sháh Kamrán's sons, Sháhzádeh Syf-ool-Moolk, was declared heir-apparent, and appointed to head the expedition. It had been intended that the Sháh should command in person, but His Majesty's infirmities prevented his leaving the city. At the same time Envoys were despatched in all directions for the purpose of collecting troops, and the plain between Sulzáwar and Furráh was named as the place of rendezvous. Preparations were thus made for a campaign which had long been contemplated and to which the Vuzeer had been strenuously urged by his immediate dependants and repeatedly invited by the disaffected in Sháh Shoojáh's dominions. The available means at the Vuzeer's disposal for such an expedition were, however, utterly inadequate to the end in view, even supposing that the present garrison of Kándáhár could not be reinforced.

5. There are but few Chiefs on whose fidelity the Vuzeer can rely in the event of a contest with His Majesty Sháh Shoojah-ool-Moolk, assisted by the British Government. Those of his own family, on whose influence and courage he has hitherto chiefly depended, have of late become

the objects of his jealousy, and have been deprived of their lands and followers. The principal of these, Sirdár Deen Mahomed Khán and Sirdár Sooltán Mahomed Khán, have had the whole of their property confiscated and have been in strict confinement by order of their cousin, the Vuzeer, for the last five months. The only remaining individual of the family possessed of character or influence, Sirdár Futteh Khán, has been harshly treated in consequence of his known attachment to the English, and does not possess the Vuzeer's confidence in the slightest degree. The Dooránnee tribes who occupy the plains of Furráh and Subzáwár, and who took an active and honourable part in the late defence of Herát against the Persians, have been disgusted by the excessive exactions of Yár Mahomed Khán since the conclusion of the siege, and profess to detest his authority; but the prospect of plunder would induce them to follow his standard until the first reverse. These, with the Vuzeer's immediate retainers, the whole amounting to about 2,000 horses, would form the *elite* of his army. The Hazarehs and Jumsheedees might increase the Vuzeer's force by 2,000 horse, but the Chief of the former and more powerful tribe, Kurreem Dád Khán, a discontented and ambitious man, is jealous of the power of Yár Mahomed Khán, and has good cause to distrust and fear him. On the present occasion this Chief will probably send his brother with a contingent of two or three hundred horse; and in this case the Jumsheedee Chief, Mahomed Luman Khán, fearing to expose his country to the inroads of his rival and enemy, the Hazareh, would not join the Vuzeer's camp with more than four or five hundred followers. Two or three hundred badly-equipped and wretchedly mounted horse might be collected from the other Rimauk tribes; but no assistance would, I think, be rendered by the Vazbegs of the Charbilayet, the Symunees, or the Sustaunees, who have reason to dread the Vuzeer's power and to be dissatisfied with his rule. The Ishakzai Chief of Laush, Sháh Pusund Khán, an unsuccessful rival of the Vuzeer, whom he fears and hates, will probably remain in his stronghold and be guided by the progress of events. One of his sons is at present a hostage in Tehrán and another is in the service of the Prince Governor of Kandáhár.

6. The Vuzeer's force available for a foray in this direction would not thus amount to more than about 3,000 horse, and these could not, in my opinion, be collected on the plains of Furráh in less than twenty days from this date. A body of about twelve hundred badly-armed and half-disciplined infantry would be left to garrison Herát. The Vuzeer will, I think, look for assistance chiefly from the disaffected in Sháh Shoojáh's dominions, and will probably make a rapid foray into the territory between the Khaush and the Helmud. This he might execute without coming into contact with any regular troops, and he would return with the *eclat* of having made a successful *chappow*. This is, I believe, the extent of the danger to be immediately apprehended.

7. The position which we have held at Herát since the close of the late Persian siege, though maintained at an enormous expense, has been, as I have frequently had the honour to bring to your notice, extremely insecure, and experience has proved the uncertain tenure on which it was held. The people with whom we had to deal regarded a treaty merely as an instrument of deceit, to be kept or broken as it served their ends, and looked upon the pecuniary assistance voluntarily afforded by the British Government as a blind to cover the ultimate designs which it was supposed to entertain. It was evident that so long as Herát remained independent, its Government would continue to intrigue with foreign states, either from fear of our power or in the hope of being bribed into forbearance, and the vicinity of this rallying point for the disaffected subjects of Sháh Shoojáh would ever be an obstacle to the tranquil settlement of our ally's dominions. Assuming that the possession of a commanding influence at Herát is absolutely necessary to carry out fully the policy of our advance beyond the Indus,

it is evident that this influence must be acquired by other measures than those which we have hitherto adopted. The re-annexment of Herát to Cábul has always appeared to be the best mode of attaining the end in view, but had the Government of Herát understood the obligations of a treaty and been contented with the solid benefits they derived from it, our object would have been gained, and the measure which now seems forced upon us would have been uncalled for and unnecessary.

8. If it be granted that the re-annexment of Herát to Cábul is the only safe and politic course to be pursued under present circumstances, it seems clear that delay will only increase the expense and the difficulty of carrying the measure into execution. The force employed for this purpose should, if possible, reach Herát in the early part of June before the harvest, which promises to be abundant, is ripe. Should the season unfortunately be lost, no grain will be sown in the valley or in any part of our route for the ensuing year. The harvest of Furráh and Bukwa is reaped about a month earlier than that of Herát, but the whole of the crops of these places will doubtless be consumed or destroyed by the rabble troops of the Vuzeer. Supplies of grain even for a day's consumption of such an army as would be required for the attack of Herát could not be depended on at any place on the route beyond our own depôts.

9. The presence of one of Sháh Shoojáh's sons with an army proceeding against Herát would be highly desirable, and I may add that the character of His Majesty's eldest son, Sháhzadeh Tunoor, which is I believe deservedly high, would give popularity to the expedition and would tend greatly to facilitate the future settlement of this important province.

Should hostile operations be determined on, the deputation of intelligent officers, acquainted with the Persian language, to Sustanee, Mymunna, and the Tymunee country, would doubtless be attended with advantage.

10. It is possible that the Vuzeer, before commencing open hostilities, may despatch an envoy to this place to ascertain the terms which we are yet willing to grant, but at present he is openly making arrangements and inviting assistance for a hostile movement on the territories of H. M. Sháh Shoojáh; and whatever may be the line of policy ultimately pursued towards the present Government of Herát, it behoves us, I think, to be prepared for and to punish such an act of aggression.

I have the honour to be, &c.,

(Signed) E. D. A. TODD,
Political Agent, Herát.

Girishk, 26th February 1841.

LETTERS

FROM

LIEUTENANT POTTINGER.

Herát, 10th September 1838.

To
W. H. MACNAGHTEN, Esquire,
Political Secretary, Supreme Government,
Calcutta.

Sir,—Thanks be to the almighty God I have the honour to report the cessation of hostilities in this quarter for the information of His Lordship the Governor General. In consequence of the Persian King having agreed to the message brought to him by Lieutenant-Colonel Stoddart from Her Majesty's Envoy at Tehrán the Persian army yesterday broke up from their quarters and commenced their retreat towards their territory.

Colonel Stoddart, as soon as Mahomed Shaul moved off, having taken leave, left the Persian army and returned to the city. I have hitherto been unable to report my knowledge of his arrival in the Persian camp owing to the strictness of the blockade, the want of confidential messengers, and of cash. This, however, is of little consequence, as the information I had was so vague and uncertain that I would not have ventured to report more than that he had arrived. Along with this that gentleman will also write.

I hurry this letter off to apprize you of the state of things here and shall write in detail as soon as future measures have been decided on by this Government, which professes itself most grateful for our support and entire devotion to our cause. I, however, consider it necessary to mention that it is reduced to such a destitute condition that without the promptest and most energetic support it will be impossible to keep it from sinking.

In compliance with the instructions I received from His Excellency, Mr. McNeill and Captain Burnes, I have assured the A'ghans of our assistance to repair the damage of this war, and in compliance with your letter of 15th November 1837 to Mr. McNeill, declared the intention of the British Government is to uphold the sovereignty of the Sudozy clan and assert the integrity of the A'fghán territory.

Requesting to be honored with instructions for my future guidance, and beg to subscribe myself,

Yours, &c.,
(Signed) E. POTTINGER,
Lieutenant.

Letter from Lieutenant POTTINGER to Captain BURNES, dated Hirát, 7th March 1838.

My dear Burnes,—I despatched a Kásid on the 27th ultimo to Leech and by him sent a statement of the events up to that date, also a letter to Mr. Macnaghten directed under a flying seal to you. The Vazir has this moment sent a Mirza to tell me that one of his followers will depart this evening for Kábul and that if I have any letters to send he will forward them. I therefore take advantage of the opportunity to give you information of the state of things up to this time.

In that despatch I mentioned the Kujars having on the 26th completed the investment of the city. One point is however still unguarded though from being visible to their posts it can only be made use of at night. On the 1st the enemy finished the investment of the posts occupied. On the 26th ultimo commenced approaches from two points, one opposite the gate of Mulik and one opposite the gate of Kudve Chok. The former resting on the buildings about the Mesulla and the latter on a garden called the Husht Bihisht, which they have fortified. These points, they have, however, left unconnected, trusting the safety of the communication to a high mound called the Halle-bung, which extends between these. On the same day they opened a battery of three guns against the wall of the citadel, which being on a mound, can be seen near to the bottom over the rampart of the Arkineo. The garrison on its part was not idle. It sank a covert way within the *faussebraye* of the Arkineo, completely traversed that work, widened the ditch of the threatened points, constructed covered places of arms of masonry on the level of the water, whose musketry flanked the whole ditch, destroyed the parapets of an untenable post, the N. W. angle of the Arkineo, and occupied two strong posts outside, one about a hundred yards in front of the gate of Kudve Chok and the other about triple the distance from the N. E. tower (Boorji Shah Kurumbeg).

On the night of the 2nd the enemy made a rush on the post at the N. W. angle of the Arkineo, where fifteen sharpshooters had been posted to keep down the fire of the three-gun battery. They were in great force, and as the post had been completely dismantled, the occupants thought discretion the better part of valour, and firing a volley took to their heels. They had neglected to send out scouts and were nearly all asleep when the enemy came on. As soon as the Vazir heard of the affair he came down to the point and directed a sortie for the recovery of the post. This however failed. These accidents drew on a heavy fire, which lasted uninterruptedly till daylight. The other posts of the enemy, whether fearing a general assault or for amusement, took this up and fired nearly as briskly as those at the point of attack did. Notwithstanding this tremendous expenditure of ammunition only four casualties took place in the garrison. I suspect, however, the enemy must have suffered severely as they were in a great measure exposed and uncovered, while the garrison by the aid of blue lights was able to take deadly aim from the loopholes of the ramparts and *faussebraye* some parts of which were not sixty yards from the point attacked. Strange to say, though they had a gun bearing on the post not two hundred yards from it, they never once fired it.

Asof-ud-Dowla has not yet returned from the Turkestan side of the mountains. He is encamped in a plain called the Chumun-i-bed, about 18 parasang from this. The Khán of Argunj is at Merv. If he be as long coming here as he was in arriving there from Khiva, he will not be here for two months more. If he be in force, his approach will, I suppose, detain the covering army on that side of the mountains, and in that case I do not fear the force, but with such careless dogs as the troops of the garrison to deal with it is impossible to calculate. If the enemy had a head the city must have fallen long ago. I do not think the Argunj army will be able to cope with Asof-ud-Dowla's force; but if it be, the remedy is as bad as the disease nearly. The country is totally and utterly ruined; for the next year there is neither seed to sow nor cattle for ploughing. I really fear if the Persians were forced to retreat without our interference that the unfortunate Shigas will be sold in a mass.

The Persian army now being undisturbed by the forays of the garrison, cavalry will be better able to subsist than before, and their cattle by the return of the spring will get in a better state.

In the city great distress must begin in the course of another month, as besides the fear of being plundered by their tyrannical masters, few calculated on the siege lasting more than a few weeks. Consequently the greater portion of the populace are even now hard pressed.

We are beginning indeed to feel the pressure in consequence of the investment. Sheep have almost become unknown in the city, and the supply of water being stopped, the public reservoirs and cisterns have become nearly too foul for use. There is however no fear of a scarcity of this necessary of life, as the whole city is built on a strata of alluvium lying on a quagmire, the water of which, though not so good as that of the aqueducts, is by no means bad.

I have no communication with Stoddart and so can give no trustworthy account of the Persian army. I have no objection to your forwarding a copy of this letter to Government if you think proper.

I forgot to say the three-gun battery destroyed one of the towers of the citadel (the outside). As soon, however, as they could find an entrance from the outer court (it was in the Huram) the garrison filled up the inside, which, as soon as the enemy saw, they ceased firing. In fact the fire was entirely thrown away as the place is isolated by a deep ditch and surrounded by strong works situated lower than it. The only reason I can guess for the fire is that they hoped to terrify Kamrán into a surrender by knocking the bricks about his ears.

Yours, &c.,
(Signed)   E. POTTINGER.

Extracts of letters from Lieutenant POTTINGER *to Lieutenant* LEECH, *dated Herát, 12th and 13th March 1838.*

This protracted siege has raised the self-confidence of these people to a great height and with their usual improvidence they do not look forward to the total failure of revenue for this and, probably, next year, even supposing the Persians to raise the siege.

The Persians had nearly completed the investment. They left one corner of the city unguarded. This was protected by an entrenched building on a low hillock about 300 yards from the N. E. angle. Next day, the 8th, the enemy made a demonstration with a couple of guns and five or six hundred men against the post. The party in it panic-struck took to their heels without firing a shot and the enemy gained possession of it before the fugitives reached the *faussebraye*, till which time so bad was the look-out that the garrison had not noticed the business. Though the post is so important a point and naturally strong, the enemy from not having any immediate support to it, evacuate it at night and re-occupy it during the day. The Vazir thinking the men necessary for this post better employed elsewhere sent and had the defences and walls destroyed, so that now it is untenable by either party if attacked, though the hillock affords the enemy's picket covering from the fire of the garrison.

On the day of the Eed a sort of tacit truce took place. One of the enemy's generals, Mahomed Khán, requested an interview with Fatte Khán (who was envoy to Tehrán). They had a long conversation, in which so much have they lowered their tone that Mahomed Khán tried to impress his visitor with their having only come here to stop slave-selling, that the real object is to attack the Sikhs in Hindustán. One of the Russian deserters was present at the interview, and they told Fatte Khán his father was a Russian and his mother English. Fatte Khán, who is a fine fellow and staunch friend of ours (from the treatment he received at Tehrán), said this was enough for him and he would have no communication with him. All my letters to Colonel Stoddart have been detained, and I suppose in like manner his to me.

Except the fact of there being a great scarcity in the Persian camp I can get no certain intelligence regarding it. I judge from the frequent overtures by different chiefs that the intrigue for displacing the Vazir Haji Akasee is still going on and with increased vigour, each party being desirous to be the one through which the Afgháns may offer their submission. They little think how such an idea is scouted by the Afgháns. From Asof-ud-Dowla's camp no certain intelligence has been received. He still remains in Badghis at Siri chusma; some say at Chumun-i-bed. These two places join, if indeed they be not names of different spots, in the same one. His foragers, cut off by the Furazkohee Aimaks some eight or ten days ago, about a thousand of whom have assembled on the mountains and are amusing themselves by cutting off the grasscutters and other wanderers about the neighbourhood of the camp. The Vazir (Yar Mahomed) has summoned these heroes to their side of the mountains to foray the Shah's camp, but I doubt their coming into this exhausted country as long as they can get plunder in Badghis. Report to-day says that the king has ordered Asof to return to camp; that on his doing so some time ago that officer requested to know the meaning of the contradictory orders he was constantly receiving, one day to return one day to stay.

His Majesty summoned the Vazir. The Vazir said his Mirza must know. The Mirza not giving a satisfactory reply was put to death, and the Vazir on interceding for him was told to hold his tongue or he should share his fate. I expect on Asof's arrival he will oust the Vazir and that we shall have a general assault. The country here is in such a state that the Persians cannot keep the field without regular supplies. Convoys they scarcely understand and certainly cannot now arrange for them. Foraging on a systematic plan, even if the country afforded adequate supplies, they have no idea of, and as the whole population is inimical they cannot procure a sheep without a skirmish. The last detachment under Shamsoodeen Khán (who is personally acquainted with the country) only brought in, after ten or eleven days' search, forty or fifty khurwars of grain, though they went to a place untouched by former parties. This paltry supply even was purchased by the loss of two hundred men.

The two surprises of the 2nd and 8th had a good effect in putting the garrison more on the altert and in pointing out some useless men amongst the ones relied on. The Vazir has been ill; a Hindustáni doctor has patched him up. I write privately now but shall address a public letter to Mr. Macnaghten under a flying seal to your mission as soon I can ascertain the answers and the real feeling regarding your letter to Kamrán. I shall also send you the correspondence between the hostile parties, if I possibly can get hold of it. Of course, if you like, use the intelligence I send you in this letter when you address Government. I sent to the Vazir's most confidential Mirza to-day to notify that I was coming to return a visit he had paid me, and he sent to request I would do so alone as he had intelligence for me. The intelligence was to the purport of the end of the last paragraph of my letter to Mr. Macnaghten. Look at that. I demanded unreserved communications from the Vazir and refused to talk on the subject through a third person. I will, as soon as the interview is over, write.

(True Extract.)
A. BURNES,
On a Mission to Kábul.

MASSON'S JOURNALS.

MASSON'S JOURNALS.

To
CHARLES NORRIS, Esquire,
Chief Secretary to the Government,
Bombay.

Residency in the Persian Gulf,
Sir, Bushire, 11th September 1830.

I have the honour to acquaint you for the information of the Honourable the Governor in Council that an American gentleman of the name of Masson came to Bushire a passenger from Bassadore in the sloop-of-war "Euphrates" on the 13th June last, and was received at this Residency.

Residency, Persian Gulf.

2. Mr. Masson has acquainted me that he is from the State of Kentucky in America, from which country he had been absent about ten years, and which he must consequently have left when he was young, as he is now only about two and thirty years of age. Mr. Masson stated also that he was some time in England, France and Russia, through which latter country he passed from St. Petersburg to Teflis; and he seems to have had letters of recommendation to some persons of consequence at that place.

3. Previous to the breaking out of the war between Russia and Persia in the year 1826, Mr. Masson appears to have crossed the frontier of these two states, passing by Tabreez to Tehrán, from whence he proceeded to Resht, situated within a few miles of the Caspian Sea, and which he represents as a flourishing place.

4. From Resht Mr. Masson passed into Khorássán by Meshed and Herát. The part of the journey between Resht and Meshed seems to have been performed on horseback and in company with four or five Armenians, who had been his companions from Teflis. There are several considerable towns on this road. But he did not pass near Astrábád, having a disinclination to go towards that quarter for fear of being seized and carried off as a slave into the countries in the neighbourhood of Khiva.

5. The accompanying general observations on the present political condition of the Dooránee States, and of the countries between Herát and Sind, drawn up by Mr. Masson, may serve as a good introduction to the other memoranda and sketches he has been good enough to present to me, and which are noticed hereafter separately, some as relating to particular places, others to his personal adventures.

6. From Meshed to Herát Mr. Masson went with a few travellers, making no effort to conceal his European origin, but he wore a sort of Persian dress. He represents Herát in the accompanying memorandum as a very fine and first rate city for Asia, and spoke very confidently of the excellent road for the caffilas and troops between it and Bukhára and Samarkand, but he never travelled that road.

7. From Herát Mr. Masson proceeded to Kandáhár, which is under the rule of four brothers of the Barrackzye, a tribe which at present bears the ascendancy to the depression of the Sadoozye tribe, from which Sháh Sujáh was descended.

Note.—Mr. Masson stated that he had never, until he reached Bushire, seen Mr. Elphinstone's work relating to Kábul entire, but only extracts from it in other publications.

8. Of the Dooránee States, the political interests of Kandáhár and Pesháwar seem to be considered similar and intimately connected; those also of Kábul, Ghizni, Lughman and Jallálábád appear to be combined under the superior power and talents of Dost Mahomed of Kábul.

9. Mr. Masson was well treated at Kandáhár, as indeed he appears to have been in all large towns where his being considered an European generally proved favourable to him.

10. The route from Kandáhár to Shikárpur in Sind was next followed with the view, Mr. Masson observed, of reaching the sea and so getting home. It will be seen from No. 3 of Mr. Masson's accounts of his advantures that before he could overtake the caffila from Kandáhár, with which he intended to travel, he was robbed of his horse, and, indeed, of all the little property he had, and reduced to great want and misery. He still, however, it will also be observed, accomplished his journey to Shikárpur, which he probably would have done in perfect safety had he set out at the same moment with the caffila, as he intended; but the person who promised to acquaint him when it was about to march omitted to do so, and he was thus some days too late in quitting Kandáhár.

11. Mr. Masson seems to have suffered considerably in his health in Sind; but so soon as he was able to move about, he spent a considerable time in going as a fakir, or beggar, on foot through various parts of the country between Shikárpur, Sehwan, Suchar, &c., and No. 4 is a notice on the countries west of the Indus from the city of Deyráh Gházie Khán to Kollecbut.

12. Mr. Masson about the same time was much in the Báwalpur country, which he traversed in many directions; but conceiving Mr. Elphinstone had been there and had described the country at length, he did not take such particular notice of it as he otherwise would have done, but a short notice respecting it will be found in No. 10.

13. Mr. Masson's paper, No. 5, shows that he proceeded from Ták to Pesháwar, traversing the countries of Murwut and Bunnoo by a route that seems fruitful by nature, and only dangerous on account of the feuds that exist in the territories of the different Chiefs through which it passes.

14. On enquiring I could not learn from Mr. Masson that in his opinion any important difficulties exist to a large body of troops traversing that country by the route he did; but at all events there would be the utmost facility on passing along nearer to the river Indus than the route in question goes.

15. Pesháwar has been conquered by Runjit Sing, but is not retained in full sovereignty by him, for it only pays tribute, which is generally obtained by an army being sent annually; and it frequently happens now that it is composed of his regular troops.

16. Runjit Sing is said to have a superstitious idea against occupying permanently any conquests beyond the Punjáb; he does not perhaps consider the Sikhs sufficiently numerous, and he is much hated by such of the Mahomedans as he has overcome, for he interferes with all the outward observances of their religion, forbidding the Muzzeen to call to prayers in towns, &c., &c. With the Hindus he holds a different course, and is considered to be making numerous converts among them.

17. After reaching Pesháwar Mr. Masson seems to have passed a considerable time in wandering about between Pesháwar, Ghizni, Jellálábád, Kábul and Kandáhár.

18. One of his papers is a notice respecting Jallálábád, and another relates to the valley of Kaybur, and the Sia-Posh, regarding which he seemed most interested; but he had no personal knowledge of anything concerning them, which he hopes to obtain hereafter.

19. From Pesháwar Mr. Masson passed by Attock in the Punjáb, traversing the high road to Lahore.

20. It is much to be lamented that Mr. Masson's interesting notice respecting what he calls the city of Bucefotia on the Jhelum is so short and unsatisfactory: this may in some measure be accounted for as he mentions having lost his original papers along with a great part of his baggage. Respecting the conjectured position of this city Mr. Masson stated that on the northern side of the high road between Attock and Lahore, and close to where it crosses the Jhelum, there are two villages, the names of neither of which he could recollect; but his notice was attracted by a building in the one, on the Attock, or western side; on examining it he thought the architecture foreign, and the building, such perhaps as Greeks might be able to erect, assisted by no more expert masons than the uninstructed workmen of India. The thing which tended most to confirm his ideas of this being an ancient place was seeing a coin with a Greek impress and inscription round the neck of a child; he purchased this coin, and afterwards procured some persons to dig, by which he acquired a few more, both gold and silver. These were obviously the ruins of a tower which will distinctly mark the place, and it was in these ruins he made excavations and found the coins with the bust of Alexander, and the inscription Bucefotia, which he mentions in his memorandum. Mr. Masson's means at that time being small, he could not continue the excavations. Unfortunately he was robbed during a severe illness he had at Multán on his way back to Sind, of such of the coins as had remained in his possession: some of them however, he stated were given by him to the Chevalier Allard, a French officer at Lahore.

21. Mr. Masson stayed a short time at Lahore with the Chevalier Allard, the chief of Runjit Sing's European officers, whom he represents as enjoying a high situation and salary in that service: but the Chevalier and his companion, Mr. Ventura, who have been longest employed by Runjit, are jealous of the other Europeans now there, and particularly so of all Europeans seeking military employment. The Chevalier is looked upon as the superior of the other five or six European officers.

22. Mr. Masson did not present himself before Runjit Sing, as he had no wish to enter into his service.

23. Mr. Masson's memorandum respecting the Sikhs and Lahore will be found very interesting.

24. The river Rávce, it will be observed, is represented by Mr. Masson to be so conveniently navigable that a body of Runjit Sing's troops was passed down it from Lahore to Multán, where they were required on an emergency when he was at the former place. This was towards the end of the rainy season when the country would have been difficult to traverse for troops.

25. Respecting the general state of the navigation on the rivers of the Punjáb and of the Indus, Mr. Masson did not seem possessed of any very precise information, but he had no doubts of vessels of a considerable burthen being able to pass from Multán to the sea by the Rávce and Indus, and also by the latter river from Attock, if not for the whole year, at all events for several months of it: he affirmed confidently there were no falls or rapids in any of them below the places he mentioned; and he saw in Sind vessels 30 or 40 feet long which he knew had come from Multán. When coming down himself a part of the Indus he saw other vessels tracking up, and there are many places that have bandars or piers at which boats may lie.

26. Mr. Masson returned from Lahore to Sind, as will be seen by No. 10, passing by Multán, Ahmedpore, Kirepore (Khairpur), Hyderabad to Karáchi Bandar on the sea-coast.

27. The change in his character and condition from that of a Mahomedan fakir to a European, which although not obtruding he did not conceal, prevented his renewing his acquaintance

with his former associates in the Bháwulpore country. He now for the first time visited Hyderabad, where he had not been when before in Sind.

28. Mr. Masson represents Sind to be in a wretchedly divided and oppressed state from the numerous rulers, all styled Amirs. Meer Morád Ali, the remaining brother of the three who overturned the former government of the king of Peshawar, seems still to be looked upon as the chief Amir; but the country is portioned out among his sons and nephews and vaziers, who all appear to attend to nothing but their amusements; and hunting seems a passion among these Chiefs, from which their subjects suffer greatly, more especially from the game preserves being so very numerous.

29. The Chiefs of Sind appear, by Mr. Masson's account, to be kept in a state of extreme terror at the idea of Runjit Sing attempting to overturn their power and take the country from them.

30. Mr. Masson seems to have been perfectly recognised as a European in Sind, and conceives that that obtained him more consideration even there than any other character he could have assumed would have done; but the appellation "Firangi" seems also in Sind not unaccompanied by a feeling of fear; for on one occasion when a man who was coming out of a house used the term "Firangi" coupled with an opprobrious epithet, Mr. Masson asked him how he dared to use such language with a Firangi camp so near him. The person was abashed and silenced, and seemed to think the implied threat might not be vain.

31. From Hyderabad in Sind Mr. Masson proceeded to Tatteh, and from thence to Karáchi Bandar, where he embarked, and touching at Guader, he reached Muskat.

32. From Muskat he sailed in an Arab vessel to the town of Kishmee on the island of that name, and from thence he proceeded on a camel to our naval station at Bassadore, and reached Bushire as before mentioned.

33. As Mr. Masson had expressed to me his determination to return to the countries he has described for the purpose of gaining further information respecting them, I had written a letter communicating confidentially all that I knew concerning him to Sir John Macdonald, and most strongly recommended Mr. Masson to proceed to Tabreez for the purpose of meeting him and offering a letter of introduction, conceiving that Sir John Macdonald was peculiarly well qualified, both from his pursuits and situation, to direct Mr. Masson's future enquiries to objects in these countries that require elucidation. I conceived likewise that the envoy might have been authorized to employ individuals for such purposes and to provide them with the necessary means which I was not. The information of Sir John Macdonald's lamented death reached me after the letter had been written, and I felt somewhat at a loss in consequence respecting Mr. Masson. I however still recommended him to proceed to Tabreez, giving him the same letter of introduction to Captain Campbell in charge of the Mission as had been intended for Sir John Macdonald, and Mr. Masson accordingly quitted this Residency, where he had been living upwards of a month, for Tabreez on the 23rd July.

34. I beg to observe that the papers now forwarded were given to me by Mr. Masson with no injunctions or understanding of concealment; he is perfectly aware that I would not hesitate to communicate their contents to any of my friends. I have likewise reason to think he would be flattered by this being done, provided the merit which may be considered as arising out of them were known to be his due. I feel entirely disposed to connect his name with any fame that may belong to them; but I should not consider myself justified in communicating them without his permission for general publication. I did not think it necessary to state directly to Mr. Masson that I should send copies of these papers, some of which were drawn up at my suggestion, and avowedly to be communicated to some distinguished

individuals for the information of the Government, although he must have been aware that a public officer, situated as he knew me to be and making the enquiries I did, must have done so with a view to the good of the service.

35. With this explanation the accompanying copies of Mr. Masson's papers are now forwarded, as I have at all times deemed it my duty to take every opportunity of acquiring information that might prove beneficial to the interests of the Government I have the honor to serve, without confining my enquiries either to the local and special duties of the particular situation I might at the moment fill or to the country in which I might happen to be situated.

I have the honour to be, &c.,

(Signed)   D. WILSON,

Resident in the Persian Gulf.

Observations, Notices, Memoranda, &c., &c., &c.

No. 1.

When we reflect on the former power and extended authority of the Dooránee empire and contrast it with its present powerless condition and limited sway, we cannot but be impressed with humble ideas of earthly prosperity. The sword which had triumphantly subdued every country from Tabruz to Delhi and from Cashmeer to the ocean, which had borne away the fairest gem from the diadem of the Mogul Emperor, and which in its fullness of pride even menaced the existence of European power in Hindustán, is now only drawn within the confined sphere of the Dooránee soil, and that only in intestine commotions. The provinces whose rulers obeyed the commands of the Sháh of Khorássán and heaped his coffers with their tributary gold are now independent or reduced to subjection by Runjit Sing, who formerly appeared with closed hands in the presence of Sháh Zemáun. Yet if we look at the composition of the Dooránee State we have no occasion to wonder that such changes and misfortunes should have arisen. It was an empire founded by Ahmed Sháh, and from its composition required a long suit of sovereigns equal to that illustrious Chief in character and energy to have sustained and consolidated it. It is known that the Dooránees are divided into many tribes; the sovereign was perhaps of the most respected one, but there were many much more numerous and powerful, the Chiefs of which conscious of their strength approached the throne rather with a feeling of equality than respect, and if a request were denied or a rebuke given they retired to their castles, armed their followers and became rebels. It was evident that so imperious and puissant an aristocracy could only be restrained and kept in due obedience by a Chief of that personal character and transcendant genius which would command their homage; in short it became necessary that the monarch should surpass in all splendid qualities any of his nobles. Ahmed Sháh was such a Chief, and it is probable that had he lived he might have devised the means to have abridged the influence of the leaders of tribes; but his decease, rather premature, was followed by successors of inferior ability, and the kingdom has been rent by rebellion, and what remains under Dooránee authority is now parcelled out among the successful traitors of another tribe, while the sovereign seems destined to pass his days in exile. Mr. Elphinstone has noted in his work on Kábul the history of the Dooránees until that period when the troubles commenced which terminated in the expulsion of the king and the establishment in power of the Chiefs of the tribe Barrakzye. It is not my object to narrate the intermediate occurrences; indeed I could not follow the course of events but merely to describe the state of the provinces at the periods I visited them, say the years 1827 and 1828. I shall commence with the westerly State of Herát, thence proceed easterly, then pass down the Indus.

HERÁ'T.

Herát is at present governed by Camraun (as written by Mr. Elphinstone) or Camerodeen Khán, the father of Sháh Mahmood, formerly of some notoriety in Kábul, being reputed imbecile and incapable of supporting the regal authority. Camraun is a popular monarch and possesses a reputation for firmness and energy. His Government is very favourable to those engaged in trade or agriculture; hence his kingdom is populous, and the capital has importantly increased in wealth and consequence. An Afghán being questioned as to the state of Khorássán and would reply that it was nearly ruined, and only two places, Herát and Kábul, "ábádi" or flourishing. The king of Herát has abolished the slave trade which was formerly carried on most flagitiously in his capital. He has three sons: one holds the government of Subzewar, and the other that of Farráh. The eldest (of whom it is said he entertains some little fear) is retained near his person at Herát. Camraun is of the tribe Suddoozye, and although hostile to his expelled relatives, is the implacable enemy of the Barrakzye; yet he is so circumstanced that it is not supposed he will ever again take a part in the affairs of Eastern Khorássán: he has nevertheless still partizans as was evinced in a transaction which happened when I was in Kandáhár. The Chiefs of that place had determined on an expedition to Shikarpore; their deputy or Náib Gool Mahomed was to remain in charge of the city; the Náib of the highest influence and belonging to one of the most numerous tribes had formerly been Governor for Camraun of Kandáhár and gave it up to the Barrakzye, who besieged it, only when he had received intelligence from Camraun that he did not intend to march from Herát to relieve it. He now became apparently attached to the Barrakzye and held a real or nominal command as Governor of the city, and was esteemed next to the sovereign Chiefs the most powerful man in Kandáhár. In consequence of the projected expedition, he wrote letters to Camraun, inviting him to march and that he would deliver the city to him. His méssenger, however, was seized near Girishk, and the Náib, unconscious of the detection of his treachery, attending the Darbár as usual was made prisoner by Poor Dil Khán. The caution and fears manifested on this occasion confirm my ideas of the preposterous power of the tribe leaders. Gool Mahomed was detained during the day in the house of Poor Dil. By night he was removed in a palanquin to the inner fort, where part of the residence of Kohun Dil was appropriated as his prison. In the transport the custody of his person was entrusted to none but foreign soldiers, who alike had the charge of preventing his escape. The gates of the city were strictly guarded, and all was on the alert, it being expected that his numerous adherents would attempt a rescue. Large bodies of horse were instantly dispatched into those parts of the country inhabited by his tribe to prevent insurrection: this was the more necessary as the sons of Gool Mahomed had escaped from Kandáhár. I left the Náib in prison, and the expedition to Shikárpore that year was deferred, I have since heard that he was subsequently released and went to Pesháwar, where he was related by some marriage with Yár' Mahomed Barrakzye and with whom he suffered death, as I shall relate under the head of Pesháwar.

Camraun formerly had much to fear from the Persians, but it seems the general opinion that the occasion for it no longer exists, something like an understanding having been established and cemented by family alliances between the Princes of Herát and Meshed. If this be the case, the Chief of Herát must have little to fear from his neighbours; indeed may be supposed capable of dictating the law to them. The Mogul Chief of Turbut has every disposition to annoy, but fortunately wants the power: the Chiefs of Seisthán, although predatory, I am inclined to think acknowledge his supremacy. To the north of Herát the Tártar tribes seem to be acquiring a consistence of strength derived from their union, which (especially if the report of the capture of Meshed by these savages be true) may probably soon effect the overthrow of some of the established states in these quarters. The reputation of Camraun is not confined to Khorássán. It extends even to Lahore, and Runjit Sing, hearing of one of his Chiefs who had arrived there and was about returning to Herát, entrusted him with a complimentary letter and an elephant to be conveyed to his prince. I saw this Sirdár, Jehaundat Khán by name, afterwards at Shikárpore, where he was encamped in a garden with his retinue and elephant, but in the utmost perplexity how to act as he had advanced as far as Khelát, when he learned that the Khandáhár Chiefs had ordered the seizure of himself and the elephant. He would be obnoxious from having formerly played a prominent political part, and the elephant was equally so, being a present from the Caffre Runjit Sing to their enemy Camraun. Jehaundat Khán might probably have passed by some indirect road himself; and although his funds began seriously to diminish, he was resolved not to forego, if possible, the honor of conducting the monstrous animal into Herát, to whose good citizens it would afford abundant matter of novelty and wonder.

The military force of Camraun may be estimated at 15,000, principally horse, and esteemed of good quality; their arms I should consider better than those of eastern states, their blades being of good temper, and their fire-arms of a good description for cavalry, *viz.*, the pistol and carbine. I suspect many more than 15,000 might be raised, but they would be infantry, little prized in these countries; therefore we see in the expeditions from Herát (and the same remark applies to all other states of Khorássán) an army seldom exceeds 12,000 men. The artillery of Camraun may consist of 12 or 15 pieces. The revenue of Herát I heard generally estimated at 12 or 13 lákhs of rupees, which appeared to me a very moderate sum. Camraun is said to have a well-stocked treasury. He assumes the title of Pádisháh.

KANDÁHÁR.

The province of Kandáhár is under the authority of four brothers of the tribe of Barrakzye, *viz.*, Poor Dil Khán, Kohun Dil Khán, Rahim Dil Khán, and Meer Dil Khán. It may be here fit to notice that the celebrated Dooránee Futtah Khán Barrakzye having effected the overthrow of his sovereign was seized somewhat perfidiously by Camraun and barbarously murdered. He had numerous brothers who avenged his death and established themselves in authority over the provinces of Eastern Khorássán. The common father of Futteh Khán and his brethren was Poynder Khán, but their mothers were various; hence in the appropriation of the states the brothers have been guided by the principles of their birth, the sons by one mother uniting and residing in the same territory; hence those at Kandáhár are by one mother, those of Ghizni and Kábul by another, as again are those of Pesháwar. The four Chiefs at Kandáhár occupy the tuckt or metropolis of the Dooránees, and the elder brother Poor Dil in his communications with exterior states assumes the dignity of Pádisháh, and seems moreover to be inclined to support his pretensions by the sword. He affects a control, or perhaps rather a supremacy, over his brethren established elsewhere, which they verbally admit. This Chief although so ignorant as to suppose that Hindustán was the native country of Firangees or Europeans, is possessed of much caution and prudence, and more capable of calculating soundly than any of his family. He is remarkable for being the only prince (I mean native), and I believe I may say throughout Asia, that pays his soldiers regularly, the stipendiary in his service receiving his allowance invariably every month: his brothers in the same city do not profit by this example. Poor Dil Khán is guilty of the most extravagant oppression, and his subjects after giving him credit for punctuality and a regard to truth, heartily execrate him and affirm him to be "bisiar suckut." His own nephew, the son of the brave Timour Koolee Khán, slain in action at Pesháwar, one day lamenting the condition of Kandáhár and describing the advantages of its situation and fertility, ascribed all the misery existing to the incapacity of the rulers: and when I would ask a Dooránee what could induce a man of sense, as Poor Dil has the reputation of being, to be so intent upon exactions and the impoverishment of the country, he would reply that being aware that he was an usurper and uncertain how long he might continue in power, he was amassing as much treasure as possible while the opportunity was afforded him, as was the case with all the Barrakzye. The character of this man as the acknowledged head of the Barrakzye might materially influence the future prospects of the Dooránees; but although he be capable of decided action and prudent conduct in his affairs, and possesses a regard to truth, a rare and inestimable quality in a Dooránee prince, his avidity for money and oppression of his subjects and his consequent unpopularity, to which may be added a narrow soul, will prevent him from being the restorer of his country's glory. To maintain his ascendancy Poor Dil keeps a large force in pay; and he has been heard to exclaim "what need I care about discontents, who has so many troops." Of the other brothers Kohun Dil is most esteemed, being supposed the most warlike of the four and to have a little generosity; the two younger ones are of less consequence; but I never heard any favourable report of them. When I first arrived in Kandáhár (1826) the Chiefs were at variance and had established two Darbárs, Poor Dil holding his alone, while the others assembled at the palace of Kohun Dil in the inner fort; these considered it necessary to unite, fearing the elder brother, to whom they never went or paid any kind of obedience. At length a reconciliation was effected by mutual friends, and the day was distinguished by the three brothers paying a visit to Poor Dil, who afterwards returned the compliment; soon after a Chief named Mamoo was, by the general consent of the four, appointed Mukhtár. The first measures of this minister were popular, but he has since justly or unjustly acquired the reputation of a devil.

The city of Kandáhár is regularly built, the bázár being formed by two right lines drawn from opposite directions and intersecting in the centre of the place. It is consequently composed of four distinct portions and the whole city of as many distinct quarters; and each of the Chiefs in power has authority over one quarter. I for some time dwelt within Kohun Dil Khán's fort and had the opportunity of seeing the daily visitors as they passed to the Darbár of the three confederate brothers; among the unwilling ones were invariably from fifty to one hundred Hindus, some of them doubtlessly men of respectability and wealth, and all merchants and traders who had been seized in their houses or shops and dragged before the Darbár for the purpose of extorting money. This was not an occasional or monthly but a daily occurrence, and it was certainly afflicting to behold men of decent appearance driven along the streets by the insulting hirelings of these Dooránee despots. I have seen on an occasion of a festival the Hindus of this city assembled in gardens without the walls and displaying every sign of ease and wealth in their apparel and trinkets; nor were they the less gayful than they would have been in a Hindu kingdom. The gains of these men must be enormous, or they never could provide to the exactions of their Governors, and without such profit operating as an offset they never would submit to the indignities they are compelled to suffer, and patiently too, in every Mussalmán country from the prince to the lowest miscreant that repeats his *culma*.

I am unable to state the amount of revenue possessed by these princes individually. I have heard twelve lákhs of rupees mentioned as a sufficient sum for the gross revenue of the country, which may be thought enough, looking at the deterioration everywhere prevalent and the cessation of trade. Of this sum the larger proportion may be considered as appropriated by Poor Dil, who must also be in possession of immense treasures which he acquired on the demise of his brother, the famous Sheer Dil Khán. Neither can I exactly assign to each brother the share be holds in the division of the country. The countries of Gunnsél and Girish belong to Kohun Dil, and this prince has a son resident in the castle of the last-mentioned district. I think, too, he collects tribute from the neighbouring Hazara tribes. To Rahim Dil and Meer Dil belong all the savage districts bordering on and among the Ghilzyes. Troops are not stationed here, but at certain periods a force marches and collects a tribute yielded only through intimidation. Poor Dil reserves to himself the rich and fertile districts in the neighbourhood of the city, where the revenue is at once most productive and collected with more facility. The authority of Kandáhár is in some instances recognized at a considerable distance, as by the tribes of Kakurs, whose hills and vallies unite with the range of Solyman, west of the Indus and extend so low south as the neighbourhood of Deyráh Ghází Khán ; their dependence is limited to military service and the annual offering of a *doomba* sheep. Khán Tareek of the Ghilzyes to the south of the road from Kandáhár to Kábul also attends the Chiefs when in the field; but Khán Jeháun Khán and Shaboodín Khán, the more considerable Chiefs of this tribe, refuse any obedience over most of these wild states from which tribute is raised ; it is only by force that the object is effected, especially among the Atchukzye and Hazara. The present Chief of Beloche, that is to say, of Keelaut, in 1829 was compelled to acknowledge the supremacy of Poor Dil, to pay a small tribute, I believe of one lákh of rupees Keelaut base money, equal to about 4,000 Kandáhár or common rupees, and to bind himself down to furnish a quota of troops. The bringing this Chief to a correct understanding was a very essential measure, as the recovery of Serkárpur, which seems to be the most immediate object of Poor Dil's ambition, would greatly depend as to facility of execution on his friendship or enmity, it being necessary to march the army from Kandáhár through the Beloche country for above one hundred kos. The capture of Shikárpore would lead to a collision with the Chiefs of Sind, who, although they might assemble numerous troops, would be little dreaded by the Dooránees. Allowing that the very principle of a Dooránee Government is foreign conquest, and that it would be ever put in force when circumstances permit, still it is evident they have sufficient on their hands to keep the king of Lahore in check, who has without doubt the power to crush them, although the contest would be sanguinary ; and he constantly avows his intention of subduing Kábul, if life be granted him. It would be singular if in this age when the Hindus (who in their most flourishing eras appear not to have passed the Indus) are considered as a race in a declining state, that a warlike Chief of a new sect should plant the standard of victory, and of his Guru on the banks of the Ochees, or that the mausoleum of Ahmed Sháh should be violated by the Sikhs, who had been hunted by that conqueror in the desert of the Punjáb. The existence of so formidable a power as the Sikhs, whose exuberance of strength must fall upon Khorássán and the west, for its display on the east and partly to the south is prevented by the still more formidable British power, and to the north all has been done that can be done, the impassable mountains of the snowy Imáus being in that direction the limits of their empire ; this power, it might be supposed, would induce the brothers to preserve a cordial understanding, yet such is not the case, and Dost Mahomed, the Chief of Kábul, being almost the only man of correct feeling the family can boast of, the Chiefs of Kandáhár and Pesháwár are extremely jealous of his popularity and prosperity, and thus among this curious medley of Barrakzye princes it is held criminal in those who govern for the benefits of their subjects as well as themselves. This jealousy led to the marches of armies, and as I chanced to be present, I will briefly narrate what passed more of the character of the Dooránees being elicited from trifling anecdotes, than will be gained from the most elaborate disquisition. I have stated this instance of the want of cordiality, but I am equally certain if an invasion of the Sikhs occurred they would be united, and as soon as the danger was over return to their original differences. The policy of the respective Governments, as it is directed by no fixed principles, neither can it be reduced or estimated by any established rule or criterion, the motives are as inexplicable as the union of virtues and vices in the individual character, but I know not whether we should condemn judging by that standard which civilized states have erected, and which these people might possibly object to, especially as that peculiar delicacy of action and sentiment which refinement cherishes, is unknown in Afghánistán. Without that delicacy, however, a Doorának will perform a praiseworthy action, however roughly. In 1828 the power of Kábul attracted the attention and excited the apprehensions of the rulers of Kandáhár, and Rahim Dil, one of them, started for Peshawar; he avoided the direct road on which he would have been picked up by Dost Mahomed or some of his partizans, and took the route of Ták. He had with him 500, I have heard 800, horse, and extorted money and necessaries from every unfortunate Chief he found in his way. He at length arrived at Ták, and encamping near the town he demanded a large sum of money from the surly but wealthy Chief: this prince, however, considering that his walls were thick and high and that he had a few guns of which his Kandáhár visitor was destitute, absolutely refused; and the representative of the Khorássán dynasty was compelled quietly to decamp, and found his way to Peshawar. Here a circumstance occurred, which, although not bearing on the immediate subject, may be mentioned as noting the manners of the times. That extraordinary character at Lahore, Runjit Sing, chanced to hear of Rahim Dil's arrival and that he had with him a singular or very beautiful sword; he immediately sent his compliments to the new comer, and informed him that he must send his sword to the Punjáb metropolis. The pride of the Doorának was certainly mortified, who might perhaps justly question the politeness of the request, but as in case of refusal the arrival was feared of a small foraging party of Sikh cavalry, some 25,000 or 30,000 men, the weapon was duly despatched, and Runjit may have smiled at the helpless condition to which the once terrific race was at length reduced.

Rahim Dil returned to Kandáhár accompanied with Yár Mahomed Khán, the elder of the Peshawar chieftains and his half-brother. Matters were soon settled, and it was agreed to humble Dost Mahomed and to attack him from the east and west. In conformity to this plan Peer Mahomed Khán, the younger brother at Peshawar, invaded the small country of Bungush, and expelled the sons of Summut Khán who lived at Kábul and in the interests of its Chief. He was then to have marched on Jellálábád, but the notorious Syed Ahmed Sháh, in concert with Baram Khán and Khulil, kept Peshawar in great alarm, continually making excursions, to which they were encouraged and excited by Dost Mahomed. The Peshawar force did not therefore march. I was in the Bungush country at the period of its occupation, perhaps in March, by Peer Mahomed, and met him at a village equi-distant from the towns of Hangoo and Kahut. From thence he proceeded to Peshawar, where he stayed some time and passed Khyber, Jellálábád, and Kábul; reached Ghizni, I suppose, about August, where I found Dost Mahomed encamped with, as I was told, 6,000 men, and the Kandáhár army, stated at 11,000, seven kos in front; a battle was daily expected by the men, but I doubt whether intended by the leaders. I was most civilly received by Hadjee Khán Kakar, at this time Vizier of Kábul and a celebrated warrior. His brother commanding the contingent of the Kakar country was in the hostile army, being an ally or dependant of Kandáhár. Vakils were in the first instance despatched by Dost Mahomed, who, although the most celebrated officer in Khorásán, is yet prudent enough to effect, if possible, his objects more by fair words than by violence. These envoys demanded the reasons of the hostile array, asked if the Barrakzyes were not Mussulmen and brethren, and how much better it would be to unite their arms against the Sikhs than ingloriously employ them in combats of Dooránees against each other. They moreover asserted that Dost Mahomed was perfectly aware of the right of primogeniture of his brother Poor Dil, and that he acknowledges his supremacy as Chief of Khorásán, he occupying the tuckt. Poor Dil claimed the delivery of half Kábul and the whole of Logur and Shilgur as a provision for the young son of the deceased Sheer Dil Khán. The debates in this negotiation were conducted by Dost Mahomed and his envoys with such address, that the business was finally settled by Dost Mahomed not losing an inch of ground, but agreeing to make an annual remittance to Khandáhár of the amount of revenue of Logur, and expressed his willingness to co-operate in Poor Dil's projected invasion of Shikárpur. The troops of Dost Mahomed, although inferior in numbers, being choice men, were sanguine of success: it is further probable that in the event of an engagement, the greater part of the Kandáhár army would have gone over to the highly popular Chief of Kábul, as he is called the "Sepáhi's dostdár." The tidings of peace were announced in camp by the beating of drums, the sounding of horns (I mean cow-horns or conches), and all the melodious energy of the Afghán warlike instruments. Visits were interchanged between the two camps; my host the Vizier now received the embrace of his brother, who but for the new treaty might have cut his throat in the strife of battle. The Kandáhár troops returned to their city, and Yár Mahomed, who accompanied them to Ghizni, quietly passed to Peshawar. When these were gone, Dost Mahomed remained encamped, revolving, I should suspect, in his mind how he should compensate himself for the loss of the revenue of Logur: he suddenly struck his own tents, giving no previous notice to march. He was however soon followed, and scouring the country of the wild tribes south of Ghizni suddenly turned his course upon the lands of the Ghilzye Chief, Khán Tareek, who attended the Kandáhár forces as a vassal. This unfortunate man was harshly plundered, and, strange to say, the Kandáhár Government never interested as to the fate of its dependant; and I venture to think Khán Tareek never thought of addressing the Government for protection.

The revenue of the Kandáhár princes I have before calculated at 12 lakhs of rupees, and their military force may be estimated by the above account. The consent of the Beloche Khán to furnish his quota will, however, considerably increase the numbers. On a former occasion, when this quota was furnished to Sheer Dil Khán, it amounted to 3,000 good horse. At all events it may be apparent that the Kandáhár Chiefs might command an army, including the contribution of quotas, of 20,000 men. The artillery is equally divided among the four brothers, to each five, the total 20. Some of these are unserviceable, and among the good ones are two or three Dutch pieces, which they accurately distinguish by the name Hollandoise.

The Chiefs of Kandáhár affect no kind of pomp, and even Poor Dil is contented among his own Dooránees with the simple appellation of Sirdár. On the whole they are decidedly detested and a change is ardently desired, and one of the fairest provinces of Khorásán is daily accelerating in deterioration.

The Ghilzye.

These tribes, although not Dooránees, I mention here, as they occupy the principal space between Kandáhár and Ghizni; they are moreover the most numerous of the tribes of Afgháns, and if united under a single Chief of fine talent and energy, would become the most powerful. These people are found between Furráh and Herát; but as they are submissive to authority if they have leaders, they are seldom heard of, being of no distinction. They also occur between Kábul and Jellálábád, but being in due control, their Chiefs are never noticed. The Ghilzyes between Kandáhár and Ghizni are subject to the authority of Khán Tareek and Sháboodeen Khán. Those more to the south approaching the Beloche country are subject to Khán Jeháun. Khán Tareek I have noted is an ally or tributary of Kandáhár. I visited his country and passed the night at his fort here, called Keeláh Khán. There is a fine spring of water flowing round it, and he has planted a good garden of fruit trees. In his portion of the country there are many villages, and cultivation is more or less general. Khán Tareek enjoys a good character, and I have reason to speak favourably of my reception by him. Khán Jcháun Khán is perfectly independent, and I never heard of any expeditions against him. Sháboodeen Khán claims descent from the ancient Ghilzye princes, and is so esteemed by the tribes. This Chief is reputed brave, and sets the Dooránee rulers at defiance, alleging that his ancestors never acknowledged Ahmed Sháh and why should he respect traitors. The Ghilzyes commonly vaunt that they have from one to three lákhs of muskets among them. If Sháboodeen be asked why he does not collect the tribes and assert his rights to the sovereignty of Khorásán, he replies, he shall not do that, as being deprived of power may be the will of God, but that, if the Sikhs should march into Khorásán, he would range all the Ghilzyes in the cause of Islám. His fort is seated near the high road passing from Ghizni and Kandáhár; if troops march in force he deserts it and retreats to the hills. He has a mischievous practice of detaining passengers, perhaps for months, nay for a year, in his fort. It is impossible to pass his country without being robbed; unless, indeed; you had fifty matchlocks considered a sufficient escort. The Ghilzyes are universally robbers and men of degenerate and brutal habits. In dress, manners, &c., they perfectly resemble the Atchukzye. When Nádir Shah invaded Khorásán, Hussein Sháh Ghilzye sat on the tuckt at Kandáhár. That conqueror destroyed both the city and the Ghilzye authority; they have never been able to recover themselves, but have made some strenuous efforts.

The Hazaras.

This race occupy an immense tract of mountainous country extending from Kábul to Ghizni, thence to Kandáhár, and thence to Herát. They are found below the hills just before you reach Ghizni; also west of Ghizni to the right of the Kandáhár road they extend northerly until the frontiers of Balk, in which direction they seem to have established something like order in the government of Kundoos. They are violent Sheeahs and have some singular customs, as furnishing their women to Syeds and strangers. They are evidently of the Tártar race, having the small eye and prominent cheek-bone. I have introduced them here merely to note the relation they stand in as regards the present powers in Khorásán. Dost Mahomed levies tribute from all of them near Kábul, even I believe from the Khán of Kundoos. The Chiefs of Ghizni also collect from those near him; here are many living on the plains, having villages and forts. These are in all respects good and faithful subjects. In the neighbourhood of Kandáhár the Hazaras usually refuse to pay tribute, asserting that they would pay willingly to the king, but they do not know the Barrakzye. On this a small force is detached with one gun, and having selected a good spot among the hills, the gun is discharged and the report multiplied and prolonged by echoes. On this the Hazaras all come tumbling in with their tribute. There is never occasion to fire the gun twice.

Ghizni.

The small principality of Ghizni is under Meer Mahomed Khán, brother of the Kábul Chief. The revenue I have heard reported at two lákhs of rupees according to the king's book; but Meer Mahomed obtains another half lákh by *zúlúm* or oppression: he is nevertheless not unpopular and his soldiery and subjects seem contented. You will be told he dare not govern badly, or Dost Mahomed would take him to task. In his political views he identifies himself with his brother at Kábul.

Ka'bul.

We now arrive at the flourishing State of Kábul under the government of the brave and popular Dost Mahomed Khán, emphatically designated one of the swords of Khorássán by his brother, the *vazire* Futteh Khán. It is cheering for the traveller in these generally misgoverned regions to arrive at some spot where order and security is established, and to be able to pass through the wildest scenes, where although the ruffian inhabitants possess the desire of plunder, they are deterred by the stern arm of justice raised over them from exercising it. Dost Mahomed formerly governed in Kohistaun to the north of Kábul which then belonged to Abeebooler Khán, son of Azam Khán. This was a young man of great courage but of no capacity though popular among the multitude, as his generosity was carried to excess. Not having a political idea and naturally headstrong, he set the authority of Kandáhár at defiance and declared his resolution of acting perfectly independent of them or any other of the family. This produced a visit from Sheer Dil, his uncle, who despoiled him of all, or the greater part of the vast treasures left behind by Azam Khán. This Sheer Dil, so celebrated in Dooránee history for his valour, returned to Kandáhár with his nephew's wealth, and died a year afterwards. The Afghán beholds in this a judgment from heaven. Immediately after Sheer Dil's death, Dost Mahomed discovered that he was violently enamoured with the mother of Habeeboola, and demanded her. Habeeboola alleged every argument drawn from the consanguinity of the parties and wishing to ask what would be thought of him were he to surrender his mother to the lust of her brother, absolutely refused. This led to a war, and after much resistance Kábul was taken by Dost Mahomed, who fixed in that forgot his love for his sister. Habeeboola is now at Kábul and commands 1,000 cavalry, the horses excellent and his own property; the men consider themselves also especially in his service. Hence his jághír or allowances must be very great. He has acquired an honourable reputation for preserving his mother, and lives in apparent harmony with Dost Mahomed. The assumption of authority by this last Chief has been extremely favourable to the prosperity of Kábul; and it is generally supposed if he lives he will yet play a considerable part in the affairs of Khorássán. Whether his energies are to be displayed in the defence of his country against the ambition of the Sikhs, or exercised to establish universal sway, is not decided upon; but he is universally regarded as the only Chief capable of restoring the Dooránee fortunes. It is his fortune to be beloved by all classes of his subjects; and the Hindu fearlessly approaches him in his rides, and addresses him with the certainty of being attended to. He administers justice with a firm and steady hand, and has proved that the lawless habits of the Afghán are to be controlled. Idolized by his troops, he is perhaps the only prince in these countries who regards the quality rather than the quantity of his men. He engages none but with reference to their physical capabilities, and gives large pay. Having been but a short time in possession of Kábul, his finances are small; hence he is compelled to confine his views. I heard at Shikarpore about the end of 1829 that he had found a large treasure supposed to have been concealed by Ahmed Sháh (such discoveries of coin or of jewels are not uncommon), and moreover that he had marched an army of 18,000 men towards Pesháwar to avenge the murder of his brother Yár Mahomed by the notorious fanatic Syed Ahmed. If these relations be true, I can but rejoice at it, as Dost Mahomed with treasure and 18,000 men would be little annoyed by the jealousies of his brethren at Kandáhár. He is no less *politique et ruse* than brave, and only employs the sword as the last resource. He is remarkably plain in dress, and would be scarcely noticed in the Darbár but for his seat; his white linen raiments afforded a strange contrast to the gaudy exhibition of some of his Chiefs, especially of the young Habeeboola Khán, who glitters in gold. I had an audience of him, and should not have conjectured him a man of ability either from his conversation or his appearance; but it becomes necessary to subscribe to the general impression, and the conviction of his talents for government will be excited in every step through his country. A stranger must be cautious in estimating the character of a Dooránee from his appearance; merely a slight observer like myself would not discover in Dost Mahomed the gallant warrior and shrewd politician, still less on looking at the slow-pacing, coarse-featured Hádjee Khán, the Vazier, would be recognized the active and enterprizing officer who, in conjunction with Sheer Dil, humbled the Persians, and carried Meshed sword in hand. On the gates of that city the painter has pourtrayed the events of the storm, and from the gigantic figure intended for Hádjee Khán it is probable that posterity may entertain as big notions of him as the English do of the famous Earl of Warwick.

The revenue of Kábul, I believe, may be calculated at 14 lákhs of rupees, and may be considered likely to increase. Of his military force an idea may be formed from what has before been mentioned. Most of his infantry are clad in red jackets, and are principally Kohistánees, the best of Khorássán. He has about twelve pieces of artillery, and they are better attended to than those of Kandáhár. Of Dost Mahomed's personal views there can be nothing known, as he is too prudent to divulge them; but there would appear little to prevent his becoming the sole authority in Khorássán, the sway of his brethren being so much detested. I have heard of his putting a Suddoozye to death—a circumstance related with horror even by his friends. Again, I have heard that he is not inimical to the restoration of the king; and it is a common saying with the Dooranees, how happy we should be if Sháh Sujáh were king and Dost Mahomed vazier. The king, it is known, has a sister of Dost Mahomed in his harem; but how he became possessed of her is differently related. Some say Sháh Sujáh heard she was a fine woman, and forcibly seized her; others that she was given to him with the due consent of all parties. This prince and his brother of Ghizni are supposed to be Sheeahs, although they do not profess it, as their mother was of that persuasion.

LUGHMA'N.

The small principality of Lughmán, with the Ghilzye country between Kábul and Jallálábád, with some districts south of the last city, are held by Jubbal Khán, and produce a lákh and a half to two lákhs of rupees annual revenue. The Chief is a son of the same father as the other brothers, but his mother was a slave girl. This excellent man is at once a good prince, a brave warrior, and a pious moolláh; and enjoys an equal reputation for valour and sanctity. He is a firm ally of his brother Dost Mahomed. Jubbal Khán is remarkable for the attention he pays to the European traveller. I saw him at Jallálábád, and was kindly treated. In his camp were two companions, so singular in their union, that I mention them to elucidate the liberality of the Dooránees in religious matters. They were á Mussalmán Moolláh from Lahore and a Hindu Bráhmin from Lucknow. They had both started with the design of travelling for a few years, and having accidentally met each other had joined company. They each bore the appearance of first rate respectability, and were amply provided with all conveniences, nay luxuries of dress, equipage, &c. They had horses for themselves and servants, whether at the expense of Jubbal Khán or of themselves I know not. They paid me a visit the day I stayed in the camp, and never did I witness so much politeness in either a Mussalmán or a Hindu. The former had great vivacity, and was dressed in black silk. What with his gaiety and spirit he was not a jot behind an Abbé of the old French school. He liberally made me offers of assistance with money, clothing, &c., and much wanted me to take one of his horses. I know not his name, but I think the Hindu was nicknamed Moollah Mull.

JELLA'LA'BA'D.

This province is nominally subject to Mahomed Zummer Khán. I know not in what relation this prince stands with the other Barrakzyes; but he is not their brother. The revenue of Jallálábád, containing nine pargannás, is estimated in the king's books at 12 lákhs of rupees; but no such sum is realized by the Chief, whose authority is not acknowledged even one kos from his capital. I was entertained in this country by one Cullecle Khán, who had three forts and dependent villages about a mile from the town. He surprized me by informing me that neither he nor his neighbours acknowledged Mahomed Zummer Khán, and that they should resist any attempt he might make at levying duty. These villages have the Kábul river between them and the town, and to this circumstance I suspect they owe their independence, which may probably be the fortune of all the towns, &c., to the north of the river down the extent of the valley. Easterly to Basawul and to Dakkar at the entrance of the Khyber hills the authority of Jallálábád is established, these being to the southern side of the river, and accessible to compulsion. Mahomed Zummer Khán is esteemed very wealthy, but is unpopular and oppressive as a Governor. He is an ally of Kábul, and in fact a mere instrument of Dost Mahomed. I know not the amount of his troops; he has six pieces of ordnance stationed at Bollabrang.

KHYBEREE TRIBES.

Sheenwárrees.

These live principally to the south of Jallálábád and also occupy part of the range of hills between that province and Pesháwar. They are now perfectly independent, but are usually accounted better than their brethren the Afrédee, being engaged a little in traffic. These men have no order or government, but live like their neighbours the Sheenwárree in wild and savage independence.

Afrédee.

These men, reputed the most lawless of the savages, occupy the range of the hills between Pesháwar and Jallálábád, and also part of the plain of Pesháwar. They formerly received pay from the king, but as that has been long since discontinued, they live in open brigandage. They are sufficiently numerous, and when the Syed Ahmed Shah, who dwells in the Eusofzye country, has money to pay troops, he can always command three or four thousand men from Khyber. A nephew of the Syed, as he calls himself, resides in quality of agent at the town of Jum at the entrance of the hills 10 kos west of Pesháwar; he is named Sháh Risool Sháh. This gentleman, as well as many of the people of this town, at the time of my visit to Khyber had fled to the hills, apprehending a visit from Pesháwar. The people of Khyber during Runjit's last personal visit to Pesháwar diverted the course of the Kabul river and inundated his camp by night; in the consequent confusion they were on the alert, and secured a vast number of horses. In the morning the Dooránee Chiefs of Pesháwar were summoned, but they asserted it was not their deed, and Runjit marched towards Lahore, having made but a stay of three days; and it is probable, but for this accident, he might have remained as many months.

PESHÁWAR.

Pesháwar at the time of my visit (1827) was governed by Yár Mahomed, Sultán Mahomed, Syed Mahomed, and Peer Mahomed. These four brothers appeared to preserve a good understanding, and assembled at a common Darbár held at the house of their mother. Yár Mahomed, as eldest, was nominally the Chief, and in fact possessed the greater proportion of revenue; but Peer Mahomed, the youngest, was perhaps the more influential from the number of his troops. Syed Mahomed held the fort and district of Hasannuggur. The revenue of Pesháwar I heard computed at ten lákhs of rupees, to which must be added one lákh, the revenue of the newly-acquired country of Bungush retained by Peer Mahomed. The Chiefs of Pesháwar cannot be called independent, or rather seem to hold their country entirely at the pleasure of Runjit Sing. The circumstances which led to this dependence involve the notice of Syed Ahmed Sháh, and I shall relate them as briefly as may be consistent with clearness. The pious fanatic who announces himself the Imám Mehdi of the Korán, and that he has a divine commission to take possession of the Punjáb, Hindustán and China, came a few years since into the country of the Eusofzye and assembled above 100,000 men, avowing his design of compelling Runjit Sing to turn Mussalmán or to cut off his head. The Chiefs of Pesháwar had united themselves with the Syed, and with their troops and guns were in his camp. The Sikhs naturally were preparing to meet the threatened crisis, and Hurree Sing commanding 30,000 men was to keep them from passing the Indus until the king should arrive with a large army, including all his regulars, from

Lahore. In the Mussalmán camp all was hope and exultation; the numbers of their host, and the presumed favour of heaven, permitted none to doubt of success, and a distribution was already made of the Sikh towns and provinces. The soul of Ahmed Sháh dilated, and in his pride of feeling he made use of some expressions which implied that he considered himself the master of Pesháwar; the Dooránee Chiefs became displeased and their final defection if not occasioned is by some palliated on this account. The half of Hurree Sing's force under an old warrior Boodh Sing, appears to have crossed the Indus and entered the Mussalmán country, where they soon found themselves surrounded; they were in the utmost distress for some days, and Boodh Sing finally determined to extricate himself or perish. In the meantime he had written to the Dooránee Chiefs of Pesháwar, assuring them that if they took no part against him in the action he was about to give, their conduct in the Syed's business should not be questioned: he alluded to the immense army on the road with Runjit Sing, and pointed out that the destruction of himself and troops would not influence the issue of the contest; and they must know, he said, that the Sirkár was Zorabar. His argument decided the Pesháwar leaders, and on the morning of battle they, who with their guns were stationed in the front, at once passed to the rear. Boodh Sing invoked his guru, and with his Sikhs charged á bride abattue. The resistance of the Mussulmán was very trifling, and the Sikhs boast that each Sing that day slew fifteen or twenty of his enemies, allowing, however, that they did not fight but threw themselves on the ground. The Syed, who had assured his men that he had fixed a charm on the Sikh guns and matchlocks, did all that a brave man could do, and was forcibly conducted from the field by some Indians who made his elephant pass a river, he himself declining to fly and persisting that the infidels could not injure him. Runjit Sing arriving soon after this victory with an immense army as also Hurree Sing, the confederate troops marched to Pesháwar, where they stayed some months; it was now that Balla Hissar and part of the town were destroyed, as well as many of the gardens, and the whole country was exhausted. Runjit does not exact money from the Pesháwar Chiefs, who have none to give, but horses and the famous rice grown near Pesháwar, and he detains the sons of Yár Mahomed as hostages at Lahore. He has established a system of annual visits to that country, apparently with the intention of keeping it from the possibility of revival in consequence, and is so oppressive that Yár Mahomed in 1829 remonstrated and put the case to him that if it were his pleasure that he should continue to govern in Pesháwar the visits must cease, if not, he would retire to his brother in Kábul. Runjit told him to remain, but demanded a celebrated horse called Leila. Here a difficulty arose, for this animal cannot be delivered up without a loss of honour. Yár Mahomed affirming that if he must suffer one of two dishonours, he would rather surrender his wife than the horse. I could not ascertain on what grounds this horse is held so sacred, but heard something of an allusion to the loves of Mujnoon and Leila. Troops were despatched to obtain the horse, but Sultán Mahomed, who appeared to be in charge of the beast, swore on the Korán that it was dead. M. Ventura, an Italian officer commanding the expedition, not being so much interested in the horse as his royal master, believed the Mussulmán, or pretended to do so, and returned to Lahore. Some time afterwards Runjit was informed that Leila was alive, and the Italian was again despatched to bring Sultán Mahomed to him. In the meantime another circumstance happened which, particularly interesting the Pesháwar Chiefs, increased the positiveness of Runjit's demand for the horse. This was the arrival at the Court of Moollah Shukoor, envoy from Sháh Sujáh, wishing to make arrangements for the recovery of Pesháwar and Kábul, proposing to pay immediately 3 lákhs of rupees in money and jewels, and an annual tribute for his dominions. Runjit refused to listen to these terms, but informed Yár Mahomed of them and assured him that unless the annual presents were doubled and the horse Leila produced, the king would be sent at the head of an army to recover his states. The Italian officer had arrived at Pesháwar, when the Syed Ahmed Sháh unexpectedly issued from the Eusofzye hills, defeated Syed Mahomed and possessed himself of Hasannuggur was joined by immense numbers. This happened in October or November 1829, when I was passing down Sind towards the sea; hence my intelligence is neither full or positive. I know not whether Ahmed Sháh went to Pesháwar or not. I heard he did; however he grew so formidable that Yár Mahomed sought a conference, in which he was seized and beheaded by the Syed with some of his attendants and friends, among whom was the Náib Gool Mahomed, already mentioned in the notice on Kandáhár. On receipt of this intelligence Dost Mahomed of Kábul is reported to have marched with 18,000 men towards Pesháwar, and Runjit Sing with an immense force moved upon the Indus and the Ráwal Pindi country. From this period I know not what passed, but it is easy to suppose the Syed must have been expelled, but I cannot conjecture even on the present state of Pesháwar.

The Eusofzye.

These tribes are compelled to furnish tribute of horses to Runjit Sing, and perhaps they have been more severely treated than any people subdued by that conqueror. His vengeance nevertheless was excited by their own folly, and but for that they might have been still independent. The course of operations against the Patháns of Gunghur led Runjit on the eastern bank of the Indus, the Eusofzye on the opposite side slaughtered cows and insulted the Sikhs in the most aggravated manner. Runjit did not intend to have passed the river, and probably the Eusofzye supposed he could not from the rapidity of the current; but not able to contain his anger he ordered his cavalry to pass over, which they did, losing twelve hundred. The Eusofzye country was now ravaged and an indiscriminate slaughter made of man, woman and child for some days. The miserable hunted wretches were compelled to throw themselves on the earth, and placing a blade or tuft of grass in the mouth to cry out "I am your cow." This deed and exclamation which would have saved them from an orthodox Hindu had no effect with the Sikhs.

Ever since the expulsion of Sháh Sujáh the Eusofzye have been enemies to Pesháwar, and they now profess themselves tábedárs of the Syed Ahmed Sháh, who resides among them, the government of the country being the same as usual vested in the several Maliks. Ahmed Sháh after his grand defeat by the Sikhs being no longer able to attempt anything against them directed hostilities against the Dooránee Chiefs of Pesháwar, whom he denounced as infidels and traitors to the cause of Islám, and Yár Mahomed he called by the name of Yaroo Sing, and ordered that he should be so styled when mentioned in his camp. He accordingly, whenever he had funds, engaged troops from Khyber and other places, and issued from the hills, always in the direction of Hasannuggur. By such conduct although he achieved nothing of importance, he kept his enemies in perpetual alarm. He paid his troops in *baldi* rupees; hence many supposed him an agent of the British Government. Whence he procured his occasional supplies of money was equally inexplicable. He had with him three or four Chiefs of some repute, but discontented with the Barrakzye, as Jummer Khán, Baram, Meer Allum, and the Khalil Chief. The last grand effort of the Syed I have noticed but remain in ignorance as to his fate. Perhaps few men have created a greater sensation in their day than this Syed, and setting aside his fanaticism, his talents must be great to have succeeded in persuading so many myriads of beings, and to preserve their confidence in his mission after the reverses he has experienced. Among all the Patháns of Muckelwand and Damaun and thence to Pesháwar he is constantly prayed for, and frequently is expressed the fervent wish that God would grant victory to Ahmed Sháh. He also makes a great figure in their songs. It is generally believed he is a native of Bareilly; and it appears certain that he for some years officiated as Mooláh in the camp of the famous Ameer Khán, respected for his learning and decorum of life. At that time he made no pretensions to communications from heaven. He has continually emissaries spread over all parts soliciting the aid of Mussalmáns to support his cause; and I beheld at Ták the accredited agent of Sultán Mahomed of Pesháwar, who by the bye was also a Syed, soliciting pecuniary assistance for Ahmed Sháh, his master's enemy. This would be singular in any but a Dooránee; but I doubt not he transacted his prince's business with perfect fidelity, and with equal sincerity of feeling begged for the Syed.

CASHMEER.

This beautiful and rich province is possessed by Runjit Sing. Long it was an object of ambition to him, but his first attempts were foiled, and he once suffered a severe defeat from A'zem Khán. He at length found it unprovided with troops and made an easy conquest of it. Jubbal Khán, the present prince of Lughmán, had an opportunity of showing his spirit, 700 Dooránees encountering 11,000 Sikhs.

KUTTUCK.

This state produces a revenue of two or three lákhs, and its Chief is dependent on Runjit Sing. The former chief (be that Mr. Esaw) was one of the first that connected himself with the Sikhs; hence he was much blamed by the Dooránees. He was shot in the back with a pistol by his attendants when riding. Runjit was particularly angry.

STATES OF MAHOMED KH'AN.

On the overthrow of the Dooránee power these states became independent, and the Khán was styled a Naváb by his subjects. He appears to have been in a flourishing condition and wealthy when Runjit Sing invaded his territories. The fortress of Monkeerah made a memorable defence, but the perseverance of the besieger overcame all difficulties, and the whole of the countries east of the Indus were annexed to Lahore. The old Chief did not long survive the loss of his dominions, and his son Shere Mahomed now lives in the town of Deyráh Ismáel Khán west of the Indus, a dependent on the Sikhs.

MOOLTA'N.

I doubt whether Mooltán was ever exactly considered an integral portion of the Dooránee empire as Deyráh Gházie Khán and Shikarpore undoubtedly were. I have elsewhere recorded the fate of this country and its possession by the Sikhs.

BHA'WALPORE.

This is another state not strictly Dooránee, but which, it seems, professed an obedience to its Government; and I have reason to believe that the present youthful Khán has said, that he considers himself a slave of the Suddoozye. In the time of Saadut Khán, Sháh Sujáh passing from Loodiánna arrived at Bháwalpore intending to attempt the recovery of some or all of his dominions; the Khán supplied him with 5,000 horse, which furnished Runjit Sing with a plea for the invasion of Bháwulpore. He exacts tribute of half the revenue or nine lákhs of rupees annually. It was then the Sikhs first seized Deyráh Gházie Khán, which not being convenient to occupy, or contrary to their policy, they let to the Bháwalpore Chief for three lákhs of rupees. The young Khán submits very unwillingly to the imposition of tribute, and among the *on dit* of this part of the world is one, that he has informed Poor Dil Khán if any thing should be attempted against the Sikhs he would assist with 30,000 men. When I was at Hyderabad in Sind there was an embassy there from Hulaut in Belochistán, the object of which I heard was to engage the Sind Chiefs in an expedition against Bháwalpore. I suspect the object of the embassy was misrepresented,

Deyra'h Gha'zie Kha'n.

Held by the Sikhs and let to Bháwul Khán.

Shika'rpore.

Fraudulently possessed by the Sind Chiefs. The recovery of this city is the primary object of Poor Dil Khán's policy, and will no doubt be accomplished with facility. The Chiefs of Sind were formerly vassals of the Dooránees and would be so again if ever they consolidated their power.

Keelaut (Beloche).

This state is at present under the sway of Meerab Khán; his father did not acknowledge the supremacy of Kandáhár, but recommended the Chiefs who applied for tribute to keep themselves quiet at home or he would pay them a visit. His heir possessed not his spirit and we find him as an ally or dependent with a force of 3,000 men in the army of A'zem Khán, which expelled Sháh Sujáh from Shikárpore. As the family of Meerab Khán was indebted for empire to the generosity of the Suddoozye, it cannot be supposed he would be hostile, and on this occasion, when the armies were opposite each other, Meerab Khán declared to Azem Khán that he would not fight the Suddoozye, but was ready to obey his commands against the troops of Sind. Had an action ensued and an opportunity occurred, it is probable he would have joined the king. Some time after this Meerah Khán began to treat the Chiefs of Kandáhár with indifference, and for three or four years refused to pay tribute or acknowledge any dependence. In the spring of 1829 Poor Dil marched and the Khán of Beloche paid him a trifling sum of money and bound himself to accompany the armies of Kandáhár whenever summoned. I heard the revenue of Keelaut computed at six lákhs of rupees—a moderate sum for so large and fine a country, as Elphinstone mentions three lákhs to have been the revenue. I need only point out the existence of the large and trading bázár towns of Keelaut, Mustoong, Shall Dardur, Hadjee Shar, Bang, Gunderbaz and Rojan, with their dependent fertile districts, to disprove so low a calculation. These towns I have seen, and there are others I have not visited, and therefore do not mention. The states of Kábul, Kandáhár and even Herát have, we may almost say, but one bázár town. The capital, Keelaut, has several and of such consequence that Bang, Gunderbaz and Keelaut are rivals in size of Kandáhár, and most of the others surpass Ghizni, without estimating their commercial advantages. The country is moreover fertile, and large quantities of grain and even some inferior sugar is produced. No state possesses greater capabilities of improvement than those of Meerab Khán. Were a prince of energy to arise and assert the ancient rights of his country, he would possess the country from Brahooee to the sea. Karáchi, held by the Sind Chiefs, having once been a possession of the Beloche Chiefs. The Beloche tribes are very numerous and brave, and if their power was drawn forth, or the country under proper government, there can be little doubt but Kandáhár would become a dependent province. At present trade is little promoted, and the merchants of caravans have little encouragement to sell their goods in a country where base coin is circulated. The military force of Meerab Khán I do not suppose to exceed three or four thousand men: that he might raise a very large number I can readily conceive. His artillery consists of six pieces of ordnance at Keelaut. Belochistán is a country of which much remains to be known, and whose early history would repay the search for it.

Balkh.

It may be necessary to notice this state as having some time been dependent upon the kings of Kábul. I cannot describe the revolutions which it has undergone during the last few years, but believe it had been subdued by a prince of Bokhárá, but that it is at present an independent state governed by a *ci-devant* vazier who successfully rebelled.

(A True Copy).
(Signed) D. WILSON,
President, Persian Gulf.

Memoranda on Herát, &c.: by Mr. C. Masson.
No. 2.

The city of Herát, once so famous as the capital of Khorássán and the residence of the sons of Timur, no longer retains its ancient splendour, yet still being the seat of Government of an independent kingdom and possessing natural advantages of position and climate, preserves the rank of a first rate city in the regions of Central Asia. It is situated in a fine, rich and extensive valley, watered by a river of good size, whose direction is from north to south; it flows west of the town, and has a bridge thrown over it of very great antiquity and of admirable workmanship. This is one of the buildings of which a native of Herát would make a boast. The city is surrounded with a good wall, containing a due proportion of circular bastions, and is kept in a state of tolerable repair, to which the necessity caused from turbulent times compels the attention of the sovereign. There are a number of buildings in Herát which are termed handsome, and in fact are so, in comparison with those of other cities in these parts, as Kandáhár, Ghizni or even Kábul and Pesháwar, but infinitely falling short of the magnificent structures of Lahore and the cities of the East. There are the ancient palaces of its kings existing, but in decay, so destructive has been the hand of time upon them, that another century may witness their entire demolition. The royal masjids are, many of them although neglected, in a state of decent preservation, and although deprived of a portion of their ornaments and painted tiles, preserve sufficient tokens to enable us to form an estimate of their former state. But in most of these the summons to prayer is never heard, I believe from an objection to make use of the spot which was appropriated to devotion by an unfortunate and rejected sovereign. At Pesháwar, in confirmation of this objection, the entrances to the masjid, built under the hill on which the fort stood by the king Sháh Sujáh for his immediate use, have been actually closed with bricks since his expulsion. Masjids and tombs seem among Mussalmáns to be the objects on which most labour and expense are bestowed, and on which they principally depend that their names may live after them; as these are seldom repaired, so are they generally constructed with proportionate solidity and durable materials. The prince who builds a palace is aware that he builds merely for himself and not for his successors; hence his ephemeral production mingles with the dust soon after him who raised it. Many of the recently erected masjids in Herát, which are designated by the names of their respective founders, cannot vie with the former ones; their decorations are very flimsy, and the solidity of old times is dispensed with on account of the charges; the painted tiles no longer possess that brilliant and permanent line which distinguished the ancient ones, while the buildings on the whole are miserably deficient in size and arrangement; and we look in vain for the reservoir of water in the grand square with the baths and other conveniences which welcomed the sight in the masjids of the olden times. It were devoutly to be wished that men of wealth would employ it rather in preserving the old and stately structures from decay than in erecting new ones. There are numerous buildings in the city which were hospitals for the indigent and afflicted during the sway of the descendants of Timur, but they are occupied by the Khán or the merchants, and their funds, or revenue estranged from the original purpose. The bázár of course in so large a city is ample and extensive, although in its width and convenience it has not the advantages of Kandáhár, perhaps the best arranged city of Central Asia.

At the Chah-soo, or point in the centre where the several streets of the bázár meet, is a large covered building, under which sit a vast number of vendors of all descriptions of goods—fruits, vegetables, &c.—and here at all periods of the day is a considerable crowd collected. From the top of this erection the nagárás announce the morning and evening nobut. It is in the evening that the bázár exhibits a scene of much business and activity. All is then bustle and movement, and then is presented to the traveller the best time to make observations on the domestic trade of the people, as all their matters of sale and barter are openly and publicly transacted. Standing as an idle spectator I have often been referred to by two men disputing the value of a trifling article, and as often excused myself, and endeavoured to convey to them the meaning of the poet's line—

"Who shall decide when doctors disagree."

The concourse of strangers is moreover great. Here will be seen Persians from Meshed, Moguls from Turbut, Tartars from Bokhára, Kurds, Afgháns, Seistánees and Beloches. The number of Hindus in the city will be large, yet not comparatively so with Kandáhár and the cities to the East. West of Herát they either dare not or are not allowed to reside permanently; their avocations as dealers in the necessaries of life could not be carried on as the Sheeahs would eat nothing sold by them. As the valley of Herát is very large, the soil very fertile and its cultivation very generally and successfully carried on, the markets of the capital are well supplied, and all kinds of vegetables are abundant and cheap. The fruits are generally such as are found in Kábul, perhaps the apples and pears are finer. They have also almonds, grapes, peaches, apricots, cherries, quinces, the various kinds of melons and pisters; it is remarkable that the latter fruit, which is here much esteemed but which would appear of little consequence, is the only one which they vaunt as being superior to that of other regions, while all their other fruits they allow to be surpassed by those of more genial climates. In this city the Serais called Karavanserais* are open for the reception of the traveller, and they are pretty numerous. In Kandáhár owing to the bad Government and depression there is but one, and that never used. In Kábul they have many, as the traffic and intercourse with other parts is constant and protected by the ruler.

The general mode of building in Herát is with arched roofs, suggested by the scarcity of wood proper for the purposes of the builder. The houses derive an air of importance from these circular formations; but I fancy they would gladly be omitted by the inhabitants if they could procure wood for rafters to enable them to support flat roofs, as during the rainy season, which is their winter, vast numbers of the roofs fall in. Whether this be owing to the bricks being generally unburnt, the bad quality of the mortar, or the want of skill in the builder, or the defect of the system, I know not; otherwise they would appear substantially and neatly built, the walls of every house being of considerable thickness, as well as the roofs. The species of building just mentioned prevails over Western or Persian Khorássán, and extends to Kandáhár and fifty kos east of it, where it ceases; the roofs of the houses of the Ghulzie being flat. In the immediate vicinity of Herát are numerous large and beautiful gardens; but the universal complaint in all these countries may also be justly made here that they are either suffered to run absolutely waste, or only partially attended to. It may be questioned whether if a considerable sum did not annually proceed from the sale of the fruit, these gardens would not be deserted *in toto*. I never remember an instance of any of the Chiefs at present in authority throughout Eastern Khorássán visiting any of the royal gardens. There are no gardeners attached to them,

* The term Karavanserai intimates the origin of the English word caravan as applied to collections of travellers, &c., but I never heard it, or indeed any other word than Kaffee made use of to express these assemblages in Beluchistán; and I believe in Persia Kurrum Serai is used to denote the travellers' Serai; in Herát and Kandáhár only I heard the word expressed Karavan Serai.

unless they be called so, who are hired for the purpose of watching the fruits at a certain season of the year and gathering them when ripe, when they are sold at the gate (where a weigher and Munshi attends) to the dealers, who retail them in the bázár. The soil of the garden is wholly unproductive and remains choked with weeds. I am here speaking of the gardens planted by the kings famed in history, and at present under the control of the sovereign; those held by private individuals, and which contribute to the supply of the markets, are admirably worked, and exhibit a bright verdant aspect. Among their numerous vegetables they have many common to European climates, as cabbage (I only observed one species), spinach, lettuce, carrots, turnips, radishes and onions, the last not very fine. I should observe that at Herát, as well as at Kandáhár, Kábul, Pesháwar, and Lahore, there is a royal garden called Shalimar, the meaning of which word I could never learn from any person in any of the cities mentioned. There are also many magnificent tombs in the neighbourhood of the city, and many of the shrines of saints and Zeearuts are visited by the pious. Among the tombs is that of the celebrated poet Jami; the gardens with which it was surrounded have long since vanished. The cultivation of grain in the plains of Heárt is most successful and productive and entirely wheat, of which only in Herát bread is made; this is the case also in all countries of Khorássán, the poorest inhabitant of which will on no account eat bread made of other substances. I have noticed their fruits, which are very abundant, and much wine is made from their grapes, which are inferior to those of Kandáhár, but perhaps equal to those of Kábul. In addition to the fruits enumerated should be added mulberries and pomegranates. I am not certain whether walnuts are produced here or brought from elsewhere. Some raw silk is procured near Herát and employed in their home manufactures. The large population of Herát would naturally induce a considerable activity in the internal trade of the inhabitants were its extent limited to the supply of the individual wants of its own community; but this is much increased by the passage to and fro of caravans, and the resort of traders from the neighbouring districts to which Herát has become the mart, partly through the distraction prevalent elsewhere, and partly to the able conduct of its Chief, and the security experienced in his dominions. They have manufactures of silk, worsted woollens and carpets, but I heard of none in which they excelled. Their arms indeed are highly prized, and a blade of Herát is easily known to the connoisseur by its finely watered appearance; their pistols and carbines are also esteemed. Their cattle generally consists of *dumbás* or large-tailed sheep, from the milk of which they make krout, butter and cheese. They have few cows, which abound in no part of Khorássán. The camels are large, excellent, many of them white. Horses are generally bred throughout the country, and besides being very hardy and serviceable, are very cheap. The Chief of the State is a Mahomedan of the Sunnee persuasion, but most of his subjects are Sheeahs. Moguls are very numerous at Herát, and the bulk of the peasantry are called Parsevans, a name indicating a Persian origin. These men possess a suavity of manner and prepossessing appearance, not discoverable in the Afghán or even Tadjik of Eastern Khorássán, who also claim Persian descent. The genuine Dooránee (although the Chief is one, being a Suddoozye) always appeared to me to consider himself a stranger in this country and few have settled in it, but such as dare not go elsewhere owing to the part they had taken in the political occurrences of late years. It should be noted that the river of Herát is called Pool Mallán, from which it would seem to have derived its appellation from the bridge; there is also another smaller river immediately adjacent to the city called Yakil.

The nominal king of Herát is Mahomed Sháh Suddoozye, but owing to real or imputed imbecility, the son, Camraun, or, I suspect properly Kamerodeen Khán, has the charge of affairs, and assumes the title of Pádsháh, which is conceded to him by his subjects. There can be no doubt of the incapacity of Mahomed Sháh to act as king, the loss of Kandáhár, Kábul, and, in short, the Dooránee empire over which he once swayed being entirely the consequence of his infatuation and weakness, and it is asserted that he now stupifies himself daily with opium and other deleterious substances. The son, Kamerodeen, assumed the reins of Government with the approbation of all parties, and his administration has been highly popular and beneficial to the country. After the expulsion of Shàh Sujàh from Kàbul, he made an attempt to recover the eastern provinces; and after taking possession of Kandàhàr, advanced to Kàbul, but was compelled to return precipitately to Herát, having received intelligence of the intended delivery of that city to Sheer Dil, one of the Barrakzye, by the Governor he had left behind. Since that period the Barrakzye family have somewhat consolidated their power, and he dare not think of attacking them. While he occupied Kandàhàr he made himself remarkable for cruelty, and you still see in the garden of Shallimar the block on which every morning the wretches who excited his suspicions were decapitated, and the balcony opposite to it in which he sat enjoying the sanguinary spectacle. His barbarous execution of the celebrated but factious Futteh Khàn is an indelible strain on his character, and is ever spoken of in strong terms of horror by the Afghán. This ferocity to his enemies, in which he exceeds all other princes of the present day on the line of Meshed to the Sutledj, appears his principal blemish. In other respects he is liberal and exact in the payment of his troops, and without any idea of political economy contents himself with moderate imposts, and effectually provides that there shall be no unnecessary severity or extortion in the collection of his revenue. He is found to promote the security of travellers, and an authenticated robbery would be certainly followed by the death of the offender. To his credit the slave trade is abolished in Herát, where before his reign it was carried on to excess. I have been assured that nothing was more frequent than to invite the unsuspecting stranger to a repast or other entertainment, then seize him and give him over to the "Adam feroosh;" it was moreover perilous to sit without doors after sunset. Kamerodeen has vindicated the rights of humanity, and hangs the unnatural transgressor. The revenue of Herát I have heard estimated at twelve lákhs of rupees—a very small sum for so fine a country and infinitely short of the revenue in former times; but we must take into calculation the series of destructive wars which have lately desolated those regions, no invasion was more injurious to this country than that of the present Futteh Alli Sháh of Persia. Some years since he advanced as far as Subzewár, one hundred kos east of Herát, and finding himself compelled to quit the country, resolved to do it as much harm as he possibly could, and accordingly ravaged it in his retreat. The kingdom, however, has been recovering rapidly the last few years, as Herát has been visited by no foreign enemy. The Persians have other objects to attend to than the conquest of Eastern Khorássán; moreover an alliance has been effected with the Sháhzádáh at Meshed by the interchange of daughters. Although from the peculiar state of the governments in those countries no Chief can at present venture on remote expeditions, for their capitals are absolutely so many nests, which if they were to leave some neighbours would step in, yet the reputation of Kamerodeen is such that no one of them, or, indeed, a coalition of them would venture to attack the lion in his den; hence Herát is perfectly secure, and likely to be so from the alarms of war, and may continue her plans of amelioration without the apprehension of interruption. The military force I should estimate at 20,000 men, the greater proportion horse. I am not certain that force is actually retained in pay, but it is the number he appears to have had on foot during his advance to Kábul. He then had 15,000 with him, and I apprehend 5,000 is little enough to be allowed for the troops remaining in the countries of Herát and Kandáhár. His artillery, eight to ten pieces of ordnance. Kamerodeen has three sons arrived at years of discretion, the eldest, of whom he seems to entertain some suspicion, he always retains near his person; another is Governor of the province of Subzewár, and the third commands at Furráh.

The dominions of Kamerodeen are circumscribed on the northern side by the Tartar districts, on the southern by the province of Seistán, on the eastern by the Moghul principality of Turbut, and on the western by the desert which separates it from Girish, a dependency of Kandáhár. I shall close my notice of this state by a few remarks on the routes to Kandáhár. There are two routes, the most direct passing by the large town of Ghiraunee, which may be called the northern route; this was travelled by Mr. Forster and appears to have been a very painful one from the nature of the country and deficiency of water. Caravans, as I understood, generally prefer the longer or southern route by Subzewár and Furráh; this is the road I adopted and therefore that of which I am best enabled to speak. Leaving Herát (where it is necessary to provide yourself with provisions to suffice you for the distance of 100 kos) you proceed in a due southerly direction, and passing over a fine bold diversified country you reach the luxuriant and extensive plain of Subzewár. In the distance here passed (100 kos computed distance) there is no want of water; forage and mutton (that is to say, taking the whole sheep) may be had, but generally speaking no other articles, as although villages occur at convenient distances, the inhabitants, principally of the Geelzye tribes, do not sell, and have no dealers resident among them. Subzewár is a good town and has a large mud fort, reputed strong, and here resides a son of Kamerodeen. The country around is extremely pleasant, and the plain is watered by a clear but not considerable stream. From hence again providing subsistence for 100 kos, the distance to Furráh, you again proceed southerly over precisely the same kind of country, the plains of the general Khorássánee character, bare of grass, but covered with a whitish-leaved aromatic plant perfuming the air around, and the favourite food of the dumbá sheep, to whose flesh it is supposed to communicate its peculiar and grateful flavour. There are also many prickly plants eaten by the camel. Trees throughout the distance of Herát to Furráh are rarely met with, except a few mulberries or willows near the Chushmeh or spring of water, or in the immediate vicinity of the respective villages. The vales of Subzewár and Furráh are of course excepted, where the luxurious foliage of the numerous groves will not fail to be admired and appreciated by the traveller coming from the desert. Furráh is a considerable town, and the fort is an erection of some importance, being the frontier post on the side of Kandáhár. Here also resides a son of Kamerodeen. At this town it will be necessary to provide for 140 kos, the distance to Kandáhár. From Furráh about five kos the Furráh river or Furráhrod is crossed, wide, and the current very strong. You then enter a desert extending from 80 to 90 kos, in which water occurs at four spots, at three of them deposits of rain water which never fail, and at the other, a houz. I speak of the close of the summer, the period I crossed this plain. You then arrive at Girish, a fort belonging to Kandáhár; here are a few houses, but no great supply if any should be calculated on. A fine stream is crossed immediately before arrival at Girisk. Boats are kept here, but the river is fordable at the season of my visit, viz., autumn. The northern route from Herát viâ Ghiraunee also meets at Girisk, where duties are levied on the caravans, as they are also at Furráh on the opposite side of the desert. The fort of Girisk is small and compact and belonged to the famous Futteh Khán: to this he invariably fled and found a refuge in his disasters, and here he projected the rebellions and fomented the factions which have deprived Eastern Khorássán of its lawful sovereign, and here after his murder the brothers received from their mother the funds which enabled them to wage warfare and finally to establish themselves in the line of country from Girisk to the Indus. Here are numerous gardens, and fruits are plentiful. From hence to Kandáhár there is a tract of fifteen or sixteen kos without water. In other respects the country is populous and fertile; provisions easily obtained at all the villages. In approaching the city you have a view of beautiful meadows to the right, irrigated by a fine but narrow stream. On your left detached hills surmounted with ancient brick towers, on turning which you behold at the base the ruins of the old city of Kandáhár called Hussein Sháh's, and in front you see, at about a mile distant, the new city, or rather its western wall divided by its numerous bastions. Of Kandáhár I shall make but one observation, which is that it has been supposed to be the site of one of the Alexandrias founded by Alexander, as it is expressly stated that this city was built at the foot of the Paropamisian range which is again repeated in the speech of the Nysa Ambassadors. Kandáhár has no claim to be considered Alexandria, for the hills around it are all detached ones save the inferior ranges of the Hazarah Tartars, and it is some hundred miles from the Paropamisian range. The antiquarian desirous of fixing the position of Alexandria must be recommended to go elsewhere; perhaps a trip in the annual caravans from Kábul to Balkh might put him on the scent.

(A True Copy.)
(Signed)   D. WILSON,
Resident, Persian Gulf.

Adventures from Kandáhár to Shirkárpore : by Mr. C. Masson.
No. 3.

Proceeded alone from Kandáhár with the intention of overtaking a caravan which had left two days before in progress to Shikárpore. Although perfectly aware of the danger of travelling in those countries, particularly for a stranger, understanding that the caravan would march slowly, being burthened with women and children, and judging the danger would not be excessive within two or three days from the capital of Khorásán, I started in the expectation of reaching the kaffla the 2nd March. Arriving at the last of the villages in the neighbourhood of the city and about 10 kos distant, entered it with a view of procuring some food, but could prevail on no one to prepare it. At a slight distance from the village observed a black tent which I presumed was occupied by some of those people called Loharnee, who are in general more hospitable than the Afgháns. Thither I repaired and found a family in which no one could speak Persian, and I being ignorant of Peshto, we were mutually at a loss. However I succeeded in conveying the information that bread was the article needed, and that he should be paid for it. To this he agreed, and while his wife was kneading the dough, his attention was attracted by the sight of a drinking vessel I had purchased in Kandáhár, and he took, or rather seized, it, returning me the few pice I had previously given him. Nor did he stay here, but absolutely searched my linen, and my coin in gold which I had bound in the web cord of my pyjammas underwent his inspection, the vicinity of the village alone deterred him from making it booty. Bread was at length served. While I was eating it, I could comprehend the discourse of the family related to me, and I heard the word kaffla pronounced several times, which encouraged me to hope it was near at hand. Having smoked the chillum, as is invariably the custom in these countries after meals, I took leave of my host, enquiring by signs the directions of the high road to Shikárpore. He understood me and directed my sight to a whitish-topped peak among the distant hills, under which he asserted the road winded. Having yet two or three hours of day-light, dashed across the country—in front the hills and not a sign of habitation—came to a swamp of briny water, and had some difficulty in clearing it. At length reached a large solitary building uninhabited and in decay which had probably been a serai in former times. Here were two or three chambers in decent preservation, in one of which I took up my quarters for the night, although the doing so was not unattended with danger, as from the remains of recent fires it was evident the place was frequented, and I inferred in so sequestered a spot and distant from any path or road, it might be the resort of robbers or other doubtful characters. Recommending myself to the divine protection I resigned myself to sleep, and awoke in the morning, having had no other companions than pigeons whose numerous wings covered the vaulted roofs of the buildings and no other visitants than a few owls with their large flapping wings and discordant cries occasionally broke in upon my repose. Started and nearing the hills observed the villages on ascending ground of the district called Kooshab. The city is not visible from hence, a small detached range of hills intervening. Arrived at a kareze without water, and made for a building which I found to be a deserted flour mill. I could not from hence discover the road I was in quest of, but concluded I should gain it by following the direction of the base of sand-hill to the left, towards which I accordingly steered. Approached it, when issuing from one of the apertures, galloped a horseman, one of the wild Patháns in the uncouth garb of his tribe; he rode towards me, and I believe asked me the road to some place or other, but as I was unable either to understand him or return an answer, his vociferations were to no effect, and applying to me all the curses and abusive epithets which his language furnished, he left me and galloped off to my great satisfaction. I now descried in the distance a string of camels which were without doubt pacing the desired road, and I hoped might be the kaffla I was following. Gained a road in which were abundant prints of feet of men, horses and camels. There was no person in sight that I could ask if the road was the one for Shikárpore. However I entered it without hesitation, and proceeded five or six kos without meeting or seeing any one. Hills to the right and left; those to the right, sand principally; to the left, stone covered with the slight surface of earth, but no vestige of inhabitants. Found the camels I had seen to be return camels from Kandáhár, whither they had conveyed wood. This mortified me for the moment, as it left me dubious as to the road; but on passing those which had halted I again perceived the traces of men, horses and camels as before, and the rinds of pomegranates which had manifestly been that day only thrown on the ground encouraged me to hope the kaffla was very near. Arrived at the kareze to the right of the road. The water of bad quality and unpalatable. Continued marching with still the same signs of the caravan. When night began to overcast the horizon, at a distance of a quarter of a mile from the road observed two or three trees which, with the circumstance of the kareze before mentioned winding in the same direction, indicated the existence of a village. Found about one hundred and twenty tents arranged in a semi-circular form, in front of which were two spots enclosed with stones, which served as musjeets where the men of the village were assembled, it being the time of evening prayer. I rode up to one of these and and saluted with the usual Salám Aleekum, and was invited to sit down. When the prayers were finished, one of the men decently apparelled said to me : "Dondee kouree dil ter razee", which signifies if you will eat bread, come with me. I accepted the invitation and accompanied him to his tent, which was well furnished after the fashion of the country, and before the entrance were stationed three tolerable horses. The whole had an appearance of easy circumstances, or, indeed, of comparative opulence if the general poverty of these people be considered. Bread was cooked expressly for me, water was brought to wash my hands before eating, and I was encouraged to eat heartily. I felt perfectly at ease, and was doing justice to my entertainment, having eat nothing during the day, when another man came in and seated himself by my side. The repast being finished, my new visitant applied a rather rude slap on the cheek, at which I merely smiled, presumed it intended as a joke, and although a severe one, yet as these savages understand little of decency, and being alone among many, it was but common prudence to pass it off lightly. He then asked me for my upper garment. This I refused, still thinking him disposed to be merry. I, however, found to my cost he was not trifling, for he despoiled me of it by pure force, as well as of my head-dress, in short left me nothing but my pyjammas and shoes. He also applied two or three additional slaps on the cheek, and a liberal allowance of terms of abuse in Persian, which was all he knew of that language: this he did in ridicule of my ignorance of Peshto, which he was continually urging me to speak. During this time my worthy host, the master of the tent, encouraged and abetted my despoiler, and received some pice which were in a pocket of my upper garment. The clothes were detained by the other ruffian, who after a while conducted me to his tent, one much smaller and of mean appearance. He bade me sit down by the fire and warm myself, and in due time spread blankets on the ground by the fire side which were to serve me for a bed, and informed me I might repose myself, cautioning me, as I understood him, not to attempt to escape during the night, for I should certainly be seized by the dogs. I stretched myself on my sorrowful bed, and ruminated on my desperate situation, consoling myself, however, that it did not appear the intention of my friends to despoil me of my pyjammas, in the web cord of which I have before stated was my stock of money, and calculating on certainly reaching the kaffla the next day if suffered to depart in the morning, I should be able to repair my deficiency of raiment. Still my situation was very deplorable, particularly from the prospect of a long journey on foot, to which I had not been accustomed, as I could not hope I should be allowed my horse; yet from the fatigue of the day's march, the power of a naturally strong constitution, the presence of the fire, I shortly fell asleep, and enjoyed uninterrupted repose during the night, and awaking only in the morning when kicked by my host, who called me a Kaffree or infidel for not rising to say prayers, which ceremony he shortly afterwards performed on the very clothes of which he had despoiled me the preceding evening. I was now led into the tent in which I had been originally entertained, where several other men were assembled. Here I was beat with sticks and cords, and had some large stones thrown at me; in short, I made no doubt but it was intended to destroy me. I therefore collected my spirits and resolved to meet my fate with firmness, and betray no marks of weakness or dejection. Thanks be to heaven it was otherwise. I was asked if I was an Usbeck, an Hazarah or Beloche; the latter question was many times repeated, but I persisted in the negative, being conscious that the Beloche tribe were the enemies of these men (the Atchuckzye), and asserted that I was from Cutch Mekran, they not having the least notion of an European. This answer might have proved unfortunate, for I have since learned that the Mekranis are a Beluche tribe; but the geographical information of these savages was probably confined to the knowledge of the name of the districts immediately adjoining their own, and they stumbled over the words Cutch Mekran, without being able to divine what country it could be. At length the sun being considerably elevated, they dismissed me in the state of nakedness to which they had reduced me, telling me " Daggur lor de wurza," or take that road. I walked about thirty paces, a few stones being complaisantly thrown after me, when I was hailed by a man to return, and eat bread before I went. I was compelled reluctantly to comply, as a refusal might have involved my destruction, and the doing so again brought me in contact with the ruffians. Their consultations were again renewed concerning me, and I gathered from their discourse that it was in question to reduce me to slavery and bind me. My case now assumed a very serious aspect. I was not wholly depressed as I reflected that the road to Kandahár was large and well defined, and that any night would convey me to the Durrannee villages, where I knew they would not dare follow me. I therefore made up my mind to make the best of my situation, as to resist was impossible, and if reduced to bondage, to appear resigned and cheerful, by such means to induce my detainers to relax their precautionary measures, and avail myself of the first opportunity to escape. It now happened that I was observed by two or three aged venerable-looking men who were standing before the entrance of the tent on the extreme right of the semi-circle, which was larger than any of the others, and had before it a spear fixed in the ground, the symbol, I presumed, of authority. They beckoned to me, and I went thither accompanied by the men who had so ill-treated me, and several others. A question was put to one of these aged men, who I found was the Mulláh or priest, if it was not lawful and according to the Korán to detain me as a slave, alleging the singular reason that they had performed rites of hospitality towards me the night before. The Mulláh instantly replied that it was neither just nor lawful, nor according to the Korán, but decidedly to the contrary. Perceiving the Mulláh to be a man of some conscience, I asked him if he understood Persian. On his replying a little, I related to him how I had been treated. He expressed the greatest regret, and severely rebuking the offenders, urged them to restore my horse and clothes. This they were unwilling to do, and much debate ensued, in which being supported by the Mulláh I took a part, and ventured to talk loudly. To one of my questions to the man who had the most ill-treated me and struck me on the cheek if he was a Mussalmán, he replied—béshuk Mussalmán, or that he was one in every respect. I uttered the common eastern exclamation of "tofan" or wonderful, and the English one of "Lord have mercy upon the sinner." As if my misfortunes were never to cease, my money which until now had escaped observations was seized by one of the men who asked me what I had concealed there; the Mulláh desired him to desist, saying "oh, merely a few surafees or something of that kind, but the fellow wrenched out the net cord from my pyjammas, and with eyes glittering with delight, and a countenance, the expression of savage satisfaction which will never be obliterated from my memory, unfurled it and exposed to view the surafees. The Mulláh now assumed a stern authoritative tone, as did also the other inmates of the tent. He seized the robber by the arms, and ordered him to restore the gold and also my other property. The orders were obeyed, everything was restored, except the horse, concerning which severe contention ensued. Finding it unlikely that I should recover it, and delay being fatal to me, I begged the Mulláh to accept it, when the ruffians who would not deliver it to me felt themselves obliged to yield it to their priest. After receiving the benediction of the Mulláh I made for the high road. I might have proceeded one hundred yards or about when a man came running after me and, sword in hand, demanded my money. Observing two young men approaching with matchlocks, notwithstanding his menaces If refused to deliver it until their arrival. They fortunately understood a little Persian, and asserting that I was a stranger prevailed on the robber to depart. I asked them where they were going in the hopes of finding companions; they replied, fowling. Gaining the high road, I proceeded rather depressed in mind, as I could not conceive the ruffians of the village would suffer me to depart having had a sight of so much money, and with the almost certainty of being followed. For a considerable distance fell in with no one until I arrived at a spot where the road branched off in two directions, where was a grave newly prepared for the reception of a corpse and over which were seated fifteen or twenty men. I would have avoided their observation, but they discovered and hailed me, asking me if I had any snuff or tobacco. I replied in the negative. One of them came taking my arm led me to the grave, when I had to submit to a variety of questions, but was finally dismissed without receiving any injury. The road here gradually ascends for a short distance, and again descends. I had gained the descent when one of the men seated on the grave, who was without doubt one of the inhabitants of the village, as probably they all were, came after me and asked for my money. As he was alone and had no other weapons than stones I might have resisted him, but fearing the other men would come to his assistance, I produced the money and representing, as well as I could, that the road to Shikárpore was long and that food was requisite, I succeeded in preserving ten surafees. Chancing to make use of some expressions in which the word Mussalmán occurred, he took offence, and seizing my neck was about to proceed to acts of violence. I also assumed the defensive, deeming it as well to die fighting as passive before such a wretch, when some camels appeared on the top of the ascent with four or five attendants. He now loosed his hold as I did mine, and was about to depart, when I informed the camel-drivers of the robbery.

These men merely smiled, on seeing which he returned, and was willing to renew hostilities. It being an object with me now to accompany the camels who were going my road, and still having ten surafees and my clothing I used my endeavours to pacify him, which with some ado was accomplished. While a stone is within reach, the Patháns of these countries are never at a loss for offensive weapons. I have seen several severe wounds inflicted by these missiles. They assert that Cain killed Abel with stones, which appears to have established a precedent for their use. One of the camel-drivers told me to mount a camel, but I could not catch one. Learned that they were proceeding to Robát, having conveyed wood to Kandáhár, marched four or five kos, when they halted, and told me that they should go to Robát in the evening. I would have continued my journey, but alas! I was to encounter robbery anew. My clothing and ten surafees were now taken, and I was entirely stripped. In return for my pyjammas they gave me a ragged pair which did not cover the knees. My shoes alone escaped, being either too large or too small for their several feet. I did not part with my apparel or money very willingly or very peaceably; in fact one of the ruffians unsheathed his sword, but the others forbade violence. I appealed to them as men and Mussulmáns, but this only excited their laughter. I was still arguing with them, when two men made their appearance on the road. They now conversed with each other, conjecturing these might be companions of mine, and began looking at their means of defence. They however felt perfectly easy, being five in number and armed. These new men proved to be Hadjees, a name properly belonging to such as have made a pilgrimage to Mecca, but appropriated also by those who are going or pretend they are so. One of them had a smattering of Persian, and endeavoured, but ineffectually, to procure the return of my money, &c. As these men were proceeding to join the kaffla I accompanied them, the camel-drivers much wishing to detain me, wishing as they said to entertain me the night at Robát. I was now without money or clothing, a stranger in the centre of Asia, unacquainted with the language which would have been most useful to me, and from my colour exposed on all occasions to notice, enquiry, ridicule and insult. Still I did not despair, and although I never doubted or questioned divine providence, yet had I done so, my preservation in so many cases of extreme danger, the supply of my wants through so many unexpected channels, the continual birth of circumstances to alleviate or obliterate misery, would have removed my scepticism, and carried to my mind the conviction of the existence of an omniscient and benevolent being, who does not neglect the meanest being of his creation. It was some consolation to find that the kaffla was not far off, and in company with my new friends proceeded without apprehension of further plunder, having nothing to be deprived of, and moreover the satisfaction of being certain that any change in my circumstances must be for the better, as it could not well be for the worse. On the road first met a horseman of the Atchukzye, who desired and received the benediction of the Hadjee. This consisted in turning the back towards the Hadjee, who repeated or rather mumbled something which might or might not be Arabic, but is supposed to be so, in which the words *doneeah* or world, and *Bismillah* or God be praised were the only ones audible. At the close the Hadjee stroked his beard and gave the barbarian two or three slaps on the back, which completed the blessing. The Pathán salammed with much respect and departed well satisfied. In this rencontre I passed unnoticed. A little farther on met two men who came across the hills on foot, but tolerably dressed. They also received the benediction of the Hadjees and discoursed a short time, enquiring news of the Beloche tribes, who it appeared had but a few days before plundered the Atchukzye village. I afforded matter of mirth to these men, and they expressed themselves much surprised at seeing a man who could not speak Peshto. Until now we had been on either side surrounded by hills. They ceased here, and I discovered a plain of large extent bounded on all sides with hills utterly devoid of anything in the shape of trees, with two or three buildings in the distance, apparently the square forts—if such name they deserve—the common defensive erections of these people, and to which their skill in military architecture is hitherto confined. Beneath us on the high road, whose course being straight is visible for some distance, was a building with arched roofs after the Kandáhár mode, which on reaching found to be a houz or reservoir of rain water. The building was substantial and the water good; this is a work of utility, as there is no water between the villages. I left in the morning, and reached Robát, a distance I suppose of fifteen or twenty miles. At this houz the embers of the fires kindled by the men of the caravan who had halted here were still alive. About two miles farther on approached the assemblage of tents which are called Robát: these covered the plain to a large extent, and must certainly have comprised five or six hundred tents. My companions went to the nearest of these with the view of procuring food and lodging for the night, and directed me to a ruined fort where they told me I should find the kaffla. These Hadjees, or men representing themselves as such, are men who travel the country subsisting on charity, and as ignorance begets superstition and superstition begets dread, they are looked up to with much awe and respect by these savages, who tremble at the very name.. They are given the best of entertainments, in return for which they give blessings, or, if able to write, scraps of paper, which contain, as their credulous clients believe, preservatives, charms, and antidotes against all disasters and diseases. In these countries, where travelling to other individuals is attended with so much danger, and indeed impracticability, they proceed in perfect security and reap a rich harvest. In more civilized countries they are treated with less respect, and although their character for sanctity is not disputed, they are usually answered that Allah or God will supply their wants, and are reduced to sit in the masjids, the common resort of the destitute. On my road to the caravan was accosted by one of the Atchukzye, who asked me who I was. I replied a Hadjee, and he went his way making use of some expressions relative to the wretchedness of my condition. Found the caravan encamped under the fort wall, and joining them, it was no easy matter to satisfy the curiosity of the several individuals composing it, but this accomplished, I became an object of neglect, and I began to fear the possibility of suffering from want. Among these people I went to Kádur Khán, the most opulent man in the company, and stating my case requested his assistance during the journey. He frankly replied he would give me none. Night coming on, the fires were kindled, round which the individuals of the kaffla respectively grouped. Having no other clothing than the tattered pyjammas of the camel-drivers, and the cold being so intense that ice was found on water in the morning of thickness of perhaps three-quarters of an inch, I suffered accordingly, and ventured to approach the fires, invitation being out of the question. I did so only to meet repulses. I was rejected from all of them; some alleging I was a Kaffre; others, no reason at all. In this desperate state of affairs I was thinking of hazarding a visit to the village of Robát, when a poor but humane fellow came and led me to his bivouac. He said, he was but a poor man and lived coarsely, but that I should partake of his fare during the journey; that he had absolutely no clothing or I should not continue naked. My new friend named Mahomed Ali proved one of four associates who had two or three camels laden with pomegranates. I gladly availed myself of his offer and returned him my acknowledgments. He kindled his fire, and seated me by it, desiring me on no account to be sorrowful; that God was merciful and would provide every thing needful. I now became easy as to subsistence, and considered myself as one of the caravan, whose composition I shall here briefly describe. The principal member was Kádur Khán, one of the Barrakzye and son of Jummir Khán, formerly Hakim or Governor of Sirkárpore and now in the service of the confederated Sind Chiefs. Kádur Khán is engaged in traffic, which had led him to Kandáhár, whither he had brought his women and children. He was now escorting them back with a few horses. He had a number of attendants, and a plentiful show of tent equipage for the accommodation of his ladies. His nephew, Abdoolláh Khán, a fine young man of extraordinary height, also accompanied him. Next in importance was one they termed by way of respect Hakumzadah, who, I believe, was what is designated the Kaffla Kabashee, or director of the caravan, although Kádur Khán, or rather Abdoollah Khán, appeared to order the marches. There were also two or three Shikárpore Syeds, well mounted and apparelled, and a well fleshed jovial horseman in the employ of the Sind Chiefs; besides these a few poor traffickers who drove camels, asses, &c., laden with fruits, snuff, &c. This system of proceeding in caravans, absolutely necessary in such inhospitable countries as these, appears to have prevailed throughout the East in times of the most remote antiquity, the Patriarch Joseph, according to Moses, having been sold by his brethren to a company of travelling merchants. The same history, and at an antecedent period that of Abraham's connection with his slave Hagar, authenticates the existence of the slave trade in those early times, which is still carried on in all Mussulman countries; and slavery in some instances is deemed lawful by the Prophet. These caravans are under the direction of the bashee, who is generally some substantial man, and whose business it is to regulate the daily marches, and arrange matters with the authorities at several places where muscool or duty is collected. In recompense he receives a donation, more or less according to circumstances, from Saodágars and others benefited by his exertions. In these caravans the attendants on the camels, &c., are generally armed with matchlocks and swords, so as to be able to show face against the mere inhabitants of the countries through which they pass; but it sometimes happens that they are attacked by organized bands, when they are compelled to submit to plunder if nothing worse. A small caravan proceeding from Kandáhár to Herát was attacked by a troop of Ushees, and the whole of its members were carried off and consigned to slavery. I was seated with my new friends, when a youth, who was also travelling without means, came and said he would put me in the way of procuring food for the night. I paid no great attention to him, feeling easy on that account, but my companions told me to go with him. I therefore obeyed and was provided with a formidable long pole, for what purpose I was at a loss to conjecture, the youth and another Durannee destitute, but well dressed, being similarly armed. We then made for the village of Robát nearing which my associates commenced howling Allah, Allah, Allah, and the sticks, I found, were to keep off the dogs while the begging of bread at the several tents was carried on. The appeal for charity at no one tent was ineffectual, the inmates hastening to afford their mites, many even asking if flour or bread was needed. Our begging was carried on systematically, the youth, who appeared perfect in his part and accustomed to such scenes, going towards the entrance of the tents and stating we were Hadjees, while I and the Durrannee by plying our long poles had to contend with the dogs who assailed us on all sides as if conscious we were demanding the scraps which they considered their due. About thirty or forty pounds weight of bread was procured, of which I merely received as much as sufficed for the evening meal. The cold increasing as the night advanced I suffered much from the want of clothing. My companions on preparing for sleep furnished me with a quantity of wood to enable me to keep the fire alive during night, over which I was to sit. I did so with my knees drawn up to my chin, nevertheless the severity of the cold was severely felt. Towards morning my situation being observed by a Mogul soldier in the service of Kádur Khán, he came and threw over my shoulders a posteen, or great-coat, if I may so express myself, made of skins of doombas or sheep, the leather excellently prepared and the hair preserved. These are the general winter habits of all classes in Khorásán, and are certainly warm and comfortable. I endeavoured to rise and return my

B 1485—34

thanks, when I found what with the heat of the fire in front and the intensity of the cold behind my limbs were contracted and fixed in the cramped position in which I had been so long sitting. I now became alarmed lest I should not be able to accompany the caravan; nor should I, had it started early in the morning, as these caravans generally do, but this with a view to the convenience of the women, did not march until the sun was high above the horizon. This was a fortunate circumstance, as the solar heat gradually relaxed the stiffness of my limbs, and as I became warm in walking, the pain lessened. I know not whether to impute my misfortunes here to the presence of the fire or the cold. My legs and arms were covered with blotches, and at their respective joints were reduced to a state of rawness, while I was also afflicted with an involuntary discharge of urine. The rawness of the joints departed in a few days; the affection of the urine also ceased after some time; but the pains in the limbs continued to distress me seriously for four or five months, and have not wholly left me to this day, and probably never will. This present of the posteen was undoubtedly the means of my preservation, as I never should have been able to have passed another night, especially as for eight or ten marches the cold increased. The marches were not of extreme length, and I contrived tolerably well to keep up with the caravan, starting with the asses, who went on first, when, if unable to keep pace with them, I was sure of having the camels behind, who followed and were always considerably in the rear. In this manner I was secure from the interruption on the road by the inhabitants of the country. We made seven or eight marches, passing two extensive plains and their enclosing hills, the passes through which were none of them difficult, the country sterile and slightly inhabited. In one of our marches passed a body of men, women and children, migrating with their property to some more genial climate during the winter. The men had most of them matchlocks, but I suspect no ammunition, as they begged flints* and powder, and a small quantity of each given them elicited many thanks. Leaden bullets with the men of this country, I believe, are generally out of the question, having seen them in many instances making substitutes of mud, which they mould and dry, and with such projectiles they contrive to kill large fowls, &c. During our progress we one day fell in with a large deposit of wheat straw cut into chaff and intended as winter provender for cattle. This deposit was opened, and all the camels, horses and asses of the caravan were laden with its contents, Kádur Khán, and the basbee directing the operation and remaining with the mounted men while it was carried on. We here saw no inhabitants, although from this deposit, and the existence of water at some distance to the right, it was natural to infer there were some in the neighbourhood. I could not here help drawing a conclusion, that if these kaflas are liable to insult and extortion among these people, they in some measure deserve it. In no instance where plunder could be committed safely was it omitted. The sheep or goats that strayed into their track were invariably made booty, and if they met with but a few tents, they did not fail to procure flour, ghee, akrowt, &c., without payment, which the few inmates gave fearing worse treatment. At one of our halts by a pond of rain-water, a faquir mounted on a small horse without saddle came from an adjacent village which we did not see and demanded alms, expatiating much on the splendour of the tents and the wealth in the caravan. Abdoolláh Khán asked him for his blessing, and while he was giving it, some of the men were engaged in fixing a cord round the neck of a large-sized dog which accompanied the faquir, and they succeeded in purloining it without notice. At this halting place melons of large size were brought to the caravan for sale. The Hadjees as usual when any village was near went into it to pass the night, procuring better entertainment there than among the men of the caravan. Indeed through-

---

* Flints for the purpose of igniting the matches.

out Khorásán among the Durránees charity appears extinct, as does also, with few exceptions, the existence of any kind of social or benevolent feeling. On passing a third range of hills, on arrival at the intended halting spot, it was discovered that the heat of the season had dried up the water in the places where it was usually found. Kádur Khán was much mortified, there not being any spot so convenient for encampment among these hills, and it was necessary to pass the night among them, as it would take a day's march to clear them. Men were despatched on all sides to search for water, and one returned with a piece of ice which he exhibited as evidence of his discovery, but the water although near trickled from the crevices in the height above us, and would have been useless with respect to the animals, it being found in no place in quantity and losing itself among the rocks; moreover to encamp near it was impossible. In this dilemma two of the Atchukzye appeared; they stated they were acquainted with water very near, but would not discover it unless they received grapes, raisins, snuff, tobacco, &c., in short something of every thing they supposed might be in the caravan. Kádur Khán strove to induce them to moderate their demands, and much parley ensued. The gesticulations of the savages, had I been free from pain, would have sufficiently diverted me, as well as the stress they laid on water or "obo" as they call it, with the enormity of their demands. The Khán being unable to come to terms with them, gave the order to march forward. We now ascended a steep and difficult passage down which the water trickled in numerous rills; there was also much ice and many of the camels slipped, the women had previously been removed and seated on horses. This ascent naturally involved a troublesome descent, and we had to pass another elevation equally precipitous, on gaining which an extensive plain burst upon the sight. At the bottom of this hill we found a good place to halt in, and water from springs tolerably near. This was the only pass that could be termed difficult we had met with in our journey, and we observed another road to the left which it was supposed was more easy. In the morning continued our progress through a durrah or valley, hills on either side of inferior elevation. Here were numerous trees of the species called mimosas, from the trunks and branches of which gum plentifully exuded. This was eaten eagerly by the men of caravan, but I found it unpalatable. Arrived at a small hut constructed of the boughs and branches of trees. From this rushed two or three men who, under the pretence of examination with reference to duty, rifled all the packages carried by the asses, and forbade further progress until their claims were satisfied. These men refused either to give water or to disclose where it could be found, and only after receiving a quantity of tobacco would they give fire to enable the poor drivers to smoke their chillums. Both parties were still in full debate, when Kádur Khán and the horsemen, hitherto in the rear came up, and instantly ordered an advance, it being nonsense to hear duty talked of in such a place and by such men. I was indeed surprised at the audacity of these fellows, who were nearly naked; nor could it ever have been imagined that such miserable beings were entitled to collect duties. They were without weapons, and probably calculated on the stupidity or timidity of the ass-drivers, who they might also have thought were proceeding alone. During their search a korán received the marks of their respect, being applied to the eyes and lips. On clearing this durrah we entered the plain, to the right of which on rising ground stood a square fort, the residence of Abdulláh Khán, Chief of the Atchukzye. There were two or three trees near it—novelties in these plains—and slight cultivation of wheat and melons. Kádur Khán and his mounted men rode up to the fort for the purpose of arranging duty matters, and wished the whole of the caravan to have accompanied, but the men composing it would not consent, fearing the rapacity of the Atchukzye Chief should they place themselves in his power. We therefore, under the orders of Abdulláh Khán, the nephew, passed on, and crossed a small river, on which was a village, the houses built of mud. We then directed our course to the left making for a village, a circular tower in which was visible far off. Here we halted, the water-supplied from a pond, the river being considerably distant. Kádur Khán joined us, and expressed anger that the caravan had not accompanied him, as the matter of duty would have been terminated. The men who now came from the village to claim duty were most beggarly dressed, and without shoes. A most contentious scene occurred, their demands being exorbitant, and nothing that evening was settled. These officers of the customs stayed with us during the night, and were most oppressive visitants, admitting no refusal of anything they asked for. The next day passed also in stormy debate, and the evening approached without satisfactory result, when the Kafilaka bashee seized one by the neck and pushed him towards the horses, telling him to count them, it appearing that the number of horses in the caravan was disputed. To count twenty or twenty-five actually exceeded the raffian's numerical ability; it was necessary to count them for him. The spirited conduct of the bashee seemed to have its effect in bringing matters to a close. Money was now paid and matters were considered settled. The men did not leave us, and towards night urged fresh claims as to the asses, and they with their burthens went into the village for inspection. In the morning some fresh altercation ensued, and a well dressed youth made his appearance, who wrote Persian and officiated as secretary; nor was it until the day was considerably advanced that the kaffla was permitted fees having been given to the secretary and others. I could not estimate the degree of danger that attended our stay here, but Kádur Khán who, on the score of his family had the most to stake, was continually walking to and fro in great agitation, and frequently vented fervent ejaculations that he might safely extricate himself from the Atchukzye country. It would have given me much pleasure had I known Peshto to have learned what passed during the debates at this place, for undoubtedly much eloquence was displayed on both sides. I could glean that the Atchukzye ridiculed the menace of forcing a passage without payment of duty, and that they asserted it was much better to have Hindus to deal with, who without parley or hesitation paid five rupees per each ass, whereas they could only procure two from a Mussulmán, and that after much dispute. The two evenings we halted here the men of the village assembled in great numbers around us (for curiosity merely), and I noted that none of them had weapons, which perhaps are scarce among them. Abdulláh Khán their Chief had, I was informed, a piece of ordnance at his fort. Leaving this village our course led through a small space of jungle stocked with the jhow tree. Clearing this we halted between a village and a contiguous stream, the same probably we had before passed. The next day's march led us anew among hills, which passing arrived at another river, on the banks of which we halted, two or three villages bearing to the left with a few trees interspersed. These were inhabited by the tribe of Patháns called Alazai. During the night we halted here a robbery was committed on one of our Syeds, who suffered to the amount of one hundred rupees. His korán, which was carried off, was afterwards returned in a mysterious manner. The thieves were not discovered, but the Alazai had the credit of the robbery.

The next march was cheerfully performed, as it removed us from the country of the Patháns and brought us into that of Meeráh Khán, the Chief of Khelát. Here dangers to the same extent do not prevail, but in these semi-barbarous countries where tyranny and misrule prevail, oppression never ceases. This day I was so absolutely exhausted and my pains so severe, that I was utterly unable to keep pace with the caravan, and the camels even passed me. Leaving the river a village occurs, in which the men were employed in winnowing corn; they suffered me to pass unmolested. Beyond this is a karez of good water and a few trees (the barren mulberry), and farther on is the entrance into the small ridge of elevations which separate the Alazai from the valley of Sháll. Among these eminences I was compelled from the acuteness of my sufferings to cast myself on the earth, and truly death at that time would have been hailed as friendly. With much difficulty found my way into the plain, and in progress to the city, which is distant four or five kos, I replied to all I met that I was a Hadjee. I distributed several benedictions, consisting of a few lines from Shakespeare or any other that first entered into my head, which being unintelligible, was received with due confidence and respect, and arrived at Sháll at the close of day. Learned from one of the soldiers at the gate that the caravan was immediately under the walls of the town, and passing down the bázár, found Gool Mahomed, one of my companions, who conducted me to it. All were glad to see me again, fearing some accident had happened to me, and I amused them by relating my adventures as a Hadjee on the road. I may here observe that my situation in the caravan as regards attention and civility had become very supportable. Kádur Khán, who had refused me assistance, saluted me with congratulations the very next day when he beheld me comfortably clad in a posteen, and never passed me on the road without notice. The Kaffla Kabashee associated himself with my companions at their meals, I consequently ate with him, and was invariably treated with kindness. This man I afterwards saw at Hyderabad in Sind, where he is engaged in the military service at a salary of Rs. 200 monthly.

Before continuing my narrative I shall note a few remarks on the country and manners of the people we had just left, with some reflections suggested in my progress, which I previously omitted fearing they might break in too much upon the connection of my personal narrative. The tract of country between Kandáhár and Sháll, computed at one hundred and fifty kos of road distance, or perhaps of as many British miles direct distance, is inhabited by a tribe of Patháns called Atchukzye. This tract consists of three distinct extensive plains separated by ranges of hills possessing considerable elevation. These two first plains exhibit a series of sandy undulations, in the hollows of which are the villages or tents of the inhabitants; in the latter and more considerable plain, in which resides the Chief, the soil is more level, and better adapted to agricultural purposes. Trees are not seen in the country, if we accept a very few near the fort of Abdulah. The villages of tents are moveable, their position being governed by the supply of water and food for their cattle. The cold in this country during the winter is much more severe than at Kandáhár, where snow is very rare, yet the climate on the whole may be considered temperate. We found the heat oppressive about noon during two or three marches, but this arose from the local character of the plains we were passing. The Atchukzye have large flocks of doombas or large-tailed sheep and goats with numerous camels and a few horses. These derive their sustenance generally from the stunted herbs, &c., of their plains, among which, one of considerable fragrance, is excellent for the sheep; their horses subsist on grain and the chaff or chopped stalks of wheat, there being no grass whatever. The people themselves live nearly independent of any extraneous supply, meat being furnished by their camels and flocks, from whose milk they make a variety of preparations as ghee, krout, &c. Cheese is not in use. Their bread is made from their own wheat, which they raise only in such quantities as may suffice for their wants. Their tents appear intended as much to protect their stock as for convenience to themselves; their wheat or flour being put into carpet bags of size with reference to the burthen of a camel and piled up on three sides, the space in the centre being occupied by the family, affording but little room, when the tent is small and the family numerous. Their horses are picketed in front of their tents, and their camels, sheep, &c., are lodged for the night in enclosures to the rear defined by prickly herbs, &c. For fuel besides wood, which in some places is scarce, being procured at great distance, they make use of the dung of their camels. The tents are generally arranged in a semi-circle, the musjids or spots made to answer the purpose being always centrical. With the wool of their sheep and the hair of their camels and goats, they manufacture a variety of articles, such as rugs to repose on, Kashers or great-coats, and numerous articles of clothing made from camel hair. The beating of wool with wooden mallets into a consistence proper for their woollens is the principal occupation of the women during the day when not engaged in more urgent or culinary duties. These rugs and blankets they carry to the towns and vending them procure linen, loonghees and shoes; their ghee also forms an article for sale as do their sheep and goats. They also barter with the passing caravan for such articles as they stand in need of as snuff, tobacco, &c. The poorer class are very meanly clad, generally with skins of sheep or goats, or the coarsest specimens of their woollens. Their feet are usually naked; indeed they appear not to need shoes, as on a journey walk barefoot, with their shoes carried in their hands. Throughout Khorásán this fashion prevails. The dress of the women consists of gowns or petticoats, the covering for the breasts fancifully decorated with strips of various colours. The hair of the head is braided, and a plait of it hangs immediately down the centre of the face, to which are attached rupees or other trinkets. This has naturally the effect of producing an inversion of the eyes, a defect which may possibly be deemed a grace by the gallants of the Atchukzye. Their domestic utensils are few, the more substantial have ewers of Kaliad copper, serving as drinking vessels or for ablutions preceding prayers, perhaps a dish or two of the same metal, or of wood to contain their food. Their bread is placed in carpet bags. Water is lodged in mussacks or the skins of sheep and goats. Most of the women have their breasts and arms covered with figures traced in with blue lines; I believe indigo is employed. From whatever cause this custom may have had its origin, it appears to have been practised by all savages in all ages, by the ancient inhabitants of Europe, and at the present day by the South Sea Islanders and the colonered natives of America. Among the tribes of Patháns, such as the Atchukzye, Gulzye, Alazai, &c., it is general as regards the female portion of society, and I believe is prevalent in India and China. Owing to their regular and temperate mode of living longevity is general amongst them; the smoking of tobacco and the use of snuff are the only luxuries they allow themselves. My intercourse with them did not afford me an opportunity of ascertaining their diseases or their remedies. I remember an instance of a woman with inveterate sores in the neck, which I take to have been the scrofula or king's evil. In considering the manners of these people attention must be paid to the character of the country in which they reside, and their political situation, both of which have unquestionably an influence on their dispositions. Nature in the Atchukzye country exhibits none but harsh features, the sterile plain, and rugged mountain. Nurtured in these rude scenes of solitude, the mind receives their sullen expression, and from circumstances deprived of the benefit of education to direct the reason, it degenerates into absolute barbarism. The oppression of the Durannees who exact tribute, tends also to exasperate their minds, and the recollection of the devastation occasioned by the march of the armies, induces a spirit of retaliation, which is exercised as occasion offers. The bad conduct of the men of caravans passing keeps alive their resentments, and preserves in full energy an anger become implacable, which might probably by kind and generous treatment have been softened or subdued. Owing to these causes, and poverty, and the lack of instruction, the Atchukzye have become more infamous for robbery and inhospitable manners than any of the other Pathán tribes. In religion, if it consist in matter of faith, they are Mahomedans of the most bigoted description. On no account will they dispense with their daily orisons, the casual omission of one of which through sleep or any other circumstances would be deemed a great misfortune. Punctuality under this head, and observance of the fast prescribed by the Koran, appear to be considered by them sufficient for their salvation and to efface all their crimes of rapine and murder, which never occasion them the least concern, in fact rather furnish matter of triumph and congratulation. This strange reconciliation of crime and prayer, while it denotes a deplorable state of society, is observable in all Moslem countries, and is occasioned by the ignorance of the Mulláhs or priests, and the consequent want of religious instruction. Among the Atchukzye and other Pathán tribes, the learning of the priests amounts to the ability of repeating prayers, and relating legends and traditions of the most extravagant character. No falsehood, however egregious or revolting to reasor, is too much for the belief of these poor individuals. Tradition, which has its origin in truth, becomes adulterated in its course as the river which issues clear from its springs loses it purity by the accession of muddy and tributary streams. The narration of the Patriarch Abraham's trial of faith may be adduced as a moderate specimen of traditional distortion. This narration, as given by Moses, is clear and equal to any comprehension. The following is the version received of it in these countries: The Patriarch proceeding to put into execution the divine command, applied a bandage to his eyes, and, as he believed, cut the throat of his son, whom he had previously bound, but in reality that of a sheep which the angel had substituted. In the agony of his mind he flung the bloody knife into the air which struck a locust, descending it glanced on the hump of a camel, and thence fell into a river and wounded a fish. From that day they assert, locusts, camels, and fish became *halál* or lawful as food, which they were not before. I may also note here, as connected with tradition, the practise of shaving the hair around the circumference of the mouth in commemoration of Abraham's connection with Hagar, the mother of Ishmael.

The Atchukzye, as do all the Pathán tribes, deduce their ancestry from the Patriarch Abraham, and amid their ignorance and barbarism, look down upon all other people with contempt—a species of conceit not peculiar to them. In former times the Jews looked with horror upon the uncircumcised nations around them, the Roman citizen considered the alien as his inferior, and the country of Cyrus was deemed barbarous by the polished inhabitants of Greece. Their language called Peshto, they assert to be coeval with the religion of Mahomed, with which it took its birth. Rejecting this hypothesis I presume it may be referred to the confusion of tongues at the tower of Babel, as it has every sign of being an original one. It possesses, I conceive, some affinity with the ancient Syriac, and is undoubtedly a strong, energetic, and I judged sufficiently copious. A few words have been borrowed from the Persian, the characters of which are employed to express Peshto in writing, it having no peculiar signs or characters. This language is very difficult to acquire. It extends over an immense tract of country from Meshed to the Indus; indeed in the western parts of the Punjab it is the current language, as it is of all the Pathán nations, the Afgháns and the Hazará Tartars towards Balk and Bhokara:—Yuk, one; do, two; drai, three; soloor, four; spinz, five; spa, six; of, seven; ot, eight; no, nine; lus, ten; yolus, eleven; dolus, twelve; drailus, thirteen; soalus, fourteen; spinzalus, fifteen; spalus, sixteen; offalus, seventeen; ottalus, eighteen; nolus, nineteen; shell, twenty; ho, yes; neeteer, no; oar, fire; rora, bring; spind, white; dondee, bread; obo, water; core, home; sind, river; spoe, dog; tumla, wood; ruppie, shoes; horse, horse; willow; push, cat. It is singular that they have the same appellations for a horse and the willow tree as in the English language, and I smiled when the thought struck me that we might be indebted to Peshto for a word to describe that noble animal. The term push for a cat is similar to the English familiar one of puss.

Continuation of Personal Narrative.

The caravan halted two or three days at Sháll to arrange the affair of duty, which is collected there, and to allow men and cattle a little time, having made fifteen marches from Kandáhár. My pains grew intense, so much so that I was unable to accompany my friends, who departed. At Sháll I was very hospitably treated, lodged in a warm apartment, and provided with abundance of good provisions. My afflictions daily became less, and at length announced my ability to proceed whenever the kaffla might arrive. Two or three companies of merchants bringing horses from Khorásán passed, but

I was not allowed to accompany them, it being feared that I could not keep pace with horses. Finally a large multifarious caravan arrived from Kandáhár, which I joined, provided through the bounty of a Biccaneer Brahman with a quantity of flour for the journey. I had also received from the same man a linen dress, of which I had been before entirely destitute. The caravan was directed by one they called Beloche Khán, and consisted entirely of traders bringing fruits, &c. There were no Hindus in this or in any of the caravans I had seen coming from Khorásán. The first day's march, a short of four or five miles, brought us to the extremity of the valley, where to the right we encamped near a kareze of excellent water, but no inhabitants. Here we were joined by a migratory tribe of Beloche who were going to the warmer climate of Harree. To our right here through a pass in the hills led the high road to Mustoong and Khelát, and to our left the high road to Shikárpore, which we were about to trace. The town of Sháll is one of some extent, contains a small bázár of Hindus, and is the place of rendezvous for the caravans coming from Kandáhár and Kábul; hence its traffic is considerable. The town is enclosed with mud walls, and comprises a citadel, or inner fort, erected on a mound of earth of great elevation. The valley may be about ten or twelve miles in length and on an average three miles in breadth. It is well supplied with water, and besides good wheat, produces several kinds of choice grass. The gardens, which are numerous around the town, appear but lately planted, the trees being young. They have the vine, the fig, the plum, and the pomegranate trees, and I believe the apple and pear; they have moreover abundance of melons and mulberries. The town of Mustoong, distant sixteen kos, is particularly famous for the latter fruit. I was much pleased with the climate in this valley, the frosts during the night being gentle, and the heat of the sun being far from oppressive during the day, as is the case in Kandáhár even during the winter. The people told me in another month they might expect snow, which would continue two months, during which time they would be left to their own protection, the garrison retiring to the warmer country of Dardar; and I saw them engaged in repairing the casualties in the town walls. There is some little danger from their troublesome neighbours, particularly from those in the adjacent hills, who are notorious thieves. The outsides of the Mussalman houses in this town were covered with salted sheep, from which they extract the principal bones and extend the carcasses in the air, these serve for the winter consumption. Besides Sháll there is another considerable village on the opposite side of the valley which has also a bázár, and there may be seven or eight other small hamlets, and near the town are two or three forts or rather fortified residences of individuals, which are large. From the kareze the mussacks being duly filled with water, we proceeded for small distance parallel with hills, then striking across a plain approached the bulk of the great range of mountains which spread from China and Tartary to the ocean. We entered a durrah or valley, and after a long march halted at a spot where there was no water. The company here were highly amused by a witty fellow named Shabbadeen, who personated one of the Atchukzye and proffered to show them where obo or water could be found; he imitated their modes of expression exactly and extorted loud peals of laughter from his audience. In our next march from the hills, to our right water gushed in large volumes, and formed a splendid scene; hence the valley became well stocked with streams. We halted this day on a small table ground, opposite to us in graceful majesty stood a solitary date tree, the emblem of our approach to a warmer climate. We had hitherto seen no inhabitants, but occasional tracks across the hills seemed to indicate their existence. During the night the sentinels were particularly alert, keeping up an incessant discharge of matchlocks. Our next march continued through the valley, and after crossing a river brought us to an open space, to the left of which was a small mud village with a square tower and slight cultivation. We passed on to the right and took up our night quarters near the river just mentioned, which flowed in this direction, and was henceforward to be our companion through the valley. The following day our course through the durrah was rendered troublesome, the river winding from one side to the other, and sometimes filling the entire passage. It continued in this manner during the whole of our progress, nor ceased until we gained the plain of Dadar, where the river takes its course to the left. In this march, being as usual behind the caravan, perceived three men on the hills on a great elevation above me; they discharged their pieces, but their distance was too great to cause me uneasiness. I however received a caution not to lag behind my companions.

The magnificent pass we had now cleared is throughout its whole extent perfectly level, and the scenery in many places of the most sublime kind. It is a singular circumstance connected with it, that in the one-half of it in the cold season intense cold prevails, the standing water being ice-bound, while in the other half at the same season it is so warm that deficiency of clothing is not felt. The men of the caravan asserted the medial extent of this pass to be the point where Hindustán and Khorássán met in this direction. When I reflect on this pass and others that I have met with, I could not forbear the impression that they were intended by nature for the convenience of man, and that the Almighty who has created mountains as boundaries of states and empires, has also in his wisdom decreed these passages of communication to promote the intercourse of their inhabitants, and to afford them the power of mutually contributing to the wants and conveniences of each other.

At a short distance from the hills were seen some large old tombs and other ruinous buildings, in some of which exhibited a style of superior architecture. We passed these the next day, when our march consisted merely of a change of ground, and brought us within a mile from the town of Dadar and near the high road from it to Bhag. My feet being blistered the last day's march through the pass, I did not visit this town. It appeared in the distance to be of some extent and tolerably well built. The Hindus of the bázár resorted to the caravan to traffic. We halted here two days, duty being levied, when our company augmented by some Beloche traders, we started for Bhag. The hills in this part of the country form a vast semi-circle, the main chain stretching away to the right, while others of equal elevation bear to the left bounding the country of Dadar and approach the Indus in the neighbourhood of Sungáh and Deyráh Gházie Khán. They are inhabited by savage tribes, whose predatory habits render them a great annoyance to this part of the country, as they frequently issue from their fastnesses in great numbers and plunder and devastate the villages. From the one range to the other extends a Jubbul or small rocky chain which encloses the Dadar District. At Dadar there were numerous trees of the date and other species, and this abundance prevails along the entire base of the hills to the left. The heat here is very considerable, so much so that the unburnt bricks of the buildings have become of a red colour. Through the rocky Jubbul just mentioned our road led, the pass being perfectly level, perhaps a mile and a half or two miles in length, the elevations on either side were remarkable as having an artificial aspect. In this march I was seized with vomiting, occasioned, I believe, by the water I had drunk at Dadar. I was constrained to halt on the road, and the caravan passed me. I was lying in the shade produced by a rock when two or three horsemen of the caravan who had remained behind came up. (I may observe we marched during the night on this occasion, the distance to the halting place being considerable, and no water to be met within the intermediate space.) These men kindled a fire and smoked *charas*, an intoxicating composition in general use throughout this part of Asia. I was encouraged by them to proceed and did so for a short distance, when again assailed by my new disorder, I left the road, and found near the dry bed of a nála or small stream, and reposed a while under the shade of its bank. My strength a little renewed again, followed the road, and after four or five kos' march, arrived (being evening) near a village. Here was a river, to which I hastened to appease my thirst, and on traversing a ravine to regain the road, was attacked by a ruffian with a naked sword, who ordered me to accompany him. Clearing the ravine, he examined my posteen, and the goat skin bag which contained my provisions. Much debate ensued, he insisting I should follow him, and I unwilling to do so. I told him if he was a robber, as he was superior on account of his weapon, to take what he wanted. To this he replied by putting the forefinger between the teeth, and shaking the head, I presume significant that he was not one. I was unable to prevail upon him to suffer my departure, and was reflecting what fresh adventures my compliance might involve, when a Hindu suddenly made his appearance. Neither I nor my oppressor had before seen this man—an angel could not however have more seasonably interposed—the fellow reluctantly yielded to my departure, and I with the Hindu passed over to the other side of the ravine, when the latter made towards the village, and I took the direction of the road. The robber, who had remained stationary, on seeing me again alone called to me to come back and threw stones, a rather singular method of inducing my return. Having the ravine between us and descrying three or four men in a cultivated field adjacent, I paid no attention to him, and he shaped his course across the plain telling me to go on. My escape from this man I consider most fortunate, as he would probably have sacrificed me when at a due distance from the village, or, had he not done so, but taken me to the hills, my life would have become one of painful slavery. He may have had companions at hand, but be this as it may, there were no villages or inhabitants between us and the hills, the plain from the level character of its surface being visible the whole extent, nor could the hills have been nearer than thirty to forty miles. I now went to the men in the field and related to them how I had escaped robbery, when my tattered garments were again explored, and certainly had I had any thing worth the plunder it would have been taken here, as it was, one of the men remarked, what could be taken from you, and in the same breath asked me to exchange my shoes for a pair of chopplas. I refused, as the shoes, although old and absolutely worn out, had become convenient to my feet; yet my refusal was of no avail, and the shoes were taken from me, the men asserting that I gave them with a good will, and I, that they were forcibly taken. It was moreover promised that a youth should conduct me to the caravan which had marched about two kos in advance. On hearing this I became more tractable, intending to have detained my guide until the shoes had been restored. However on putting the shoes on his feet, the man said they were not worth exchanging, and returned them. He now put his fingers on his eyes and assured me that he was a Mussalmán and no thief, and invited me to pass the night at his house, where I should be well entertained. I might have trusted myself with him, as this application of the fingers to the eyes among Mussalmáns is equivalent to a most solemn oath, but it was my object to gain the caravan. Therefore declined, and the road being pointed out, struck into it. Night with its companion darkness coming on, repaired to some old sepulchres or Zeearuts to the right of the road, as well to elude observation if followed by any of the villagers as to await the rising of the moon, the better to find my road. By the light of the moon I proceeded, but in a short time it was evident I had quitted the high road, and being ignorant of its direction, I laid myself down on the ground, and wrapping my posteen around me, resigned myself to sleep. Arose with the break of day, and not far off, perceived a man of respectable appearance, of whom I enquired the road to Bhag, stating that I had gone astray. He lamented that I had been compelled to sleep in the open air, to which however I had become familiar, and going out of his own track conducted me to it. In a short time met a village situated on a river. I had before lost the road, which is very imperfectly defined, but was guided by the prints of the feet of camels and of the caravan. The river flows between high banks, and at this season of the year had a considerable body of water. I descended and followed the direction of the right bank, which enabled me to pass the village without observation. A little past this, I halted and took my scanty breakfast, soaking my scraps of bread like the barber of Gil Blas in the water of the stream. Here I was accosted by a youth, who also wanted to exchange shoes. He had himself a new pair, and perfectly sound. The exchange would have been to his prejudice, but I declined, and he did not insist. The brother of Meerab Khán with a party of horse was encamped near this village. From the bed of the river passed through a jungle swarming with people—the migratory tribes of Belochistán—who had recently arrived here and taken up quarters for the winter. The town where the caravan had stayed the night contained some good houses, and the domes or goomats of its musjids were seen at some distance. Found the caravan had left it early in the morning and proceeded to Bhag; enquired the road of a Hindu, who directed me, but cautioned me to go alone. I went on, having in fact become indifferent to danger. On the road was passed by three Beloche soldiers mounted on camels. One of them said to me in Persian—Ah! Ah! you are an Usbeck. I told him I was not; but he maintained that I was laughing and in perfect good humour. This was not the first time that I had been taken for one of these Tartars. In the town of Sháll notwithstanding my own asseverations, and their confirmations by some of its inhabitants that I was an European or Ferang, several believed that I was an Usbeck, and the Mulláh or priest who officiated in the principal musjeed informed a large company with an air of great self-satisfaction that I was a Turk, nodding his head and winking his eyes, as if his superior penetration had discovered an important secret. At this town I was daily visited by a woman who brought me always some little present as sweetmeats, &c., and implored my blessing. Not wishing to offend her, I went through the forms, but I could not conjecture why she considered me qualified to give benedictions, when one day I heard her tell another woman that I was the idiot from Mustoong. Idiots, who in Europe are lodged in "lespetites maisons," being held in veneration in Mussulmán countries.

Continued my route, and after a march of seven or eight miles passed a deserted fort, and a little farther on, came to a small village enclosed with walls. I passed without notice, and as night drew near came to a cluster of houses and population I presumed to be Bhag. It being perfectly dark, and not wishing unnecessarily to expose myself, I made no enquiry as to the kaffla, but quietly took up my abode for the night in a Zeearat. In the morning found that Bhag was distant about one kos, the latter part of the course led along the banks of the stream I had before seen. The country here was populous and well cultivated; indeed for eight or ten miles round this town cultivation is more or less general. The soil is fertile, producing sugar-cane and many kinds of grain, particularly jowár, of which the major part of the inhabitants make their bread. In a field of jowár there are always two species, the stem or cane of one of them having a saccharine taste little inferior to that of sugarcane. Sweet jowár is recognized by the natives on an inspection of the leaves and is eaten by them in the same manner as sugarcane. I was informed sugar could not be extracted from it. Trees are numerous, consisting chiefly of mimosas, and the tree yielding an inferior fruit called bair. We halted three or four days at Bhag, duty being again levied, and some sales were effected with the Hindu dealers, when crossing the river at a small ford, proceeded on our march to Shikárpore. We made, I believe, three marches and arrived at the last village in the Bhag District, beyond which stretches a barren uninhabited space of eighteen or twenty kos. During this part of our progress we passed immense fields of jowár, but most of the villages were deserted, the inhabitants having fled before the hill marauders who had secured the country. There is considerable danger from these mountaineers in passing the desert track which was now before us. The director of the caravan therefore determined to make one march of it, and we started at the approach of night, continued walking the whole of the night and next day passing in our track a tomb to the left, the elevation makes it serviceable as a point of direction, there being no beaten road. Once during the day a cloud of dust being observed, the caravan was halted, the men with matchlocks assembled, and the horsemen took up position in front, the dust, being merely the effect of whirlwind, subsided, and the journey was resumed. This space, on many parts of its surface, was strewed with the quills of geese and other fowl, it being during a portion of the year covered with water. Arriving at a wooded jungle and making a course of two kos, we reached Rojan in the evening. This town is subject to Meerab Khán of Khelát, although from its geographical position, and the slight distance between it and Shikárpore it would seem naturally to be dependent on that city. Here was a bázár, and around much cultivation of jowár and cotton; also species of plant yielding oil. Water is here of bad quality and procured from a series of wells of little depth immediately under the walls. The inhabitants of this town, of the Beloche tribe of Magsi, have been lately nearly exterminated by another tribe called Rind. Our next march led us to Jaggem, distant six kos, our course led through jungle interspersed with occasional villages and cultivation. Tagaum is surrounded with walls and has a good bázár. It is under the authority of Shikárpore, one of the governors of which, Cássum Sháh, a Mogal Syed was there on our arrival, and visited the caravan. Duty was paid here for the last time, and the next morning to my great joy we marched for Shikárpore, another six kos. Shikárpore is a city formerly of opulent and commercial note, the ramifications of its connections extending to the most remote parts of Asia. It was particularly celebrated for its numerous bankers and immense money transactions. It is still principally inhabited by Hindus, but the changes in the Government of these countries has injured its importance and sensibly affected its traffic. It will be remembered that the expatriated king of Kábul, Sháh Shujáh, resided here about two years, when through complicated treachery he was compelled to fly, and the city fell into the power of the Sind Chiefs. They now exercise the authority, and their deputy or governor occupies the palace of the Sháh. The annual revenue of Shikárpore and the district surrounding it for about fifteen miles under the regal sway amounted to eight lákhs of rupees; at present about two lákhs and a half can only be raised by the most oppressive extortion. Of this two-thirds is handed over to the rulers of Hyderabad, and the other third to Meer Shrob of Kirepore. The houses of the principal Hindus are distinguished by their loftiness and extent; and indeed in all countries I have seen these people appear to be more attentive to the conveniences and enjoyments of life than the supine Mahomedan, who is content to reside in a wretched dwelling and satisfy himself by stigmatizing his more enlightened neighbours as dogs and infidels. The bázár is extensive and well supplied; the principal parts of it are covered, so as to moderate the heat, which is very powerful. In this town, as common with all Indian cities, is the usual inconvenience of narrow and confined streets; nor is too much attention paid to cleanliness. There are numerous musjids, two or three of which only deserve notice. Numerous wells are interspersed within the walls, and the water is esteemed good. Shikárpore may be considered a city without defences, its dilapidated walls and crumbling bastions being no longer capable of excluding an enemy. It may be observed in all cities, however, of importance which were once subject to the Government of the Afgháns, that the fortifications have been suffered to decay and have never been maintained or repaired. This arises from the natural character of that race of men who despise fortresses and artillery and place their dependence on cavalry and the sword. The town is surrounded with numerous gardens furnishing mangoes, mulberries, bananas, melons and other fruits. Provisions were here formerly remarkably cheap; they are now equally high priced, duty being exacted at the town gates on the most trifling article of consumption. The neighbouring lands produce wheat, jowár, cotton, and an oleaceous plant. The grass is very plentiful and luxuriant, particularly towards Loll

Khonnor; hence milk and its preparations are good and abundant. The traffic in linen is still considerable. Shikárpore in former times was celebrated for the number of the caravans that visited or departed from it; at present they are but few, owing to the deteriorated condition of the various countries of Khorásán, and the introduction of base coin in Katoal and Kandáhár. Shikárpore is about eight kos from the Indus in the direction of Kirepore, sixteen kos from the fort of Bukkur and the town of Roree, and twenty-one kos from Loll Khonnor. About four kos from Shikárpore on the road to Roree is a considerable town which supplied under the Pathán authority one lákh of rupees to the revenue. It is now absolutely deserted and is the abode of thieves, who infest the vicinity of the city. In the same direction on the borders of the Indus and opposite to Bukkur and Roree is the town of Sukkur, once large and flourishing, but now also deserted and in ruins. It is lamentable to observe the change which a lapse of fifteen or twenty years has occasioned in this district, and whatever may have been the nature of the Doorannee or Afghán Government, it appears to have been sufficiently mild, and to have afforded protection to its subjects, which is vainly looked for from the Sindee sway, robbery and murder being committed under the very walls of Shikárpore. The part of Belochistán traversed in this route is subject to Meeráb Khán, whose capital is Kalort, famous for a citadel erected by Nádir Sháh; it is usually termed Brohee by the inhabitants, and is generally fertile. It formerly appertained to the kings of Khorásán, but was granted in full sovereignty by the Doorannee Ahmed Sháh to one of his generals Nasseer Khán,' father of the present ruler, on account of his valour in the field. Khelat, when mentioned by a native, is usually styled the Kalort of Nasseer Khán. The present Chief, inferior to his father in valour and capacity, acknowledges the supremacy of Kandáhár, to which he pays a small tribute. I have heard the revenue estimated at six lákhs of rupees, the military force at 5,000 men, principally horse, with six pieces of ordnance stationed at Kalort. This country I shall again more particularly notice in a memoir on Belochistán generally.

(A True Copy.)
(Signed) D. WILSON,
Resident, Persian Gulf.

Notice on the Countries West of Indus from the City of Deyráh Gházee Khán Kollecbat: by Mr. C. MASSON.

No. 4.

Deyráh Gházee Khán is a large city, formerly of great commercial note, but its importance has declined owing to the political changes in that quarter. It contains several extensive and lofty dwellings, and many of its musjids have been costly and handsome, numerous gardens are interspersed within the city and in its environs, and it is surrounded on all sides by vast groves of date trees, whose fruit forms one of its principal branches of traffic. There is a square erection in this city designated the fort, but of no consequence as a place of defence. The necessaries of life are here abundant and reasonable, as are most of the articles esteemed luxuries by the natives of these countries. The town and district of Deyráh Gházee Khán on the dislocation of the King of Kábul's authority were taken possession of by the Sikhs, who have subsequently let it to the Khán of Bhawalpore for three lákhs of rupees per annum; he, it is asserted, procures five lákhs; it formerly yielded ten or twelve lákhs. The city is seated two kos west of the river. The neighbouring lands are fertile, producing besides wheat, sugarcane and a variety of vegetables, as turnips, carrots, spinach, and even a few potatoes. Milk, ghee and butter are also plentiful, the vicinity of the river and the numerous small channels which flowing from it intersect the country being favourable to the grass of its jungles. From Deyráh Gházee Khán to Sungah, a distance of thirty kos, the road leads

B 1485—37 ←

through a jungle, more or less intense, but containing many villages and cultivated spots, Sungah, a town of small extent, has a fort, the residence of Assut Khán (Beloche), who rules this petty state. He has three pieces of ordnance and retains in pay about 1,000 troops, 700 of whom are mounted and reputed brave soldiers. The fort, considered strong in these parts, is in reality of no value as a place of defence, its walls being even falling, and it has no trench. It is built in a rectangular form, the sides containing many bastions ; those at the angles are strengthened by outworks; the entrance faces the north, in which direction the town is situated. Besides this fort Assut Khán has another within the hills about five kos distant, also reputed strong. I did not see it, but conclude it is seated near a pass in the hills through which a road leads through the country of Kákur to Kandáhár, sometimes frequented, as I afterwards learned, by caravans coming from Deyráh Gházee Khán. The revenue of the principality of Sungah may be about Rs. 1,50,000 annually, of which 30,000 are paid to the Khán of Bhawalpore, who is however under the necessity of sending an army to procure it. Sungah lies about a kos west of the river. The dependent district extends about twenty-five kos north, where it joins a small tract of country occupied by the Sikhs ; to the south towards Deyráh it may embrace ten or twelve kos. The villages throughout this country are numerous, but the dwellings are miserably built of mud. The land sufficiently fertile and the pasture abundant ; hence milk and its various preparations are plentiful and cheap. This is the case along the whole course of the Indus, large herds of buffaloes and cows being seen in all directions. The milk of the former is preferred and is procured in larger quantities from the animal. I found it extremely sweet and pleasant, while that of the cow was comparatively insipid. Turnips in these quarters attain an enormous size, and are cultivated generally as food for cattle. Forty kos north of Sungah is the town of Deyráh Futteh Khán, which, with a small portion of country on either side, is held by the Sikhs. The town is small, but the bázár neat and well supplied. About a kos west of Deyráh Futteh Khán is the fort of Gerong. I did not see this structure, but agreeably to report its walls are of considerable thickness and are garrisoned with some pieces of artillery. This is the only tract of country retained in absolute possession by the Sikhs to the west of the river, they appearing generally averse to the establishments on that side, Deyráh Gházee Khán belonging to them being let to the Bhawalpore Chief, while tribute only is exacted from the conquered countries as far north as the Pathán State of Ráwul Pindee. The retention of so strong a fortress as Gerong appears to have caused them to deviate from their general plan. The district moreover is very fertile, and from its flourishing condition affords the evidence of being under a mild and protecting Government. From Deyráh Futteh Khán, tracing the banks of the river, we arrived after forty kos to Deyráh Ismáil Khán, the country, as usual, consisting of jungle and occasional villages ; but these are not so numerous, nor is the cultivation so general as in the more southern lands. The ancient town, or we may perhaps say city, of Deyráh Ismáil Khán, was seated on the bank of the river, and is reported to have been very large and to have contained some capital buildings. It was washed away by an inundation two or three years since, and so complete has been the destruction, that scarce a vestige of its existence remains. The new city is built two kos from the river and will probably be of a large size. The bázár is spacious and of convenient breadth—an improvement in the general plan of Indian cities, whose bázárs are usually of all parts the most narrow and confined. On the casualty to the old city, the little village of Morally became of consequence, and the new city being built about two kos from it, it will probably in time be incorporated with it, buildings and serais for merchants and their effects already nearly stretching over the intermediate space. Deyráh Ismáil Khán is one of the greatest marts on the Indus and is the entrepôt for the merchandize of India and Khorásán passing in this direction, the duties levied on which form the principal part of its Chief's revenue. The new fort is not one of strength, the Sikhs forbidding a substantial erection. It is small, of a rectangular form with circular bastions at the angles, on which are mounted six pieces of ordnance taken in an engagement with the troops of Ták. The walls are lofty without a trench. There is a minor fort which contains the residences of the Chief and his family, protected by a trench, and its faces are defended by jungles. The district immediately dependent on Deyráh Ismáil Khán extends about forty kos in a northerly direction and about twenty-five kos to the southern. Its Chief, moreover, exacts tribute from most of the petty rulers around him, such as Durrahbund or Drabind, as here pronounced, lying off the Deyráh District and between it and the hills Kolychee, also in the same direction north of Durrahbund, and from Esau or Issa Khéte, and Kolybah on the banks of the Indus, as well as from the Patháns of Murwut. The father of the present Chief or Naváb, as he is styled, possessed an extensive tract of country on the opposite or eastern side of the river, to wit, the fertile and populous districts of Monkurah and Ducker, while on the western side his authority extended to Sungah. He was dispossessed of his country by the Sikhs, to whom he made a brave resistance and died shortly after. They have assigned the son, Sheer Mahomed, the present Naváb, a slip of land west of the Indus, for the support of himself and family. His revenue may be about three lákhs of rupees annually, derived principally from the duties collected at Deyráh on the transit of merchandize. This includes also the several sums received from tributary Chiefs. The Sikhs take one-half of the gross amount. I know not the number of troops retained in pay, but on an expedition that it was found necessary to make to Murwut, 2,500 were assembled, of whom 2,000 were horse, furnished, I should suppose, principally by those who hold lands on condition of service. The artillery consists of six cannons, four of them serviceable. Seven kos northwest of Deyráh is the small town and fort of Kooyah, containing a garrison of about fifty men. This is the frontier post on the side of Ták. Twelve kos north is the town of Sarpore, situated under the hills. Besides these there are no other villages deserving the appellation of towns, if we except Morally, which I have before mentioned. The water at the new city is supplied by wells, and but of indifferent quality. Did the ruler of this country possess the means or the spirit requisite for the undertaking, the supply of water from the contiguous river would be highly advantageous to his capital, and its vicinity would become productive and populous. Near Kooyah also are streams which are never dry, whose waters might be conducted through various channels for the benefit of the cultivators of the land. The country in the neighbourhood of the city is extremely level and would yield a luxurious cultivation had it but the necessary supply of water. The jungle is generally slight, consisting principally of the Karectah tree, which with its handsome red flowers assumes a very gay appearance at certain periods. In the vicinity of the villages are invariably a few bair trees, the fruit of which is generally eaten, and occasionally a few trees of the Palma recinus, from the nuts of which castor-oil is extracted. This plant is very ornamental, and its tufts of crimson blossoms are superb. Our garden flower, the stock, is indigenous in these parts, and is found of diminutive size. The district of Durrahbund is subject to the authority of Amir Khán. His revenue I should suppose about 60,000 or 70,000 rupees annually, of which he pays 20,000 to the Naváb of Deyráh. This Pathán Chief generally resides at Gunderpore, a large village, but the capital is Durrahbund, romantically situated on the very elevated banks of a hill stream which flows beneath it. This town has a small bázár and has some large houses, deserted and in decay, the inhabitants (Hindus) having fled. The water of the stream is reputed unwholesome, the townspeople drinking that of a small cut north of the town. The neighbourhood of this town is agreeable, and the heat is not so intense as the Deyráh. The bulk of the hills may be about two kos distant, ravines or broken ground intervening. A few vines and fig trees are in the gardens of Amir Khán, who has a house here; and apples are produced in some of the adjacent villages, small in size and few in quantity. The cultivation, which is principally wheat, is generally distant from the villages; and at the harvest season the bulk of the inhabitants abandon their dwellings until crops are collected. At such times there is considerable danger from the Vizeerees, who issue from the hills, and murder as well as plunder. Durrahbund has been frequently visited by these marauders. The villages in the district of Durrahbund amount to thirteen; these would not supply the revenue of its Chief, which I have stated at Rs. 60,000 or 70,000 rupees per annum, but as a considerable portion of it is derived from the Loharnee or migratory tribes of Khorásán, who annually visit and remain in these countries during the cold season. These tribes settle more or less along the tract west of the Indus and between it and the hills. In Durrahbund they are particularly numerous, and as in other places, pay a certain sum for the sufferance of their settlement. In this district, at the close of the cold season, all the tribes assemble; their traders who have proceeded to the various parts of India arriving by the routes of Bhawalpore, Multán and Lahore. When in a collective body they proceed through the district of Ták, and paying an impost to its Chief, collected at the fortress of Durburra, they enter the hills, and forcing a passage through the hordes of the Vizeeree that infest them, proceed to their several destinations, when the merchants spread themselves over the adjacent regions, even to Turkistán and Bokhára, vending their merchandize and procuring horses for the ventures of the ensuing year. Omer Khán retains 180 foot soldiers in pay. Kochee district, enclosed by the lands of Ták to the north, by the Deyráh and Durrahbund domains to the east and south, and by the grand chain of mountains to the west, is governed by Muzuffer Khán. The town of Kochee is very commercial and has a large bázár. The revenue of this district may be perhaps a lákh of rupees, of which 20,000 are paid to the Naváb of Deyráh. The number of troops retained in pay I know not, but suppose 200 or 300 men. In the Deyráh Chief's expedition to Murwut, Mozuffur Khán, as his dependant or ally, proceeded with a force of 700 men. This number will not coincide with the amount of his revenue, but he probably on this occasion drew out the strength of his country, in which the major part of the proprietors of land hold it on conditions of service. Moreover, it must be remembered that all the men of these countries consider themselves as the servants of their respective princes, and from their warlike dispositions they are easily assembled. In noting the military strength of these and other Pathán states it must be held in memory that the number of troops retained in pay do not only constitute it, which in fact consist of their levies *en masse*. By these, when speaking of their numbers, the natives always calculated, and their statements usually exaggerated as to the stipendiary soldier, may approach the truth if applied to the levy *en masse*. Kolychee district does not include a great number of villages, the eastern portion of it being scantily supplied with water, and the western extending to the hills consisting of ravines and thick jungle, and liable to incursions from the robbers of the Vizeerees. In these jungles wild hogs are numerous, and are objects of chase to such of the opulent as follow that amusement. Melons, which are common in all these countries, are particularly fine at Kolychee. North of Kolychee, encircled by hills to the west and north and by the lands of Deyráh to the east, is the country swayed by Serwar Khán, the Chief of Ták, who from the amount of his wealth and the extent of his authority, is generally termed a Naváb. This district is well watered, having two or three considerable streams; consequently its produce is abundant. In all these regions the soil being fertile water is the desideratum. The town of Ták is surrounded with a mud wall and has numerous gates; the wall is neither of any height or breadth. Within the walls is a citadel, in which resides the Chief, which is large and protected, or I should say strengthened, by a broad and deep trench. The walls are very high and constructed with bricks; the bastions at the four angles are ample and provided with twelve or thirteen pieces of artillery. The interior of this fortress is very intricately disposed, and the present Serwar Khán, who planned it, appears to have been determined to place it out of the power of his neighbours to drive him out of his nest. It is the most regular and massive piece of defensive erection in these countries, if Gerong perhaps be excepted, which I have not seen. Ták is famed for its fruits, which are plentiful and cheap; its gardens furnish large quantities of grass, oranges, citrons, plums, apples, &c. East of the town is an immense grove of Shahtoot trees, which have attained a size superior to any I have elsewhere seen. The bázár of this town is not large, nor is its commerce very extensive. The revenue of Serwar Khán is estimated at one lákh to one lákh and a half of rupees annually, the Sikhs occasionally paying him a visit and exacting a portion of it. He is represented as having hoarded much wealth in coin and jewels during the early part of his reign. He was the sole proprietor of the lands in his country, the peasants being merely his slaves; hence he derived the profit on the whole produce. The history of this Chieftain is singular and may deserve notice. He had scarcely seen the light, when his father, who also ruled at Ták, was slain by a traitor who usurped the authority, and to confirm himself therein slew all the family of his former prince with the exception of Serwar, who, an infant four or five days old, was placed by his nurse in an earthen jar and carried out of the town on her head, she asserting at the gates that she was conveying a jar of milk. She succeeded in clearing the country, and brought up the young prince as her son. When he arrived at the years of discretion, she informed him as to the circumstances of his birth. He thereupon presented himself to the king of Kábul and demanded an armed force to enable him to recover the possession of the lands of his ancestors. This was granted, and he in turn slew the usurper with all his relatives; then placing their heads in a heap he seated himself thereon, and summoned the several leaders in the country, demanding if they were willing to recognize him as their lawful ruler seated on the musnud. He repaired, or, I may say, rebuilt the town of Ták, and arranged the fortress with a view both to security and pleasure, and appears to have devoted himself to the amassing of wealth and the gratification of his sensual appetites. His zenana contains about two hundred females, and he and his family freely indulge in the luxury of wine, although he forbids its use by others on the score of morality and obedience to the precepts of the Korán. When I saw the costly decorations of his residence, the disposition of his gardens filled with flowers of a thousand herbs, the lakes of water on which were floating hundreds of geese and whose bosom reflected the image of the orange and citron trees with their glowing fruit waving on their margins, I could not but pay homage to his taste, and there needed but the presence of the ripened beauties of the harem to have presented a complete picture of Eastern magnificence. As it was, my mind was filled with astonishment in beholding such a display in so obscure a part of the world. Serwar is now advanced in years, and his eldest son, Alládát Khán, is useful to him in the direction of affairs. This young man may be considered a drunkard, yet is much beloved in the country for his valour and generosity. In a war with the Deyráh Naváb, four or five years since, Alládát commanded the Ták troops, about 4,000, the greater portion Vizeeree auxiliaries or mercenaries. These fled at the commencement of the action, leaving the guns exposed, which were captured. Alládát highly distinguished himself, working two of his guns after it had been deserted by its attendants, and standing by it until two cuts of the sword had been made at him by Serin Khán, the commander of hostile force, who recognized him; then only was he induced to mount his horse and provide for safety. Peace was purchased by the payment of one lákh of rupees. Besides Ták there are two or three large villages and several which have small bázárs. The fortress of Durburra belonging to Ták is situated in the mouth of a pass of the hills seven kos from the capital; its walls are surprisingly lofty and have a singular effect when seen from the distance. In the immediate vicinity of the town the villages are very numerous and the cultivation general. Towards Kooyab and Deyráh they are less so, but the cotton plant is plentifully raised. The country between Koondee, the frontier post on the Bunnoo side, and the hills which immediately divide it from Bunnoo, is uninhabited and consists merely of ravines. The troops retained in pay I should compute 500 men. The artillery, I have before stated, at thirteen pieces, which may be increased, as Alládát Khán has acquired the art of making cannons. Ták is deemed insalubrious, particularly to strangers. The water with which the town is supplied is said to be very pernicious and impure. The Naváb and family make use of that from a stream about two kos distant, which is a good sanative. The insalubrity of Ták may be accounted for by the extreme heat and its local situation, as well as in the quality of its water. The approach to Ták from the Deyráh side for about two miles leads through an avenue of full grown trees, principally mimosas, from which gum is collected. The common fruit-trees called bair are spread over all this country. The inhabitants throughout the space of country here described speak the same languages—a dialect of Hindustáni, here called Indee, and sometimes Peshto or Pathán. Their usages and manners are also nearly similar; those of the north being perhaps more hospitable than their countrymen in the south. In religion devout but ignorant, they entertain a deadly enmity to the Sikhs, whom they regard as their particular antagonists from the circumstances of the *báng* or summons to prayers being inderdicted to Mussalmán, in all countries under Sikh control. Diseases of the eye, particularly cataract, are very prevalent, and arise from the extreme heat and its reverberation from the white surface of the soil. In the Ták country an inflation of the abdomen is frequently imputed to the bad quality of the water. Beyond Deyráh Ismáil Khán, distant forty-five kos is the town of Issa Khéle, belonging to Ahmed Khán, who pays tribute to Deyráh. This Chief has a few horsemen in pay. The town is seated on the banks of the river and has some fine gardens. Kolybah is also a small town north of Issa Khéle, famous for its mountains of salt. Its Chief pays tribute to the Naváb of Deyráh, and I believe also to the Sikhs.

(A True Copy.)

(Signed)   D. WILSON,
Resident, Persian Gulf.

Adventures in a Journey from Ták to Desháwar through the unfrequented Countries of Murwut and Bunnoo, the Valleys of Angoo, Kivort: by Mr. C. MASSON.

No. 5.

The more secure road from this part of the country to Desháwar leads along the banks of the Indus to Kolybah, famous for its salt mountains, and from thence to Kivort, or as it is also called Bungush; but as this route had before been traversed by Mr. Elphinstone, I resolved to pass by the dangerous one of Murwut and Bunnoo. Such is the reputation of the Patháns inhabiting these countries, that faquirs even are deterred from entering them. Placing my trust in divine providence I resolved to commit myself among them, and accordingly left Tak alone towards the evening. After a course of about five or six miles northerly, the clouds gathered and threatened rain. I made to a village where I seated myself under the shade afforded by a Kareetah bush. The rain descended and continued more or less until the approach of night, when I left my quarters and entered the village to procure a place to repose in. Repaired to a company of individuals who were seated in a small hut or shed. Entered into discourse with one of them, who questioned me as to my country and religion. I answered him a European (for of an American they have no notion) and a Christian, when he informed the company that our Saviour or Hazrut Esau was an *usseel* or genuine Pathán. This information made me an object of much curiosity; a fire was kindled that they might the better observe my features. The best entertainment that the village afforded was produced and in such quantities that I was compelled to cry quarter. The informant, who I found was a Syed, made himself particularly busy, and provided me with a snug place to repose in and plenty of warm clothing. In the morning four or five kos cleared one of the villages of Ták, and I steered direct across the country towards a point in the encircling hills through which I was given to understand the road led to Murwut. Arriving at a cultivated spot with outhouses, where some people were engaged in cutting the corn, and enquiring of them as to the road, they strongly urged me not to proceed, for alone I should infallibly be murdered. Their representations were so forcible that I was induced to take their advice, and proceeded on a westerly direction with the view of gaining a small town and fort called Kundi, which they designated, and from which the high road led to Murwut, and where I might possibly find companions for the journey. In my progress to this place was met by a man who drew his sword and was about to sacrifice me for an infidel or Sikh. I had barely the time to inform him that I was a foreigner or European, when he sheathed his weapon, and placing his arms around my waist conducted me to a village near at hand, where I was hospitably entertained. Learned that Kundi was still a kos distant, to which I continued my route. Near this town an old man tending goats seized a small bundle I carried in my hand; he had merely a stick and I could certainly have vanquished him, but shame deterred me from striking so aged and enfeebled a being, Other persons made their appearance and obviated the necessity of a violence. The old man swore on his faith as a Mussulmán that he did not intend robbery, and alleged that he supposed I was a Hindu. I was now led into the village, and refreshed myself with bread and butter milk. I was here informed to my great satisfaction that a party was then in the village who would proceed in the morning by the route I intended to go, their destination being Peshawar. I found this party to consist of a Syed of Peshawar and his attendants by a Munshi of Serwar Khán, the Chief of Ták, who had two fine camels in charge as present to Sultán Mahomed Khán, one of the four brothers of the Barrackzye in authority at Peshawar. I was politely received and my new companions promised to attend to my wants during the journey. Kundi had a fort, the residence of Ahmed Khán the Governor, who commands a garrison of one hundred men, this being the frontier post on the Bunnoo side. This garrison I found was necessary, for towards evening the alarm was beat and the soldiers hastened to the plain, the marauders of Bunnoo having issued from their hills and approached this place. They however retired, and Ahmed Khán before re-entering his fort exercised his few mounted attendents in firing and throwing the lance. The greater part of his soldiers were on foot—men of small stature and clothed in black. I know not to what race or zát they belong, but they are peculiar to these parts. We were provided with a repast of fowls in the evening and early the next morning proceeded, accompanied by a guide, for Murwut. A march of about seven kos, the road tolerably good, brought us to the mouth of the pass, when our guide solicited his dismissal, urging his dread of proceeding farther. The passage through these hills, which are of small elevation, was generally wide and convenient. About midway were a number of wells, or natural reservoirs of water in the rocks, where numbers of people—men and women—were engaged in filling their mussucks or skins, which they transport on asses and bullocks. They had come hither five and six kos, belonging to the villages on the plain of Murwut. The water may be good and wholesome, but was rendered unpalatable, having imbued a taste from the numerous mussucks continually plunged into it.

On gaining the ascent of the last hill in this range, on which was an extensive burial place, the plains of Murwut and Bunnoo burst upon the sight, the numerous villages marked by the several groups of trees, the yellow tints of the ripe corn and the fantastic forms of the surrounding mountains in their union presented a splendid scene. The distant mountains to the west surmounting the inferior ranges exhibited a glorious spectacle from their pure whiteness and azure tints. To these must be added the beauty of an unclouded sky. I was lost in rapture on the contemplation of these still and serene beauties of nature, and awoke from my reverie only to lament that villainy of man should make a hell where nature had created a paradise. These moments of real enjoyment belonging exclusively to the man of taste and reflection are one of the benefits derived from intellectual improvement. Such moments I have often experienced in the course of my peregrination, when I have set at defiance the perils that environed me, and exulted in my temerity which has afforded me the opportunity of beholding scenes of beauty and wonder denied to many. Often have I exclaimed in the words of Addison: "My toils repaid by such glorious sight." Three or four kos brought us to the first of the villages which we passed and successively several others. During this part of our route I went to some reapers at a little distance from the road to ask for water. In learning that I was an European, they put themselves to the trouble of fetching some which was cool and lying under the shade. At length entered a village where we found the people in a group seated on an elevation of earth raised near the masjid, engaged in discourse and smoking the chillum. Similar erections are found in all the villages of Murwut and appropriated to the same social purposes. Buttermilk was brought to our party. The houses were neatly constructed, principally of reeds, the heat of the climate and the scarcity of rain rendering more substantial dwellings unnecessary. In each village were two or three Hindu traders. An additional march of two kos, during which we passed a large pond of rain water, brought us to a village where we halted during the heat of the day which was very oppressive. I was here civilly treated, and attracted much notice. I was conveyed to the masjid, which was neatly and commodiously built on an elevation; a cot also was given me to repose on, and large supplies of bread and milk were brought. Moreover the village barber was produced and cut the nails of my fingers and toes, and my friends continued their various attentions, until I signified my wish to take a little rest, when they left me. At noon left this town for Lukkee, a town distant about six kos, to which the plain gradually descends, a river flowing in the hollow. At a small distance from the village descended into a ravine of surprising depth. On this passage so intense was the heat that perspiration was copiously excited, and I could not help thinking that had a Homer or a Virgil been born in these rigions, this spot would have been the entrance to their infernal mansions. Arrived at Lukkee towards evening—two or three villages with much cultivation extending to the left. This is a town with a bázár of some extent situated on a fine stream; it may be said to have no fortress, the residence of the chief authority or Mulláh as here called not meriting that appellation. We were here provided with fowls for our evening entertainment, and in the morning were allowed a guide mounted and armed with sword and spear to conduct us to the villages of Bunnoo. Crossing the river, which at this season of the year (I believe about the month of May) was but knee-deep, we ascended the gentle rise of the opposite plain, on which was situated a village, into which our Syed did not think prudent to enter. Our guide however went there to obtain some information relative to our route before we attempted it. This gained, we proceeded across a barren uninhabited plain, in extent about ten kos, speckled with small stunted trees and bushes, generally thorny mimosas. On one spot were two or three holes containing muddy water, sufficient to allay the thirst of the casual passenger, but not so for the wants of large parties. Passed a large burial ground and neared the villages of Bunnoo. It may be noted that in all Mussalmán countries, or at least such as I have visited, the burial-grounds are invariably at a considerable distance from the habitations, and, if possible, eminences are selected for their sites.

Although in general the dwellings of the living are not conspicuous for splendour of decoration or even convenience, the abodes of the dead are often constructed with much expense, and it is on them that their taste in architecture is chiefly displayed. On arrival at a place where were deposits of muddy water, we found six or seven thieves. They did not however attack us, our party being protected by the sanctity of the Syed. I was about helping myself to water from the deposit near to which they were standing, when they pointed out another spot where the water was more pure. The river of Murwut and Bunnoo was again passed; its course was very rapid over a stony bed, the depth shallow, and gained cultivated ground near the villages. We halted at a town called Nuggur, of tolerable size and walled in; but its defences were considerably injured by time. The bázár I did not see, but conclude it pretty large from the number of Hindus I observed. We were duly provided with lodgings, and the Mulláh came and sat with us bringing his musicians and hawks. He was a young man dressed in silk and directed much of his attention to me, and what I would wish to eat in the evening. He further wished that I should write him something that he might wear round his neck as a charm, and on my assuring him that I possess no supernatural power or secret, our Syed scribbled on a scrap of paper probably a verse of the Korán, which was received by the Mulláh with all due reverence. The giving charms and antidotes against diseases is one of the modes employed by Syeds and others in these countries to impose upon the credulity of the ignorant. Matters were going on very amicably when a soldier recognized in the horse of the Ták Munshi or Vakíl an animal that had been stolen from him. Much altercation now ensued, the Bunnoo people insisting upon the delivery of the horse and the Munshi refusing, asserting that his master had purchased it. This dispute detained us the next day, nor were we suffered to pass the following one until papers were given, and it was agreed some one should proceed to Ták to receive the value of the horse. This animal was singular and named by the people the European horse, being branded with numbers and a cross and had been, as they asserted, rejected from the British cavalry service in India. The affair arranged, we again started, and in our progress were saluted by all we met with a cordial shake of the hand, and the Peshto greeting of *Urkorlar rashur*, or are you come happy. I knew not how to reconcile this friendly reception with the character for ferocity I had heard of these people. This day marched I suppose about ten kos, the country well watered and cultivated; the water conducted through artificial channels, and attention to its due distribution appears the principal duty of the agriculturist. In the plains of Bunnoo every house is a fort, and it would appear that the mutual enmity existing among the inhabitants renders it necessary. The advocate of anarchy in contemplating such a lamentable state of society might learn to prize the advantages conferred by a mild and well regulated government, and might be induced to concede a little of his natural right in preference to existing in a state of licentious independence as the savage of Bunnoo, continually dreading and dreaded. Near the houses or forts were generally small gardens of mulberry trees and occasionally a few plum trees and vines. We halted this day at another good-sized town, and were kindly received by the Mulláh. He was very civil to me, and greatly wished me to stay some time with him and repose myself, pointing out the toils which would attend the long march through the hills in front which he thought I should not be able to accomplish, my feet being already blistered. He assured me every attention should be paid me, and a goat should be furnished every day for my food. In the evening he ordered some of his men to practise firing at a target for my diversion. We occupied the principal masjid, in which the effects of the party were lodged, and the saddles of the camels which were plentifully garnished with silver ornaments covered with cloth the better to elude observation. The men of the party had gone to the Mulláh's house, leaving a youth of twelve or fourteen years of age in charge of the property. I was also

b 1485—39

reposing there. The youth closed the doors of the masjid and fastened them inside, refusing admittance to some persons, who it proved were weavers of linen, and accustomed to lodge their machinery in the house of God. They insisted an entrance; the youth was stedfast in his denial, and we were assailed by stones ejected through the appertures in the walls for the admission of air. These raiued in upon us so plentifully that the urchin opened the door, when the camel saddles were uncovered and the silver decorations exposed. The youth was severelly beaten by two or three of them, and he in turn spying the Munshi's sword unsheathed it and compelled his assailants to fly. He followed them into the town. As matters thus stood, the Syed and his companions returned, one of whom was instantly despatched to inform the Mulláh of the outrage, but it proving that no offence was intended, the affair terminated. The people were particularly anxious that I being a stranger should be convinced that no robbery was designed, and that the saddles were uncovered merely to satisfy curiosity. The next morning provided with a guide to conduct us through the mountains, a small horse being presented by the Mulláh to our Syed, we continued our journey. Two or three kos brought us to the entrance of the hills where we found natural reservoirs of excellent water. The whole of this day's march was passed in the ascent and descent of mountains of great elevation. We passed two or three houses of the Vizeeree, and halted a while at a spot where were two or three vines hanging over a spring of good water; Here we were joined by several persons, although we did not see their habitations. We did not consider ourselves among these hills in particular danger, having the Syed with us, as the Vizeeree, although notorious robbers in common with other barbarous tribes, look upon the descendants of their Prophet with peculiar awe and respect, and esteem themselves happy to receive their benedictions, which they (the Syed) liberally bestow, as they cost them little, We at length passed under the hill, on which is seated the ancient fortress called in the countries Kaffre Kote, or the fort of the idolaters. Similar edifices exist in the valley of Khyber. On the ascent of the hill opposite to this fortress the rock was so arranged that I was doubtful whether it was the office of art or the sportive hand of nature. They had the appearance of decayed buildings, while on the verge of the hill was a parapet of stones, so regular that I could not absolutely come to a decision as to its origin, and I much regretted my being unable to stay to have satisfied myself. Kaffre Kote is asserted by the natives to have existed before the Mahomedan invasion of India. The stones employed in its structure are represented of immense size. I have been told by a gentleman who visited it that he did not consider it so ancient, as there are embrasures for artillery in the bastions, but this is no evidence of a recent foundation, as the Mussalmáns assure you they have been since added. The fort has been abandoned some years, the water being procured at some distance. Night approached and we were still among the hills. We however cleared them to our great joy and passing perhaps two kos over a broken and stony plain, in which I found the white pink growing abundantly in a state of nature, arrived after the period of the last prayer at a village seated under another range of hills, where we halted and were entertained the night. This march my friends computed at twenty-four kos of road distance, and from its difficult nature my feet became exceedingly painful, although I had occasionally been seated on the horses and camels. At our entrance into this village our guide from Bunnoo took his leave, sayiug that the people here were his enemies; he hoped we were satisfied with him and shook all our hands in turn. With the break of day ascended the hills, our route over which was visible from the village. We passed three successive grand elavations and crossing a small stream took a northerly course, hitherto our road leading west, and halted at a small village under the hills to the right during the day. In these hills pomegranate and other fruit-trees were general. The valley we were now passing leads to Angoo and Kivort, its scenery extremely diversified, and the trees, many of them of the flowering species, were numerous. There were two or three villages under the hills to the left, built of stones, as are all the houses in this valley. Fruit-trees were always found near the villages—the vine, the plum and the peach. I was so exhausted this day that I lagged behind the party, the man in charge of the camels having declined to allow me to ride although solicited by the Syed. It may be noticed that on passing the stream this day the party refreshing themselves with the water, a tin vessel was given to me by the Syed, who afterwards replenished it and handed it to one of these camel-drivers, who refused to drink from it as I had used it, asserting I was not a Mussulmán. The Syed smiled. I always found that in all large cities, the low and ignorant, especially such as had visited Inda, would reject any vessel I had touched, alleging that Europeans eat swine and moreover dogs, jackals &c. With men of sense and condition I was always treated with perfect equality and heard of no such indecent remarks. I am speaking of those of the Suni persuasion. The Sheeas are more tenacious. The party preceded me, and ignorant of the name of the town in which the night would be passed, followed the main road and arrived at a spot where the road branched off in two directions. I was here directed by a shepherd to take the right direction who had been instructed by my friends to point it out to me. I was soon overtaken by an armed man, but I could understand little of what he said, he making use of the Peshto dialect. In company with him arrived at a village where I found the Syed and his party and where we passed the night. It was named Mudkozah and there were a few Hindus resident. From this village marched in the morning along the level valley, the road bearing parallel to the hills on the left; two or three villages were seated to the right, and the cultivation was more or less general. Along the road passed occasionally small groves of mulberry and other trees where musjids were erected, which had each its dependent well of water, serving at once for places of repose and refreshment to the weary traveller, and for devotion, the union of these two objects I judged extremely decorous and commendable, and as reflecting credit on Mussalmán manners and hospitality. On the extreme summit of a lofty hill was a white tomb, visible at some distance, arriving under which in a recess of the hills was the small town of Angoo with numerous gardens or orchards of fruit-trees in its vicinity. My friends had passed on as I was unable to keep pace with them. I was here conducted to the Chief Suddoo Khán, the son of Summut Khán, who resided at Kábul. He received me courteously and gave orders for my entertainment. I accepted his invitation to repose a day or two, the road not being now so dangerous, and should recover my effects which were with the Syed on arrival at Pesháwar. Angoo has a small bázár, the houses of which are built of mud. The fort was built of stones and defended by a few jinjals. The situation of this little town is very pretty, and it is supplied with water which issues from the rocks contiguous and forms a stream which winds through the valley in the direction of Kivort. Here were the apple, the plum, the peach, the mulberry and sheettoot trees. I also descried the bramble or blackberry bush scrambling over the hedges. Suddoo Khán had a small flower garden, which he tended himself. The young man was a devout Mussulmán, and one of the few that I have met with that I could consider sincere in his devotions. My entertainment was of the best description. Two or three days after my arrival intelligence was received of the approach of a hostile force from Pesháwar. Suddoo Khán collected the revenue of his country and proceeded to Kivort, where his elder brother Ismáil Khán resided, but finding it impossible effectually to resist, he returned with the brother to Angoo, and taking all his effects, jinjals, &c., with him, evacuated the country and proceeded by a mountain route to Kábul. With Ismáil Khán were two or three elephants, and a numerous zenana. I now left Angoo, and proceeded along the valley. The scenery was extremely beautiful and diversified with large quantities of mulberry trees in all directions. Villages occasionally occurred, in all of which I was kindly received. Met a reconnoitring party from the Peshawar force; was asked a few questions, but the Chief politely assured me he had no intention to molest me, being a stranger. At a small village called Lo was induced to stay a day by a Syed who would not admit refusal. Here were abundance of springs of excellent water and gardens of plums and vines. In this as in all the other villages the Hindus had deserted their dwellings, having paid the year's impost to their former ruler and fearful of being compelled to pay it anew. From this village continued my route and meeting with another party of mounted men was searched so roughly that my linen was torn. I appealed in strong terms against such usage, and addressed myself to the Chief, who expressed his regret that my linen had been rent. He ordered his foot attendants to escort me to Peer Mahomed Khán, one of the four brothers in authority at Peshawar, and who commanded the invading force. The Doorannee troops were encamped near at hand under the shade of the mulberry trees, and I was led before the Chief, who returned my salute, the man with me informing him that I had been met on the road and had no papers. This man was dismissed, and I was taken to the Darbár. Peer Mahomed appeared very sulky and did not address a word to me, but at times taking a minute survey of me. The various Sirdárs however were very civil and supplied me with fruits. During the audience several messengers arrived, all announcing the departure of the two brothers from Angoo. Peer Mahomed hypocritically expressed his satisfaction that they had taken to the prudent part and declined a battle, observing that they were his relatives and Mussalmáns. Shukkoor Khán, the second in command, a frank young man and a good soldier, seated me by his side and gave me his hookah to smoke. The darbár being closed, a repast being announced in the tent of Peer Mahomed, the son of Abdoolah Khán, a principal Chief, seized my hand and led me to his bivouac, telling me I must spend the day with him. I did so and was treated with much attention. Next morning the troops marched for Angoo, artillery being discharged in honor of the conquest of the country, and took the direction of Kivort. This spot was situated midway between the two towns, being six kos distant from each. There was a petty village seated round an eminence in the midst of the small valley, on the summit of which was a well-built tomb. After about three kos the valley opened and discharged a large plain, in which stands the town of Kivort. Here I was received at the house of a Mulláh or priest. This town is seated principally on a lofty eminence, and is walled in. Its appearance is very ancient. The citadel is small and weak, serving for the abode of the Chief. The bázár is pretty considerable. There were many vines in the neighbourhood, and in a garden was a mango tree, the only one of its species so far north on this side of the Indus. The principal masjid is a handsome edifice, and adjacent to it are public baths, the water pure and delightful, issuing from the rock on which the masjid stands. The water of Kivort is particularly esteemed for its sanative qualities; that of Angoo, although beautifully clear, reputed unwholesome. The districts of Kivort and Angoo belonged to Summoo Khán of the family of the Barrackzye, who resided at Kábul, and his two sons exercised the authority. The revenue of Kivort is estimated at Rs. 80,000, that of Angoo at Rs. 20,000, annually. About this time the Chiefs of Kandábár and Peshawar jealous of the prosperity and growing power of Dost Mahomed, their brother in Kábul, had concerted a plan to attack him on either side. In furtherance of the combination the Peshawar troops were to seize Kivort, the proprietor, Jummut Khán, being in the Kábul interest, after which they were to march on that city by the Jallálábád road, while the more considerable army from Kandáhár advanced on Ghiznee. The plains of Kivort and valley of Angoo are well cultivated and populous, producing besides rice and wheat a species of excellent jowár, from which excellent white bread is prepared. Large quantities of melons are raised, and fruit is particularly plentiful. There are few streams of water, and the scenery of the Angoo Valley is extremely picturesque. The climate appeared genial and temperate. The plain of Kivort appears on all sides surrounded by hills, on the summit of one of which to the left is seen a tower by which the road to Peshawar leads. The ascent to this is long and difficult and said to be dangerous, the adjacent hills being inhabited by desperate tribes who are not Mussalmáns. I however started from Kivort alone, and passing a durrah in which the Peshawar troops had encamped, ascended the hill and arrived in safety at the tower, leaving which the descent leads into a small valley. Down this road was overtaken by a man, who said nothing but walked by my side. He offered me a piece of bread, which, fearful of giving offence, I accepted. He then picked up a blade or two of grass which he twisted, and still preserving silence repaired a casualty in one of my shoes. We arrived at a pond of water which I was passing when my companion, who I had begun suspect dumb, asked me if I could not drink. I did so and went on alone, he taking another course. Arrived at a village built on the ascent of the hills to the left, went up to it and reposed a while. The water here is procured from wells in the rocks at a still higher elevation. Then passing through a confined passage across which a once substantial bund, now in decay, made an open space, to the left of which, under the encircling hills, stands a village with three or four towers. Thither I repaired and found a Doorannee soldier with his servant. He informed me the village I had passed belonged to him. I was here hospitably entertained, and the Pathans of the village invited me to stay a day or two. I was lodged in a house which serves for the accommodation of travellers, and where in the evening the old and young assemble to converse and smoke the chillum. Here was hung up a musical instrument for the use of such as possessed skill enough to set its strings in motion. This circumstance reminded me of the stanza of Moore:

> When the light of my song is o'er,
> Oh take my harp to yon ancient hall,
> Hang it up at that friendly door,
> Where weary travellers love to call, &c., &c.

The water of this village was excellent, but procured at some distance. The hills here produce a kind of flax, which is beaten, and of this the people construct chapplas, or a substitute for shoes. Ropes and baskets, and other trifling articles are also made from this plant. The men of the village who were employed in the harvest went out fully armed with matchlocks, sword, and shield. The plain was rocky, but generally cultivated with wheat. From hence the road winding through a small stony passage leads into another plain, in the extreme right and left of which is respectively situated a village with numerous assemblage of trees. I was proceeding along the high road when two horsemen galloped towards me issuing from a small grove at some distance, and while I was considering what might be their intention, one of them dismounted his horse and embraced my feet. I found in him a Doorannee of Peshawar who had formerly been in my service when travelling under more prosperous circumstances in the countries of Tárbát and Herát. He much lamented to see me in so sad a plight and on foot, and insisted so strenuously that I should return with him to Kivort, that I was induced to do so. A day or two residing here, Peer Mahomed Khán returned from Angoo, and as I was taking my evening walk, he observed me and rode towards me. He was now extremely civil, having learned, I presume at Angoo, that I had no further connection with Suddoo Khán than as a stranger partaking of his hospitality. He ordered that I should be brought to the darbár in the morning, and promised me that all and everything I might need should be supplied. The brother of my former servant proved to be the master of the horse to Peer Mahomed. I was accommodated at his quarters, was as comfortable as I could wish for the present. Two or three days had passed when news arrived that the Syed Ahmed Sháh, of great notoriety in these countries, had come from the hills of the Subzee and advanced on Hirrar, a fort ten or eleven kos from Peshawar. The troops were instantly in motion, and marched in the evening. I was assigned a place on the elephant of Peer Mahomed, and on the back of that animal arrived at Peshâwar in the morning, having marched twenty-four kos. As it was night I could not make such observations on the country as I could have wished. However on leaving the plain, on which I have mentioned I met my old servant, we passed a ruined fort of some extent to the left, beyond which for about ten or twelve kos stretches a barren uninhabitable space intersected with ravines, to the west of which is the great plain of the Afreedee Pathâns. To the east the hills are nearer, but the intermediate tract alike barren and uninhabited. Passing this, villages and cultivation occur successively and generally until our arrival at the city.

The country of Murwut cannot justly be considered independent, its inhabitants being compelled to pay tribute by the Navâb of Deyrâh, whose right of supremacy is not however acknowledged. Wheat appeared to be the only grain cultivated, and goats their principal stock, there being few sheep or cows. Horses are very few. The heat is very intense and the climate more forward than that of Peshâwar. A great evil in this country is the want of a due supply of water, being procured at great distance from the villages, and inapplicable to the purposes of irrigation of the land. There is no single authority in Murwut, the several villages being independent of each other, although they combine in cases of invasion. Runjit Sing, the Râja of Lahore, invaded Bunnoo with an army of 25,000 men; he encamped at Lukkee, and exacted 30,000 rupees, but did not think it prudent to attempt a permanent retention of the country as he had originally contemplated. The country of Bunnoo from its advantages of water might be rendered very productive, the soil being also capable of yielding any kind of produce. As it is, wheat, rice and a little sugar with melons constitute its produce. To the north of the plain are large groves of date, indubitable evidences of fertility in these countries. The people of Bunnoo are remarkable for entertaining what the French call "esprit de pays", and the exclamation of my own dear Bunnoo is frequently heard among them. The authority in their two towns is vested in a Malik, whose revenue is derived from the duties levied on the Hindus, who are the only traders of the country. Without the towns each occupier of a fort is his own master and neither pays or acknowledges submission to any one. The hills surrounding Bunnoo to the west are inhabited by a race of savages called the Vizeeree who occupy the range of mountains for about sixty kos; their country also extends considerably inwards. They are lawless depredators, and the Loharnee, or migratory tribes of Khorâssân who proceed through their country, are frequently compelled to fight their way. They are represented as very numerous; their weapon chiefly swords and spears, fire-arms being very scarce amongst them. Some of them I have seen in the various towns on the banks of the Indus were men of gigantic proportions, and I learned that many of them possess this uncommon stature. I once fell in with a party of them near Kolychi; they were all mounted with swords and long lances, clothed in red frocks lined with yellow, and had a gay appearance. They have immense flocks of sheep and goats, and a fine breed of hardy horses. These men acknowledge no supremacy, and live in a state of savage independence. I am not certain whether they have any town. I have heard of one called Nanni, which occurs in a route from Tâk to Kâbul, and am inclined to suppose it belongs to them. In many parts of their country considerable cold prevails; hence their complexions are sufficiently blanched as to bear comparisons with Europeans. It is singular that among these hills Hindus are to be found; these wretched people, for the sake of gain, being contented to submit to all kinds of scorn and contumely.

(A True Copy.)

(Signed) D. WILSON,
Resident, Persian Gulf.

Notice on the Province of Jallálábád and on the Seeaposh: by Mr. C. Masson.

JALLA'LA'BA'D.

No. 6.

The district or province of Jallálábád is situated between Pesháwar and Kábul, bounded to the north and west by the mountains of the Seeaposh and of Luckman, and to the south and east by the hills of Khyber and the plains of the Shinwári. It is divided into nine parganás, which denote as many towns of some consequence. Its extent from east to west may be estimated at sixty kos, from north to south continually varies, but in no instance exceeds twenty kos. It consists of a beautiful valley through which flows a fine stream, and from the variety of mountain, foot and water scenery, it may with some propriety be denominated the Switzerland of Khorássán. It is extremely fertile, producing abundant crops of rice and sugarcane of great sweetness. The date-tree occurs in this valley and is not seen farther west. Grapes, figs, plums, and excellent pomegranates are plentiful. The climate, however, is not so forward as that of Pesháwar, as the fig which had passed out of season before I left had not attained maturity here. Some is produced in this country in small quantities. Its towns are generally a collection of square forts, in which the agriculturists and Hindu dealers reside. The capital Jallálábád is not large and is surrounded with walls of considerable thickness; but their defences have been neglected, and are in a ruinous state. Among the small elevations to the south of the valley copper ore of excellent quality is abundant; in fact the hills absolutely consist entirely of it; yet no advantage is taken of this metallic treasure, and the Government so far from suspecting the existence of copper ridicuously impute the yellow appearance of the ore to the presence of sulphur. Indeed such is the supine disposition, and total absence of active enterprize in the Mussulmán, that were the mountain bursting with gold he would not take the trouble to extract it. If he observed the pure substance lying at his feet, he might possibly condescend to pick it up. The political condition of this country is very deplorable; the nominal Chief Mahomed Zummer Khán is far from popular, nor is his authority universally acknowledged. Within a mile from the city of Jallálábád are several forts and villages, the occupiers of which are wholly independent of him, and in case of warfare side with his relatives and enemies of Pesháwar. He is represented as wealthy, and in his political views is an ally of Dost Mahomed Khán of Kábul. Ten kos from Jallálábád is the fortified town of Ballabang, perhaps more flourishing than it. Here the artillery, I believe six pieces of ordnance, is stationed. South of this place are hills of a semi-transparent white stone, which yields easily to the knife. The only use I discovered to which it was applied was the formations of cups and topees or tops for chillums. The mountains in this part, as indeed generally throughout Khorássán, are extremely rich in metallic and mineral substances; but their treasures are neglected, and will continue to be so while these countries are under Mussulmán sway. The immense and inexhaustible stores of coloured marbles, jasper and porphyry are resorted to merely by the solitary mechanic, who with his little hammer supplies himself with sufficient quantity to make a *tusbee* or string of beads. An enlightened ruler in these countries might have it in his power to make the boast of Augustus that he found "his cities wood and left them marble." In noting the produce of this country, indigo and tobacco must be included. The pomegranates called Beedanas are particularly esteemed, and remarkable as containing no stones or seeds. The revenue of this province is generally estimated at twelve lákhs of rupees, but in its distracted condition the half of it I should suppose is not collected. A long passage through the heart of the hills which confine the river on its southern side about the midst of the valley may be mentioned as a natural curiosity. Among the various species of trees here the willow is abundant and bears the same name in the Peshto or natural dialect of the country. It also occurs in the plain of Pesháwar, and from thence is seen all over Khorássán. Lizards of immense size, but esteemed innoxious, are frequent among the hills and mud buildings.

The inhabitants employ their fat or grease medicinally. The hills immediately north of Jallálábád are inhabited by a race of men who on many accounts deserve notice. They are here called Seeaposh, alluding to the nature of their costume, or sometimes in the Hindi dialect *bhitta kaffres*, white infidels. These people from the traditions in these countries, and I understood also from their own accounts, are descendants of some of Alexander's soldiers who settled in these parts. The character given of them is various : the Mussulmán, to whom they are decidedly hostile, it would seem on the score of circumcision particularly, asserting them to be a most ferocious race, binding their prisoners and placing their food behind them. The Hindus who resort during the month of Tir to the boundary of their country for the purpose of traffic and barter, and who have therefore more claims to credence, assuring that they are perfectly gentle and that the Mussulmáns belie them. From what I could learn of their customs they appear to have preserved many of the usages of their ancestors. They are represented as assembling towards evening in companies, each bringing his stool (for they do not sit on the ground), and amusing themselves with singing, while the bowl freely circulates. Their wine is stated of excellent quality and is sometimes procurable. Their grapes are said to be of large size. Their bowls or basins the Hindus represent to be of gold. Their houses are built of wood, and reported to be highly decorated. The males lead a life of indolence, all the toils, even of agriculture, devolving on the female portion of society. The men shave their heads, leaving a tuft on the crown. Their weapon, principally bows and arrows. The Hindus assert they perform poojah on altars; it would be singular if the ancient Yoagan mythological rites should have been preserved by the people. The houses of the Mussulmáns are contiguous to the dwellings of the Seeaposh, whose women are sometimes carried off; their beauty is the theme of much praise. The same reputation for fine forms and beautiful countenances is allowed the men. They have no salt in their country, for which they are indebted to the Hindus, who during the month of Tir proceed to their frontier. During other periods the route is represented as inaccessible from the quantity of water collected in the approaches. They clothe themselves principally with skins of sheep dyed black; hence their name Seeaposh. The more wealthy avail themselves of linen and longees. I could gain no information as to the nature of their government or extent of country. This stretches nevertheless a considerable distance, as I have heard that the Patháns of Rawul Pindi who inhabit the two sides of the Indus north of Attock are in the habit of making incursions among them and carrying off their men and women as slaves. A Syed now dead who resided in Khouah, one of the eastern divisions of Jallálábád, became possessed of one of their women, and he was held in high reputation amongst them. I was told that the people of Lakhman who live in the country west of them could understand the Seeaposh. The people at Jallálábád assert it would occupy three days to gain the dwellings of the infidels.

(A True Copy.)
(Signed) D. WILSON,
Resident, Persian Gulf.

Passage through the Pass of Khyber, and Notice on the Countries West of the Indus from Deyráh Gházi Khán to Koltibah or Kolibah.—Passed through Khyber in July.— Was in the countries West of the Indus from Christmas, I suspect, to April: by Mr. C. MASSON.

No. 7.

From Peshawar to Kábul there are three distinct routes, all of them leading through the vast chain of mountains to the west, viz., those of Khyber, Abkonnur and Krapper, the former decidedly the preferable from its level character and directness, but the most dangerous from the predatory habits of the lawless tribes who inhabit it. It is therefore seldom frequented, and only by faquirs or bodies of troops who march in force, the caravans of merchants and others passing by the more difficult and tedious, but at the same time the more secure routes of Alkonnur and Krapper. Having determined to attempt the Khyber passage I divested myself of my clothes and other property, and clad myself in garments of little worth, as did also a Pathán of Momunzye who volunteered to accompany me. This man was serviceable and indeed necessary from his knowledge of the Peshto or Pathán dialect. I took leave of my friends at Pesháwar, who strove to induce me to change my determination by setting forth the dangers of the road, the ferocity of the inhabitants and the inevitable fate that awaited me, being a European. But as I had taken my resolution and the spirit of adventure having got the better of prudential calculation, moreover of opinion that my European birth which I intended not to conceal would not operate to my prejudice, I started with my companion before the break of day, taking with me besides my mean apparel nothing but a small book, and a few pice or half-pence which were put in a small earthen water vessel, the better to escape observation. My Pathán had two or three cakes of bread and a knife which he concealed in the bands of his pyjammás or trousers. From Pesháwar marching about three kos we cleared the villages in its neighbourhood, and struck across a large space of ground overspread with stones; perhaps five kos in breadth, though this barren tract was the bed of streams at this time without water, and midway was a small Doorannee Chauki or guard. To the right was a large artificial elevation of earth called the Pádsha's topee, near which the last battle was fought between Sháh Sujáh and Azam Khán, the brother of the Vazir Futteh Khán, where the former being defeated fled to the hills of Khyber. Nearing the hills approached the small town or village of Jum, which has a wall of stones cemented with mud but no bázár. We did not deem it prudent to enter this town, but halted during the heat of the day at an enclosed zeearat or burial-place of a Syed or some other saintly character which we found a little to the right. Here was a musjid, a grateful shade from the trees and a well of indifferent water. When the fervour of the sun abated, we continued our march and entered the hills, taking a foot-path, the main road, which is practicable for artillery, bearing to our left. Ascending and descending a variety of hills we fell in with the high road leading through a valley supplied with a fine stream of clear water. Hitherto we had neither met nor seen any person. Arrived at a spot, where the water gushes from the rock to the left, which supplies the stream just mentioned, I slaked my thirst in the living springs, and such was the delicious and refreshing coldness of their waters that I envied not the gods of Homer their nectar. Immediately adjoining this spot were assembled under the shade of the rocks about twenty men, most of them elderly and of venerable appearance. Our salutes were acknowledged, and after replying to their enquiries as to who we were, where we were going, and on what business, they invited us to pass the night with them, telling us that we should find a village a little farther on, but nearly bare of inhabitants who had come hither with their flocks, as is their custom during a certain portion of the year, to this village they belonged. I became an object of much curiosity, and as I had conjectured on leaving Pesháwar my European birth did not prove to my disadvantage. These men spoke nothing but Peshto. I therefore was compelled to keep up my conversation with them through the medium of my Pathán or interpreter. The news of the arrival of a European or Firangi soon spread and several persons came who were afflicted with disorders or wounds, many with ophthalmia. I could not forbear regretting that I had no knowledge of medicinal remedies, as it would have afforded me the highest satisfaction to have administered to the wants of these poor people whose reception of me had so fully belied the reports of their neighbours. I asserted my ignorance of the art of healing, but was not credited, and finding it impossible to avoid prescribing or to be considered unkind, I took upon myself to recommend in the ophthalmic cases ablutions with lukewarm milk and water in the morning and during the day frequent splashes of old spring water. I moreover arranged a shade, which simple contrivance was much admired and esteemed a singular effect of ingenuity. In the cases of wounds, which were three or four in number and inflicted with the sword, I proposed injection of sweet oil, or, in default of which, butter or honey, strongly urging cleanliness and absolutely forbidding the use of cotton rags, which have the tendency to irritate and influence the sores, and directed leaves to be applied in their stead. It is the custom in these countries to apply to wounds a mixture of mud and salt. I know not whether this be judicious, but conclude not from the number of accidents of this kind I have seen in which the wounds were still open owing, as I supposed, to the repulsive agency of the dirt and cotton bandages.

I received many thanks for my advice and sat with my Khyber friends until the approach of night, smoking the hookah and listening to their conversation, at which I appeared to be much pleased although I understood but little of it. They pointed to an eminence above the springs, on which they assured me Sháh Sujáh passed the night after his defeat in the plains of Peshálwar. We now ascended the mountains, and on the tabular summit of one of them found the inhabitants of the village in a bivouac. There were but three cots or bedsteads of these countries among them, and one was provided for me, it being alleged that I was an European and had prescribed medicines; my companion received a mat. As night advanced, bread was brought with the addition of ghee and milk. The chillum also was furnished, and three or four young men came to sit with me until I felt disposed to sleep, and on receiving their leave of departure asked me if during the night they should bring the chillum. Such was the attention I received from these savages, and I am gratified to relate it as it affords an opportunity of doing justice to hospitality and kindness, and opposes a pleasing contrast to the treatment I have experienced among the barbarous and inhospitable tribes. Awaking in the morning I beheld my friends anxious to anticipate my wants ready with the never-failing chillum and a bowl of fine butter-milk. My departure that day was moreover very unwillingly permitted. Proceeding through the valley or durrah met two men of the wildest appearance running armed with matchlocks, the matches of which were lighted. They were without covering to their heads and were in search, as they said, of their enemies who had paid them a visit during the night. Passing these we were soon overtaken by another man, also armed with a matchlock, who came running after us. We were at first dubious as to his intentions, but it proved that he was come to beg me to look at a sister who was lying ill in the village, to which we were now very near. I could not but consent, and found a miserable being in the last stage of declining nature; learned that she had been three years in that state. All I could do was to recommend attention to her regimen and obedience to her wishes whatever they might be, that the few days of her earthly existence might pass serenely as possible under the circumstances of her case. This village was small and had a tower substantially built of large stones. Leaving it we entered a plain, of perhaps two miles in circumference, on which I counted twenty-four circular towers, which denote as many family residences, each house having its dependent defensive erection, for such I understood was the nature of society among the inhabitants of the Khyber valley, that when not united for any foreign excursion or plunder, they carry on an internal warfare from tower to tower, and that they consider each other as enemies. They may serve to secure their properties and families in case of invasion on the march of troops. In our road from the village we were accosted by two youths who accompanied us and begged to proceed to a house to the left of the road. We were there civilly received by a sturdy young man, who immediately produced a cake or two of bread and as usual the chillum or hookah. He also had heard of my arrival in Khyber, and was overjoyed that I had come to his house. My medical skill was again put into practice. The skin of my new client was plentifully covered with eruptive blotches of pimples. He appeared extremely anxious for my advice, yet had manifestly a delicacy in asking it, fearing I should not confer upon him so great a favor. After an inspection of his disorder, and telling him that I thought something might be done for him, he was almost frantic with joy, and expressed his gratitude with much earnestness and eloquence. His father now arrived—a man of respectable appearance and benign features: he was glad to see me, and asked what I considered the nature of his son's disease. I replied that the eruption on the skin was probably occasioned by the heat and impurity of the blood, and that his son must take medicines to purify it when the blotches would gradually disappear, to which also a hot application might be serviceable. The old man seized my hand and asked me if I was certain of his son's disease. I told him nearly so. He was extremely delighted, informing that it was believed in the valley that his son had the bad Firang or venereal distemper; that he was shunned as unclean by his neighbours, who would neither associate with him nor smoke the same chillum, and that his wife, the daughter of the occupier of an adjacent tower, had been taken from him. I positively assured him that the disease was not the bad Firang and recommended the use of brimstone internally and externally. I had to prepare on the spot a mixture of ghee and powdered brimstone, and directed my companion (the Pathán of Peshawar) to anoint the patient. He did so, and rather roughly, for he tore down the skin with his nails and then rubbed in the ointment. I asked for some honey, which is plentiful among the hills, and mingled with it a proportion of brimstone, directing it to be taken night and morning. I further ordered him to drink water impregnated with the same substance, and ventured to promise him a speedy cure. We were treated with the greatest kindness by the old man, whose name was Khair Mahomed, and after taking a comfortable repast of good bread and fine butter took our leave about noon. We had scarcely gained the road when we were hailed by some people seated under a tower to the right. We repaired thither, and my advice was solicited for a pain in the abdomen by one of the hailers. This exceeded my Æsculapian ability; nevertheless I directed the use of the seeds of paneer, a plant which grows in large quantity among these hills and is much prized for its medicinal qualities in many countries I had visited. I had also found it serviceable in a similar affliction. A man was despatched to procure some seeds and soon returned; these people, I discovered, were ignorant of its virtues. We again took the road, and approached the last house in the plain which had no tower, but was enclosed with mud walls and had a somewhat better appearance than any of the others. Observing three or four persons seated at the entrance, we went towards them, deeming it advisable that it might not be supposed we were clandestinely passing. We saluted with the customary Salám Aleekum and received the invariable responsive greeting of Aleekum Salám. We found this to be the abode of Aládát Khán, one of the most influential men in Khyber He said he recognized me to be a European in the distance by my step. He farther asserted that his country would some day be under European control, and he begged to remember of it if it so happen in his or my time. I had here to officiate as a physician for the last time. My patient was either the wife or the sister (I know not which) of Aládát Khán; she was lying in a deplorable state of decline. I was asked if I thought it probable she would recover. I replied in the negative as the disorder had become superior to medicinal remedies, and the vital principle was nearly extinct. My host, who was a man of sense, agreed with me, and after smoking the chillum I took my leave. At a small distance from this house were met by a man, who observing the water vessel of my companion asked for water (it will be remembered in this vessel were the few pice we carried with us). My Pathán first told him that his people were near, and that we had a distance to go in which we might not possibly find water; but he insisted on drinking. Other reasons were urged, and finally that the water belonged to me, who was a Kaffre or infidel; he then swore he would drink if it killed him. My Pathán desired him to place his hand under the mouth, into which he poured the fluid, and with such care that the money was not discovered. The fellow drank and went satisfied away. I know not however how this water, in which thirty or forty pice had been lying for above thirty hours, may have afterwards agreed with his stomach or digestive powers. In this small plain is another of those monuments called the Pádasháh's Topee; it is in good preservation and consists of a solid rectangular base surmounted with a dome, erected on the summit of an eminence. I have noticed the existence of another in the plain of Pesháwar, and I have heard of another in the Punjáb. The inhabitants here refer the structure of these edifices to Ahmed Sháh, but I judge their antiquity to be more remote. The stones employed in the Khyber monument are of very large dimensions, and the whole has a grand and striking aspect.

From this plain passed through a burial-place and a little broken ground, then making a turn in the hills, we entered another plain, of much the same extent inhabited by the Sheenwáree tribe of Patháns, the former being occupied by the A'fredee tribe. The houses here were enclosed with walls of cemented stones, these being substituted for the circular stone towers of their neighbours. We left these houses to the right and were proceeding down a descent which leads from the plain into the valley beneath, when two men rushed from the rocks and stopped our progress; our clothes were searched, and a chadder or long piece of linen I wore loosely hanging on my shoulders was taken, in one corner of which was my book tied; this I asked them to return, asserting it was religious book or kitáb of the Mulláh. They did so. From my Pathán they took a small pocket knife. The earthen vessel which contained our pice had been placed on the ground. One of the ruffians who was particularly exact in his search took out a twist of grass, which inserted in its mouth served as a stopper, and actually examined it minutely; finding nothing he replaced it and the pice escaped. This fellow put me to a severe search, and contented with stroking his hands down the various parts of my body, he untied the strings of my trousers. My companion expressing his anger, rather too honestly, and comparing our treatment with that received from the A'fredee, swords were drawn; but I desired the Pathán to cease compliments as they were useless, and we departed. I was tolerably satisfied with this mishap as my book was preserved, and our loss was trifling. I was however much surprised, as from all previous accounts the A'freedee were most to be dreaded, it being asserted that the Shinwáree from their commercial pursuits were not so savage as their neighbours. These people breed a vast quantity of mules, and are engaged in the carrying on of trade. We had not gained the valley when we were hailed by another armed man tending goats, and had we not been plundered before, we must have resisted or submitted to it here. In our course along the durrah arrived at a spot where a little rice was cultivated. Here was excellent spring water. We were ordered to halt by some fellows on the top of the hills to our left, but they were too distant to cause us apprehension or induce us to comply. About this spot the valley considerably widens, and we passed the ruins of a fort built on an elevation in the midst of it; it appears to have been a very solid structure. Near it are a quantity of wells of slight depth, or reservoirs of water, in two or three of which only we found a little water. Throughout the whole extent of the valley or pass of Khyber, on the crests of the enclosing hills, are the remains of ancient forts, whose neatness and solidity of structure evince their founders to have been much more enlightened and opulent than the present inhabitants of these countries. The usual reply to any question as to their origin is that they were built by infidels, or sometimes that they were raised by demons. There are some of them of very large extent, and must in their periods have been very important works. I regretted much the impossibility of a close inspection of some of them. There are also among these hills a great number of artificial cavities which may have served as places of refuge, or may have been the abode of human beings in the rude and infant state of society. The latter part of our route through the valley was sandy and so continued until our arrival at Dakkar, a small fort and town dependent on Jallálábád, and seated on a fine stream. The pass of Khyber I suppose to be about fifteen kos or nearly twenty-five British miles in extent; the intermediate passage, it will be observed, is slightly inhabited. I know not however to what degree the hills may be so, which enclose it in either side. The two tribes of Khyberi Patháns, the Afreedee and Shinwáree, formerly considered themselves in the employ of the kings of Kábul, from whom they received an annual stipend on conditions of service. On the destruction of the regal authority and the consequent convulsion of the Doorannee empire, these tribes have assumed independence; and the several Chiefs of the Barrackzye being either unwilling or unable to continue their former allowance, they have become absolute robbers and decided enemies to those countries they once served. It is Peshawar where the predatory habits cause most mischief, for they not only are prone to plunder caravans passing through their valley, but have sometimes intercepted those passing by the other routes of Abkhonnur and Krapper. In some instances, when some arrangement can be made, caravans passing pay a duty of two rupees for each mounted and one rupee for each dismounted member. Yet such is the dread entertained of these savages and the distrust of their good faith, that no halt is made even to cook their victuals. In the march of troops they evacuate their houses and retire to their hills. I have heard that the Afreedee tribe could muster forty thousand fighting men: this may be true if into the calculation be taken the number of males among them capable of bearing arms; but on two or three occasions when they have assembled in force, their numbers have not exceeded three to four thousand men. Their weapons are matchlocks, swords and shields. Many of them carry knives of a foot and half or two feet in length. It must be understood that the inhabitants of the valley form but a small portion of the tribe of Afreedee, the bulk of them residing under the hills to the south-west of Peshawar, where, from the number of trees visible in the distance, I should suppose their residences are more convenient and the cultivation cheap and general. In the valley wheat is raised only in sufficient quantities for the immediate wants of its inhabitants. The water is excellent and I believe procured at some distance from the houses, as it is preserved in mussacks or the prepared skins of sheep or goats. It may be noted also that the bulk of Sheenwáree tribe reside on the western or Kábul side of the hills, where their rectangular forts are very numerous, and have a fine effect seen from the Jallálábád district, the ground gradually ascending until it unites itself with the hills to the south.

(A True Copy.)
(Signed) D. WILSON,
Resident, Persian Gulf.

Discovery of the sites of the ancient Cities of Bucephalia and the presented Tomb of Bucephalus, the Charger of Alexander the Great: by Mr. C. MASSON.

No. 8.

Among the events connected with the early history of Hindustán and the adjacent countries to the west, the invasion of Alexander the Great deserves particular notice, and is a subject to which the attention of any traveller visiting those countries should be particularly directed. Of the expeditions of Bacchus and Sesostris we merely know that they occurred. Indeed they are so mysteriously announced that we may be excused if we doubt the testimony concerning them. It is far different with the gifted warrior of Macedon. His exploits are related in detailed and authentic records, and he has left behind him in all countries that he visited the imperishable evidences of his progress by the foundation of cities and monuments from the Egyptian Sea to the banks of the Hydaspes. Had the poet and historian been silent respecting him, his genius would have secured immortality, as he has bequeathed us ocular proofs of his victories and conquests, and in those regions his memory is consecrated by tradition. His historians have been very precise in their relations of his progress, even to the detail of his marches; but as the names, which are almost always invariably Grecian, differ so essentially from those current amongst the natives, the grand object is to recognize and identify them. It is well known that his progress in the East terminated on the banks of the Hydaspes, which river I believe is supposed by Major Rennell, and all others who have written on the geography of India, to be the present Ravee. I arrived in the Punjáb under unfortunate circumstances, having lost all my books and other property some time before, and my memory, although it retained the grand features of Alexander's memorable expedition, failed me as to the minute details which would have been most serviceable in conducting an investigation. Nevertheless I was so fortunate as to make a discovery which may be interesting to the lovers of antiquities and important as elucidating the ancient geography of the Punjáb. On the bank (the western) of the river Jhelum is a monument which the people there suppose to have been constructed by demons, as they usually suppose all such with whose origin they are not acquainted. It struck me that its architecture, although I could not refer it to any known species, was assuredly foreign, and that its antiquity must be remote. In the course of my enquiries among the oldest people in a small village near, I learned that there had formerly existed two cities, one on each bank of the river. I repaired to the spot pointed out as the site of one of them and found abundant vestiges of a once large city, but so complete had been the devastation of time, that no distinct idea of its form or architecture could be gleaned. I set people to work in the ruins, and their exertions were rewarded by the discovery of coins in gold, silver and copper of Alexander the Great, in all twenty-seven, with the same figures and inscriptions, excepting one. On the one side was the bust of Alexander and on the reverse a dismounted lancer with the inscription BUCEPHALIA. The coin that differed had an inscription on which were plainly observed the letters NERO. I could not suppose this to be a coin of the Roman Emperor, but if my small knowledge of Greek does not mislead me the word *neros* has reference to the confluence of waters. It was evident that there were other letters obliterated by time. I now remembered that in an action on the banks of the Hydaspes Bucephalus was wounded and died in consequence thereof, and that Alexander in commemoration of his much-prized charger founded two cities which he named after him, at least so writes Plutarch. I therefore had no difficulty in supposing the cities which once stood here to be the ancient cities of Bucephalia, and that the present river Jhelum is the Hydaspes of the Greek historians. The monument I moreover conjectured to be the tomb of the favourite horse, into which I found it impossible to penetrate, it being closed on all sides without any appearance or sign of an entrance.

Encouraged by this discovery I began considering other points connected with this expedition and remembered that Major Rennell is at a loss to account for the position of Oornus, a fortress particularly designated by Alexander's historians, that veteran geographer asserting that there is no place in the Punjáb that coincides with the description given of it.

The fortress is represented as having been built upon an isolated and almost inaccessible mountain with no other hills near it, and in those days enjoyed a reputation for impregnability. The Grecian hero ever for glory, and anxious to undertake what others deemed impossible, quitted the high road which was the course of his march, and marching I believe seven or eight days presented himself before it and summoned it to surrender. He received for reply that had his soldiers wings, he had done well in bringing them there. Alexander formed the siege and in fifteen days became the master of the place by assault.

Having made particular enquiries if such a position could be now found, I was led to believe that the hill named at present Gun-Ghur is the identical Oornus of the ancients, with whose description it exactly agrees, if it should appear that Alexander quitted the course of his march soon after his conquest of Porus. The high road I make no doubt was the same in the days of Alexander as at the present time, its course and position being dictated by the natural character of the country. The intelligent Mr. Forster who has published an account of his travels in these countries, will probably have made some remarks on the marches of Alexander. I have read the first volume only of his works which brings him to Cashmere, and in hazarding an opinion as to the course of that march, I do so with all deference and humility should I differ from so respectable an authority. It appears to me that proceeding on the high road from Persia to Hindustán he struck to the north to destroy the murderers of Darius who had collected an army, and having vanquished them passed by Balk, the ancient Paropisarmus, and passed by the route of Kundooz to Kábul, when descending by Jallálábád passed through the valley of Khyber and crossed the Indus at Attock, in fact following the high road which was the same then as at the present day. The evidence of his progress through the valley of Jallálábád is confirmed at this day by the existence of a white people who inhabit the hills which bound the valley to the north, and who agreeably to their own accounts and tradition of the country are the descendants of some of his soldiers who settled here, probably in the valley, whose situation is very delightful and the soil fertile, and on the Mahomedan invasion of that country were compelled to resort to the hills, where they maintain their independence and appear to have preserved many of the customs of their ancestors. I shall mention these people again in another notice. In the valley of Khyber is a monument named the Pádsháh's Topee and others are in the plain of Pesháwar and the Punjáb. These, though referred to Ahmed Sháh, are obviously more ancient, and I indulge the idea of their connection with the expedition of Alexander.

From the tradition also in the Punjáb it would seem almost certain that Alexander visited the fortress called at present Kangrah in the hills north of Lahore, where they have a hill which retains his name, but I must inform myself more particularly on the details of his historians before I venture to credit this tradition which is, I think, at variance with their accounts, which agree in fixing his progress to the banks of the Hydaspes.

There is a history of Alexander or Secunder Zoolkurna, or Alexander with the one horn in the Persian language, entitled Secunder Námeh, but its relations are grossly exaggerated and fabulous. I know not whether the appellation of Zoolkurna had any connection with the typi-

---

N.B.—Gunghur is about seventy or eighty miles from the city of Attock, and was brought under subjection by Runjit Sing of Lahore about four or five years since. The Patháns who inhabited it repulsed his generals twice or thrice owing to the strength of their position.

fication of Alexander by the Prophet Daniel, who designates him as the ram with one horn, that destroys the beast with many heads, or the king of Persia.

(A TrueCopy.)
(Signed) D. WILSON,
Resident, Persian Gulf.

Memoranda on Lahore, the Sikhs and their Kingdom and Dependencies: by Mr. C. MASSON.

No. 9.

Lahore, the capital of the Punjáb and of the territories of Runjit Sing, is a city of undoubted antiquity, and has been long celebrated for its extent and magnificence. The extravagant praises bestowed upon it by the historians of Hindustán must, however, be understood as applicable to a former city, of which now only the ruins are seen, to which also must be referred the current proverb which asserts that, Isfáhán and Shiráz united would not equal the whole of Lahore. The present city, is nevertheless very spacious and comprizes many elegant and important buildings. Among these the Masjid Pádisháh and the Masjid Vazier Khán are particularly splendid; the Sonara Masjid also commands attention from the attraction of its gilded cupolas. The Masjid Pádisháh is substantially built of a red friable sandstone, and from its size, the loftiness of its minarets, the dimensions of its cupolas, and the general grandeur of the whole, is an edifice worthy of its founder, the mighty Aurangzebe. Lahore is indebted for this building to the following circumstance: the Emperor commanded the Vazier to raise a masjid for his (the Emperor's) own devotions which was to surpass all others then known; the minister accordingly at an immense expense erected a masjid, and having announced its completion, the Emperor proceeded to inspect it, and as well to pray. On approaching it he heard it circulated among the crowd—"Behold the Emperor who is going to the Masjid of Vazier Khán." The emperor retraced his steps, observing that his design had been frustrated, inasmuch as the masjid had acquired not his name but that of his minister, and then personally commanded the construction of another, superintended its progress during the building, and succeeded in connecting his name with it. The masjid of Vazier Khán is a sumptuous building, distinguished by minarets of great height, and entirely covered with painted tiles, which present a gorgeous appearance; it is said that the whole of the Korán is written on the walls and various parts of this building. Contiguous is a small bázár, the house-rents of which were formerly allotted to the repairs of the masjid, and to support the necessitous who frequented it. These funds the Sikhs have otherwise appropriated. The Sonara Masjid, independently of its gilded cupolas, is a handsome and extensive edifice. There are also many other masjids and serais deserving attention, and many Hindu temples very splendid. The streets are very narrow, as are the bázárs, which are numerous and distinguished by the names of the occupations chiefly carried on in them; hence the Goldsmith's Bázár, the Cloth Bázár, &c. There are some exceedingly lofty, bulky mansions, well built of burnt bricks (of which the entire city is generally built), many of them recently erected. These have no exterior decorations, exposing their vast extent of dead walls, in which are inserted a few apertures scarcely observable. Among the most conspicuous of these for size is the abode of a Sikh Khoosial Sing, a Bráhmin renegade, raised by Runjit Sing from the rank of scullion in the kitchen to that of a general. The sons of Runjit Sing have each of them a large palace within the city, and Runjit Sing in his occasional visits to Lahore resides in the inner fort or citadel, which, as well as his residence, contains extensive magazines of warlike stores and manufactures of muskets, cannon ball, &c. Lahore seated near the Ravee, is not dependent on that river for water, which she obtains from numerous wells within her walls, and I believe of very good quality. Lahore is surrounded with a substantial brick wall of fair height, say twenty-five feet, and of such thickness that a piece of ordnance may turn on it. It has bastions circular, and bastions of many sides inserted at regular distances, and is provided with many gates, as the Moorchee Derwáza, the Delhi Derwáza, the Láhore Derwáza, the Attack Derwáza, &c. Runjit Sing has moreover surrounded the city with a good trench, and carried handsome works and redoubts along the entire line of circumference, which are plentifully garrisoned with heavy artillery. At the Láhore Derwáza is a large piece of brass ordnance termed the Bungee, much prized for its dimensions. A traveller at Lahore, had he never before seen tigers, might gratify his curiosity by going to the gate to the right of the Moorchee Derwáza, where some three or four are enclosed in sufficient cages; and at the inner fort, where Runjit Sing resides, is a numerous collection of animals, and among them one presented by an Ara envoy, which may or may not be supposed to be the mysterious unicorn. This animal has a graceful head resembling the horse, with a beautiful straight spiral horn issuing from the forhead. The body is alike of just proportions, but unfortunately its legs are preposterous and clumsy and have more analogy to those of an elephant than to the horse. Without the walls are scattered on all sides, the ruins of the ancient city, which although in many places cleared away by the express orders of Runjit Sing, and also for the construction of cantonments and exercising ground for the troops of the French Camp, and the constant diminution of their bulk in furnishing materials for new erections, are still wonderful, and convey a vast idea of the extent of ancient Lahore. Numerous tombs and other buildings are still standing, some of them nearly entire, and such is their solidity that they seem if not to baffle old time, to give ground very slowly. North-west of Lahore, perhaps half a mile distant, is the very beautiful and far-famed Mokubberah Jehangier, or tomb of the Emperor Jehangier. This superb edifice is seated immediately on the western banks of the Ravee and is classed among the four objects of wonder which adorn their country by the natives of Hindustán. Under the domination of the barbarous and tasteless Sikhs this delightful specimen of Indian skill, labour and ingenuity is neglected and falling into decay, and its fine gardens are waste and desolate. It will be remembered that the Táj Mahál at Agra was built by Jehangier, and although I have not seen this building, yet from a print I have met with, the advantage in exterior appearance decidedly lies with the Mokubberah at Lahore. The interior decorations I believe are on the same principle, therefore he only who has seen both structures can testify as to the superiority of either. Runjit Sing assigned this building as a residence to a French gentleman in his service, who caused its chambers to be cleared of their accumulated filth; the alleys of the garden were swept, and the Mokubberah was assuming a gay appearance, when alas he died. The Mussalmáns did not fail to attribute his death to his temerity and impiety in daring to profane so sacred a spot by the presence of an infidel, and asserted that the Emperor actually appeared to him and announced his death as the punishment for his crime. Another building towards the west of the city and east of the river some few yards is the tomb of Anarkullee, remarkable for its appearance and solidity, and for the unfortunate fate of the person it covers. Anarkullee was a youth of extreme personal beauty, and the favourite and the constant attendant of an Emperor of Hindustán. On occasions when the prince would be in company with the ladies of his harem, the favourite page would not be excluded. It happened that one day the Emperor seated with his women in an apartment lined with looking glasses, beheld from the reflected appearance of Anarkullee who was behind him, that he was smiling. The Emperor's construction of the intent of a smile proved so melancholy to the smiler that he was ordered forthwith to be interred alive. This command was obeyed by building around

B 1485—43

him with bricks, and an immense superstructure was raised, the expense of which was defrayed, as the tradition relates, by the produce of one of the bangles or ornaments which were bound on his legs. There were formerly extensive gardens, and several buildings connected with the sepulchre or mausoleum, of which not a vestige can now be traced. This tomb was formerly occupied by Kurruk Sing, the eldest son of Runjit Sing, but has been subsequently given to a French officer, who has converted it into a harem. Adjacent to Anarkullee's tomb is the magnificent house of the two principal French officers of Runjit Sing's service, on the left and front of which are the well built cantonments of the regular troops, that is to say, a portion of them. Around Lahore are many large and delightful gardens. The fruit trees and flowering shrubs and plants are such as are probably general in Hindustán and the East, not being of characters and species prevalent in the West. The fruit trees here are the mango (mangifera), the plantain (musa), the apple (pomus) of indifferent quality and small size, the peach (persica), the jaman (eugenia jambolana), the fig (ficus agustis), the karonda (carissa carandas), the quince, the orange, the lime, both acid and sweet; date trees are pretty numerous but the fruit so bad as to be scarcely eatable. Pomegranates are moreover plentiful, but not prized, and occasionally may be seen a few vines. The flowers are in no great variety, but cultivated chiefly with reference to the odour. Chaplets are made of the blossoms and sold in the bázárs. The jasmine (white) is very common. The gardens here, as in all eastern countries, are not closed to the admission of individuals, who may, preserving due respect for the fruits, &c., freely enter and stroll about them; but the mean practice prevails of selling the fruits and flowers, from which sale the proprietor of a garden, be he king or subject, derives a profit. About three or four miles east of Lahore is the extensive and once delightful garden of Shalimar. Here are still the marble tombs and dry fountains with splendid machinery which once ejected water in every direction. The gay summer houses and other buildings which directed this immense garden have suffered not so much from the dilapidations of time as from the depredations of Runjit Sing, who has removed the greater quantity of the marble and stone of which they were composed to employ them in his new constructions at the favoured city of Umritsur and also at Govindghar. Still in its decline of splendour, Shalimar has sufficient beauties to interest and delight a visitor, whose regret will be powerfully excited that desolation should be suffered to destroy the noblest garden which belonged to the imperial family of Timur. Among other gardens surrounding Lahore at near distances and deserving notice are those of the sons of Runjit Sing, the one of the late Diván Misser Chund, General of Artillery, and which retains his name, with those of the two principal French gentlemen. In describing Lahore, a small village, or it may perhaps be styled a town, as it contains a bázár and is tolerably sized, named Noa Kote, should be noticed, as well from being very ancient as from its connection with the capture of Lahore by Runjit Sing. The city and destined capital of a powerful Sikh kingdom, was then occupied by four Sikh Chiefs, each perfectly independent of the other, and engaged in internal warfare. While affairs thus stood, Runjit presented himself before the place with 700 horse. The common danger united the four Chiefs of the city, which they prepared to defend. The young invader, unable from the description of his troops to make any impression upon a town defended with a substantial wall, took up a position at Noa Kote, whence he harassed the vicinity, and prevented the egress or ingress. He remained some months, adhering to the plan he had adopted, when the cultivators of the garden grounds which immediately surround Lahore, and whose operations were necessarily suspended, became reduced to extremities to procure subsistence, and seeing no probability of a termination to the evil, they applied to Runjit Sing and volunteerd to conduct him into the city by some unguarded or neglected entrance. This was effected at night, and after the usual slaughter on such occassions, Runjit became master of Lahore.

and hence may be dated the downfall of the independent Sikh Chiefs, and the consequent supreme authority of their conqueror. Noa Kote has been granted by Runjit Sing as a provision for Yacoob Sháh, the brother of the unfortunate Sháh Sujáh. I shall leave Lahore with a plan of its situation, which will be very imperfect as drawn from memory, and very deficient, as I have only noted such places of whose positions I am certain.

To mention the Sikh, as relates to their sect and opinions as sectaries, might be deemed superfluous, as the subject has been before treated by Sir John Malcolm, who not only (I believe) has visited the Punjáb, but could procure information of the very best description from the Sikh seminaries at Benáres. My notice of these points will therefore be brief. The sect is new and originated with one Nánnock. This person lived contemporary with the famous Aurangzebe, by whom he was persecuted, and to whom (as the Sikh's say) he predicted, that his empire would be wrenched from his successors by the men who visited Hindustán in large ships. Nánnock, in the foundation of his new sect, appears to have contemplated the restoration of Hindu power by removing the causes which have unquestionably produced its decline, and which as certainly as long as they exist must prevent its revival. His doctrines, therefore, completely destroy the distinction of caste, inasmuch as Brahmins are admitted to be Sikhs. He has further instituted a new military race of Hindus, and by permitting conversion (another attack on the principle of caste), he has opened a road to their unlimited increase. He plainly saw the evident decrease of the Hindu population of India through the exercise of Mahomedan power, and the calls of interest and convenience, which must have induced so many to abandon the faith of their ancestors, which had become a reproach and ridicule, to embrace that of their rulers and secure worldly advantages and security from insult and contumely. Although he may not have hoped to convert the fierce and bigoted Mahomedan, he may have expected or intended his system to operate among the other classes of Hindus, who would of necessity become soldiers and ultimately be enabled to reject the imposed sway and to assert their independence and supremacy. By removing the various prohibitions of the orthodox Hindus, and allowing a reasonable latitude in articles of food, in fact forbidding nothing but actually the cow, and allowing the unqualified indulgence of wine, he may be considered to have had in view the improvement of the physical force and energies of his followers, an object of primary importance to the military man. Whether absolutely owing to this or other natural causes the Sikhs of the present day are remarkable for their capabilities of supporting excessive toil and fatiguing expeditions. Nánnock, like most founders of new religions or sects (for all generally adopt the same principle but differ in their modes of doing it), must needs forbid something; he has therefore proscribed tobacco, which none of his adherents are permitted to smoke, nay, not so much as touch; but as he equally well knew that the practise of smoking the ill-fated herb was general among Hindus, and aware that tenacity of old customs, and reluctance to dispense with established enjoyments were characteristics in human nature, he wisely enacted that such circumstances might not prove obstacles to his favorite plan of conversion, that any Hindu on being admitted a Sikh who had previously been accustomed to drink wine and smoke tobacco might still employ, according to his pleasure, the glass or the hookáh. In his character as a prophet it became him to prophesy; he has done so, and in his various prophetical legacies, his followers view the predictions of the capture of Multán, Kashmere, Monkurah, Peshawar, in short of every success that has happened to them. What yet remains to be fulfilled is their subjection to British authority for one hundred and forty years (which they suppose will commence on the demise of Runjit Sing), after which they are to repel it, become masters of Hindustán, and carrying on the war beyond seas, to destroy the famous fort of Lunká. The books I have seen containing these prophecies are decorated with many uncouth pictures, and this event is depicted by a number of monstrous-looking men with maces knocking off the towers placed on the head of another man equally disgusting in appearance. Agreeably to my intention of brevity as regards their religious ceremonies and opinions, I close my notice of them in observing that they employ the rosary or string of beads in common with the most rigid Mussalmán or most devout Catholic.

It was long since foretold by a celebrated traveller (Mr. Forster) in the reign of Timur Sháh of Kábul that the Sikhs would become a powerful nation so soon as some chief more enterprising than the rest should unite them in one body by destroying the independence of the very numerous petty chieftains who respectively governed them. This has been accomplished by Runjit Sing, and the Sikhs under his sway have become, as predicted, an independent and powerful nation. The system of numerous and independent chiefs was agreeable to the sanction of their Guru Nánnock, with whom I believe it even originated; his notions of government appear to have been purely patriarchal, and he merely enjoined them, when their faith should be attacked, or, in any particular crisis, to assemble their collected forces at the holy city of Umritsur. Hence the assumed authority of Runjit Sing must be considered as an usurpation and infraction of the sacred and fundamental laws of the Sikhs; and although that authority has been rendered agreeable to the majority of the community by advancing them to wealth, power, and command, in consequence of his numerous and splendid conquests, yet its establishment was long strenuously opposed, and was effected only by the destruction of the chiefs attached to the old system. Runjit's policy has led him to make an entirely new creation of chiefs and leaders, selecting them generally from the low classes, thereby subverting every principle of aristocracy, and forming a set of men attached to himself and the new order of things to which they owe their elevation. That the usurpation of Runjit Sing has been favorable to the increase of Sikh power no one can doubt, for anterior to that period, so far from having any common object or bond of union, they appear to have been engaged in perpetual strife with each other. That the condensation of their power and subjecting them individually to the operation of acknowledged laws has improved the state of society among them and excited a regard for reputation which did not before exist, is equally undeniable. Time was, that a Sikh and a robber were synonymous terms. At this period few thefts are heard of, and if the inclination still remains, the restraints of justice prevent its indulgence. At this day the operation of the laws is so effectual, that there are few eastern countries in which the solitary traveller might pass with more safety than in the Punjáb.

In the reign of the celebrated Doorannee Ahmed Sháh the Sikhs were prodigiously increasing the number of their converts, and were excited by all the phrenzy and confidence of new sectaries That great prince gave it as his opinion that it were prudent not to attack the Sihks until the fervor of their religious zeal had abated. Zemáun Sháh, in pursuance of his determination to invade Hindustán, several times entered the Punjáb, and was extremely anxious to reduce the Sikhs under his authority. He appears to have adopted conciliatory measures, and was so far successful, that the several chiefs, and even Runjit Sing, who was then powerful and pursuing his plans of sole rule, were finally induced to visit Lahore and acknowledge the supremacy of the Kábul Government. In one of the expeditions of Zemáun Sháh, Runjit Sing with numerous troops sought refuge at Putteeála, and repaid the Rájáh for his asylum by the seizure of many of his guns, implements of warfare, with which he was before unprovided. During the reign of Máhmud Sháh the Government of Kábul were too much occupied at home to attend to the Sikhs or the affairs of the Punjáb; they appear to have been engaged in intestine conflicts, while Runjit was steadily and successfully pursuing his ambitious plans, and the capture of Lahore about this period would seem to have been followed by the submission of his countrymen and the universal acknowledgment of his authority. It is certain that in the early part of the following reign of Shán Sujáh the Sikhs called him Pádisháh or king. The confusion in the countries west of the Indus and the expulsion of the king presented opportunities of aggrandisement too favorable to be neglected by Runjit Sing. He accordingly possessed himself of Attock and the countries west of the Indus, and after many attempts succeeded in reducing Kashmere, the fairest province under the Doorannee sway. Elated by this conquest, and full of zeal, and the desire of retaliation on Mahomedans, he proceeded to Multán, which after two or three repulses he carried by storm, the city was delivered to plunder, and the treasures, represented immense, of the Chief Mozuffer Khán, fell into the hands of the conqueror. He next successively reduced the town and country of Monkirah, which was, as well as Multán, tributary and dependent on Kábul, and took possession of Deyráh Gházi Khán, which formed an integral portion of the Doorannee country. While he was thus employed in the south and west, he was equally industrious and successful in the north and north-east among the native and independent Hindu states, subjecting Jummu, and establishing his claim to tribute from the several hill Rájáhs as Mundoye, &c. He moreover obtained the strong hill fort of Kote Kangrah from the illustrious Rájáh Sensar Chund of Sujauhanpore, previously driving away an army of Gurkás that besieged it. On the demise of this prince, about two years since, he invaded the dominions of Sujauhanpore on the most unjustifiable plea and annexed them to his own, the son of Sensar Chund seeking an asylum in British Hindustán. Runjit has also invaded Bháwulpore under pretence that the chief had assisted his enemy Sháh Sujah, and exacted a tribute of nine lákhs of rupees per annum, or one-half of the entire revenue of the country. The fertile province of Pesháwar has also been devastated by the Sikhs, who not only require annual tributes of horses and rice, but send large bodies of troops to ravage the country, apparently with the view to prevent its ever reassuming political importance. The country of the Eusofzye Patháns has alike been ravaged by Runjit Sing, who ordered an indiscriminate slaughter of the inhabitants. From this devastated country annual supplies of horses as tribute are enforced. Among the Eusofzye resides the notorious fanatic named Syed Ahmed Sháh. This man announced himself as the Imám Mehdi predicted in the Korán, and that he had arrived from Mecca with orders from heaven to take possession of the Punjáb, Hindustán and China, and that either he would make Runjit Sing a Mussulmán or cut off his head. He was enthusiastically received among the wild, ignorant and barbarous tribes of Patháns, and assembled immense numbers, some say 150,000 men; but as they were badly armed and acted under no kind of order, they were easily defeated by 15,000 Sikhs commanded by a gallant old veteran Boodh Sing, since dead. The Syed persisted that success would ultimately crown his views, and being unable to wage direct war with the Sikhs from his scanty means and resources, directs his hostilities against the Doorannee Chiefs of Pesháwar, whom he stigmatizes as infidels, they having moved to the rear in his action with the Shiks. Yar Mahomed the elder brother, he speaks of with the Hindu appellation of Yaru Sing. He keeps these chiefs in perpetual alarm by inroads into their possessions; and I heard on leaving the Punjáb that he had succeeded in the capture of Hissar or Hasannuggur and Pesháwar, and having seduced Yar Mahomed to an audience, he cut off his head and those of the Sirdárs who attended him. He would not however be able to maintain himself in Pesháwar, as the Chief of Kábul, Dost Mahomed and brother of Yar Mahomed, immediately marched on Pesháwar with a powerful force, while Runjit Sing marched 50,000 men from Lahore. If he escaped being taken, he is still probably a vagabond in the mountains of the Eusofzye.

Reverting to the countries tributary to Runjit Sing must be included the whole of the petty states between the Indus and the range of Soliman west of it and on the banks of that river to the parallel of Attock. The mode of collecting their several tributes is peculiarly vexatious and appears intended as an insolent display of power and to impoverish the countries. The tribute does not appear even to be fixed, but to be perfectly arbitrary; and in the instance of the petty states I have mentioned, dependent upon the will of Hurri Sing, who commands for Runjit in the countries east of the Indus. A numerous body of horsemen, say 60 to 100 men, without any previous notice, arrive at the residence of a chief and demand 40,000, 50,000, 60,000 rupees, as the case may be, and while this sum, which to such men is excessive, will be preparing, these men are living perhaps six months at the expense of the state. At Peshawar this evil is seriously felt, where 10,000 or 20,000 men sometimes march and destroy the whole cultivation. On the eastern side Runjit Sing cannot pass the Sutledje without violating his treaty with the British Government in Hindustan; on all other sides he is at liberty to act, and contemplates the conquest of Kábul and Sind. From the latter country he has been in the habit of receiving annual presents since his invasion of Bháwalpur, when he advanced as far as Subseldah Kote, the frontier town of the Sindee or Serai States. The amount of his revenue I believe accurately estimated at two crores and a half of rupees. This sum is small, viewing the very large and fertile countries belonging to him, but from the barbarous policy of the Sikh conqueror in carrying fire and sword through all vanquished countries, the value of his conquests has much diminished; and the beautiful province of Kashmere, the very commercial Suba of Multán, as well as Monkira, &c., by no means supply the revenue they contributed to their former masters. Neither is the revenue I have mentioned to be considered the whole absolute revenue of the country at large, which would produce much more, but a large portion of it is held in jághirs by his officers and troops, there being scarcely a Sikh who is not a jághirdár; and from lands so granted no benefit accrues to the king's treasury. Shaum Sing, a considerable chief, holds one hundred and fifty towns and villages in jághir, which yield a revenue of three lákhs of rupees. This is not the largest of the Sikh jághirs, those held by the minister Dyan Sing, Hurri Sing, Futteh Sing, Khusial Sing, &c., Sirdárs of high consideration, are probably much more important. I suppose four crores of rupees annually would not fall short of the annual revenue of the Punjáb were the amount of the jághírs carried into the computation, which perhaps it should strictly be, as the king receives the benefit of it in the pay and maintenance of the larger portion of his troops. Of the two crores and a half revenue actually coming into the king's possession, it is supposed that after paying the charges of Government and foreign troops, as natives of Hindustán proper, Gurkhás, Patháns, &c., he is enabled to place in deposit one crore of rupees. It is further believed that he has already in his treasury ten crores of rupees in money, and his various magazines of musquets and military stores are annually increased in a certain ratio.

The military force of Runjit Sing next demands attention, and the number of men I believe may, in round numbers, be estimated at 70,000, of which perhaps 20,000 are disciplined after the French mode. The Sikhs themselves universally assert, in their manner of expressing the number of bunduks or matchlocks among them, to be at least equal to three lákhs, which supposes 300,000 men; but this is obviously an enormous exaggeration, for we are only to ask the question where are these men to be found, to be convinced of the fallacy of the assertion. I do not pretend to speak positively as to the position and numbers of the Sikh troops, but generally speaking the following particulars may be depended on:—

		Rs.	
In Kashmere	... ...	10,000	Under orders of Shivprasád, Bráhmin.
With the King	... ...	3,000	
Kurruk Sing	... ...	2,000	
Sheer Sing	... ...	3,000	Sons of the King.
Tarrah Sing	... ...	1,500	

		Rs.	
Rájáh Dyan Sing	... ...	5,000	Prime Minister.
Hurree, Sing including various Sikh Chiefs under his orders.		10,000	In command of the frontier on the Indus.
Khusial Sing	... ...	3,000	Renegade Bráhmin generally near the King.
Shaum Sing	... ...	800	One of the ancient Chiefs.
Futteh Sing	... ...	500	In authority towards the Sutledje, I believe at Alloa.
Gundee Sing, commanding troops at Multán.		1,000	
Officer commanding troops at Monkira	...	500	
Runjit Nujjibs	... ...	1,000	First raised Regiment of Runjit's.
Chevalier Allard's Cavalry	... ...	3,000	Comprising 1 Regiment Lancers, 2 Regiments Dragoons.
Monsieur Ventura's Infantry	...	4,000	Comprising 2 Battalion Regiments, 1 Regiment Light Infantry, and 1 Regiment Gurkhás.
Monsieur Court's do.	...	1,000	Battalion Regiment.
Monsieur Avitabile's do.	...	1,000	Do.
Mr. Mevires's do.	...	1,500	Do.
Mr. Campbell's Cavalry	... ...	1,200	This officer dismissed Regiment Light Cavalry.
Mr. Garron's do.	... ...	600	Do. do.
Dowkul Sing's Pultan	... ...	1,000	Battalion Regiment.
New raised Regiment Infantry	...	1,000	Not yet provided with muskets; marching about with sticks.
Troops forming the Camp of the late Monsieur Amise Infantry	...	4,000	These Battalion Regiment.
Cavalry	... ...	2,000	These Light Cavalry.
Artillery men, reckoning broadly 10 men to every gun, supposing 200 guns, principally Horse Artillery	...	2,000	
Allowance for troops of Rájáh Guláb Sing of Jummu and the various petty Sikh Chiefs who entertain from 10 to 200 followers on a liberal computation	...	10,000	
	Total ...	73,600	

(Regulars bracket encompasses Chevalier Allard's Cavalry through Artillery men entries.)

The disciplined troops of Runjit Sing have a highly respectable appearance, are well clothed and equipped, and appear to be in want of no necessaries. Their value in the field remains yet to be ascertained. On the few occasions they have seen service, their enemies have been too contemptible to establish a criterion. The regiments are indiscriminately filled with Mussalmáns and Sikhs, and wear for head dress the puggree of the Punjáb, each regiment adopting a distinguishing and particular color, as red, blue, green, &c.; in other respects they are clothed similarly to the native troops in the British Indian service. The regiment of Gurkhás alone wear caps. As soldiers, the natives of the Punjáb are extremely patient of fatigue and capable of making prodigious marches with apparent ease, of which indeed they pride themselves, and evince not only willingness, but pleasure, and mutual emulation in learning military exercises. But they are much addicted to plunder, and it is invariably their custom at the close of a march to separate over the country (even in their own territories) for perhaps four or five miles armed with short sticks or cudgels, and make booty of any thing that comes into their way. They have frequently been known to employ violence. As men, physically speaking, the natives of the Punjáb have a much more manly aspect than the natives that I have seen of Hindustán proper. Their limbs are muscular and well proportioned, and they have a stoutness in the leg and solidity of calf seldom seen, in the Hindustán. Instances of tall stature are rare, the general standard being the middle size. These observations apply particularly to the more considerable or Mussalmán portion of the population. The Sikhs taken collectively are certainly a fine race of men, and many of them have a fairness of complexion not discoverable among the Mussalmáns, their neighbours. Many of their men are remarkable for stature and a majestic gait, and models of masculine beauty may frequently be met with among them. Their women being not permitted to go abroad I can scarcely speak decidedly concerning them, but the some five or six I have by chance met with would justify the supposition that the Sikh ladies were not deficient in personal charms. They wear extraordinary high conical caps which produce a most curious effect; they also wear trowsers. The dress of the men is peculiar, but not inelegant, consisting of the Punjáb puggree for the head, a vest or jacket made to fit close to the body and arms, and large bulky trowsers terminating and gradually lessening beneath the knee, the legs from the calfs being naked. Chiefs however occasionally wear full trowsers. Over the shoulders a scarf is usually thrown. Generally speaking these articles are white, and I never saw a Sikh with dirty linen. The scarf will be trimmed with some colored silk, or sometimes shawls of scarlet or other showy colors are employed. A mounted and gaily dressed Sikh, well armed, riding against the wind with his scarlet scarf streaming behind him, has a fine effect. Such a sight has often reminded me of the first line of a popular song—"A knight of a gay and gallant mien." The Sikhs, I have before said, are almost exclusively a military race, few of them applying to agriculture, and such as do, considering themselves in a double capacity. They pay much attention to the breed of horses, and there is scarcely any Sikh who has not one or more of these valuable animals. Hence among the irregular cavalry, to which service they are most partial, every man's horse is *bonâ fide* his own property; and even in the regular cavalry a very trifling proportion of the horses is the property of the king. The Sikhs, it must be confessed, are barbarous as far as the want of information and intelligence can make them; yet they have not that savage character which makes demons of the wild tribes of western Asia. They are frank, generous, social and lively. The cruelties they have practised towards the Mahomedans in the countries they have subdued ought not, I think, to be alledged against them as a proof of ferocity. They were urged to them through a spirit of retaliation. Heaven knows, the fury of the begotted Mahomedan is terrible, and the unhappy and persecuted Sikhs had been literally hunted like beasts of the field. At present flushed by a series of victories and conquests, the Sikhs have a high buoyancy of spirit, and a zeal almost amounting to fanaticism. Morality, I believe, is scarcely recognized amongst them; and chastity, I have been told, is neither observed nor expected to be observed by their women. But the infringements on the rules of propriety must be made by themselves and among themselves when they are not thought criminal. Liberties taken with strangers would be esteemed as crimes and punished accordingly. Should the Sikhs continue an independent nation, when it may be supposed that civilization will gradually remove those features of barbarism which are now visible, the Sikh will become a very amiable nation. Though professed converters, they are perfectly tolerant, and though singular in some of their customs, they never require you to imitate them. On the whole having been long among the ferocious tribes of Khorásán, or the degraded race of Sindees and Daoudpootres, I was much pleased with the Sikhs; and the general ignorance which prevails among them is more a misfortune than a crime, and to that I conceive their deviations from decorum and other foibles are chiefly imputable.

The Sikhs I have mentioned are principally cavalry, and they have a peculiar kind of exercise, at which they are very expert. In action their reliance is not so much upon the charge, it is upon a desultory species of warfare, to which they are well trained. It consists in advancing on their enemies until their matchlocks can take effect, discharging them, and immediately precipitately retreating, then reloading and again advancing. They are considered sure shots ; and their plan has hitherto answered, as they have had to encounter no opponents provided with strong divisions of artillery. Among the irregulars they have a peculiar set of fanatics called Byarulleah, who clothe themselves in black and carry round the head a circular steel ring with a rim, perhaps an inch broad, the edge of which is very sharp. I at first supposed this appendage to the head dress was intended to frustrate the stroke of a sword, but afterwards learned that it was an offensive weapon thrown by the hand, and was assured that these men could eject it with such force, and that too at a great distance, that they would cut off the leg of a horse or even of an elephant.

The pay of the troops holding jághírs is of course very variable, and no standard can be fixed. The pay of the regular infantry is professed to be (to the private soldier) one rupee more than is given by the British in Hindustán. The pay of the officers is also fixed, but is not regular, as those made by king himself receive extravagant allowances, while those promoted by the officers commanding troops receive only the fixed stipend, which is comparatively trifling. The forces are not regularly paid, but they are certain of receiving all arrears once during the year. The Sikhs are allowed every year the indulgence of leave for three months to visit their homes, and on their return at the period of Dussera, the king reviews the assembled force of his empire. Umritsur is usually the spot selected for this review. The Sikhs being permitted the free use of wine, it is much to their credit that during the nine months they are present with their regiments the greater part of them religiously abstain from it, and make up for their forbearance during the revelry of the liberty season.

I shall terminate this brief notice with a few remarks on Runjit Sing and his personal character. Runjit was the son of one Maha Sing, and was born at a small town, I believe about sixty kos from Lahore on the road to Peshawar. In his early infancy he manifested a predilection for war, and all his amusements had reference to that art. Such was the barbarity of the Sikhs at this period, that the young son of a chief was not taught to read or write—accomplishments which he has never since acquired. On the demise of his father he became possessed of two thousand horse and the town of his birth. He immediately commenced the grand object of aggrandizement. It was one of his first objects to raise a foreign regiment of foot, a singular proof of sagacity in a country where every one was a horseman ; this battalion, called the Nujjib Pultan, was of eminent service to him, is still kept up by him, and enjoys peculiar privileges. He was some years employed in the reduction of his own countrymen, and finally by taking advantage of the disorders in Kábul, he has become a powerful prince and the only absolutely independent one that exists in what may be called Hindustán. Runjit owes his elevation entirely to his own ability and energy. He has always acted on the impulse of his own mind and never consulted a second person. Although at present surrounded with ministers and officers, he takes no opinion on important state affairs. As a general, setting aside his good fortune, he has exhibited decisive proofs of great personal valor, quickness of conception, and promptitude of execution; he exemplified in the investment of Multán an acquaintance with stratagem, and in the siege of Monkira remarkable perseverance and a possession of resources to meet difficulties, which would have done honour to any General. In his relation with his troops he appears to great advantage, enjoying the general esteem which his kindness and generosity have secured. Not a day passes without thousands of fervent aspirations for the continuance of his life. He is equally popular among the generality of his subjects, and rules with an equal hand both Mussalmáns and Hindus. The only hardship of which the former can justly complain is the interdiction of báng or summons to prayer; but they should recollect that the sceptre has passed from the princes of Islám and flourishes in the hands of the sons of Brahma. His devastation of countries on their first subjection, a measure injurious to his own interest, would not seem to originate in a wanton delight of cruelty, or callosity of feeling, but in obedience to a barbarous system of warfare long established in those regions. The annual terrific visit to Pesháwar and other dependent tributary states is evidently with the political view of keeping those states depressed and preventing the possibility of a reaction. Although himself illiterate, on the only occasion which ever presented itself to him of showing his respect for literature, during his first entry into Pesháwar, he availed himself of it, and issued positive orders as to the preservation of the extensive library of the Mussalmán Saint at Chumkunnee. That the library was afterwards injured, and by the Sikhs, was not the fault of Runjit Sing. This prince must be deemed charitable, if we may judge from the large sums daily lavished upon Fakeers and others. He is doubtlessly extremely liberal in his actions, as evinced in his behaviour to his Mussalmán subjects; they are admitted to all posts and ranks, and his favored physician is Fakeer Assizuldeen. Although he has elevated some of his menial servants to the highest commands in the state and army, it must be admitted they have proved men of high merit: Witness Hurri Sing, and Khusial Sing. His Minister Meer Dyan Sing was found a stripling in the jungle on some ravaging expedition; he has not proved deficient in talents, although much so in moral excellence, unless he be belied. Runjit Sing has three sons. The eldest, Kurruk Sing, is of a placid and quiet disposition, much inclined to justice, and has often remonstrated against some of his father's violent measures, particularly the occupation of Sujauhaunpur. Shir Sing the second, partakes of the warlike character of his father, and is very popular with the army. The third, Tarra Sing, is still young. These sons are by different mothers. It is foreseen already, even by the Sikhs, that the succession will be disputed; and on the death of Runjit this circumstance, and the inevitable revolt of the Mussalmáns, will involve the Punjáb in all the horrors of anarchy. In person Runjit Sing is a little above the middle size, and very thin; his complexion fair; his features regular and nose aquiline; he carries a long white beard, and wants the left eye. Though apparently far advanced in years, I believe he has not completed sixty. On the right side of his neck a large scar is visible, probably the effect of a wound. In his diet he is represented as abstemious. For some supposed ailment he makes daily use of laudanum. Simple in his dress, which is white linen, he wears on his arm the celebrated diamond Kohinoor, of which he deprived Sháh Sujáh. His attendants, I mean his domestics, &c., are clad splendidly, and display a profusion of gold and ornaments. Although Runjit in his political relations with the Mussalmáns to the west assumes a high tone and the name of Pádisháh, yet at home he simply styles himself Sircar. The principal fault of this prince is ambition, "the glorious vice of kings," which sometimes leads him into unjustifiable measures, of which the most flagrant was the expulsion of the rája of Sujauhanpore, on no better plea than that he would not consent to disgrace his rank and descent by giving his sister in marriage to the Minister Dyan Sing, a man of low caste and questionable character. To sum up his character, he is a prince of consummate ability, a warrior brave and skilful, possessed of many shining virtues, and his few vices are rather the consequence of the barbarous period at which he was born than inherents in his nature. If there be a prince of antiquity to whom he may be compared, I think it might be Philip of Macedon, and perhaps on a comparison of their actions, their means and advantages of birth, it may be conceded that the more splendid course has been run by the conqueror of the Punjáb.

(A True Copy.)
(Signed)   D. WILSON,
Resident, Persian Gulf.

Lahore viâ Multán, Ooch, Kirepore, Hyderabad and Tatta, to Karáchi and the Ocean: By Mr. C. MASSON.

No. 10.

There are two routes from Lahore to Multán, one used during the dry seasons, and the other, which is also the longest, made available in the wet season. Having traversed both in progress to and from Lahore, I shall proceed to make such observations as my recollection may furnish concerning them. In the dry season the route of Syed-walla and Commallea is taken, computed at 120 kos, being

to Syed-walla	40
to Commallea	40
to Multán	40
	120

On leaving Lahore you proceed by Noa Kote, and keeping the river on your right hand you march twelve kos, where the river making a detour to the east is crossed and you take the road to Syed-walla, the river now flowing to your left. In this first march after leaving Noa Kote the country gently rises, and you see the stream winding in the plain beneath. Your elevated position gives the opportunity of beholding a most magnificent and extensive view of the valley of Ravee, which exhibits a fine scene of verdure and cultivation. Destitute of any striking features of mountain crest or foaming torrent, it possesses the charms of placid beauty and repose, and amid the mingled associations of thoughts to which it gives rise none was in my mind more prevalent than admiration of the sovereign whose protecting sway has enabled his subjects in a very few years to become prosperous, and even to change the face of nature. It were needless to observe, leaving so great a capital as Lahore, that numerous villages occur in this march, and a large one is seated on the northern or Lahore side of the Ravee at the point you cross it. You now *enchemin* to Syed-walla about 28 kos pass a rich, luxuriant, highly cultivated tract of country, interspersed with an abundance of villages, large and small. In most of these you observe the peculiar square brick-built towers of the Sikh chiefs of former days, and you may be able to appreciate the state of society among these petty lords or tyrants ere Runjit Sing's superior genius destroyed their authority. The bér tree (Zizyphus jujuba) is universal throughout this space, nor is it confined to the neigbourhood of villages. It attains so great a size, and so much sweetness, that I felt almost inclined to rank it with other fruit-trees. I cannot here forbear remarking how strongly the ancient accounts of the surprizing fertility and population of the Punjáb appear confirmed at the present day. Nor is it less calculated to excite surprize how singularly the country has been able to recover in some degree, and that suddenly, from the desolation in which it had been plunged ever since the demise of Aurangzebe, both by the internal ravages of the independent Sikhs and the Afghán invaders. Syed-walla is a considerable walled town, with spacious and excellent bázár. Two or three hundred yards east of it is a sound fortress with trench. From hence to Lahore I must not omit to mention the very general cultivation of a plant called bugglár, and in Persian nakoot, with the seeds of which they feed horses, and of the flour make bread for themselves. The bread is perfectly sweet, but not white; I prefer wheat. The seeds are also eaten parched and sold in every bázár. From Syed-walla the road leads through a delightful country (although not with exactly the same clusters of villages) until you arrive again at the Ravee, and for a considerable distance you trace a parallel course. The high road runs a little distance from the river, but you may follow a secondary path immediately on its banks which are embellished with groves of date trees, in which you meet at intervals with wells shaded by the branching peepul. The opposite bank is decorated in the same manner and the view upon the river on either side is extremely fine. You again cross it at a spot perhaps 30 kos from Syed-walla, after which the country is not so cultivated or populous, and jungle commences ten kos; four or five villages being passed on the road, brings you to Commallea, a town with bázár. It appears a very ancient town, and built with burnt bricks. Here is a small fort, the residence of the Sikh Chief, who has a good garden. From hence to Multán 40 kos, villages are few generally speaking, but many wells are occasionally met with where the cultivator or owner of cattle fixes his abode, and here the traveller may obtain liberty to pass the night. This tract is inhabited by a tribe called Jats, who have but an indifferent character, nor is it deemed prudent for single travellers to pass. I did so, and escaped unhurt or unmolested. But I believe on one occasion the display of firmness prevented an attack. On approaching Multán, and at a distance from it of about three miles to the east of the road, is a considerable mud fort; a little farther on a large building, alone on the desert plain, attracts attention with its lofty minarets, and proves to be an ancient masjid. Soon after this you have a view of the city which you enter passing over the ruins which surround it. This road I travelled in the month of April coming from Sind, and before noticing Multán particularly will describe, as well as I can, the other route adopted in the wet seasons, and which I passed in the month of August. The first march is the same as in the former route to the banks of the river, when instead of crossing you trace a course more or less parallel with its eastern bank. In this route for four or five marches the country may be called populous, although not so much so as on the other side of the river, villages being found generally at short distances, and some of them large; one of them, Santghurra, had a fine Sikh fort, and occurred in the third or fourth march. In this part of the country the villages are principally occupied by Sikhs, and the greater portion of it being pasture land of excellent herbage, is favourable to the rearing of horses, to which they pay much attention. I suspect that with little exception the villages seldom extended beyond the line of our march and that on the eastern side spread a thick and intense jungle, perhaps to the border of the Sutledge. We must have marched at least seven marches when we arrived at a small place where there was a high dilapidated fort, a small pond or lake of water, and a detached eminence to the west surmounted with ruined edifices. This place had some fame for sanctity among the Mussulmáns on account of some fakeer who had resided here in recent days, and we were shown an immense circular stone perforated with a hole, which it was said served the saint for a bangle. He appears to have been a man of depraved appetite as to food, which consisted, say his Moslem admirers, in dirt. This spot however is of higher importance as connected with a tradition of the existence of a city here at a very remote period which was destroyed in a peculiar manner by the immediate orders of Heaven in consequence of the sins in which the inhabitants indulged. On other eminences south of the present fort and village which lie in the plain are the evident traces of former buildings, and fragments of bricks, &c., are scattered around in all quarters and for great distances. From the eminences you have an extensive view of the country on either side; to the west, after a short distance, open the course of the Ravee distinguished but the stream not visible; to the east intricate jungle as far as the eye can reach. The grass at this village was particularly luxuriant. We ascended the latter-mentioned emiences to pass the night that we might avoid a species of stinging fly called mutchar, which we were told was still troublesome, but our precautions were vain, the horses of our party were absolutely mad, and we were compelled to march the night. (I may here note that I was in company with a Sikh chief and a party of 100 horse.) Towards two or three o'clock we arrived at the small village of Chicha Wutnee, and again saw, not I believe the Ravee but a large branch of it. We found a large boat here, and in the evening were rowed up and down the river; the Sikh Sirdár had his band of musicians and singing men. From Chicha Wutnee made a long march, I believe 15 kos, in which once came in contact with the stream. Another day's march brought us in a line with and about a mile from Tooloomba, a large fortified town. Near our encampment was the ruin of a fort, the walls immensely high and thick, and the inner dispositions alike massy and surprising. Its antiquity is said to be very great, and undoubtedly was a wonderful edifice. The country the last two or three days was absolutely an unproductive jungle; hence to Multán four days' march. The jungle is not so thick and the country is inhabited principally by men who erect temporary villages and keep large number of cows paying to the Government a duty of one rupee per head annually for the privilege of grazing. The soil is sandy, and as you approach Multán, the villages (that is, stationary ones,) commence. In each of these is the distinguishing boorj or tower. The distance of this road may be 180 kos, but it is perfectly dry and convenient. The latter part is unsafe for the individual. I think we made it in 14 marches. Multán has a good effect in the distance, which it loses on our near approach. It is walled in, and its bázár, narrow and extensive, exhibits but little of that bustle or activity which might be expected in a city of so much reputed commerce. The citadel, if not a place of extreme strength, is one on which more attention seems to have been bestowed than I have observed in any fortress not constructed by European engineers. It is well secured by a deep trench neatly faced on its sides by masonry, and the defences of the entrance appear to much advantage. This fort comprises the only buildings worth seeing in the town, the battered palace of the last independent Chief and Zeárats, the fine and lofty gomuts or domes of which are the principal ornaments of Multán. Although miserably decreased in trade since it fell into the hands of the Sikhs, its bázár continues well supplied. There are numerous bankers, and many manufactures are carried on, particularly printing of coarse linens, &c. It also still supplies a portion of the cloth which the annual caravans carry into the countries west of the Indus. The ruins in the vicinity are very extensive, particularly to the south; and gardens, some of them very large, abound well stocked with fruit-trees, particularly mangoes and oranges. On the north stands the well preserved Zeárat of the celebrated Shummuz Tabreez, who was, agreably to the tradition here, skinned alive. To a malediction of this personage the excessive heat of Multán is attributed, and the sun, it is asserted, is nearer to it than to any other place. Shummuz in his agony calling upon that orb to revenge him, claiming an affinity at least in name, when it obligingly quitted its sphere and approached the unfortunate town. The articles of consumption as flour, rice, sugar, &c., are very plentiful and cheap at Multán. It lies two or three miles east of the Ravee, where there is what is termed a bandar or port, or in this instance expressive of a boat station, whence it has a communication with the Indus, and consequently with the sea. This however is seldom used, there being little or no trade from Lahore to Multán. Also in the wet season there is a passage on the Ravee, but I never heard of its employment, but for the expedition of troops. Multán at the period of its capture by the Sikhs was in the hands of Mozuffer Khán (Pathán) with the assumed title of Naváb. Runjit Sing had made two unsuccessful attempts on the town, but had devastated the country. The third time of his approach, having made a feint to attack Khanghur, a fortress 20 kos distant, the Pathán Chief threw the better part of his troops into it when the Sikhs countermarched and invested Multán. The defence was very obstinate, and on the final assault Mozuffer Khán lost his life and his sovereignty together, while his daughter, celebrated for piety and learning, fell over a heap of Sikhs she herself had slain. At present a Brahmin Soand Mull resides here as governor for the king with the title of Soobáhdár. He has under his orders one Gunder Sing commanding 800 troops. The peasantry express themselves indulgently used, and consider themselves leniently taxed at one-third of the produce of their lands. From Multán proceeding southerly 20 kos the country dry with jungle and occasional villages arrive at Sujáhbád, a large fortified town, from

B 1485—46

its lofty and ancient battlements more picturesque than Multán. Here is an admirable bázár, I thought in nowise inferior to that of the latter city. I question also if Multán can much surpass it in size. It has a garrison and a few guns mounted. Near this place are some very large gardens, particularly one bearing the name of Mozuffer Khán. There is a very large cultivation of sugarcane here, extending 2 or 3 kos from the town; hence the road leading easterly and again southerly conducts to Peer Jallálpore, the distance of 18 kos, and the intermediate space diversified for the first 5 or 6 kos; good cultivation for 4 or 5, grass jungles, and then a sandy jungle; reaching the town a manufacture of saltpetre is passed. Peer Jallálpore is a good town held by the Sikhs with sufficient bázár. It derives its destination of Peer Jallálpore from containing the tomb of some Mussalmán saint, a handsome erection standing north on entering the town; it is covered with painted tiles, has its minarets, and a fine dome. There is another large village called Chota or Little Jallálpore in the direction between this place and Sujáhbád, and singularly, although surrounded by Sikh territory, belongs to the Khán of Bháwalpore. Travellers coming from Sujáhbád must be particular in asking for Peer Jallálpore, otherwise they may be directed (as I was) to the other Jallálpore, which is out of the direct road, but not seriously. From Jallálpore about half a mile we arrive at a large cut or arm of some river which was fordable in April, wading up to the chin, and not so in September or perhaps October. A boat is stationed here. This water forms the boundary of the Sikh and Bháwalpore territories. A mile south of it a village distinguished by its groves of date trees, as I should have noted, is Peer Jallálpore. From this village viewing on all sides the traces of villages and cultivation, arrive on the banks of the Gurrar river, skirting which about a kos and a half cross it at a ferry and a course of about 8 kos conducts you to the towns of Ooch embosomed in an immense assemblage of date trees. There are now two Ooches seated contiguous and in the same line, the eastern one is small, but contains a celebrated Zeárat, a building, very old, large and handsome. The other Ooch is termed Peer-ki Ooch, the revenue being applied to the benefit of Peer Nusserdeen, who resides here. You enter this town indeed by gates, but there are no walls. It is wonderfully ancient, and the bázár, covered so as to exclude the solar rays, is very extensive. I was surprised to notice that the bulk of the shopkeepers were sellers of sweetmeats, but an acquaintance and relish for dainties might perhaps have been expected in the episcopal city of a powerful Mussalmán prelate. South of these two towns lie the immense ruins of former periods, and the prodigious number of date trees and venerable peepals prove the fact of the extent of the ancient city and also the Hindu faith of its inhabitants. Many of the buildings are at this time in that state that a very little expense might render them habitable—* so solid was their structure; and they are all of them in the very best style of Hindu architecture. A great number of wells are interspersed among the ruins, some of them still worked. Although aware that the grounds I was traversing had been rendered classical by the expeditions of Alexander, and also that I had seen at Multán, the capital of Malli, my knowledge did not enable me to divine that in the ruins at Ooch I beheld those of the capital of the Oxydranee, or their interest would have been increased in a high degree. Leaving Ooch, its antiquities, and sacred groves, we immediately pass Mogul-ka-Shar, a little ruined hamlet so called from a Mogal colony that formerly settled here, and 3 short kos bring us to Ramkully, also evidently an ancient place. Here are large remains of burnt brick buildings and those of a very substantial mud fort; this appears to have been destroyed in late

---

* Writing this, reminds me of the existence of ancient buildings at Jallálpore which sufficiently attest its antiquity, not so extensive as those of Ooch; its prosperous period must be carried to the same era, the same style prevailing in the buildings.

years by the first Bháwal Khán, grandfather of the present Chief of Bháwalpore. The traditions of the natives authenticate the antiquity and former opulence and extent of Ramkully. At present it may have a dozen houses inhabited. Among them is a Hindu dealer. It has numerous scattered date trees about it, the indubitable evidences in these countries of fertility of soil, population, and antiquity. From Ramkully we pass 2 or 3 kos through fine pasture lands with many small villages, then pass a tract of sandy jungle with low bushes, and four or five kos bring us to a small but apparently commercial little town called Chunny Khan-ka-Kote; hence 4 kos through alternate jungle and cultivation to a small fordable stream, which is crossed, and you pass to Allahabad, a town distinguished by its groves of trees at some distance. From Ooch to Allahabad by this route is computed 14 kos. There is another southerly road leading from Ooch for a long distance pacing the bank of a broad watercourse, but generally dry (in October). In this passage there are numerous villages and extensive cultivation. At 6 kos from Allahabad is a very large village and 2 kos further a good town with bázár called Googujerwalla; 4 kos from hence is Allahabad. This is a pleasantly situated town with bázár. It is 20 kos west of Ahmedpore, the head-quarters of the Bháwalpore Khán's forces, and 40 koses from Bhawalpore, the capital. From Allahabad there is a distance of 20 kos to Khánpore, one of the most commercial towns in the state. The country all this road is fine and populous, especially to the left. To the right extends sandy jungles, which terminate in the absolute desert of Jeselmere. The neighbourhood of Khánpore is famous for indigo and rice; the quantity, however, is more surprizing than the quality. From Khánpore passing 4 or 5 kos we pass into a less cultivated country, but containing villages at reasonable distances. A course of 40 kos leads to Chota Ahmedpore, having passed numerous large and small hamlets and the town of Nushara. Ahmedpore had once a wall, and in the judgment of those people may be supposed to have one still, but it is useless in point of defence. It has also a new erection, which may be called the citadel; the bázár is comparatively good, and the town is garrisoned with a regiment of 350 infantry and provided with six pieces of ordnance, it being the frontier post on the side of Sind. Five kos from Ahmedpore is the castle of Fazilpore with a garrison of 100 men. This is a massive structure with lofty walls and huge bastions, but gradually crumbling into decay. East of it is at all times a large deposit of water, and at the period of the inundations of the Indus it becomes with its dependent small hamlet entirely isolated. Here formerly stood a very large town called also Fazilpore. Its walls, 360 in number, are still in the jungle, but scarcely another vestige of its existence is observable. It was destroyed by the Indus but a few years since, and a garden of fruit trees north of the present fort was in being but four years since. This also has been destroyed, and a solitary date tree remains in evidence of the fact. I did not before know that fresh water as well as salt was fatal to trees. The inundations of the Indus have sensibly increased latterly, and in these parts so completely is the country covered with water that at certain periods the communication with Khánpore is kept up through the medium of boats, Khánpore being from the banks of the Indus 57 kos. The high road into Sind leads from Chota Ahmedpore to Subseldáh Kote, a distance of 7 kos through jungle. But it may be as well before entering Sind to make a few observations on the country we are about to leave. Bháwalpore, or the country known by that name, is one of considerable dimensions; for instance, a line drawn from Goodiana, the frontier on the Putteeála side, to Fazilpore, the frontier post on the Sind quarter, produces about 300 miles direct distance, and another from the Bikkáneer frontier to Deyráb Gházie Khán furnishes about 200 miles, the former line being from the north-eastern to the south-western extremity, and the latter from the north-western to the south-eastern extremity. Of this extent of country there are some marked distinctions as to soil, character, and produce. The portion leading to Goodiána from the capital I have not seen but have heard it spoken of in glowing terms as to fertility and population : these it would seem entitled to possess, as its fertility would be secured by its bordering on the Gurráh river, and fertility would induce population; indeed I suspect this portion to yield to no other in the state for natural advantages. Immediately east and south-east of Bháwalpore (I mean the city) is the desert, the northern part of what is termed the great desert of Sind. This is of course but little productive although containing amongst others the forts and towns of Mozghur, Mooroot and Pooleráh. Delore, a fortress 18 kos south-east of Ahmedpore, is the spot where the treasures of the Khán are kept, and where in fact he resides a good deal. In the line from Ooch to Deyráh Gházie Khán there is a good quantity of jungle, but nevertheless a large number of villages, seven or eight towns, and much cultivation even of sugarcane. From the capital to Khánpore the cultivation is good although confined to the south by the sandy jungle, and from Khánpore to Ahmedpore (Chota) the face of the country changes and becomes more adapted for grazing owing to the greater moisture. It is in the immediate centre of the country that the most luxuriance prevails, including the districts of Ooch. Here are produced in great quantities rice, wheat, and indigo, all of which are largely exported. The Bháwalpore country is at once one of the most productive and cheapest in the world. The seasons here are divided into two only, the hot and the cold; but in the cold during the day the heat is very oppressive. It seldom or never rains. This deficiency is in nowise felt in respect of the cultivation, there not being any part of the country exempt from the operation of the inundations of the Indus or those of the tributary Punjáb streams. Vegetables of numerous kinds are very plentiful, as are some fruits as mangoes, plantains, oranges, pomegranates, &c. There are also dates for which Deyráh Gházie Khán is particularly famous, and they are so plentiful that they are retailed at one pice the puckah ser or lb. The reigning prince of Bhawalpore is of a tribe called Daud-pootre, signifying the sons of David. They formerly lived about Shikárpore, but becoming numerous and perhaps refractory, they were expelled that territory, and passing the Indus possessed themselves of the country they found, where they established separate independent states, and many of them built towns to which they gave their respective names; hence Bháwalpore, the town of Bháwal, Ahmedpore, the town of Ahmed, Fazilpore, the town of Fazil, and Subseldáh Kote, the fort of Subsel. I know not how long they may have continued in this state, ; but Bháwal Khán, the grandfather of the present Khán, reduced them all, and made himself absolute. He died full of years and glory, and was succeeded by his son Saodut Khán, who, after acknowledging the supremacy of Runjit Sing and consenting to pay a tribute of nine lákhs of rupees annually, died, and was succeeded by his son, the present Bháwal Khán ; this is a young man of very prepossessing appearance, and I believe is generally popular. He has a reputation for possessing a manly spirit, but he is clogged by an all-powerful minister, who, it is supposed, is sold to the Sikhs; this man's name is Yákub Mahomed. A Hindu named Mooti Rám is his minister of finance, and one Mahomed Khán, a kind of superintendent and paymaster to the forces, who, when they go on service, are generally under the orders of Yákub Mahomed. The troops consist of 7 Regiments of Infantry at 350 men each, amounting to 2,450 men. Each regiment has 6 guns attached, which may suppose 400 Artillerymen. He has besides foot companies of 50 men, 100 men, 200 men, &c., all Patháns and Rohillás, under their immediate officers, who may have 1, 2, 3 or more flags, as the case may be. Such sort of troops may be estimated at 1,000. He has moreover his horse, which I cannot think to be more than 3,000 men, making a total of 7,000 men, the native accounts say 14,000, but I never could ascertain where the men were. The annual revenue to the state is computed at 18 lákhs of rupees, one-half of which is paid to the Sikhs, from whom the Khán rents the territory of Deyráh Gházi Khán for 3 lákhs of rupees. It is said by this he gains two lákhs.

Arrived at Subseldáh Kote, which has been noted, belonging at present to Sind and its frontier station. This town was wrested from the Bháwalpore sway in the time of Sohdut Khán. It is of good size and walled in; has 3 guns mounted on the ramparts. The bázár is comparatively good. From this place there are two routes to Kirepore, an easterly one followed generally in the dry season, and a westerly one tracing for the latter part of it the Indus, or rather a branch of it. I have marched both and would prefer the western route at any time. In some parts they are blended, as Meerpore and Muttayleh are visited in both roads. On the western the country is more cultivated and consequently open; on the eastern there is continual jungle and liability to err in the direction from the multiplicity of small paths. Recommending the river route, in which I do not remember the names of places; I give the eastern one, which I have preserved:—

Subseldáh Kote.	Kos.	
Kirepore	10	Good town and bázár.
Meerpore	4	Do. do.
Muttayleh	10	Small do.
Sultánpore	8	Large village do.
Doober	14	Very small town do.
Roree	8	Large town do
	54	Kos.

In the route here noticed there is nothing particular to be noted in the road, the country being of the same jungle description, intersected by numerous water-courses. The pasture is good, and large numbers of buffaloes are everywhere seen. Wild hogs are particularly numerous. Both routes united at Roree, distant 8 kos from Kirepore. Here we find on a rock in the river the fortress of Bucker, which is supposed to have been the Soghodi of Alexander's historians. I fancy of the local identity there may be no doubt, but I would suggest that the term be transferred to the town of Roree, the fortress being a comparatively recent erection of the Emperors of Hindustán; nor is the surface of the rock so extensive as to have furnished space for a large city, which we must suppose the capital of the Soghodi to have been. That Roree was once of immense extent is evident from the ruins of very large buildings spread over the rocky eminences behind the present town. Among these are some very curious columns. The same species of ruins and columns are scattered over the opposite bank of the river, whence we may suppose the city of the Soghodi occupied the two sides; the deserted town of Sucker at this day remains in evidence. As in no map I have seen, not even in the recent map of India, is any notice taken of Roree, nor does its existence seem to have been known to Dr. Vicent, I will from memory trace a representation of the relative situation of it, Bucker and Sucker. This spot, which appears never to have been visited by Europeans, is, I think, the most remarkable place of Sind, as it is decidedly the most picturesque.

The fortress of Bucker stands on a rocky island, the walls tracing the very skirts. It is of no consequence as a fort, being entirely commanded by the heights and detached hills; exhibiting a large extent of wall, it has an imposing appearance, and assists the general effect of the beautiful scenery at Roree with its intended battlements. The Zeárats I have noted are truly splendid from their gorgeous fronts covered with painted tiles of the most brilliant colours. As buildings, they are extensive, lofty, and well arranged. Every traveller will be delighted at Roree; I not only stayed there two days on my first visit, but could not forbear going back from Kirepore. Leaving Roree we pass through a wilderness of date trees and gardens for perhaps 3 kos. Another kos brings you to the small and pleasant town of Bha, thence 4 kos to Kirepore. This place originally intended merely as cantonments has gradually increased in importance, and has become the capital and residence of Meer

Shrob, the Chief, or as he is called the Meer of this part of the country. The bázár is considerable as to size, but miserably built. The residence of the Meer is in the centre of the bázár. We might wonder why a prince possessing so magnificent an abode as Bucker should be content to live in the centre of the Kirepore bázár; but we cease to be so when we learn that his presence is necessary for the purposes of plunder and extortion on those engaged in trade of which Kirepore is the emporium. Meer Shrob's territory extends southerly, and on the eastern side of the Indus for about twenty kos; he also takes a third of the revenue of Shikárpore. He has given large portions of his country to his sons—the eldest Meer Rustom, the second Meer Mobarrak. Meer Shrob is very old and infirm; his tyrannies and exactions have made him very unpopular. He is at all times obedient to the princes of Hyderabad, to whom he is related; they do not however interfere in the internal administration of his country. I do not know the exact revenue of this country nor the number of troops, but all questions of this nature may be referred to the calculations of Hyderabad, which suppose for all Sind one crore of rupees revenue, about 20,000 troops kept on foot, whether at Hyderabad, Loll Khonnor, Kirepore, Shikárpore, &c., of which 4,000 are horse; guns without scarcity, but few mounted. The troops of Sind may be increased by a levy *en masse* to 80,000 men, the greater part without matchlocks. From Kirepore to Hyderabad is estimated 100 kos. I have not traversed this road, but have no doubt of its being a convenient one, with plenty of towns and cultivation. If it be wished to sail down the river to Hyderabad, you must, on leaving Kirepore, proceed to Loll Khonnor, 16 kos. At 12 kos you gain the river and 4 kos further the town of Loll Khonnor, situated on a cut apparently, which joins the Indus to the Aral River, a river which flows through Beluchistán. Loll Khonnor is 21 kos from Shikárpore, a populous and commercial town under the Government of Willea Mahomed, a Beluchi, who rules here absolutely with the title of Vizier of Sind; his authority extends half the distance to Shikárpore northerly, and southerly if we include a little district under his brother to within 4 kos of Sehwán, or 36 kos distance. This man is very popular and exercises no kind of oppression. Sailing down the river 40 kos, or half distance between Loll Khonnor and Hyderabad we arrive at Sehwán, a place of considerable note among Mussulmáns as containing the tomb of Loll Sháh Abbás, but more important as being the presumed capital of the Musikani. The traveller by land might easily see it, although it is seated on the opposite and western bank of the river, in fact a kos from it, by expressing a wish to visit the Ziarut of Loll Sháh Abbás, which would be deemed a very sufficient reason for deviating from the road and obviate any suspicion. The present town is small, as is the bázár, but the houses are large, and the whole has evidently an antique appearance. Another 40 kos brings you to Hyderabad, or rather at its part, if I may use the expression, a small village on the eastern bank, from which the city lies east 2 kos. It is built on a small elevation of a calcareous kind of stone running at first north and south. In this direction the city is built. It then takes a sweep in the direction of the river, on which are situated the tombs of Goolám Sháh Koloro, Meer Kurmalli and others of the past and present reigning families. The city is very mean, the bázár occupies one long street, that is, the entire length of the town, and a great deal of commerce is evidently carried on. The fort, built at the head of the city, is a large irregular building, its walls confirming to the irregularities of the eminence on which they stand; they are very high, and the whole fort is a handsome erection. It is built of burnt bricks. Here the several Meers have their residences, and strangers are not permitted to enter. The last sole prince of Sind was Koloro of Abyssinian extraction; he was slain by three of his Sirdars—Futtehalli, Kurmalli and Moradalli. These, who were brothers, usurped the authority and assumed the title of Meer. The two former are dead; the latter is still living. There are now at Hyderabad five Meers, viz., Moradalli, his son, Nusseer Khán, Meer Sohdat, and Meer Mahomed, I believe sons of Futtehalli and Meer Taarah—I rather think of the ancient family of Kalhora. Meer Moradalli may be said to govern the country. He is utterly detested, and in no country perhaps is oppression more general than in Sind; but I never heard of any cruelties, tortures or other amusements of some tyrants. The revenue I have already stated at one crore rupees and the troops at 20,000. From Hyderabad to Tatta 24 miles. If you pass by water you land 4 kos distant from it, seeing half way on the western shore the Beloche town of Rahmut, and farther on the eastern Almah-ka-Kote. If you travel by land you cross the river at once to Kotelie on the western bank which is traced the whole distance. Tatta, the Puttala of the Greeks, is still in its decay; an evidence of its former extent and the solidity of its ancient edifices attest the wealth and magnificence of its inhabitants in those periods. The elevations west of it are covered with the most superb tombs, which, as they are Mussulmán, prove the opulence of this city at no very remote period. Indeed until the last fifteen years it was the grand mart of cotton linen, but was ruined on the recent introduction of the superior British manufactures. Tatta is pleasantly situated in a country naturally fertile, and is very complaisantly spoken of by the natives of Sind, particularly the Hindus, who are aware of its antiquity. From Tatta we pass four kos partly over a tableland gained on ascent of the elevation to the west, which gradually declines into the plain on which we find the small town of Gujer. Hence proceed through a sandy jungle and pass immense deposits of rain, and some hills are approached which abound in the most curious remains of imbedded shells. Then arrive at a small hollow in which flows a stream of salt water, and ascending the circumscribing sandy jungle enter the town of Garah. There were three doongees in this water which has a communication with Karáchi. From Garah we proceed over a sandy, then a hilly country, in which no village occurs for 15 kos, after which 5 kos a troublesome march, in some places over sand, leads to Karáchi, where we have the pleasure to behold the ocean. Karáchi, though not a large town, is one of much trade. The bázár is small but good. The town is surrounded with a wall and strengthened by bastions and has a few guns mounted. The suburbs are very extensive, inhabited by fishermen and those connected with the shipping. Karáchi has 100 vessels of all sizes belonging to its harbour, and its doongees venture to Muskat, Bombay, Daman and Calicut. Karáchi harbour cannot I believe be entered by large ships, but it is evidently very commodious for the small craft belonging to it, and it is very spacious, extending about two miles inwards, the distance of the town from the mouth of the harbour. On the right going out is a high hill on the summit of which Meer Moradalli has erected a fort mounting many guns, and on the sands beneath a little to the right is a circular tower with fort, both works intended to defend the entrance. On the left going it is a sand-bank, dry at low water, and immediately beyond five detached rocks. Karáchi enjoys a very cool climate, and may claim some little notice as being the Krokala of Nearchus, and the first harbour in the Indian seas visited by a European fleet:—

	Kos.
Lahore to Multán	120
Multán to Ooch	53
Ooch to Ahmedpore	74
Ahmedpore to Kirepur	57
Kirepur to Hyderabad	100
Hyderabad to Karáchi	56

460 = 690 miles from Lahore to the sea.

(A True Copy.)

(Signed)   D. WILSON,
Resident, Persian Gulf.

NARRATIVE OF A JOURNEY

FROM

THE TOWER OF BA-'L-HAFF, ON THE SOUTHERN COAST OF ARABIA,

TO THE

RUINS OF NAKAB-AL-HAJAR,

1835.

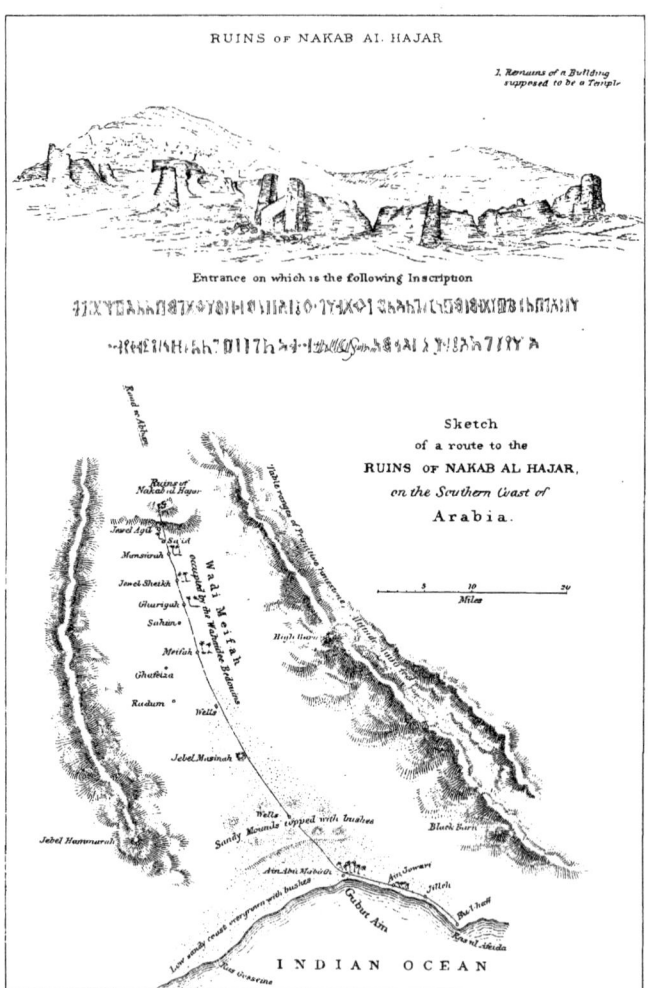

RUINS OF NAKAB AL HAJAR

1. Remains of a Building supposed to be a Temple

Entrance on which is the following Inscription

Sketch
of a route to the
RUINS OF NAKAB AL HAJAR,
on the Southern Coast of
Arabia.

INDIAN OCEAN

NARRATIVE OF A JOURNEY

FROM

THE TOWER OF BA-'L-HAFF, ON THE SOUTHERN COAST OF ARABIA,

TO THE

RUINS OF NAKAB-AL-HAJAR, IN APRIL 1835.

BY LIEUTENANT WELLSTED, INDIAN NAVY.

During the progress of the survey of the south coast of Arabia, by the East India Company's surveying vessel the *Palinurus*, while near the tower called Bá-'l-ḥaff, on the sandy cape of Ras-ul-Aseïdà, in lat. 13° 57′ north, long. 46¾° east nearly, the Bedowins brought us intelligence that some extensive ruins, which they described as being erected by infidels, and of great antiquity, were to be found at some distance from the coast.

I was in consequence most anxious to visit them, but the several days we remained passed away bringing nothing but empty promises on the part of Hámed* (the officer in charge of the tower,) to procure us camels and guides; and at length, in the prosecution of her survey, the ship sailed to the westward.

On the morning of her departure, April 29th, 1835, some hopes were held out to me that if I remained, camels would be procured in the course of the day, to convey us to some inscriptions, but a few hours' distance from the beach; and in this expectation I remained behind with Mr. Cruttenden, a midshipman of the *Palinurus*, and one of the ship's boats.

Towards noon the camels were brought, and I was then somewhat surprised to hear, after much wrangling among themselves, the Bedowins decline proceeding to the inscriptions, but express their readiness to accompany me to the ruins I had before been so desirous of visiting. For this I was then unprepared; I had with me no presents for the Sheïkhs of the different villages through which I had to pass, and only a small sum of money; but what (as regarded our personal safety) was of more moment, Hámed, who had before promised to accompany me, declined (on the plea of sickness) now to do so.

It was, however, an opportunity of seeing the country not to be lost, and I determined at once to place myself under their protection, and proceed with them. Accordingly, I dispatched my boat to the vessel with an intimation to the commander that I hoped at the expiration of three days, to be at the village of 'Aïn, on the sea-coast, when he could then send a boat for me.

Having filled our water skins at 3 P.M., accompanied by an ill-looking fellow (styling himself the brother of Hámed), and another Bedowin, we mounted our camels and set forward.

The road after leaving Bá-'l-ḥaff extends along the shore to the westward. On the beach we saw a great variety of shells; among them I noticed (as the most common) the Pinna fragilis, the Solen, the Voluta musica, and several varieties of Olives; fragments of red tubular coral, and the branch kind of the white, were also very numerous.

---

* An abbreviation for Ahmed or Mohammed.—F. S.

Under a dark barn-shaped hill, which we passed to the right, our guides pointed out the remains of an old tower, but as we were told there were no inscriptions, and as its appearance from the ship indicated its being of Arab construction, we did not stay to examine it.

At 4 h. 50 m. we passed a small fishing village called Jilleh, consisting of about twenty huts rudely constructed with the branches of the date palm. Along the beach above high-water mark, the fishermen had hauled up their boats, where they are always (unless required for use) permitted to remain.

In their construction they differ in no respect from those which I have described in other parts of the coast.

At 7 h. 20 m. we left the coast, and wound our way between a broad belt of low sand-hills, until 8 h. 30 m., when we halted for about two hours, about three miles from the village of 'Aïn Jowári, to which one of our guides was dispatched, in order to secure a supply of dates, the only food they cared to provide themselves with. Directly he returned we again mounted. At 11 h. the loud and deep barking of some dogs announced to us that we were passing the village of 'Aïn Abú Mabúth,* but we saw nothing of the inhabitants, and at 1 h. A.M. we halted for the night.

We were now in the territories of the Diyabí Bedowins, who, from their fierce and predatory habits, are held in much dread by the surrounding tribes. Small parties while crossing this tract, are not unfrequently cut off,—and we were therefore cautioned by our guides to keep a good look-out for their approach. But after spreading our boat cloaks in the sand, we were little annoyed by any apprehensions of this nature, and slept there very soundly until the following morning, Thursday, April 30th.

The Bedowins called us at an early hour, and after partaking of some coffee which they had prepared, we shook the sand (in which during the night we had been nearly buried) from our clothes, and at 5 A.M. at a slow pace we again proceeded on our journey.

At 7 h. we ascended a ledge about 400 feet in elevation, from the summit of which, we obtained an extensive but dreary view of the surrounding country. Our route lay along a broad valley, either side being formed by the roots or skirts of a lofty range of mountains. As these extend to the northward they gradually approach each other, and the valley there assumes the aspect of a narrow deep defile. But on the other hand, the space between our present station and the sea gradually widens, and is crossed by a barrier about thirty miles in width, forming a waste of low sandy hillocks;— so loosely is the soil here piled that the Bedowins assure me that they change their outline, and even shift their position with the prevailing storms. How such enormous masses of moving sand, some of which are based on extensive tracts of indurated clay, could in their present situation become thus heaped together, affords an object of curious inquiry. They rise in sharp ridges, and are all of a horse-shoe form, their convex side to seaward.† Our camels found the utmost difficulty in crossing them, and the Bedowins were so distressed that we were obliged to halt repeatedly for them. The quantity of water they drank was enormous. I observed on one occasion a party of four or five finish a skin holding as many gallons.

At 8 h. we found the sun so oppressive that the Bedowins halted in a shallow valley under the shade of some stunted tamarisk trees. Their scanty foliage would however have afforded

---

* So pronounced, but probably 'Aïn Abú Ma'bad.—F. S.

† The same formation of sand-hills was found by Pottinger in Belúchistan, and by Dr. Meyen in 1831, in the Pampa grande de Arequipa.—E.

us but slight shelter from the burning heat of the sun's rays, if our guides had not with their daggers dug up or cut off the roots and lower branches, and placed them at the top of the tree. But having done so, they quietly took possession of the most shady spots, and left us to shift the best way we could. Although we were not long in availing ourselves of the practical lesson they had taught us, I began to be far from pleased with their churlish behaviour. Every approach I made towards a good understanding was met by the most ungracious and repulsive return.

They now held frequent conversations with each other apart, of which it was evident we were made the subject,—and they not only refused fire-wood or water, in other quantities than they considered sufficient, but they watched our movements so closely, that I found it, for a time, impossible to take either notes or sketches.

I have no wish to drag forward anticipated dangers, but it was impossible but that I should feel if these men played us false, our situation must have been a critical one. I know that the natives of this district were reported to be especially hostile to those of any other creed than their own, and that they had some years ago (by seducing them with promises from the beach) cut off the whole of a boat's crew of the only vessel that had previously touched on their coast, and I could not but attribute to myself some degree of rashness, in thus venturing with no better pledge, than their fidelity, for our safety. There was however but little time for such reflections, and without evincing in my manner any change, or mistrust, I determined to watch their conduct narrowly, and to lose sight of nothing which might be turned to our advantage.

At 10 h. 30 m. continued our journey on the same sandy mounts as before. At 1 h. 30 m. we passed a sandstone hill called Jebel Másinah. The upper part of this eminence forms a narrow ridge presenting an appearance so nearly resembling ruins, that it was not until our subsequent visit to them that we were convinced to the contrary. We had now left the sandy mounts and were crossing over table ridges elevated about 200 feet from the plains below, and intersected by numerous valleys, the beds of former torrents, which had escaped from the mountains on either hand. The surface of the hills was strewn with various sized fragments of quartz and jasper, several of which exhibited a very pleasing variety of colours.

In the valleys the only rocks we found were a few rounded masses of primitive cream-coloured limestone. Placing the existence of these in conjunction with the appearance of the mountain on either side, I have no hesitation in pronouncing them to be of this formation—which is indeed the predominant rock along the whole southern coast of Arabia.

A few stunted acacias now first made their appearance, which continued to increase in size as we advanced.

At 4 P.M. we descended into Wádí Meifah, and halted near a well of good light water. The change which a few draughts produced in the before drooping appearance of our camels, was most extraordinary. Before we arrived here, they were stumbling and staggering at every step; they breathed quick and audibly, and were evidently nearly knocked up—but directly they arrived near the water, they approached it at a round pace, and appeared to imbibe renovated vigour with every draught. So that browsing for an hour on the tender shoots of the trees around, they left as fresh as when we first started from the sea-coast, notwithstanding the excessive heat of the day, and the heavy nature of the road.

It may appear strange that these animals should have been so much distressed in crossing a tract of only forty miles. Camels however differ in Arabia, in point of strength and speed, more than is generally supposed. These with us at present bore about the same resemblance to those on which I journeyed from 'Aden to Láheji, as a first-rate hunter would to a post-horse in England.

During the time we remained here, an Arab brought several fine bullocks to water. They have the hump which we observe in those of India, and to which in size, the stunted growth of their horns, and their light colour, they bear otherwise a great resemblance.

Arák trees are here very numerous, but they are taller, larger, and seem a different species to those found on the sea-coast. The camels appear very fond of those we found here, but unless pressed by hunger, they, never feed on the latter.

The arák tree* is common to Arabia, to Abyssinia, and to Nubia; is found in many places along the shores of the Red Sea,—and the southern coast of Socotra abounds with it. Its colour is of a lively green, and at certain seasons it sends forth a most fragrant odour. The Arabs make tooth-brushes of the smaller branches which they take to Mecca and other parts of the East for sale.

Tamarisk and acacia trees are also very numerous, and the whole at this period were sprouting forth young branches, and their verdant appearance, after crossing over such a dreary waste of burning sand, was an inexpressible relief to the eye.

At 5 P.M. we again mounted our camels,—our route continued in a west-north-westerly direction along the valley. It is about one and a half mile in width; the bank on either side, and the ground over which we were passing, afford abundant evidence of a powerful stream, having but a short time previous passed along it.

The country also begins to assume a far different aspect. Numerous hamlets, interspersed amidst extensive date groves, verdant fields of jowári, and herds of sleek cattle, show themselves in every direction,—and we now for the first time since leaving the sea-shore fell in with parties of inhabitants. Astonishment was depicted on the countenance of every person we met, but as we did not halt, they had no opportunity of gratifying their curiosity by gazing for any length of time on us. But to compensate for such a disappointment, one of our party remained behind, to communicate what he knew of us. In answer to the usual queries, who we were? whether we were Musselmans? and what was the nature of our business here? his reply was, that we were Káfirs going to Nakab al Hajar in order to visit, and seek for treasure. Others he gratified with the intelligence that we arrived here to examine and report on their country, which the Káfirs were desirous of obtaining possession of. In vain I endeavoured to impose silence on him, he laughed outright at my expostulation; while our guides, either disliking to be seen in our company, or having some business of their own, left us the instant we arrived near the village.

They returned shortly after sun-set, and we were in the act of halting near to a small hamlet, when the inhabitants sent a message to them, requesting they would remove us from the vicinity of their habitations. Remonstrances or resistance (except on the part of our guides, who remained quiet spectators of all which was passing without an attempt at interference) would have been equally vain, and we were consequently obliged to submit.

It was now dark, and it soon became evident that our Bedowins had but an imperfect idea of the road, for we had not proceeded more than three or four miles, when we found ourselves climbing over the high embankments which enclose the jowári fields.

---

* Salvadora Persica, called also *siwák* and *miswák* by the Arabs. It is probably a plant of African origin, being found throughout tropical Africa. From Siwák, pronounced Suag by Dr. Oudeney (Denham's Travels, p. 31), and called nyotút in Senegambia (Adanson's Travels, p. 290), the Arabs have formed the verb *sáka*, he brushed his teeth, and *siwák* or *miswák*, a tooth-brush. Its fruit, when unripe, is called *berir ;* when ripe *kebáth*. It is well described by Forskål(Flora Arabica, p. 32) under the name of Cissus Arborea. It is not the Rák of Bruce (Appendix, pl. 44), which is the Avicennia nitida (Delile, Voy. en Arabie de Léon la Borde, p. 81).

The camels fell so frequently while crossing these boundaries, that the Bedowins at last lost all patience, took their departure, and left us with an old man and a little boy, to shift for ourselves. I should have cared the less for this, if before they left, they had had the goodness to let us know to what quarter they had intended to proceed,—but this they had not condescended to do, and we were consequently preparing to take up our quarters in the fields when we unexpectedly came across an old woman, who without the slightest hesitation, as soon as she was informed of our situation, promised to conduct us to her house. We gladly followed her, but had wandered so far from the path, that we did not arrive there till eleven in the evening.

We found our guides comfortably seated in a neighbouring house, smoking their pipes and drinking coffee. I was excessively annoyed, but it would have availed me nothing to have displayed it.

It appears we had arrived at a sort of caravansera, one or more of which are usually found in the towns of Yemen, as in other parts of the East.

A party had arrived shortly before us, and the house was filled with men, who were drinking coffee and smoking. We therefore requested the old lady (whose kindness did not abate when she heard we were Christians) to remove the camels from the courtyard, and there, after a hearty supper of dates and milk, we slept very soundly until about three o'clock, when we were awakened by finding our guides rummaging our baggage for coffee. At any other period I should probably have been amused at witnessing the unceremonious manner in which they proposed helping themselves, as well as the nonchalance they exhibited in piling, without ceremony, saddles, baskets, or whatever came in their way, upon us. But men are not in the best humour to enjoy a practical joke of this nature, when snatching a hasty repose, after a fatiguing day's work—and I, therefore, with as little ceremony as they used to us, peremptorily refused to allow them to remove what they were seeking for. As we anticipated, they took this in high dudgeon, but their behaviour, unless they had proceeded to actual violence, could not have been much worse than it had been hitherto, and I therefore cared little for such an ebullition.

Friday, 1st May.—Although it was quite dark last night when we arrived here, yet we could not but be aware, from the state of the ground we had passed over, that there must be abundance of vegetation, yet we were hardly prepared for the scene that opened upon our view at day-light this morning.

Fields of dhurrah,* dokhn,† tobacco, &c., extended as far as the eye could reach; their verdure of the darkest tint. Mingled with these we had the soft foliage of the acacia, and the stately, but more gloomy aspect of the date palm,—while the creaking of the numerous wheels with which the grounds are irrigated, and several rude ploughs, drawn by oxen in the distance; together with the ruddy and lively appearance of the people (who now flocked towards us from all quarters)—and the delightful and refreshing coolness of the morning air, combined to form a scene, which he who gazes on the barren aspect of the coast could never anticipate being realized.

At 6 A.M. we again mounted our camels. We passed in succession the villages of Sahún, Gharígah, and Jewel Sheïkh, and at 8h. 30 m. arrived at another small village, where we had hitherto been led to anticipate we should find the Sultán; but, to our very great joy, we found upon inquiring for him, that he had set off yesterday for Abbán, and we accordingly pushed on.

Several people stopped us on the road to inquire who we were, and where we were going? They saluted us with much civility after the Arab fashion, and appeared perfectly satisfied at the answer our guides now thought proper to give to them, that we were proceeding to their Sultán on business.

---

* Sorghum vulgare.   † Sorghum saccharatum.

We met the only man who recognized us in the course of our journey as Englishmen. He was a native of Haḍramaut, and had heard of the English at Shaḥer. He was impressed with a belief that we were proceeding to purchase Hasan Ghoráb from 'Abdul-Wáḥid.

At 9 h. we passed Manṣúrah, and Sa'id and at 9 h. 30 m. arrived at Jewel Agil, one of the largest hamlets of the group. Leaving several other villages to the left, we now passed over a hill about 200 feet in height, composed of a reddish-coloured sandstone. From the summit of this, the ruins we sought were pointed out to us.

As their vicinity is said to be infested with robbers, we were obliged to halt at a village, in order to obtain one of its inhabitants to accompany us to them. Our guides, as usual, having gone to seek shelter from the heat of the sun, had left us to make our breakfast on dates and water, in any sheltered spot we could find. The sun was nearly vertical, and the walls of the houses afforded us no protection.

Seeing this, several of the inhabitants came forward, and offered with much kindness to take us to their dwellings. We freely accepted the offer, and followed one to his habitation. Coffee was immediately called for, and it was with some difficulty, by promising to return if possible in the evening, after we had visited the ruins, that we prevented his ordering a meal to be immediately cooked for us.

This, combined with several other instances which came before us on our return, convinced me that if we had been provided with a better escort, that we should have experienced neither incivility nor unkindness from this people.

About an hour from this village we arrived at the ruins of Nakab al Hajar,* and a rapid glance soon convinced me, that their examination would more than compensate for any fatigue or privations we had undergone on our road to them.

The hill upon which they are situated, stands out in the centre of the valley, and divides a stream which passes, during floods, on either side of it. It is nearly 800 yards in length, and about 350 yards at its greatest breadth. The direction of its greatest length is from east to west. Crossing it diagonally, there is a shallow valley, dividing it into two nearly equal portions, which swell out into an oval form. About a third of its height from the base, a massive wall averaging, in those places where it remains entire, from thirty to forty feet in height has been carried completely round the eminence. This is flanked by square towers, erected at equal distances. There are but two entrances by which admission can be gained into the interior. They are situated north and south from each other, at the termination of the valley before mentioned.

A hollow square tower, each side measuring fourteen feet, stands on either hand. Their bases are carried down to the plain below, and they are carried out considerably beyond the rest of the building. Between these towers, at an elevation of twenty feet from the plain, an oblong platform has been built, which extends about eighteen feet without, and as much within the walls. A flight of steps apparently was formerly attached to either extremity of the building, although now all traces of them have disappeared. This level space is roofed with flat stones of massive dimensions, resting on transverse walls. It is somewhat singular that we could not trace any indication or form of gates. The southern entrance has fallen much to decay, but the northern remains in almost a perfect state. The sketch on the map will illustrate its appearance and dimensions better than any verbal description.

---

*Nakabu-l-hajar signifies "the excavation from the rock."

Within the entrance of this, at an elevation of ten feet from the platform, we found the inscriptions, which are also given. They are executed with much apparent care, in two horizontal lines on the smooth face of the stones of the building. The letters are eight inches in length. Attempts have been made, though without success, to obliterate them. From the conspicuous situation which they occupy, there can be but little doubt, but that when deciphered, they will be found to contain the name of the founder of the building, as well as the date, and purport of its erection.

The whole of the wall, the towers, and some of the edifices within, have been built of the same material, a compact greyish-coloured marble streaked with thin dark veins and speckles. All are hewn to the required shape with the utmost nicety. The dimensions of those at the base of the walls and towers, were from five to six and seven feet in length, from two feet ten inches to three feet in height, and from three to four in breadth. These decrease in size with the same regularity to the summit, where their breadth is not more than half that of those below. The thickness of the wall there, though I did not measure it, cannot be less than ten feet, and, as far as I could judge, about four at the summit, notwithstanding the irregularity of its foundation, the stones are all without deviation, placed in the same horizontal lines. The whole has been carefully cemented with mortar, which has acquired a hardness almost equal to that of the stone. Such parts of the wall as remain standing, are admirably knitted together, others which by the crumbling away of their bases incline towards their fall, still adhere in their tottering state without fracture. And those patches which have fallen, lay prostrate on the ground in huge undissevered masses.

There are no openings in these walls, no turrets at the upper part,—the whole wears the same stable, uniform, and solid appearance. In order to prevent the mountain torrent, which leaves on the face of the surrounding country evident traces of the rapidity of its course, from washing away the base of the hill, several buttresses of a circular form have been hewn from that part, and cased with a harder stone. The casing has disappeared, but the buttresses still remain.

We must now visit the interior, where we arrived at an oblong square building, the walls of which face the cardinal points. Its largest size, fronting the north and south, measures twenty-seven yards. The shorter, facing the eastward, seventeen yards. The walls are faced with a kind of free-stone, each stone is cut of the same size, and the whole is so beautifully put together, that I endeavoured in vain to insert the blade of a small penknife between them. The outer surface has not been polished, but bears the mark of a small chisel, which the Bedowins have mistaken for writing.

From the extreme care which has been displayed in the construction of this building, I have little doubt but it formerly served as a temple, and my disappointment at finding the interior filled up with the ruins of the fallen roof, was very great. Had it fortunately remained entire, we might have obtained some monument which would possibly have thrown light on the obscure and doubtful knowledge we possess concerning the form of religion followed by the earlier Arabs.

Above and beyond this building there are several other edifices, but there is nothing peculiar in their form or appearance.

From a stone which I removed from one of the walls, the inscription was copied.

Nearly midway between the two gates, there is a well of a circular form ten feet in diameter, and sixty in depth. The sides are lined with unhewn stones, and either to protect it from the sun's rays, or to serve some process of drawing the water, a wall of a cylindrical form, fifteen feet in height, has been carried round it.

On the southern mound we were not able to make any discoveries. The whole appears an undistinguishable mass of ruins. Within the southern entrance, on the same level with the platform, a gallery four feet in breadth, protected on the inner side by a strong parapet three feet in height, and on the outer by the principal wall, extends for a distance of about fifty yards. I am unable to ascertain what purpose this could have served. In no portion of the ruins have we been able to trace any remains of arches or columns, nor could we discover on their surface any of those fragments of pottery, coloured glass, or metals, which are always found in old Egyptian towers, and which I also saw on those we discovered on the north-west coast of Arabia.

Although, as I have before noticed, attempts have been made to deface the inscriptions, yet there is no appearance of the building having suffered from any other ravages than those of time; and owing to the dryness of the climate, as well as the hardness of the material, every stone, even to the marking of the chisel, remains as perfect as the day it was hewn.

We were naturally anxious to ascertain if the Arabs had preserved any tradition concerning their buildings, but they refer them, in common with the others we have fallen in with, to their Pagan ancestors.

"Do you believe," said one of the Bedowins to me, upon my telling him that his ancestors were then capable of greater works than themselves, "that these stones were raised by the unassisted hands of the Káfirs? No! no! they had devils, legions of devils (God preserve us from them!) to aid them." This we found was generally credited by others.

Our own guides followed us during the whole of the time we were strolling over the ruins, in expectation of sharing in the golden hoards, which they would not but remain convinced we had come to discover; and when they found us as they supposed unsuccessful in the search, they consoled themselves with the reflection that we had not been able to draw them from the spirits, who, according to their belief, keep continual watch over them.

The ruins of Nakab al Hajar, considered by themselves, present nothing therefore than a mass of ruins surrounded by a wall; but the magnitude of the stones with which this is built, the unity of conception and execution, exhibited in the style and mode of placing them together, —with its towers, and its great extent, would stamp it as a work of considerable labour in any other part of the world. But in Arabia, where, as far as is known, architectural remains are of rare occurrence, its appearance excites the liveliest interest. That it owes its origin to a very remote antiquity (how remote it is to be hoped the inscription will determine) is evident, by its appearance alone, which bears a strong resemblance to similar edifices which have been found amidst Egyptian ruins. We have (as in them) the same inclination in the walls, the same form of entrance, and the same flat roof of stones. Its situation and the mode in which the interior is laid out, seem to indicate that it served both as a magazine and a fort,—and I think we may with safety adopt the conclusion that Nakab al Hajar, as well as the other castle which we have discovered, were erected during that period when the trade from India flowed through Arabia towards Egypt, and from thence to Europe, and Arabia Felix, comprehending Yemen, Sabá, and Haḍramaut, under the splendid dominion of the Sabæan or Homerite[*] dynasty, seems to have merited the appellation she boasted of.

The history of these provinces is involved in much obscurity, but Agatharchides, before the Christian era, bears testimony, in glowing colours, to the wealth and luxury of the Sabians, and his account is heightened rather than moderated by succeeding writers.

---

[*] The ancient people called Himyarí by the modern Arabs were probably called Homeïrí by their ancestors, as their territory corresponds with that of the Homēritæ of Ptolemy (Geogr. vi. 6).

This people, before Márbe* became the capital of their kingdom, possessed dominion along the whole of the southern frontier of Arabia. We are expressly informed that they planted colonies in eligible situations for trade, and fortified their establishments.

The commerce was not confined to any particular channel; on the contrary, we learn from an early period, of the existence of several flourishing cities, at, or near the sea-coast, which must have shared in it. We know nothing of the interior of this remarkable country, but there is every reason to believe, as is most certainly the case with Nakab al Hajar, that these castles will not only point out the tracks which the caravans formerly pursued, but also indicate the natural passes into the interior.

The inscription which it has been our good fortune to discover, will, there is every reason to believe, create considerable interest among the learned.

This character bears a strong resemblance to the Ethiopic,† which in many respects approaches the Hebrew or Syriac,—and when the inscription from Hasan Ghoráb was shown to a learned Orientalist in Bombay, he at once proved the justness of the suggestion, by pointing out an exact similitude between several of the letters. I am not sufficiently versed in Oriental literature to pursue the subject further,—and these few remarks arising out of what has come before me, are offered with much diffidence.

Nakab al Hajar is situated north-west, and is distant forty-eight miles from the village of 'Aïn, which is marked on the chart in latitude 14° 2' N. and long. 46° 30' E. nearly. It stands in the centre of a most extensive valley called by the natives Wádí Meifah,—which, whether we regard its fertility, its populousness, or its extent, is the most interesting geographical feature we have yet discovered on the southern coast of Arabia. Taking its length from where it opens out on the sea-coast, to the town of 'Abbán, it is four days' journey or seventy-five miles. Beyond this point I could not exactly ascertain the extent of its prolongation,—various native authorities fixing it from five to seven days more throughout the whole of this extent. It is thickly studded with villages, hamlets and cultivated grounds. In a journey of fifteen miles along it, we counted more than thirty of the former, besides a great number of single houses.

The date groves become more numerous as we approach towards the sea-shore, while in the same direction the number of cultivated patches decrease. Few of the villages contain more than from one to two hundred houses, which are of the same form, and constructed of the same material (sun-baked bricks) as those on the sea-coast. I saw no huts, nor were there any stone houses, although several of the villages had more than one mosque, and three or four Sheiks' tombs.

More attention within this district appears to be paid to agricultural pursuits than in any other part of Arabia I have seen. The fields are ploughed in furrows, which for neatness and regularity would not shame an English peasant. The soil is carefully freed from the few stones which have been strewn over it, and the whole is plentifully watered morning and evening by numerous wells. The water is drawn up by camels, (this is a most unusual circumstance, for camels are rarely used as draught animals in any part of the East,) and distributed over the face of the country along high embankments. A considerable supply is also retained within these wherever the stream fills its bed. Trees and sometimes houses are also then washed away, but any damage it does is amply compensated for by the muddy deposit it leaves,—which

---

* The Mariaba of the Greeks (Strabo, xvi., p. 778).

† It also has some similitude to the undeciphered characters on the Lát of Firóz Sháh at Dehlí (As. Res. vii., pl. 7—10).—F. S. Similar characters may also be seen on the pedestal of a small statue in the museum at Bombay.

although of a lighter colour, and of a harder nature, is yet almost equally productive with that left by the Nile in Egypt. But beyond what I have noticed, no other fruits or grain are grown.

Having now made (during the short time we were allowed to remain) all the necessary observations on the ruins, and the surrounding country, our Bedowins, as evening was approaching, became clamorous for us to depart.

About 4 P.M. we finished packing our camels, and travelled until near sunset, when we halted near one of the villages.

Our reception here was very different from that which we on our journey from the well experienced at the first village. About fifty men crowded around us; their curiosity, though much heightened by all they saw about us, was restrained within the bounds of good taste. Such questions as they put to us respecting our journey were proposed with a degree of delicacy, which surprised and pleased me. Milk, water and firewood were brought to us almost unsolicited, for which we had nothing to return but our thanks. I much regretted on this occasion being unprovided with some trifling presents, which we might have left as a memorial of the Englishman's sojourn among them.

What a different impression we might have formed of this people, had we drawn our opinion from our guides or our first reception amidst them!

Saturday, 2nd May, we started shortly after midnight, and travelled until four, when finding we had lost our way, we halted until day-light. At this time a heavy dew was falling, and Farenheit's thermometer stood at 58°; it was consequently so chilly, that we were happy to wrap ourselves up in our boat cloaks.

At 8 h. we again halted at the well to replenish our skins, previous to again crossing the sandy hillocks, and then continued on our journey. From 9 A.M. this morning until 1 h. 30 m. we endured a degree of heat I never felt equalled. Not a breath of wind was stirring, and the glare produced by the white sand was almost intolerable. At 2 h. our guides were so much exhausted, that we were obliged to halt for an hour. At 5 h. 30 m. we arrived at the date groves, near to 'Ain Abú Mabuth, where there is a small village and some fountains of pure water about fifteen feet square and three deep.

At 7 h. we arrived at the beach, which we followed until we came opposite to the vessel. It was, however too late to care about making a signal to those on board for a boat, and I was moreover, desirous, from what we overheard passing between the Bedowins, who were with us to defer our departure until the morning. Any disturbance we might have with them had better happen then, than during the night. We, therefore, took up our quarters amidst the sand-hills, where we could light a fire without fear of its being observed by those on board.

It will readily be believed that if we felt fatigued, it was not without reason. We had been but seventy hours from our station at Bá-'l-ḥaff, during which we had been forty-four hours mounted on our camels. The whole distance, 120 miles, might have been accomplished, on a quick camel, in half that time,—and it was the slow pace during the excessive heat of the weather at this season which formed the most toilsome and tedious part of the journey.

May 3.—We were discovered at an early hour this morning from the ship, and a boat was immediately dispatched for us. Strengthened now with the boat's crew, we settled with the Bedowins, without any other demand being made on us, and in the course of a few minutes we were on board the vessel, where we received the congratulations of all on our return. Considerable apprehension had been entertained for our safety, when it was discovered that Hamed had not accompanied us,

The success which has attended this brief journey to the interior will, it is hoped, prove an inducement to others to follow up our researches. Had I been differently situated, I should have proceeded on to 'Abbán, on the road to which there are at a village called Eisán, ruins of nearly equal magnitude with Nakab al Hajar. But independent of these ancient monuments, in themselves—far more than enough to repay the adventure,—the condition, character, and pursuits of the inhabitants, the productions, resources, and nature of the country, severally furnish subjects of peculiar interest, and would, there can be no doubt, amply repay the curiosity of the first European who should visit them.

I imagine, to proceed, nothing more would be necessary than for an individual to procure a letter from the British Government to the Sheïkh of 'Abbán. A guard could there be sent to escort him from the sea-coast, and he could from thence be forwarded to the next Sheikh by a similar application.

By the assumption of a Mohammedan or even a medical character, and by sacrificing every species of European comfort, he might, I have very little doubt, penetrate to the very heart of this remarkable country.

ACCOUNT

OF

AN EXCURSION IN HADRAMAUT

BY

ADOLPHE BARON WREDE.

ACCOUNT OF AN EXCURSION IN ḤAḌRAMAUT

BY

ADOLPHE BARON WREDE.

COMMUNICATED BY CAPTAIN J. B. HAINES, INDIAN NAVY.

As you take great interest in all that promotes the cause of science, I beg to communicate to you the brief outline of a journey—from which I have very recently returned—to the very interesting part of Arabia, which on our present maps bears the name of Haḍramaut, and being that portion which separates the desert of El Akkaf from the Indian Ocean.

The endeavours of former travellers to penetrate South Arabia have always been unsuccessful from the very strong religious fanaticism which animates all the inhabitants, more especially those of the towns.

Lieutenant Wellsted, in his valuable work on Arabia, suggests the propriety of subsequent travellers adopting the Mohammedan costume, the better to escape observation, which I accordingly did under the name of Abd-el-Hud, and in that disguise I left Aden on the 22nd of June, 1843, and sailed for Osurum; from whence I travelled by land to Makalla. Being afraid of drawing upon me the attention of those inhabitants who are acquainted with Europeans, I hurried my departure as quickly as possible, and left the latter place on the 26th of June for the interior, under the protection of a Bedowin of the powerful tribe Akábre. The celebrated Wadi Doân was the end of my first journey, which I reached after a march of 8½ days: our stages were generally very short, as we had to pass a ridge of steep hills; the actual time consumed on the road was 49 hours and 18 minutes; the general direction N.-W. The first day's journey lay through a continued succession of deep and narrow dales, bounded by bare granitic mountains which elevate their serrated summits about 2,000 feet above the level of the sea. A great many chalybeate springs, the heat of which indicated 100° to 130° of Fahr., rose from the sides of the mountains, the waters of which proved good and drinkable, as they contained no trace of sulphur. Although the broken ground of the dales is apparently infertile, yet a great many trees and plants are to be seen luxuriantly flourishing, and which supply sufficient food for the camels of the numerous caravans passing along this road. The traveller too enjoys the shade of the rich foliage of the lofty trees which shelter him at noon from the scorching beams of the sun. As a perfect calm prevails in these valleys from 10 A.M. till 4 P.M., the temperature rises to the height of 150° to 160° of Fahr. The road passed through many villages, and there were others at a short distance from it. On the 4th day's journey I ascended the mountain of Sidara, which rises about 4,000 feet above the level of the sea. The sides of this mountain are covered with aromatic plants: on arriving at its summit I found myself at the foot of two peaks, called Chareibe and Farjalat, which on the right and left rose perpendicularly to the height of 800 feet above my position, and being hardly 10 minutes[*] asunder, they looked like the colossal pillars of a gigantic gate. Iron-sandstone now appears to cover the before-mentioned granite. The thermometer had fallen, and, after the fatiguing march of the day, the night was sensibly cold. The following day I ascended some terrace-like ridges

---

[*] The Baron gives all his distances in time, by which we are probably to understand the time required to walk over them.—ED.

B 1485—52

rising one above the other, the highest of which is named Gebel Drôra. From the commencement of this day's journey I observed the iron-sandstone to be overlaid by a sandstone having a fine granular texture, yellow in colour and very hard. I was now about 8,000 feet above the level of the sea, and my view from W. to N.-E. ranged over a yellowish plain of immense extent, on which rose every here and there conical hills and ridges. In the E. the summit of the colossal Kar Seban towered beyond the plain. Towards the S. is seen a labyrinth of dark granitic cones, and the view is lost in the misty atmosphere of the ocean. From this point the road continues to follow the level ground, while on the right and left many Wádis meander through the plain in narrow defiles conveying the rain-water to the lower regions.

At the point where these defiles commence the traveller meets with a few stunted acacias, which afford a little shelter and scanty food to the camels. Every 6 or 9 miles there are cisterns, but neither bush nor village interrupts the monotony of this immense plain. The temperature on this elevated plateau was very agreeable in the day-time, the thermometer never rising above 80° Fahr.; but the nights were intensely cold, the thermometer sinking to 50°. The sudden appearance of the Wádi Doân took me by surprise and impressed me much with the grandeur of the scene. The ravine, 500 feet wide and 600 feet in depth, is enclosed between perpendicular rocks, the debris of which form in one part a slope reaching to half their height. On this slope towns and villages rise contiguously in the form of an amphitheatre; while below the date-grounds, covered with a forest of trees, the river, about 20 feet broad, and enclosed by high and walled embankments, is seen first winding through fields, laid out in terraces, then pursuing its course in the open plain, irrigated by small canals branching from it. From the description you will, I trust, form a correct idea of the Wádi Doân, of the extent, situation, and character of which travellers have given such contradictory statements.

My first view of the valley disclosed to me four towns and four villages within the space of an hour's distance. The road that leads down into the Wádi is a very dangerous one, particularly in its upper part; on the right, in some places, are precipices from 300 to 400 feet in depth, whilst a rocky wall on the left nearly stops up the road, leaving it scarcely 4 feet in breadth; and to add to the difficulty it is paved with pebblestones, which, having been constantly trodden by men and animals, have become as smooth as a looking-glass. No kind of parapet or railing whatever has been constructed to prevent accidents.

At Choreibe, one of the towns of the Wádi, I was received with all possible hospitality by Sheïkh Abdalla-Ba-Sudan, a man celebrated for the influence he has in the country, and for the reputation of sanctity he has attained. From Choreibe I directed my course towards the S.-W. to copy the incriptions subsisting in the Wádis Uebbene and Maifaah. I was not permitted to visit Nakab el Hadjar, Eisan, and Habalen; I however discovered in the Wádi Uebbene, an himiaritic inscription on a wall which encloses, as it were, the valley. About 6 English miles distant from Nakab el Hadjar I was stopped by a band of Bedowins who forced me to return to Wádi Doân. The country of Habahn was in open insurrection, as the former Sultán, Achmed-ibn-Abd-el-Wachet, had been dethroned by his nephew and imprisoned, together with his brother. On the road from Wádi Doân to Wádi Maifaah, at the distance of 5 days' journey, is the fertile Wádi Hagger, where immense forests of date-trees are watered by a continually running stream, that rises 4 days' journey N.-W. from the town of Hota. One day further down this Wádi is called Giswuel, and 2 days' journey more downwards it is called Wadi Mefah, under which name it reaches the sea near the village of Bir-el-Hassi, eastward of Ras-el-Kelb. By a more northern route, passing the Wádi Reide-Eddin, I reached Choreibe in 8 days, having been 20 days absent from the town. Wádi Doân changes its name several times; it is called Choreibe, Wádi Nebbi; from thence Wádi Doân; from Gahdun Wádi Hajarin; from Hora,

Wádi Kasr; and from Kubr el Hud, Wádi Missile, under which name it reaches the sea near Sah-Hud. After resting a few days I set out in a N.-W. direction, and two days' long and fatiguing journey brought me to Wádi Amt, which I followed in a northern direction. It is equal to the above-mentioned Wádi in extent, and resembles it in form and in the proximity of its towns. From Hora, where the Wádi Amt joins the Wádi Hajarín, I again ascended the high table-land, and taking a westerly direction arrived in 4 days at the town of Sáva in the Wádi Ráchie. This Wádi is not so populous as the two before-mentioned Wádis, most part being covered with sand. It runs 8 days N. from Sáva, above Terim, into the Wádi Kasr. Here I was told that the desert El-Akkaf was only a day's journey distant, and that that part which extends 8 days along its borders to Kubr-el-Hud, was inaccessible, and was called Bahr el Saffi; that the whole space was full of *snih spots*,* in which anything which happened to fall would perish. The place derived its name from King Saffi, who starting from Bellad Sabba Wadian and Ras el Ghoul, attempted to march an army through this desert, in the midst of which his troops perished. On the following day I set out for that place, in order to convince myself of the truth of the statement which I had received. After a 6 hours' journey in a N.-W. direction I reached the borders of the desert, which is about 1,000 feet below the level of the high land. A melancholy scene presented itself to my astonished sight! Conceive an immense sandy plain strewed with numberless undulating hills, which gave it the appearance of a moving sea. Not a single trace of vegetation, be it ever so scanty, appears to animate the vast expanse. Not a single bird interrupts with its note the calm of death, which rests upon this tomb of the Sabæan army. I clearly perceived three spots of dazzling whiteness, the position and distance of which I measured geometrically. "That is Bahr el Saffi," said my guide to me; "ghosts inhabit those precipices, and have covered with treacherous sand the treasures which are committed to their care; every one who approaches near them is carried down, therefore do not go." I of course paid no attention to their warnings, but requested to be led to those spots in accordance with the agreement I had made with my Bedowins. It took my camels full 2 hours' walk before we reached the foot of the high plateau, where we halted at sunset, in the vicinity of two enormous rocky blocks. On the following morning I summoned the Bedowins to accompany me to the places alluded to above, but they were not to be induced; and the dread of ghosts had obtained such complete mastery over them, that they scarcely ventured to speak; I was therefore determined to go alone, and taking with me a plummet of ½ a kilo's weight and a cord of 60 fathoms, I started on my perilous march. In 36 minutes I reached, during a complete lull of the wind, the northern and nearest spot, which is about 30 minutes long and 26 minutes broad, and which towards the middle takes by degrees a sloping form of 6 feet in depth, probably from the action of the wind. With the greatest caution I approached the border to examine the sand, which I found almost an impalpable powder; I then threw the plumb-line as far as possible; it sank instantly, the velocity diminishing, and in 5 minutes the end of the cord had disappeared in the all-devouring tomb. I will not hazard an opinion of my own, but refer the phenomenon to the learned who may be able to explain it, and restrict myself to having related the facts.

The following day I returned to Sáva where I visited a himiaritic tomb, which was only 15 minutes distant from the town. The fanaticism of a Sheikh had unfortunately destroyed

---

* The subsequent context will show the nature of these spots. It appears probable, from the author's want of sufficient acquaintance with the English language, he knew of no better term than the one he has used, and which, we believe, means those accumulations of drift snow that are found in the hollows of rocky regions, and into which the unwary traveller sinks.—ED.

the inscription that had formerly existed on the entrance. The next day I started on my return to Choreibe, which I reached after a 4 days' march. Having remained four days at this hospitable place, I left it in order to visit the country of Kubr el Hud, which historically and geologically is highly interesting; two sons of my host and the celebrated Habib Abdalla ibn Haidum accompanied me. We rested the first night at Grein, a considerable town on the right bank of the Wádi Doân, and on the following day I arrived at Seef, about an hour after my companions who had preceded me.

An immense multitude of people had assembled in the town to celebrate the feast of the Sheïkh Said ben Issa ibn Achmudi, who was buried in Gahdun, situated in the vicinity of Scef. As soon as I had arrived among the crowd they all at once fell upon me, dragged me from my camel, and disarmed me; using me very roughly, they tied my hands behind my back and carried me, with my face covered with blood and dust, before the reigning Sultán Mohammed Abdalla ibn ben Issa Achmudi. The whole of my captors raised a horrible cry and declared me to be an English spy exploring the country, and demanded my instantly being put to death. The Sultán being afraid of the Bedowins, on whom he, like all Sultáns of the Wádi, is dependant, was about to give orders for my execution, when my guides and protectors came in haste and quieted the Bedowins' minds by means of the moral influence they had over them. In the meantime I remained confined to my room with my feet in fetters. I was imprisoned for 3 days, but provided with every necessary; on the evening of the third day my protectors came to me with the news, that they had pacified the Bedowins under the condition that I was to return to Macalla, and that I should give up all my writings. At night I concealed as many of my papers as I could, and delivered only those which were written in pencil, with which they were contented. After my notes were given up, the Sultán wished to see my luggage, from which he selected for himself whatever pleased him. The next morning I set out on my return to Macalla, which town I reached on the 8th of September, after a journey of 12 days, and thence took a boat for Aden.

MEMOIR

OF

THE SOUTH COAST OF ARABIA

FROM

THE ENTRANCE OF THE RED SEA TO MISENAT

1839.

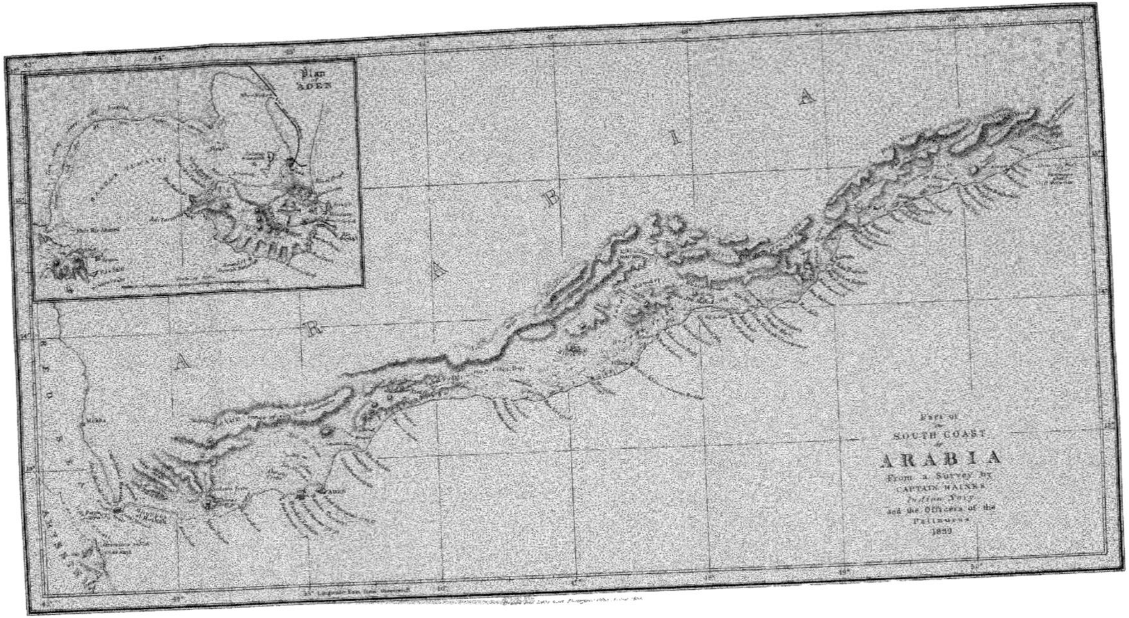
Plan of ADEN
A R A B I A
Part of the SOUTH COAST of
ARABIA
From a Survey by
CAPTAIN HAINES
Indian Navy
and the Officers of the
Palinurus
1839

MEMOIR

OF THE

SOUTH COAST OF ARABIA FROM THE ENTRANCE OF THE RED SEA TO MISENA'T, IN 50° 43' 25" E.

BY CAPTAIN S. B. HAINES, INDIAN NAVY.

RAS BAB-EL-MANDEB, or the Cape of the Gate of Affliction, is a prominent cape which forms the south-western extremity of Arabia, and the north-eastern shore of the entrance into the Red Sea. When seen from the eastward the land assumes the shape of a wedge of gunner's quoin, and is visible from a vessel's deck, on a clear day, at the distance of 35 miles. Its highest peak, named Jebel Manhalí, rises to 865 feet, whence it slopes to the southward, and terminates in a low point on the sea.

Before proceeding with the narrative, I may be permitted to state that, in the following pages, it is proposed to give a description of about 500 miles of the southern coast of Arabia—hitherto almost unknown—and such an account of its population, government, and commerce, as was obtained, during the survey of these shores, by myself and the officers of the E. I. Company's ship *Palinurus*, in the years 1834, 5, and 6 :—premising that the longitudes were determined by meridian distances, measured from the flag-staff at Bombay, assumed to be in 72° 54' 26" E., by the means of 5 and also of 8 chronometers, at different times, and by quick and direct measurements.

I am happy to have the opportunity afforded me of expressing my thanks to Rear-Admiral Sir Charles Malcolm, who has ever proved himself a generous promoter of scientific pursuit; also to my friends Lieutenant Sanders, Assistant Surveyor, Lieutenants Jardine and Sheppard, Messrs. Smith, Cruttenden, Grieve, Ball, Rennie, Stevens, and Barrow, for their cheerful assistance during the survey. The late Dr. Hulton also proved a valuable auxiliary, and, I lament to add, fell a victim to his unceasing exertions throughout the progress of a tedious and trying service.

The peak of Jebel Manhalí[*] is in lat. 12° 41' 10" N., and long. 43° 32' 14" E. Off the extremity of the Cape Báb-el-Mandeb, numerous rocky points, projecting about half a mile from the mainland, form shallow bays, affording shelter to boats and small vessels; and here the boatmen from the opposite coast of Abyssinia land their sheep and drive them to Mokhá, to spare themselves a tedious voyage back against southerly winds.

About 1½ mile to the north-eastward of Jebel Manhalí is a small range of hills, named Jebel Heïkah, extending about 3 miles in a N.N.W. direction of less elevation, and of an

---

[*] The orthography of the names of places has been altered according to the standard adopted in the Geographical. Journal :—*i.e.*, the consonants are to be sounded as in English, and the vowels as in Italian, or as in the English words father, there, fatigue, cold, rude. *See* vol. vii., p. 245.—ED

irregular outline. The intervening land is low, sandy, and barren; but in the valley a few bushes and spots of grass may occasionally be seen, and on this scanty food I found beautiful antelopes subsisting. A little to the eastward of the cape is a square dark hill, named Turbah, on which are some ruins and near it an old village, possibly the site of the ancient Ocelis: the steep rocky points here form a sheltered anchorage. In a valley are some old date-trees and a well of brackish water, at which the wandering Bedowins of the Ṣubeiḥi tribe occasionally water their camels.

Jebel Manhalí and the other hills would seem to be of volcanic origin; on its summit I found the needle of my theodolite deflected several degrees from the magnetic meridian. To the northward and eastward of this small hilly district the land is low and sandy.

Returning to the straits, a small spot named Pilot-Island lies about half a mile distant from the Arabian shore.

Perim, or *Meyún*, a bare rocky island, about 4½ miles long by 2 broad, rising 230 feet above the sea, lies at the distance of 2 miles from the coast of Arabia; and forms, between it and Pilot-Island, a good channel, known by the name of the Small Strait, its least breadth being 1½ mile. It possesses a good harbour on the south-western side, with an entrance half a mile wide. Here are a tank, the ruins of a rudely-constructed pier, &c.—traces of the British occupation in 1801. The needle was here deflected 3° on the rocky part of the island. Variation 5° 42′ W., in 1836. Lat. of south point of island 12° 38′ N., long. 43° 28′ 40″ E. High water, on full and change, at noon. Rise of tide about 6 feet.

Rás Seján, a cape on the Abyssinian shore, forms the southern point of entrance into the Red Sea. It is a gloomy-looking peak, about 380 feet high, projecting to the northward from the coast, with which it is connected by a piece of low land 700 yards wide, having a swampy bay, surrounded with mangrove-bushes, to the westward. The northern face of this cape is rocky and steep, but, from a small bay to the eastward, a bank runs out about 1 mile, with from 5 to 6 fathoms on its outer edge.

The distance from Rás Seján to the nearest point of the Arabian coast is exactly 14½ geographical miles, which is therefore the extreme breadth of the Strait of Báb-el-Mandeb: this is divided into two, as before-mentioned, by the island of Perim; and between the south point of this island and Cape Seján, forming the southern entrance, or Large Strait, the breadth is exactly 11¼ miles. This channel is again narrowed by a cluster of islets, called *Jeziratu-s-sab'ah*, or Seven Islands, commonly known to the English by the name of "The Brothers": they are named the "Eight Brothers" by Horsburgh[*]; but it seems more correct to describe them as six rocky islets, extending 5¼ miles in an E. and W. direction; the highest, or north-eastern, lying 6½ miles due E. of Rás Seján, and 9¾ miles S. of the southern point of the island of Perim.

The high Brother forms a conspicuous peak rising about 350 feet above the sea, with a small bay on its northern side abundantly supplied with turtle and fish of various kinds. The position of the peak is in 12° 28′ N., 43° 28′ 50″ E. A low rocky island to the westward is the only part which may be considered dangerous.

The western island is distant only 4,624 yards from the coast of Africa, and the easternmost 7¼ miles, with soundings the whole way, varying from 6 to 25 fathoms, and a safe channel, although the currents and tide are rapid and irregular, with a rise and fall of 7 feet: the anchorage good.

---

[*] Indian Directory, Vol. i., p. 233.

The *Brothers* are of a brownish colour, the most western is certainly volcanic: they are of considerable height, and five out of the six islands may be seen from 20 to 30 miles in clear weather; the highest, perhaps 29 miles; the second from the westward, 26' miles; and the westernmost, 22 miles; giving a height of about 350, 300, and 250 feet respectively.

The soundings in the Small Strait vary from 8 to 14 fathoms; in the middle of the Large Strait we had no bottom with 120 fathoms of line.

The coast of Abyssinia from Rás Seján to Ras el Bir extends in a S.S.E. direction about 20 miles, being low and sandy, and covered with mangrove and brushwood; towards the interior are three or four ranges of flat-topped limestone mountains, named Jebel Ján, which reach a great elevation, and form the northern boundary of an extensive plain covered with thicket, opening out to the westward on a range of mountains named Jebel Tejúrah, which continues parallel to the sea-coast in a southerly direction. At the back of the southern bluff of Jebel Ján I discovered the remains of a large Bedowín encampment, which had been deserted by a party of the Danákilí* tribe of Somális, who, like the Ṣubeiḥï Arabs on the opposite coast, probably leave the sea-shore during the months of June, July, and August. The few inhabitants we here met with were wretched-looking beings of this tribe; and from them we learnt that the only fresh water was to be found near the hills, from 10 to 12 miles distant from their present habitation. Here are some jackals, foxes, and hyænas; and among the feathered tribe I saw the ostrich, pelican, flamingo, curlew, and plover.

The little village situated inland is named Tejúrah. The territory of the Danákilí tribe extends some distance along the coast, and for many miles inland. The only instance on record of a female chief being placed at the head of this tribe, occurred in 1836. The neighbouring tribes hold the Danákilí in great disrepute, generally considering them cruel, treacherous, and inhospitable.

To return to the coast of Arabia:—as before-mentioned, the land to the northward of the hilly tract of Heïkah is low: the coast from Rás Báb-el-Mandeb extends in a north-easterly direction about 7 miles, when it turns abruptly E.S.E. for about 25 miles, as far as Rás A'rah forming, in the bight, the bay of Ghubbet el Heïkah, which affords a convenient and smooth-water anchorage to ships working up to the straits against the strong north-westerly winds in June and July. At Sekeyyah is a group of palm-trees, and 2 miles to the eastward a well of good water; fuel is abundant. *Jebel Hejáf* is a low range of hills extending for about 16 miles in the same direction as the coast, from which they are distant about 8 miles: they are of a dark aspect, irregular in their outline, and terminate in a bluff to the westward. *Jebel ' A'rah* (Chimney-peaks of Horsburgh) is a remarkable range of lofty mountains extending in a N.-W. by N. direction for about 18 miles, with an irregular outline, being a continued chain of peaks, terminating to the S.-E. in a barn-shaped hill, with a peak in its centre: they have a dark, gloomy aspect, and are bounded to the N. by a higher range of distant mountains.

Along this coast are small projecting rocky points, forming little bays, with a sandy beach; towards the interior, the land, as it rises towards the hills, is covered with bushes.

We met a few fishermen, looking wretchedly poor; and on one occasion a party of Ṣubeiḥï Bedowíns, fully accoutred for war. During our little excursions from the coast we saw some

---

* That is, people of Doukolah.—F. S.

antelopes and hares; and it is amusing to observe the former cooling themselves on the sea-shore during the day—at sunset they disappear.

Rás' A'rah, the southern cape of Arabia, is a very low sandy rounded point, in lat. 12° 37' 30" N., long. 44° 1' 40" E., and is one of the most dangerous capes on the coast, being in the direct route for vessels proceeding to or from the Red Sea, and having a bank of hard sand, extending nearly 3½ miles off-shore to the eastward of it, with one or two dangerous rocky patches with only 9 feet water. In 1836 a fine Dutch ship was wrecked here, and during my service on this coast several vessels have been lost. This bank, which extends as far as Khór 'Amrán, is the more dangerous as the water suddenly shoals from 15 fathoms; indeed a ship with good headway could hardly get a second cast of the lead before touching the ground. It is advisable by day not to approach nearer than 15 fathoms, and by night into not less than 20 fathoms water.

In the bight of the small bay to the westward of Rás 'A'rah are a few date-trees and a supply of fresh water; the bay also affords shelter against the strong winds during the N.-E. monsoon: the coast immediately around it is rather steep.

Khór 'Omeyra is a remarkable inlet situated 13½ miles E. by N. from Rás 'A'rah, 4½ miles long from E. to W. by 2½ broad: it is almost land-locked by a narrow spit of sand which projects from the eastern shore and forms its southern boundary, leaving a very narrow entrance to the westward, with only 6 feet water; nor does this depth increase for 2 miles, when it opens out into a fine basin, having from 3 to 6 fathoms water. At high water the low southern spit of sand is nearly covered.

Jebel Kharaz, or the Highland of Sant' Antonio, reaches the height of 2,772 feet above the sea at its northern peak, while its southern bluff in lat. 12° 41' N., long. 44° 16' E., rises 2,085 feet almost immediately to the north of the basin of Khór 'Amrán. On the western side of the summit of the north peak we found a ruin of roughly-hewn stone without date or inscription but sufficiently remarkable to give a name to this mountain, which is called Jebel Jinn, or Genii-Hill, on account of some mysterious tale attached to this building. The mountain is chiefly composed of limestone; I also saw some granite.

Rás Ka'ú is a projecting cape, lying 17 miles E. by N. of the entrance of Khór 'Amrán, which, from its dark appearance, is commonly known by the name of the Black Cape: it is in lat. 12° 39' 45" N., long. 44° 32' 30" E. Three miles inland to the N.-N.-W. is the remarkable saddle-hill named Jebel Ka'ú, rising 798 feet above the sea; three other small hills occur to the south-west of it, near the coast. Between this cape and Khór 'Omeyra a very dangerous sand-bank with overfalls extends, at one point reaching 4 miles off-shore: no vessel should approach nearer than to 15 fathoms water by day, and 20 fathoms by night, and even then great attention must be paid to the lead.

The whole of this coast is low and sandy with a few bushy shrubs, while here and there a rocky point breaks the desolate monotony of the scene. To the eastward of Rás Ka'ú the coast is still flat and sandy for 18 miles, as far as Rás 'Amrán, forming a bay nearly 5 miles deep: the land towards the interior is low, and covered with ragged wild bushes. Antelopes, hares, plovers, partridges, bustards, and various small birds of beautiful plumage, were seen. At Rás 'Amrán the territory of the Ṣubeïḥi tribe of Arabs terminates: these people, though numerous, are little known: from the slight intercourse we had with them, I should consider them kind and communicative, and well adapted by figure and constitution to endure hardships. We had some difficulty at first in making acquaintance with them; but when they gained confidence, they accompanied two of the officers of the ship, Messrs. Ball and Grieve, to the summit of Jebel Jinn, where they found the ruins before alluded to, which may possibly be of the same date as those of Nakab el Hajar,* Hisn Ghoráb, &c. The Ṣubeïḥí tribe are said to number 12,000 persons: they are Mohammedans, and are governed by their principal chiefs, who are absolúte. The women are, generally speaking, delicately formed, with very dark eyes and long beautiful hair. Their territory is for the most part barren, yet on a few productive spots they cultivate coffee, fruits, &c. Cattle may be always found in large flocks, and camels in great numbers.

Rás 'Amrán, in lat. 12° 43′ 30″ N., long. 44° 49′ 40″ E., is the S.-W. extreme of a small rocky island, divided from the mainland by narrow channels, almost wholly filled up with rocks: off its western side are three small rocks of considerable elevation, with deep water close outside them. The cape of the mainland is a rocky promontory, rising 712 feet above the sea, which projects, including the island, about $2\frac{1}{2}$ miles in a S.S.W. direction from the general line of coast, and forms the western limit of the bay which lies to the eastward.

Bander Feïkam is a bay about 5 miles broad by 2 miles deep, formed by the projecting land of Rás 'Amrán on the W. and Jébel Ilasan on the E.; near its centre is a small round island, with a rock, barely covered with water, about 800 yards to the E.S.E. of it, with from 5 to 6 fathoms water between it and the island, to the N.-W. of which a shoal-patch extends a short distance. On the western shore of this bay is the tomb of Sheïkh Sammarah, surrounded by a few fishermen's huts. Projecting to the S.-E. is a small dark-coloured peak called Jezirat Abú Shammah, and to the westward of it are two anchorages for small boats. The land surrounding the bay is a low, dreary, swampy tract of sandhills, so much so, that at high water each cape appears like an island. The soundings in the bay are regular, and the bottom of sand or mud.

Jebel Hasan is a mountainous mass of granite, which forms a peninsular promontory, 6 miles long from E. to W., by 3 miles in breadth: its highest peak, in the form of a sugar-loaf, reaching 1,237 feet above the sea. This promontory has numerous projecting rocky points, to each of which the Arabs give a name: to the S.-W. are Rás Feïkam and Rás Alargah;† the most southern, called Rás Mujallab Heïdi, is in lat. 12° 43′ N., long. 44° 59′ E., and forms the western limit of the small bay named Bander Sheïkh. Rás Abú Kiyámah divides this bay from Khór Kádir. On the southern and eastern sides of this promontory are nine rocky islets, nearly connected with the main at low-water springs; two of these islets lie in the middle of the entrance to Khór Kádir; another is situated off the S.-E. point called Rás Sáliḥ; and five of them off the N.-E. bluff, about one mile from the shore.

The white tomb of Sheïkh Kádir is about 1,100 yards to the northward of the extreme point of Rás Abú Kiyámah; near this spot the 'Akrabís deposit coffee, cotton, and a few other articles of merchandise, in readiness for the small trading-boats lying in Bander Sheïkh and Ghór Kádir, the only two ports belonging to the 'Akrabi tribe.

At the eastern end of this mountainous promontory is a remarkable double peak of granite 700 feet in height, which from its peculiar shape is commonly known by the name of the Ass's Ears. The outline of the whole of Jebel Hasan is very picturesque: a deep ravine winds through the hilly tract from Bander Feïkam to the little bay of Bander Sheïkh. The land to the northward is low, and immediately at the back of the mountains a deep inlet, named Khór Biyar Aḥmed, or Seïlán, extends 3 miles to the westward, almost insulating the promontory of Jebel Hasan.

Biyar Ahmed, a small fort and village situated about 3 miles from the beach and $6\frac{1}{2}$ miles due N. of the Ass's Ears, contains about 250 inhabitants: it is the residence of the chief, or Sultán, as he is called, of the 'Akrabi. About 2 miles to the N.-E. of Bíyar Ahmed is the village of Seïlán.

---

* Described in Journal, vol. vii., p. 20.—Ed.   † From the Portuguese "alarga"?—F. S.

The territory of the 'Akrabí tribe does not exceed 20 square miles, with a population of 600 males, a fine body of men, who keep their more quiet neighbours in a constant state of alarm. Their chief is named Ahmed ibn Meïdí, who in person conducts his followers through every kind of war and rapine, and has for many years supported himself in independence, until forced to pay a tribute to a neighbouring chief in consideration of the freedom with which he is permitted to spoil the adjoining tribe of Abdáli. This chief is noted for his treachery, and it was not without some difficulty that we established any communication with him; but at length he allowed two of the officers, Messrs. Cruttenden and Grieve, to visit his village, and received them very civilly. The women of this tribe are generally pretty, of a slight, elastic, healthful form, which, added to great cheerfulness, creates a charm not often awakened by the tawny inhabitants of a tropical and desert country. This territory is bounded on the N.-E. by the Abdálí and Haushábí, and to the westward by the Ṣubaïhí tribes. The chief produce of the soil is jowári (millet), of which they export great quantities; large flocks of sheep and goats are seen browsing, tended by the watchful eye of the pretty Bedowín shepherdess: in the interior are thick forests of thorny acacia, affording a retreat to the antelope from the scorching rays of the sun; doves also are numerous, and occasionally may be heard the lively chirrup of the Bayah, or Hottentot crested sparrow, and the warbling of a small beautiful bright yellow bird with crimson legs. Indeed, notwithstanding the usually arid appearance of the country, much may be found here, as well as elsewhere, to enliven the traveller as he passes on, or to break the monotony of a minute nautical survey of a little-frequented coast.

Bander Tuwayyí, or 'Aden West Bay, (the 'Aden Back Bay of Horsburgh), is formed by the projecting headlands of Jebel Hasan on the W. and Jebel Shamshán on the E., enclosing a bay 8 miles broad from E. to W., by 4 miles deep, with an entrance between Rás Salíl on the W. and Rás Társhein on the E., exactly 3 miles 750 yards wide. The peninsular promontory of 'Aden is almost divided from the mainland by a creek on the eastern side of this bay named Khór Maksá, similar to that behind Jebel Hasan on the opposite side of the bay, which gives these lofty promontories—not very unlike in appearance.—the aspect of two sentinel islands guarding the approach to the magnificent bay they enclose. A ship may anchor in any part of this bay, the soundings gradually decreasing from 5 fathoms towards the shore, with a clear sandy bottom. In going into the inner or eastern bay it is requisite to keep over on the starboard or southern shore, as a flat runs off ½ a mile to the southward of the small islands of Alikah. Probably just past Flint Island or Sheikh Ahmed would be as good an anchorage as any: of course with a westerly wind the smoothest water will be on the west side. The tides in the bay are strong and irregular, owing to the influence of the outside currents: by several observations the rise of tide at full and change was 8½ feet between the hours of nine and ten. Variation of the compass 5° 2′ W. in 1836.

Jebel Shamshán, so called from the turreted peaks on its summit, is a high rocky promontory of limestone, the most elevated point of which reaches 1,776 feet above the sea; it extends 5 miles from E. to W. by 3 miles in breadth, its southern point Rás Sinailah, the Cape 'Aden of our charts, being in lat. 12° 45′ 10″ N., long. 45° 9′ E. Numerous rocky points project from this mass of mountains forming small bays and shelter for bagalás or boats.[*] Commencing on the inner or north-western side, the point of Hejáf forms the southern and western limit of the inner bay; immediately off it lies the rock of Jeramah, and 1 mile due N. of it are the two islands of

---

[*] Captain Haines' Memoir is accompanied by a beautiful plan of 'Aden, and of the adjacent bays on the scale of one inch to a mile; with several spirited outline sketches of the highland forming Cape 'Amran, Jebel Hasan and Jebel Shamshán or Cape 'Aden, which give a much better idea than can any description of the numerous peaks and varied outline of these remarkable mountains.—ED.

Jám 'Alí and 'Alíyah; but, as before-mentioned, a flat, dry at low-water spring-tides, runs out $\frac{1}{4}$ a mile to the southward of these islands, thus narrowing the passage into the inner bay to $\frac{1}{2}$ a mile, with $2\frac{1}{2}$ fathoms water in the mid-channel. Within this bay are five small rocky islands: the eastern and principal one, named Jezírah Sawáyíh, is 300 feet high, and almost joined to the mainland at low-water spring-tides. The others are named Marzúk Kebír, Keïs el Hammán, Kalfetein, and Firinjí. Proceeding to the westward, nearly $\frac{1}{2}$ a mile from Hejáf, is the rocky point of El 'Aïnah, and $\frac{1}{4}$ of a mile beyond the Flint rock or small island of Sheikh Ahmed; 500 yards further W. is the small point of Rás ibn Tarsheïn; rather more than $\frac{1}{2}$ a mile beyond is Rás Marbút, and the same distance again brings us to the extreme W. point of this promontory, named Rás Tarsheïn; the high peak about $1\frac{1}{2}$ mile at the back of which reaches 988 feet above the sea. Turning thence to the S.-E., the same bold coast continues for $2\frac{1}{2}$ miles as far as a round island named Jezírah Denáfah, 1 mile beyond which is Rás Sinaïlah, the southern point of this peninsula.

Rás Marshigh, 2 miles farther E., is a narrow projecting cape forming the south-eastern point of the promontory, and affording shelter to the anchorage called Bander Darás, lying between this latter cape and Rás Taïh.

'Aden, once a populous town, now a ruined village of 600 persons, is seen immediately on rounding Cape Marshigh, lying on a plain little more than $\frac{1}{2}$ a mile square, encircled on the land-side by singularly-pointed hills, with its eastern face open to the sea, while immediately in front is the rocky fortified island of Sírah. The position of the N. point of this island, which may be taken as that of the town of 'Aden, is 12° 46′ 15″ N. lat., by means of numerous observations of sun and stars on shore; and 45° 10′ 20″ E. long., being the mean of eight chronometers measured from Bombay, the flag-staff there, as before-mentioned, being assumed at 72° 54′ 26″ E. This island commands the eastern bay and town of 'Aden: it is a triangular rock about 430 feet high towards the southern end, $\frac{1}{3}$ a mile long by 600 yards broad. Of late years the sand has filled up the small creek which used to separate it from the mainland, consequently at low-water it is now joined to the coast of Arabia.

On the summit of the island is an old fort with a wall which reaches down to the round tower on the other side, the only fortification now perfect. But if these were all put in repair, a mere handful of men could defend it; three reservoirs for water still remain, but one of them is almost entirely filled up with sand and stones.

Between the island and Rás Marshigh the curve of the land forms a small sandy bay named Bander Hokat, and another to the northward between the N. point of the island and Rás Kutam.

The anchorage in the eastern bay of 'Aden is very regular, so that a vessel may choose her own position, from 5 to 10 fathoms. During the easterly winds a heavy swell rolls in, but from June to August, with the wind from the westward, good anchorage and smooth water may be always found close under the island. The hot dry gusts blowing from over the hills are usually strong and disagreeable.

There are several mosques in 'Aden, but the only one kept in repair is that lying immediately to the southward of the town, being the mosque and tomb of Sheikh Idris. To the S.-W. the Wádí Kubbeh, or Tomb Valley, extends among the numerous pointed hills that enclose the plain; to the N.-W. a track leads through a pass in the hills, at an elevation of 226 feet, and descends upon the shore of the western inner bay, and on the sandy isthmus which joins this rocky peninsula to the mainland. And here we are indebted to the perseverance of the late Dr. Hulton, our surgeon, and Mr. Cruttenden, of the *Palinurus*, for the discovery that what has hitherto been vulgarly termed a Roman road is in fact the aqueduct of Soleïmán the Magnificent, extending in a general N.-W. direction upwards of 8 miles into the interior. It is built of red brick and stone, about 4 feet 6 inches wide, and the enclosed water-course measures 19 inches by 16 : there are no remains of arches, the ground not requiring them ; and its general appearance is that of a mound about 5 feet high, and bricked over. Commencing at the northern extremity of the peninsula, just inside the ruined wall named Dureïb-el-'Arabi, which extends from sea to sea entirely across the isthmus, only 1,300 yards wide at this part, the aqueduct for the first mile curves slightly to the eastward, whence it assumes a N.-W. direction as far as the village of Biyar Amheït, a distance of 16,320 yards along the line of aqueduct. Here was the source that supplied the various reservoirs placed at certain distances along its side : the well is 60 feet deep, and near it are the ruins of a small fort. The white tomb of Sheïkh 'Othmán is conspicuous on the right side of the aqueduct about $2\frac{1}{2}$ miles before reaching Biyar Amheït : and a bridge on the line is thrown across the north-eastern end of the inlet of Khór Maksá, where it joins a large swamp. The labour and expense employed by the Turks to ensure a plentiful supply of water, one of the prime necessaries of life in this arid and burning clime, are highly praiseworthy. Besides the magnificent aqueduct above mentioned, there are numerous hanging tanks, if the term may be allowed, formed by excavations in the limestone rocks, which receive the mountain stream and have a deep hollow beneath prepared to receive the surplus water overflowing from that above. There are also several tanks of great size around the town, and about 300 wells lie towards the plain, many of which are hewn out of the solid rock, from 60 to 125 feet deep. Another fine tank just beyond the before-mentioned wall was exclusively intended for the use of vessels in the harbour. Such magnificence in works of public utility bears the strongest evidence to the former state of opulence and prosperity of 'Aden : indeed, we know that scarcely two centuries and a half ago this city ranked among the foremost of the commercial marts of the east. In the time of Constantine it was considered a Roman emporium and celebrated for its impregnable fortifications, its extended commerce, and excellent ports, in which vessels from all the then known quarters of the globe might be met with. But now what a lamentable contrast ! Its trade annihilated, its governor imbecile, its tanks in ruins, its water half brackish—deserted streets and still more deserted ports—yet these latter remain as nature made them, excellent, capacious, and secure.

The remains of several old fortifications and other buildings are met with along the rugged paths of Jebel Shamshán. In 1838, accompanied by Lieutenant Swan, Dr. Arbuckle, and Mr. Hamilton, officers of the *Palinurus*, I ascended this mountain, and discovered, to my surprise, that an excellent road had already been made from its base to its summit, built in a zig-zag direction, from 10 to 12 feet broad, and in some places raised to the height of 20 feet. Centuries have elapsed, probably, since this great and skilful undertaking was completed ; yet it is extraordinary to observe how slightly it has suffered from the destructive effect of time.

Another object here of some interest to the historian is a Turkish cemetery on the S. side of the plain of 'Aden : many of the tombs are constructed of white marble, and the head-stones inlaid with jasper tablets, on which are inscriptions surmounted by the cap and turban. At 'Aden also are 3 long brass guns, probably relics of Soleïmán the Magnificent, perhaps brought here by his fleet in 1530. The longest measures $18\frac{1}{2}$ feet, and would probably carry a shot of 80 lbs. ; the inscription on this could not be deciphered ; the second measured 17 feet, and bore upon it "made by Mohammed ibn Hamzah," in the year of the Hijrah, 701 [?]. The third is highly ornamented, and measures 15 feet 7 inches, and the only trace of inscription is " Soleïmán ibn Selím, 901 " (A.D. 1523).

The peninsula of 'Aden bears much resemblance to the rock of Gibraltar, and could easily be rendered as impregnable; but its rocky heights are more elevated and much more peaked in their outline than those of that celebrated European fortress.

The present Sultán of the Abdálí territory, in which 'Aden is situated, is an indolent and almost imbecile man, 50 years of age, who resides at Lahaj. He is named Al Hasan ibn Fudhl Abdu-l-Karim, and has seven sons, the eldest aged 22. The Abdáli tribe is said to number 10,000; yet this chief permitted the Fudhlí in 1836 to ransack the town of 'Aden, and carry off 30,000 dollars (6,000*l.*), and afterwards, in order to make peace, consented to pay a tribute of 365 dollars, 365 mansúríes,* and 40 camel-loads of jowári (millet).

At 'Aden good water may be procured (but it requires care); fire-wood, vegetables, and fruit are scarce and dear; in August and September grapes and pomegranates may be had; bullocks and sheep are plentiful, and occasionally poultry.

Of its present population of 600 persons 250 are Jews, 50 Banians, and the rest Arabs: here is a dowlah, or Assistant-Governor, a Collector of Customs, and a guard of 50 Bedawí soldiers. The exports consist in coffee and jowári in small quantities; the imports, of cotton cloths, iron, lead, rice, dates, and occasionally cattle and sheep from Berberah, Bander Kásim and Zeila', which afford the Arabs an opportunity of improving their breed of cattle. The revenue is derived from a heavy duty on both exports and imports, and a land-tax of 25 per cent. and amounts, I believe, to about 12,000 dollars (2,500*l.*) annually; yet the dowlah contrives to increase this sum by his extortions on every occasion. The Sultán possesses 3 small vessels.

But, as before-mentioned, the superiority of 'Aden is in its excellent harbours, both to the E. and to the W.; and the importance of such a station, offering, as it does, a secure shelter for shipping, and almost impregnable fortress, and an easy access to the rich provinces of Hadramaut and Yemen, without the long voyage to Mokhá, is too evident to require to be insisted on.

Lahaj is a dirty, populous town, about 18 miles N.-W. of 'Aden, in lat. 13° 2′ N., long. 45° 0′ 30″ E., standing in a wide plain, surrounded by gardens and date-trees. This is the residence of the Sultan of the Abdáli, and his palace, built of stone and mud, is situated on the W. side of the town, and guarded by a host of armed slaves. The population of the place may be 5,000, among whom are a few Jews and Somális. The bázár is filled with inferior silks, cotton cloths, dates, butter, tobacco, &c. A great portion of the land in the neighbourhood is cultivated, and produces some flowers and fruits, among which I observed the melon, lime, mango, almond, plantain, and jessamine, which last is very highly prized by the Bedowin girls, who link it into wreaths to adorn their raven tresses. On the road from 'Aden to Lahaj the traveller passes through several scattered villages, thinly peopled; Darab, Mahallah and Misderah, are mere collections of rude huts made of mats, each village having a tower for its protection in the centre. The spoils of a shipwreck which had recently occurred bedecked the persons of their wretched inhabitants.

The Abdálí appear to be strict Mohammedans.

Quitting Cape 'Aden, which is perhaps the most remarkable feature on the S. coast of Arabia, the land turns suddenly to the N.N.E. for 19 miles, then again to the eastward for 12 miles, reaching to Rás Seilán, a low, round cape. The shores around this bay, which is called Ghubbet Sellán, are flat and sandy, gradually improving as you advance to the eastward. A low plain extends into the interior covered with stunted bushes and patches of the cotton-tree

---

* Mansúri, a small copper coin, bearing the impress of Mansúr, one of the Imáms of San'á. 365 of these equal a German crown at Lahaj, and answer to the Komásí of Mokhá.

and acacia, which latter thrives luxuriantly in this arid soil. The soundings in this bay are irregular: the shoal water extends to a considerable distance off-shore, and vessels should, if possible, avoid it, owing to the difficulty they might experience in getting out of the bay when blowing hard from the eastward. A ship was wrecked here in 1836, and two bagalás narrowly escaped sharing the same fate.

This part of the coast is inhabited by the Yáfa'í, a numerous tribe, said to amount to 20,000 persons, spread over an extensive tract of country, and reaching inland to the high mountains called from them the Jebel Yáfa'i: this range, which rises about 6,500 feet above the sea, extends in an E. and W. direction, generally speaking, about 30 miles from the shore, but the bight of the bay of Ghubbet Seïlán approaches it within 20 miles. The Yáfa'í territory on the coast lies between the Abdáli to the S.-W., and the Fudhlí to the N.-E.: in the interior it is mountainous with numerous fertile valleys, producing coffee, wheat, and millet* in abundance. It formerly extended for 40 miles beyond Rás Seilán; but during the years 1837-8 the Fudhlí have been too powerful for them, and have obtained possession of this fertile tract of country, which has long been a cause of altercation between them and the Yáfa'i on account of the abundant produce of the cotton-trees; the last victory gained by the Fudhlí was in 1837, when they took possession of three towers erected a short distance from the coast, for the protection of this fertile tract, expelled the Yáfa'ís, and are still, I believe, the unquiet possessors of it, being constantly subject to the invasions of their rivals; 500 Bedawís are always kept in readiness to repel an attack.

Ghább Wáli, a village about 5 miles N.-W. of Rás Seïlán, is situated near the above-named towers; and during my visit to it preparations were in progress, on the part of the Yáfa'i, for the renewal of hostilities against the Fudhlí, as a year's truce which they had made would expire on the 18th January, 1838. Seven hundred matchlocks were already collected, and the cotton gathered in and forwarded to the interior, to be conveyed to Hadramaut for sale, as the Yáfa'í have no vessels.

Sultan 'Alí ben Gháleb, chief of the Yáfa'í tribe, is a bold and resolute Bedawí with a daring, yet handsome expression of countenance. His family consists of several sons and daughters; the eldest girl is married to the chief of the Fudhlí, but this does not prevent their constant feuds, notwithstanding which, presents are constantly exchanged between father and daughter.

The principal residence of the Sultan is at El Gharrah, a town about 100 miles, or 5 days' journey, from Sughrá. From the little intercourse we had with the Yáfa'ís they seemed to partake much of the character of their chief. They possess large flocks of goats and sheep, numerous camels, and a few horses.

Rás Seïlán is a low, round, sandy point, in lat. 13° 3′ 30″ N., long. 45° 28′ 30″ E.: a few date-trees grow near the cape, with some larger trees to the N.-W. About 1¼ mile to the westward of the cape is the village of Sheïkh Abdallah ben Marbút, containing one square building and a few huts: it forms the present limit of territory between the Yáfa'i and the Fudhlí. From Rás Seilán the coast runs in an almost straight N.N.E. line for 20 miles to Sughrá, with a sandy beach the whole way. The bank of soundings off Rás Seïlán extends 10 miles off-shore, dropping suddenly from 40 to 100 fathoms at that distance: the 20-fathom line of soundings averages a distance of 5 miles from the coast. Sand, shells, and broken coral is the usual nature of the bottom along this portion of the shore.

---

*Jowárí of the Hindús, dhurrah of the Arabs; i.e., sorghum vulgare or saccharatum.—F.S.

Al-ṣáliḥ is a small town 10 miles to the N.-E. of Rás Seïlán, and about 2 miles from the coast. It contains 200 houses, 40 of which are built of stone—its population about 500; the country immediately around is well watered and cultivated. The trade of this place is in the hands of a few Banyans, among whom is the Sultan's agent. We were received here with civility, and good faith was evinced in their transactions with us. A few partridges were shot. To the S.-E. of Al-ṣáliḥ the tomb of a Sheïkh lies near the beach, and close to it the fishermen draw up their boats. About 6½ miles to the westward, towards the interior, is a village named El Kho'r, surrounded by low hills, on which small towers have been erected for the purpose of its protection: its inhabitants are chiefly agriculturists, and the soil amply repays the trouble bestowed on it. Here, and at Al-ṣáliḥ, the nephew of the Sultan governs as a lesser Sheïkh.

Barrow Rocks, so named from the discoverer, are two dangerous rocky reefs, with only 6 feet water on one: they lie 1¼ mile apart, and 2 miles distance from the coast rather more than half-way between Al-ṣáliḥ and Ṣughrá, from which latter place the northern reef bears S.-W. 4⅓ miles distant. The best direction for clearing them is to keep in 15 fathoms water, while the dark saddle-shaped hill called *Kermin Kálási* bears on any point between N.N.E. northerly to N.N.W. This hill, which is about 1½ mile from the beach, bears N. by W. 3 miles from the northern reef. There is a channel between the reefs and the shore 1¼ mile wide, with 6 fathoms water.

Sughrá[*] the principal port of the Fuḍhlí district, is a village of 200 persons, with a stone building called a castle, being the residence of the Sultan for several months of the year. This castle lies in 13° 21' 30" N., 45° 46' E., and is situated about a quarter of a mile from the beach, on the borders of a plain commencing at the foot of Jebel Kharaz, which is its eastern limit, having the valley leading to Wádí Bahreïn, and a barn-shaped hill with a peak on its western end, to the north; and a number of granite hills, terminating in a small eminence, forming a point to the westward at some distance from the sea, probably the Black Point of Horsburgh.[†]

Much millet is cultivated, and here is also a large grove of date-trees in the immediate vicinity of the village.

A break in the reef of rocks, which girts this part of the coast at a distance of ½ a mile forms a small harbour or shelter for bagalás, with 1, 2, and 3 fathoms water. The *Palinurus* anchored in 9 fathoms water, muddy bottom, 600 yards from the edge of the reef, the Sheïkh's castle bearing N. by W.; high water on full and change at 7 o'clock; rise of tide from 8 to 9 feet; the flood-tide sets to the westward, variation 5° west in 1837. Good water, bullocks (similar to those of Súrat, and at a moderate price), sheep, poultry, onions, and pumpkins may be easily procured. The *Palinurus* was probably the first European vessel ever anchored on this part of the coast, and it was amusing to see the general curiosity excited, particularly when the guns were fired; the exclamations of surprise knew no bounds. Our reception, after the first shyness had been overcome, was very cordial. The Sultan, as he is called, is named 'Abdallah ben Ahmed ben Fuḍhlí, and in 1837 his family consisted of three sons and three daughters, whose mother is the daughter of the Yáfa'i chief before mentioned. 'Abdallah is far from prepossessing in appearance, of slight proportions, but resolute and determined in character, and much respected and feared by his neighbours: the Fuḍhlí tribe is reckoned at 15,000 persons, 4,000 of whom are said to be capable of bearing fire-arms. The territory is stated as extending northerly to the distance of 80 miles, bounded on the E. by Makáteïn and the Urlají tribe, and reaching as far as Rás Seïlán on the W., comprising about 70 miles of

---

[*] By corruption often pronounced and written Shugra. [†] Vol. i., p. 259.

coast. The country is chiefly mountainous, Jebel Kharaz, a high range 16 miles N.-E. of Ṣughrá, reaching 5,442 feet above the sea. The Wádí Baḥreïn winds through this range of mountains, abundantly supplied with streams which flow into an extensive lake, whence the valley takes its name. The largest village in this district is Meïn, with a population of 1,500, said to lie 36 hours' journey to the N.-W. of Ṣughrá. Many of the natives are said to inhabit caves in the mountains. The Fuḍhlís are a fine, bold-looking race of men: the women are the prettiest we have seen in all the parts of Arabia we have visited. Their religion is a lax state of Mohammedanism; the fast of the Ramazán almost passes unnoticed. The import and export duties are valued at 600 dollars annually. At the time of our visit, a dollar, or 4s., would buy 12 lbs. of coffee, 150 lbs. of millet, and 24 lbs. of g'hí or clarified butter.

From Ṣughrá eastward to Makáteïn, a distance of about 44 miles, the coast becomes irregular. For the first 13 miles it is flat, and then gradually ascends from the sea to the heights of Jebel Kharaz; advancing to the eastward we suddenly lose the bank of soundings which extends from 'Aden rather beyond Ṣughrá, and find from 20 to 30 fathoms close in-shore.

Jebel Kharazí, or Fuḍhlí, is a range of lofty mountains extending for about 20 miles nearly E. and W., about 5 miles inland from the coast, which follows the same direction. Its summit is singularly broken into gables, peaks, and bluff points. The most conspicuous gable is rather to the W. of the centre of the range, and rises 3,900 feet, and is remarkable for an opening like a great embrasure, or cleft, which gives it, from the eastward, the appearance of a double peak, whence it descends almost abruptly towards the sea. The highest point of the range is to the westward, and reaches 5,442 feet: from this it declines slightly to the eastward, when a barn-shaped mountain reaches 3,950 feet above the level of the sea. The structure of this range is, I believe, limestone, but we were not able to land to examine it: the valleys appear well wooded.

Makáteïn* is an anchorage formed by a slightly projecting rocky point of the coast, resorted to by trading vessels for shelter during the N.-E. monsoon: the cape lies in 13° 24′ 30″ N., 46° 32′ E., whence some rocky islets project to the southward about 500 yards, and a reef to the distance of 1¼ mile.

Makáteïn may easily be known by two black hills immediately to the eastward, and close on the sea. There are others 3 or 4 miles farther E., but not so distinctly separate as the former; when arriving from the eastward, they resemble one long hill; 500 yards to the N. of the point of the cape is a black ruin. High-water here on full and change at 9 h.; rise of tide 6 feet; variation 5° 12′ W., in 1835. Five miles W. of this spot is the best anchorage off Makáteïn-Ṣeghir, or the lesser, formed by a projecting point. Six miles to the eastward of Makáteïn is the small rocky point named Sambeh, and for 13 miles beyond, as far as Howaïyah, a low sandy coast with rocky points prevails: throughout this distance the bank of soundings extends about 6 miles off-shore.

Howaïyah is a town of about 600 houses, situated on a wide plain, 5 miles inland, bounded on the N. by hills, the principal house in lat. 13° 28′ 45″ N., long. 46° 47′ 25″ E. This is the residence of Náṣir ben Abú Bekr, chief of the Urlájí tribe, who received us civilly, and supplied the officers who visited him with horses to ride through the adjoining hamlets, the population of which, including the town, may amount to 5,000 persons, chiefly employed in agriculture. We here got some fine bullocks, with an abundant supply of good water and excellent fish.

---

* Commonly written and pronounced Mughatain, k being sounded like g.

Nasál, a town of the Urláji tribe, seven days' journey, or about 200 miles, from Haur, is said to be populous, and the soil to be fertile. *Maghná* is another small town situated in a secluded spot 4 miles farther inland.

The Urláji territory extends about 55 miles along the coast from Makáṭeïn on the W., to Wádi Ṣanam on the E., and is said to reach 200 miles into the interior. The coast is flat, but about 35 miles inland is a high mountainous range of very irregular outline. We are told that the tribe can muster from 7,000 to 8,000 fighting men.

Rás Urlajah is a low sandy cape: the soundings off this part of the coast, and for some distance to the eastward, are regular, the 20-fathoms bank reaching about 2 miles off-shore with sand and coral, and 160 fathoms at 6 miles' distance. Twenty-one miles farther E. is the tomb or ḵubbeh of the Sheïkhah Hurbah, a female devotee, who is said to have perished from voluntary starvation, imagining that it would be a meritorious act in the sight of her Maker and of Moḥammed, as she believed, his prophet. This ancient shrine is very conspicuous, being covered with white chunam.*

Twenty miles to the eastward is the mosque of Sheïkh 'Abdu-r-raḥmán Baddás, standing on a low, round, sandy point, and a village inhabited by a few fishermen. Two banks, with 40 fathoms water, are reported to lie at some distance off-shore at this part of the coast, but we were not successful in our search after them.

Rás Safwán is a slightly projecting point thinly covered with bushes, on its extreme edges in lat. 13° 48′ N., long. 47° 42′ E.; almost immediately N. of it is the southern peak of the *Jebel Hamari*, which range forms the leading feature on this part of the coast: it extends from 25 to 30 miles in a N.-E. direction, its highest central peak, about 16 miles N. ¼ W. of Rás Safwan, rising 5,284 feet above the sea. This range is apparently of limestone, and, when seen either from the eastward or westward, its summit resembles the roof of a barn. The aspect of the whole range is very dismal and rugged. The peak lies in 13° 3′ 30″ N., long. 47° 37′ 30″ E. A little more than 1 mile N.-E. of the cape is the village of Haurá, of about 100 persons: it is only noted as the residence of a patriarch of the Dujábí tribe.

Jebel Mukánati is a projecting bluff on the coast, 4 miles N.-E. of Haurá, forming a small bay for boats to anchor in: the cape is moderately elevated, perhaps 200 feet, and white with dark veins. Close off it lies a small island, and inland it terminates in sand hills; from the summit of the cape several villages may be distinguished in the valleys of this territory; the extensive valley of Wádi Meïfah lies at the eastern foot of the Ḥamari range; fine large groves of date-trees add much to the beauty of the scene.

It is to the northward of this range, and apparently in a prolongation of the Wádi Meïfah, that the remarkable ruin named Nakab el Hajar is situated, which was visited by two of the officers of the *Palinurus*, Lieut. Wellsted and Mr. Cruttenden, in April 1835: unfortunately, Dr. Hulton, who volunteered his services to be one of the party, could not then be spared from the duties of the ship.†

Rás al Ḵosaïr, a low rounded sandy cape, 7 miles farther to the N.-E., has two large trees on the edge of the shore; a conspicuous gable-shaped hill rises in the distant range of mountains, with a bluff both to the E. and to the W. of it; the centre of the gable, or barn, bears from

---

* Chunam is the Hindú word chúná (from the Sanskrit chúrna) with the Portuguese nasal termination *m*. It signifies lime, particularly shell-lime, and thence a white plaster made of it, which takes a fine polish.—F. S.

† Captain Haines' Memoir is accompanied by a sketch of these ruins by Mr. Cruttenden, with a ground plan, and a copy of the inscriptions; the latter differs in five of the characters from the copy published in the London Geographical Journal, Vol. VII, p. 32.—Ed.

this cape N. by W. about 40 miles distant. This is the eastern boundary of the Diyabí territory, which extends about 36 miles along the coast. They are a tribe much feared, and bear a bad character. From this point as far as Rás el 'Aṣidah, a distance of 22 miles, the coast forms a bay 6 miles deep, named *Ghubbet 'Ain*; on its shores are situated the villages of 'Aïn Abú Ma'bad and 'Aïn Jowári; the former consists of a mosque and about 100 huts, the latter, of 70 huts; springs of water, (as their names denote,) date-trees, and jowári, (sorghum or dhurrah,) abound. Farther to the eastward is the fishing hamlet of Gillab, inhabited by 50 abject-looking Baddás Sheikhs, who are permitted to live unmolested, owing to the sanctity of their descent.

Rás el 'Aṣidah,[*] the eastern cape of this bay, is very conspicuous, from having at its extremity a dark, rocky, conical hill, 160 feet high, and not unlike a haycock: it lies in lat. 13° 57' N., long. 48° 15' 20" E.[†] This cape forms three projecting rocky points; in a small bay to the westward is the tower of Ba-'l-háf, so named from a Sheikh whose burial-place is contiguous. The bay affords fair shelter during an easterly wind; but a good look-out must be kept in the event of its changing to the westward: the bottom is clean and the soundings regular. It is high water on full and change at 8 h. 30 m.; the rise of tide from 5 to 6 feet; the variation 5° 23' W. in 1835. The tower is garrisoned by two or three Wáḥidí soldiers, who levy dues on the goods landed here for 'Aden, Makallah, &c. Here is no fresh water but what is brought from a distance.

To the eastward of Rás el 'Aṣidah the coast takes an E. by N. direction for 30 miles, as far as Rás el Kelb; for the first half of the distance the shore is irregular, with rocky projecting points. Rás Roṭl is a remarkable round cape, considerably elevated, perhaps 400 feet, with a deep hollow, apparently like a crater, in the middle; on each side of the cape is a bay for boats.

Jebel Hiṣn Ghoráb, 5 miles farther E., is a square-shaped dreary-looking brown hill, 464 feet in height, with steep sides, its eastern point lying in 13° 59' 20" N., 48° 24' 30" E. It was here that the late Dr. Hulton and Mr. J. Smith, officers of the *Palinurus*, discovered, in the course of their indefatigable and successful rambles, that a narrow pathway led to the summit, and, as no difficulty ever deterred them from attempting an object attended with any prospect of success, they forthwith climbed up, and found the remains, which may be compared to those of Nakab el Hajar. Much time and labour must have been employed in the construction of the road, which in some parts is nearly 10 feet broad. On a second visit, these officers effected a more minute examination, measuring with care, and making plans of each separate portion. It was here that the inscription, in characters similar to those above-mentioned, was found, carved on the smooth face of the solid rock, and whence it was copied by Dr. Hulton.[‡] He described the inscription as being very slightly impaired by the lapse of years, and not one character seemed effaced. The tanks, together with the ruins of several walls, were composed of cement as hard as the rock itself. I am indebted to Lieutenant Sanders, who afterwards became my Assistant-Surveyor, for a plan of these remarkable remains. I will not attempt to draw any conclusion as to the period in which a city may have flourished here, nor venture an opinion concerning the supposed unknown character of the writing, as a copy has already been sent to

---

[*] Cape Porridge.—F. S.

[†] "Not" observes Captain Haines, "in 46°¾E., as published in the London Geographical Journal, vol. vii., p. 20."—Ed.

[‡] See Bengal Asiatic Journal, for 1834.

those more competent to come to a correct decision on this point; * but I may briefly mention that an Arab tradition states that this spot was originally peopled by a tribe called Kúm-Harmás, whose descendants still dwell near Makallah, and also by the tribe of Wádí Misenát (to the westward of Sihút); the former constitute a separate and distinct tribe, now bearing the name of Beni Seibán, who have insensibly become incorporated, and many of them will be found dispersed among other nations. The Wádí Misenát tribe still maintain a desolate and exclusive mode of living, and are known by the opprobrious epithet of 'Abíd el 'Ibád,† or the slaves of Somális. This appellation arose from their assimilation with the slaves of Africa. On the N.-E. side of the continent of Africa, there is a district called Samhá, containing the populous towns of Makdishá and Jubah, bordering the river of that name, known by the natives of Bráwah as Wewendah.‡ This river rises, it is said, in Abyssinia, probably in the Mountains of the Moon. The language of the people inhabiting these towns is wholly unlike the Sawáhilí§ spoken in Zingibár; and it will be remembered that, when the Portuguese took possession of this coast in the 15th century, they found the villages, &c., from Makdishá to Ṣofálah, governed by Mohammedans, differing in dialect, person, and character, from either the Arabs or Africans. The causes which have led to so great a dissimilarity in people who occupy almost the same spot of land I leave to those more versed in such inquiries: one thing, however, appears certain, that there was an established facility of intercourse with Abyssinia; and since the tide of population from that part of the world flowed down the Jubah, and there exists an affinity between the languages, the presumptive intimacy of the two nations acquires double weight. Possibly a clue might thus be traced to elucidate the name and origin of the tribe who are said to have occupied this station, and then proceed towards solving those hitherto undeciphered inscriptions. At whatever time the buildings around Hiṣn Ghoráb were erected, I consider their discovery of great importance; the fort having, doubtless, been intended to protect the harbour on its eastern side, independently of the town beneath, which, judging from the size and extent of the ruins, must have been considerable. Its position would point it out as a sea-port of some consequence, and the citadel on the hill might be the grand depôt for its commercial resources.

Bander Hiṣn Ghoráb, a small, secure, and well-sheltered bay and harbour 1½ mile wide by 1 mile deep, lies immediately to the eastward of the black hill of Hiṣn Ghoráb. Off the eastern side of the bay a rocky reef reduces the entrance to 1,700 yards, or half its width, and must be carefully avoided. At the bottom of the bay is the square tower and hamlet of Bír 'Alí, or the Well of 'Aḵ, and several adjoining hamlets, containing each about 50 Wáḥidís. In standing into the bay the square tower must not be brought to the northward of N. by E. ½ E. (magnetic.)

Haláni island, a rocky limestone plain, ¾ of a mile long from N. to S. by ½ a mile broad, lies about 1 mile S.S.W. of Hiṣn Ghoráb Point, separated by a shoal channel; between it and Rás Mafrádah, 2 miles to the westward, is a tolerable shelter against easterly winds.

Sha'rán is a circular table-topped sandstone hill 300 feet high, lying 3⅕ miles E. by N. of the point of Hiṣn Ghoráb, and close to the sea, remarkable for a cavity or crater-shaped hollow within, filled with water, the edge of which is fringed by an overhanging bank of mangrove-trees; the diameter of the cavity is about 2,500 yards, and is reported by the Arabs to be

---

* A copy of this inscription, as well as of similar inscriptions found at Nakab el Hajar and at San'á, has been forwarded to Professor Gesenius at Halle. See also several letters on the subject of the Ikhkilí or Himyaritic language, by M. F. Fresnel, at Jiddah, in the 'Journal Asiatique,' for July and Dec. 1838.—ED.

† Literally slaves of slaves.—F. S.

‡ The plural of Wendah in the Sawáhilí language.—F. S.

§ Sawáhil, plural of Sáhil, signifies "coasts;" the "coasters," or inhabitants of the shore, are therefore called sawáhilí, often spelt *sowyly* by travellers.—F. S.

fathomless. We had no means of ascertaining its depth in the centre, but at 8 yards from its western bank it was already 11 fathoms deep. The water is very salt, and on analysing it I found it to contain sulphuretted hydrogen. This sheet of water is named Kharíf Sha'rán, and, having heard strange reports of it, I determined to visit it. Accompanied by Lieut. Sanders and Dr. Hulton, I landed early one morning, and, in spite of the superstitious feelings of the Arabs, but almost suffocated with heat, we scrambled up to the summit of the sharp circular edge that forms the bowl, whence we had a romantic and beautiful view: before us that deep dark water of Kharíf Sha'rán, girt by a belt of mangroves; immediately around rocky heights frowning over fertile valleys which bloomed beneath; and in the distance the dark blue and ever-beautiful ocean, reaching away to the distant horizon, only broken by a few rocky islets, and perchance a solitary sail spread to catch the first breath of the ever-welcome sea-breeze. As before mentioned, this hollow resembles a crater, but I do not conceive it to be of volcanic origin. Our guides pointed out a level plain to the N. called Maïdán,* and said that a number of iron rings and pegs, commonly used to picquet horses, had been found there; but we could see nothing. We returned on board by noon, well pleased with our trip, but suffering much from the heat, which was oppressive in the extreme.

The Kadhreïn islands, or rather rocks, lie about 1 mile offshore, nearly S.S.E. of Rás Khadá, a rocky point at the foot of the hill of Sha'rán.

Sikkah or *Jibús*, is another small island, rising 450 feet above the sea, and lying 5 miles due S. of Rás Khadá, in lat. 13° 54′ 40″, long. 48° 28′ 20″ E., and may be seen at a distance of 30 miles: its summit is flat and white, owing to the excrements of numerous flocks of birds which resort thither, and keep up an abundant supply of this manure, so valuable to the agriculturists. This island is called Sikkah by the natives of the coast, and Jibús by Arab navigators, from its outline resembling the Kítár,† a musical instrument of the Indians.

Rás Makdahah is a dark, moderately elevated cape, being the southern termination of a range of hills which extend 10 miles inland in a northerly direction: it forms the eastern limit of the Bay of Makdahah, affording an anchorage sheltered from easterly winds; the only danger is a sunken rock ½ a mile off-shore on the N.W. side. The village of Makdahah, consisting of a mosque, one stone and mud building, a few huts of matting, and a population of 60 persons, lies in the eastern angle of the bay, close under the hills. It affords no supplies, and indifferent water; yet, notwithstanding its poverty, it is the chief residence of the sultan· or chief, Mohammed ibn Abú Bekr, a tributary of 'Abdu-l-Wáḥid, who derives the principal part of his revenue from traffic in the aforesaid manure. He is a fine-looking man, and visited me on board the *Palinurus*, where he behaved very courteously.

Baraghah Island is a lofty and precipitous limestone rock without a vestige of vegetation which lies off Rás Makdahah, between which is a safe channel about 1 mile wide, with 15 fathoms water. It lies in lat. 13° 58′ N., long. 48° 32′ 40″ E.

Khárijah‡ is a town said to contain 3,000 inhabitants, about two days' journey inland from Makdahah, between the first and second range of the Wáḥidí mountains. It is in a fertile country abounding in date-groves and excellent pasture-land, affording food for numerous herds of cattle, which enables the natives to export large quantities of g'hí, &c.

---

* 'A plain.'—F. S.   † Either the parent or offspring of our word guitar.—F. S.

‡ El Khárijah, "the exterior," as the principal town in the Oasis of Thebes, is called El Khárijah, vulgo *El Chargé*.—F. S.

Rás el Kelb (Cape Dog) is a low, round, sandy cape in lat. 14° 1' 40" N., long. 48° 46' 50" E., lying 13 miles E.N.E. of Rás Makdahah, the intervening coast being also low and sandy. This cape is considered dangerous, many boats and bagalás having been wrecked upon it, and thence it is said to derive its name. But if the lead be attended to, the soundings will give due warning of any danger.

From Rás el Kelb the shore turns abruptly in a N.E. direction for 40 miles as far as Makallah : the first part of it is wretchedly waste and sombre in aspect; sand-hills extend inland for some miles. The distant mountains in the interior appear equally sombre, yet relieved by a very irregular outline, assuming the form of peaks, bluffs, &c., and rising almost precipitously to the height of from 2,000 to 4,000 feet above the sea.

Rás Rehmat, the next cape, is elevated perhaps 300 feet, of limestone, and of a dark peaked outline; on its south-western face the sand from the plain has been swept up into a great heap by the strong S.W. monsoon: it takes its name from the effects experienced by the bagalás in running up the tadhbíreh, the Arabs considering that, if they rounded this point in the S.W. monsoon, the extreme violence of the wind had abated : it signifies " lull of the wind," a term frequently used by the Arabs when it falls calm. From seaward this cape is remarkable as being the commencement of the bold, rocky land extending from hence to the N.E. for 17 miles. Here is the eastern limit of the Wáhidí territory, which has a coast-line of 60 miles in extent; its only two ports are Bá-'l-háf and Hisn Ghoráb. The Wáhidí tribe consists of several thousand persons, and, it is said, can muster 2,000 match-locks in case of war. They are a brave, hospitable race, much respected and feared by their neighbours. The sultan Abdu-l-Wáhidi is said to be an upright chief, and possesses great influence on account of his noble descent. ' Abbán is his usual residence, and that town and Meïfah are said to be equal to Makallah in size and in the number of their inhabitants.

Rás Assasah, or Asr el Hamrá (Red footstep), is a rocky point, being the termination to seaward of a rugged range of hills which extend some distance inland : this cape is 6 miles N.E. of Rehmat, and in the valley between lies the town of Al Ghaïdhar, embosomed in luxuriant date-groves, at about 4 miles from the shore.

Rás Burúm, 8 miles farther, is a bold, dark, craggy cape, chiefly of limestone, the highest point of which I have seen at 38 miles' distance; the cape lies in 14° 18' 30" N., 49° 3' 25" E. Between this point and Rás el Ahmar, or the red cape, the coast forms a small bay called Ghubbet Kulún, and again to the S.W. another small bay, in the bight of which was a hamlet of about 40 miserable-looking people of the Berishí tribe.

The village or town of Burúm lies at the N.W. angle of a small bay which forms to the N. of Rás Burúm: it is surrounded by date-trees, and situated immediately at the foot of an offset of the range of hills which here extends down to the shore and forms a bold and rocky coast. In 1835 its population was about 450, the huts and houses wretchedly built; but we obtained good supplies of water, wood, and stock. The natives were very civil to us. This village, as well as Fuwah, Al Ghaïdhar, &c., is under the Sheikh Mohammed Safali, chief of the Berishí tribe; he has also several smaller tribes tributary to him. Ijilli, a white mosque erected on an eminence a short distance from the beach, may be plainly seen by vessels passing along-shore; it was erected by a pious priest of the name of Sheïkh Wúlí, who is also patron saint of the village. The valleys inland hereabout are rich and beautiful, producing large quantities of millet; they are bounded by the purple-streaked mountains which rise from 5,000 to 6,000 feet above them, whose summits in the cold season, we were told, are at times covered with snow. Heavy and continuous rains fall in November and December, July and August; and even in April and May I have seen rain for three days following. The variation here in 1834 was 4° 44' W.

From the bluff of Radham, the N. cape of Bander Burúm, to Makallah, a distance of 15 miles, the coast is low and sandy, forming a slight bay, with high mountains in the distant background. About half-way from Burúm is the town of Fuwah, containing about 500 inhabitants, who were not very courteous to those of our party who visited them. The soundings throughout this extent are regular.

Rás Makallah is a low neck of land projecting about 2 miles in a S.S.E. direction from the base of the hills, which here extend from the interior close down to the shore; its S. point is in lat. 14° 29' 40" N., long. 49° 14' 20" E., with a rocky shoal with only 4 fathoms on it, lying ½ a mile to the S. Three-quarters of a mile W.N.W. of the cape is Rás Marbát with a ruined fort; and 2 miles to the N.W., and within the bay, lies the town of Makallah, the principal commercial depôt of the S. coast of Arabia, partly built on a narrow rocky point, projecting about ¼ of a mile to the S., and partly at the foot of a range of reddish limestone cliffs, rising about 300 feet, immediately at the back of the town, and on which are 6 square towers for the protection of the place. Almost directly above this remarkably level range of cliffs the flat-topped summit of Jebel Gharrah, composed of beautiful white limestone, rises 1,300 feet above the sea, and may be seen at a distance of 42 miles. The northern portion of the town is built on ground sloping from the base of the hills to the bay, and enclosed on the W. side by a dilapidated wall extending to the shore, with only one entrance-gate, constantly guarded by a few Bedowins. The Nakíb or Governor's house, a large square building, is in lat. 14° 30' 40" N., long. 49° 11' 48" E.; the other buildings are chiefly cajan huts, intermingled with a few stone houses and two mosques. The population of the town may be about 4,500, being a motley collection of the Beni Hasan and Yáfa'i tribes, Karáchíes, and Banias, with foreigners from nearly every part of the globe. On either side of the projecting point on which the town is built is a small bay; that on the W. side is sheltered from the W. by a rocky reef, nearly dry at low-water spring-tides, and forms a haven much frequented by Arab boats and coasting vessels. I have observed 20 of these arrive in the course of a day, and some from 100 to 300 tons burden. The custom-duties are 5 per cent. on goods from India. The exports consist in gums, hides, large quantities of senna, and a small quantity of coffee; the imports, chiefly of cotton cloths, lead, iron, crockery, and rice, from Bombay; dates and dried fruit from Muskat; jowári,* bajri,† and honey, from 'Aden; coffee from Mokhá; sheep, honey, aloes, frankincense, and slaves, from Berberah, Bander Koṣaïr, and other African ports. Much coasting trade is also carried on. Traffic in slaves exists to a frightful extent; I have seen 700 Nubian girls exposed at once in the slave-market here for sale, and subject to the brutal and disgusting inspection of the purchasers; the price varies from 7l. to 25l. a-head. The duties here in 1834 amounted to about 800l., but in 1836 to upwards of 1,200l.; the chief part of the trade is carried on by the Bania merchants. The present Nakib or chief Moḥammed ben 'Abdu-l-'Abid, is a young man of firm and upright character, and is much respected: commerce has greatly revived since his reign. A ship in want of supplies will find Makallah the best port on the coast for procuring them: the water is good, but it requires watchfulness here as well as elsewhere on this coast to obtain it pure; there is none in the town; it is brought from a distance of 1½ mile, and furnishes a means of subsistence for many of the poorer class.

---

* Millet, or sorghum, of various kinds.—F. S. † Or bájará,—Panicum spicatum.—F. S.

The anchorage in the bay is good, from 8 to 10 fathoms, sandy bottom, with the flag-staff on the Governor's house bearing N.N.E. from ¼ to ½ a mile off-shore. A rock with only 1½ fathom water lies 700 yards due W. of the extreme S.W. point of the town, and must be carefully avoided. High-water at full and change at 8 h. 30 m., rise of tide 7 feet. Variation 4° 30', W. in 1834.

While we were at Makallah an excellent opportunity for exploring the interior of the province of Haḍramaút occurred, but on account of the expense it would have entailed I was obliged to decline it. The journey was to have been made in company with a respectable and wealthy merchant named Ṣáliḥ ben 'Abdallah ben Sáil, who, having been wounded in the arm by a musketball, had come to the coast in hopes of meeting with some European surgeon who could extract it for him: this was kindly and immediately done for him by Dr. Hughes, then a passenger on board the E. I. C. ship the *Hugh Lindsay*, and, in gratitude for the relief from violent pain, this merchant offered to conduct any officer safely to the interior on his return home; but, as before stated, we were obliged most unwillingly to decline it. Ṣáliḥ ben 'Abdallah described his intended route as follows:—the first day's journey to Túkam; the second to Jebel'Akár; the third to Wáṣel; the fourth to Raïdah, a place of considerable extent belonging to the Yakís; the fifth day arrive at Sá'ah, of the Yabarí tribe; the sixth day at 'Abd al Betí, inhabited by Al Tatamín Eïwarmás; the seventh, Tarbál; the eighth, Sihún; both the last possessed by the Yáfa'ís. Allowing 20 miles a-day for the camel's journey, this would be 160 miles' journey from Makallah; a courier can accomplish it in 4 days. The usual estimate of the distances from Sihún, the capital of Haḍramaút, to the different towns, is said to be as follows:—to Dau'an 36 hours; to Tarím 6 hours; to 'Aïnát 26 hours; to Shibám 24 hours: the whole province is represented as fertile, the towns and villages populous, abundance of water and date-groves.

The appearance of the natives of Haḍramaút that we saw was favourable; handsome features, slight made, active men, well armed with matchlock and krís, ornamented with gold or silver.

From Rás Makallah the coast extends to the N.E. in an almost unbroken line of low sand for 40 miles, as far as the cliffs of Hámi; the edge of the 20-fathom bank of soundings generally lying about 2 miles off-shore, and dropping to 100 fathoms, at 4 miles' distance; clear bottom of sand and shells. Immediately to the N.E. of Rás Makallah the small anchorage of Bander Roweiní affords shelter for bagalás against the S.W. monsoon. Two miles farther is the village of Rághib, with a large ancient mosque; this coast abounds with fish, and the whole of the inhabitants of the village appeared to be fishermen.

Bú Heïsh, 3 miles beyond, is a village surrounded by date-trees in a well-watered valley, about 1½ mile from the shore.

Shehr, once a thriving town, but now a desolate group of houses, with an old fort, lies close to the shore in lat. 14° 38' 30" N., long. 49° 27' 35" E. This was formerly the residence of the chief of the Kaṣáïdí tribe, but the village has now dwindled to about 300 persons, chiefly fishermen.

Súku-l-Baṣir is a small town lying inland, about 4 miles N.W. of Shehr; it is said to contain 4,500 inhabitants: its mosques may be distinctly seen above the date-groves from the sea, and the valley appeared extremely luxuriant. Much tobacco, plenty of vegetables, good dates, and pure water may be obtained here. Five miles farther to the N.E. the oblong, table-topped hill of Jebel Dheb'ah (Hyæna Mount), entirely separate from all other hills, rises close to the shore: as it is visible at some distance, it forms a good landmark for making Makallah from the eastward.

Zakfah is a pretty village surrounded by date-groves, on the shore, 4 miles farther E., and Máyariyán, 2 miles beyond, is a ruined village, abundantly supplied with water.

Shehr, the chief town of the district of this name, extends one mile along-shore, with a fortified castle, the residence of the sultan, on an eminence near the centre, in lat. 14° 43' 40" N., long. 49° 40' E., and is visible from seaward before any other object in the town. Here is a mosque and a custom-house; the town is built in the shape of a triangle, and, though the dwellings are much scattered, they are tolerably spacious and comfortable; the population is about 6,000. Supplies may be easily obtained here, but the water is not good. Shehr is a place of much trade; its manufactures are chiefly coarse cotton cloths, gunpowder, implements of war, &c. The duties on exports and imports amount to about 5,000l. annually.

The anchorage off Shehr is only an open roadstead; clean bottom of sand and shells in 7 and 8 fathoms, from ¾ to 1 mile off-shore.

Four miles N.E. of the town is the hill of Yakalif, on which are the remains of a wall and a terrace: this hill forms a good landmark for making the place.

The sultan of the Hamúm tribe, Sheïkh 'Alí ibn Násir, is a young man under 30 years of age, and is very superior to the generality of Arab chiefs: he is able to muster 7,000 matchlocks in case of war.

The Hamúm tribe is subdivided into the following lesser tribes:—

Beït 'Alí (Tent of ' Alí),	Beït Subhí,	Barwákhi,
—Aghraf,	—Hamúdíyah,	Sa'il,
—Ghoráb,	—Sheneïn,	Hakkam,
—Bú Salíh,	—Karzet,	Hur.

We were also given the names of the following towns and villages in this territory, besides those already, or to be, described:—

Defeïghah,	Karadah,	Zaghafah,	Mayán 'Abáduh,
Sewán,	Taballah,	Sa'íd,	Ma'du',
Nagkar,	Wásalat,	Dau'an,	Ararah,
Ariyah,	Arab,	Meyú,	Musayyid.
Tiklidah,	Bú'ísh,	'Arif,	

Hámí, the next village, 13 miles farther to the eastward, lies just below the dark double hill of the same name, in a picturesque ravine, with a date-grove and cultivated ground near the beach; its population is about 500; supplies are not easily obtained; fishing seems the chief occupation of the inhabitants. Hot-springs are numerous near Hámí; those I examined stood at 140° Fahr.

Between Hámí and Rás Sharmah, 9 miles farther E., the coast forms a bay 2 miles deep with sandy bottom and regular soundings; in the bight of the bay, on a rocky eminence ½ a mile from the coast, stands the ruined fort of Hisn el Misenát, and between this point and Rás Sharmah lies Sharmah Bay, considered the best on the coast for shelter during the N.-E. monsoon. Along the shore of this latter bay are the ruined fort of Mughrá, the ruined mosque and village of Kalfah, and El Gharm, a small fishing village; while inland at 2 miles distance is the walled town of Dís, containing 1,000 persons and some hot springs. In 1836 the Daulah or Governor here was named Aïwás ibn Aḥmed, who was very civil to the officers who visited him, but the legitimate chief is Moḥammed 'Omar ibn 'Omar, the owner and captain of a fine ship, which command he prefers to that of an unsettled government.

Ḍhabbah, a village 4 miles farther inland, surrounded by date-groves, is noted for its hot springs of peculiar efficacy in rheumatic complaints.

Rás Sharmah is a small headland projecting to the S.-W., and forming the eastern limit of the bay; the point lies in 14° 48′ 30″ N., long. 50° 2′ 30″ E., immediately N. of it a hill named Chehár Saber* rises 170 feet above the sea; and 700 yards W. of the extreme point of the cape lies the small rock called Jezírah Sharmah, 70 feet high. It is high water here on full and change at 9h.; rise and fall 8 feet; variation in 1835 was 4° 39′ W. From Rás Sharmah the coast runs nearly due E. for 8 miles, presenting a succession of limestone and chalky cliffs rising almost precipitously 400 feet above the sea.

Rás Baghashú', a rocky cape 300 feet high, is the eastern termination of this bold shore, and lies in lat. 14° 49′ 10″ N., long. 50° 9′ 30″ E.: a miserable village of the same name stands a little to the eastward; and 4 miles to the westward, in a gap of the cliffs, is another small village called Ḍhafghán. About 3 miles to the northward is Jebel Hamúm, a hill, near which we found some inscriptions in the same character as those of Hiṣn Ghoráb,† &c. Here also are several springs of good water and considerable cultivation.

A lofty range of mountains extends in the direction assumed by the coast, varying from 10 to 15 miles' distance from the sea: commencing to the eastward of Makallah, they bear the name of Jebel Jambúsh, then Jebel ibn Shamáyik, with a remarkable bluff towards its eastern end on a still more distant range: then follow Jebel Asad, (Mount Lion,) which stretches away to the north-eastward towards Rás Fartak.

The Beït 'Alí sub-division of the Hamúm tribe have great influence along this part of the coast; their Sheïkh, Ḥasan ibn 'Alí, is a man of ability and courage, and commands 1,000 matchlocks, a force sufficient to make a chief much respected and feared by his weaker neighbours.

Thirteen miles of low sandy coast in an E.N.E. direction bring us to the sandy cape of Rás Koṣaïr; and 1 mile due N. of the point is the small town, or rather village, of Koṣaïr containing several stone buildings, but chiefly huts; its population is estimated at 300 of the Beït 'Alí and Beït Ghoráb tribes. The highest house in the centre of the village is in lat. 14° 54′ 40″ N., long. 50° 21′ 50″ E. The natives have a few boats, and catch abundance of sharks, the fins and tails of which find their way, *viâ* Maskaṭ and Bombay, to the Chinese market, and fetch good prices.

Half a mile to the N.-W. of the village is a ruined square fort and a date-grove, and 2½ miles in the same direction is the scattered hamlet of Koreïn. Immediately to the S.-W. of the cape a rocky shoal extends for ½ a mile.

For the next 30 miles the same description of low, sandy coast continues to the north-eastward, forming a slight curve, in which the chief place is.

Raïdah, a small town of 700 inhabitants on the sea-coast, only noted as the residence of the Sultán, 'Alí ibn Abdallah, &c., a descendant, it is said, of one of the principal chiefs of

---

* This is a Persian, and therefore not the native name.—F. S.
† See London Asiatic Journal for 1838, p. 91.—Ed.

Southern Arabia. The present chief is a man of about 50 years of age, and is much respected; he is of the Kaṣáīdí sub-division of the Hamúm tribe, and his territory extends from Rás Baghashú' to Misenát, a sea-coast of about 35 miles. Frankincense, aloes, ambergris, and sharks' fins are the chief articles of export. Here are about 30 boats.

The villages of Raidah, Seghir, or Serrár, of 80 people; of Harrah, conspicuous for its round tower; and the ruined fort of Huseïn el Katherí, lie on the coast between Koṣair and Raïdah.

Misenát is an old ruin on the coast, 13 miles E. by N. of Raïdah, and lies in lat. 15° 3′ N., long. 50° 43′ 25″ E. Here is a spring of excellent water, but the land is swampy and abounds in mangrove-trees. The remains would indicate the site of a town of some size, and we were told that coins and other things have been picked up here, and amongst them a pair of scales. It is melancholy to find this interesting coast, which in former days was probably fertile and populous, now almost entirely desolate; and the few inhabitants that remain nearly always at strife with their neighbours.

At this place a party of officers, consisting of Lieut. Sanders, Dr. Hulton, and Mr. Smith left the *Palinurus* and proceeded about 10 miles inland to Wádí Sheikháwí, 3 miles distant from the village of Mayokí, where they discovered some inscriptions similar to those found at Hiṣn Ghoráb,* &c. The valley is said to be fertile and to contain numerous villages. Wádi Sheikháwí may be easily distinguished by a remarkable gap in the mountains that encompass it.

The coast between Misenát and Sihût is low and dreary, with a gradual ascent to the Sheikháwí mountains, the eastern termination of which forms the western side of Wádi Masellá.

The Mahrah territory here commences and continues to the eastward nearly as far as Marbát.

'*Abdu-l-Kúrí*, or *Palinurus* Shoal, a dangerous patch lying off this part of the Arabian coast, was unknown to both Arab and European navigators till this survey in 1835; an old fisherman, who had lived many years in this neighbourhood, pointed it out to me as a place where I should be likely to catch plenty of sharks, and it was not until after a difficult and tedious search, and struggling against a current running 3 miles an-hour, that we were able to take soundings upon the shoal spot. The shallowest part of this newly-discovered shoal is a pointed rock with only 4 fathoms water on it, and lies in lat. 11° 54′ 50″ N., long. 50° 45′ 20′ E., determined by observations made on the spot by Lieut. Jardine (an excellent and accurate observer) and myself, and agreeing by trigonometric and chronometric measurements within a few seconds. The variation of the compass, by means of twenty-three observations in 1835, was 4° 26′ westerly.

The shoal extends for 1,850 yards in a N.N.E. and S.S.W. direction, and is from 300 to 600 yards broad, with a bottom of alternate rock and coral. The soundings round the shoal cannot be relied on, as they vary suddenly, and do not always decrease on approaching it. The nearest land is at the old ruin of Misenát, distant 8½ miles, and bearing N. by W., being almost in a transit bearing with the eastern bluff of Sheikháwí Gap. From the shoal the sandy beach on the mainland is not visible.

The fishermen assured me that forty years ago there was more water on this spot, and at that period no coral could be perceived at the bottom. The soundings, measured from the shoal

---

* See London Asiatic Journal for 1838, p. 93.

spot, gave 80 fathoms at 1 mile distance to the S.-W., and 64 fathoms at 2 miles distance to the S.-E.; in every other direction they exceeded 100 fathoms at this distance; at 2 miles distance from the shoal spot towards the shore the soundings were 120 fathoms.

From the accounts we received of it, and the opinion we were enabled to form, I strongly recommend navigators wholly to avoid this spot, either by keeping the land well aboard, and so passing between it and the shore, or else to keep a good offing, say from 12 to 15 miles from the coast, as there seems reason to believe that the shoal is gradually becoming more shallow.

Subjoined are the chief positions determined during the survey.

Name of Place.	Exact Point.	N. Lat.	E. Long.	Height in feet.
		° ′ ″	° ′ ″	
Ras Bab-el-Mandeb	Manhalí Peak	12.41.10	43.32.14	865
Perím Island	Pyramid at N.-E. angle	12.39.20	43.28.50	230
Rás Sejan	Summit of centre	12.28.22	43.22.50	380
Jeziratu-s-sab'ah [Brothers]	Summit of High Brother	12.28.00	43.28.50	350
Rás 'Arab	Low point of Cape	12.37.30	44.01.40	
Jebel Kharaz [St. Antonio]	Southern Bluff	12.41.00	44.16.00	2,085
Rás Ka'ú [Black Cape]	Cape	12.39.45	44.32.30	
Rás 'Amrán	S.-W. point of island	12.43.30	44.49.40	
Jebel Hasan [Sugar-loaf]	Highest point	12.44.50	44.58.40	1,237
,, [Ass's ears]	Eastern peak	12.44.35	45.01.00	700
Rás Mujallab Heidí	Point	12.43.00	44.59.00	
Jebel Shamshán	Summit	12.45.30	45.03.00	1,776
Rás Sinailah [Cape Aden]	South point	12.45.10	45.09.00	
'Aden (town)	N. point of Sírah Island	12.46.15	45.10.20	
Lahaj (town)	Centre of west side	13.02.00	45.00.30	
Rás Seilan	Low eastern cape	13.03.30	45.28.30	
Sughrá (village)	Sheikh's castle	13.21.30	45.46.00	
Jebel Kharázi, or Fudhli	Western summit	13.31.30	45.59.00	5,442
Makátein	Point	13.24.30	46.32.00	
Howaiyah (town)	Sheikh's house	13.28.45	46.47.25	
Jebel Hamari	Summit of peak	14.03.30	47.37.30	5,284
Rás el'Asídah	Hill at point	13.57.00	48.15.20	160
Jebel Hisn Ghoráb	Eastern point	13.59.20	48.24.30	464
Sikkah, or Jibús Island	Centre	13.54.40	48.28.20	450
Rás el Kelb	Low cape	14.01.40	48.46.50	
Rás Burum	North rocky cape	14.18.30	49.03.25	
Makallah (town)	Governor's house	14.30.40	49.11.48	
Shehr (town)	Centre	14.43.40	49.40.00	
Rás Sharmah	Point	14.48.30	50.02.30	
Rás Baghashú'	Cape	14.49.10	50.09.30	300
Kosair (village)	Centre	14.54.40	50.21.50	
Misenát (ruin)	Centre	15.03.00	50.43.25	
'Abdu-l-Kúrí, or *Palinurus* Shoal	Shoalest spot	14.54.50	50.45.20	

NARRATIVE OF A JOURNEY

FROM

MOKHA' TO SAN'A' BY THE TARIK-ESH-SHAM.
OR NORTHERN ROUTE

IN

JULY AND AUGUST

1836.

Sketch of
the Northern Route from
MOKHÁ TO SANÁ,
by
J. G. Hulton, M.D. and C. J. Cruttenden
Indian Navy
1836.

5 10 20 30 40
English Miles

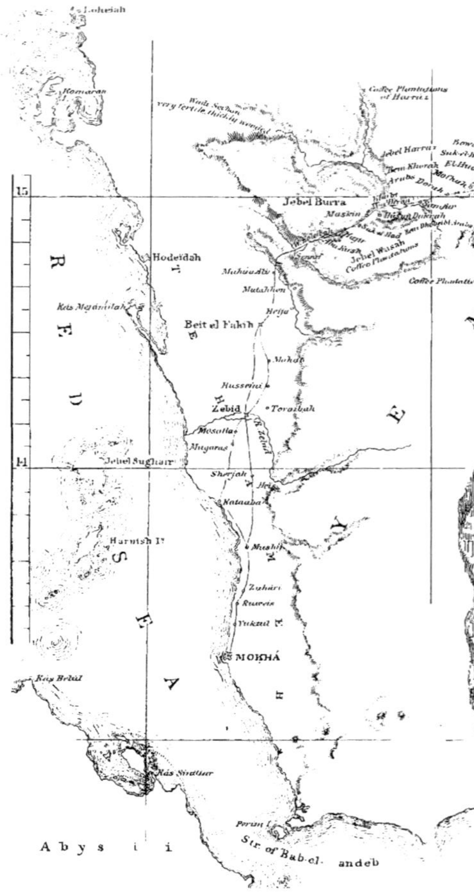

Found at Saná.

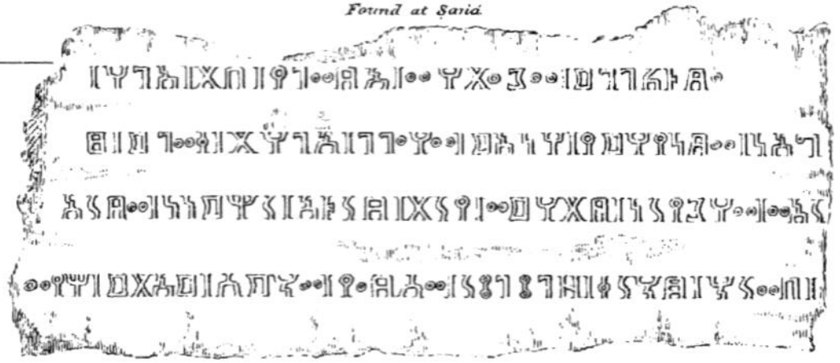

On Marble found at Saná.

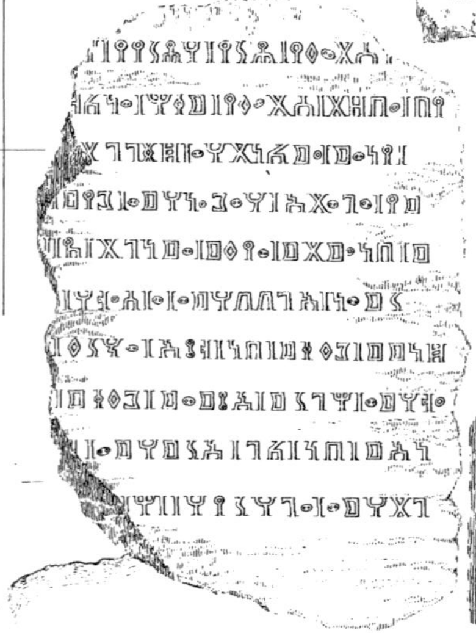

Found on a detached Stone at Saná.

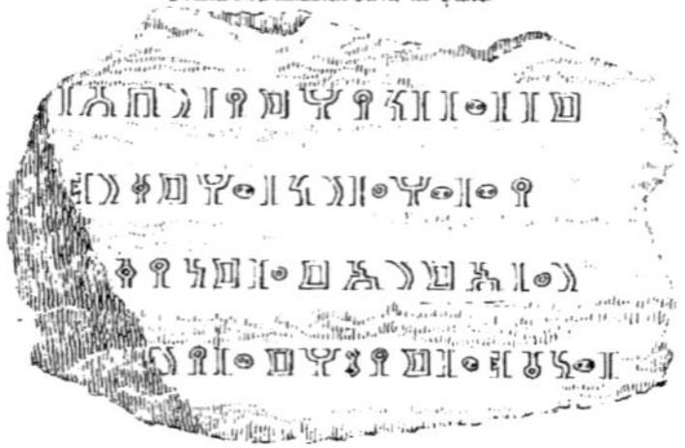

On the side of a house in the Bazaar Saná.

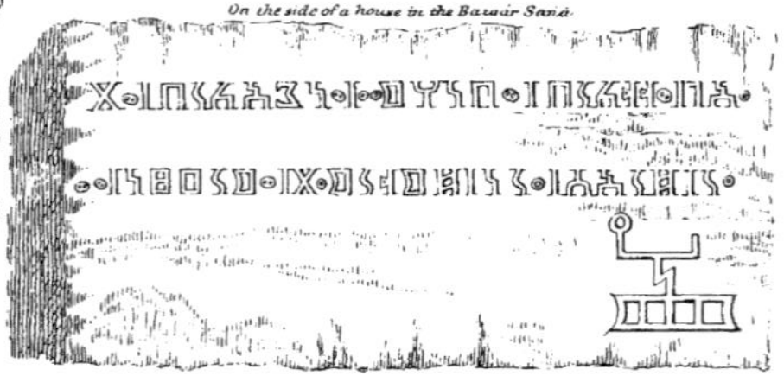

NARRATIVE OF A JOURNEY

FROM

MOKHA' TO SAN'A' BY THE TA_{RIK}-ESH-SHA'M, OR NORTHERN ROUTE, IN JULY AND AUGUST 1836.

BY Mr. CHARLES J. CRUTTENDEN, INDIAN NAVY.

During the time that the East India Company's surveying brig *Palinurus* of the Indian Navy was employed at Mokhá in making a plan of the roadstead, Dr. Hulton, the surgeon of the vessel, and myself, took advantage of the opportunity thus offered to endeavour to penetrate as far as Ṣan'á. We had previously made the attempt from 'Aden, on the south coast of Arabia, but, owing to the suspicious temper of the Sulṭán, were unable to effect our purpose.

Lieutenant Wellsted, I. N., has already, I understand, laid before the Geographical Society copies of inscriptions found at Nakabu-l-Hajar,[*] and the Royal Asiatic Society have, I believe, published those found at Ḥiṣn Ghoráb, on the southern coast of Arabia, and our pleasure was, of course, great in finding the very same characters in Ṣan'á. We were the more surprised at this discovery, as Niebuhr says he could hear of none at that place, though the buildings on which we found these were, by the accounts of the townspeople, at least seventy years old.

My original intention was merely to offer to the Geographical Society the copies of the inscriptions, and an account of the place where they were found. As, however, I understand that a narrative of my journey to Ṣan'á may be acceptable, I have given a few rough notes made during our progress across the mountains, which may serve to show the nature of the country, and the principal towns.

The inscriptions were found in the neighbourhood of the most ancient part of Ṣan'á, near the foot of Dár-el-Ṭawáshí, or the "Abode of the Eunuchs:" it is also sometimes called Bakhírí. It is the eastern extremity of the town, and in former days was the part appropriated to the Jews. The letters are about 2½ inches long; three of the inscriptions are in relief, and the fourth is cut into the marble.

These inscriptions are exactly in the same characters as those found at Ḥiṣn Ghoráb, about 70 miles to the westward of Makullah, on an almost insulated rock, on the south coast—as those at Nakabu-l-Hajar, in 14° 30′ N. long. 46° E.—and as those of Nakhl Mayúk and Koṣaïr, about 70 miles to the eastward of Makullah—but the two latter are said to be in red paint.

Several of the principal merchants in Ṣan'á assured us that these stones had all been brought from Máreb, which was about two long days' journey distant; and, in reply to our questions, told us that it was less expensive to bring these ready-cut stones from Máreb than to prepare them in Ṣan'á. The fact of Máreb being still called by the natives "Arḍ-es-Sabá"

---

[*] Journal, vol. vii., p. 20.

(*i.e.* the land of Sheba),* leads to the supposition that this might be the ancient Saba, but of this hereafter.

We determined to adopt the native costume as being better adapted for travelling, and, through the kind assistance of a wealthy Persian merchant at Mokhá, we found no difficulty in procuring a guide and eight mules to take us to Ṣan'á. We were particularly anxious to take the eastern road, or "Ṭarik el Yemen," by "Ta'ez and Dhamár," but the intestine feuds of the Bedawí Sheïks in that part rendered travelling impracticable, and indeed this road has been blocked up for eleven years.

July 13, 1836.—We quitted Mokhá at sunset, as, the hot season having commenced, we were compelled to cross Tehámeh by night, and travelled along the shores of the Red Sea in a northerly direction, about two miles from the beach. Our party consisted of Dr. Hulton, myself, two servants, who also acted as interpreters, and four muleteers, all well armed, as even in Tehámeh travelling by night is not considered altogether safe.

In that tract the caravan-seraïs, or, as they are here called, the "Mekháyehs,"† are generally divided into several small apartments, each sufficiently furnished with rude wooden bedsteads, and small three-legged stools for coffee, &c. In the evening the inhabitants of these several chambers have their beds carried outside into the square court-yard, which forms the centre of the building, and placed in the open air, the weather being too oppressive to admit of any one's sleeping under cover.

The dews at night fall like rain, but, if the precaution is taken of covering the face with a light linen cloth, no evil effects result from the exposure, owing to the absence of trees; and the sensation of perfect refreshment that is experienced on rising is indescribable.

The "Mukawwí,"‡ or coffee-housekeeper, supplies his guests morning and evening with curdled milk and a coarse cake of Jowárí§ bread, which weighs about a pound, and is commonly called by the natives by the name of "one man's share." The whole cost of supper, breakfast, and a night's lodging, did not exceed a third of a dollar, or 1*s*. 6*d*., and there are stated prices for every article of food. At this time grain had risen greatly in price, owing to the continued drought that had prevailed for nearly four years.

The scenes of misery and wretchedness which we witnessed on our passage across Tehámeh were dreadful. In Mokhá it was no uncommon thing to see dead bodies lying unheeded in the streets, victims of famine, and this, added to the grinding tyranny and brutal oppression of the Egyptian troops, rendered the condition of these poor people almost insupportable.

Our first stage was about fifteen miles to the small village of Ruweïs,|| where we halted till three o'clock on the following day. Thermometer in shade at 1 P.M. 96° Fahr.

July 14.—We pursued our route for about twenty miles, gradually diverging from the shore as far as Múshij, or Maushij,¶ a large village, containing perhaps eight hundred inhabitants, and celebrated for the quantity of "yásmin," or jessamine, which grows there; its flower, stripped of its stalks, and strung upon thread, is daily carried to Mokhá, where it is eagerly purchased by the women as ornaments for their hair. In each thicket of jessamine there is

---

* Máreb was the capital of Sabá. "Sabá cujus metropolis Márab, Mariaba: Strabo. Plin, &c., paulo plus triduo distans á Sanaa." Golius in Alphergan, p. 86.

† Properly Meháyí, plural of Mahyá; a living-place.

‡ The furnisher of refreshments. This word is not derived from Kahweh, coffee.

§ Sorghum vulgare, called *dhurrah* by the Arabs.

|| Little Head.   ¶ Also called Maushid, Niebuhr's Descr., p. 224.

a well of pure and sweet water, so that these bowers form a very delightful retreat during the intense heat of the day.

The mosque at Múshij is noted as being the favourite resort of the Imám 'Ali, son-in-law of Moḥammed, who is believed to descend nightly in an invisible shape, and perform his devotions.

Múshij is under the dominion of Sheïkh Huseïn bin Yaḥyá, whose character is so extraordinary, that it deserves to be more particularly noticed.

This chief owns the tract of land about three miles in length, by fifteen average breadth, extending from the back of Mokhá as far as Múshij, including the mountains bordering on Tehámeh. His influence with the neighbouring tribes of Bedawís is so great, that Moḥammed Alí, the Páshá of Egypt, is glad to purchase his alliance, or, more properly speaking, his neutrality, at the rate of eight or ten thousand dollars a year. He is absolute in his own territory, and his commands are obeyed with the blindest devotion. His nominal residence is at the fortress of Heïs, situated in a deep ravine eighteen miles N.-E. of Múshij, but it is never certainly known where he is. He is held in such dread by the peasantry, that they scarcely mention his name but in a whisper, and he bears the highest character for impartial but strict justice. For several years his alliance has been courted by the Imám of Ṣan'á, who is naturally anxious to secure his co-operation in defending the country from an invasion of the Turks; but the Sheïkh persisted in remaining neuter, till the continued encroachments of the Governor of Mokhá roused him. He then at once renounced all friendship with Moḥammed Alí, and, in company with Sídi Kásim, the exiled uncle of the Imám of Ṣan'á, invested the fortress of Ta'ez, where there were two regiments of Egyptian infantry, and which, as we understood, he succeeded in reducing.

The latest accounts we had, stated that he had furnished the exiled Sidi Kásim with troops; and that, in company with the tribes of Do Mohammed and Do Husein, whose territories lie in the neighbourhood of Dhamár and Ebb, Sidí Kásim had dethroned 'Alí ben 'Abd-allah el Manṣúr, the reigning Imám, and established himself at the head of the Government. Thermometer in shade at 1 P.M., 95° Fahr.

July 15.—Our next stage, of eight hours in a north-north-east direction, to the hamlet of Sherjah, was of little interest, the country being nothing but an arid sandy plain, covered with a coarse kind of grass and stunted bushes, here and there intersected by the dry bed of a mountain-torrent. Thermometer in shade at 1 P.M., 95°.

July 16.—From Sherjah to Zebíd, six hours and a half, in the same direction, the country presented a better appearance, being in many places carefully cultivated. This valley is mentioned by Niebuhr as the "largest and most fruitful in the whole of Tehámeh;" and in a prosperous season it certainly would deserve that appellation. Four years of continued drought had, however, completely burned up the soil, and the husbandman could not but despond when he had placed the grain in the ground, and saw no prospects of a return for his labour.

Wádi Zebíd is in many places covered with a thick brushwood of tamarisk, which affords shelter to numerous wild guinea-fowl. We shot several, and found them quite as palatable as the domestic birds bred in England.

We did not reach Zebid till midnight; and, the gates of the city being closed, we were obliged to search for accommodations in the suburbs, which, after some difficulty, we found.

Zebíd is a city of moderate size, not quite so large as Mokhá. It had a peculiarly gloomy appearance, owing to the dark colour of the bricks with which the houses are built, and the ruinous state of many of them. It is, I believe, considered as being the most ancient town in Tehámeh. The Arabs have a tradition that it has been three times washed away by floods, with the exception of the Mesjid el Jámi', or principal mosque, which certainly wears a venerable appearance.

That edifice is very large, and has an octagonal menáreh, which is ornamented with a light net-work of stone, giving it a very elegant appearance. The interior is the same as in other mosques, and consists of one large room, with the kiblah pointing out the direction of Mekkah, and several small adjoining oratories branching off in different directions, containing, the tombs of deceased " welís," or saints. The " súk," or market, is remarkably well arranged and divided into three compartments for fish, flesh, and vegetables. The supplies are ample for the garrison of 700 men, and the inhabitants, who may amount to 7,000 persons.

With the exception of a few rusty 24-lb. carronades at the principal gate Zebíd is destitute of artillery. Like many other Arab towns, the number of tombs and mosques outside the walls render it practicable to march an invading force within 100 yards of the town without the slightest exposure. So long as the Arabs have no artillery the Egyptian troops are safe in Zebid. In that case the town is well adapted for defence, the walls being high and crowned with numerous towers with loopholes for musketry. The town is well supplied with water; indeed, on our return, we found the road impassable from the overflowing of a mountain-torrent.

In many parts of Arabia, and particularly in Socotra, the marks of very heavy mountain-torrents are evident, but with one exception I never witnessed the effects of one at the time; this was on our return from San'á when, crossing a broad mountain-stream, a sudden rush of water took place that carried a donkey on which I was mounted off his legs, and drowned him before we could succeed in catching him, nor did I land without much difficulty; ten minutes afterwards the stream was impassable, and the remainder of our party that had not crossed it were compelled to wait patiently till it had subsided. This must account for the numerous rivers that we see marked in old maps of Arabia; and in no place would a person be so easily deceived regarding their permanency as in Tehámeh, where the water always takes its old bed, and where the ravines are always clothed with thick underwood.

I have, in the small map, traced the river at Zebid as it appeared on our return, but it must not be supposed that it is thus throughout the year. Four years, as I before stated, had elapsed without a drop of rain, and many persons may have been to Zebíd in the interim and found everything dried up, as we did on our first arrival. With the exception of that of Zebid, all the streams I have laid down are perennial, generally of small size, but the best proof we have of their duration is the fact of their having many fish. Therm. in shade at 1 p.m. 96°.

July 17.—We left Zebíd in the afternoon, and after a very long and fatiguing stage of nine hours and a half, or nearly thirty miles, in a north-easterly direction, we reached the city of Beït el Fakíh,* an hour after midnight. The country we had passed over was, if anything, more arid and barren than any we had hitherto seen, and we heard with much satisfaction the assurances of our guides that this was our last stage in the plains of Tehámeh, and that the following night would see us, " In shá állah !" (please God), across the Turkish frontier and in the dominions of the Imám of San'á.

We found Beït el Fakíh a large town of 8,000 persons, with a citadel of some strength in the centre of it. The town itself was unwalled, and consisted generally of a large kind of

---

* Lawyer's house.

house, built partly of brick and partly of mud, and roofed with branches of the date-tree. It is the frontier-town of the Egyptian Government, and as such is of some importance, it being the emporium for all the coffee that comes from the interior. The principal articles of trade in Zebíd and Beït el Fakíh are piece-goods from India, consisting chiefly of coarse blue and white cloth, English shawls, which are in great request, spices from Java, and sugar from Mauritius, which are bartered for money, wax, gums, and frankincense, and a small quantity of coffee that the neighbouring Bedawís bring down in preference to sending it to the San'á market. Indian Banias are the principal merchants in the place; they are very numerous, but they have to pay a very heavy tax to the Governor, and one of them declared, with tears in his eyes, that they could not make near so much profit as in India under the Government of the English. A heavy duty is here levied upon all káfilahs (caravans) of coffee that arrive from San'á on their way to Hodeïdah, or Mokhá, and so vexatious are the continual demands upon the Sa'ná merchants that it will end, in all probability, in their carrying their coffee to 'Aden, more especially as it is now under the English flag. The distance is nearly the same, and we frequently heard while in San'á that the merchants contemplated changing the route, if practicable; though of course, when this was said, they knew nothing of the treaty since formed by the Bombay Government with the Sultán of 'Aden.

Beit el Fakíh is, without exception, the hottest town we found in Tehámeh, the thermometer being at noon 102° in the shade and 141° in the sun. The land between the city and the sea is higher than that on which the town stands, which prevents the sea-breeze from cooling the air. In fact, we found the wind so heated in its passage across the dry sandy plain that lies between Hodeïdah and Beit el Fakíh, that it was less oppressive when it was calm. The fort is governed by a bimbáshí,* or sub-captain, and the garrison consists of about 500 men. The Governor was extremely civil, but evidently thought we were going to the court of the Imám, to set on foot a treaty regarding the expulsion of the Turks from Yemen. He pointed out to us the numberless dangers of the road, and strongly advised us not to go; finding, however, his remonstrances of no avail, he no longer endeavoured to make us relinquish the attempt, and allowed us to depart with a good grace.

July 18.—We left the city at 6 P.M. and travelled in a north-east direction for eight hours immediately towards the mountains, the base of which we had for the last two days been skirting. After an alarm of robbers, on passing through some thick underwood at the foot of the hills, which made us alight and prepare for an attack, but which proved groundless, we reached a pass, and, crossing over a low shoulder of the mountain, descended, by a densely-wooded ravine, into the beautiful valley of Senníf.† Dark as it was, it was evident that the scene was changed. Tall, majestic elm-trees mingled with the wide-spreading tamarind, and forming a natural avenue, met our view. The bubbling of a brook was heard, and the sound of our footsteps was lost in the grass. To us, who for six days had been travelling in a comparative desert, the change was delightful in the extreme.

July 19.—At 1 A.M. we reached the village of Senníf, and were soon established in a comfortable seráï, or meháyé, with a temperature comparatively so much lower that we were glad to sleep under cover. The village was very full, owing to its being the day of the " súk," or market, and we in consequence could not procure beds till an hour before daylight, when we retired to rest much fatigued.

On rising in the forenoon we found Senníf a large village, built entirely of conical straw huts, with the exception of the sheíkh's house, which was a large barn-like building. Its

---

* Bing-báshí : *i. e.*, head of 1,000 ; a Turkish title.
† This cannot be the Sennef of Niebuhr, Voy. i. 334.

population may be 1,000 persons. The sheïkh sent us a fat sheep as a present, and offered us every assistance in his power. We found not only the appearance of the country but the dress of the natives totally altered; the men wearing conical straw hats and the women wide blue cotton trousers drawn tight round the ankle, their head-dress consisting of a handkerchief profusely ornamented with steel chains; they were also fairer than the peasantry of Tehámeh, owing probably to the greater coolness of the atmosphere in the mountains. In Socotra we found the Bedawís of Jebel Hajjiyeh much fairer than the town-Arabs, and attributed it to the same cause.

The valley of Senníf has the shape of a horse-shoe, and is as carefully cultivated as the lands of India; wheat, jowári (Sorghum vulgare), and barley, flourished in great luxuriance, with several small patches of Indian corn, and some indigo.

Senníf is a market-town, and is also called "Súk el Jum'ah," or Friday-Market. There are seven market-towns between this place and Ṣan'á, in each of which the market is held on a different day of the week, and they are a night's journey distant from each other. The sheikhs of the different villages levy a tax upon all merchandise, and take the merchants under their protection for the time.

We here first saw the Bedawís of the mountains; they are very slightly but elegantly formed, and their average height is five feet six inches; their colour is lighter than that of the Bedawis on the southern coast, and they have long, black, curling hair. The dress of the higher classes among them consists of a blue frock or shirt, with very wide sleeves, bound tight round the waist by the belt of their yambé' or dagger, and no sash, or, as it is termed in India, " kamar-band." The dagger is different from any other that I have seen, being much longer and nearly straight. Their turban is of blue cloth, with several folds of cotton of the same colour bound round it, the Bedawí disdaining to wear the straw hat used by the cultivators of the soil. They carry a short sword with a very broad, spoon-shaped point, if I may use the term, and a long matchlock. When on horse-back they carry a very long spear, having a tuft of horse-hair close to the steel head. They appear to be very quick in taking offence, but their quarrels seldom last long. I have seen a man deliberately draw his sword and endeavour to cut down another with whom he was disputing, nothing but the folds of his turban saving his life, and I have been surprised to see the very same men quietly smoking their pipes together on the evening after the quarrel. We found them inquisitive, but not impertinently so. They would collect round us when we halted and listen to our accounts of "Wiláyat,"* or England, or to what they infinitely preferred, the musical box which we had with us. Some, indeed, after hearing the box for a minute or two, would exclaim, "'Audhá Billah min Sheiṭán e rájim!"†—"God preserve us from the power of the devil!"--and walk away, but they were generally laughed at for their folly. They all expressed the utmost detestation of the Turks, or " El Aḥmarán" (the red men), as they designated them, and laughed at the idea of their endeavouring to penetrate into the interior through the intricate mountain-passes.

Our party was here increased by the addition of the leader of a large káfilah, which was awaiting us about twenty miles further on, and two Ṣan'á merchants, mounted on two very beautiful Abyssinian mules. Therm. in shade at 1 P.M. 88°.

July 20.—As the intricacy of the passes would not admit of our journeying by night, we left Senníf at daylight and proceeded through a very romantic valley called Wádi Koleibah, on our way to Hajír, which was to be our halting-place for the night.

---

* The (foreign) country; hence Wiláyetí, corrupted by the Bengalese into Biláïtí.
† " 'Audháṇ billahi min Sheitan er rájim," lit. (I fly) for refuge to God from Satan the stoned.

As we gradually ascended, the scenery hourly became more striking and magnificent. The hills were thickly clothed with wood, and we recognised several trees that we had formerly seen in the Jebel Hajjíyeh of Socotra. The villages became more numerous, and, the sides of the mountains being in their natural state too steep to admit of grain being cultivated, they are cut away so as to form terraces, which in many places gives them the appearance of an immense amphitheatre. The hamlets are generally built of loose stones with flat mud roofs, and, perched upon overhanging rocks as they generally are, they add considerably to the romantic beauty of the scene. After a halt of an hour during the hottest part of the day at one of these villages called Abu Kirsh, as its latitude, we again pursued our way up a steep ravine where we had to dismount. We here observed many large trees, one in particular, of a spongy nature, the stem about two feet six inches in diameter, and the leaves very large and of a leathery texture. It is called by the natives the " Tolak-tree," (Ficus Bengalensis) and is generally covered with the nests of the " baia," * a small kind of sparrow. I have seen upwards of 300 nests upon one tree. They are of a pear shape, having a long funnel-like aperture at the base, and the interior divided into two compartments, one for the male and the other for the female and her progeny.

Partridges (the red-legged species) and Guinea-fowl are plentiful, though wild, and we also observed the jungle-cock of India.

A very fatiguing ascent of three hours brought us to a large fortified seráï, or, to use the mountain term, " simsĕrah," on the ridge of a mountain, and commanding the pass on both sides, and this we found was our halting-place for the night. The simsĕraht of Hajír was a large square building about forty feet high. Round the interior were two stories of cells, and the central space was appropriated to the beasts of burden. We found the temperature here 79°, which, to us, who had not forgotton the heat of Beït el Fakíh, was very low, and we were glad to creep into our cells, though we soon discovered that we were not the sole occupants of them.

On another ridge immediately above Hajír is a fortress of considerable strength belonging to the Beni Dhobeïbi‡ tribe, though nominally one of the frontier garrisons of the Imám. We found, however, that of late years his authority has been much curtailed, and the Bedawí tribes now levy an arbitrary tax upon all káfilahs of merchandise, whether going or returning, that pass through their territories, in return for which they furnish them with a guard. We here found a large káfilah of goods from Hodeïdah, bound to San'á, and an escort of about thirty men from the fortress to attend them, accompanied by Sheikh Gházi Naijí in person. We joined their party, and whether they did not think it worth while to demand a tax from us, or whether they were in fear of the Imám, we knew not; they received us civilly, and said we were welcome to join them. Hajír is about 1,200 feet above the sea.

July 21.—We started at sunrise, and, descending the ravine on the east-north-east side of Hajír, pursued our way through a broad and well-cultivated valley, gradually increasing in width as we approached Huṣún§Dikarah or Dakrah, a very strong hill-fort on a conical-shaped mountain, belonging to the same tribe. The valley called Wádí Ṣeiḥán here opened out into a broad plain, increasing in size till it was lost in Tehámeh, some miles to the northward of the parallel of Hodeïdah.

---

* Baiah ?
† Not found in this sense in the dictionaries, but Simsár, " a broker," or " valuer ;" one who assists strangers in making bargains, gives a clue to the meaning of samsareh or simsereh, " the place of brokerage."
‡ Probably the Beni Doleibi.—Niebuhr, Descr., p. 248.
§ Huṣún, the plural, is commonly used by the Arabs for the singular, Hiṣn.

The mountains on the north side of this plain are known as Jebel Harráz, and on the other side they are called Jebel Burra'. On both these mountains are coffee-plantations, but those on Jebel Burra' are small and insignificant, while Jebel Harráz produces very superior coffee. It is likewise celebrated for the variety and abundance of its fruit.

In many places in the vicinity of our road we found large enclosures of several kinds of grain, but were cautioned not to straggle from the main body of the party, as a small tribe called the Bení Khórah, who reside in the ravines bordering on Jebel Harráz, were in the habit of waylaying any unfortunate straggler, and, contrary to the usual custom of Arab banditti, murdering their captives. A party had been seen in the valley that morning, and our escort accordingly received an additional reinforcement from Huṣún Dakrah. This dreaded part of the plain is known as 'Khubt ibn Deran,* and we were shown several graves which remained as monuments of the cruelty and ferocity of these miscreants.

We now crossed over an undulating country for several miles, much more barren than that we had left; and, shortly after fording a broad stream that runs down Wádí Ṣeihán, we reached the village of Samfúr at noon.

We here found another large káfilah from Ṣan'á bound to Mokhá with coffee, and, therefore, our guards left us to take back this party, and made us over to the charge of Sheikh el Jerádí, who was to see us safe as far as Mofhak, or two days' journey towards Ṣan'á. The village of Samfúr may contain about 20 houses or huts. Therm. 82° in shade.

July 22.—On leaving Samfúr the next morning, we found several people by the road-side with baskets of fruit from Harráz, amongst which we saw the peach and apricot, several kinds of grapes, walnuts, and a small species of pear, like the stone-pear of England.

The Harráz mountains are at least 1,500 feet high from the plain on which they stand, and by our estimate about 3,000 above the level of the sea. They are apparently composed of a species of trap-rock. They afford a residence to many tribes of Arabs, who are nominally under the dominion of the Imám. but, like all the other tribes, pay no tribute beyond the tax which is levied upon their coffee as it passes through the gates of Ṣan'á. The coffee of Harráz is very superior, but not of the best kind, the trees from 'Uddeín, the "'Uddeíní," being much larger than the others, and about twelve feet high.

The valley now became much narrower, in many places not exceeding twenty yards in width, while the mountains on either side rose to the height of 1,200 or 1,400 feet above the plain, thickly wooded to within 200 feet of their summit, where they presented a barren sheet of grey limestone rock. Under a huge mass which had fallen and completely blocked up the valley, we found a coffee-house and two or three small huts. Understanding that there was a coffee plantation in the neighbourhood, and of the very best quality, we gladly availed ourselves of the suggestion of Sheikh el Jerádí, and halted there for the day. A scrambling walk over the before-mentioned rock, by means of steps cut in it, brought us to the coffee-plantation of Dórah.† It was small, perhaps not covering half an acre, with an embankment of stone round it to prevent the soil from being washed away.

The coffee-plant is usually found growing on the side of any valley or other sheltered situation, the soil which has been gradually washed down from the surrounding heights being that which forms its support. This is afforded by the decomposition of a kind of clay-stone, slightly porphyritic, which is found irregularly disposed in company with a kind of

---

* Probably the Khobt Derham (Drachm-plain) of Niebuhr.—Descr. 149.
† Coffee-plantage Eddóra.—Niebuhr, Reise, i. 433.

trap-rock, among which, as we approached Ṣan'á basalt is found to predominate. The clay-stone is only found in the more elevated districts, but the detritus finds a ready way into the lower tract by the numerous and steep gorges that are visible in various directions.

As it is thrown up on one side of the valley, it is there carefully protected by stone walls, so as to present the appearance of terraces.* The plant requires a moist soil, though I believe much rain is not desirable. It is always found growing in the greatest luxuriance when there is a spring in its vicinity; for in those plantations where water is scarce the plant looks dry and withered. The bean is gathered twice a-year, and we were told that one of the Dórah trees, though of the smallest quality, ought to produce in the two crops at least ten pounds, or a Ṣan'á " maund."†

We found the fig, plantain, orange, citron, and a little indigo, growing among the coffee. A stream of water from a neighbouring spring was drawn through the garden, and we were told that the roots of each plant were regularly watered every morning and evening. The plant is said to live six years; three of which are requisite for bringing the tree to perfection, for three it bears, and then dies and is rooted up. Therm. in shade 75°.

July 23.—The following morning, accompanied by the Sheïkh and his party, we left Dórah and took the road to Mofhak‡ travelling for nine hours in an east-half-north direction. The country was more open and highly cultivated. Barley seemed to be the principal grain, though there were many enclosures of Indian corn and wheat. In this stage particularly, we observed many of the trees found in Socotra. I had (when Captain Haines of the *Palinurus* was employed in surveying that island) accompanied Lieut. Wellsted, and was on the island for nearly two months; a great part of which time was spent among the rocky ranges of Jebel Hajjiyeh. At that time, Dr. Hulton, my present companion, was of opinion that they were peculiar to the island, but I have since seen them on the mountains, at the back of Dhofár, and also on the hills of Yemen, especially the dragons-blood-tree, and the lubán or frankincense-tree, which we at first thought was not to be found in Socotra, but, on comparing the sabhúr tree§ of Socotra with a specimen of the lubán that I procured on the southern Arabian coast at Hásek, they were found to be exactly the same.

The valley of Dórah, through which we travelled in an E.N.E. direction, opened, after three or four miles, upon a large plain, in the midst of which was the village of Ṣeiḥán.∥ The country was the same as that we had hitherto passed through, though not so mountainous. At three we reached the village of Mofhak, and found good quarters in a simsereh. This village of 50 huts is situate on the crest of an oblong hill, about 300 feet high, the sides of which are too steep for any beast of burden to ascend. It presents the appearance of an immense fort, and with a little care might be rendered impregnable. We here found another plantation of coffee of the 'Uddeïní sort. The trees were about twelve feet in height; but, owing to a scarcity of water in the immediate neighbourhood, looked sickly and faded.

Our Arab guards here left us, as no further danger was to be apprehended. A piece of white cloth and a little gunpowder made the old sheïkh quite happy, and we parted good friends. The lat. of Mofhak, deduced from a mer. alt. of the sun taken seven miles west of the village, is 15° 8 N.; therm. in shade 74°.

---

* See Niebuhr, Voy. I. Pl. lxiii, lxv.
† Man, pronounced maun by the Bengalese, whence the English "maund" an Indian measure introduced by merchants, as kírsh, in the plural kurúsh, from the Turkish ghurush, is derived from the German grosch, and used as the name of the piastre.
‡ Niebuhr, Descr. p. 250, Voy.
§ Sabhúr?   ∥ Sehân, Niebuhr, Voy. i. 432.

July 24.—On the following morning we made a short stage of four hours, in an E.N.E. direction, to the village of El Hudheïn,* and here we sent on a courier to Ṣan'á with a letter to one of the principal merchants, which our Mokhá friend, Háji 'Abd-er-Rasul, had kindly provided us with. Thermometer in shade, 73°; temperature of a spring, 64° (Fahr.).

In the immediate vicinity of El Hudheïn are several villages, and the inhabitants of these, hearing that two white men had arrived, crowded round us to beg we would tell them if any rain was coming. For some days the appearance of the weather had been threatening, and we therefore told them that rain would come, and they departed, quite satisfied that we knew all about it.

July 25.—At 6·30 started for Motteneh, distant eight hours and a half, in a general E.N.E. direction. At 3 m. we passed the village of Súk-el-Khamís; at 7 m. reached the village of Bowán, where we found a neat stone bridge thrown across the stream that flows to the Wádí Ṣeïhán; at 13 m. passed Yazil, a hamlet of about 30 houses. On leaving El Hudheïn we ascended gradually for about two hours, when we reached the ridge of the mountains; and from the summit a most magnificent view burst upon us. The hills formed an immense circle, like the crater of a huge volcano, and the sides of which, from the top to the bottom, were cut regularly into terraces. I counted upwards of 150 in uninterrupted succession; and the *tout-ensemble* was most extraordinary. At the bottom of this basin ran a small stream,† which, from the height at which we were, looked like a silver thread.

Small hamlets, each with its little white mosque, were scattered over the sides of the mountains, and added greatly to the beauty of the scene.

We skirted the edge of this natural amphitheatre, and shortly afterwards reached a long table-land, very barren and stony, that extended to the village of Motteneh.

We had now attained our extreme elevation, and I do not think we were less than 5,000 feet above the level of the sea; and, as this was the last stage before we reached Ṣan'á, I will here introduce a few hasty notes made by Dr. Hulton before illness rendered him unequal to any exertion:—

"The hills in the neighbourhood of Sennîf are not high, and seem to be composed of a species of trap-rock of various kinds. Hills of the same kind prevail as far as Samfúr, where the compound becomes more crystalline, and partakes of the character of granite. Here the hills assume a remarkably varied appearance. Stupendous masses are heaped one on the other to an immense height, and others have rolled down of such dimensions as almost to obstruct the road through the valley.

"Near Mofḥak this rock disappears, and a mixed kind then prevailed, with a large proportion of hornblende, aluminous matter, and quartz.

"From El Hudheïn the clay predominates; and from this bed it would seem that the chief part of the soil deposited in the valleys is washed down. After surmounting the lofty hills beyond Khamís,‡ the country is less mountainous, and appears to be more of a volcanic nature, large masses of cellular trap and scoriæ lying scattered on the plain."

During our stay at Motteneh we had a most terrific storm of thunder, lightning, and rain. It lasted about three hours, and washed down many of the huts in the village. We were told that it was the *first rain that had fallen for three years* and the event was celebrated by a kind of festival. Therm. in shade, at 8 P.M., 72°; at 2 A.M., 53°. Population of village 250 persons.

---

* Hadeïn, Niebuhr, Voy. i. 431.
† The Wádí Ṣeïhán, according to Niebuhr's map. ‡ Suk-el-Khamís (Thursday market). Niebuhr, Voy. i. 431.

July 26.—On the following day we left Motteneh at seven A.M., and continued over a table-land, in a N.-E. direction; at 10 h. we passed the village of Lalwá, and at noon reached that of Assúr, seated at the eastern verge of this plateau, and saw the city and beautiful valley of Ṣan'á* stretched before us.

My first sensation was that of disappointment; but it soon gave way to a more pleasant feeling. We quickly descended about 1,200 feet into the valley, and at three o'clock entered the suburbs of the city by the "Báb Ká'-el Yahúdí,"† or the Jews' Gate.

The first thing that struck us on entering the city was the width of the streets and their cleanliness. This, however, did not last long, as we became more acquainted with the town. The suburb of Bír el 'Azab, through which we were passing, is now walled round, although it was not so in Niebuhr's time. We saw no guns on the fortifications.

Proceeding through the Jewish town, we were met by Ismá'il Walání, our Ṣan'á friend, to whose care we were consigned. He received us very cordially, and conducted us to a very neat house in the Bir el 'Azab, where preparations had been made to receive us. We were now told that our sudden arrival had caused great uneasiness to the Imám, as he imagined we were nothing more than Turkish spies. We hastened to convince Ismá'il of the error, and were shortly after waited upon by the Vizier, Moḥammed Sa'di, who had a long conversation with us, and having ascertained that we were British officers, welcomed us formally, in the Imám's name, to Ṣan'á.

The etiquette of not allowing strangers to receive visits, which existed in Niebuhr's time, is still in force: we were therefore carefully locked up for the remainder of the day; but everything we could wish for was brought to us, and, with the exception of not being allowed to walk about the town, we did as we pleased. On the following day the Vizier again called, and told us that the Imám had provided another house for us in his own gardens, and accordingly we were conducted thither. Shortly after our arrival we were summoned to attend the Imám in his palace of Bustán el Metwokkil.‡

We found His Highness in a large saloon, very splendidly furnished,§ sitting on a raised throne of richly-carved wood, with a silk canopy overhanging it. By his side stood his uncle Seyyid Moḥammed, or the Seïf el Khalifah.∥ The Imám wore a white turban, with a skull-cap of cloth of gold, a rich crimson silk robe reaching to his ankles, and a Kashmír shawl. His dagger, which was quite a blaze of jewels, had a gold hilt and scabbard. He received us kindly, ordered two chairs to be brought in for us, and accepted the presents we had to offer him. He repeatedly asked if we were not French, and seemed pleased at our declaring ourselves to be English. Dr. Hulton prescribed for some imaginary pain that he complained of and we were then told that our audience was at an end.

A present of five sheep, some wax candles, and a bale of Persian tobacco, followed us; and we were besieged on all sides for a "Bakhshísh," or present of money, by the eunuchs who brought them. We were permitted to walk through the gardens, where we found many English fruits in great luxuriance; but there had been a great scarcity of rain here, as well as on the mountains, and everything looked dry and withered.

---

* Capital of Yemen, or Arabia Felix.

† Báb-el-ká'el Yahúdí, *i.e.* Jews' Plain Gates. Yahúdí, also called 'Oseir, was a separate town in Niebuhr's time. Descr. p. 232.

‡ Properly Mutewakkil. El Mutewakkil billah (he who trusts in God) is a title assumed by the Imáms of Ṣan'á.

§ Luxury seems to have crept in since Niebuhr's time. *See* Voy. i, pl. lix.

∥ The Khalif's sword.

A large fountain played in front of our house, overshadowed by a huge vine that almost broke under its load of fruit. Walnuts, figs, and plums were plentiful; and the trees were the resort of a great number of black monkeys, which I suppose had been settled there for the Imám's amusement. We went out in the evening; and, though the people crowded about us in great numbers, no insult was offered, and we were allowed to do as we pleased. As, however, a daily journal of our movements here would be tedious, I will endeavour to describe the city and the court of the Imám as we found them in 1836. In Ṣan'á we adopted the English costume, as it was already known there, and, having proclaimed ourselves English officers, we thought it best to appear in our uniform.

The Imám of Ṣan'á has two large palaces with extensive gardens adjoining; the whole walled round and fortified. The first and largest is called Bustán el Sulṭán, or the Garden of the Sulṭán; the other, which is the most ancient, Bustán el Metwokkil. They are built of hewn stone, plastered over with a grey-coloured mortar, having the windows and cornices of a bright white colour, which gives the house a very light and airy appearance. Fountains appear to be indispensable in the houses at Ṣan'á, and in the Bustán el Metwokkil there are several. The Imám has a stud of very fine horses that are always piqueted in front of the palace. They come from the desert of Jóf, to the north of Ṣan'á, and for the first four years of their life rarely taste anything but dates and milk. They are larger than the "Nejdi" breed, but I believe are not considered as inferior to them in symmetry or speed.

At daylight every morning the levee takes place, and by eleven o'clock the Imám is no longer visible. 'Alí Manṣúr, who was the reigning prince during our stay (though since deposed), was much addicted to drinking spirits, and in fact was rarely sober after midday. He was a young man, born of a Nubian mother, and with a peculiarly disagreeable expression of countenance, owing to a cast in his right eye. As a Zeidí in faith, the use of tobacco was forbidden to him; but it can hardly be supposed that a man who would disregard one precept of the Korán would hesitate to break another. His days were consumed in smoking and drinking with the lowest of his servants, who plundered him in all directions. We were twice invited to join him in his house during these hours of recreation, but were too much disgusted to repeat the visit.

On Friday the Imám goes in state to the mosque, and the procession we witnessed was very splendid. Troops were called into the town to assist at the ceremony, and during the time of the procession the city gates were, as usual, closed. About fifty armed Bedawís formed the commencement of the cavalcade. They walked six abreast, and sang in chorus. The principal people of the town followed, mounted on horseback, each carrying a long spear with a small pennon. The Imám next followed on a splendid white charger, and very superbly dressed. He held in his hand a long spear with a silver head, having the shaft gilt. His left hand rested on the shoulder of a confidential eunuch, and two grooms led his horse. A very magnificent canopy, much like an umbrella in form, was carried over his head, having the fringe ornamented with silver bells.

The Seïf el Khalífah came next, having a canopy held over his head likewise, but smaller and less costly. The commander of the troops and the Imám's relations and principal officers followed, and about 100 more Bedawís closed the procession.

On reaching the square in front of the palace, the footmen ranged themselves round it, and the Imám, followed by his nearest relations, galloped repeatedly round the square, brandishing his spear, and making a feint of attacking the nearest horseman. After this had lasted some minutes, the Imám stood still in the centre of the square, and the people rushed from every quarter to kiss his knees. He then retired towards the palace, and as he passed under the archway, a gun was fired to give notice that the ceremony was at an end.

The government of Ṣan'á under an Imám is, we were told, to be dated from the time that the Turks in the reign of Suleïmán, commonly styled "the Magnificent," were driven from that part of the country about 210 years since. The greater part of the fortifications in the old city of Ṣan'á were built by them, and there are the remains of a noble aqueduct yet existing, said to be their work. The first Imám was Kasim Abú Moḥammed, a "sheríf" or descendant of the Prophet, of the family of Imám Hádi—Abú Moḥammed's son took the name of "Met. wokkil Allah," God's Vicegerent*—and this is now common to all the Imáms, as well as that of "Manṣur,"† or Conqueror. The Arabs of Ṣan'á have a tradition that a descendant of the Imám shall assume the name of "El Hádi," the Regenerator,‡ and carry every thing before him, when, having taken the name of "El Mahadí," and converted all nations to the religion of "Eslam," the world will come to an end.

Sidi Kásim, uncle of the reigning Imám, who was banished during our stay, all his property having been confiscated, soon after our departure assumed the title of El Hádi, and so worked upon the superstitious fears of the Arabs, that he was enabled, through their assistance, to dethrone the Imám, and, under the name of "El Mahadí," assume the government himself.

The valley of Ṣan'á lies about 4,000 feet above the sea; it is from 6 to 9 miles broad, extending northward as far as the eye can reach; it is bounded on the east by low table-land and a mountain called Jebel Nagam, rising about 1,500 feet above the plain: to the west it is bounded by the table-land of Asár and Lúlúwah, about 1,200 feet in height; while to the south, at 7 miles' distance, it contracts into a narrow valley called Tarik el Yemen.

The population of Ṣan'á is great, perhaps 40,000, and I should say that in the four towns in the valley, viz, Ṣan'á, Ródah,§ Wádí Dhar, and Jeráf, there are not less than 70,000 people. The old city of Ṣan'á is walled round, and, including Bír el Azab, is 5½ miles in circuit: it has some guns, but in a very bad condition. The houses are large, and the windows of those of the higher classes are of beautiful stained glass. A handsome stone bridge is thrown across the principal street, as in wet weather a stream of water runs down it. The streets are narrow, though broader than those of Mokhá and Zebid. Great hospitality was shown us on entering their houses; we were always pressed to stay, and never allowed to go without taking a cup of coffee, or rather of an infusion of the coffee husk called "Keshr"; for, strange to say, though in the heart of the coffee country, coffee is never taken as a beverage, being considered as too heating. The infusion of the husk is very palatable; and we found it much more refreshing, and nearly as powerful a stimulant as the infusion of the bean itself.

The merchants form the principal body of men in the town. They are generally wealthy and live in good style.

The Banias are also numerous, but they are compelled, like the Jews, to conceal what they really possess, and however wealthy they may be, to put on an outward show of abject, poverty.

The principal trade is of course in coffee, but the Ṣan'á merchants are so fearful of trusting their goods to the Turkish government, that they prefer filling their warehouses with it in Ṣan'á to sending it to Mokhá.

---

* "The Truster in God."
‡ "The Guide, or Leader."
† "Aided by God;" thence "Victorious."
§ Rauḍhah or Rauḍah, i.e. Garden.

The whole cost of transporting a camel-load of coffee from Ṣan'á to Mokhá is forty-four dollars, upon which the merchant clears a profit of three dollars and a half. It is brought into the Ṣan'á market in the months of December and January, from the surrounding districts. The nearest place to Ṣan'á where the coffee grows is Haffásh, about a short day's journey south-east of San'á. Attempts were made by the last Imám to cultivate the plant in his own garden, but without success, owing, it appears, to the cold. The varieties of coffee are "Sharjí" (the best), "Uddeiní," "Maṭari," "Harrází," "Habbat," "Haimi," and "Shirází;" of these the Sharjí and Habbat are the smallest and best. Keshr (husk), being more in demand at San'á, obtains a higher price. The best is the 'Anezi (Habbat), and is sold at twelve dollars for the hundred pounds; the inferior sorts at four, five, and six dollars for the same quantity. The imports are principally piece-goods and Persian tobacco, with dates from Tehámeh; and a great quantity of thread, or rather twist, for weaving. The import duties in San'á are very light, and indeed almost nominal. Glass is in great request, and the demand is supplied from Egypt. Very magnificent silks and velvets are exposed for sale in the bázár, as well as spices, sugar, &c., &c.

The principal artisans are the Jews; these amount to about 3,000 persons, and live in a quarter of the city appropriated to them. As infidels, they are exposed to many exactions and repeated insults. Each man pays twenty-five komásís per month, or about *a dollar* per year for permission to reside in the city. A sheïkh is appointed, who is responsible for the regular payment of this impost, and of the heavy taxes that are likewise laid upon their vines, gardens, &c. They subsist chiefly by the sale of silver ornaments, gunpowder, spirituous liquors, and many by working as common artisans, such as shoemakers, &c. The mosques in San'á, about twenty in number, are very splendid, many of them having their domes gilt, particularly those containing the tombs of the Imáms. The baths are also very good, and on the same plan as those in Egypt: they are a favourite resort of the merchants, who meet here to discuss the state of trade and the news of the day, over their cup of keshr and their never-failing ḥukkah. The San'ánís are very much addicted to chewing the leaf of a tree which they call "kát." It appears by their account to exhilarate and produce appetite; it also causes great thirst, and if taken in large quantities, will bring on spasms. It is the never-failing accompaniment to the breakfast or dinner; and, from long use, appears to be indispensable. The wealthy merchants on week-days generally ride a very fine-spirited kind of donkey, much larger than the English ass, and very strong and fleet. These donkeys are similar to those from Baḥreïn, in the Persian gulf. On Fridays, all who can afford it, appear on horseback to join the procession of the Imám to the Mesjid el Jámi'.

About five miles N.N.W. of Ṣan'á is the town of Ródah, which is much cleaner and neater than the capital, being the residence of nearly all the merchants, who retire to their country-houses after the business of the day is over. The gardens at Ródah and Wádi Ḍhár, another town five miles to the west of the former, are very fine, and the vineyards beautiful. The vines are trained over a trelliswork about four feet from the ground, and are very extensive: the best kind of grapes are "el Bedá," a small white grape without a stone, and the "'Ayún," a large black one very richly flavoured. Peaches, apricots, plums, &c., were abundant, and indeed formed the principal food of the lower classes. The town is well watered by several small streams: on the banks of one of these I saw the only gum Arabic tree which we had seen during the journey: there was an immense quantity of gum dropping from and incrusted on the bark, but it appeared to be considered as of no value by the town-Arabs. Half way between Ródah and Ṣan'á is the town of Jeráf, built much in the same style as the former places, and furnishing vegetables chiefly, for the Ṣan'á market. Each of these towns is governed by an Amir, who levies the government taxes in the name of the Imám.

The climate of Ṣan'á is too dry to be healthy: there is rarely any dew at night, and the wind produces a feverish feeling in the hands and face. In average seasons, rain falls three times a year, *i.e.* in January, in very small quantities, and frequently not at all; in June for about eight days: by this time the seed is sown and the cultivator looks forward to this season with great anxiety. Lastly, it falls in the latter end of July, when it is in the greatest abundance: a few farmers defer sowing till this period; but this is not commonly done when they can reasonably expect rain in June. In July the wind from the south-east prevails during the day, but, declining in force during the afternoon, it is met by a current of air from the north-west, and the two strata of clouds meeting in different states of electricity, thunder, lightning, and rain are the result. Thus it is that rain is never known in these regions at this period without being accompanied by vivid lightning and loud peals of thunder.

For nearly four years preceding our visit they had hardly had a drop of rain, which was the cause of incalculable distress to the people in the vicinity. This long drought had added considerably to the general unhealthiness of the country. The people on our first arrival were dying at the rate of 150 per day, from the effects of a malignant fever which was raging with great violence, and which generally carried off the sufferer in four days. The famine was also dreadful here,* and dead bodies were seen in every corner of the streets awaiting the compassion of some one to afford them the means of burial. Many of the wealthy merchants fed a stated number daily, and boasted loudly of their charity. On inquiry, however, we found that the food furnished consisted merely of refuse grapes, such as were literally of no use. The Imám, too much engaged in his favourite amusements of smoking and drinking, thought little of the distress which his people were enduring; and though the incessant funeral chant, as the bodies passed under his windows on their way to the burying-ground, ought to have roused him from his gross sensuality, he heeded it not: the consequences fell heavy upon him. In a month from that time he was dethroned, insulted, and immured in a dungeon, while his uncle, who supplanted him, wisely endeavoured to secure the affections of the people by relieving their distresses with a liberal hand.

During our walks through the city we discovered the accompanying inscriptions,† and forthwith copied them on the spot. On close inquiry we found that the stones had been brought from Máreb, about two days' journey distant to the N.E.,‡ and that there were many more to be found there. The longest inscription was on a slab of white marble, and, when we saw it, served to cover a hole in the roof of a mosque. A bribe of a dollar had a magical

---

* To give an idea of the great scarcity experienced in 1836, and at the same time of the usual fertility of the soil in this part of Arabia Felix, I subjoin an account given to me by one of the principal Banian merchants in the town. Wheat, which in time of plenty is sold at 1*s*. 6*d*. the gaddá of 54lbs., was now selling at 3 dollars or 13*s*. 6*d*. the gaddá. Barley, usually sold at 6*d*., was now 8*s*. the gaddá. Jowárí, usually 9*d*., now 9*s*. the gaddá. Beans, usually at 8*d*., now 12*s*. the gaddá. Ghí, or clarified butter, usually sold at 4*d*., now 1*s*. per lb.

† That these inscriptions are specimens of the *Musnad* or ancient Himyarí character, will hardly be doubted by those who have read M. Rœdiger's learned paper in the *Zeitschrift für die Kunde des Morgenlandes* (Gœtt. 1837, 8vo., p. 332), though the corresponding alphabet given by him from an Arabic MS. may be fairly set down as one of the many literary frauds with which the half-learned in Asia have endeavoured to raise their reputation at the expense of truth; such, for example, are '*Ancient Alphabets*' and the late Mr. Price's interpretation of the *Persepolitan Inscriptions*, from a Persian MS. The striking resemblance, at first sight, between these Himyarí characters and those on the ancient Bactrian coins deciphered by Mr. Prinsep in the *Calcutta Asiatic Journal*, did not escape Mr. Cruttenden's notice; and it is possible that a further acquaintance with these characters will prove their identity: if so, the happy conjectures of Dr. Lepsius, in his tract on *Indian palæography*, will receive an extraordinary and unexpected confirmation.—F.S.

Professor Gesenius, to whom all our inscriptions have been sent, has, we understand, deciphered the words, " King of the Himyarites."

‡ Between seventy and eighty miles, according to Niebuhr's calculation.

effect on the scruples of a servant, and the stone was brought to our lodgings that night to be copied, and carefully replaced before daylight. The Jewish workers in gold assured us that frequently square gold coins were brought to San'á by the shepherds of Máreb for sale, and a Banian merchant corroborated this account, adding also that jewels, particularly pearls, are found there usually, after heavy rains, when the people closely search the water-courses, and generally find something to repay them for their trouble. In the Imám's garden I one day found a marble head, and on inquiry learned that this also came from Máreb: to my great mortification I was told that the figure arrived at Ṣan'á perfect, but was immediately broken by order of the Imám, as a relic of ancient idolatry, and I was unable to find the other parts of the statue: the head, however, I secured, after some demur on the part of the gardener, and brought it to England; it is the only specimen of sculpture that I have ever observed in Arabia Felix, and as such I esteemed it a curiosity.

Hearing so much about Máreb we forthwith determined to go there, and for that purpose sent for a sheikh who lived in that part of the country. The Imám, however, now became jealous of our proceedings, and for six days we were not allowed to leave our house in the garden. Our agent Ismá'il also gave us strong hints that we had better go at once, as the people in San'á were becoming troublesome, and the Imám attributed it to the "Christians." At this time the uncle of the Imám, Sidi Kásim got timely warning that his head was in danger, and escaped that night, accompanied by about forty of the Imám's servants and guards, mounted on his best horses. We now found that we could do nothing: our garden-door was always locked, and what with disappointment and anxiety, my companion's health began to decline, and he soon was in a state that precluded all possibility of travelling.

After nearly three weeks of severe illness, Dr. Hulton thought himself strong enough to return to the vessel. As travelling on horseback was out of the question, I constructed a kind of palanquin out of an old litter belonging to the Imám, and procured twelve men to carry it.

I also went to take leave of the Imám, who sent us two fine horses and some shawls, as a parting present. On the 20th of August therefore we left Ṣan'á, having been resident in the town nearly a month.

The thermometer during our stay reached 75° as the highest and 55° as its lowest point, between the 26th of July and the 20th of August.

The crowd collected in the streets on the occasion of our departure was immense, but so far from insulting us, many appeared to commiserate the emaciated appearance of Dr. Hulton. All our friends assembled to see us depart, and accompanied us to the gates of the city, when we bid them farewell, and pursued our way slowly to Mateneh. Our journey to the sea was of course slower than it had been upwards, but on our arrival at Sennif my friend Dr. Hulton was sufficiently strong to travel on the back of a donkey; and in fourteen days from our leaving Ṣan'á we reached the gates of Mokhá.

Nothing worth notice occurred during our way down, except the demand of a few dollars made by the Arabs as toll for the passage of the escort across the Wádi Ṣeihán, and the improved appearance of the country, owing to the great fall of rain that had taken place during our residence at Ṣan'á. We found the ship still anchored at Mokhá, and all our friends very uneasy at our protracted absence. I hoped that the return to the sea would restore Dr. Hulton's health, but it was too late, and he died very shortly after he reached the ship.

In closing this brief Memoir of our journey into Yemen, I can only regret that the task has not fallen into abler hands than mine: I am well aware that an account drawn up by a man of such general attainments, and especially in geology, as Dr. Hulton, would have been far more valuable and satisfactory.

NARRATIVE

OF A

JOURNEY TO SHOA.

B 1485—C4

NARRATIVE

OF

A JOURNEY TO SHOA.

JOURNAL.

> I had heard of battles and I longed
> To follow to the field some warlike lord.—"*Douglas*," *by Home*.

A similar feeling induced me to give up the command of the "Euphrates" (a ten-gun brig) and to accompany the party, under Major Harris of the Bombay Engineers, proceeding through the wild deserts of the Dankali to the court of the Christian King of Shoa with costly presents from the Indian Government.

Never shall I forget the feeling with which I, for the first time after a period of nearly thirteen years' uninterrupted service, found myself freed from that strict restraint so necessary in naval service. I indeed felt free! But little did I then think of all the dangers, the difficulties we had to encounter in crossing perhaps the most inhospitable desert on the face of the earth, exposed during the day to the scorching rays of a tropical sun, and at night to the lurking crease of the midnight assassin. Verily part of the prophecy has been fully carried out in these wild sons of the desert, for their "hand is indeed against every man."

And but too soon we experienced its reality; but of that hereafter. I shall not attempt to describe the innumerable annoyances we had to suffer before we could procure the necessary number of camels to carry the costly presents with which we were intrusted, nor the many difficulties we had to encounter in conciliating the various petty chieftains, who had all conspired to plunder us as much as they could.

We at length commenced our journey on the evening of the 1st of June 1841, the anniversary of one of our greatest naval battles, and hence we considered that we had launched into the desert under rather favourable auspices.

Our party consisted of Captain Harris of the Bombay Engineers, Lieutenant Charles Douglas Graham of the Bombay Native Infantry, Assistant Surgeon R. Kirk, Dr. Röth, naturalist, myself, an escort of ten European soldiers, volunteers from the Bombay Artillery and Her Majesty's 6th Foot, and a motley assemblage of all nations. The presents and our baggage required a string of 180 camels, and besides we had 35 mules and 17 horses.

We had also a Native escort, of whom the Chief was Izakh, brother of the wily old Sultan of Tajura, all of whom were sworn to conduct us in safety: the sequel will show how they did so.

Our course for the first two marches lay along the sea-beach, the schooner "Constance," commanded by my old friend Lieutenant Christopher of the Indian Navy, keeping company with us from station to station. It was not, however, till midnight of the 4th of June, that we took our final departure from the coast. The signal gun was fired from the schooner exactly at midnight. Great was the confusion and uproar for the space of nearly two hours. The last camel then moved off, and the utmost quiet succeeded to the Babel-like confusion. The moon was near the full; not a cloud was to be seen, not a sound heard except the washing of the sea against the pebbly beach, the almost noiseless tread of the camels on the sand, and the creaking and groaning of the wheels of our gun-carriage, which was drawn by mules. We had not proceeded far, however, before we reached the foot of the hills, where the ground became so bad that it was found necessary to dismount the gun, and having selected two of the stoutest of our camels to carry it, we transferred it to their backs: this piece of ordnance was a brass three-pounder field-piece. We had plenty of ammunition of all kinds, and 150 British muskets, all presents for the King. When we placed it on the backs of the camels I declare the animals moved on so stately that they appeared proud of their load! At about eight o'clock on the morning of the 5th we reached our destined halting-place on the elevated table-land forming the northern boundary of Gobaad Kharab, about 1,500 feet above the sea—a most barren desolate place;—not a tree, not a shrub to be seen: nothing to keep off the glare, which was very distressing to the eye. To add to our discomfort, a hot south-west wind blew the whole day, which was felt the more as we had but a limited allowance of water, and that of the most indifferent quality.

During the night the Ras-el-Kafilah awoke me to say that the "Bedoos" had threatened to attack the camp unless they were well supplied with blue cloth, warning me to have all the muskets loaded. He was assured that we were well prepared. He came again a second time but received a similar answer. After some time he again called, and assured me that he had taken upon himself to present the said worthies with the cloth demanded; and the night passed off in peace.

Here we remained till three o'clock the following morning, when we resumed our march. At the distance of a few hundred yards we commenced our descent of the Ra-Eesah pass, a place every stone of which could tell its tale of midnight murder. Woe to the unfortunate traveller who should venture through this pass alone, or have the temerity to halt here! In this pass the Eesah, who inhabit the south side of the Bay of Tajura, are always at enmity with the Dankali. A few years back they suffered a most sanguinary defeat from their hereditary foes. The story was thus related to me. The Eesah, at the voice of their chiefs, assembled suddenly in great numbers and made a descent upon the lands of the Dankali, and penetrated to the remotest corners thereof, carrying everything before them. Flushed with success, they were returning laden with spoil, when a resolute few of the Dankali attacked them in this pass: seized with a panic, many of them threw themselves from the cliffs into the sea rather than fall by the hands of their bitterest foes. The slaughter was complete, for scarce one of them returned to tell the dreadful tale.

We descended by a narrow winding path scarce wide enough to admit of the camels passing in single file. As the day dawned we had just cleared the pass, and found ourselves once more on the sea-coast on the verge of Gobaad Kharab; we again ascended over a mass of lava and volcanic remains which divides the waters of Gobaad Kharab from Bahr Assal, or the Salt Lake. There was not a breath of wind, and no sooner had the sun risen above the hills than the heat was most oppressive, almost overpowering. At length, at eleven o'clock, we reached our halting-ground on the borders of the lake, six hundred feet below the level of the sea, but not a tent near; the camels were still in the rear, nor did the whole of them arrive till a late hour at night.

Here we found Lieutenant Christopher, who had succeeded in beating the schooner up Gobaad Kharab, and who had gallantly come across with a small party to receive our last despatches.

Never shall I forget this day. The heat was indeed fearful, the glare oppressive; in vain we looked for shelter, a few stunted acacias, scattered here and there as if in very mockery of nature, was all that could be obtained, and even there we were not allowed to remain under in peace, for both camels and mules, throwing off their accustomed fear of the "lords of the creation," crowded together and were with difficulty kept off.

I mentioned that Lieutenant Christopher had come over from his vessel to receive our last despatches. One of his men, an Englishman, on returning, fainted and sunk down on the way; his companions were compelled to leave him and proceed to the vessel for assistance. A party was instantly sent in quest of him, but he could not be found, so they came to our encampment, and one of the natives volunteered to return with them. On the road back the unfortunate man was picked up quite exhausted, and, notwithstanding that every means was resorted to for his recovery, he lingered but for a few hours and in great pain, and then, in the emphatic language of Scripture, "was gathered unto his fathers." He was buried at Tajura, the first victim on this side to African discovery. Lieutenant Christopher remained with us till about ten o'clock in the evening, and then returned to his vessel.

This was a night that will never be forgotten by any of our party, a night of great suffering. While at Tajura a number of skins had been purchased, to furnish us, as we thought, with a never-failing supply of water on our march. They were all new, and to make them watertight were thickly coated on the outside with rancid butter, and on the inside with some vile mixture, a compound of herbs and the bark of trees, which gave to the water a most disgusting flavour. Many of these skins had burst, so that, bad as it was, we had taken only a scanty supply. I had been on short allowance of water at sea, and compelled to drink water collected in tarpaulins, savouring strongly of all that is unpleasant; but what would I not have given for one single pint of it now!

After much delay and discussion among the chiefs of the caravan, we at length, at eleven P.M., departed from this furnace, leaving the baggage and everything else in the hands of the worthy Ras-el Kafilah, or sender of the caravan, and had not proceeded far before man and beast began to sleep by the wayside from sheer exhaustion; in vain every encouragement was held out, their sufferings were too great.

Our road lay over a broken mass of lava for some distance, and again we gradually ascended, till as the day dawned the foremost of our party arrived at some small pools of water the most refreshing man ever tasted. A supply was instantly sent back to the sufferers, and the party pushed forward, descending again to the south-east corner of the Salt Lake. We there crossed over a mass of salt hard as ice, and at length reached our halting-place about eight o'clock in the morning. The whole party, however, did not get up till late in the afternoon.

Had it not been for one good Samaritan amongst the Dankali, I do not think one of us would have survived to tell of the horrors of that night; his name deserves to be recorded— Mohamed Ali, the son of Ali Abbi, of the tribe of the Wulasma, one of the principal sub-tribes of the Dankali.

While encamped on the borders of the Salt Lake intelligence had been received that a small quantity of water was to be found on the hills around. It was immediately proposed by Mohamed Ali that we should proceed there forthwith; this was objected to by all the others, who exclaimed that we should drink it all up, and none would be left for them. "Better that the infidels should die than that we should suffer" was the exclamation.

Mohamed Ali, however, grasping his spear and calling two or three of his followers, exclaimed, "I will take them there; they shall not perish." We accordingly followed him; he, however, did not take us to the water, but sent some of his followers in advance with empty skins, which were filled and brought out to us; for he was afraid if we once saw the water we should not be persuaded to quit the place.

Of our numerous party, about forty individuals and seventeen horses and thirty-five mules, all arrived safe at Goongoonteh, our halting-place above the lake. For two days and a half our cattle had not tasted a drop of water; one dog perished on our dreary march.

B 1485—65

Goongoonteh is situated in a deep ravine, down which the water in the rainy season pours with great velocity to the Salt Lake. It appears to have been split apart, cliffs towering up almost perpendicularly several hundred feet on either side. A small stream of water issuing from some hot springs in the head of the ravine was murmuring along when we arrived: nothing could restrain our animals from making to it: they would not wait to have their bridles removed.

Owing to the narrowness of the ravine our encampment was rather scattered, but we took, as well as we could, every precaution against being surprised. A portion of our Native escort was stationed some yards in advance, and an English sentinel kept watch and ward in our immediate vicinity. All passed quietly that night.

On the 8th, our party having suffered so much in crossing from the coast to this place, it was determined to halt here another day to refresh ourselves. During the day we found shelter in some caves by the side of the ravine, and passed a fearful day though we had plenty of water. In the evening we moved down by our last night's encampment, and observed the same precautions as on the previous night. All passed quietly till about three o'clock on the morning of the 9th, when we were startled by a loud scream from one of our followers, cook to the English escort. Only a short time before two of the party were awake and talking, remarking how beautifully the moon sailed through the heavens,—and indeed had but just lain down again. We were not long in ignorance of the cause of our being disturbed, for the poor cook had been stabbed in the stomach, and two of our soldiers lay weltering in their blood. Accursed deed! It would appear that three of the dastardly savages had crawled along the sides of the ravine among the broken masses that had been hurled down by the mountain torrents, and, watching when the sentry's back was turned, had accomplished their murderous intentions.

When the alarm was given they were seen for a moment and then they disappeared behind the rocks. Our unfortunate men were murdered merely for the sake of murder; no attempt was made to steal. One was lying on the right side; he had the carotid artery severed on the left—a cut not half an inch long; he must have passed from sleep unto death. The other was stabbed to the heart. The poor cook lingered a few hours, and was buried on the line of march.

When the alarm was first given suspicion fell strong on the camel-men, for after their conduct at the Salt Lake we could repose no confidence in any save Mohamed Ali.

"It is related of the Taifabæ," says Gibbon,[*] "one of the tribes of the Goths (in the latter part of the fourth century), whose military renown was disgraced by the public infamy of their domestic manners, that the youth could only prove their manhood by slaying in single combat a huge bear or wild boar of the forest." These wild savages of the nineteenth century have a more atrocious method of evincing their manhood, namely, by slaying a male of their own species and after having mutilated the person, displaying the disgusting trophy to the admiring gaze of their savage countrymen. It is this that renders their country so dangerous to the stranger; they dare not slay a man of one of the tribes, for fear of establishing a blood-feud; but whom has the unwary traveller to revenge his death?

This suspicion, however, soon wore off from the deep sympathy they evinced. I have observed that three individuals were seen hurrying away; they were pursued but without success. Graves were prepared by the camel-men and our Native escort, to which, as the day dawned, the remains of our slaughtered companions were consigned, our leader reading a portion of the burial service.

---

[*] *Decline and Fall of the Roman Empire*, cap. xxvi, p. 437.

We were anxious to quit a spot fraught with such dire disaster at even this early stage of our wanderings, but some of the camels had strayed away in the confusion, and were not recovered until about eleven o'clock in the forenoon. Loud and bitter were the curses heaped upon their hereditary foes the Eesah by our camel-men and Native escort. "It is they who have done this accursed deed," they exclaimed. "Did you not observe the skulking villains as they went past with their flocks? They are infidels, the descendants of infidels."

As we wound up this valley of death the road became much worse. In one part in particular huge masses of rock, which had been washed down by the last torrent, obstructed the way to such an extent that we were obliged to unload the camels—there being no room for them to pass with their burdens—and to carry the bales and boxes through. We were cautioned not to straggle. As we ascended the ravine again widened out. It was a dreary march—every one was buried in his own thoughts. At last we reached our halting-ground, at Aloolie, signifying fresh water.

To us this place appeared a perfect paradise after what we had suffered in crossing the Tehama, a large pool of water teeming with wild duck, which ere long garnished our table.

We had now better encamping-ground, and got the gun mounted, due notice whereof was given to all evil-disposed persons that might be lurking about at eight o'clock. A stronger watch was also set, namely, an officer, two soldiers, a horsekeeper, and one of the servants, who relieved one another every hour, firing a musket.

Our Native friends were loth to quit so pleasant a place, so we were detained the following day with the usual excuse that a camel had strayed. It was a very warm day, the wind blowing in fitful gusts from the south-west. We managed, however, to shoot several gazelles which proved a most agreeable addition to our by no means luxurious fare.

Near midnight the order was given to be up and stirring, and after a lapse of nearly two hours we moved on over a low, broken range of hills, crossed a dry water-course, and then ascended to the plains of Hender Addi Dowar and Gurguddi; the latter plain we were three hours in crossing. We then again passed through the dry bed of another water-course, and encamped on the elevated plain above it, at a place called Bedi Kurroo Ruff. Nothing to relieve the eye; the same desolate appearance in every direction. During the march I frequently entered into conversation with our Native escort. One young man in particular was very talkative, a nephew of the Sultan of Tajura. With regard to the Eesah, those of the sea-coast, said he, are inoffensive, but those of the hills are devils incarnate. They are constantly wandering about, more for the sake of murder than plunder, in parties of from three to ten travelling night and day without suffering either from heat or cold.

About a year ago a return caravan of the Dankali from Abyssinia lost one young man. It appears that, being tired, he had halted behind a rock for a while, when he was attacked by six of the Eesah and killed; his cries, however, had been heard by his companions, who gave chase to and succeeded in capturing the whole six, one of whom was immediately put to death— "life for life;" the remainder, despoiled of their arms, were released.

But a few years back the road between Tajura and Abyssinia was closed for the space of three years by the repeated incursions of the Eesah on the south and the Mudaitoo on the north, until Johita ibn Ibrahim, Akil or Chief of the Debeni, assembled his clan, and drove the robbers on either side back to their fastnesses, since which all has been quiet, and the Eesah in particular are better disposed owing to their intermarriages with several families of the Debeni.

On the 12th of June, at half-past three o'clock in the morning, we again moved on, the country still of the same desolate character; the heat still dreadful, the thermometer showing

111° Fahr. in the tents. And thus we marched on from day to day; to give particulars of each day's journey would be tiresome.

June 16th.—We had been detained to receive a visit from the renowned Chief of the Debeno mentioned above; he did not, however, make his appearance till dusk. A short description of him may prove interesting. His height was about five feet ten, his age about thirty-five; he had a very determined look, bright twinkling eyes, hair rather scanty and well coated with grease. His only dress consisted of a filthy rag reaching from his loins to his knees, and a pair of sandals made of cowhide; he wore no head-dress. His only ornament was an armlet of buffalo horn above the right elbow; he carried also a crease or dagger, a spear and a shield. The spear had several brass rings about it, in token of his being a great warrior. His crease, a formidable-looking weapon for close quarters, was about fourteen inches long, curved, very broad, and double-edged. Be it observed that the crease is used for all purposes—for slaying, whether man or animal, eating with, shaving, cutting wood, &c., &c.

Acknowledged, nay dreaded, as a chieftain of great power, a mighty warrior, yet he dared not accept even a small present of cloth and trinkets for the sharp eyes of his myrmidons, but waited till the hour of darkness arrived, when, watching a favourable opportunity, the said presents were clutched—I can use no other expression—with a greedy grasp, and instantly concealed beneath his only garment. He departed, as he came, without salutation of any kind. It was amusing to observe the deference paid to him by our Tajura friends—Izakh, brother of the Sultán and leader of the caravan, in particular was respectful even to servility. Mohamed Ali was the only one who appeared at his ease, laughing and joking;—by the by, that was all on his side, for I do not think the Chief moved his lips except to smile at some joke, but sat there in sullen dignity.

June 17th.—To-day we shifted our encampment four miles to the bed of a water-course, where there are some ponds of water to be found by digging in the sand. We filled up all our water-skins, for at the next stage there is no water. Here for the first time since leaving Goongoonteh we saw several flocks of the black-headed sheep so common about Berbera and its vicinity, tended not by pretty shepherdesses, but by old fat and ugly wenches whose sole covering was a kind of leather kilt from the waist to the knees, well saturated with grease, and which appeared to have been handed down for several generations. The nights are now becoming cool, though the days are still warm; thermometer in the tents 108°.

On the 19th we halted at a place called Dah-way-la-kayl, where we found a pool of filthy water, but we were glad to get even that. We passed a herd of wild asses, too wild for us to get a shot at them. On one occasion I observed that in passing a certain spot each of the Dankali picked up a stone and throwing it towards a pile by the wayside exclaimed " Aooz bellah el Shitan el Rajeem! " " I fly for refuge to God from Satan the stoned! " Tradition says that an old man was here stoned to death for incestuous intercourse with his daughter, since which period all travellers observe the custom above alluded to. Judging from the appearance of this pile, not only many years must have elapsed, but many travellers must have passed by it.

By slow and tiresome marches we at length arrived at the Wady Kilulloo, where we were detained till the 30th. This is one of the principal resorts of the various tribes of the Aysomauli, Debeni, Wulasma, and even the Eesah and Mudaitoo; for during the dry season it is the only place where water can be obtained for many miles around. Innumerable flocks and herds were driven in during the day.

While detained at Kilulloo, the weather being threatening, we pitched our rain tents, of painted canvas. These were very small for three persons. One evening at dusk my servant had just made my bed in one of these tents on the ground, when, unluckily, one of the savages who had cast an evil eye on my blanket stole up to the tent, and quietly slipping his hand underneath managed to withdraw the article and was off like a shot. He really deserved to succeed, it was so dexterously managed.

Many were the disputes to be settled here, that had arisen on the line of march from Tajura, between Mohamed Ali and the brother of the Sultán of Tajura and their respective parties. The most noted chieftains appealed to were Mohamed ibn Hagaioo (Oogass) and Ali Abbi, uncle and father respectively to Mahomed Ali, and Ibrahim Ibn Mohamed, Akil or Chief of the Aysomauli, each of whom sent presents of sheep, bullocks, &c., and in the evening, as soon as it was dusk, honoured us with a visit, partook of tea, coffee, dates, and snuff, and then according to what appears their universal custom, rose up and departed without a word or ceremony of any kind.

During our stay here there was no end to their continued consultations, and, "by way of keeping their hand in," the savages managed to establish a few quarrels. Blood was drawn freely, but I do not think any lives were lost.

One day in particular we were disturbed by hearing a great noise which originated in a "tale of love." It appears that one savage, some years previous, had run away with the betrothed of another. The injured man had long waited for a convenient time to have his revenge, but he was disappointed of his victim by the interference of the others, only laying open his scalp from the crown to the temple. It was verily a dreary time, and annoying in the extreme to see hoary-headed old men squatted in groups, endeavouring to arrange matters between the disputants; at last all was settled, and we moved forward six miles on the 30th, when we were again detained one day to fill up our water skins, as for three days' journey we should find no water.

On the evening of the 1st of July proclamation was made that Ibrahim ibn Hagaioo, Oogass of the Wulasma, had lost his spear, and those concerned in the abstraction thereof were called upon to restore it. On the 3rd, 4th, and 5th we made very fair marches of sixteen, eighteen, and twenty miles. Road much better, weather cooler. On the 6th we arrived at Toor Erain Murroo. Here there is a large pool or basin of water, to which we descended by a gradual slope and encamped immediately under the bank, which rose almost perpendicularly behind us, the pool of water being about a hundred yards in front.

Many were the tales we heard of the ferocity of the tribes in the vicinity. Seldom indeed did a caravan halt by the side of the pool, but encamped on the ground above, for fear of the Galla and Mudaitoo. The former in particular are much dreaded, and described as infidels who fear neither God nor man; the latter were said to be nominally Mussulmans, yet some of them are cannibals!

Notwithstanding all we had heard, we passed the night without alarm, but the following morning Izahk, about ten o'clock, became very fidgetty, hurried the loading of the camels, and begged that every man would have his musket loaded, as he had heard we were to be attacked. His fears were not at all alleviated by the sudden arrival of three horsemen in the camp, wild-looking savages of the Takyla tribe. We cleared the ground, and soon gained the summit of the table-land to the westward, where the caravan was drawn up in close order, and moved forward as we arrived at the head thereof, in double file, when a body of twenty-five or thirty men was seen marching towards the pool with spears erect, but on seeing the caravan they made instantly towards it. A halt was called, and the camels huddled close up together without much order; each of our camel-men together with our so-called Native escort, grasping spear and shield, hurried forth to meet the advancing party. We were requested to draw up on the opposite

B 1485—66

side to await the result. Our party out-numbered theirs in the proportion of three to one. The parties passed within a short distance of each other, and one from each side advanced to a parley. The strangers gave out that they were on a foray against the Galla, for whom they took us at first, but rejoiced that they had met friends instead of foes. Had the wily savages outnumbered our party, or caught us unprepared at the pool below, doubtless they would have attacked us.

We continued our march over a very level country and passed several herds of antelope. We encamped on the eastern bank of the river Hawash on the morning of the 10th. As we approached its banks the country gradually improved, and game became abundant. Here on its banks the vegetation was most luxuriant, and our weary animals at length, for the first time since quitting the coast, had abundance of grass.

The Hawash takes its rise in the country of the Garagin, situated to the southward and westward of Shoa, and empties itself into the lake Oussah. The rainy season had only just commenced, and we found the river at this period a dirty muddy stream flowing at about two miles an hour, about fifty yards wide and eight feet deep, with precipitous banks twenty-five to thirty feet high. Early on the morning of the 11th we commenced crossing the river on rafts, floated by inflated water-skins, and got all across by about four o'clock in the afternoon, and took up our abode on its western bank: we lost one musket and a few trifling articles.

One of our followers, a washerman, had been furnished at Tajura with an ass to carry himself and chattels. The poor beast partook too freely of the waters of the river, to remedy which its owner tied a rope to its hind legs, at the suggestion of some mischievous wag, and suspended it to a tree, as he said to let the water run out of its mouth; the consequence was that the poor animal was suffocated. Our party, with the exception of Dr. Kirk, had gone to one of the small lakes to the north of the river, to try to get a shot at a crocodile or hippopotamus, when we were startled by loud shouting in the direction of the camp. We instantly returned, fearing an attack had been made upon the camp, when, behold! the unfortunate ass was found suspended by the heels from the bough of a tree, and the shouting proved to have been caused by the united lungs of the European and Native escort, in their exertions to remove the unfortunate animal from his unenviable position, and although he was immediately lowered, life was extinct. During the night we were much disturbed by the laughing and cackling of packs of hyenas, which had come down attracted by the smell of the dead ass, lying just beyond our encampment. We watched, but in vain; not one would venture within range of our guns, so we gave it up in despair. The following morning not a vestige of the animal was to be seen, not a hair or a bone—all had been carried off. About four hundred yards to the westward of our encampment is a small lake, apparently deep, swarming with crocodile and hippopotami, and again still further to the westward there is another lake, the waters of which have a very sulphureous taste.

After crossing the Hawash the country again displayed much the same character as to the eastward, a barren desert, with, however, this advantage, that the climate is now much cooler. On the 14th of July we at length arrived at the frontier station of his Most Christian Majesty's dominions, but not a soul was there to greet our arrival, or offer us a welcome: this did not please us.

Mahomed Ali, however, having volunteered, was despatched with a letter to the Reverend Mr. Krapf, a missionary resident in Shoa, and we unloaded the camels to dry our tents and baggage, for we had had a smart shower during the night.

At about noon we had almost completed our arrangements for resuming our march, when the Wulasma Mohamed Abogaz, hereditary Governor of the Eastern Frontier, with a disorderly retinue of about three hundred spears, made his appearance and halted about a hundred yards from our encampment.

He sent a message to say that the King's orders were that we were to stop here till a guard of honour arrived to conduct us into his country ; and shortly after he condescended to pay us a visit, accompanied by the Wulasma Moosa and his wild retinue.

As we had much to do with the worthy Wulasma Mahomed Abogaz, a short sketch of him is necessary. He is about forty-five years of age, rather stout, and has the appearance of one who has led a very dissolute life. He has a most unprepossessing countenance, with small deceitful eyes ; his head is shaved, he wears no head dress ; his clothing consists of short loose unmentionables, a waistband, and a long cloth of Abyssinian manufacture hanging from his shoulders downwards to the ground—no sandals. After the defeat of the great Mohamedan invader of Ethiopia, Mohamed Izakh, by the Portuguese auxiliaries of the Christian king in the sixteenth century, several of the chiefs of the defeated army seized upon certain portions of the frontier, which they were permitted to retain, owing to the weakness of the Abyssinians, and from one of the most powerful of these Mohamed Abogaz claims his descent.

He holds his lands for military service to the King of Shoa, to whom, at certain periods, he has to pay his respects. In addition to the important post of Governor of the Eastern Frontier he is the keeper of the state prisoners. Alas for the barbarity of the customs ! the sole crime of many of them is that of being related to the reigning monarch ! A follower of the false prophet, as his name indicates, as bigoted as he is ignorant, and possessing to the utmost extent the Moslem's contempt for the Nazarene, the more so that he is compelled to acknowledge one for his lord and master, it may be supposed that he looked with no friendly eye on the arrival of the white Christians, and this he with difficulty kept from showing on every occasion.

When he paid his visit he was, as I before mentioned, accompanied by the Wulasma Moosa and a host of his followers ; one bore his sword of state—an unwieldy straight blade, much resembling the old Roman falchion, with a silver sheath ; another bore his shield and spears.

The shield formed of the hide of the Baza (oryx, *Antilope Leucoryx*),· an animal forming as it were the connecting link between the cow and the antelope, having straight horns about two and a half feet long, the body shaped like that of the antelope, with long spindle legs, a cow's head and tail, and the cow's gait in running. It is an animal very common in the Dankali country (the only one I ever saw killed weighed 216 pounds). The whole surface of the shield was covered with symbols in silver and brass, the Cross and the Crescent predominating—an unseemly association.

The Wulasma Moosa wore a silver-sheathed sword curved like a reaping-hook, and the extremity of the sheath formed of a fluted silver knob. He formed a striking contrast to his superior ; the one was bloated and surly-looking, the other thin and all smiles ; yet there was something unpleasant in his appearance also. Of the two I should rather have trusted Mohamed —his countenance could not conceal the working of his mind; the other would smile and stab. Notwithstanding, he was no match for his gruff superior, who some months afterwards caused him to be disgraced, and his silver sword and office taken from him.

The Wulasma repeated what he had before sent by a messenger, that we were to wait here for the King's gunmen ; so there was another weary night of watching ; for since that night at Goongoonteh we had never ceased to keep a vigilant watch.

Verily, I do think there is not a more inhospitable desert than that we have just traversed. *On one occasion only*, on the banks of the Hawash, did we ever have grass, wood, and water ; at the same time out of seventeen horses one only was in a state fit to mount; our mules were almost as bad, for, poor animals! on several occasions they were two and even three days without water. All that can be said of the country is that it is worthy of its possessors, a wild race whose hand is against every man, who fear neither God nor man—indeed, whose whole life is spent in bloodshed, murders of the most atrocious kind being of daily occurrence. Nature appears to have set her curse upon the country and its inhabitants, for it is scorched and burnt up, the greater portion having been at one time subject to volcanic action, as thermal waters are to be found scattered all about the place. The inhabitants are liars and murderers from their youth.

Our encampment, two thousand feet above the level of the sea, was at the foot of the lofty mountains of Shoa, which towered some six thousand feet above us. It was not a well chosen place; however, with a thorn fence we fancied ourselves pretty secure against wild animals; hyenas in particular were prowling about the whole night.

On the morning of the 15th we moved our encampment to Denel Melei, about five miles; this is the place where all customs are levied.

About noon the Reverend Mr. Krapf and Mr. Beke came down from the capital to us with orders from the King that we were to be feasted and assisted in our march towards the capital, and instantly large quantities of bread were furnished by Mohamed Abogaz, together with two bullocks, and jar after jar of a kind of meal called by them "tej," and a kind of beer, *small, very small indeed*, called "tulla." This day we made our first good meal since quitting Taj, a period of forty-five days, so that ample justice was done to the Chief's good cheer.

In the evening the sound of musical instruments, discharging of matchlocks, and the voices of the multitude proclaimed the approach of Itoo Kotama, General of the Gunmen, and shortly after of Itoo Woldo Lanna, Governor of the capital (Ankobar), who instantly came over and paid their respects to the Ambassador, bringing words of welcome from their renowned master. On the following morning, after much wrangling, we moved on to Fari, about two miles distant only, where the baggage was delivered over to the King's people, after many vain attempts on their part to ascertain which was the King's; had they been told, ours would doubtless have been left behind.

And now we were within the dominions of Sehela Salassie, King of Shoa, Efat, and the Galla—a high-sounding title!

On the 17th, having delivered over all the baggage to the authorities, to be carried on men's shoulders, the country being too hilly for camels, we set out at eleven o'clock in the forenoon for the village of Alio Amba, where we arrived at 5 P.M. What a contrast to the country we had just left! Our road wound round the sides of the mountains, across running streams of the most clear and delicious water—a great treat to us—the hills crowned with villages whose inhabitants greeted us with loud shouts of joy, for we were "the King's strong strangers," and accompanied by the royal troops, the principal of his Governors, and the General of the Gunmen. Our hearts felt quite light as we wound our way cheerily along, for all around smiled peace, and the country had a refreshing appearance. They had had a few showers, though the rainy season had not fairly set in, which caused the green grass to show itself; we heard the warbling of birds; verily it appeared to us a perfect paradise. Who has not read of the happy valley in Johnson's Rasselas? We fancied that he had chosen this very spot for the scene of his tale.

However, instead of being ushered into comfortable houses, we were huddled up into wretched barn-looking places, swarming with vermin of every kind, where we were destined to remain till the 1st of August. And a very tedious time it was; for on the day after our arrival the rains set in in earnest, so that we could not come out; the nights were cold, and even during the day we were glad to have a fire in the room, and had to endure all the discomforts of the smoke, besides being pestered with visits from people from all quarters of the country. It appears that His Majesty half repented him of having invited so large a body of "gipsies," as they honourably termed us. Many were the tales told of our conquests of foreign lands; which our Dankali friends took good care to exaggerate, and place in the most unfavourable light. "True they are few in number," said they, " but they have with them guns, and fire (alluding to the rockets) which, if thrown upon the ground, will destroy whole armies."

And then the several nobles were afraid that we should make the King too strong for them. Prophecies were quoted and invented, one that the country would be visited by red men from the East, who would seize upon the country, and destroy all the inhabitants. Another prophecy, however, was favourable. The late monarch had dreamt that during his son's reign, men from Egypt (from whence the term "gipsy") should come bringing with them presents such as their fathers never even pictured, and still greater presents should be brought during the following reign.

The only compensation we had for all our vexations was the beautiful scenery around, but this also became tiresome from its sameness.

Below, as far as the eye could reach, extended the inhospitable plains of the Adel; bounded on the north by the volcanic mountains of Ayaloo, to which is attached many a strange tale, and to the south by mountains of the Eto Galla, and about the time of the sun's rising the Hawash might be seen rapidly filling with the rains poured down from the mountains—winding its tortuous course towards the great lake at Oussah, also the smaller lakes of Abhibbah and Laahdoo.

To the north-east, distant about eight miles, is the hill of Gouchoo, on the summit of which is the stronghold of the Wulasma Mohamed, surrounded by a triple stockade, and accessible only on one side. There, in vaults, are confined the state prisoners of the kingdom of Shoa including the male relatives of the reigning monarch.

To the north the mountains of Emameret, or Mother of Mercy, towered some two thousand feet above the adjacent hills (many a legend is attached to this also), where the King is said to have concealed the riches of his kingdom.

To the westward is the capital, Ankobar, situated on the summit of the range. It was beautiful in the early morning to see the clouds rolling up from the valleys below, and to cast one's eyes around and observe the innumerable cascades in every direction, but all tending to feed the still thirsty Hawash, or still more thirsty plains of the Adel.

It should be observed that the term Dankali is applied to the whole of the tribes inhabiting the plains below; the Adel, or Adaiel, is the principal tribe in this part, and therefore the country is frequently called the land of the Adel.

At a subsequent period it was my destiny to dwell alone in the place for three months; so that hereafter I shall give a more particular account of it. Suffice it that we felt quite a relief when instructions were at length given, on the 1st of August, to prepare for an audience with the monarch of this most *Christian* people, who at length had conquered all his scruples, and determined to receive us at his private residence at Muklewans, only about three miles from this, and about the same distance from his capital.

However, delays were still made, for, instead of proceeding at once to the monarch's residence, we were compelled to halt for the night in some rude huts on a farm still more uncomfortable than our residence at Alio Amba.

The following day set in with repeated showers of rain; we, however, moved forward attended by the King's gunmen firing their matchlocks loaded with ball, in a most indiscriminate manner (it was really a wonder no one was wounded), and at length arrived at some tents that had been pitched for us, within a few hundred yards of the royal residence.

About two o'clock in the afternoon, all being prepared, we at length set out for the palace, all in full uniform, which led some of the troops to observe that it could not be true that the "gipsies" had come to take away all the gold out of the country seeing that they had brought more in than had ever before been seen or the country could produce.

But even now, after we had entered the enclosure round the palace, more delay was necessary to show the dignity of the monarch. "He might be sleeping;" so we were ushered into a dark room which had recently been used as a granary, where we were gazed at by all the court menials, until at last it pleased His Majesty to send for us.

We were ushered into the royal presence at last. The apartment was a rude thatched building. In a sort of alcove reclined the monarch, immediately surrounded by his pages, and squatted on the floor on either side of the throne were the several nobles of the kingdom all bare to the waist—for none of his subjects dare appear in the "presence" otherwise; and in immediate attendance, as master of the ceremonies, stood the Boulder Abbul, or introducer, with a green rod as the symbol of his authority. Immediately opposite the King was a similar recess adorned with "kitchen materials;" the walls around were hung with the royal shields, about forty in number, somewhat similar to that described as belonging to the Wulasma Mohamed, and several matchlocks, with a few double-barrelled percussion guns.

I have observed that the King reclined in a sort of alcove (which was raised about four feet from the ground); he was supported by silken cushions, had a silken canopy overhead and a splendidly embroidered footcloth under him; some old Persian carpets were spread in front of the throne. Doubtless he had been anxious to make an impression. The monarch had no headdress or covering for his feet; his hair was frizzled up and well greased; he had silken small-clothes, and the usual Abyssinian robe but adorned with several broad red stripes at each end and also in the middle. He had evidently determined to receive us with reserve, and as we entered he glanced at each of us with his one eye (be it observed, he has lost the use of the other), returned our salutation in a scarce audible tone, and then begged us to be covered and seated:—we had previously sent our chairs, which were placed in front of the throne.

The European escort had been left behind with the little gun, which, after they had fired a royal salute in our own honour, they brought up in front of the door.

After the letter from the Bombay Government had been delivered, and the usual compliments, and after the Ambassador had replied to each of the many anxious questions of the monarch of How are you? Are you quite well since your journey? and a host more to the same purport, the presents were at length called for.

A magnificent musical clock, musical boxes, a Brussels carpet, dress swords, silks, muslins, Delhi scarves, *ad infinitum*, were displayed before the King, to each of which the answer given was "May God reward thee! May God restore it unto thee!" with the utmost gravity.

The escort then made their appearance, and went through the manual and platoon exercise. At the moment when the movement was made to receive cavalry, the King exclaimed "Ah, that will do here, but would they thus kneel before the cavalry of the Galla?" They retired and brought in the muskets; hitherto the King had retained his gravity, but about the time the hundredth musket, with its bright polished bayonet, was laid before him, he gave vent to his feelings in a prolonged shrill whistle. Ye gods! what an unkingly act! Shortly after we took leave, and were that evening regaled with all the luxuries the royal kitchen afforded. Upon the whole I was disappointed with the appearance of the King; although only forty, he appeared to be full fifty years of age, caused by the very dissolute life he has led: his eye, it is said, was lost by disease.

On the following day we had a private audience of His Majesty, that is to say, only the immediate retainers of the king were present; the remainder of the costly gifts were then spread out for His Majesty's acceptance, with the ammunition and the three-pounder field-piece. To initiate him into the use thereof we had some artillery practice in the evening, at which he appeared perfectly delighted.

In the evening the King's confessor, a dwarf three feet six inches in height, aged about fifty, was sent with a speech from the throne which was to the following purport:—"During the reigns of seven kings" (the limit of the present dynasty) "travellers have from time to time arrived from far countries bringing with them strange things but none have ever brought such things as you this day have given to the King, none have wrought the wonders that you have this day performed. May friendship, lasting friendship, exist between your Queen and me! saith Sahela Selassie; from this day ye are my children, Sahela Selassie is your father." A suitable reply of course was returned. Beeroo, the favourite page, a lad of about twelve years of age, son of one of the nobles, was sent some time after dusk with a huge pie from the royal table highly seasoned with red pepper, and bearing a salutation from the King: "May my children sleep well!"

Wednesday, August 5th.—Having had another private audience we took leave, and proceeded towards Ankobar, winding round the sides of the hills, along very narrow pathways, and after a ride of about an hour and a half arrived at Ankobar, amidst the universal greetings of the inhabitants, who were loud in their praises of the munificence of "the King's strong strangers."

Here we were shown to a house certainly superior to any we had yet seen, the roof of which had suspended from it the inner fly of a tent, and the walls surrounded with its "*kunnauts*" thus dividing off separate apartments. We fancied ourselves tolerably comfortable. The night was very cold, the thermometer 48 Fahr, everything very damp from the continual rain. In looking at these Abyssinian dwellings one is reminded of the saying that man's first attempt at architecture was in imitation of the birds. Verily, these people have made but little improvement thereon. Here there is no attempt at laying a foundation, no levelling the ground beyond the removal of a few stones perhaps, that may be inconveniently in the way; but, having chosen the spot on which to build his dwelling, the Shoan commences by driving into the ground, in a circular form, a number of stakes of the requisite dimensions: these are bound together at intervals with ropes made of green twigs: this forms the interior. Another circle similar to the other is formed six to ten feet beyond the former one, and is generally plastered over with mud, having gaps here and there to answer the purpose of windows. If two doors are required, they are invariably placed opposite each other. A conical roof is generally prepared, the frame of which rests upon the stakes, and projects some four or five feet beyond the outer wall. It is also supported by a beam laid across them, on which there is a pole to support the centre. The houses are in general well thatched. The inner court is inhabited by the master and mistress, the outer indiscriminately by slaves employed in grinding wheat, cooking, &c., and by animals—mules, horses, sheep, &c. Fires, which one can hardly dispense with, are a great nuisance, inasmuch as there is no way for the smoke to escape otherwise than through the doors or the so-called windows.

A Shoan requires but little furniture, and of cooking utensils still less. A cot of rude manufacture, no mattress, but merely strips of cowhide laid across and across, a wicker table, formed something in the shape of an inverted hat, and chairs (esteemed too great a luxury to be used as with us) of sufficient height to eat from when seated on the bare ground. Leathern jars for their beloved beverage "tulla," or very small beer, a few horns to serve for drinking-cups, comprise nearly the whole of the former; and as for the latter, among a nation who generally live on raw meat, it cannot be supposed that they have made great advancement in their *cuisine*; a few earthen pots, and a flat baking-pan sometimes made of iron but more commonly of clay, are found more than ample. Bedding they have none, the long robe worn in the day answering the purpose both of sheets and coverlid at night.

And these were the dwellings we were destined to occupy for several months.

But a brief sketch of the history of this once famous province of the mighty empire of Ethiopia will not be uninteresting.

The monarchy of Shoa is of comparatively modern date, the present being the seventh king from the founder. They trace their pedigree to the "queen of Sheba" who went to Jerusalem "to hear the wisdom of Solomon," and who, they say, was queen of Ethiopia. It would appear that the wisest man that ever lived, not content with his "seven hundred wives, princesses, and three hundred concubines," became enamoured of this queen, and, to show how much he was flattered by the visit of so great a sovereign, gave unto her all that her heart could desire, even "whatsoever she asked," "so she turned and went to her own country, she and her servants," and the Abyssinians look with great respect on their monarchs, considering them as the lineal descendants of Solomon by the queen of Sheba.

It is well known that the Ethiopians were a mighty nation, that they conquered a great portion of Arabia, and even attempted the conquest of its "Holy City," but "the Lord rained hail upon them from heaven, each stone as big as a pigeon's egg, and utterly destroyed their army." (See Sale's Koran.) The fate of Ethiopia was similar to that of the Roman empire: attacked on the south and west by fierce tribes of the Galla—those Goths and Vandals of Africa—and on the east by the followers of the false prophet under Mohamed Izakh, whose descendants dwell at Aussa, in the country of the Dankali, they were at length compelled to give way. Assistance was asked for and obtained from the Portuguese. Their successes, though brilliant; were but of short duration. The fate of Ethiopia was sealed; each chief endeavoured to secure for himself some portion of the dismembered empire; and we find at the present day the northern province, with its ancient capital, Gondar, of which Ras Ali is Chief, and Tigré, of which Wabi is Chief; then in the extreme west, Gojam and Damot, of which Beeroo is Chief. The plain between Shoa and Gondar is inhabited by the Wooloo Galla, who have become converted to the Mohamedan faith; and, lastly, there is the southern portion, Shoa, of which Sahela Selassie is the Chief.

Still the Christian portion all acknowledge the supremacy of the high priest at Gondar in all ecclesiastical matters. He is appointed by the Greek patriarch at Alexandria.

In the south-west portion of Shoa there is the ancient city of Tegulet. It is built on a table-capped hill accessible only on one side. This was for a time the capital of Ethiopia, in its wars with the southern Galla: it was here that the Portuguese embassy was received; now it is a mere heap of ruins.

Sahela Selassie, whose name signifies "the Bounty of the Trinity," was twelve years of age when he ascended the throne, and at the time of our arrival had reigned twenty-eight years. He makes three expeditions yearly against the Galla, and has conquered a considerable portion of the lands lost by his ancestors to these wild people. There are stated periods for these expeditions, which remind one of the saying of Scripture " at the time when the king went forth to battle."

Though a despot he is not cruel, at least to his subjects,—only one, a person of some distinction in the country, having been put to death since his accession. The career of this person is not without some romantic incidents. Itoo Metookoo, for such was his name, had been raised from one post of distinction to another by his sovereign, for his valiant conduct in the field, until he was made governor of the conquered Galla to the south-westward of the capital, and as such became the most powerful subject in the kingdom. He had the temerity to propose allying himself with the monarch by marrying one of his daughters, for which he was sentenced to be confined in Gouchoo, the state prison before alluded to, but from which he managed to effect his escape, and fled to the seat of his government.

Having collected a large army he determined to depose the King and seize upon the throne himself. One of his sons informed the King of his father's intentions, but was not believed, and was compelled to join his father from the ignominy with which he was treated by his sovereign.

The King upon subsequent information prepared to meet the danger, and surrounded Angollala, where he was then residing, with a rude wall, sufficient, however, to keep off the Galla horsemen, and then, having assembled his forces, marched forth to meet the rebel army which was approaching.

The King halted in the plain of Angollala, in a well chosen position, and had pits dug and stakes driven into the ground to check the advance of the enemy; a severe battle was fought, in which the King was victorious, and the rebel leader made prisoner and again sent to Gouchoo, from whence he a second time managed to effect his escape, but, instead of flying from a country in which he had so much to fear, he proceeded to the royal residence, where the King was sitting in judgment, and there braved the resentment of the monarch. He was seized—but not till he had killed and wounded several persons—and, in accordance with the sentence passed by the assembled nobles, was stoned to death. He is described (this occurred only about seven years before our arrival) as having been a tall muscular man, and one much respected for his valour, as well by friends as foes. His sons are still living, and one of them has been promoted to great honour—he who gave the first intimation to the King—but it is said that Sahela Selassie secretly fears him. The King has gained much power by this timely defeat of so renowned a warrior, yet the unfortunate rebel is always spoken of with respect.

His Majesty's principal residences are Muklewuns, Ankobar, Angollala, and Debra Berhan or the Monastery of Light.

They are all built on the summit of conical hills, and well fortified by stakes around, or stockades. The description of one will serve for a description of all; so I shall just give an idea of Ankobar. The ascent to it is by steps cut in the sides of the mountains, and at the surface there is a cleared space or courtyard, surrounded by the royal kitchens and outhouses; in this place the King's workmen are employed under his own eye, he being generally seated in a balcony commanding a view of the whole court.

Here also he sits in judgment daily for a certain portion of time, being assisted in the distribution of justice by the *four chairs*, men who are privileged to sit in the "presence" on iron chairs; he can, however, overrule their decision.

Every morning we were disturbed at an early hour by loud cries of " Abiet!" " Abiet!" proceeding from the stentorian lungs of the middle-aged, combined with the shrill accents of the *softer sex* and children, and the feeble voice of the old man, lifted up against the oppressor. At a given signal the gates are thrown open, and the crowd sent into the "presence," where they immediately prostrate themselves to the earth, bare to the waist.

At length order is restored, and each individual in turn is permitted to state his grievances. Some cases were trifling indeed, and it was laughable to observe the air of wisdom adopted by the sages "the chairs," and the patience with which they listened to each trivial case.

A burly-looking savage would step forth and state, with much action and energy, how his mule had been fastened in its place and by some strange accident had got into his neighbour's field, who had seized it, and refused to restore it until compensation was made for the injury his crop had sustained. "Sahela Selassie eniot! (May the King die!) I did not send it there." The other in reply would say: "Sahela Selassie eniot! this neighbour's mule has done me injury to the value of several pieces of salt, which he, the owner, refuses to pay me." Then after the monarch's brief judgment, "Pay him," another pair are brought forward, and so on.

It is a singular custom that of swearing by the life of the King, but it prevails throughout the kingdom; their greatest asseveration, however, is "Be Sahela Selassie Umbus! By Sahela Selassie's God!" He himself swears "May Woosun Juggut die! (his father, who has been dead this long time.) In the villages the people swear by the life of the Governor of the district in the same way. The custom even prevails amongst his Mohamedan subjects.

We were detained at Ankobar, scarcely ever moving a yard from the house, until the 23rd of September, when we were invited to pay his Majesty a visit at Debra Berhan, to be present at a review of a portion of his troops. After the usual wrangling and squabbling about mules, baggage, &c., and being half-deafened by the repeated cry of "Sabela Selassie eniot!" from old and young,—man, woman, and child,—we at length made our escape, and after a ride of about an hour descended some fifteen hundred feet to the valley of the Chaffa, through which the river Izabra, flows to add its mite to quench the burning thirst of the plains below. Having crossed it (it is a miserable river, or rather a brook; the meaning of the name is "He shall not be pardoned"), we scrambled up the mountains of the Chaka to an elevation of some fifteen hundred feet above Ankobar.

On gaining its summit an extensive plain lay before us, extending as far as the eye could reach to the westward, the ground slightly undulating, covered with fields of various grains; the tall grass moving to and fro in the wind gave it a wave-like appearance reminding one of old times at sea.

To the north-eastward the peak of Emamaret reared its black summit almost to the skies, and to the eastward the contrast was very striking—a waste, a desert, a howling wilderness; and as the wind bore along huge columns of sand it appeared that "the Spirit of Evil" was still at his post. The Dankali when they meet any of these flying columns of sand, cut at them with their creases or daggers, exclaiming "Aooz bellah el Shitan el Rajeem!" "I fly for refuge to God from Satan the stoned!"

After halting here a short time to admire the prospect, we again pushed forward to Debra Berhan, where we arrived at about 3-30 P.M.; it is twenty miles W.N.W. of Ankobar.

September 25th.—At about eight o'clock in the morning we were summoned to the "presence," whither we accordingly proceeded in full dress.

The King was seated in the porch of the palace, surrounded by his courtiers. A Persian carpet was placed at the foot of the steps, and several hassocks for seats for our use. Our escort performed the manual and platoon exercise, and fired several rounds of blank cartridge. The King appeared much pleased with the rapidity with which they loaded.

Here we found tents prepared for us about half a mile from the palace, which was built on a rising ground, surrounded by a loose stone wall, and four rows of stockades, rendering it thus a stronghold against the Galla.

The surrounding country is highly cultivated, and bears testimony to a long reign of peace; but there is a great sameness in the appearance, scarcely a single tree or aught else to diversify the scene for miles.

Towards evening people flocked in from all quarters, either to take part in or to be spectators of the review.

Debra Berhan is in latitude 9° 42' 11" N., Ankobar in 9° 34' 47" N.

A short time afterwards Itoo Lestowald appeared with his troop of menials, four hundred in number. These are attached to the royal household, and are generally employed to convey messages to and fro, and to act as spies for the monarch, being placed with strangers on their arrival in the kingdom to act as "Janissaries." They are styled Aferoch Phual Afresol.

These men came in dancing, shouting, and capering about like madmen, each furnished with a rod of green rushes. On entering the " presence," at a given signal, they all made a most terrific shout, and threw their rods down at the foot of the temporary throne and then squatted down in four rows.

Shortly after, a horseman rode in, fully accoutred for war, who as he gallopped up and down between the seated Aferoch. kept shouting out "Ana gaita folaje!" " I am the King's slave?" and shaking his spear at the imaginary foe dared the Gallas to the combat. At this period the Aferoch jumped up and gave a loud roar, probably intended to imitate that of the lion.

He retired and a foot-soldier next appeared, went through the same antics, and retired also. Then the order was given to clear the court, and His Majesty dismissed us by telling us we had better go home and get something to eat. We returned to the tents, but found that our worthy Abyssinian servants had devoured all that had remained from the previous day.

In about half an hour the head blacksmith, Itoo Habti, who appears to act as master of the ceremonies in the introduction of all foreigners, and has the confidence of the king, being one of the principal men in the kingdom, came to usher us once more into the royal presence. Following him, we were shown into a small tent which had been prepared for us close under the walls, and to the left of a temporary throne erected on the walls, where His Majesty was seated. surrounded as usual by the pages and others of the household; at the foot of the throne was spread the Brussels carpet hanging down over the wall, and all were dressed in their best. The gun was placed near a pole some three hundred yards in advance of the King.

We were graciously received and accommodated with bread, raw meat, and mead in abundance. The review commenced by Itoo Kotama bringing forth his gallant band of gunmen, in number about six hundred, chanting forth songs in praise of the " Bounty of the Trinity," and shouting defiance to his enemies, the worthy General, in his cracked voice, screaming " Behold in me the King's great warrior! I have slain the Galla till their blood flowed like water! I am the King's slave!" to which his worthy followers replied by a loud shout of " Wo-Wo-Wo!" in a kind of chant. Having discharged their muskets and matchlocks in what might truly be called "independent" firing, they advanced to the foot of the throne, bared themselves to the waist, and fell prostrate to the earth. They then arose, and marched past, shouting and singing as they came, and their General gallopping up and down their ranks screaming as if he were frantic.

These are the King's favourite troops, and were the only portion allowed to come up to the very foot of the throne, the others not being permitted to approach nearer than three hundred yards. Itoo Kotama was clad in silken small-clothes, his "loins girded up" with some sixty or eighty yards of cloth, wearing a particoloured chintz waistcoat, and the skin of the lion buttoned round the neck and hanging over the left shoulder. He had a silver-sheathed sword, his shield (carried by a young man, his shield-bearer) was studded with silver devices, the Cross predominating. On his arm he wore a silver gauntlet, and armlets of the same metal and ivory above his elbow, and his appearance altogether was the very type of the savage warrior.

Itoo Kotama is by birth a Galla, but taken prisoner in one of the King's early expeditions, his youth and his comely appearance pleased the monarch, and he was spared the brutal infliction of the knife, which is indeed but too common among the Amhara, and subsequently, for his fidelity and bravery, he was advanced to his present post, and enjoys no small share of his sovereign's confidence. Thirteen Governors passed by in the same order as the gunmen, with their several contingents, varying from six hundred to a thousand each, mostly cavalry, and lastly the Galla cavalry, under Itoo Maretch, which had been drawn up on one side of the ground.

These were the finest body of men, in number about two thousand. They came forward at a hard gallop in a double line, and pulled up so suddenly that their horses were almost thrown upon their haunches. "I have slain men!" shouted forth Itoo Maretch as he approached to make his obeisance; he then gallopped off along the line of his followers, and returning shouted 'I am the King's slave! Behold in me the Father of Warriors!'" and then throwing his spears at some immaginary foe (which were nimbly picked up by his shield-bearer) and throwing his sword, his men gave a loud shout, then gallopped past, and were soon lost in a cloud of dust.

Itoo Maretch was habited much after the manner of Itoo Kotama, excepting that hitherto he had disdained to accept of any of the silks or satins brought by the "Gipsies," and in addition to the ornaments worn by the latter he had the "Akoo Dama," which is worn only by the bravest of the brave." It is a silver bar which is fastened across the forehead, and to which there is appended a row of silver chains reaching below the eyes, and at each extremity of the bar down to the shoulders, imparting a peculiarly wild appearance to their swarthy features. There were several Governors who had been honoured with this royal mark of distinction, but none did it become so well as Itoo Maretch.

Shortly before the approach of Itoo Maretch with his contingent we were requested to take our places by the gun, in order that "the King's strong strangers" might be seen, and to fire the gun quickly.

We fired about thirty rounds, till the little gun danced about in fine style. These valleys had never before been disturbed by the roar of cannon. Great astonishment was depicted in every countenance.

During the review a messenger arrived from Tajura bringing us letters, &c., amongst others a very peremptory one commanding my *immediate* return to Aden. I had before this volunteered to proceed to Harrar, and had obtained our Chief's sanction, so that I was not much put out by it.

At about three o'clock in the afternoon all was over, and we departed to our tents. I should think at least twelve or fifteen thousand men must have passed by: the effect was striking, and gave one some idea of the power of the Christian King.

We were feasted liberally, and in the evening we astonished the surrounding thousands with the display of a few rockets, doubtless to the great dread of the distant Galla.

The following day all rested from their labours, and at an early hour the day after we accompanied the King to another of his "palaces," Angellala, distant about five miles south-west.

His Majesty was escorted by about a thousand cavalry; he rode on a mule in advance, and, had a crimson umbrella carried on either side of him, the sign of royalty. Our road lay over undulating ground and, as we advanced, troops of horsemen joined the cavalcade. As soon as they approached within two or three hundred yards of the umbrellas, they dismounted and fell prostrate to the earth, in which posture they remained till the King passed by. One wild horseman rode in front of the King curvetting backwards and forwards anglewise with the road.

We passed the spot where the daring rebel Itoo Metookoo in one night slew a thousand of the King's subjects, and also the site of the great battle wherein the rebels suffered so severe a defeat. Tents were prepared for us here as at Debra Berhan; these tents are made of a kind of coarse black woollen cloth, and are similar to those used by the Gipsies in England, having a pole to support each end, and one along the centre, the sides being pegged down to the ground.

Monday, 27th.—We had a private audience with His Majesty, who has now got over all his fears, and treats us with confidence. Immediately on entering his palace he dismissed all his attendants, and throwing off all reserve seated himself beside us on a couch. This is the only stone building in the country, and was erected by an Albanian named Demetrius.

After he had expressed his great admiration of all our guns we offered them for his acceptance; he set aside three from which to select one, and as we took leave he said "You are all my children; I will show you my country. Sahela Selassie will give you great things. May Woosun Juggut die!"

28th.—His Majesty, accompanied by two hundred men, took us out to show us his country. In passing a pool of water the escort were directed to take up their position around, and we were invited to see the royal sport of this mighty monarch, namely, shooting wild duck! To his annoyance, more fell by the hands of the "Gipsies" than by his own; no one else dared to fire.

We returned in the afternoon to our tents, the weather delightfully cool.

On the 29th it was intimated to the King that I had been ordered to return to my country and his assistance was requested in forwarding me by Harrar, to which he gave his consent and promised me a letter of introduction to the Emir, or Prince, of that country.

While in command of the "Euphrates," and after that, I had received a good deal of information regarding Harrar, and it had long been my wish to visit the place. Prior to my recall I had received permission from Major Harris to go there.

On the 1st we returned to Ankobar, the mission to prepare for the approaching expedition against the Galla, and I for my journey to Harrar. A proclamation was made prior to our quitting Angollala to the effect that the King had enemies and would defeat them. Certain of the Governors were cited to appear with their several contingents at a certain spot, with provisions for twenty days. Eighteen days was the time allowed them to prepare for the expedition against the enemies of the King, and the concluding part of the proclamation was that he who failed, his family, slaves, and property should be confiscated to the mighty monarch, and remain his for seven years. I now commenced making preparations in earnest, and on the 3rd of October went to Alio Amba to one Abdool Liki, Chief of the Harrargi, an individual whose acquaintance I made at the review at Debra Berhan, and who on that occasion was suffering from ophthalmia. I therefore supplied myself with the necessary medicines, hoping to gain his favour, and thus be enabled to carry out my long-cherished wish of paying a visit to his country.

I was received with much kindness by Abdool Liki, and spent the day with him. In the course of conversation I mentioned that the King had given me permission to quit Shoa, and had promised to furnish me with a letter of introduction to the Emir of Harrar. He replied that if the King sent me it would be well, but at the same time tried to dissuade me from attempting the journey. I returned to Ankobar in the evening.

October 7th.—A messenger arrived from the King saying that he was anxious to see me before I left his country, and that he would do great things for me.

October 9th.—The Reverend Mr. Krapf having kindly offered to accompany me to Angollala to take leave of the King, we quitted Ankobar at 7-20 A.M. Descending to the valley of the Chaffa, our course lay W.N.W., along the left bank of the river Irahra ("He shall not be pardoned"), which we crossed about six miles from its source, at a narrow part and a very tolerable ford, and from thence ascended the Chaffa. There are four roads over this mountain, the northernmost is the *King's own road;* we pursued the one next to it. The ascent was very gradual to the height of about fifteen hundred feet above the level of Ankobar, or nine thousand five hundred feet above the level of the sea.

Having attained the summit, we had an extensive view of the surrounding country. The sky was beautifully clear, and the sun shone forth in all his glory, which was very desirable, inasmuch as there was a bleak north-easterly wind.

To the eastward, as far as the eye could reach, extended the inhospitable and parched up plains of the Adaiel, bounded in the extreme distance by the mountains of Ayooloo and Haybooti; the lakes of Aihibulloo and Laahdoo were very distinct.

To the north-east about five miles, still towering several hundred feet above us, stood the frowning black mountain of Emameret, or Mother of Mercy.

To the westward, a striking contrast to the plains of the Adaiel, lay those once belonging to the pagan Galla, but now to the Christian King of Shoa, in a state of high cultivation, the token of a long reign of peace. It was indeed as it were a moving sea, the crops waving to and fro with the wind, the ground gently undulating with a gradual descent to the south and west; here and there might be seen a solitary tree, marking the spot where once stood a Galla village. The religious ceremonies, if so they may be termed, of these people are always performed beneath the shade of a tree. After having halted for a short time to admire the surrounding scenery, and to refresh ourselves and our animals, we again continued our journey, and at two o'clock in the afternoon arrived at Angollala, the distance from Ankobar being about twenty-five miles. About an hour after our arrival Itoo Habti, Chief of the Blacksmiths, Introducer of Foreigners, and one of the most confidential of the King's advisers (if the despot can be said to have advisers), called to see us, bringing a present of two loaves of bread, ten eggs, some dried meat, &c., besides which we received the usual "dirgo" or daily allowance from the King's kitchen, and a tent was pitched for me close to Mr. Krapf's house.

After the usual compliments had passed, Itoo Hahti rose to take leave, saying as he quitted the tent " All is arranged; the King will send you away with great honour."

On the following day, being anxious to pay our respects to His Majesty, we waited till near noon (for Itoo Habti had promised to call early to usher us into the King's presence), and then proceeded to the palace, in the outer court of which the worthy individual was having his hair dressed, so we had to wait some time, until the last finish had been given to it, when he condescended to lead us to the "presence." The King was seated in the porch of the palace. After the usual salutations and inquiries had passed, Mr. Krapf told his Majesty that I had called to take leave of him, and to request a letter of introduction to the ruler of Harrar. To this he replied "My son, why do you wish to leave my country, having been here only a few days? You must accompany me to the expedition against the Galla, which will only last ten days? after that I will let you go, and will give you many things. My son, why do you leave my country?" It was explained to him that I had been recalled, and that my Queen would be angry if I did not return soon. To which he replied: "Say to your Queen that Sahela Selassie would not let you go; he wished you to see his country."

Monday, 11th October.—We were awoke at dawn this morning by the loud cry of "Abiet! Abiet!" proceeding from the stentorian lungs of about thirty of His Majesty's liege subjects appealing for justice against their oppressors. His Majesty holds a court daily, and he dare not refuse to listen to the complaint of the meanest subject, lest his *name should be destroyed*. He generally sits in a kind of verandah. The four Judges, or as they are called the Wambewateh or Chairs (being privileged to sit on iron chairs in the "presence"), are seated immediately below him, and try each case in succession. The King confirms, modifies, or cancels their decision.

Even when the King has been out riding I have frequently observed people throwing themselves on the ground before him and crying out "Abiet! Abiet!" He would sometimes settle the matter at once, at others appoint a time for hearing it.

After innumerable vexatious disappointments, the King at length consented to my departure from his kingdom, that is, he permitted me to go towards the frontier to make preparations for my departure, presented me with a mule, and sent a message to the Governor of the frontier to assist me. As will, however, hereafter be seen, the Governor did not pay that strict attention to the King's wishes which the generality of his subjects were in the habit of paying.

The 18th of October is a day ever to be remembered by me. At the earliest dawn there was an unusual bustle and confusion; we had all assembled at Angollala, Major Harris, Graham, and the other members of the mission in readiness to accompany the King on his expedition against the Galla, myself to obtain final permission to leave the country, and once more to brave the dangers of the desert in order that I might return to civilised life.

This was the day appointed for the assembling of the King's army at a place called Waloc, about five hours' journey to the south-westward of Angollala; Governors, Deputy Governors, freemen and slaves, and even women and children, were seen in all directions, as if actuated by one and the same mind, rushing forward to the appointed rendezvous to swell the hosts of the Christian despot.

It was a stirring sight to see with what spirit the royal commands were attended to. At last the royal trumpets gave warning that the King was leaving the palace, and it became necessary for me to part from my fellow-travellers. In a few moments they were gone. I stood alone gazing in vain to catch a last glimpse of them, for they were soon lost in a cloud of dust, and I felt for the first time alone in a strange land. We had shared dangers and much hardship; the kindness of two individuals in particular I shall never forget: long may they live to enjoy the society of their numerous friends! Who could know the author of "Wild Sports in Southern Africa,"—that mighty Nimrod, that fearless traveller,—and not admire his character, and not feel at once a desire to be considered the friend of such a man?

My ride back to Ankobar was a solitary one; I had not even a servant with me. I could have cried from very bitterness of soul, and then the thought passed through my mind, Shall I ever again see those from whom I have just parted? Shall I ever see my own country again? Shall I ever be able to pass in safety through that desert, dreary and inhospitable, the abode of thieves and murderers? My answer to all these questions was, as it would be now: Thy will, O God, be done! I *did* pass in safety through that dreary desert; I *have* seen those friends again; but my country, England, the pride of the universe, am I ever again to visit *thee*? Thy will, O God, be done! I still say.

And now from this day my trials commenced in earnest. I did not arrive at Ankobar till late in the afternoon. Our house was deserted; but this was not a time for vain regrets. It was necessary for me to "be up and doing." On the following day I rested, and the day after proceeded to Alio Amba, where the principal market is held every Friday, and there took up my abode to make preparations for the journey. As soon as I had obtained lodgings and got all my baggage removed from Ankobar, I determined upon visiting the Wulasma Mohamed Abogaz, hereditary Governor of the Eastern Frontier, to ascertain what instructions he had received from the King.

October 21st.—Having obtained the assistance of one Hajji Sayad as an interpreter, I proceeded at an early hour towards Gouchoo, the residence of the Wulasma, about six miles distant from Alio Amba. Our road lay over a hilly country intersected with numerous ravines, and crossed by three inconsiderable streams, namely, the Jami, Dinki, and Wamburroo; the last-named flows round the foot of Gouchoo, and all flow eastward. At this period they had only about sixteen inches water in each, and varied in breadth from thirty to eighty yards. The hill of Gouchoo is only accessible on one side, and that is very steep; the residence of the Wulasma is at the very summit, and surrounded by a triple stockade, each about 12 feet high—for here, as mentioned in a former part, are confined the male relatives of the reigning monarch. It was near the harvest-time, and the whole country was groaning under the hand of all-bountiful Nature. Grain of various descriptions were almost ready for the reaper. *Jowári (Holcus spicata)* appeared to be the most abundant, and grew to a great height.

We were about three hours on the journey, but our ride was a very pleasant one. Game rather scarce:—indeed we saw but a few of the small kind of antelope generally known by the name of Salt's antelope, and some few beautiful specimens of the feathered tribe. We found the Wulasma, truly *à l'Abyssine*, squatted on a stone by the roadside a few hundred yards in front of his dwelling with about twenty of his immediate followers, dispensing justice to all who chose to demand it. After the usual salutations, and on his inquiring to what he might owe the honour of this unexpected visit, I told him that I was about to leave the country, and wished to know if he had received any instructions from the King about me? He made no reply, but after a while inquired if I were a follower of Islám? On my replying in the negative, he begged I would go to his house and refresh myself (it was the month of Ramazán). I accordingly proceeded thither, and was warmly welcomed by his wife and daughters. Food was instantly set before me, and having satisfied my inner man the young ladies became very inquisitive, asking me all sorts of questions, and examining every part of my dress. All this took place during the absence of their mother, the wife of the Wulasma. Immediately on her return they resumed their occupation, spinning with true Mussulman gravity. The wife of the Wulasma was about thirty-five years of age, well formed, and with some pretensions to beauty; she had five daughters, the youngest of whom, about thirteen years of age, was decidedly beautiful, a brunette with dark eyes, and long dark eyelashes, arched eyebrows, well-formed lips and mouth—indeed the prettiest girl I had seen for some time. She was, as is the case with most beauties, fully aware of her charms, and withal very coquettish.

Her mother again quitting the room, she came to me and said in the most piquant manner imaginable, "You Captain, I am told that all white people are exceedingly clever, and have great knowledge of medicine; my eyes are weak, pray give me something to do them good." Although she pretended to be displeased at my answer; it was evidently what she expected: "Your eyes are only too beautiful, and are more likely to cause harm to others."

Opposite the door by which I entered was a long passage, which was crowded with the attendants of the unfortunate prisoners; this passage led to a staircase communicating with the vaults below, where their masters were confined, and for what crime?—I am tired of repeating it—merely that of being allied to the reigning monarch.

I was shortly after again summoned to the presence of the Wulasma. I found him at the same spot, attended only by one of his nephews, by name Jalee; after conversing upon various subjects, he at last told me that he had received instructions from the King about me, and that I should be forwarded immediately. Alas! I was detained three months. Upon the whole my visit was satisfactory, for before leaving I presented the Wulasma with a shawl, a box, &c., and we parted on very friendly terms. And now I set to work in earnest to prepare for my journey. It would be tedious to relate what passed daily; I shall therefore allude only in general terms to my residence here.

In the first place I hired a hut belonging to a Mohamedan woman, a native of the place, a widow with two children; her husband had been killed on his way to Harrar by the Adaiel. Her name was Miriam; she acted as my housekeeper, so that I had not the trouble of attending the markets. The hut was nearly circular, with a sort of box attached to it about ten feet in diameter; my bed was placed in the box or recess. There was a rude court on one side for visitors, the kitchen on the other side; so that it at once formed bedroom, parlour, and kitchen. It was so scantily thatched that it would keep out neither wind nor rain—quite a Jack Straw's house.

A few evenings after I had taken up my abode there, Hajji Sayad being in the hut, my worthy hostess, having prepared coffee and burnt frankincense, asked Sayad to say a prayer; he quoted part of the Koran, and concluded with "May the Most High God protect and preserve him from all his enemies, and may he return to his father's house in peace!" my hostess continually repeating "Ameen, Ameen." I was indeed much affected, for they both appeared to be sincere. During a sojourn of three months I experienced many acts of kindness from these poor people; verily they acted the part of good Samaritans.

Many people called to see me, so that, what with preparing for the journey, &c., my time was fully taken up. On the 27th of October I received a visit from Imeeat Dajah, a Mohamedan devotee, one of the most unprepossessing creatures I ever saw—in fact, ugliness itself—about five feet ten inches in height, old and wrinkled, with filthy rags about her person, and an immense number of charms, packed up in red leather bags attached to each other and suspended round her neck in the form of a necklace, reaching considerably below her waist. I really never saw anything so frightful, such a fiendlike specimen of humanity. She said that hearing I was about to depart alone to brave the dangers of the desert, and to tempt the ready daggers of those midnight assassins the Adaiel, she had called to give me her blessing. Having come for so charitable a purpose I could not do less than make her a present, and accordingly gave her four pieces of salt, upon which she arose and with uplifted hands blessed me and said, in a sort of prophetic tone, that by the grace of God I should return in safety to my country. The instant she quitted the hut Miriam and Sayad kissed my right hand, and the former said, "The Lord be praised that caused you to behave as you did towards that woman! she has blessed

B 1485—70

you, and her words never fall to the ground. Now I know that you will return in safety to your country." Better this, certainly, than that she had cursed me. It appears that her father was a very devout Mohamedan, and died when she was very young, since which she has taken up her abode at his tomb, living on the charity of strangers. She is about sixty years of age and a virgin. Scarcely a caravan arrives or departs without a collection being made for her. On the following day I was sitting alone in my hut and meditating upon what I had seen and heard the day before, when I received a message from one Alee Arab, a Tajuran, begging me to come and see his slave-girl, who was very sick. I went to his house, about half a mile off, and saw her, a poor child of about ten years of age, a native of Garagin. They told me that she had not eaten anything for many days, that she had no pain but would scarcely answer the questions put to her. Poor thing! she appeared to be actually pining away. She was brought here but a few weeks back, and no doubt she was fretting for parents, sisters, and brothers. I recommended that she should be treated with kindness, and that attention should be paid to her slightest wants, so that, if possible, she might be led to think less of her home and friends.

On the 31st of October, hearing that the King had returned to Angollala, I left at daybreak to pay my respects to him, and also to see how it fared with my countrymen. I arrived at Angellala at four o'clock in the evening. Itoo Habti brought me a message from the King "My son, why did you remain behind? you did not act well in remaining. Did I not tell you I should be away only ten days? Have my people behaved well?" I replied that I had difficulty in procuring beasts of burden, and that his people had behaved well; and I sent my congratulations to His Majesty on his success.

The following day I had an interview with the King, who assured me that he had given orders that I was to receive every assistance from the Wulasma Mohamed and his people, and that I might depart from his kingdom as soon as I wished. I returned to Alio Amba the same evening, a pleasant ride of about seven hours.

The King had been very successful in his expedition; the unfortunate victims were the Finfinny tribe of Gallas, who inhabited a fertile valley about fifty miles to the south of Angollala. The royal forces fell upon them by surprise, and it is said slew about four thousand men, women, and children, drove off all their cattle, to the number of nearly twelve thousand, and destroyed the whole of their crops by fire.

The barbarities committed by this Christian people almost exceed belief. There is a savageness in Abyssinian warfare unheard of in other parts of the globe I believe—I trust so, for humanity's sake. It is that having slain their foe, they proceed to mutilate the body, the virile member of which they cut off and exhibit as a proof of the undaunted courage of the warrior. Fifteen thousand of these disgusting trophies were exhibited before the King the day after the battle—battle forsooth! it was like a battle between wolves and sheep; there was little or no resistance.

Imagine the scene the day after the battle. The King, having caused a sort of temporary throne to be erected, sat in state to receive the accounts of the acts of prowess committed by his loyal subjects. The brave warriors rode past in succession, each, as he approached the throne, shouting forth the praises of the King in general and his own in particular, in something like the following words; "I am the King's slave. The King is a warrior; I also am a warrior. Behold in me the King's strong soldier! I have slain men." On this he raises his arm as if in the act of spearing some one, and exhibits the disgusting trophies hanging from his waist, Who can boast of the superiority of human nature after witnessing a scene like this? And what is the close of the day's proceedings! A night worthy to follow such a day, a night spent in the grossest debauchery. Verily a handful of brave men would have crushed the hosts of the Christian despot in a few hours. Christian did I say? Ay, Christian, but only in name. No wonder that the surrounding nations should prefer, ay, the *light* of paganism to such *dark* Christianity! One anecdote and I have done with this subject. In the midst of rejoicing and congratulations, a message was brought to the monarch that a Galla had been discovered in a tree, which was instantly surrounded by hundreds of the Amhara. The King thought this a fitting opportunity for his friends the "gipsies" (or English) to show their valour, and requested Harris to go and shoot the unfortunate man. Upon his declining so great an honour the King himself went to the spot with his rifle, and, taking deliberate aim, shot him in the leg. The poor fellow dropped to the ground and was about to be speared by the Amhara, but the King stayed them—a solitary instance of mercy. He had adjured the King by the "life" of Woosun Juggut (the King's father, dead some twenty-eight years) to spare him, and he *was* spared. The morning after I returned to Alio Amba, namely, the 2nd of November, I was disturbed by a great noise between Miriam, my worthy hostess, and her uncle. It appeared that during the night my mules had got loose and committed trespass by breaking through the hedge surrounding his dwelling. He had taken great offence at Miriam's receiving an *infidel* into her house, and thought this a good opportunity of showing his contempt; however, I did not interfere, for Miriam had much better assistance in one of her own sex, the wife of a Mohamedan priest living next door, and between the two the old man was completely driven out of the field, and compelled to retreat. Marvel not; the tongue was the weapon.

In the evening the priest came to see me, and we had a long chat; he was very friendly and said "Don't let that old man's words disturb you; I have plenty of room at the back of my house; tie your mules there." This man became to me quite a companion, and tended much to while away the time. By birth an Edjou Galla, when young he had professed Mohamedanism, and I believe was sincere in his profession: he was one in whom there was no guile. He had seen but little of the world, yet was not an ignorant man, and he had less bigotry than any Mohamedan I have ever met with.

One morning, the 6th of November, I was on the point of setting out for Ankobar to visit my friends there, when I was called to visit one of the Harrargi who had received a severe wound on the head in a drunken row the preceding evening. It was of no avail my declaring my total want of surgical skill; the only answer I got was "All white men are skilled in surgery;" so I had to do what I could. The wound was on the left side, from the crown to near the left temple, inflicted by a sharp crease or dagger. I plastered his head up, bid him live quietly, and in about a fortnight he was quite well. The person who had bestowed this mark of regard on him was sentenced to pay a German crown as the price of blood; he had also to pay five pieces of salt, or a quarter of a dollar, to the Governor of the town, and the same sum to Abdool Liki, Chief of the Harrargi. Had the man died there could have been no compromise, but life for life. This is only one of the many disputes that occurred during my sojourn here. From my treatment of this individual my fame spread far and wide, and I was daily visited by many people for medicine for real or imaginary diseases, protection against the "evil eye" being the most common demand.

On the 14th of November I received a visit from Jalee, nephew of the Wulasma Mohamed. As it is said he has great influence with his uncle, I made him a present of a few dollars, a looking-glass, &c. He declared in the most solemn manner that I should be forwarded on my journey as I desired, that his uncle had sent for guides, and that I should depart in six days.

His six days were exactly two months. One of the principal Harrar merchants called, and promised every assistance, but I afterwards found out that it was merely done to ascertain whether I really intended going to Harrar or not; for from this day reports were put constantly in circulation regarding the dangers of the road, and the hatred that the Emir of Harrar had against all strangers, but particularly against "infidels."

On the 18th I went to Ankobar, and this day the King made his triumphal entry. Not having my uniform with me I could not witness it. For the first time the glorious ensign of Old England was displayed at the *Residency*. I returned in the evening to Alio Amba. On the 22nd I paid a visit to the King with the intention of obtaining his signature to a letter of introduction to the Emir of Harrar. The courtyard was thronged with workmen of every description, busily employed under the eye of the monarch. Some of the principal people of the kingdom were in attendance on the monarch—Itoo Melkoo, Master of the Horse; Itoo Kotama, General of the Fusiliers; the Alafa Wolda Geosgis, Head of the Church. The King was evidently in a bad humour, so I did not present the letter, deeming the time unfavourable. It appeared he had asked one of the members of the Embassy to give his rifle, but received a pistol instead. I again returned to Alio Amba.

23rd.—My fame is now completely established as a master of medicine, much against my own will, for should a man die I should have the credit of having killed him: I have therefore to be extremely cautious. To-day the Deputy Governor of the village called on behalf of his brother, an old man about fifty years of age. "My brother," said the applicant, "in former years was a great orator, so much so that when he rose up to speak men marvelled at his eloquence, but the hand of fate had fallen heavily upon him, he had been smitten with disease, caused no doubt by the evil eye of some envious person falling upon him. He was sick for about a year, nigh unto death, but at last recovered, and from that day his speech failed him! he became a silent man." Now I imagined that he had become dumb, but to my great astonishment the individual himself shouted out: "But it is not always so with me: there are times when I can speak as before, but at others, when my heart is full, the tongue refuses to perform its part." This I was obliged to declare beyond my comprehension altogether. The old man departed, evidently much displeased and disappointed. From the Wulasma there was a message received by the Harrargi to the effect that he had sent to the chiefs of the Adaiel to prepare guides for them, and that he expected they would be in readiness to depart in six days, and that I should accompany them; whereon a general meeting was called in the market-place, and a great discussion arose as to the propriety of my travelling with them, one old man saying "Have not the Adaiel sworn to murder any Feringhee that shall attempt to pass their road? Will not *our* lives be endangered by his presence? And even granting that we escape and arrive in safety at Harrar, who will be answerable to the Emir for having brought a stranger into his kingdom?" It was decided that I should not accompany them.

Another greybeard then arose and said "Who has shown the Captain this road? Who has purchased his mules and asses for him? Who has purchased his provisions for him? Is it not Hajji Sayad? Behold, there he stands!" Whereupon the whole assembly shouted out "Hajji Sayad is the man." "At this moment," said Hajji Sayad, for he it was that told me all this, "I could have died with fear, for they are a bad people; however, Abdool Liki took my part, and said that I had done no evil:" the meeting then broke up.

On the following day, accompanied by Hajji Sayad and my servant Adam, I proceeded to Gouchoo, in order to acquaint the Wulasma with all that the Harrar people had said. He appeared to be much enraged with them and said "Who are they? they came not here neither can they depart hence without the assistance of the tribes. Fear not; you shall go with them; the day after to-morrow I will see the King, and all shall be arranged satisfactorily." Having partaken of refreshments as before, I took leave. He sent a guide with me to show me the tombs of his ancestors (nothing remarkable in them, by the bye, no inscriptions), and also the King's " garden," as it is called, in which there are a few plantain trees and sugarcanes; why it is called a garden I am at a loss to understand. I returned to Alio Amba in the evening.

In the morning I set out for Ankobar to tell His Majesty also the determination that the Harrar people had come to. He tried to dissuade me from attempting the journey, and begged I would remain in his country; but at length, finding me determined, he carefully perused the letter to the Emir of Harrar which had been written in Amharic, having a translation in Arabic, ordered his seal to be brought and attached it to the document. The letter was as follows, as translated by the Reverend P. L. Krapf: " May this letter from Sahela Selassie, King of Shoa, Efat, and the Galla, reach the hands of Aboo Bekr, the Ruler of Harrar! How are you? Are you well? Are you quite well? I am well. The bearer of this letter is Captain Barker; he is an Englishman and commands a vessel in the sea of Tajura. He has been ordered by his Queen to return soon to his country; now, in order that he might do this, he wished to return by the nearest road, and begged of me a letter of recommendation to you. I am thinking of him very much; and I wish that on his road, and when he passes through your country, nothing should do him harm. I therefore wish that you should protect him perfectly, and assist him in all that he wants. The love which you show to him I will consider as shown to myself, and it will give me pleasure to hear that he has reached the sea-coast in safety by your assistance. He came to me by order of his Queen, and I am in great friendship with her; if you will show kindness to him, my name as well as yours will be honoured beyond the Great Sea. A traveller when in a far country has no father, no mother, no relations; it is therefore becoming in the watchmen of kingdoms, in the Kings and Rulers of Provinces, that they should protect travellers and assist them in all that they desire. If they do this they will be blessed by God and honoured by men. I command you this; I command you this." The seal was attached to the lower corner; it is in Arabic characters, for the Emir of Harrar is a Mohamedan. In writing to Christians he has a seal in the Amharic character.

Having obtained the above document I returned to Alio Amba with a lighter heart than I had had for a long time, thinking that before such a weighty document all difficulties would vanish. But alas! man is doomed to suffer disappointments at the time when he least expects them. No sooner had I quitted Alio Amba in the morning than the Harrar people seized my interpreter, Sayad, and gave him a sound beating, for having gone with me to Gouchoo, and as they expressed it, shown me the way to Harrar. He could hardly walk from the bruises he had from the sole of his foot to the crown of his head. I wanted to set out and complain to the King, but he begged me not to do so, for if any of them were punished they would kill him.

What with preparing for the journey and attending to my patients my time is fully occupied. On the 4th of December accounts were received that there had been several disturbances on the frontier, and that more murders had been committed at Tajura. On the 8th I sent my interpreter and Adam to the Wulasma to beg of him to assist me on my road; they returned with a civil answer. When is all this to end? When shall I get away? On the 10th of December the Wulasma came to Alio Amba, and took up his abode there for the night. The following morning, at an early hour, he sent for me; I proceeded to his house with Sayad and Adam. He received me kindly, and placed me on his right hand beside him. The principal people of the village called to pay their respects, and a great number of the Harrar people. The Fat'hah or opening chapter of the Koran was read, and after that coffee and a small piece of bread were handed round to each person present.

The Wulasma then pointed to one of the Tajura people present, and said to me "That man will convey you in safety to Tajura." I then declared that I would not go that road; that he was aware of the vile murders that had been committed in the valleys of Goongoonteh; that I could never pass that spot; that the blood of my slaughtered countrymen called for justice; that I had no doubt this would be obtained in due time, but that rather than return by that route I would beg my bread from door to door in Abyssinia. I then produced the King's letter; the seal he acknowledged was the King's, but said that the letter could not be his. On this I rose up and retired, leaving him with the Chief of the Harrargi.

In the afternoon I had again a private audience with him, his nephew Jalee being the only one present besides Sayad and myself. They both swore in the most solemn manner that I should go the road I wished. I told him that unless I left soon I should die, that I was at the mercy of bands of savages, that my servants had been beaten, that indeed my life was a burden to me.

I occasionally went to Ankobar to see my friends there; once during my absence there my servant Mohamed, an Arab lad about sixteen years of age, was beaten by the townspeople for discharging one of my fowling-pieces. At another time a man rushed at Adam with a crease (they had had some words); one of the bystanders in attempting to lay hold of the man's arm caught the crease instead, and was severely wounded. The sight of blood prevented all further disturbance. However, I thought I had waited patiently long enough, so I determined upon sending the King a letter, which I was enabled to do through the kind assistance of the Reverend P. L. Krapf, and which was presented by Captain Harris on the 2nd of January 1842.

The letter was thus worded:—"May this letter from Captain Barker come to the hands of Sahela Selassie, King of Shoa, Efat, and the Galla! Are you well? Are you quite well? I am well. May you bear me in love! You know that I have been ordered by my Queen to return to my country. You consented to my going by way of Harrar, and gave me in kindness a letter of recommendation to the ruler of that province. I have now been detained nearly three months at Alio Amba; no kafilah has left during that time. My heart is very sore; will you therefore, as a kind father, take away my distress, and give orders that I may accompany the kafilah which is to leave in about fifteen days, should you not furnish me with a special guide before that time. My ship is waiting for me at Zeyla. If I do not return soon they will think some evil has befallen me, and my Queen will be angry. I beg of you therefore to give orders that I may accompany the first kafilah to Harrar. I know that you can and will do this." About the same time I received a message from the Wulasma to hasten my preparations for the journey, as he had procured me a guide. I asked for what road; he replied "even to Tajura." So I said to the messenger. "Return to the Wulasma and say ꞏ you have promised in the most solemn manner, calling the Most High God to witness, that you will forward me to Harrar; now if you cannot do this say so; I will go to my country by way of Gondar.' Tell the Wulasma he has sworn to forward me, and he must do it. Shall I have to say that in Shoa they are all liars? These are my last words to the Wulasma."

January 4th.—Proceeded to Ankobar. The King returned a verbal answer to my letter through Major Harris that he had been very angry with the Wulasma for having detained me so long upon the frontier and issued orders that I should be forwarded on my journey immediately.

January 7th.—The Wulasma being at Ankobar I called upon him. He said "Why did you write to the King? He has been very angry with me." I replied that I had remained quiet too long, that I was compelled to write to clear myself in the eyes of my Government for having remained so long after I had been recalled. He said, "Well, now the day of your departure is nigh at hand; go to Alio Amba, prepare your provisions, I have a good guide for you." I accordingly repaired to Alio Amba, gave the necessary instructions for the purchase of provisions, and returned to Ankobar in the evening.

On the following morning I waited on the King to take leave. I assured him that I was fully sensible of his kindness to me and my countrymen, that it was not of my own will that I was about to leave his country, but that, as he was aware, I had been recalled. I wished His Majesty a long and prosperous reign, that he might be victorious over all his enemies, and that his name might spread throughout the world as a great king and conqueror. In return he wished me a safe and speedy journey. I then took leave and went to Alio Amba.

Sunday, January 9th.—Yesterday there was a meeting of the Harrar merchants, at which it was decided that they would not travel with me, that if I went their road they would remain behind. Haji Sayad was well-nigh getting a second beating; yet they are all friendly in their manner towards me, especially the principal people.

I was one day going to Ankobar when I was thrown from my mule; some of those who saw it came immediately to my assistance, and caught the mule for me, offering me the loan of one of theirs—the one I was riding was a borrowed one, my own being out grazing—and indeed on all occasions treated me with great deference. The Wulasma came to Alio Amba, as he had promised, told me not to care about the Harrar people, that he had a good guide, and that I must come to his house to be introduced to him.

I accordingly set out for Gouchoo on the morning of the 10th of January. On arriving there I was treated, as at other times, with the greatest kindness and hospitality. The Wulasma had been detained on the road by some appeal from the villagers, and did not arrive till the evening; my guide arrived about noon. Sayad immediately recognised him as the " protector " of a kafilah of Harrargi some three years back, who were plundered as soon as they were out of his " protection," because he had demanded a hundred and eighty pieces of cloth and they would only give him eighty. The kafilah was attacked by his people; he himself did not appear:—scarcely a soul escaped to tell the tale. A pleasant fellow for a guide certainly!

The name of this individual is Datah Mohamed, Chief of the Seedy Habroo, one of the sub-tribes of the Debeni. His height is five feet ten inches, his age forty-five years; he has small twinkling eyes, deep-arched wrinkles over either eyebrow, meeting at the bridge of the nose; thick, bushy eyebrows; one of his front teeth black, apparently decayed; hair thin but long, and sticking out stiff like porcupine quills, just turning grey. His dress consists of merely a filthy rag secured round his loins by the narrow leather belt of his crease or dagger, and barely reaching to the knees, and an equally dirty rag thrown carelessly over the shoulders; add to this dirty black nails, a roll of tobacco stowed away under the upper lip, and the most villainous expression that ever disgraced the human visage, and the picture is complete.

He had a shield, spear, and crease; his only ornament was a black horn armlet worn above the elbow. The dagger was about fourteen inches long, well curved and sharp, double-edged and much worn. In the evening the Wulasma arrived and introduced me to the worthy I have been endeavourng to give a sketch of; he then presented a sheep to us, which we were both to partake of together. In a marvellously short time the sheep was killed, and a considerable portion of it simmering in an earthen vessel over the fire with just sufficient water, by the bye to keep the pot from burning—for water has to be brought from the foot of the hill, about a mile and a half distant—and before it had time to be well warmed through I found myself seated on the ground endeavouring to partake thereof. I was obliged to eat a little, well seasoned with red pepper; my new "protector," however, enjoyed himself amazingly. All present were invited to the feast of friendship, my servants even. Adam I instructed to pay due attention to the worthy. (It is considered a joint compliment here to cut off a titbit and force it into the mouth of an individual you may delight to honour.) He did so almost to choking him. Coffee was afterwards served. However I had friends in camp, who, as soon as it was dusk, brought me something much more palatable, in the shape of fine white bread, sausages, and other dainties, from the Wulasma's table, and some "tej" or hydromel, far superior to any we ever received from the King's kitchen. I had made a great friend of the Wulasma's youngest son, by giving him a little powder and one or two gilt buttons. He was a fine young lad, about ten years of age, evidently the spoilt child of the family, and he was continually backwards and forwards bringing me something. The most welcome gifts were a couch and a new Abyssinian cloth large enough to form bed and covering into the bargain. So that my first night spent (I trust I shall never have to spend another, notwithstanding) in the state prison of the King of Shoa passed off agreeably enough.

In the morning we all assembled in one of the inner rooms, a private room of the Wulasma's, and made the final arrangements with my guide. The Wulasma on his part was to give him certain presents now, and others when he received intelligence of my safe arrival at the coast. I was also to give him a present of cloth; a horse, a spear and shield he was to get in my name from the Wulasma.

The Wulasma said: "This is the best guide I can procure you; all the Adel are bad people. He knows his interest and will protect you." He told me the same story that Sayad had told me regarding him, with this addition, that two of his children, a son and daughter, some months after the transaction, venturing to the frontier village of Fari to purchase grain, were there seized and conveyed to the prison at Gouchoo. On the receipt of this intelligence the tribe were for setting out at once and rescuing them by force, but the old man said "Nay, I will rescue them." He waited a short period, and then proceeded to Fari with a present of a few bullocks for the Wulasma, and was immediately forwarded on to Gouchoo. The Wulasma, much surprised to see him, taxed him with the attack on the Harrar kafilah. He stoutly denied the charge and said "Had I done so do you think I would have ventured here? I have brought a small present for you; release my children, for what have *they* done? do to *me* as you please; put me on the fire and roast me." The Wulasma, struck with the boldness of the man, immediately ordered the release of his children, and having feasted them and their father permitted them to return to their native wilds.

"Now," said the Wulasma as he finished his tale, "they have tasted the air of Gouchoo, and you know how dearly the 'Bedoo' loves the free air of the desert; so fear him not." By this politic act the Wulasma has gained a much greater ascendancy over these wild sons of the desert than he would have done by harsh measures.

In the afternoon I returned to Alio Amba to make final preparations for my departure, and from thence proceeded to Ankobar to say goodbye to my countrymen.

On the 14th of January, having completed everything for my journey as far as my very limited means would allow, I addressed a petition to Captain Harris, of which the following is a copy:—

"*Alio Amba, January 14th, 1842.*

"Sir,—I have the honour to report my approaching departure from this kingdom, having at length obtained a guide to take me to Harrar.

"The Wulasma Mohamed Abogaz, in obedience to instructions from the King, came to this village on the 9th instant, for the purpose of sending me on with the people of Harrar, but they one and all declined to proceed with me, on the plea that the Emir would probably confiscate their property, and perhaps kill the leading members of the kafilah, for bringing a stranger into his kingdom. On hearing this I told the Wulasma that I had not asked the Harrargi to take me on; that I looked to *him* to carry out the instructions of the King; all that I required was a guide. He consented to furnish me with one, and begged I would accompany him to Gouchoo on the following morning.

"I cannot divest myself of the idea that my proceeding to Harrar will be greatly to the advantage of British interests in this country, for I feel assured that a speedy communication with the sea-coast is all that is wanting to render the residence of the British mission at the Court of Shoa of the greatest importance towards carrying into effect the humane intentions of all well-disposed persons relative to the abolition of slavery and the civilisation of Africa.

"On the 10th instant, accompanied by a relative of the Wulasma, I proceeded at an early hour to Gouchoo, where, on my arrival, I was treated, as at other times, with the greatest kindness and hospitality. The Wulasma did not arrive till the evening, when he introduced me to Datah Mohamed, brother of Bedur, one of the chiefs of the Debeni, a tribe of the Adaiel, as the person he had selected for me as a guide from hence to Emier, and Bedur is to forward me from thence to Harrar. All arrangements being concluded, the Wulasma presented us with a sheep, which was immediately slaughtered, it being the custom among the Adaiel, at the conclusion of all arrangements of this nature, to slaughter an animal, of which both parties—indeed, all present—partake.

"On the morning of the 11th we again talked over my approaching journey. Datah Mohamed declared that I should be forwarded with a strong band, the Wulasma assuring him that as soon as he heard of my safe arrival on the coast he would handsomely reward him.

"I am at a loss to account for the extraordinary behaviour of the Harrargi, many of whom had promised to accompany me, and in fact assisted me in making preparations for the journey; probably they thought I did not intend to go, but finding me determined they have not only refused to go with me, but by repeated threats have so frightened Hajji Sayad that he also has declined to travel with me. I am the more provoked at his conduct, as up to yesterday, he constantly assured me of his determination to accompany me wherever I went, and I am now unable to obtain another person in his room; consequently but little information can be gained on the road, from my total ignorance of the language of the tribes.

"I beg, however, to bring to your notice the great assistance I have received from the Wulasma Mohamed Abogaz and his people in general, more especially his nephews Jalee and Johar. My limited funds would not allow me to reward them as I wished; I therefore recommend them to you. Nor must I forget Abdool Liki, Chief of the Harrargi, who on all occasions treated me with great kindness, but who, unfortunately, had not the power to overrule the prejudices of the majority of his countrymen. A most absurd story was put in circulation that he had received a bribe of two hundred dollars from me to betray his country: no doubt these reports will be conveyed to the ear of the Emir.

"It is my intention to quit this early to-morrow morning, and I trust that I shall quit Chanoo (the frontier) the following day. Notwithstanding the difficulties thrown in the way of my proceeding, by the ill-feeling displayed by the majority of the Harrargi, and the defection of Hajji Sayad at this the eleventh hour, I am still sanguine of succeeding in gaining the consent of the Emir of Harrar to the establishment of a safe and direct route between Teejlol and Shoa.

I have the honour to be, &c.,
W. C. BARKER.

To Captain W. C. Harris,
  Bombay Engineers,
    On special duty at the Court of Shoa."

And now before taking my departure from Alio Amba, I will endeavour to give some account of a place where I spent a weary time of three months, and in so doing will copy my official letter on the subject to Captain Harris, dated 7th January 1842.

" The village of Alio Amba is situated about five miles to the E.S.E. of Ankobar, and is built on an elevation of about three hundred feet above the adjacent valleys, inaccessible on the eastern side. Two insignificant streams wash the base to the south and north, dignified with the appellations of Alio Amba Wah and Jami.

" Eastward, as far as the eye can reach, extend the inhospitable plains of the Adaiel, bounded on the north by the Ayaboo and adjacent range, and on the south by the mountains of the Eto Galla. The lakes of Laahdoo, or 'water yet distant,' and Ailihullo, are plainly distinguishable and towards the close of the rainy season the river Hawash may be seen, but only about the time of the sun's rising.

" To the north-east, about four miles, is the hill of Gouchoo, on the summit of which is the house of the Wulasma Mohamed Abogaz, beneath which, in vaults, are confined the state prisoners of the kingdom of Shoa, the only crime of many of whom is that of being related to the reigning monarch, and for which they are condemned by a barbarous policy to a life of perpetual confinement.

" To the north the mountain of Emameret rears its proud summit some fifteen hundred feet above the adjacent range; according to legend it once towered to the very skies.

" Southward about three miles, is the village of Abder Russool, the grand slave-market of Shoa.

" The surrounding country is highly cultivated, producing various kinds of *jowári*, wheat, barley, &c., and a grain called 'teff' by the natives, and which, made into bread, forms the principal food of the lower classes. The *jowári* in the more secluded parts grows to the height of from fifteen to eighteen feet, a height I have rarely seen it attain in other countries.

" The innumerable villages which crown every rising ground give to the country a pleasing appearance, which would be greatly heightened by the presence of a few trees, but in this particular Abyssinian, or rather Shoan, scenery is, generally speaking, deficient. The village of Alio Amba consists of about three hundred houses or huts—for they hardly deserve the name of houses—and contains a fluctuating population, amounting at present to about eight hundred souls, chiefly Harrar merchants and Angola, with some few Amhara.

" The principal market of the kingdom of Shoa is held here every Friday, when the villagers supply their wants for the ensuing week; all kinds of grain, horses, mules, asses, horned cattle, and sheep, hides, cotton, cotton cloths, zinc, copper, beads, &c., &c.,—in fact, every article of domestic economy, as well as for the use of the merchant, is sold. The bustle and din of human voices on this day is particularly striking; during the rest of the week the village has almost the appearance of being deserted, except when its quiet is disturbed by some drunken brawl. At an early hour people of both sexes may be seen hurrying to and fro, while from every quarter people from the adjacent villages may be seen pouring in—Galla, Amhara, Angola, and Adaiel—all in wild confusion. The market is held on a clear space to the west of the village, where the Governor and his myrmidons may be observed availing themselves of the scanty protection against the sun's rays afforded them by an almost withered and solitary tree. About noon the confusion is at its height, and by 5 P.M. the village subsides into its usual quiet. Until within a few days Alio Amba was governed by a Christian (who is now in confinement for embezzling the royal revenue), but the present ruler is a Mohamedan, an Angola by birth, by name Aboo Bekr. It may be as well to mention that the Mohamedan subjects of Sahela Selassie are called generally Angola, in contradistinction to the Christians, who are called Amhara. The Angola are the principal inhabitants of the adjacent villages, and hence towards the eastern frontier.

"As above mentioned, Alio Amba is chiefly inhabited by Harrar merchants, who reside here until they have disposed of their merchandise, and then return with slaves to their native country, a fresh swarm taking their place.

"Having once taken up their residence here they are loth to quit for some time, which is not at all surprising when it is considered that with the produce of their merchandise brought from Harrar they purchase slaves at Abder Russool, which they take to Gedem, a journey of only two or three days, and there dispose of at a profit of from thirty to fifty per cent. There they buy the 'amoolee' or salt money at the rate of twenty-three to twenty-five per German crown which they sell here at from eighteen to twenty. The hire of an ass for the trip is five 'amoolee;' having made a few such profitable trips they are enabled to purchase prime slaves, with which they proceed to their country, and from thence to Berbera or Zeyla.

"That it costs them such a mere trifle to live comfortably, according to their rude ideas of comfort, is also another reason for their remaining here. The morality of both sexes is at so low an ebb that but few resort to marriage, and even that is only a slight check upon them. On the departure of their liege lords, the women live in open adultery, and even during their husband's residence here it is said are not at all sparing of their favours, an indifference existing on the part of the men as to the conduct of their wives which is most surprising, more especially when it is considered that they are Mohamedans, who are usually rather particular on this score.

"The marriage ceremony is merely a mutual agreement between the parties in the presence of the Kazi, when the bridegroom settles a certain sum upon the bride, which is hers in case of divorce. A hundred pieces of salt, or five German crowns (about one guinea), is considered a large sum; the parties then retire, but not to rest, for the friends of each, both male and female, assemble to converse with them for several nights in succession.

"The knot which when once tied it is so difficult a matter to loose in more civilised countries, costs but little trouble to untie here, for it is only necessary for the husband to repeat three times in the presence of the Kazi 'I divorce thee,' to pay the sum agreed upon at their marriage, and the matter is settled.

"The Mohamedan law is rather curious on these points. The prophet, as a check to the too frequent resort to the 'triple divorce,' ordained that the parties should not marry again until the lady had married and been again divorced, so that in the event of a man in a moment of anger saying to his wife 'I divorce thee by the triple divorce' and repenting of it in his cooler moments, he has only to procure a 'dullal' or agent, to whom the wife is married, and with whom she must retire and remain alone one entire night, the said 'dullal' for a consideration abstaining from all intercourse. Instances have been known, however, where they have not been able to resist, where the spirit has been willing but the flesh weak,' and as she has become the wife of the 'dullal' no one can compel him to divorce her.

"One 'amoolee,' value twopence halfpenny, is generally given each market day by those who are not married, to the women in whose houses they live, which is sufficient to purchase provisions for both parties for the ensuing week. Occasionally a quantity of flesh is bought in addition to the above, about eight pounds for one 'amoolee,' which is cut into strips and dried: most of their houses are ornamented with this dried meat, which is called 'inantah.' They have only two methods of cooking, either grilling on the coals, or making a sort of stew highly seasoned with red pepper.

"'Tulla', or beer, of which they are very fond, is made from barley-water fermented, six jars of which, each containing about two gallons and a half, is sold for one 'amoolee.' Weak, unpalatable trash as it is to the taste of Europeans, yet, as above mentioned, these people are very partial to it, drinking it night after night till they become intoxicated.

"I was called one morning and saw a repetition of the case of the Harrar man I cured of a severe wound caused by the *potency* of their favourite beverage.

"Many instances of the kind occurred during my stay. It appears that the Harrargi are very fond of drawing the crease; they do not, however, seem desirous of killing, but merely of marking for life. The so-called Governor has not the power to prevent the frequent occurrence of such disturbances, and perhaps he secretly rejoices over them.

"The Chief of the Harrargi at this place is duly appointed by the Emir of Harrar: the present man is Abdool Liki. At Debra Berhan, at the review, he applied to me for medicine for his eyes, which were very weak. On returning to Ankobar I found him laid up with fever; a little opening medicine soon restored him to health, and cold applications cured his eyes. This was my first acquaintance with the Harrargi. I privately related to him my intention of visiting his country. He advised me strongly against attempting such a step, but at last allowed that backed by a letter from Sahela Selassie there would be no danger; at the same time he assured me of his friendship, but said he was afraid to assist me in the matter. Abdool Liki will remain here till another person is sent to relieve him; he has full power to settle all disputes between his countrymen, and can chastise and fine them; from his decision they dare not appeal except to the Emir.

"The Angola are generally employed in weaving; their machinery is of very inferior construction; the cloth is, however, well made and cheap. The men wear short loose inexpressibles. The Harrargi more generally wear a 'fatah' or striped cloth around the middle, reaching to the knees, and over all the Abyssinian cloth or 'shumah.' None but Hajjis, or those who have performed the pilgrimage to the holy city Mecca, wear turbans. The women wear a kind of chemise, very loose, which reaches the ground. They permit their hair, which they plait, to grow long (contrary to the practice of Amhara), and it hangs down below the shoulders. Both Mohamedan and Christian women practise the absurd custom of shaving their eyebrows. The former are distinguished not only by allowing the hair to grow, but also by a red cloth laid over the head lightly and buttoned under the chin.

"Both sexes are exceedingly superstitious, and, notwithstanding their avowed contempt for the white strangers, are obliged to confess that these strangers are superior to themselves in several points. Many were the visits I received from persons residing at a great distance who came to be cured of real or imaginary diseases, or to procure medicines for their relations. One man begged earnestly for medicine for his daughter, residing at Angollala, upon whom the 'evil eye' had fallen, and many others consulted me for equally absurd things (here will perhaps be recollected the case of the man whose speech had failed him). There were others with more reasonable complaints; these I had pleasure in relieving.

"The following story will give some idea of the skill of the Galla as physicians. A native of Harrar on his way to this place fell sick of a fever; a Galla of the Eto undertook to cure him. Having made him insensible by means of some powerful herbs or drugs, he, with the assistance of several others, cut and burnt him from the crown of his head to the sole of his foot. A more miserable object I never beheld; his whole body was covered with scars. He was one of those who came to be cured, complaining that he could neither eat nor drink without pain. No wonder! his skin was so drawn up, by the innumerable cuts that had been made in it, that it had actually become too 'taut' for his body. It is scarcely necessary to add that the skilful Galla physician waited not for his patient to recover, but decamped without his fee.

"To return to my narrative. The yearly revenues of Alio Amba cannot be less than three thousand German crowns in cash besides the value of about two thousand in kind. Salt money alone pays an import duty of twenty per cent. As before mentioned, the slave-market is held at Abdar Russool; for each slave a head-tax is paid to the King of four "amoolee" or pieces of salt. When it is considered that the Berbera, Zeyla, Harrar, and Tajura markets are chiefly supplied from this, as well as Gedem, from whence they are sent to Gondar and Massowa, the annual import of slaves cannot be estimated at less than three thousand: they are principally brought from Garagin and the Galla countries to the south-west. Girls of from eight to fourteen years of age are sold at from twenty to forty dollars a head, boys of the same age at from twelve to twenty; above the age of fourteen the price of both sexes decreases.

"The merchants from Tigré and the north generally resort to Abder Russool. It is worthy of remark that though the Galla are mostly hostile to Sahela Selassie, yet they never molest the traders; persons can proceed singly from hence to any of the surrounding countries of the Galla, and even to Massowa, a journey of about thirty days for a messenger, without fear. Not so through the country of the Adaiel or Adel; this is frequently closed for months, and it is seldom safe for persons to journey alone either to Harrar or Tajura. I have endeavoured to ascertain the cause of the long detention of the Tajura and Harrar kafilahs. It would appear that it is really fear of the Adaiel, who at the close of the rainy season are to be met with in large parties along the road, but who again retire towards the highlands on either side as water and pasturage become scarce. The merchants would rather suffer all the inconveniences arising from a limited supply of water than expose themselves or their slaves to the knives of the blood-thirsty savages.

"It may not be out of place here to mention that during my residence at this town I have had several opportunities of confirming the account of Harrar I forwarded through you to Government on the 17th of September last, by the testimony of one Ali, an Egyptian, and several others.

"I also received the following account of the route from Kilulloo to Zeyla from Deeni, a native of Tajura, who pursued that route in the months of August and September 1840, being unable to proceed to Tajura for fear of the Mudaitoo, who were then at war with the Adaiel. The kafilah with which he travelled consisted of about fifty camels, carrying provisions for the slaves and people of the kafilah, altogether amounting to about two hundred and fifty souls, of which nearly two hundred were slaves, mere children, of both sexes.

"They quitted Kilulloo under the guidance of Sayad ibn Gagaioo, and on the morning of the tenth day arrived at Zeyla. The first day's march was over a hilly country and through the Wady Hoombelli, a stream of brackish water, and from thence over tolerable ground to Jebel Warrah Ambili (this hill is marked in the Trigonometrical Survey of the Bay of Tajura), one day's journey from Taccoodah, which is about four miles to the south-west of Zeyla. As it was the rainy season they had water in abundance the whole way. During the dry season there are but four watering-places. Quitting Kilulloo they marched one day without water; at the close of the second day they arrived at a place called Hurrohwah, good water: the third day there was no water; the fourth day good water at Metta; the sixth day hot springs, called in the Eesah language Biya Karrah, or bitter water; the eighth day at Hoombelli, the ninth day at Warrah Ambilli, the tenth day at Taccoodah; he could not remember the names of the intermediate halting-places.

"The road is safe, as the Eesah fear the Emir of Zeyla on the one side and the Woemah on the other; with the latter they frequently intermarry.

"I also obtained the following information of the route hence to Massowa from one Hajji Mohamed, a native of Tigré (uncle to Hussain, the bearer of presents from the King of Shoa to the British Government in September 1840). He had just arrived from the country of the Wooloo Galla with the ostensible object of inquiring after his nephew, but from his very short stay at Alio Amba and from certain reports here I am led to suppose that he was sent by Beeroo, the Mohamedan ruler of the country, to seek for medical aid for that prince, and to ascertain the object of the residence of the British Mission at the Court of Shoa. He frequently alluded to the illness under which Beeroo laboured, a disease only too common in Abyssinia, and from which neither king nor peasant appears to be exempt.

"The following are the names of the halting-places between this and Massowa:—Bagotk Agamooti Shurikoorgi, Gooje Amba, Johivaha, Wesper, Jendoo, Majetti, Woola-hiya: thus far through the territories of the King of Shoa. Then Bowkoonoo Ancharoo, the principal market of the Galla; Antoori Kutli, through Beeroo's country; then Mursa Goorah, through the country of Ali Malla; from thence five days to Antalow, through the country of the Areeah Galla, who are represented as being, much after the manner of the Adaiel, divided into petty tribes, each under its own chieftain. From Antalow to Massowa thirteen days, or a total of thirty-three days from Alio Amba, the greater part through a thickly populated country. Massowa is about 240 miles from Alio Amba; this would give an average of about thirteen miles a day.

"I regretted much that the man made so short a stay at Alio Amba; he is one of those Mohamedans who gain their livelihood by trading from place to place, and has visited Tajura, Aussah, Massowa, Gondar, and the Lake T'znai, and no doubt could give much interesting information about those places.

"In conclusion I have only to remark that I trust the time of my departure is now near at hand. The Harrargi are preparing for the journey. Having heard it rumoured that the Wulasma did not intend to allow me to depart before the arrival of Mohamed Ali, I addressed a letter to the King, which Mr. Krapf kindly translated for me into Amharic, and which, as you are aware of its contents, and of the King's answer thereto, I need not more than allude to.

"It is due, however, to myself to bring to your notice, for the information of Government, that no kafilah has left since the twenty-fifth of October. I would readily have availed myself of the first opportunity of returning to Aden, for my situation here has been truly an uncomfortable one, located amongst a set of savages in a rude hut barely affording shelter from the inclemency of the weather, and cut off from the society of my countrymen.

"I have the honour to be, &c.,
(Signed) W. C. BARKER.

"To
    Captain W. C. HARRIS, Bombay Engineers,
      On special duty at the Court of Shoa."

January 15th.—At an early hour I commenced packing for my weary journey. I really felt dispirited at the thought of leaving this place; it is true I had met with much opposition but at the same time I had also experienced much kindness. The man whom I thought I could place full confidence in, whom indeed I had considered indispensably necessary during the journey I was about to enter upon, had, alas! deceived me. Coming, after the evening meal and prayers, to the hut in which I lived, he threw himself at my feet, and with tears in his eyes endeavoured to dissuade me from carrying out my determination to start on the morrow; not being successful, he then declared to me that his countrymen had sworn to kill him if he accompanied me. I told him to be gone, that I wanted not the services of such a coward.

Of a truth, the reports brought up by the Adel were anything but pleasing. A party of two Turks and three Arabs, who had quitted some fourteen or fifteen days before, had, it was said, been attacked, and some of them murdered, and that the "Bedoos" had sworn that no Feringhee should pass through their country. This it was that had alarmed Hajji Sayad, and not him alone, for one of my servants, a stout, burly African, also refused to accompany me. Him, however, I would not allow to leave me, and as he was in my debt I went to the Governor of the village and told him that the man owed me money, and that unless it was paid me I should make the debt over to him, to be recovered for the benefit of the poor. The sum I had advanced to the man was no less than five German crowns, about a guinea, and for four German crowns I offered him to the Governor; at the same time, to show that I was not mercenarily inclined, I begged the worthy Governor to distribute the money amongst the poor. This was neither more nor less than offering him as a slave, at which he was so terrified that he was glad to brave all the dangers of the desert than become most probably a slave for life.

This matter being adjusted, to my own satisfaction at all events, at about eight o'clock in the morning we took our departure from the village of Alio Amba, accompanied for several miles by the villagers, who evinced great sympathy with us, many of them crying bitterly. Shortly after we were joined by Jalee, the nephew of the Wulasma, who accompanied us to Fari, furnished us with a house, and took charge of our cattle for us.

Sunday 16th.—The Wulasma arrived about noon, and sent me a present of five large loaves of bread.* I called upon him in the evening, showed him the King's letter, and requested a similar one from himself to the Emir of Harrar, which he promised should be ready by the following day. At about noon of the 17th, having concluded all arrangements with my guide, the Wulasma presented him with a spear, shield, and Abyssinian cloth, also the horse and cloth I had purchased for him; we then took leave and proceeded to Dabharah.

Fortunately for me, as will appear in the sequel, a çaravan quitted at the same time for Tajura, consisting of about fifteen of the natives of that place, who had with them fifty camels laden with provisions for the journey, about fifty male and twenty female slaves (mostly children of from six to ten years of age). This caravan was under the guidance of Ibrahim ibn Burantoo, who accompanied our party to Shoa, and always gave the orders for loading and unloading, &c., but we knew not then that he was our Ras-el-Kafilah (leader of the caravan). Owing to his generally disagreeable behaviour, he did not receive anything from the Mission on our arrival in Shoa.

---

* Let it not be supposed that when I speak of loaves of bread I mean the small loaves used in more civilised countries. These were on a much larger scale, circular, about eighteen inches in diameter, and about three inches thick, made of beautiful white wheaten flour.

This individual, a short time after the Wulasma had left, accused me of being the cause of his not having received a present, "for," said he, "you were the mouthpiece of the Commander (Harris). You loaded Izakh Kashim, the son of Ali Abi, and others, with presents, but to me you have given nothing. Now we shall see; you think to pass through the country of the 'Bedoos;' we shall see. I have as it were a knife in my stomach, which is continually cutting me; this knife you have placed there; but, Inshallah (God willing), it is now my turn; I will be quits with you; you don't know me." I replied: "It is true, I knew not that you were the leader of our caravan. You say that you have as it were a knife in your stomach; I can remove that knife. Those that treat me well shall be rewarded. Now I am about to return to my country. There, the Lord be praised! I have the means of rewarding my friends; those that treat me ill shall also receive their reward." Knowing that this man had it in his power to do me much mischief, I determined to gain him over to my interests. Accordingly, there being a young man in the caravan who spoke Arabic fluently, and who, moreover, was indebted to me for some medicines and a few trifling presents while in Shoa, I took him apart and begged of him to assist me as interpreter in the first place, and in the second quietly to explain to Ibrahim that he would gain much more by civility than the reverse, that if he treated me well I would reward him, if not, a line or two dropped to my friends at Aden would be sure to cause him misfortune. To this he readily consented, and soon induced Ibrahim to change his behaviour.

We were detained at Dabharah till the morning of the 19th, owing to one of the mules of the Ras-el-Kafilah having strayed, when we resumed our journey. As we pursued the route traversed by the Embassy it is needless for me to give a description of it; I shall merely remark that the country at this season assumes a much more lively appearance, grass being abundant. I observed also that there was much gum acacia on the trees by the roadside, which was gathered by the people as they passed.

At noon we halted under the shade of some venerable acacia trees, having been travelling since 7 A.M. Here we met six Bedouins of the Woemah tribe, who were going to Shoa; they gave an account of the disasters that had befallen the party that had preceded us. It appears that they were attacked by a party of the Takyle, an Arab boy was killed, and the rest were plundered of all they possessed. One man, an Arab, being mounted escaped, but they could not tell us whither he had gone, the remainder were taken under the "protection" of the Chief of the tribe. They further stated that a party was lying in wait for us on the banks of the Hawash. Two of my servants, my friend the African and a Greek servant of Captain Harris's, both large of carcass but small of heart, were for retracing their steps to Shoa, but I persuaded them to go on another day's journey, when I would be guided by circumstances, and doubtless their reports were exaggerated.

My guide proposed that, as we were all mounted, we should make a dash for it, but this was overruled by the Ras-el-Kafilah. The guide then sent off to one of the neighbouring tribes for assistance, and we pursued our journey to the lake Laahdoo (water yet distant).

The following morning the requisite assistance arrived, consisting of about twenty-five stout-looking savages well armed with spear, shield, and dagger, and we again continued our journey, passing numerous deserted villages, until we approached the Hawash, where we found several villages the inhabitants of which had not yet retreated towards the heads of the watercourses, as is their wont when pasturage becomes scarce. We crossed the Hawash, about waist-deep, at 3 P.M., but saw no signs of our anticipated enemies. Both banks of the river swarmed with herds of cattle. We journeyed on till 5 P.M., when we halted at the extremity of the plain of the Hawash, about one mile eastward of a small pool of water.

At daylight of the 23rd my guide's horse was missing, owing to his confidence in the honesty of the people. Several times when it had strayed during the night my servants had tied it up for him, but he had loosed it as often to feed, remarking that no one would steal it. On my endeavouring to console him for the loss of so noble an animal he replied: "Never mind, I know who has stolen it; but God willing, I'll steal the best of his camels. My cousin that was with us yesterday is the thief; he has stolen it because I refused to give it to him." A short time afterwards I observed one of the Bedouins walking away in the quietest and most leisurely manner with the old man's saddle, and pointed him out. Chase was given immediately and the man, finding there was no chance of escaping, quietly stood still, and on delivering it up said: "Why, of what use is your saddle to you now that you have no horse?" It was taken from him, however, and given to another man.

Having settled with our escort, we bade them adieu and resumed our journey. The Ras-el-Kafilah having become very friendly with me, we frequently rode side by side. In the course of conversation he told me one day that it was absurd my trying to go to Harrar, that the "Bedoos" would kill me; "indeed," he said, "I will not let you remain behind; you must accompany us to Tajura." On my replying that I had not provided myself for so long a journey, he offered to share all he had with me, and as another inducement for me to accompany him to Tajura he remarked: "Have you not observed the longing eye your guide is continually casting towards your baggage?" I had indeed, and I took the hint by causing it to be distributed amongst the kafilah people, who promised to take care of it for me.

When we encamped, there being an unusual scarcity of water, I had contented myself with some parched grain, not having sufficient of the precious liquid to make bread* with. Datah Mohamed, however, supposing that my servant had secreted his usual portion, became exceedingly angry, and a dispute arose between him and Adam, which I had some difficulty in allaying.

Having lost his horse, he insisted on having one of my mules, as he said he was an old man and could not walk; and indeed he began to be so very troublesome that I reflected on what Ibrahim had told me, and determined on giving up the idea of going to Harrar.

As we resumed our march at daylight on the morning of the 23rd, Datah Mohamed requested the loan of two mules, in order, as he said, that he and his friend might ride forward and prepare the people to receive me in a friendly manner. I lent him two, and they departed, but shortly after he returned to change the mules, saying I had given him the two worst: of course I was obliged to comply.

About noon we arrived at the lake Yoor Erain Murroo, where we fell in with a great number of Bedouins, who were watering their cattle, to the amount of at least three thousand head of horned cattle, and sheep innumerable. Datah Mohamed was seated under the shade of a spreading acacia. I joined him, and was introduced to the savage band as his guest and the friend of the Wulasma Mohamed Abogaz.

A huge bowl of fresh milk was produced for me, and a similar one for my servants, which was very refreshing, for the day was exceedingly warm. Shortly afterwards Datah Mohamed and his friends quitted us, and we prepared our encampment for the night.

On the following morning the whole of the caravan people, as well as myself and servants, were invited to the village of Datah Mohamed to partake of his hospitality and be present at

---

* Bread.—Flour and water mixed together in a frying pan, then beaten out between the hands to somewhat of the shape of a pancake but much thicker, and baked dry in the pan. This was a luxury! (Memo.—Very like tough leather.)

his marriage festivities, for the old man was about to take unto himself another wife. We accordingly set out thither, and found him, with the principal people of his tribe, seated under the shade of a venerable acacia, indulging in a luxurious feast of raw beef. Six bullocks were slaughtered immediately on our arrival, and we were desired to "eat and be merry."

The village consisted of about sixty huts arranged in a circular form, with an open space in the centre for the cattle, and the whole surrounded with a thorn fence, to keep off the wild beasts. The huts are formed merely of four curved sticks, their ends resting in the ground, covered with mats, of an oval shape, about fifteen feet in length, eight feet broad, and five feet high.

We encamped at a short distance from the village, and failed not to keep most diligent watch and ward, for bitter experience had told us that our *friends* were not to be trusted. We were feasted abundantly with *raw meat* and milk *ad libitum*, and as the sun set, a fine young camel was led out in front of the village and slaughtered for the good of all, and as a mark of great favour.

As soon as it was dark, Datah Mohamed came to me, and the old man began : " My son, you have as yet given me nothing; the Wulasma gave me everything. My horse has been stolen. I want a mule and much cloth." I told him that it was myself that gave him the horse and cloth, but he interrupted me by saying "No, no, my son, the Wulasma is our father; he told me that he gave them to me, and he said that you would give me great things on arriving at my village. My son, the Wulasma would not lie!!" I confess I felt the full force of the complaint, and was about to make an angry retort, when he was called away.

25th.—Early in the morning we were summoned to the dwelling of Datah Mohamed; Ibrahim ibn Burantoo, Deeni, myself and servants, and one or two others, quite a hutful. Here we beheld the unfortunate victim to his brutal passions, a young girl who appeared the very picture of misery. I could almost fancy that she had but just been rescued from the grasp of some ferocious monster; the tears poured down her cheeks in torrents, and her bosom heaved as if it would burst at every throb.

I can fancy her having been a comely maiden, well formed and of moderate stature. Her age was about fourteen. She was seated on a wicker frame about six inches from the ground. After the opening chapter of the Korán had been recited by a venerable sage, to which all devoutly responded " Ameen," a large bowl of sour milk was produced, thickly sprinkled with red pepper, not at all savoury in smell or pleasing to the eye. What was the surprise of the old man when I declined partaking thereof! Not drink sour milk! "There is no God but God! God is great!" he exclaimed; however, he had the civility to send for a bowl of fresh milk, and I partially regained his favour by the ample justice I did to this, almost equal to the relish evinced by my Tajuran friends to the former bowl. Fresh ghee (clarified butter) was then handed round, with which all anointed their bodies, and we then took our departure.

The Dankali have an idea that fresh milk is unwholesome, but they are very partial to sour milk, drinking large quantities of it daily.

A short time after, the wily old Chief returned my visit and said to me : " My son, you see I have treated you with great honour. I have feasted you with meat and milk in plenty ; now I want a mule and plenty of cloth, for all my people want cloth and as yet you have given me nothing." I became angry, and told him that I had given him the horse and cloth, &c.; he smiled and said "Yes, I know that, but I want a mule; my horse has been stolen." He also said he wanted some blue cloth, and he took a great fancy to my Arab cloak, my only covering at night. My portmanteau being torn, he thrust his fingers in between the outer leather and the lining, and said, with a most avaricious grin, " What have you here ?" Upon this I arose and said, " I see now that you are no longer my father. The Wulasma Mohamed said you would be kind to me; is this your kindness?" He begged pardon, and said, "Don't be afraid, my son; I will take nothing but what you give freely. People have been telling you bad things of me, but don't believe them. I am an old man now, and have given up plundering people."

It now became necessary to ascertain what Datah Mohamed's intentions were regarding me, for I had been intrusted to his charge, and I was fearful he might make some objection to my going on with the Tajura people. I found that I had been most miserably deceived in Shoa, for there I was told that my worthy guide was the brother of Bedar, one of the principal chiefs of the Adaiel, and that he resided at Errur, both of which statements were false.

Datah Mohamed told me that his marriage festivities would last seven days, after which he proposed forwarding me to the renowned chieftain Bedar, who would act as he thought fit in forwarding me on to Tajura or Harrar.

Vexed and disappointed that I should have suffered so much to no purpose, I felt compelled to give up all hope of reaching Harrar. By remaining with the Bedouins I should but be bandied about from one Chief to another, and the constant demands of Datah Mohamed for tobacco, cloth, &c.,—in fact, for all that his covetous eyes lighted upon—did not give me any encouragement to trust myself with him after the departure of the Tajurans.

Besides, on leaving Shoa the Mission treasury was at so low an ebb that I had only the small sum of three German crowns with me: however, as it was currently reported that Mohamed Ali was on the frontier, and we knew of his having been upwards of two months of the road with a fresh supply of cash, I anticipated meeting him and obtaining as much as I wanted to carry me from Harrar to Zeyla. But he was at Kilulloo, some days still in advance.

The Tajurans also all begged of me not to think of remaining with the Bedouins. "Think not of your property alone," cried out Ibrahim, "but also of your life and the lives of your servants. Remember the belly of the 'Bedoo' is never filled. Come on with us; we will share with you our provisions and travel with speed." So I gave my consent, and to my delight the old man made no objection.

Again, as soon as it was dark, Datah Mohamed came to me, and asked for a mule and all the cloth I had! Seeing that he was determined to have a mule—for had I refused to give him one I felt assured he would steal all, so as to make sure of having the best—I deemed it prudent to make a virtue of necessity. I therefore said to him "Listen to me. My father, you have treated me kindly; you have feasted me with milk and have slain bullocks for me. You have asked me for a mule: I will give you one, but remember, should any of my countrymen pass through your country at any time you must be kind to them and assist them." To this he replied in the affirmative, but on my pointing out the mule for his acceptance he said, "I will not have that one;" in fact, he would only be satisfied with the best, the one I rode. Then he demanded cloth; I gave him all I had, and had to borrow three pieces from the kafilah people before he was content. At last, near midnight, he took his departure, leaving the mule for me to take care of till the morning.

26th January.—At earliest dawn Datah Mohamed came for his mule, but it was a long time before he could make up his mind which one to take. He then demanded more cloth. I had none to give him. He then demanded my Arab cloak, which I refused to give him, as it was bed, coverlid, everything, during the night, and during the day formed a rude kind of tent, to keep off the scorching rays of the sun. He at last departed with his mule.

I had, however, but a short respite, for in less than an hour he returned, bringing with him a very particular friend of his, who had come a long distance on purpose to see me. I fully understood the drift of this, expressed my sense of the honour his friend had conferred upon me, and regretted much my inability to prove it otherwise than by words, as he himself had received my last cloth; "however," I continued, as I observed the old man's brow darken, "I will try and borrow a cloth for your friend." Deeni, who was present, after some little difficulty, got me one, which was rejected as being too coarse. I then exclaimed: "You see my dress, this cloth is better than what I myself wear; but here, take my turban." This had the desired effect; the cloth was accepted, and I retained my turban. The old man dared not *plunder* me; he could only take what I *freely gave* him! What an odd mixture of good and evil is to be found in the Bedouin character! Had we not feasted together at Gouchoo, had we not eaten salt together, this man would assuredly have plundered me, aye, and have thought as little of murdering me as of killing any animal by whose death he would have been benefited! Yet he dared not infringe the rites of hospitality; the "sacred salt" was my safety. At 2 P.M. the welcome order was given to load the camels and prepare once more to move forward. We were detained a short time by the parting speech of the old man, who gave me over to the charge of the leader of the caravan in a most impressive manner, conjuring him to watch over me by night and by day, "for I was unto him as a son," and then giving me his blessing. Most heartily did I join in the "Ulhumdilillah! ("Praise be to God!") of the Tajurans as soon as we were once fairly on our journey.

Notwithstanding that the Galla and Eesah are said to be the hereditary foes of the Adaiel, yet during our short sojourn the village was visited by several of both these tribes. The Eesah are a fine race of people, subsisting chiefly on wild fowl and by the use of the bow and arrow (in war they use poisoned arrows*); they are said to be good marksmen, and very persevering in the chase: these people had several hides and skins for sale. The Galla brought with them tobacco and coffee to barter for the brass wire, beads, cloth, &c., of the kafilah people.

27th.—We were on the point of resuming our march, when two of my mules ran away; chase was instantly given, and we succeeded in catching them after a run of about an hour. The whole of the people of the kafilah were loud in their congratulations that I had been persuaded to give up the idea of going to Harrar, and were very civil and obliging. At nine o'clock, as the sun was getting very warm, we halted at Coduitoo; the country bears marks of having been densely populated during the rains, but at present, owing to the scarcity of water, not a soul was to be seen.

While at Murroo we had filled up our water-skins for a journey of two days to Doomi, but on the Ras-el-Kafilah telling me he had heard that at that place the Bedouins were as numerous as the hairs of his head, "and many of them were his relations and would want much cloth," it was deemed advisable to make a détour to the south, and proceed to Harrah Ambili, where there was plenty of water to be obtained from wells in the valley, and where, owing to the scarcity of pasturage, we were not likely to be troubled with many of these gentry. So, starting forward again at 3 P.M., we continued our journey to the Wady Boondeerah, where we halted at 9 P.M.; from thence we proceeded at 4 A.M. the following morning to Geera Dohiba, where we halted at 11. We again pushed forward at 4 P.M. through a dry watercourse, the road very bad, through Madeera Dubbah, the "place of lions" (we did not see any, however) till 10 P.M., halted at Hagaioo Geera Dubbah; no water yet. This was formerly the dwelling-place of Hagaioo, Chief of the Woemah; the rude inclosures for the cattle still remain, made of loose stones piled one on another. The Eesah surprised them by a night attack and swept off the greater portion of their cattle, since which time the place has been deserted.

---

*The arrow poison of Eastern Africa is obtained from the *Waba* plant, a toxicodendron.

The slaves were now beginning to feel the effects of the journey, more especially the last march; several of them were obliged to be tied on to camels. From the scarcity of water I was obliged to content myself with parched grain and a wee drop of coffee.

29th.— At daylight we continued our journey to Harrah Ambili, where we arrived about noon, having passed an encampment of the Eesah, with their pretty maidens tending their flocks.

Here we had plenty of water, but not of the best quality—indeed in some of the wells the water was quite brackish, and several were hot springs—wild fowl in abundance, besides antelope and wild boar. Here I obtained intelligence of Mohamed Ali, who was in charge of the presents, &c., for the embassy that we had left at Tajura. It appears that on the 18th he halted at Kilulloo and sent his camel-men to Aussa to purchase grain, and while they were absent a dispute took place between some of his people and the Eesah, and a man was killed on each side; immediately on the return of his camels he quitted Kilulloo and proceeded to Errur.

A kafilah from Tajura passed by this day. I took the opportunity of sending letters to my friends in Abyssinia, giving them all particulars connected with my journey. Mohamed ibn Burantoo, one of our kafilah, presented me with a sheep, which of course I was only too glad to accept, but it was near being the cause of a misunderstanding between the Ras-el-Kafilah and myself. It appears that there was a grudge of long-standing between them, so when he heard that I had accepted the sheep he said to my servant Adam, "Is it well for your master to take presents from other people? If he wanted a sheep why did he not ask *me* for it? We shall see." Adam replied: "Don't be angry; my master did not ask for the sheep; it was given to him, and has just been slaughtered; I was looking for you to distribute it among the people. Further, if my master hears what you have said he will be angry, for he wishes to be friendly with everybody, and for that reason accepted the sheep." This quieted him.

In the evening I had a long conversation with the Ras-el-Kafilah, and endeavoured to persuade him to accompany me on to Tajura, leaving the kafilah to follow; but to this he objected, saying that it would not be safe for us to go on from here, but that he would accompany me from Dahwaylakal, three marches in advance. He also gave me a sheep, which, like the other, was slaughtered *pro bono publico*.

Remained at Wassah Ambili during the 30th, to allow the slaves to recruit their strength and at 1 P.M. of the 31st broke ground and marched till 9 P.M. to Bussoo Ruddah; passed several small parties of the Eesah.

February 1st.—We marched from 4 till 11 A.M., when we halted in the valley of Fiahloo; grass abundant, but no water. At 3 P.M., we again moved forward. In crossing the plain of Ahmahdoo some men were observed in the distance marching towards us; the alarm was instantly given of "the Eesah!" and all were ordered to close up. The slaves were all placed in the centre, and the camels drawn up around them. The men threw aside their upper garments, girded up their loins and prepared for battle, then, like true believers, with their faces towards Mecca, said their prayers. As the strangers approached, two valiant warriors accompanied the Ras-el-Kafilah a short distance to the front. Doubtless to the joy of both parties, they proved to be friends, and we went on our way rejoicing, many of the young men boasting of what they would have done had the party turned out to be the cowardly Eesah instead of their own most particular friends the Aysomauli. We halted about eight o'clock in the plain of Dahwaylakal.

2nd.—At daylight, accompanied by three of the kafilah people and two of my servants, I rode on in advance of the kafilah to water our mules and give them some rest at Dahwaylakal, where we arrived about an hour before noon, and found the Bedouin women watering their herds from a small well in a ravine:—a little hollow is made in the ground by the well-side, and the water baled up by one of them. Our mules were so knocked up for want of water that they rushed in the most frantic manner towards it alarming the damsel in the well, who instantly set up a shrill cry. Hitherto we had seen only one of the rougher sex, but in a moment we were surrounded by about twenty savages, fierce-looking fellows, armed with spear, crease, and shield, who claimed the well as their own ; and as we were not in a position to dispute their right to it, we moved further up the ravine, till at the distance of about one mile we came to a pool of water the filthiest I have ever seen, black as ink, containing the concentrated essence of all that is vile. Thirsty as we were, we could not touch it. Our mules, poor things! were not so fastidious, for, ere we had time to remove the bits from their mouths, they rushed into it in the most frantic manner: they had not tasted water for upwards of two days.

We again moved down the ravine, and found the kafilah had just arrived, and, what was more gratifying, that the inhospitable "sons of the desert" had taken their departure, so, that we were now in a position to retaliate, if we felt so inclined, upon any newcomer. From hence I determined upon setting out for Tajura, leaving all my baggage with the kafilah people. A sheep was purchased and boiled for our journey, and one mule selected to carry such things as we actually needed, which consisted of a very small quantity of coffee, parched grain, and a little flour, a coffeepot and a frying-pan, and a change of clothing for each; this mule was taken in tow (to use a nautical phrase) by one of my servants.

At 3 P.M., the whole of the kafilah people assembled to see us off, and to wish us "God speed." The party now consisted of Ibrahim, the Ras-el-Kafilah ; Deeni, the interpreter ; a Bedouin of the Assoubah tribe (a sub-tribe of the Adaiel) who rejoiced in the designation of "Adam the Black ;" John, a Greek ; Adam, an Indian ; Mohamed, an Arab (my servants) ; and myself; altogether seven, all mounted on mules and well armed.

We started off at a good pace, but had not proceeded far before we came up with a party of the Eesah who were tending their camels : they appeared much alarmed at our approach. We rode on in peace, Adam the Black telling them that we were a party of the Assoubah proceeding to the coast with letters from the King of Shoa. At 7 P.M., we arrived at a retired place where grass was abundant, having been four hours in the saddle; and after tying the mules' forelegs together, to prevent their straying, we lay down to rest.

February 3rd.—Before one o'clock, we again saddled our mules, and pushed forward at a rapid pace till four o'clock, when we halted for about half an hour, and had each a cup of coffee *à l'Arabe* (not much more than a large thimbleful) and a handful of parched grain, and again went onward. At daylight we came up with an encampment of the Debeni. Loud and shrill were the cries from the fair damsels driving their flocks out to graze; Adam the Black proceeded to pacify them and we rode on. We halted at 8 A.M., at the Wady Rummoo-delly to water the mules and fill up our water-skins, and at 10 A.M., having arrived at a convenient place, we halted for breakfast, after having been nearly nine hours in the saddle.

Our breakfast consisted of parched grain, a cup of coffee as before, and some of the meat we had remaining from yesterday.

At noon we moved forward again, and at about 3 P.M., arrived at a pool of water called Mushahr, in the Wady Dalaboyeh, where we refreshed ourselves with a wash, and indulged in the luxury of some bread made in the most primitive manner,—indeed mere flour and water. After an hour's rest we continued our journey through the Wady, passing several encampments of Bedouins, and a little after dusk descended to the plain of Gingaddi.

As we had to pass near several encampments, the fires of which we could see in the distance, we halted and sent the Bedouin "Adam the Black" forward as a scout, to ascertain whether they were friends or foes. Dismounting from his mule, stripping himself perfectly naked, and grasping his crease or dagger in the right hand and his shield in the left, the wily savage crept along on his hands and knees.

We awaited in breathless suspense the return of our scout: at last Ibrahim whispered to me "They have found him out; let us go forward: he is a 'Bedoo' and will take care of himself." We had moved but a few yards, however, when he was in the midst of us— he had approached so cautiously. The encampment nearest to us, he said, was one of the Debeni. Although a friendly tribe, it was deemed advisable to pass them as quietly as we could. We succeeded in doing so without disturbing one of them, and having got a respectful distance by half-past eight we halted in a clear space, so that we could see any one approaching.

Ibrahim begged me not to light a fire, but I was quite done up, and longed for a wee drop of coffee; so collecting a few sticks we made a fire, covering it all round with our shields, which as soon as the coffee was prepared was extinguished and covered over with sand.

We slept for about five hours, keeping watch alternately—that is, my servants and myself; as for our worthy companions, they are too confirmed fatalists to think of taking any such precaution.

February 4th.—At 3 A.M., we resumed our journey, and at half-past four, coming to a good patch of grass, halted to let our poor mules have a feed, as they had nothing yesterday, and indulged ourselves with a cup of coffee; time was precious, however, as we had yet a long journey before us, so after a halt of about an hour, we again pushed forward at seven o'clock, and arrived at Allooli—the station this side of the abominable and never-to-be forgotten valley of Goongoonteh,—where we watered our mules, and then, instead of pursuing the route by which the Embassy came across the Salt Lake, we struck off to the right, over broken masses of lava and volcanic remains, and had a splendid view of the lake from the summit of the hills. At one o'clock I found the heat so very oppressive that I was obliged to halt for a couple of hours under the shade of some detached rocks. The wind was blowing with such violence that it considerably retarded our progress, so that we did not arrive at Dahfurri till sunset. Here we found a large pool of fresh water, clear as crystal; this we must have passed, on going to Shoa, within a few hundred yards, at a time when we suffered so much from the want of water, and only four miles from our halting-place at the Salt Lake. However, Ibrahim declared to me that at that time it was a mere pool of filth, but that the late rains had filled it as we found it now.

Having filled our water-skins, we retired to some distance from the pool, and kept a most vigilant watch till one o'clock next morning. We had a slight adventure in the early part of the day. Conceiving that none but ourselves could be wandering in such a desolate place, we had omitted to observe the usual caution of keepping together. Ibrahim, deep in thought had got some distance in advance. I was walking alone, my mule following me, my servant, some distance in the rear, when I was startled by a man jumping-up suddenly from behind a rock just after Ibrahim had passed it. As he was coming towards me, I half drew my sword,—my pistols were in the holsters; he placed his hand on his crease, and thus we passed within a yard or two of each other. At this moment Ibrahim turned round and exclaimed : "The Lord preserve us from Satan the stoned! Did I not tell you now, Captain, to keep together?" and as I approached him he said "That man is one of the fellows who killed your people at Goongoonteh." My mule had just come up to me, so I seized my rifle; a rock just covered him, but the impulse was so great that I am certain had he not at that moment been shut from view I should have shot him.

However, he fell in with Deeni and the Bedouin in the rear, who had wandered after some stray camels which this villain had stolen from Tajura—at least that was their story; so they stripped him, beat him, and drove off the camels, taking also his spear and shield.

February 5th.—At one o'clock in the morning we started again so as to clear the Ra Esa pass before daylight, as we had heard at Dahwaylakal that the Bedouins were hovering about there, on the look out for their customary toll from the kafilah.

As we wound up this dreadful pass the barking of dogs betrayed the vicinity of the Bedouins—indeed they were encamped but a short distance above us. Not a word was spoken, but each urged his mule forward by sundry kicks, and as the day dawned we ascended to the elevated plain of Wady Lissan, where we halted for about two hours, and shared the last of our provisions —about a handful of parched grain, and a cup of coffee! Indeed we were so hard pushed that we were glad to eat some *jowari* or millet we had kept for the mules.

Ibrahim was so completely done up that he could proceed no further, at least at our rapid pace, so he begged us to go on and he would follow at leisure.

We had not proceeded far before we caught sight once more of the sea. How delighted I was! "All danger is over now!" I exclaimed; "now I am at home!" At eleven o'clock we reached Sagullo, on the sea-shore. Ibrahim came up about three hours afterwards, and we had a feast of mutton and milk, or here we were among friends. At three in the afternoon we proceeded to Ambaboo, arriving there at sunset. We were kept in suspense for about a quarter of an hour while the elders deliberated; they then came forward, welcomed me to their village, prepared a house for me, and sent over an immense bowl of boiled rice and a quantity of milk, with some grilled mutton and a bag of dates; in fact, they treated me and my servants with the greatest hospitality. When we had satisfied the cravings of hunger, by no means an easy task, the elders came to hear our adventures, and were astonished at the rapidity of our journey, exclaiming "Wonderful! wonderful! God is most great! Verily, God was with them!" They soon left us to the repose we so much needed.

At an early hour the following morning, Sunday the 6th of February, I set out for Tajura where on my arrival I was received with demonstrations of joy by both rich and poor. The Sultan invited me to his house, whither all the people flocked to welcome me on my return; but he, with much consideration, after I had taken a cup of coffee, sent them all away till I had rested, he himself keeping watch at the door. My rapid journey from Dahwaylakal, and the constant excitement I had laboured under from the time of quitting Shoa, had almost worn me out, and I soon fell asleep—*the first refreshing sleep I had had for a period of eighteen days!* At about eleven o'clock, hearing the door open, I started up and found the old Sultan creeping in softly to see if I was awake, to announce breakfast, which was immediately produced by his woman-servant, who first brought me water to wash my hands. I know not when I enjoyed a meal so much—not that any great delicacies were provided; for it was simple enough, consisting of some very nicely boiled rice, fresh, clear ghee, and some boiled mutton, after which coffee was served.

In the afternoon the people again flocked to the house, and at the head of them the Kazi, who after having recited the Fat'hah, or opening chapter of the Koran, offered up a thanksgiving to God, "the only one God," for having protected me during my journey, and for having enlightened my mind and understanding, whereby I had been led to avoid the cruel and bloodthirsty people of Harrar, and to return to my country through that of *my friends* the Dankali.

Old Izakh, the brother of the Sultan (who had charge of the first detachment of the Embassy), and several others of distinction were there, and responded most loudly "Ameen, Ameen." I was indeed quite unprepared for so much kindness. All were desirous of presenting me with something; one brought eggs, another milk, and others honey, ghee, fish, rice, &c., &c., so that, verily, I felt that I had fallen among good Samaritans. The Sultan asked what my intentions were, whether I would remain at Tajura till the arrival of the vessel from Aden, or whether I would hire a boat. I replied that my desire was to return instantly to Aden, but that I had neither funds nor food, and further that the Bedouin objected to going across to Aden and I had not the means of paying him. Upon this the Sultan said:

"Do as seems best to you: the town is yours if you wish to stay; if you wish to go, there is Aboo Bekr's* boat at your service; and as for the Bedouin, I will advance what you require for him. Your food I will also care for, and if you go to Aden I will take care of your mules till you return or send for them." The sum of ten dollars was instantly advanced, with which I paid the Bedouin, and urged Aboo Bekr to get his boat ready quickly, telling him I would settle with him at Aden. In the evening, however, a larger and better boat arrived from Berbera, intimation of which I received from Aboo Bekr, who said: " I am as fond of money as most men, and that, I dare say, you know, Captain (his boat had been employed by me in the Survey); but you are anxious to return soon to Aden; so, if you wish it, hire the other boat, she sails faster than mine. Aboo Bekr says so!" As I knew that the old man spoke the truth, in this instance at least, I engaged the other boat.

I remained at Tajura till the 10th, as the boat had cargo to discharge and ballast to take in and was treated with every kindness and consideration by all classes. Whenever I went out I was accompanied by some of the villagers, and I was fed, aye, and clothed by them. One in particular, the wife of a man I had frequently received visits from while in Alio Amba, and to whom I had given some trifling presents, sent me word that her husband had desired her to provide me with all that I wanted, and that I had but to intimate to her what I required and it should be given me. I went to see her and to thank her for the kind offer, and declared that the Sultán had supplied all my wants, but she insisted on my accepting milk, honey, and ghee, and during my stay at Tajura she sent me daily a supply of fish that her son had caught. I confess I would not have given the people credit for so much kindliness of disposition.

On leaving Abyssinia I was annoyed at a dog, belonging to a neighbour, following me. I tried to drive him back but he would not leave me; the poor creature had attached himself to my fortunes: whenever I lay down he always lay at my feet. The boatmen objected to take him on board, so I was obliged to leave him with the Sultán. In the morning, just as we were starting, we again saw the poor creature, who had managed to get loose and come down; he howled most piteously. He was afterwards stolen.

On the 10th of February I quitted Tajura with the land wind early in the morning, and about noon anchored in Mersa Munger Duffa, on the opposite coast, to collect firewood and to barter with the natives.

In the evening I went on shore to bathe. A number of the Eesah had collected, and were disposing of their goods, to the no small advantage of the Tajurans. The instant they saw me they shouted out "The Lord preserve us from Satan the stoned!" and were seized with such a panic at the sight of a white man that they one and all took to flight, and it was some time

---

* Aboo Bekr was surnamed by his countrymen Denah-bilu, or "The Liar,"—rather a flattering title, particularly when it is considered that the whole of his tribe are notorious for the same moral infirmity. There is not one who can be depended upon; it is their nature to depart from the truth; indeed their adherence to truth in any one instance would be pronounced most marvellous, and the result, must assuredly, of accident, not of design.

before they could be persuaded to return. The following morning, the 11th of February, we set sail, and at noon anchored under Ras Gomahli, where we remained till the following morning, when we proceeded to Zeyla, where we arrived about noon of the 12th of February. The Governor of the place sent off to invite me on shore; on my landing I was received with all due honour by the "Captain of the Port," and the garrison of the place, who conducted me to the presence of the Governor, firing matchlocks, &c. Immediately I entered the room where the Governor was seated he rose to meet me, welcomed me in the warmest manner, and seated me on his right hand. Hookahs and coffee were instantly brought in, and indeed I was treated with every consideration, the Governor assuring me over and over again that the town was mine to do aught with that my heart desired, &c., &c. On quitting I was accompanied, as before, to my dwelling by the garrison of the place.

I took up my abode in a house belonging to Ali Shermaki, of Berbera, who had sent instructions to his agent here, in the event of my arriving, to see that I wanted nothing. In the evening the Governor sent me a present of a sheep and a large quantity of fresh milk, and I sat down to what would have been a very comfortable repast were it not that the exposure and excitement I had undergone had almost worn me out. I retired, but passed a most fearful night.

Early the following morning I found myself burning with fever, which lasted, without intermission, till 4 P.M. I tried to persuade the boatmen to take me on board and put to sea, but they were not ready.

I was visited by the Governor of the town and several of the people, all bringing presents of sheep, milk, &c., and expressing great anxiety about my sickness. The Governor recommended a quiet, and offered me his house; he also presented my Arab servant with a suit of clothes, which the poor boy much needed.

14th February.—The fever returned with great violence. At daybreak I was carried on board, being quite unable to walk, and we soon put to sea with a fair wind for Berbera. Indeed we could have stood across to Aden, but such is not the custom of these people. Their forefathers when travelling by land had their regulated days' journeys and their established "mauhalia" or halting-places, which are still adhered to. So with their voyages: from time immemorial vessels from Tajura at this season of the year coast it thence to Kurrum, from whence they cross over to Aden, the prevailing wind being easterly; but should a westerly wind set in they would remain there till it veered to the eastward. At 6 P.M. of the 15th February we anchored at Berbera. Ali Shermaki no sooner heard of my arrival than he came off to the boat, and had me carried to his house, where he made every exertion to make me comfortable.

16th February.—At sunrise I was carried again on board the boat, and with much difficulty I persuaded the crew to put to sea. All this while the fever was raging violently and there was nothing to alleviate it. At 2 P.M. the wind freshened so much that our timid sailors bore up for Berbera again! Early on the morning of the 17th I sent for Shermaki to beg he would get me another boat. He had me removed to his house, for I was perfectly helpless, and if kindness could have cured me I should soon have been well. Shermaki could not get me another boat till the 21st; I believe the people were afraid that I should die in the boat. I was indeed quite worn out; the burning fever, and the absence of all means to alleviate or check the disease had reduced me to a living skeleton; moreover, chicken broth and tamarind water had been my sole nourishment since the commencement of my illness at Zeyla.

On the evening of the 21st I embarked in one of Shermaki's boats; he told the Nacodah (master) and the crew to obey my orders implicitly. We moved down to the mouth of the harbour, ready to start with the land wind.

The mere circumstance of an Englishman being in the boat induced one of the Banians (Indian Merchants) to bring two thousand dollars in a bag, and in the most public manner ask Shermaki to send it over to Aden; usually all money transactions are conducted with great secrecy. The money was received. About midnight a brother of Shermaki's came alongside in a canoe and persuaded the Nacodah that Shermaki and the Banian had disputed about the freight, and that they were both waiting on the beach to receive back the money. Accordingly, the stupid man, getting into the canoe, handed the bag to the brother of his master, who kindly offered to take care of it, and away they went to the shore, the brother to look after Shermaki, the Nacodah remaining with the boat. He waited in vain, and at last in despair returned to his vessel and acquainted me with what had occurred. At this moment a fast-sailing boat was seen to glide by; a suspicion instantly crossed my mind that this boat contained the *brother* and *robber*; so off we went in pursuit, and, ill as I was, I got together all my firearms and loaded them, for I knew if we overtook the robber he would not give up the money without a fight. The instant the men in the other boat saw they were pursued, they got their oars out and pulled in for the land, which we determined to prevent; they then tried first one tack and then another, but finding they were cut off from the land they made for sea. Shortly after the moon set, and as I felt assured their making for sea was only a feint, we returned with all haste, and when off the harbour's mouth sent the canoe in with one man to give notice to Shermaki; we then stood along the coast westward.

As the day broke we observed the villains plying their oars and making every effort to get in with the land. Off we went in pursuit, and presently observed a fast-rowed boat filled with armed men coming out from Berbera; it soon passed us, but it was of no avail; the robber had beached his boat and was off, having seized a camel long before the other boat could come up, and so got away into the interior.

During the excitement of the chase the fever appeared to have left me, but as soon as it was over the malady returned with tenfold violence. Towards evening I became delirious, and indeed from this time till my arrival at Aden I scarcely knew what occurred; I only feel deeply sensible of the kind attention shown to me by my domestics.

Early on the 25th we anchored under Seerah southward of Aden. I had so far rallied that I was enabled to land and walk up to the house of the Political Agent, Captain Haines. I was quite worn out, and this, together with the fact of my having adopted the Turkish costume, and presenting a wild appearance from not having allowed the razor to touch my face for upwards of ten months, prevented his recognising me for some time. For many subsequent days and nights I could not sleep. It is impossible to describe the state of mind I was in from the constant excitement of the past five weeks.

NARRATIVE OF A JOURNEY TO SHOA.

APPENDIX.

Route from Tajura to Ankobar pursued by Major HARRIS in 1814.

Names of Stations.	Distance. Miles.	Distance. Furl.	Supply of Water.	Elevation above the level of the sea.	Latitude and Longitude.
Tajurah	...	...	Well	......	Lat. 11° 46′ 35″ N. Long. 43° 0′ 20″ E.
Ambabo	3	4	Do.		
Dullool	7	...	Do.		
Sagullo	2	4	Do.	......	Lat. 11° 40′ 15″ N.
Wady Lissan	14	...	None	1,697	
Bahr Assal	16	...	Do.	Below 570	Lat. 11° 37′ 30″ N. Long. 42° 33′ 6″ E.
Goongoonteh	16	...	Stream.		
Allooli	9	...	Pool	228	
Bedikurroof	16	...	Do.		
Suggadéra	8	...	Do.	......	Lat. 11° 19′ 3″ N.
Murrah	4	...	Well	......	Lat. 11° 17′ 3″ N.
Duddee	15	...	Pool.		
Gobaad	12	...	River	1,057	Lat. 11° 0′ 54″ N.
Sunkul	4	...	Pool.		
Suggagídan	7	...	None	......	Lat. 10° 53′ 0″ N.
Dahwáylaka	9	4	Pool.	1,228	
Oomergooloof	8	4	None.		
Amádoo	7	4	Pool.		
Fiáloo	3	4	Do.	1,605	
Barúrudda	15	...	None.		
Kilulloo	12	...	Pool.	1,542	Lat. 10° 34′ 33″ N.
Waramilli	7	...	Do.	1,752	
Naga-koomi	15	...	None.		
Meinha-tolli	15	...	Pool.		
Madéra-dubba	15	4	None		
Sultélli	17	...	Do.		
Mároo	13	...	Lake.		
Moolu-Zughir	13	...	None.		
Burdúdda	9	...	Pool.		
Háo	15	...	None	......	Lat. 9° 39′ 13″ N.
Hawash River	11	...	River	2,223	
Azbóti	12	4	Pool.		
Dathára	12	4	Stream.	2,944	
Dinomali	5	...	Do.		
Fárri	1	4	Do.		
Alio Amba	13	...	Do.	5,271	
Ankóbar	5	...	Do.	8,200	Lat. 9° 34′ 45″ N. Long. 39° 54′ 0″ E.
Total Distance	370	...			

By the passage of the polar star over the meridian the magnetic Variation at Ankobar was observed, with the aid of a well-regulated chronometer, to be 7° westerly.

The longitude was determined both by a series of lunars and by the eclipses of Jupiter's satellites, the mean of upwards of 150 observations being taken.

INDEX

―: o :―

A

	PAGE.
'Abbán	...195, 199, 201, 227
Abbás ...	55
Abbás Khán Hirátee	59
Abbás Meerza	38
Abbás Mirza	36, 37, 53, 56
Abbe of the old French School	116
Abbott, Captain	87
'Abd al Betí	229
Abdálí territory, the—	220
„ Sultán of—	219
„ tribe, the	...216, 219
'Abdalláh ben Ahmed ben Fudhli, Sultan of the Fudhli	221
Abd-el-Hud	205
Abder Russool	286, 287, 289
Abdool Aziz	63
Abdool Kaháb Khán	63
Abdoolah Khán	134, 156
Abdoolláh Khán	133, 134
Abdool Liki, Chief of the Harrárgi	273, 274, 279, 280, 285, 288
'Abdu-l-Kúri or *Palinurus* Shoal	...232, 233
Abdulláh Khán : Chief of the Atchukzye	135, 136, 137
Abdu-l-Wáhidi, Chief of the Wáhidi tribe	196, 227
'Abdu-l-Wáhid : Mohammed Ibn Abú Bekr, a tributary of—	226
Abeebooler Khán ...	114, 115
Abel ...	131
Abbibba : Lake of—	265
'Abídel 'Ibád	225
Abkonnur	160, 165
Aboo Bekr	301
„ Governor of Alio Amba	287
„ Ruler of Harrár	281
Abraham	133, 139
Abu Kirsh	243
Abú Mohammed	249
Abyas ...	55
Abyssinia	194, 211, 225, 259, 282, 301
„ and Tajura : Road between—	259
„ Coast of—	213
Abyssinian cloth	288
„ dwellings	267
„ extraction: Koloro, Prince of Sind of—	186
„ or Shoan scenery	286
„ shore	212
„ warfare	278

b 1573—1

	PAGE.
Abyssinians, the	263
Abyssinians : Superstitions of the—	288
Acacia tree	194
Achikzyes, the	14
Achmed-ibn-Abd-el-Wachet, Sultán of Habahn	206
Achumuclee, the	39
Adaiel, the—	...277, 285, 287, 289, 290, 295, 296, 298
„ Chiefs of—	280
„ Feast of friendship amongst—	283, 284, 285
„ Plains of—	274, 286
Adam ...	280, 281, 282, 284, 293, 297
Adam feroosh	125
Adam the Black	298, 299
Adel ...	284
Adel or Adaiel, the	265, 291
„ Inhospitable plains of the—	265
'Aden (Aden)	193, 205, 208, 216, 217, 218, 219, 222, 224, 228, 233, 237, 241, 290, 292, 301, 302, 303
„ Account of—	219
„ Captain Haines, Political Agent at—	303
„ The peninsular promontory of—	216
„ Treaty between the Bombay Government and the Sultan of—	241
„ West Bay	216
Adraskán, the	10
Aferoch Phual Afresol	271
Afghán costume	10
„ invaders	179
Afgháns, the	5, 8, 11, 12, 13, 17, 22, 40, 41, 75, 97, 100, 108, 113, 115, 123, 124, 125, 127, 139
„ and the Persians : Wars between —for the conquest of Herát	9
„ believe in the Gospel	14
„ Character of—	14
„ Power of—	36
„ Remarks of Mahomed Hoosain about—	75
„ Staple food of—	14
„ State of the fortifications under the Government of—	144
Afghánistán	111
„ (Western)	90
„ Civil wars in—	16
„ Dispute among the sons of Timour for the throne of—	16

INDEX.

	Page.
Afghánistán: Government of —	17
,, Persian party in—	40
Afrédee	117, 165
,, Patháns	158
,, tribe	164
Africa	212, 285
,, Goths and Vandals of—	268
,, Slaves of—	225
African discovery	257
,, ports	228
Africans, the	225
Aga Khán, Governor of Kerman	69
,, Mahomed	53, 73
,, Sayed Mahomed ...	73
Agamooti	290
Agatharchides	198
Agaum	30
Aghráf	230
Agra	169
Agriculture	199
Ahmahdoo	297
Ahmed	184
,, ibn Meídi, Chief of the Akrabi tribe	216
Ahmed Khán	150, 151
,, Sháh ...13, 14,27, 63, 107, 113, 115, 145, 164, 167, 172
,, ,, Dooránee ...	35, 41
,, ,, Mausoleum of—	111
Ahmedpore 105, 183, 184, 187
Ahmud Sháhee	72
Aihibulloo : Lake of— ...	274, 286
'Aïn	191, 192, 199
,, Abú Ma'bad	224
,, ,, Mabúth	192, 200
,, Jowári	192, 224
'Aïnát	229
Aiwás ibn Ahmed	231
Akábre : Tribe of— ...	205
Akchu	38, 39
Akhmand Moola Rúsheed ...	73
Akhwundzada Abdool Kureem	75
Akoo Dáma (kind of ornament)	272
'Akrabis, the	215
Akrabi Tribe : Territory of the—	216
Aládát Khán	163
Alafa Wolda Geosgis, Head of the Church...	280
Alazai, the	136, 138
Albanian	273
Alee Arab	278
,, Khán Bukhtiyaree ...	69
Alexander the Great ...11, 13, 58, 182, 185
,, City of Herát, supposed to be built by— ...	8
,, Coins with the bust of— found in the Punjáb	105
,, Invasion of Hindustán by— ...	166—168
,, Tomb of Bucephalus, the charger of—	166—168
Alexander's soldiers	160
Alexandria	127
,, the Greek Patriarch at—	268

	Page.
Alexandrias	127
Al Ghaïdhar	227
Al Hasan ibn Fudhl-Abdu-l-Karim, Sultán of the Abdali territory	219
'Ali	230, 289
Ali-abad	3
Ali Abbi	257, 261, 292
'Ali (Beït)	231
'Ali ben 'Abd-allah-el Mansúr ...	239
'Ali ben Gháleb (Sultán) Chief of the Yáfái tribe...	220
Ali Malla	290
'Ali Mansúr	248
Ali Shermaki of Berbera ...	302, 303
'Ali : The well of—	225
Alikah : Island of—	216
Alikzyes, the—	15, 16
Alio Amba ... 264, 265, 273, 276, 301, 304
,, Account of— ...	286—290
,, and Massowa : Route between—	290
,, Morality of the male and female sexes at—	287
,, Narration of the events during the residence of Lieutenant Barker at—	277—284
,, Revenues of—	289
'Aliyah : Island of—	217
Alizyes : The tribe of—	11
Alkonnur	161
Alla Dád Khán Burdooránee ...	70, 71, 72
Alladát Khán	149, 150
Allahábád	183
Allah Koolee Beg	56
,, Khán	56
Allard Chevalier	105, 175
Alla-zar-Khán (Asefoodaulah)...	54
Alloa	175
Allooli...	299, 304
Almah-ka-Kote	187
Aloolie...	259
Al-sálih	221
Al Tatamín Eïwarmás	229
Amádou	304
Ambaboo	300, 304
Ameer Dost Mahomed Khán of Kábul	53, 69
,, Dost Mahomed Khán : Mahomed Hoosain's proposal to the Sháh of Persia to send a confidential person to— ...	65, 66
,, Dost Mahomed Khán : Presents from the Sháh of Persia to— ...	66
,, Dost Mahomed Khán proceeded to Peshawar to oppose the Sikhs ...	53
,, Hoosain	56
,, Hydar Gházi	56
,, Khán	119
,, Mahomed Khán	72
America : Coloured natives of ...	138
,, The state of Kentucky in—	103
Amhara (tribe) ... 272, 279, 286, 287, 288
Amharic characters	281
Amir Khán	147, 148

INDEX.

	Page.
Amirs	106
Amise, Monsr.	175
Amoolee or salt money	287, 288
'Amran : Cape of—	216
Anarkullee : Tomb of—	169, 170
Andhoe	53
Andkho	38, 39
Angola,	286, 287, 288
Angollala	269, 273, 274, 275, 278, 288
Angoo	150—158
„ Conquest of—by the Peshawar army.	156
„ The valley of—	150
Ankobar	...265, 267, 269, 270, 271, 273, 274, 276, 279, 280, 281, 282, 283, 284, 286, 288, 304
„ Itoo Woldo Lanna, Governor of—	264
„ Triumphal entry of the King of Shoa in—	280
Antalow	290
Antelope	276
Antonio St. : The Highland of—	214
Antoori Kutli	290
Aqueduct of Soleiman the Magnificent	218
Arab, the—	14, 192
„ (village)	230
„ banditti	244
„ guards	245
Arabia	194, 198, 199, 205, 240, 268
„ Bullocks of—	194
„ Felix	198, 247, 252
„ Lt. Wellsted's work on—	205
„ Memoir of the South Coast of—	209—233
„ Narrative of a journey from the tower of Ba-'l-haff, on the southern coast of—to the ruins of Nakab-al-Hajar	189—201
„ South Coast of—	237
„ (Southern) Chiefs of—	232
„ Survey of the South Coast of—	191
Arabic characters	281
Arabs, the	5, 39, 194, 198, 215, 219, 225, 226, 227
„ of San'á	249
„ Religion of—	197
„ (Subeïhï)	213, 214
Arachasia	13
Arachotus (river)	12
Ara envoy	169
Arák trees	194
Aral (river)	186
Ararah	230
Arbuckle, Dr.	218
Ard-es-Saba	237, 238
Areeah Galla,	290
Arghandáb (river)	12, 13, 15
Argunj : The Khán of—	98
Aria of the Greeks	8
Ariapolis	11
'Aríf	230
Ariyah	230
Arkassan (river)	12

	Page.
Arkineo	98
Ark-i-no	22
Armenians	103
Arms of Herát	124
Army of the King of Persia	64, 65
Asia	9
„ (Western) : Wild tribes of—	176
Asifoodaula	57
Asof-ud-Dowla	98, 100
Asr el Hamrá	227
Assafœtida	4
Asses (wild)	5
Assizuldeen, Fakeer	178
Assoubah tribe	298
Ass's Ears	215
Assúr (Asúr)	247, 249
Assut Khán	146
Astrábád	103
Asuf-ood-Dowlah	89
Atchikzyes (Atchukzye), the	...24, 26, 111, 114, 129, 131, 132, 135, 136, 137, 138, 139
„ and other Pathán tribes : Origin of the practice of shaving the hair around the circumference of the mouth amongst—	139
„ „ Religious education amongst—	138, 139
„ country	136
„ Manners of—	137, 138, 139
Attock	105, 160, 167
„ Derwaza	169
„ taken by Runjit Sing	173
Augustus	159
Aukun Ladáh Mahomed Dáood	83
Aurangzebe	168, 171, 179
Ausef-ood-Dowlah	79
Aussa	268, 297
Aussah	290
Avaz	7, 8
Avitabile (Avitable), Monsr.	7, 10, 16, 17, 175
Ayaboo, the	286
Ayaloo : Mountains of—	265
Ayooloo : Mountains of—	274
Aysomauli, the	260, 297
„ Ibrahim Ibn Mohamed, Chief of—	261
Ayún (grapes)	250
Azam Khán	114, 115, 120, 161
Azboti	304
Azbuks, the	57
Ǽzem Khán	120, 121
Azeres	17
Azeris	8

B

Baba Wullee	13
Babel	139
Báb-el-Mandeb Strait	211, 212
Báb Ká'-el-Yahúdi	247
Bacchus' expedition to Hindustán	166
Baddás Sheikhs	224

Badghis	100
Badirzye, the	24
Bag : Fort of—	64, 66
Bagotk Agamooti Shurikoorgi...	290
Bahoristán (poem) dedicated to Sultan Hussain Bookára	8
Bahr Assal or the Salt Lake	256, 304
Bahrein	250
Bahr-el-Saffi	207
Baia : Nests of the—	243
Bák : Fort of—	66
Bakhírí	237
Bakora...	11
Bakwa	26
Bá-'l-háf	227
„ The tower of—	224
„ Narrative of a journey from the tower of—to the ruins of Nakab-Al-Hajar	189—201
Balkh ... 9, 38, 39, 114, 121, 127	139, 167
„ Kilick Ali Beg, Chief of—	39
Ball, Mr.	211, 214
Ballabang : Town of—	159
Balla Hissar	29, 118
Balta Koolu Beg	58, 64
Bamiyan	40, 54, 55
Bampoor : Fort of—	69
Bander Burum	228
„ Darás	217
„ Feikam	215
„ Hisn Ghoráb	225
„ Hokat	217
„ Kásim	219
„ Kosair	228
„ Roweiní	229
„ Sheikh	215
„ Tuwayyí	216
Bang	121, 150, 178
Banians	219
Banias, the	221, 228, 241, 249
Bani-kazals, the	5
Baraghah Island	226
Báram...	119
Baram Khán	112
Bareilly	119
Barızye branch of the Noorzyes	24
Barker, W. C., Captain ...273, 275, 276 285, 288, 289, 302, 303	
Letters to Captain Harris from—284—290	
Letter to the King of Shoa from—	282
Narrative of a journey to Shoa by—.	255—304
Narrative of the events during the residence of—at Alio Amba.	277—284
Reception of—by the people of Tajura	300, 301

Barker, W. C., Captain : Remarks of—about the family of Wulasma Mohamed Abogaz	276, 277
Baronsky, Mr.	64
Barrakzyes, the 9, 12, 14, 17, 25, 26, 41, 103, 107, 108, 109, 110, 111, 112, 114, 116, 119, 125, 132, 151, 156, 165	
Barrow, Mr.	211
Barrow Rocks	221
Barúrudda	304
Barwákhi	230
Basawul	116
Bassadore	103, 106
Batal	4
Bayah	216
Baza	263
Bazars in Indian cities	146
Beads	172
Bedar	295
Bedi Kurroo Ruff	259, 304
Bedoos, the 256, 284, 291, 292,	293, 295
Bedouins (Bedawis), the 191, 194, 195, 197, 198, 200, 205, 206, 207, 208, 212, 213, 220, 228, 238, 239, 241, 242, 243, 248, 292, 293, 295, 296, 297, 298, 299, 300, 301	
Bedouin girls	219
„ shepherdess	216
„ soldiers	219
Bedur : Datah Mohamed, brother of—	285
Beedanas	159
Beeroo	267, 268, 290
Behrám Khán Kyánee	36
Beila	47, 49
„ the Chief of—	49
Beit 'Ali (Tent of 'Ali), sub-tribe of the Hamum tribe	230, 231
Beit el Fakih : The City of—	240, 241, 243
Beke, Mr.	264
Bellad Sabba Wadian	207
Belooks	36
Beluchees (Belochees), the 5, 6, 7, 11, 13, 15, 36, 48, 50, 70, 113, 121, 123, 129, 131, 140	
„ Chief of—	111
Beluchee country	113
„ traders	141
„ tribe of Magsi, the—	144
Beluchistan	12, 121, 145, 186, 192
„ The migratory tribes of—	143
„ Road for troops through—	45
Benáres : Sikh seminaries at —	171
Beni-Assad	5
Beni Dhobeibi	243
Beni Hasan	228
Beni-Kafodges,	5
Beni Khorah	244
Beni Seibán	225
Berbera 219, 228, 260, 287,	289, 301, 302

	PAGE.
Berbera : Ali Shermaki of—	302, 303
Berdooranees, the	35
Berishí tribe, the	227
Besoot	40
Bha	185
Bhag	141, 142, 143
Bháwal	184
„ Khán	121, 183, 184
Bháwalpur	104, 106, 120, 148, 174, 183, 184, 185
„ Chief or Khán of—	145, 146, 182, 183, 184
„ Expedition against—	120
„ invaded by Runjit Sing	173
Bhitta Kaffres	160
Bikkáneer (Biccaneer)	183
„ Brahman	140
Bing-báshí	241
Bír ' Alí	225
Birdján	3, 4, 7
„ Kind treatment of Major Neil Campbell by the Governor of —	7
Bír el 'Azab	247, 249
Bir-el-Hassi	206
Birgind	37
Bix Barrik : The mountains of —	3
Biya Karrah	290
Biyar Ahmed	215, 218
Black cape, the	214
„ Point of Horsburgh, the...	221
Blankets	137, 138
Blessings by the Hadjees	132
Bokhára	7, 8, 9, 39' 53, 54, 55, 57, 73, 122, 123, 139, 148
„ Ameer (king) of—	38, 54, 55, 122
„ and Herát : Road between—	103
„ Embassy to the king of Persia and the Sultan of Turkey from the Ameer of—	56, 57
„ Interview of Mahomed Hoosain Káshee with the Ameer of—	55, 56
„ Kabil Beg, the Elchee of—	66
Bokharians, the	54
Boldár (Baldi) rupees	119
Bollabrang	117
Bombay	187, 199, 211, 217, 228, 231
„ Kafillah from—	49
Boodh Sing	118, 173
Boonia Khán	8
Boorji Kafirán or the tower of infidels	58
„ Shah Kurumbeg	98
Boostam	64, 66
Bootlchak	29
Boulder Abbul	266
Bowan	246
Bowkoonoo Ancharoo, the principal market of the Galla	290
Brahmins	171
Brahooee	121
Bráwah : Natives of—	225
British Ambassador at the Court of the King of Persia	68, 69

	PAGE.
British authority : Sikhs' subjection to—	171
„ Government	54, 174
„ Mission at the Court of Shoa	290
„ „ to the Persian Government.	84
„ officers in Persia : Kind treatment of Mahomed Hoosain Káshee by the—	66—69
„ power	111
„ troops in Hindustán paid less than the troops of Runjit Sing	177
Brohee	145
Brothers, the (Islands known as Eight Brothers)	212, 213
Bucefotia : Masson's notice of the city of—	105
Bucephalia : Discovery of the sites of the ancient cities of —	166—168
Bucephalus : Tomb of—	166—168
Buchahod Shahabadeen	27
Buchni Moghool	55
Bucker	185, 186
„ Fort of —	145, 185
Buckwa	84
Bugglar	179
Bu Heïsh (Bú'ísh)	229, 230
Buhmun (Shábzada)	67
Buildings in Herát...	122, 123
„ „ Khorássán	123
„ of the Ghulzie	123
Bukwa	93
Bullets	134
Bullocks of Arabia and India	194
Bund	89
Bungee	169
Bungush	112, 117, 150
„ invaded by Peer Mahomed Khán...	112
Bunnoo	104, 150—158
Burdúdda	304
Burial grounds	152
Burnes, Captain	53, 63, 75
„ Alexander, Mr.	71, 72, 73, 74, 75, 97, 100
„ „ Notice on Herát by—35—41	
Burúm	228
„ Town of—	227
Bú Salih	230
Buseriah	4
Bushire	103, 106
Bussoo Ruddah	297
Bustán el Metwokkil : Palace of—	247, 248
„ Sultán	248
Byabanck	25
Byarulleah : Head dress of the —	177

C

Cábul (see Kábul).	
Cain	131
Calicut	187
Camels	139, 193, 194
Campbell, Captain	106
„ Major	48
„ „ Itinerary from Yezd to Herát and from Herát to Kábul *viá* Kandáhár by—	3—17

b 1573 - 2

INDEX.

	PAGE.
Campbell, Mr.	175
Camraun or Camerodeen Khán, Chief of Herát	7, 8, 9, 17, 23, 35, 36, 37, 38, 99, 100, 108, 109, 124, 125, 126
Camraun or Camerodeen Khán: Administration of Herát by—	125
Camraun or Camerodeen Khán: Army of—	109
Camraun or CamerodeenKhán: Dominion of.	125, 126
Camraun or Camerodeen Khán : Present from Ranjit Sing to—	109
Caravans	133
Caravanserais	3
Carpets	37
Carvan Cazee	24
Cashmeer (See Kashmere)	
Caspian Sea	103
Cássum Sháh	144
Castes : Nannock's doctrines regarding—	171
Catholic	172
Cattle in Herát	124
Caves (Cavities)	165, 222
Central Asia	35, 82, 122
Chaffa: Valley of the—	270, 274
Chah-Soo	123
Chaka: The mountains of the—	270
Chalybeate springs	205
Chanoo	285
Chardeh	28
Chár Sú	13
Char Viláyut	85
Checkaub	24
Chehár Saber	231
Chehl Buchagan	28
Chehl Zeena	12, 58, 70
Chesgoo	17
Chicha Wutnee	180
Chikzyes	24
China	117, 138, 140, 173, 231
Chontoram	6
Choriebe	205, 206, 208
Chota Ahmedpore	183
„ Jallálpore	182
Christian despot, the	275
Christianity	14
„ among the people of Shoa	279
Christopher, Lieutenant	255, 256, 257
Chuchaktoo	39
Chukunsoor	36
Chulakzyes, the	24
Chumkunnee: Library of the Mussulmán saint at—	178
Chumuni-bed	98, 100
Chunam	223
Chunny Khán-ka-Kote	183
Churkh	55
Coduitoo	296
Coffee-plantations	244, 245
Coffee: Varieties of—	250
Coins: Greecian—found in the Punjab	105
„ in Kandáhár	15
„ of Alezander the Great	166
Commallea	179, 180
Connolly, Captain (Lieutenant)	24, 25, 26, 87

	PAGE.
Constance, the (ship)	255
Constantine	218
Cooking: Methods of—in Alio Amba	288
Copper (Kaliad)	138
„ mines	4, 8, 159
Corsica	4
Cotton linen	187
Court, Monsr.	175
Cow	171
„ killing	119
Crops	5
Crusaders	53
Cruttenden, Mr.	191, 211, 216, 217, 223
„ C. J., Mr.: Narrative of a journey from Mokha to San'á by the Tarik-esh-Sham or Northern route by—	235—252
Culleele Khán	116
Customs duty: Levy of—in the Atchukzye country	135, 136
Cutch Gundava	45
„ Mekran	129
Cyrus: The country of—	139

D

Dabharah	291, 292
Dadar (Dardar)	121, 140, 141
Dahfurri	299
Dah-way-la-kal	260, 297, 300, 304
Dakkar	116, 165
Daman	187
Damann	119
Damot	268
Daniel	168
Dankali (tribe)	213, 255, 256, 257, 259, 260, 265, 270, 294, 300
„ Character of the—	213
„ Country of the—	255, 263, 268
Danville	12
Darab	219
Dár-el-Tawáshi	237
Darius	167
Dash Kulla	87
Dat	11
Datah Mohamed	284, 293, 294, 295, 296
Datah Mohamed, Chief of the Seedy Habroo, one of the sub-tribes of the Debeni	283, 285
Dathara	304
Dau'an	229, 230
Daudpootres	176, 184
Daulah or Governor	231
David: Daudpootre signifying the sons of—	184
Davlatabad	10, 24
Debeni (tribe)	260, 283, 298, 299
„ Datah Mohamed, brother of Bedur, one of the Chiefs of the—	285
„ Johita ibn Ibrahim, Chief of the—	259, 260
Debra Berhan (the Monastery of Light)	269, 270, 271, 273, 274, 288

INDEX.

	Page.
Deeni	289, 294, 296, 298, 300
Deen Mahomed Khán	92
Deewalik	27
Defeíghah	230
Deh Koundee	40
Dejisk	7
Delhi	107
Delhi Derwaza	169
" Firoz Sháh of—	199
Delore : Fortress of—	184
Demetrius	273
Denel Melei	264
Derind	4
Deyrah	150
" Futteh Khán	146
" Gházie Khán	15, 104, 111, 120, 121, 141, 145, 146, 160, 173, 183, 184
" " to Kollecbat : Notice by Mr. C. Masson on the countries between—.	145—150, 160—165
" Ismail Khán	120, 146, 147, 150
" Naváb of—	147, 148, 149, 158
Dhabbah	231
Dhafghán	231
Dhamár	239
Dhofár	245
Dhurrah	195
Dih-Zunghee	40
Dilaram	26, 84
Dinki (stream)	276
Dinomali	304
Dís : Town of—	230
Diván Misser Chund	170
Divorce system amongst the Mahomedans in Alio Amba	287
Diyabí Bedouins	192
" tribe	224
Djami, the poet	8
D'Jenghis Khán	8
D'jun hills	8
Dog, cape	227
Dohor hills	11
Dohosi	11
Dokbn	195
Dominies Khail	27
Do Mohammed and Do Husein : Tribes of—	239
Doober	185
Doombás	124, 126, 137
Doomi	296
Doorannee Chauki	161
" Chiefs	117, 118, 119, 173
" Empire (States)	103, 104, 107, 124
" fortunes, the	115
" Government	145, 173
" servant of Mr. Masson	157
" troops	156
Doorannees, the	14, 26, 27, 28, 92, 107, 110, 111, 112, 113, 116, 120, 121, 124, 133, 138, 165
" Character of—	115
" Charity of—	135

	Page.
Dooranees: Masson's observations regarding—	107
" Metropolis of—	109
" Tolerance of—in religious matters.	116
Dooshaukh	25
Dórah	244, 245
Doree (river)	12
Dost Mahomed, Ameer, Khan, &c., of Kábul	40, 55, 63, 64, 70—75, 104, 111—117, 119, 156, 159, 173
Dost Mahomed Khán and the other Dooranee Chiefs : Settlement of the dispute between—	112, 113
Dost Mahomed Khán and the other Dooranee Chiefs : Army of—	116
Dost Mahomed Khán called the "Sepáhi's" dostadár	113
Dost Mahomed Khán : Character of—	115, 116
Dost Mahomed Khán conquered Kábul	115
Dost Mahomed Khán invaded the country of Khán Tareek	113
Dost Mahomed Khán marched against Syed Ahmedsháh	119
Dost Mahomed Khán : Troops of—	113
Doutuluh	35
Dowkul Sing	175
Dragon's-blood-tree	245
Dress amongst the Abyssinians	288
Ducker	147
Dudd	304
Dugha	54
Dughdrab	39
Dujábí (tribe)	223
Dullool	304
Durburra : Fortress of —	148, 149
Dureïb-el-'Arabi	218
Durrahbund (Drabind)	147, 148
Durya-i-Koower	81
Dussera : The review of the Sikh troops on—	177
Dutch guns in the Kandáhár army	113
Duties : Levy of—on goods	241
Dyan Sing	174, 175, 178
Dyeing seeds	9

E

East India Company	191
" Surveying brig Palinurus of the—	237
Ebb	230
Ecchdakan	4
Ecchkidur	4
Eedzil Canal	9
Eesah (tribe)	256, 259, 260, 290, 296, 297, 298, 301
Egypt	198, 200, 250, 265
" Mohammed Ali, the Pásha of—	239
Egyptian Government: Beït el Fakih, the frontier town of the—	241
Egyptian ruins	198
" sea	166

	Page.
Egyptain towers	198
" troops	238, 240
Eïsán	201, 206
El Ahmarán	242
El' Aïnah	217
El Akkaf	205, 207
El Bedá (grapes)	250
El Gharm	230
El Gharrah	220
El Hádi	249
El Hudhein	246
El Khór	221
El Mahadi	249
El Mutewakkil billah	247
Elabousails (tribe)	5
Elephant: Story of certain ignorant persons of their knowledge of—	53
Elliott, E. K., Lieutenant	84, 89
Elphinstone, Mr.	104, 107, 121, 150
Elphinstone's work on Kábul	107, 108
Emameret or Mother of Mercy: Mountains of—	265, 270, 274, 286
Emaum Reza: Tomb of—	3
" Teiralabadeen	29
Emier	285
England	103, 193
" (old): Display of the glorious ensign of—at the English Residency at Ankobar	280
English: Ameer Dost Mahomed Khan's negotiations with the—	74
" Intrigues of Yar Mahomed Khán for the ejectment of the— from Herát	79, 80
Englishmen	196
Engoonzik	4
Errur	295, 297
Erzeroom	84
Esau	147, 150
Esaw, Mr.	120
Eshan Khoja	39
Ethiopia	268
" Mohamedan invader of—	263
Ethiopic characters	199
Eto	289
Eto Galla: Mountains of—	265, 286
Etymander, the	25
Eunuchs: Abode of the	237
Euphrates (ship)	103, 255, 273
Europe: Trade from India to—	198
European comfort	201
" fleet: Karáchi, the first harbour in the Indian seas visited by a—	187
" fortress	219
" power in Hindustán	107
" travellers	116
Europeans, the	17, 56, 109, 161, 185, 205
Eusofzye (tribe)	119, 120
" country	117
" hills, mountains, &c	119, 173
" Patháns	173
Eusofzyes: Slaughter of the by the Sikhs	119

F

	Page.
Fakeer Mahomed, Chief of Nal	47
Falahies (tribe)	5
Faredoon Mirza (Prince)	64
Fari	264, 284, 291 304
Farjalat	205
Farráh	8, 10, 11, 108
Fazi	16
Fazil	184
Fazilpore	183, 184
Feelee (tribe)	53, 63, 68
Feerozkohee (tribe)	38
Fennel of Corsica	4
Fiahloo: The valley of—	297, 304
Firangis	46, 49, 106, 161
Firauz (Firooz) Khán mountains	10, 11, 12
Firinji	217
Firoug	10
Fish	139
Flagstaff at Bombay	217
Flint Island	216
" rock	217
Ford	27, 28
Forster, Mr.	26, 126, 167, 172
Foster	12
Fountains	248
Fourk	7, 8
" Castle of—	4
France	103
French	247
" Camp	169
" Officers of Ranjit Sing	170
Fresnel, M. F., Mr.	225
Friendship: Feast of—amongst the Adaiels.	283, 284, 285
Fruits of Herát	123
Fudhli district: Sughra, the principal Port of the—	221
" territory	220
Fudhlis	219, 220, 221, 222
Furazkohee Aimaks	100
Furráh (fura)	24, 25, 37, 91, 92, 93, 113, 125, 126
" Government of	35
" river or Furráhrod	126
Furrookh Khán	66, 68
Futeh Alee	56
Futtehalli	186
Futteh Alli, Sháh of Persia	125
Futteh Khán (Fatte Khán or Futtah Khán).	17, 25, 87, 92, 99, 109, 114, 125, 126, 161
Futteh Sing	174, 175
Fuwah	227, 228
Fyfool Moolk	25
Fyz Mahomed Khán	79, 80, 83, 86 87, 91

G

Gadhar Ghar	28
Gabdun	206, 208

INDEX.

	Page.
Gaistuddeen	8
Galen	63
Galla (tribe)	261, 262, 266, 268, 271, 272, 273, 274, 287, 289, 290, 296
Galla (Edjou)	279
„ Expeditions of the king of Shoa against the—	268, 269, 273, 275
„ Finfinny tribe of—	278
„ horsemen	269
„ physician	289
Gallas and the army of the King of Shoa: Battle between the—	278, 279
Garagin	262, 278, 289
Garah	187
Gardens	123, 124
Garidj	3
Garron, Mr.	175
Gauz: Province of—	10
Gawridean Dynasty	8
Gazun: Ruins of—	4
Gebel Dróra	206
Gedem	287, 289
Geera Dohiba	296
Genii Hill	214
Georgian	16
Gerong	149
„ Fort of—	146
Gesenius, Professor	225
Ghább Wáli	220
Ghag (stream)	10
Gharígah	195
Ghilzye (Gheelzye, Gulzye, Geelzye) 15, 16, 27, 30, 110, 111, 113, 114, 123, 126, 138
„ Chief of the—	16
„ Chief, Khán Tareek	113
„ country	116
„ Masson's memo. regarding—	113, 114
„ Nativity of the—	113
Ghiraunee	126
Ghizni (Guznee, Ghuznee, &c.) 16, 28, 29, 40, 72, 104, 109, 112, 113, 114, 116, 121, 122, 156
„ Chiefs of—	114
„ imprisonment of Major Campbell and others by the Governor of—	16, 17
„ Masson's memo. regarding—	114
„ to Kábul: Stages for caravans from—	17
Gholam Hyder Khán, a son of Ameer Dost Mahomed Khán	28
Ghoráb (tribe)	230, 231
Ghore	25
Ghorian	24, 36, 37, 79, 80, 85, 89
Ghor Kádir	215
Ghubbet 'Ain	224
Ghubbet Kulún	227
„ Seilan	219, 220
Gibbon	258
Gibraltar	219
Gillah	224
Gingaddi	298
Gipsies	265, 266, 272, 273

B 1573 – 3

	Page.
Girishk	10, 11, 12, 25, 81, 85, 86, 89, 90, 91, 108, 110, 126
„ Fort of—	84, 126
Giswuel	206
Gloondee	28
Gobaad	304
Gobaad Kharab	256
Godin Komber	6
Goher Shah	8
Goidez	17
Gojam	268
Gold: Traces of—in the earth of Posht—Badam	4
Gondar	268, 282, 289, 290
Goodiana	183
Googujerwalla	183
Gooje Amba	290
Goolám Sháh Koloro	186
Goolkoo mountain	12
Goolkun (mountain)	16
Gool Mahomed	108, 119, 137
Gocnabad	37
Goongoonteh	257, 258, 260, 263, 304
„ the valley of—	282, 299
Goordewan	39
Goorgan	58
Goorzerja	8
Gosk	5, 7
Goths	258
„ and Vandals of Africa	268
Gouchoo	276, 281, 283, 284, 285, 296
„ hill	265, 286
„ State prison at—	269
Gour: Province of—	11
Gouzherab	9
Govindghar	170
Gownabad	3
Graham, Charles Douglas, Lieut.	255
„ Mr.	275
Grapes	9, 124
Grazing fee	181
Greece	139
Greek architecture	105
„ historians	166
„ patriarch at Alexandria	268
Greeks	4, 15, 39, 105
Grein	208
Grieve, Mr.	211, 214, 216
Guader	105
Guinea-fowl	243
Guisk	4, 5, 70
Gujer	187
Guláb Sing, Rájáh	175
Gum	4
Gunderbaz	121
Gunderpore	147
Gunder Sing	175, 181
Gunghur	119, 167
„ Patháns of—	119
Gunneemurgh	24
Gunnsél	119
„ Countries of—	119

INDEX

	Page
Guns (brass)	218
Gurdun Deewar	55
Gurguddi: Plains of—	259
Gurkás...	173
Gurmah	84
Gurmal	84
Gurmee	84
Gurmser	70
Gurráh river	184
Gurrar river	182

H

	Page
Habahn	206
Habalen	206
Habeebóola	115, 116
Habib Abdalla ibn Haidum	208
Hadjee Khán	115
Hadjees (see Hajis).	
Hadramaut	195, 198, 219, 220, 229
„ account of an excursion in—by Adolphe Baron Wrede	203—208
Haffásh	250
Hagaioo, Chief of the Woemah	296
„ Geera Dubbah	296
Hagar...	133, 139
Haines, J. B., Capt...	205—208, 245, 303
„ Memoir of the South Coast of Arabia from the entrance of the Red Sea to Misenat by—	211—233
Háji Abd-er-Rasul...	246
„ Agasee, minister of Foreign Affairs, to the King of Persia	64, 65, 66, 67, 68, 69
„ Dost Mahomed	70
„ Khán	115
„ „ Kakar...	112
„ Mohamed	290
„ „ Hoosain Isfahanee	71
„ Sayad	276, 277, 280, 283, 285, 286, 291
„ Shár	121
Hajír	242, 243
Hajis	131, 132, 133, 134, 137, 288
Hakim-ben-Hasheen	11
Hakkam	230
Hakumzadeh	133
Haláni island	225
Halle	225
Halle-bung	98
Hamari range	223
Hámed	191, 200
Hámi	229, 230
Hamilton, Mr.	218
Hamoo	36
Hamúdiyah	230
Hamum tribe	230
„ „ Beit 'Ali, sub-division of the—.	231
„ „ Kasáidi, sub-division of the—	232
Hangoo	112
Hao	304
Harrah	232
„ Ambili	296, 297
Harrar...	272, 273, 275, 277, 282, 284, 285, 287, 289, 293, 295, 296, 300

	Page
Harrar, Account of—	289
„ Emir of—	274, 280, 285, 286, 288, 291
„ Journey to—	289
„ Kafilah	284
„ Letter of introduction to Lieutenant Barker from the King of Shoa on the Emir of—	280, 281
„ Lieutenant Barker's intention to go to—	280, 281, 285
„ merchants	280, 283, 286, 287
Harrargi	280, 288, 290
„ Abdool Liki, Chief of the—	273, 274, 279, 282, 285, 288
„ Behaviour of the—towards Captain Barker	285
Harráz mountains	244
Harree...	140
Harris, Captain (Major)	255, 273, 275, 279, 282, 286, 292
„ „ Letters from Captain Barker to—	284—290
Hasan ibn 'Ali	231
Hasannuggur	117, 119, 173
Hásek...	245
Hassan Khan	24
Haur (Haura)	223
Haushábi	216
Hawash (river)	262, 263, 265, 286, 292, 304
Haybooti: Mountains of—	274
Hazara country	9
„ Tartars	127, 139
Hazaras	28, 38, 39, 40, 54, 55, 92, 110, 111, 129
„ Chiefs of the—	79
„ Masson's memorandum relative to the—	114
„ of Taloda Hoojooristán	40
Hebrew	199
Heeroonees (tribe)	5
Heikah...	213
Heis: Fortress of—	239
Hejáf	216, 217
Helmund (river)	11, 12, 25, 26, 36, 92
Hender Addi Dowar: Plains of—	259
Herát	7, 9, 13, 14, 16, 71, 91, 92, 103, 113, 114, 121, 124, 126, 133, 157
„ Abolition of the slave trade in—	125
„ Account of the city of—	8, 9, 21, 22
„ Administration of—by Camraun (Kamerodeen Khán)	125
„ Allowances to the King of—	83, 86, 87, 88
„ and Bokhára: Road between—	103
„ „ Kabul: Roads between—	39, 40
„ „ Persia: Negotiations between the Governments of—	91, 92
„ „ Persian Governments: Alliance between the—	125
„ „ Sind: Countries between—	103
„ „ Yezd: Country between—	5
„ Army of—	125
„ Attack on—by the Persians	36

INDEX. xi

	PAGE.
Herát: Bázárs in—	122, 123
,, British influence in—	92, 93
,, Buildings in—	122, 123
,, Chief of—	37, 108
,, City of—supposed to be built by Alexander the Great	8
,, Civil war in—	8
,, Direction of the route from Yezd to—.	3
,, Expedition to—	66
,, Fruits of—	123
,, Garrison at—	35
,, Government and Politics of—	35, 90, 91
,, Intrigues of the ruler of—	79, 80
,, Itinerary from Yezd to—	3—17
,, Lieutenant Pottinger's letters regarding the state of affairs at—	97—100
,, Mahomed Sháh Suddoozye, king of—.	124
,, Major D. Todd, Envoy to—	83, 84, 89
,, ,, Todd's letters regarding—	79—93
,, ,, ,, negotiations with the Government of—	80, 81, 85—88
,, ,, ,, proposals for insuring British influence in—	82, 92, 93
,, Masson's memorandum regarding—	108, 109, 122—127
,, Military force at—	125
,, Notice on—by Captain Burnes	35—41
,, People of—	54
,, Reannexment of—to Cábul (Kábul)	93
,, Revenue of—	36, 109, 125
,, River called Pool Mallán	124
,, Siege of—by the Persians	36, 92, 97—100
,, State of affairs at—	79, 80, 81—89, 92, 93
,, to Kábul : Routes from—	9, 10
,, ,, ,, vid Kandáhár: Itinerary from—	3—17
,, ,, Kandáhár : Route from—	26
,, ,, Simla : Report of a journey from—	21—31
,, ,, Yezd: Unsafe condition of the route from—	6, 7
,, Translation of a note from the Vuzeer of—to Major Todd	89
,, Valley of—	9
,, Westerly state of—	107
,, Withdrawal of the British Mission from—	84—91
,, Yar Mahomed Khán of—	79, 80, 81
Heri (river)	9
Herirood (river)	23
Heriz	8
Himyari	198
Himyaritic language	225
Hindu architecture	182
,, Koosh	40
,, population : Decrease in the—owing to the influence of the Mahomedan power.	171
,, power : Nánnock's project for the restoration of the—	171

	PAGE.
Hindus	4, 13, 104, 110, 111, 115, 116, 119, 123, 136, 140, 141, 142, 143, 144, 147, 151, 152, 153, 155, 156, 158, 160, 177, 187
,, The Sheeahs do not eat things sold by the—	123
Hindustán	109, 117, 141, 173
,, Early history of—	166
,, Emperors of—	185
,, Proper : Natives of—	176
Hirrar	157
Hisn el Misenat : Fort of—	230
,, Ghoráb	196, 199, 215, 225, 227, 231
,, ,, Buildings around—	225
,, ,, Inscriptions at—	232, 237
Hissar	173
Hissaruk	29, 30
Hodeidah	241, 243
Hog and Tiger hunts	49
Homer	152, 161
Homerite dynasty	198
Hoombelli	230
Hoosain	47
,, Ali Mirza, Prince of Khorássán	8
Hora	206, 207
Horsburgh	212
,, The 'Aden Back Bay of—	216
,, Chimney peaks of—	213
Horses: Climate of Seistan not congenial to—	37
,, of the Imám of San'a	248
Hota : Town of—	206
Hoteekee branch of the tribe of Ghilzye	27
Hottentot crested sparrow	216
Houlliads	13
Houz (reservoir of water)	23
Houzi Muddudkhán	26
Howaiyah	222, 233
Huft Kothul	29
Hugh Lindsay (ship)	229
Hughes, Dr.	229
Hulaut in Belochistan : Embassy from—to Hyderabad	120
Hulton, Dr.	211, 217, 223, 224, 226, 232, 237, 238, 245, 246, 247, 252
Hunuf Koolee Khán	57
Hur	230
Huram	99
Hurree Sing	117, 118, 174, 175, 178
Hurrohwah	230
Husein el Katheri : Ruined fort of—	232
Husht Bihisht	98
Hussain, the bearer of presents from the King of Shoa to the British Government	230
Hussein Sháh	114
Husún Dikarah or Dakrah	243, 244
Huzaras (see Hazaras).	
Huzrutgee	13
Hyæna Mount	229
Hydaspes, the	166, 167
Hyderabad	105, 106, 120, 186
,, Princes, rulers, &c., of—	144, 186

xii   INDEX.

	PAGE.
Hyderabad : Routes from Láhore to—	179—187
Hyderee	38

I

Ibrahim (name of a stream)	11
„ ibn Burantoo	291, 292, 294, 295, 298, 299, 300
„ „ Hagaioo	261
„ „ Mohamed Akil or Chief of the Aysomauli	261
„ Joee (river)	24
„ Khán D'Jamshed : Palace of—	8
„ Khán-i-Sheerazee	68
Idiots	143
Idolaters : Fort of—	154
Ijilli	227
Ikhkili or Himyaritic language, the	225
Ils	39
Imak tribe	7
Imám 'Ali, son-in-law of Mohammed	239
„ Hádi	249
„ Mehdi	117, 173
„ of San'á	241, 243, 244, 247
„ Roza : The tomb of—	8
Imáus : Mountains of—	111
Imeeat Dajah	277, 278
Insntah	288
Indee language	150
India	4, 14, 15, 40, 228, 241, 242
„ Bullocks of—	194
„ People of—	63
„ Routes from Kandáhar to—	15
„ Russian expedition against—	9
„ Trade from—	198
„ Workmen of—	105
Indian corn	242, 245
„ Empire	82
„ Government	255
„ Navy	205, 237
„ Ocean	205
Indus, the	12, 15, 40, 92, 105, 111, 117, 118, 119, 120, 126, 139, 141, 145, 146, 148, 150, 160, 167, 181, 183, 184, 185, 186
„ Countries west of—taken by Runjit Sing	173
„ Deyráh Ismail Khán, one of the greatest marts on—	146
„ Masson's notice on the countries west of—	104, 145—150, 160—165
„ Navigation in—	105
Infidels	164
Inscriptions at Hisn Ghorab	237
„ Nakabu-l-Hajar	197, 199, 237
„ Nakhl Mayúk and Kosair	237
„ San'á	237, 251
Ira'ıra (river)	274
Irak	66
Isl a'kzai chief of Laush, Sháh Pusund Khán	92
Ishikaghassee Abdoomheem Khán	88, 89
Ishuk Aghassee	85

	PAGE.
Iskunder Shahzadeh	23
Ismá'il	139, 252
„ Khán	155
„ Waláni	247
Ispahan	6, 17, 30, 168
Issa Khéle	150
Issa Khéte	147
Itinerary from Yezd to Herát and from Herat to Kábul viá Kandáhár	3—17
Itoo Habti	271, 274, 278
„ Kotama	264, 271, 272, 280
„ Lestowald	271
„ Maretch	272
„ Melkoo	280
„ Metookoo	269, 273
„ Woldo Lanna, Governor of Ankobar	264
Izabra (river)	270
Izakh	255, 260, 261, 301
„ Kashim	292

J

Jagatars	28
Jaggem	144
Jagharra	84, 87
Jaghooree	40
Jahánábád	36
Jahazán	57
Jakera	35
Jálee; nephew of the Wulasma Mohamed Abogaz	277, 279, 282, 285, 291
Jallálábad	30, 79, 83, 85, 104, 112, 113, 116, 117, 165, 167
„ and Peshawar: Routes between	30, 31
„ Government of—	30
„ Masson's memorandum regarding	116, 117, 159, 160
„ road	156
„ valley : Tribe of white people of Greecian origin in the—	167
Jalloogeer	27
Jám 'Ali : Island of—	217
Jami (poet) : Tomb of—	124
„ (stream)	276, 286
Jamsheedee Kimaks (tribe)	38
Janissaries	271
Jankira	39
Ján Mahomed Khán	29
Jardine, Lieutenant	211, 232
Jats	180
Java	241
Jazarjurchees	30
Jebel 'Akár	229
„ Árah	213
„ Asad	231
„ Burrá	244
„ Dheb'ah	229
„ Gharrah	228
„ Hajjíyeh	242, 243, 245
„ Hamari	223, 233
„ Hamúm	231
„ Harráz	244

INDEX.

	PAGE.
Jebel Hasan	215, 216, 233
,, Heikah	211
,, Hejáf	213
,, Hisn Ghoráb	224, 233
,, Ibn Shamáyik	231
,, Jambúsh	231
,, Ján	213
,, Jinn	214
,, Káû	214
,, Kharaz	214, 221, 222, 233
,, Makánati	223
,, Manhali	211, 212
,, Masinah	193
,, Nagam	249
,, Shamshán	216, 218, 233
,, Tejúrah	213
,, Warrah Ambili	289
,, Yáfa'i	220
Jehangier: Tomb of the Emperor—	169
Jeháundat Khán	109
Jehaun Khán	113
Jendoo	290
Jeráf	249, 250
Jeramah: Rock of—	216
Jerusalem	268
Jeselmere	183
Jessamine	219, 238
Jewel Agil	196
,, Sheikh	195
Jewish workers in gold	252
Jews	139, 219, 237, 249, 250
Jews' Gate	247
Jezirah Denáfah	217
,, Sawáyih: Island of—	217
,, Sharmah	231
Jezirat Abu Shammah	215
Jeziratu-s-Sab'ah	212, 233
Jhelum (river)	105, 166
Jibús	226
Jiddah	225
Jilleh	192
Jóf desert of—	248
Johar: Nephew of the Wulasma Mohamed Abogaz	285
Johita Ibn Ibrahim, Akil or Chief of the Debeni	259, 260
Johivaha	290
John	298
Johnson's Rasselas	264
Joseph, Patriarch	133
Jowar	143
Jubah	225
Jubbal Khán, Chief of Lughman	116, 120
Jubbar Khán	55, 73, 75
Jubbul	141
Juhma Mirza	53
Julduk	15, 27
Jum	117, 161
Jummer Khán	119
Jummir Khán, Governor of Shikárpur	132
Jummu	173, 175
Jummut Khán (Summut Khan)	156

B 1573—4

	PAGE.
Jumrood	30
Jumsheeddees	92
,, Chiefs of the—	79
Jungle-cock of India	243
Juzailchees	54

K

Kaband: Salt spring of—	5
Kabashee	133
Kabil Beg	58, 64, 66
,, the 'Kurawool Begee'	56
Kabis or Kermania, the great desert of—	3
Kábul	14, 15, 16, 17, 28, 29, 30, 35, 39, 40, 48, 53, 54, 55, 57, 69, 71, 72, 73, 74, 75, 82, 90, 97, 104, 108, 109, 111, 112, 113, 114, 116—119, 121—125, 127, 140, 155, 156, 158, 159, 160, 167, 173, 174, 177
,, (river)	17, 29, 30, 116, 117
,, Account of an embassy to the King of Persia from the Ameer of—53—59, 63—75
,, and Herát: Roads between—	39, 40
,, and Kandáhár: Roads between—	28, 29
,, Attempts of the Kandáhár Chiefs to dissuade Kumbur Alee Khan from proceeding to the Ameer of—	71, 72, 73
,, Bool	29
,, Combination of the Kandáhár and Peshawar Chiefs against Dost Mahomed of—	156
,, Deputation of Kumber Alee Khán by the King of Persia to the Ameer of—	66
,, Dost Mahomed Khán, Ameer of—	40, 65, 66, 111, 159
,, Elphinstone's work on—	107
,, Evil designs against Dost Mahomed of—	156
,, Government	172
,, Itinerary from Herát to—	3—17
,, Kandáhár Chiefs jealous of the Ameer of—	71, 72, 73, 111, 112
,, King of—	145, 149, 165
,, Mahomed Hoosain Khán Kashee's interview with the Ameer of—	53, 54, 73—75
,, Masson's memorandum on—	114—116
,, Re-annexment of Herát to—	93
,, Report of a journey from Herát to Simla viâ—	21—31
,, Revenue of—	115
,, Route from Kandáhár to—	15
,, Sháh Shujáh, King of—	144
,, Sir W. H. Macnaghten, Envoy to—	79
,, Stages for caravans from Guzni to—	17
,, taken by Dost Mahomed	115
,, Timur Sháh of—	172
,, to Herát: Routes from—	9, 10
Kadhrein islands, the	226
Kádur Khán	132—137
Káfila Kabashee	133, 137
Káffre Kote	154

INDEX.

	PAGE.
Káfir-Kála	9, 17
Káfir Kilar	39
Káfirs	198
Kagis	4
Kahreez	28
Kahut	112
Kajars	58
Kakurs	111, 112, 146
Kalfah	230
Kalfetein	217
Kalhora: Ancient family of—	186
Kaloo	55
Kalert (Khelat)	145
Kálposh	57
Kamerodeen Khán (See Camraun).	
Kamran (See Camraun).	
Kandáhár ... 3, 5, 8, 9, 12, 26, 35, 37, 38, 40, 54, 70, 71, 72, 73, 74, 80, 84, 87, 88, 103, 104, 108, 110, 111, 112, 113—116, 119, 121, 122, 123, 124, 125, 126, 127, 137, 140, 145, 146	
,, and Kábul : Road between—	28, 29
,, and Sháll : Masson's remarks on the manners of the people of the country between—	137, 138
,, Army in—	14, 15, 113
,, Chiefs or rulers of—	14, 15, 92, 108, 109, 110, 111, 112, 113, 121, 156
,, ,, Army of the—	113
,, ,, dissuade Kumbur Alee Khán from proceeding to the Ameer of Kábul	71, 72, 73
,, ,, Expedition against Shikárpur by the—	108
,, ,, Extortions by the—	110
,, ,, jealous of the Ameer of Kábul	71, 72, 73, 112, 113
,, ,, Mahomed Hoosain's arguments with the—for allowing Kumber Alee Khán to proceed to Kábul	71
,, ,, Presents from the King of Persia to the—	67, 69
,, ,, Revenue of the—	113
,, City of—	13, 110
,, Coins in—	15
,, Commerce of—	15
,, Description of the city of—	26, 27
,, Fears for being rich in—	15
,, Females of—	13
,, Fortification of—	13
,, Government	113
,, Intended attack of the Herátees on—	91
,, Major Todd's suggestion for concentrating British troops at—	82
,, Masson's memorandum on—	109—113

	PAGE.
Kandáhár: Pir Dil Khán, one of the rulers of—	12
,, Population of—	13
,, Products of—	13
,, Report of a journey from Herát to Simla viá—	21—31
,, Revenue of—	110
,, Road for troops from—to the sea	45
,, Road from Girishk to—	12
,, Route from Herát to Kábul	10
,, Routes to—	126
,, Siege of—by Nádirsháh	13
,, to Kábul : Route from—	15
,, to Shikárpur: Masson's adventures from—	127—145
,, to Shikárpur : Road from—	15, 104
,, Weather at—	13, 14
Kangrah : Fortress of—	167
Karabagh	28
Karáchi	121, 187
,, Bunder	105, 106
,, the first harbour in the Indian seas visited by a European fleet	187
,, Naomull Seth of—	49
,, Routes from Lahore to—	179—187
Karáchies (tribe)	228
Karadáh	230
Karavanserais	123
Karek	10
Karez	5
Kargan : Scarcity of grain in—	66
Karkar hills	48
Karon	12
Kar Seban	206
Karzet	230
Kasáídí (tribe)	229, 232
Kashan	53, 67, 68, 69
,, Shahan	53
Kashee	53
Kashmere	15, 63, 107, 120, 167, 171, 174
,, taken by Runjit Sing	173
Kasim Abú Mohammed	249
Kasserman	10
,, Pass	11
Katoal	145
Kauf and Kayu : The unsafety of the route between—on account of the plundering Turkomans	7
Kava Bagh	40
Kayu (Kayin)	3, 5, 7
Kayu : Governor of—	37
Kázar : Fort of—	55
Kázee : Fort of—	69
Kázim	55
Kázi Mulláh Mahomed Hussein	83, 86, 87, 88
Kazunees	5
Keeláh Khán (fort)	113
Keisel Hammán	217
Kelat-i-Ghiljee	27, 29
Kelat-i-Nahsir Khán (Khelat-i-Ghilzie)	15
Kelmond	4
Kentucky : The State of—in America	103
Kerman	6, 69, 70
Kermania : The great desert of—	3

INDEX.

	PAGE.
Kermin Kálási	221
Keshr	249
Khaf	36, 37
,, Chiefs of—	38
Khail-i-Akhoond	27
Khails	26
Khair Mahomed	163
Khájeh Ourieh	23
Khak-i-Chaupan	26
Khak Teezee	29
Khaleefa Sofee Islam	56
Khalif's sword, the	247
Khalil Chief	119
Khamis	246
Khán Dejun	6
Khandenur, the author of an abridged Universal History	8
Khanghur	181
Khán Huzrut, Chief of Khyva	87
,, Ján	36
,, Jeháun Khán	111, 113
Khanjuen	4
Khanjuerkan	4
Khánpore	183, 184
Khán Tarcek of the Ghilzyes	111, 113
Kharam Segan	7
Khareez	28
Kharif Sha'rán	226
Khárijah	226
Kharuck	24
Khaush (river)	89, 92
Khaushrood (river)	25, 26, 36
Khawer Taneh : District of—	27
Khelát (Kelat or Keelat)	109, 111, 121, 140, 145
,, Capture of—	45, 46, 48
,, Chief of—	111
Khelat-i-Nadiree	57
Khelát : Meeráh Khán, Chief of—	136, 144
,, Saed Mahomed Khán, Chief of—	57
,, to Sonmeani : Narrative of a journey from—	45—50
Khiva	53, 82, 87, 98, 103
Khivans, the	36, 38
Khogianees	30
Khojee Chist	40
Khok	4
Khonah (river)	84, 160
Khondil Khán	14
Khooda Buksh Khán	29
Khoollum	55
Khoord Kábul	29
Khoorshnakhood	26
Khooslik	79
Khór 'Amrán	214
Khorássán	3, 7, 9, 37, 38, 103, 108, 109, 111, 113, 114, 115, 116, 122, 123, 124, 125, 126, 127, 135, 138, 139, 140, 141, 145, 146
,, dynasty	112
,, Ferocious tribes of—	176
,, Husain Ali Mirza, Prince of—	8

	PAGE.
Khorássán: Jallálábád denominated as Switzerland of—	159
,, Kuhruman Mirza : Ruler of—	54
,, Migratory tribes of—,	148, 158
,, Prince of—	7
,, Sháh of—	107
,, Winter dress in—	133
Khór Biyar Ahmed, or Seílan	215
,, Kádir	215
,, Maksá	216, 218
,, 'Omeyra	214
Khower Taneh	27
Khubeloollá Khán, father of Aga Khán	69
'Khubt ibn Deran	244
Khulil	112, 119
Khuramabad	63
Khusial Sing	168, 174, 175, 178
Khyber	112, 117, 119
,, hills	116, 159
,, Masson's notice on the passage through the pass of—	160—165
,, Monument	164
,, Pass	160—165
,, Valley	104, 154, 165, 167
,, ,, People living in—	162
Khyberi Patháns	165
,, Tribes	117
Khyrabad	39
Kila-i-Nan	36
Kilick Áli Beg, Chief of Balkh	39
Killa Dookhter	23
Killa-i-Khalekdad Khán	27
Killa-i-No	38
Killa-i-Pisr	23
Killa Rohee	37
,, Suffeed	24
Kilulloo	260, 295, 297, 304
,, to Zeyla : Route from—	289, 290
Kirepore	105, 145, 186
,, Meer Shrob of—	144
,, Routes from Láhore to—	179—187
Kirk, Dr.	255, 262
Kishmee	106
Kitár	226
Kivort	150—158
Kizilbashis (Kuzzilbash)	35, 40, 55, 56, 58, 63, 64, 73
Kobis : Desert of—	6
Kochan	3, 6
Kochee district	148
Kohinoor	178
Kohistan	114
Kohistanees	116
Kobun Dil Khán	67, 68, 69, 70, 71, 73, 108, 109, 110
Kola-tool : Fort of—	13
Kolibah	160
Kolk	12
Kollecbat	104, 145
,, Notice by Mr. C. Masson on the countries from Deyráh Gházee Khán to—	145—150

	PAGE
Koloro, the last sole prince of Sind	186
Kóltibah (Kolibah): Notice by Mr. Masson on the countries from Deyrah Ghazi Khán to—	160—165
Kolybah	147, 150
Kolychee	147, 148, 158
Komási of Mokhá	219
Kon	4
Kondemir	11
Koon	7
Koondooz: Moorood Beg of—	39
Koorham: The festival of—	83
Koorrum	27, 28
,, Khán	29
Kooshab	128
Kooshbegee, Vazir of the Amir of Bokhara	54, 55
Koosh-i-Nakhúd or Khoorsh Nakhood	12, 26
Kooyah (Kooyab)	147, 150
Korán	173
Korein: Hamlet of—	231
Korook Subzawaur	21
Kosair	231, 232, 233
,, Inscriptions found at—	237
Kosháb (river)	11
Koshroud (river)	11
Kotali Onnee	55
Kote Kangrah	173
Kotelie	187
Kou-Doug	11
Kouroot (a kind of curd)	14
Krapf, Reverend	255, 262, 264, 274, 275, 281, 282, 290
Krapper	160, 161, 165
Krokala of Nearchus	187
Kubr-el-Hud	207, 208
Kudve Chok	98
Kufnak	53
Kuhruman Mirza, ruler of Khorassan	54
Kujars (tribe)	97
Kulla-i-Azmi Khán	27
Kulla-i-Hazee	29
Kulla-i-Jaafferee	28
Kulla-i-Nader	26
Kulla-i-No	79
Kulla-i-Ramazan Khán	27
Kum	68
Kumber (Kumbur) Alee Khán	67, 69, 71, 72, 73
Kumher Alee Khán: Deputation of—to Ameer Dost Mahomed Khán	65, 66
dissuaded from proceeding to the Ameer of Kábul	71—73
,, Reception of—by Kohun Dil Khán	70
Kúm-Harmás	225
Kumuruk	55
Kundi (Koondi)	150, 151
Kundoos	114, 167
Kurds	123
Kurmalli	186
Kurokh	36
Kurreem Dád Khán, Chief of the Hazaras	92

	PAGE
Kurruk Sing	170, 174, 178
Kurrum	302
Kusar	39
Kuttuck	120
Kuzabak	16
Kuzzaks (tribe)	87
Kyánee	36

L

Laahdoo: Lakes of—	265, 274, 286, 292
Lahaj	219, 233
Láhejí	193
Lahore	105, 109, 112, 116, 117, 118, 120, 122, 124, 148, 167, 172, 173, 177, 181
,, Conquest of—by Rungit Sing	170, 171
,, Derwaza	169
,, Gardens of—	170
,, Masson's Memorandum on—	105, 168—178
,, Rungit Sing, King of—	111, 158
,, to Karáchi: Routes from—	179—187
,, Zoological collection at—	169
Lakhman: People of—	160
Lalpur	31
Lalwá	247
Languerd: Valley of—	17
Largebur Kahreez	24
Large Strait	213
Lasgurd	67
Lásh	37
,, Shah Pusund Khan, Chief of—	35
Lát of Firóz Shah	199
Laush	92
Lead mines	4, 9
Leech, Lt.	97, 99
Leila (name of a horse)	118
Library of the Mussulman Saint at Chumkunnee	178
Lindsay, Mr.	64
Lion (Mount)	231
Lizards	160
Lo (name of a village)	156
Loaves	291
Locusts	139
Login, Dr.	89
Logur	29, 112, 113
Loharnee	127, 148, 158
Loll Khonnor	145, 186
Loll Sháh Abbás: Tomb of—	186
Londgerd	17
Loodiana	31, 120
Loot	37, 70, 73
Loveday, Lt.	86
Luban or frankincense tree	245
Luckman	159
Lucknow	116
Lughman	104, 120
,, Masson's Memorandum on—	116
Lukkee	152, 158
Lúlúwah	249
Lunka: Fort of—	171
Lur	25
Lyari	49

INDEX.

M

	PAGE.
Macdonald, John, Sir	106
Macedon: Gifted warrior of—	166
,, Philip of—	178
Macnaghten, W. H., Sir, Envoy and Minister at Kábul	79, 83, 85, 90, 97, 100
Madeera Dubbah	296, 304
Ma'du'...	230
Maeevend	12
Maghuá	223
Magnificent: Suleïmán, the—	249
Magsi: the Beloche tribe of—	144
Mahallah	219
Maha Sing	177
Mahmoodabad	38
Mahomed	56, 223, 282, 298
,, Abogaz	263, 264
,, Akber Khán, a son of Ameer Dost Mahomed Khán	30, 71
,, Ali.	257, 258, 260, 261, 262, 290, 295, 297
,, ,, Hospitality of—to Mr. Masson.	132
,, ,, Khán	57
,, ,, Mirza	53
,, ,, (Alee), Nazir of the Minister for Foreign Affairs to the King of Persia	67
,, ,, Páshá of Egypt	239
,, Ameer Khán	72
,, ben 'Abdu-l-'Abid	228
,, Daood	88
,, Haleem Khán	24
,, Hoosain Káshee	53
,, ,, ,, Account of an Embassy to the King of Persia from the Ameer of Kábul by—	53—75
,, Hoosain Káshee and Hajee Agásee: Enmity between—	66
,, Hoosain Káshee argues with the Kandáhár Chiefs for allowing Kumber Alee Khán to proceed to the Ameer of Kábul	71, 72
,, Hoosain Káshee detained at Merv by Neaz Mahomed Khán	56, 57
,, Hoosain Káshee: Interview of—with the Ameer of Bokhara	55, 56
,, ,, Interview of—with the Ameer of Kábul	53, 54, 73—75
,, ,, Interview of—with the King of Persia	63—68
,, ,, Intrigues of the officers of the King of Persia against—	66—69
,, ,, Mahomed Zaman Khán's endeavours to take his revenge on—	54, 55

	PAGE.
Mahomed Hoosain Káshee refused to accept the supply of money from the Sháh of Persia for expenses	66
,, ,, returned to Kábul	73
,, ,, suspected of negotiating with the English for the Afgháns	67, 68
,, Hosen Khán Murnee	68
,, Hussan	45
,, ibn Abú Bekr, a tributary of 'Abdu-l-Wáhid	226
,, ibn Burantoo	297
,, ibn Hagaioo (Oogass)	261
,, ibn Hamzah	213
,, Imám 'Ali, son-in-law of—	239
,, Izakh	263, 268
,, Khán	53, 99, 120, 184
,, ,, Begler-Begee	38
,, ,, Kuráee	38
,, Luman Khán, Chief of the Jumsheedees	92
,, Mirza	36
,, 'Omar ibn 'Omar	231
,, Omarkhán	25
,, Omur Khán	72
,, Oosman Khán	25
,, Rahim Khan Ameen-ul-Mulk	53
,, Ruza Khán, Governor of Seestán	70
,, Sa'di, Vizier of the Imám of San'á.	247
,, Sháh	8, 9, 12, 17, 24
,, ,, King of Persia	10, 53, 54, 55, 56, 57, 71, 73, 74, 82, 91, 97, 172
,, ,, son of Timour	16
,, ,, Suddoozye, King of Herát	124
,, Shaul (See Mahomed Shah).	
,, Siddik Khán	25, 70
,, Zaman Khán	54, 55
,, Zummer Khán	116, 159
Mahomedan costume	205
,, invader of Ethiopia	263
,, prejudices	14
Mahomedans	104, 171, 219, 225
,, Cruelties of the Sikhs towards the—	176
Mahommed or Mahommud (See Mahomed).	
Mahrah territory	232
Maïdan	17, 29, 226
Maimuna	38, 39, 40, 53, 93
Maintenance in Alio Amba: Cost of—	288
Majetti	290
Makalla or Makallah	205, 208, 224, 225, 227, 228, 229, 230, 231, 233, 237
Makateïn	221, 223, 233
Makateïn-Seghír	222
Makdahah	226
Makdisha	225

B 1573—5

INDEX.

	PAGE.
Makullah	237
Makur ...	15
Malcolm, Charles, Sir	211
,, John, Sir	171
Maliks...	119, 158
Malli ...	182
Malyar...	29
Mamoo, Muktyar for Kandáhár	110
Mango tree	156
Mansur	249
Mansúrah	196
Mansúri	219
Manufactures of silk, woollens, &c., in Herát.	124
Marbát...	232
Márbe ...	199
Máreb ,...	237, 238, 251, 252
Mariaba	199
Market towns between Senníf and San'á	242
Mároo ...	304
Marriage ceremony in Alio Amba	287
Marzúk Kebir	217
Masjid (Mesjid) el Jámi'	240, 250
Masjid Pádisháh	168
Masjid Sonara	168
,, Vazier Khán	168
Masson, Mr., an American traveller in Central Asia	103, 104
,, Adventures from Kandáhár to Shikárpore by—	127—145
,, Adventures in a journey from Ták to Pesháwar by—	150—158
,, in Sind	104
,, Memorandum on the discovery of the sites of the ancient cities of Bucephalia by—,..166—168
,, Memorandum on Herát by—.122—127
,, Memorandum on Lahore, the Sikhs and their kingdom and dependencies by—	168—178
,, Memorandum on the routes from Lahore to Karáchi by—	179—187
,, Notice on the countries west of the Indus by—. 145—150, 160—165
,, Notice on the Province of Jallálábád and on the Seeaposh by—	159, 160
,, Observations of—on the political condition of the Dooránee States and of the countries between Herát and Sind	103
,, Treatment of—at Kandáhár	104
,, Wilson's letter to the Government of Bombay regarding—	103—107
Masson's Journals	103—187
,, skill in medicine	161, 162
Massowa	289, 290
,, and Alio Amba: Route between—	290
Mateneh	252
Manlama Jalaloodin Roomee	53
Maund...	245
Mauritius	241
Manshid	238

	PAGE.
Mayán 'Abáduh	230
Máyariyán	230
Mayokí: Village of—	232
Mazinduran: The plain of—	57
McNeill, John, Mr., Her Majesty's Envoy at the Court of Persia	21, 97
Mecca	131, 173, 194, 240, 288
Meer Afzul Khán	70
,, Ali Naghee Khán, Governor of Toon	37
,, Allah	23
,, Allum	119
,, ,, Khán	37
,, Daood (Daoud or Dooad)	10, 23, 88
,, Dil Khán	14, 109, 110
,, Kázim	55
,, Khail	29
,, Kurmalli	186
,, Mahomed	6, 186
,, ,, Khán	114
,, Mobarrak	186
,, Morád Ali	106, 187
,, Rustom	186
,, Shrob	144, 185, 186
,, Sidick Khán, Chief of the Berdooránee tribe in Berát	35, 88
,, Sohdat	186
,, Taarah	186
Meerab Khán, Chief of Khelat or Kalort... 121, 136, 143, 144, 145
Meerpore	185
Meerza (See Mirza)
Meháyí	238
Mehrab Khán	46, 49
Mehr Dil Khán	67, 70, 71, 72, 73, 74
Meifah...	227
Meimaneh: Khán of—	8
Mei-moneh	7
Meïn	222
Meinha-tolli	304
Mekháyehs	238
Memkhán, Chief of Noorzyes	24
Memla...	30
Memoir of the South Coast of Arabia from the entrance of the Red Sea to Misenat.209—233
Mersa Munger Duffa	301
Merv ...	38, 54, 56, 57, 98
Meshed	...3, 6, 8, 9, 37, 38, 53 56, 57, 65, 66, 79, 80, 81, 83, 86, 87, 89, 90, 91, 103, 108, 115, 123, 125, 139
,, Family alliances of the princes of Herát with those of—	108
,, to Bulkh: Road from—	39
Mesulla	98
Metals...	4, 15
Metta ...	290
Metwokkil Allah	249
Mevires, Mr.	175
Meyen, Dr.	192
Meyú ...	230
Meyún...	212
Military force of Runjit Sing	174—177
Minerals	159
Mir (See Meer)

INDEX.

	Page.
Miriam, a Mahomedan woman, with whom Lieutenant W. C. Barker had put up at Alio Amba	277
Mirza	63
„ Abbas	68
„ Abdool Hoosain Khán	69
„ „ Hussun Khán	84
„ „ Kasim, Vazir Toork	53
„ „ Sumee Khán	54, 73
„ Agásee	64
„ Alee Akbar Khán	73
„ Hádee Khán	69
„ Imám Verdee	73
„ Mahomed Tukeo	65
„ Muhdee	68
„ Musnod (Masood), Minister for Foreign Affairs to the King of Persia... 59, 63, 64, 65, 68, 84	
„ Rajik Khán	4
Misderah	219
Misenát	232, 233
„ Memoir of the South Coast of Arabia from the entrance of the Red Sea to—	209—233
Mizrab Khán, an Uzbek of the tribe of Wun.	38, 39
Mofhak	244, 245, 246
Mogul Emperor of Delhi	107
Mogul-ka-Shar	182
Mogul principality of Turbut	125, 126
Moguls	123, 124
Mohammed (See Mahomed).	
Mokhá	211, 219, 228
„ Governor of—	239
„ to San'á by the Tarik-esh-Sham or Northern route: Narrative of a journey from—by Mr. Charles J. Cruttenden	235—252
Mokubberah Jehangier	169
Momund tribe	31
Momunzye	161
Monkira (Monkeera or Monkurah)	147, 171, 174, 175, 177
„ Fortress of—	120
„ taken by Runjit Sing	173
Mooknee	15
Mookoor	15, 16, 28
„ Khail	30
Moolla Budroodin	54
„ Dauran Kakuree	54, 55
„ Jubbar Achukzaees	72, 73
„ Mahomed Omar	88
„ Mull	116
„ Rusheed Akhunzada	71, 72, 73
„ Shukoor, Envoy from Sháh Sujáh	118
Moolu Zughir	304
Moon: Mountains of the—	225
Moorád Beg of Koondooz	39, 40
Moorakee	28
Moorchee Derwáza	169
Moorcroft	39
Mooree	55
Moore: Stanza of—	157
Moorghab and the Soonee Huzaras	38, 39

	Page.
Mooroot	184
Moosa Beg	79
„ Hola: Mosque of—	8
Mooti Rám	184
Moradalli	186
Morality of the male and female sexes at Alio Amba	287
Morally (name of a village)	146, 147
Morgah, the	8
Moscow	53
Moses	133, 139
Mother of Mercy: Mountains of the—	265, 274
Motteneh	246, 247, 252
Mozghur	184
Mozuffer (Muzuffer) Khán	148, 173, 181, 182
Muchnee	31
Muckelwand	119
Mudaitoo (tribe)	259, 260, 261, 289
Mudkozah	155
Mughrá: Ruined fort of—	230
Mujuoon and Leila	118
Mukawwí (coffee house-keeper)	238
Muklewans	265, 269
Mulberries	124
Mulik Gate	98
Multan (Mooltan)	105, 120, 148, 171, 174, 175, 177, 181, 182
„ conquered by Runjit Sing.	173
„ Routes from Lahore to—179—187	
Mundoye	173
Munsoor Khán Barukzan	68
Murrah	304
Murroo	296
Mursa Goorah	290
Murwut	104, 150—158
„ Expedition to—	148
„ The Pathans of	147
Musayyid	230
Mushahr	298
Mushed	3, 6, 8, 9, 56, 57
Múshij or Maushij	238, 239
Musicians	180
Musíkani	186
Muskat	106, 187, 228, 231
Musnuvee (name of a book)	53
Mussulmán Saint at Chumkunnee: Library of the—	178
„ subjects: Runjit Sing's behaviour to—	178
Mussulmans	160, 172, 176, 177, 180, 186
„ Revolt of the —	178
Mustoong	121, 140, 143
Mutewakkil	247
Muttayleh	185
Muttee	31
Muzdooran	57
Muzuffer Khán (See Mozuffer Khán).	
Muzzeen	104
Mydan (See Maidan).	
Mymunna (See Maimuna).	

INDEX.

N

	PAGE.
Nádir Sháh	...9,13, 14, 22, 35, 39, 63, 114, 145
Naga-koomi	304
Nagkar	230
Nahkop	7
Náib Gool Mahomed	119
Nakab-Al-Hajar	196, 199, 206, 215, 225
„ Description of the ruins of—	196—198
„ Inscriptions found at—	237
„ Narrative of a journey from the tower of Ba'.l-haff on the Southern Coast of Arabia to the ruins of—	189—201
„ Ruins of—	223, 224
Nakabu-l-hajar (See Nakah-Al-Hajar).	
Nakeb-el-Hadjar (See Nakab-Al-Hajar).	
Nakhl Mayúk : Inscriptions found at—	237
Nakih	228
Nakoot	179
Nal	45, 48, 49, 50
„ : Fakeer Mahomed, Chief of—	47
Nánee	16, 28
Nanni	158
Nánnock, the founder of the Sikh sect	171
„ Notions of—about Government	172
Naomull Seth of Karáchi	49
Naoor	12
Nasál	223
Násir ben Abú Bekr, Chief of the Urláji tribe	222
Nasseer Khán of Kalort	145
Navigation on the rivers of the Punjáb and Indus	105
Nawab Jubber Khán	17, 67
Nazarene	263
Nearchus	187
Neaz Mahomed Khán	56
Nejdi breed of horses	248
Nero	166
Niebuhr	237, 239, 241, 245, 246, 247
Nile (river)	200
Nimrod	275
Nishápur	38
Noa Kote	170, 171, 179
Noodseezan	13
Nooree	29
Noorzyes (tribe)	10, 11, 23, 24, 26
Norris, Charles, Mr.	103
North, Lieutenant	86, 89
Northern route : Narrative of a journey by Mr. C. J. Cruttenden from Mokha to San'á by the—	235—252
Nubia	194
Nubian girls	228
Nuggur	153
Nujjib Pultan	177
Nujjoo Khán	81, 83
Nujuf Ali Khán	57

	PAGE.
Numzand	25
Nurmsher	69
Nushara	183
Núshki	12
Nusroola Khán	66
Nusseer Khán	186
Nusserdeen (Peer)	182
Nussur Collab Teimoree	37
Nysa Ambassadors	127

O

Obé	36, 38, 40
Obeh (Oba)	28
Ocelis	212
Ochees (river)	111
Olives	191
Omer Khán	148
Oms, Mr. : Imprisonment of—by the Persians	7
Onnee	55
Ooch	182, 183
„ Routes from Lahore to—	179—187
Oogass of the Wulasma	261
Ooloos	38
Oomergooloof	304
Oornach, the	48
Oornus	167
Orghan Mirza	8
Orgunge	53, 54
„ Allah Koolee Khán, ruler of—	56
„ Army of the Governor of—defeated by the son of Saed Mahomed Khán	57
Orientalist	199
'Oseir	247
Osurum	205
Ouch	105
Oudeney, Dr.	194
Oussah lake	262, 265
Outram, Captain	90
„ „ Narrative of a journey from Khelát to Sonmeani by—	45—50
Oxus (river)	82
Oxydranee	182

P

Pachemour	12
Pádsháh	124
Pádsha's topee	161, 164, 167
Palinurus, the	191, 211, 217, 218, 221, 223, 224, 226, 232, 237, 245
„ Shoal	232
Pampa grande de Arequipa	192
Paogan	39
Parkoo	47
Paropamisan mountains	15, 127
Paropisarmus	167
Parsevans	124
Parthanils	4
Parthian kings : Tombs of the—	4
Partridges	243
Patab	13

INDEX.

	Page.
Pathans ... ... 137—139,	184
„ Character of the—	131
„ of Gunghur	119
„ of Momunzye	161
„ of Muckelwand and Damaun ...	119
„ of Rawul Pindi	160
Pathan States: Military strength of the—...	148
Patriarch Abraham	139
Peasantry of Herát	124
Peer Dil Khán (*See* Poor Dil Khán).	
„ Jallálpore	182
Peer-ki Ooch	182
Peer Mahomed	117
„ „ Khan ... 54, 112, 117,	156
	157, 158
„ Nusserdeen	182
Penalties for wounding or killing a man ...	279
Perim or Meyún 212,	233
Persia 15, 35, 38, 40, 41	
	56, 90, 91, 167
„ Account of an Embassy from the Ameer of Kábul to the King of—53—59, 63—75	
„ Advantages from Herát remaining in the hands of—	9
„ and Russia: War between— ...	103
„ Deputation of Kumber Alee Khán to the Ameer of Kábul by the King of—	66
„ Designs of—against Herát ...	35
„ Embassy from the Ameer of Bokhara to the King of— 56,	57
„ Females of—...	13
„ Futteh Alli, Sháh of—	125
„ Her Britannic Majesty's Envoy at the Court of—...	21
„ King or Sháh of— ... 36, 91, 97, 168	
„ Mahomed Hoosain Kashee's interview with the King of— ... 63—68	
„ Russian influence in—	82
„ Sháh Sultán Hussein, King of— ...	6
Persian Army ... ... 97—100	
„ costume	10
„ Court at Tehrán	7
„ General: Interview with Fatte Khán of a—	99
„ Government: British Mission to the—	84
„ Gulf Residency	103
„ invasion and ascendency in Herát: Effects of— 40,	41
„ language	139
„ tobacco	250
„ travellers	3
Persians... 5, 7, 8, 13, 14, 22, 23, 56, 92, 108,	
	115, 123, 125
„ and the Afghans: Wars between the— regarding Herát	9
„ and the Herátees: Negotiations between the— 91,	92
„ and the Heratees: Union between the—	
	79, 80, 125
„ Attack on Herát by the— ...	36
„ believe in dreams and astrology ...	14
„ Siege of Herát by the— ... 92, 97—100	
B 1573—6	

	Page.
Persians took the fortress of Bag from the Turkumans	64
Perso-Russian Frontier	82
Pesháwar ... 14, 53, 54, 74, 104, 105, 106,	
	108, 109, 112, 113, 115,
	117—120, 122, 124, 150
	—162, 164 , 165, 167,
	171, 173 174, 177, 178.
„ and Jallalábád: Routes between— 30,	31
„ and Kandáhár Chiefs: Combination of the—against Dost Mahomed	112
„ Army	156
„ Chiefs of— ... 111, 117, 156,	173
„ conquered by Runjit Sing ...	104
„ Masson's adventures in a journey from Ták to— ... ...150—158	
„ rice (Bara) of— 69,	118
Peshto (Pushto language). ... 129, 131, 139,	150
Pharnacotes (river)	11
Pharsacs	3
Philip of Macedon	178
Phra	11
Physicians (Galla)	289
Pilau	5
Pilot-Island	212
Pinna fragilis	191
Pissaruk	29
Pistachio 9,	10
Plato	63
Plundering habits of the people between Kandáhár and Shikárpur	134
Plutarch	166
Pomegranates	124
Pooleráh	184
Pool-i-Malán	9
Pool Mallán 23,	124
Pooralloo (mountain)	48
Poor Dil Khán of Kandahár, 12, 14, 108—113, 120,	121
„ Character of —... 109,	110
Poosand	25
Pootee	15
Populzyes (tribe)	14
Porridge, Cape	224
Portuguese, the 225,	268
„ auxiliaries of the Christian King of Shoa	263
Porus	167
Post-horse in England	193
Pottinger, Colonel 45, 49, 86,	192
„ Letters from— ... 97—100	
Poynder Khán	109
Products of Herát 123,	124
Prophet	249
Pul-i-Malaum (*See* Pool Mallán)	
Pul-i-Shaikabad (bridge)	29
Punjáb, the ...104, 105, 111, 117, 139,	
	164, 166—168, 171
	—173, 178, 179
„ Navigation on the rivers of the— ...	105
„ Report of a journey from Herát to Simla *viâ*— ... 21—31	
„ soldiers, the 175,	176
Punjdeh	38

INDEX.

	PAGE.
Purali (river)	49
Pusht-Bodam or Posht-Bodam	4, 6
Puttála	187
Putteeála	183
,, Rája of—	172

R.

Radbam	228
Ra-Eesáh Pass	256, 300
Rághib	229
Rahim Dil Khán	67, 70, 109, 110, 112
Rahmut	187
Raïdah	229, 231, 232
Rájáh Sensar Chund of Sujauhanpore	173
Ramazán: The fast of the—among the Fudhlís	222
Rámdil Khán	14
Ramkully	182, 183
Rás Abú Kiyámah	215
,, Alargah	215
,, Alí	268
,, 'Amrán	214, 215, 233
,, 'A'rah	213, 214, 233
,, Assásah	227
,, Bab-El-Mandeb or the Cape of the Gate of Affliction	211, 213, 233
,, Baghashú'	231, 232, 233
,, Burúm	227, 233
,, el Ahmar	227
,, ,, 'Asídah	224, 233
,, ,, Bir	213
,, ,, Ghoul	207
,, ,, Káfiláh	256, 257
,, ,, Kelb	206, 224, 227 233
,, ,, Kosair	223, 231
,, Fartak	231
,, Feïkam	215
,, Gomahli	302
,, Ka'û	214, 233
,, Khádá	226
,, Kosair	231
,, Kútam	217
,, Mafrádah	225
,, Makallah	228, 229
,, Makdahah	226, 227
,, Marbát	228
,, Marbút	217
,, Marshigh	217
,, Mujallab Heïdi	215, 233
,, Rehmat	227
,, Retl	224
,, Sáfwán	223
,, Sálih	215
,, Salil	216
,, Seïlán	219, 220, 221, 233
,, Seján	212, 213, 233
,, Sharmah	230, 231, 233
,, Sináïlah	216, 217, 233
,, Taïh	217
,, Társhein	216, 217
Ras-ul-Aseidá	191
Rás Urlajáh	223

	PAGE.
Ravee (river)	105, 166, 169, 180, 181
,, The valley of—	179
Ráwal Pindi	119
,, Patháns of—	146 160
Red Sea, the	194, 238
,, to Misenat: Memoir of the South Coast of Arabia from the entrance of—	209—233
Rég Shuturán: Sandy mountains of—	3
Rehmat	227
Rendzye Endgousht	11
Rennell, Major	166, 167
Rennie, Mr.	211
Resht	103
Rimauk (tribe)	79,92
Rind (tribe)	144
Road for troops from Kándáhár and Shawl through Beluchistán to the sea	45
Robad	5, 6
Robad Khán	6
Robát	131, 132, 133
Ródah	249, 250
Rodrinjoe	45
Rohillás	184
Rojan	121, 144
Roman Empire, the	268
,, Emporium: 'Aden was considered a—in the time of Constantine	218
,, road	218
Romans, the	139
Rood-i-Adruscund	23
Rood-i-Guz	23
Rood-i-Helmund	25
Room: Sultan of—	56
Roostam Khán, an Uzbeck Chief	39
Roree	145, 185
Rosary	172
Röth, Dr.	255
Route: The direction of the—from Yezd to Herát	3
Ruby mine	9
Runjit Nujjibs	175
Runjit Sing, the Rája of Lahore 40, 41, 54, 63, 66, 71, 74, 104, 106, 107, 109, 111, 112, 117—120, 158, 167, 168, 171, 172—187
,, at Peshawar	117
,, Chevalier Allard, Chief of the European officers of—	105
,, Conquest of Lahore by—	170, 171
,, demanded of Yár Mahomed of Peshawar his celebrated horse called Leila	118
,, Dominion of—	173
,, European officers of—	105
,, Masson's remarks about—	177, 178
,, Military force of—	174—177
,, Revenue of—	174
,, sent an army against the fanatic Syed Ahmedsháh	117—119
Runjit Sing's expedition to Peshawar	118

INDEX.

	Page.
Runjit Sing's vengeance on the Eusofzye for cow-killing	119
Russia	53, 56, 63, 103
,, and Persia : War between—	103
,, Mahomed Hoosain Káshee went to—	53
Russian deserters	99
,, expedition against India	9
,, Frontier	87
,, slaves	87
Russians, the	74, 75, 82, 91
,, Struggles of Abbas Mirza with—	53
Rustam, the Hercules of Persia	10, 24
Ruweïs	238

S.

Saadut Khán	120
Sá'ah	229
Sabá	198, 238
Sabæan Army	207
,, dynasty	198
Sabhúr tree	245
Sabians, the	198
Sadant	25
Saed Mahomad Khán (See Sayad Mahomed Khán)	
Saffi	207
Sagullo	300, 304
Sahbis, the	5
Sahela Salassie, King of Shoa, Efat and the Galla	264, 267, 268, 275, 281, 282, 287, 288, 289
Sah-Hud	207
Sahúu	195
Sa'id	196, 230
Saifoola (Sháhzáda), Governor of Lasgurd	67
Sa'il	230
Sakzye Dooránee	37
Sálih ben 'Abdallah ben Sáil	229
Salt	160
Salt Lake	256, 257, 258, 299
Salt money	270, 287
Salt mountains	150
Salt spring of Kaband	5
Saltpetre	182
Salvadora Persica	194
Samaritan	257, 277, 301
Samarkand and Herát : Road between—	103
Sambeh	222
Samfúr	244, 246
Samhá	225
San'á	225, 240
,, El Mutewakkil billah, a title assumed by the Imáms of—	247
,, Famine at—	251
,, Government of—	249
,, Imám of—	239
,, Inscriptions at—	237
,, Mansur, one of the Imáms of—	219
,, merchants	241
,, Narrative of a journey from Mokha to—by Tarik-esh-Sham or Northern route, by Mr. C. J. Cruttenden	235—252
,, Palaces of the Imám of—	248

	Page.
San'á : Visit of the Imám of—to the mosque on Fridays	248, 249
Sanders, Lt.	211, 224, 226, 232
Sandhills	192
Santghorra	180
Saodágars	133
Saodut Khán	184
,, Chief of the Momund tribe	31
Sar : The plain of—	11
Sardar Kohimdilkhán	25
Sarpore	147
Sáva	207
Sawábili language, the	225
Sayad Ahmed Sháh	112, 115, 117—120, 157
,, ,, and the Sikhs : War between—	173
,, ibn Gagaioo	289
,, Mahomed	117, 119, 247
,, ,, Khán	57, 79, 87
,, Mirza	55
,, of Khonah	160
,, Oman Oollah	88
,, Walla	179, 180
Sayads	45, 47, 114, 154, 281—283
Sayid (See Sayad)	
Scythians	11
Se Abbase	66
Seals of the King of Shoa	281
Secunder Námeh	167
Secunder Zoolkurna	167
Sedik	7
Seeaposh (Sia-Posh)	104, 160
,, Masson's notice on the province of—	159, 160
Seedy Habroo : Datah Mohamed, Chief of the—	283
Seef : Mohammed Abdalla ibn ben Issa Achmudi, Sultan of—	208
Seerah	303
Seestán (Seistan)	5, 6, 10, 11, 36, 37, 70, 73, 85, 125
,, Chiefs of—	108
,, Fort of—	70
,, Revenues of—	81
Seestannees, the	92, 93, 123
Seghir	232
Sehwan	104, 186
Seïfel Khalifah	247, 248
Seihán	245
Seïlan	215, 219, 220
Seistan (See Seestan)	
Seján Cape	212
Sekeyyah	213
Sennif	241, 242, 246, 252
Sensar Chund, Rájáh of Sujauhánpore	173
Serais	123
Serai States	174
Scrin Khán	149
Seripool : Chief of—	39
Sernman	3
Serrár	232
Serwar Khán, Chief of Ták	148, 149, 151
Sesostris' expedition to Hindustán	166
Seven Islands	212
Sewán	230

INDEX.

	Page.
Seyyid (*See* Sayad)—	
Sháhábad	10
Sháh-Abbas	3, 5
Sháh Beg	23
Shahboodin (Shahabadeen or Shaboodin)	140
Shahboodin Khán	27, 28, 111, 113, 114
Shahbund (stream)	26
Shahdost of Nal	45
Shah Dukteran	13
Shaher	196
Sháhghassee Painda	71
Shah Hossain : Daughter of —	13
Sháh Kamrán	81, 82, 91
Sháh Maeesoond mountains	12
„ Mahmood	108
„ Maksúd	13
„ Namah of Firdose	11
„ Pusund (or Saloo) Khán, Chief of Lásh	35, 37, 92
„ Risool Sháh	117
„ Rode	66
Sháhro Khán	69
Shah Sujah (Shooja)	27, 53, 81, 82, 83, 86, 91, 92, 93, 103, 116, 118—122, 125, 144, 161, 162, 171, 173, 178
„ Envoy from—to Runjit Sing	118
„ Masjid of—	122
Sháh Sultan Hussein, King of Persia	6
Shahtoot trees	149
Sháh Wullee Khán	39
Sháhzada Mulik Kossouree : Garden of—	8
Sháhzádeh Iskunder	23
„ Syf-ool-Moolk	91
Sháh Zamoon	16
„ Zemáun	107
„ Zumán	39
Shakespear, Lieutenant	87
Shákhábad	10
Shaknápur : Fortress of—	6
Shall	121, 137, 139, 140, 143
„ and Kandáhár : Mr. Masson's remarks on the manners of the people of the country between—	137, 138
„ Dardur	121
„ The valley of—	136
Shallimar	124, 125, 170
Shar	121
Sha'rán	225
„ Hill of—	226
Sharmah Bay	230
Sharoot	64
Shaum Sing	174, 175
Shawl : Road for troops from—to the sea	45
Sheba : The land of—	238
„ The Queen of—	268
Sheeas (*See* Shias)	
Sheel, Mr.	67, 68
Sheenwárrees (Shinwari)	117, 159, 164, 165
Sheep of Herát	124
Sheer Dil	3, 115, 125
„ Khán	14, 110, 112, 113

	Page.
Sheer Hajee or Sheeradah	22
„ Mahomed	147
„ „ Khán	24, 87
„ Sing (Shir Sing)	174, 178
Shehr	229, 230, 233
Sheik el Jerádí	244
Sheikh Abdalla-Ba-Sudan	206
„ „ ben Marbút	220
„ 'Abdu-r-rahmán Baddás, mosque of—	223
„ Ahmed : Island of—	216, 217
„ 'Ali ibn Násir, Sultan of the Hamúm tribe	230
„ Gházi Naíji	243
„ Huseïn bin Yahyá	239
„ Idris : Tomb of—at Aden	217
„ Kádir : Tomb of—	215
„ Mohammed Safali, Chief of the Berishi tribe	227
„ 'Othmán : The white tomb of—	218
„ Said ben Issa ibn Achmudi	208
„ Sammarah : Tomb of—	215
„ Wúli	227
Sheikhuh Hurbah, a female devotee	223
Sheïkháwí mountains	232
Sheikhs	191, 221
Sheikh's Castle	221
Shekabad	17
Shenein	230
Sheppard, Lt.	211
Shere Mahomed	120
„ „ Khán	35, 40
„ „ „ Huzára	36, 38
„ „ „ of Killa-i-no	38
Sher Guz	70
Sher-i-Soofa	15
Sherjah	239
Shermaki	302, 303
Shia Bactiara	6
„ Dera	4
„ Nagree	4
Shias, the	7, 14, 35, 40, 114, 123, 124, 155
Shibám	229
Shibbergam	38, 39
Shield of Mohamed Abogaz	263
Shigas (tribe)	98
Shikárpur (Shikárpore)	80, 104, 109, 111, 115, 120, 121, 127, 140, 143, 144, 145, 184, 186
„ Account of—	144, 145
„ Expedition to—	108
„ Jummir Khán, Governor of—	132
„ Masson's adventures from Kandáhár to—	127—145
„ Poor Dil's invasion of—	113
„ Road from Kandáhár to—	15, 104
Shilgur	112
Shiráz	168
Shivprasád	174
Shoa	262
„ Abder Russool, the grand slave market of—	286
„ Account of the origin of the monarchy of—	268

INDEX.

PAGE.

Shoa: Administration of justice in the Court
 of the King of— ... 269, 270, 275
„ and Teejlol : Route between— ... 286
„ British Mission at the Court of— 285, 290
„ Career of the King of— 269
„ Christian King of— 255
„ Cruelties of the people of— 278, 279
„ Description of the palace of the King
 of— 266
„ Expeditions against the Galla by the
 King of— 268, 269, 278, 279
„ House-building in— 267
„ Interview of the English Ambassadors
 with the King of— ... 266, 267, 270, 273
„ Interview of Lt. Barker with the King
 of— ... 278, 279, 280, 281, 283
„ Itoo Metookoo defeated by the King
 of— 269
„ King of— 263
„ Letter from Capt. Barker to the King
 of— 282
„ The Mahomedan and the Christian sub-
 jects of the King of— 287
„ Narrative of a journey to— 253—304
„ Place of confinement of the State pri-
 soners of the kingdom of— ... 265
„ Presents to the King of— 266, 267
„ Review of the Army of the King of—271, 272
„ Salt, a piece of coin in the kingdom
 of— 270
„ State prisoners of the King of— 277, 286
„ Swearing in the kingdom of — ... 270
Shoan : Furniture in the house of a— ... 268
Shooja-ool-Moolk 37, 70
Shooráwuk 84
Shrondanes (tribe)... 5
Shuhr-i-no 38
Shukkoor Khán 156
Shukoor (Shukroo) Beg 55, 56
Shummuz Tabreez... 181
Shumsoodeen Khán ... 36, 72, 100
 „ „ Populzye 35
Shurikoorgi 230
Shurukhs 38, 39
Shusgao 29
Shutr Gurdun 31
Sia-Posh (See Seeaposh) ... ...
Sidara : Mountain of 205
Sidi Kásim 239, 249, 252
Sihún 229
Sihút 225, 232
Sikh Chiefs 179
„ Jaghirdárs 174
„ Power : Rise of the— ... 172—175
„ Seminaries at Benáres 171
„ Troops: The review on Dussera holiday
 of the— 177
„ women 176
Sikhs ... 53, 54, 99, 104, 111, 112, 114, 115,
 117—121, 145—147, 149—151,
 172, 176, 180, 181, 182, 184
„ and the Mahomedans : Encounters
 between the— ... 117, 118

B 1573—7

PAGE.

Sikhs and Syed Ahmed Sháh : War between
 the— 173
„ and their kingdom and dependencies :
 Masson's memorandum on the—105,
        168—178
„ Origin of the— ... 171, 172
„ System of warfare of the— ... 177
Sikhs' subjection to British authority ... 171
Sikkah... 226
„ or Jibús Island 233
Silk 124, 159
Silver ore 4
Simla : Report of a journey from Herát to— 21—31
Simnau ... ... 66—68
Sind ... 105, 106, 109, 119, 120, 121, 174,
    180, 183, 184, 185, 186
„ and Herát : Countries between— ... 103
„ Chiefs of— ...106, 111, 120, 121, 132,
        133, 144
„ Condition of the Province of— ... 106
„ Oppression in— 187
Sindees 176
Sindee sway 145
Sinjer D'jun hills 8
Siráh : Island of— 217
Sirdár Futteh Khán ... 84, 86, 87, 89
Siri Chusma 100
Siripool 38, 39
Siwák 194
Slave market 286, 289
„ trade ... 38, 99, 108, 125, 133, 228
Slavery 285
Slaves 7, 225, 287
Small Strait 212, 213
Smith, Mr. 211, 224, 232
Soand Mull 181
Socotra ... 194, 240, 242, 243, 245
Sofálah 225
Sofer 8
Sogan 6
Soghodi 185
Sohdut Khán 185
Sohrab (Shorab) 45, 48, 72
Soleïman the Magnificent : The aqueduct
 of— 218
„ ibn Selim... 218
Solen, the 191
Soliman 173
Solomon 268
Solyman mountains 111
Somális (tribe) 219
„ the Danákili tribe of— ... 213
„ slaves of— 225
Somnee 58
Sonmeani: Narrative of a journey from
 Khelát to— ... ... 45—50
Sooltan (See Sultan) ... ...
Soonees (Sunees) ... 7, 14, 35, 40, 124, 155
Soor (tribe) 68
Soorab Khán 69
Soorkhoud (stream) 29, 30
Sorbagh 39
South Sea Islanders 138

	Page.
State prisoners of the kingdom of Shoa	265
Stévens, Mr.	211
Stoddart, Col.	65—68, 86, 97, 99
Stones (for chaplets)	13
St. Antonio : The Highland of—	214
St. Petersburg	103
Suadat-ool-Moolk	24
Subeïhi (tribe)	215, 216
,, Arabs	213, 214
,, Bedowins	212, 213
Subhi	230
Subjezyes (tribe)	11
Subsel	184
Subseldah Kote	174, 183, 184, 185
Subzawaur (Subzewar)	23, 25, 36, 91, 92, 108, 125, 126
Subzee	157
Suchár	104
Sucker	185
Sudarzye (See Suddoozye).	
Sudavzye (See Suddoozye).	
Suddoo Khán	155, 157
Suddoozye (tribe)	15, 16, 35, 37, 97, 103, 108, 116, 120, 121, 124
Suddoozye princes in Afghánistán	35
Suffeed Karh	30
Suggadera	304
Suggagídan	304
Sughrá	220—222, 233
Sujáhbád	181, 182
Sujauhaunpur	178
,, Sensar Chund, Rajah of—	173
Súk-el-Jum'ah or Friday Market	242
Súk-el-Khamis	246
Sukkúr	145
Súku-l-Basir	229
Suleïmán, the Magnificent	249
Sultán	195
,, 'Ali ben Ghaleb, Chief of the Yáfa'i tribe	220
,, Hussain Bookara	8
,, Hussan Mirza Bairam	8
,, Ibrahim Roza : Tomb of—	4
,, Mahomed	28, 117, 118, 120
,, Mahomed Khán	92, 151
,, ,, Bárukzái	89
,, Mohammed Abdalla ibn ben Issa Achmudi	208
Sultánpore	185
Sultélli	304
Summoo Khán (See Summut Khán).	
Summut Khán	112, 155, 156
Sunees (See Soonees).	
Sungáh	141, 145, 146, 147
Sungan	38
Sungcharuk	39
Sung Hissár	12
Sunkul	304
Surat	221
Surcushma	55

	Page.
Surukhs	57
Sustanee (See Seestannee).	
Sutledje (river)	125, 174, 175, 180
Swan, Lt.	218
Sydabad	29
Syed (See Sayad).	
Syfoola Mirza	57
Symunees, the	92
Syriac language, the	139, 199
Syud (See Sayad).	

T.

Taballah	230
Tabas Khilike	4
Tabien (Tahren)	4
Tabos (See Tubbus).	
Taccoodah	289, 290
Tadjik (tribe)	124
Ta'ez and Dhamár	238
,, Fortress of—	239
Tagaum	144
Tahren	4
Taifabæ (tribe)	258
Taj	264
Tajee	15
Tajik families	38
Táj Mahál	169
Táj Mahomed Khán	68, 69, 72
Tájurah	213, 256, 257, 261, 262, 272, 281, 282, 289—291, 293, 295, 297, 298, 300, 302, 304
,, and Abyssinia : Road between—	259
,, Brother of the Sultán of—	261
,, Journey to—	289
,, Kind reception of Capt. Barker by the Sultán of—	300, 301
,, Sultán of—	255, 259
,, Trigonometrical survey of the Bay of—	289
Tajurans, the	278, 295, 296
Ták	104, 120, 147—150
,, Chief of—	112
,, Munshi of the Chief of—	153
,, to Pesháwar : Masson's adventures in a journey from—	150—158
Takli	8
Takyla (tribe)	261, 292
Taloda Hoojooristán	40
Tamarisk	194
Tamerlane	5, 8, 12
Tanim Damer Ail : The rebels of—	90
Tanjiks	28
Tanks (hanging)	218
Tarhál	229
Tárbát (See Turbut).	
Tareek Khán	113
Tarik-el-Yemen	238, 249
Tarik-esh-Sham : Narrative of a journey by Mr. J. Cruttenden from Mokha to San'á by—	235—252
Tarim	229

INDEX.

	Page.
Tarrah Sing	174, 178
Tártár districts	125
Tartars, the	8, 16, 108, 114, 123
Tartary	140
Tatta, the Puttala of the Greeks	187
„ Routes from Lahore to —	179—187
Tatteh	106
Teejlol and Shoa : Route between—	286
Teer Andaz	27
Teermáh	71
Teflis	103
Tegulet, capital of Ethiopia	268
Teháméh	238—243, 250, 259
Tehrán	7, 17, 36, 55, 64, 66—69, 92, 103
„ Her Majesty's Envoy at—	97
Teimuneer (See Teimunees).	
Teimunees (tribes)	37, 40
Teimurees (See Teimunees).	
Tein Khán	29
Teizee	29
Tej (kind of meal)	264
Terendjebin, a sort of gum	4
Terim	207
Tiger hunts	49
Tigré	268, 290
„ Merchants from—	289
Tijend (river)	38
Tiklidah	230
Timoor Sháhzadeh	93
Timour	16
„ Koolee Khán	109
Timur (Tamerlane)	16, 122, 170, 172
Tir: Month of—	160
Tobacco	195
„ Sikhs prohibited from using—	171
Tobas (See Tubbus).	
Todd D'arcy, Major : Letters from—regarding Herát	79—93
„ Report of a journey from Herát to Simla viâ Kandahár, Kabul, and the Panjáb by—	21—31
Tokhees	27
Tolak-tree	243
Tombs	153
„ at 'Aden	218
Tomb Valley	217
Toolfkar Shere	39
Tooloomba	181
Toon	3, 4, 5, 37
Toor Erain Murroo	261
Toorshish	37
„ Chiefs of—	38
Tooth-brushes	194
Toot-i-Gusserman	24, 25
Top	29
Topchee Bashee	85, 86, 89
Torkis	3
Trade from India	198
Travellers in Arabia	205
Travelling : Advantages from—	53
Treaty between the Bombay Government and the Sultán of 'Aden	241

	Page.
Treaty of Runjit Sing with the British Government	174
Tributes	174
Tubbus	3—5, 37, 38
Tubrez (Tabreez)	66, 103, 106, 107
Tubrezee wheat	58
Túkam	229
Tukht-i-Khatoom	39
Tukhya	72
Tulla (kind of beer)	264, 268, 288
Tull-i-bunjee	22
Tull-i-Kumân	24
Tumah: The lake of—	26
Tung-i-Khoord Kábul	29
Tung-i-Lullunder	29
Tung-i-Sheer	29
Tunoor (Timoor)	93
Turbut (Toorbut)	38, 123, 126, 157, 212
Turbut-i-Shakh Jam	33
Turbut : The Mogul Chief of—	108
Turkastán	36, 82, 98, 148
Turkey (Room) : Embassy from the Ameer of Bokhara to the Sultan of—	56, 57
Turkish cemetery	218
„ Frontier	240
„ Government	249
„ Spies	247
Turkomans (Toorkmans), the	5, 7, 36—38, 54, 57, 58
„ defeated by the Persians	64
„ Mahomed Hoosain Kashee's remarks about the —	65
Turks, the	14, 218, 239, 242, 249
„ Expulsion of— from Yemen	241
„ Struggles of Abbas Mirza with—	53
Turnuk (river)	12, 15, 16, 26
„ Valley	27, 28
Tymunee	85
Tymunees	92, 93
T'znai, lake	290

U.

'Uddeín	244
'Uddeini sort : Coffee of the—	245
Ufshur Toork (tribe)	39
Ulmar	39
Umritsur	170, 172, 177
Undiri, a sub-tribe of the Ghiljees	23
Urghundáb (stream)	26
Urghundee	29
Urláji (tribe)	221, 223
„ Násir ben Abu Bekr, Chief of the—	222
Uruz Beggee	85, 89
Usbeck	129, 143
Ushecs (tribe)	133
Uzbegs of the Charvilayet	92
Uzbeks	39

V.

Vandals of Africa	...	...	268
Vazbegs of the Charbilayet	...		92
Vazir Haji Akasee...	...	...	100
" (Vizier) of Sind	...	...	186
Ventura, Monsr.	...	105, 118, 175
Vhooramábád	...	...	53
Vicent, Dr.	...	...	185
Virgil ...	...	...	152
Vitkievitch	...	...	74
Vizeerees (tribe)	...	148, 149, 158
Voluta Musica, the...	...	...	191
Vorachenk	...	...	11
Vuzeer of Herát	...	...	79—93

W.

Wabi, Chief of Tigré	...	...	268
Wádi (Wady) Amt	...	...	207
" Bahrein	...	221, 222
" Boondeerah	...	...	296
" Dalaboyeh	...	...	298
" Dhar	...	249, 250
" Doân	...	205, 206, 208
" Hagger	...	...	206
" Hajarin	...	206, 207
" Hoombelli	...	...	289
" Kasr...	...	...	207
" Kilulloo	...	...	260
" Koleibah	...	...	242
" Kubbeh	...	...	217
" Lissan	...	300, 304
" Masellá	...	...	232
" Meïfah	...	193, 199, 206, 223
" Misenát: Tribe of—	...	225
" Missile	...	...	207
" Nebbi	...	...	206
" Ráchie	...	...	207
" Reide-Eddin	...	...	206
" Rummoo-delly	...	...	298
" Sanam	...	...	223
" Seihán	...	243, 244, 246, 252
" Sheikháwí	...	...	232
" Uebbene	...	...	206
" Zebid	...	...	239
Wáhidi Mountains...	...	...	226
" soldiers	...	...	224
" territory	...	...	227
" (tribe)	...		225, 227
Walls: System of erecting—round villages for protection		...	16
Walnuts	...	...	124
Waloo	...	...	275
Wambewateh or chairs	...	...	275
Wamburroo (stream)	...	...	276
Waramilli	...	...	304
Wardeks	...	...	29
Warrah Ambilli	...	...	290
Warwick: Earl of—	...	...	115
Wásalat	...	...	230
Wásel	...	...	229
Washeer	...	...	25, 84
Wassah-Ambili	...	...	297

Watch-towers	...	...	7
Wellsted, Lieut.	...	205, 223, 237, 245
" Narrative of a journey from the tower of Ba-'l-Haff, on the Southern Coast of Arabia to the ruins of Nakab-al-Hajar by—		...	191—201
Wesper	...	...	290
Wewendah	...	...	225
Wheat cultivation in Herát and Khorássán			124
White infidels	...	...	160
Wiláyat or England	...	...	242
Wilayuts	...	...	36
Wild animals	...	...	5
"Wild sports in Southern Africa": The author of—		...	275
Willea Mahomed	...	...	186
Willoughby, J. P., Mr.	...	...	83, 90
Wilson, D., Captain, Resident, Persian Gulf. 107, 122, 127, 145, 150, 158, 160, 165, 168, 178, 187
" Letter from—to the Government of Bombay, regarding Mr. Masson, an American traveller in Central Asia			103—107
Wiltshire, General...	...	...	45
Woemah (tribe)	...	290, 292
" Hagaioo, Chief of the —		...	296
Woola-hiya	...	...	290
Wooloo Galla	...	...	268, 290
World: Advantages from the knowledge of the —		...	53
Wrede, Adolphe Baron: Account of an excursion in Hadramaut by—		...	203—208
Wudd: Wully Mahomed, Chief of —		...	45, 50
Wulasma (tribe)	...	...	257, 260
" Ibrahim ibn Hagaioo, Oogass of the—...		...	261
" Mahomed	...	265, 266
" " Abogaz, hereditary Governor of the eastern frontier ... 262, 263, 276—286, 290—295
" " Abogaz: Remarks of Captain W. C. Barker about the family of—.276, 277
" Moosa	...	...	263
Wully Mahomed of Wudd	...	45, 49, 50
Wun (tribe)	...	...	38
Wurzeh	...	...	30

Y

Yabari (tribe)	...	...	229
Yacoob Sháh	...	...	171
Yáfa'í (tribe)	...	...	228, 229
" Sultan 'Ali ben Ghálib, Chief of the—			220, 221
Yahúdi	...	...	247
Yakalif: Hill of—	...	...	230
Yakil (river)	...	...	124
Yakís (tribe)	...	...	229
Yakoobees (tribe)	...	...	5
Yákub Mahomed	...	...	184
Yar Mahomed Barrakzye	...	...	108

	PAGE.
Yár Mahomed Khán (one of the Peshawar Chieftains) ... 100, 112, 113, 115, 117 —119, 173	
Yár Mahomed killed by Syed Ahmedsháh...	119
Yár Mahomed Khán Alckozye... ...	35
Yár Mahomed Khán, Vuzeer of Herát ... 79—81, 83—88, 90—92	
Yaru Sing	173
Yazil	246
Yek Nuffer Adum	89
Yemen... 195, 198, 219, 241, 245, 247, 252	
Yezd 6, 8, 69	
,, and Herát : Weather, produce, &c., of the country between —...	5
,, to Herát: Direction of the route from—	3
,, ,, Distance from — ...	3
,, ,, Itinerary from — ... 3—17	
,, ,, Unsafe condition of the route from —	6, 7
Yoagan mythological rites	160
Yokoa-bung	40
Yoor Erain Murroo, lake of —... ...	293
Yuhuya Khán	70
Yuzdan Bukhsh	55

Z.

	PAGE.
Zaghafah	230
Zainool Abideen	57, 58
Zakfah...	230
Zdedum	37
Zeárat...	181, 185
Zebíd ... ... 239—241, 249	
Zeidí	248
Zeïla	219
Zemáun Sháh	172
Zeri Lake	9, 11
Zerisk	5
Zeyla 219, 282, 287, 289, 295	
,, Captain Barker's reception by the Governor of —	302
,, Emir of —	290
,, Route from Kilulloo to— 289, 290	
Zindea (tribe)	68
Zingibár	225
Zoological collection at Lahore... ...	169
Zourmal : The salt lake of —	16
Zurrah (lake)	36

B 1573—8

BOMBAY : PRINTED AT THE GOVERNMENT CENRAL PRESS.

UNIVERSITY OF CALIFORNIA AT LOS ANGELES
THE UNIVERSITY LIBRARY
This book is DUE on the last date stamped below

JUL 18 1977

REC'D ED-URB
QL SEP 26 1977
15 1977
Chd 9/5

NON-RENEWABLE

JUN 03 1997
ILL
DUE 2 WKS FROM DATE RECEIVED

Form L-0
20m-1,'41(1122)